SOCIETY, CULTURE, AN

IN THE MIDDLE EAST

PHILADELPHIA

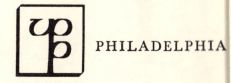

SOCIETY, CULTURE, A
IN THE MIDDLE EA

CHANGE

Golden River to Golden Road

BY RAPHAEL PATAI

Third, Enlarged Edition

UNIVERSITY OF PENNSYLVANIA PRESS

Second edition 1967

Third enlarged edition 1969

Library of Congress Catalog Card Number: 70–84742

SBN 8122–7289–7

Printed in the United States of America

Preface

From the Golden River, the Spanish colony of Río de Oro in West Africa, to the Golden Road leading from Khurasan to Samarkand in Turkestan, immortalized in English literature by Flecker, stretches the huge land mass of the Middle East. The distance from the Golden River to the Golden Road is roughly five thousand miles in a west-easterly direction, while from the Black Sea coast of Turkey in the north to Aden and Sudan in the south is about two thousand miles. The land area of the Middle East is about 7,324,815 square miles, or almost two and a half times that of the continental United States. Its population, however, is only 189 million, as against 202 million in the United States.

This huge territory, though inhabited by peoples speaking many different tongues and exhibiting many different physical features, is nevertheless the domain of one basically identical culture. The core area of the Middle East, stretching from the Nile to the Tigris, is the locale of the oldest recorded history of mankind. From here, in successive waves, cultural influences spread in all directions, reaching their climax thirteen centuries ago when the new Islamic variety of Arabian culture became superimposed on pre-existent cultural layers all over the Middle East, resulting in the characteristic pattern still predominant to the present day.

To the southwest, Muslim conquests have brought the entire northern third of Africa under the rule not only of Arab dynasties, but also of Arab culture, which rapidly spread from Arabia across North Africa to the territory of Río de Oro on the Atlantic coast. To the northeast, the Golden Road has for centuries been traversed by men who were carriers of Middle Eastern culture, which has become dominant in areas today held by the Soviet Union, notably the former Khanat of Bokhara and the Turkoman Republic.

Basic cultural identity, of course, does not mean surface homogeneity or monotony. On the contrary, upon closer inspection significant local differences can be discerned in each part of the

Middle East that give its culture areas a coloration and character of their own. But beneath localized developments and variants, the observer familiar with the whole of the Middle East recognizes the same basic pattern, the same fundamental features whose presence sets Middle Eastern culture apart from the cultures of contiguous world areas.

Cultural characteristics do not always coincide with international boundaries. It happens, therefore, that part of a country belongs culturally to the Middle East while another part of it extends beyond the limits of this world area. Such countries are the Mali Federation and the Republic of Sudan; the northern parts of both of them belong culturally to the Middle East, while their southern parts show very close affinities with the great Negro cultures of Africa. To the east, one finds that beyond the borders of Iran and Afghanistan peoples very similar culturally and in mode of life inhabit the western part of West Pakistan, which traditionally goes by the name of Balujistan, while the eastern part of West Pakistan belongs culturally to the Indian subcontinent.

The present volume deals with three interconnected topics. The first of these is Middle Eastern culture in general, including a discussion of the problems presented by the delimitation and subdivision of the Middle Eastern "culture continent." The second treats of a number of significant aspects of Middle Eastern social organization. The third is devoted to an analysis of the vital sociocultural changes taking place at present in the Middle East.

Most of the material contained in this book is printed here for the first time. Several chapters, however, are based on my previously published studies or on papers presented to scholarly conferences and utilized here in a rewritten and expanded form. Thus a shorter version of Chapter 1 was first published in the Winter 1952 issue of the *Middle East Journal* under the title "The Middle East as a Culture Area." The substance of the first part of Chapter 2, never published, was presented at a supper-conference of the Wenner-Gren Foundation for Anthropological Research on May 2, 1952. Some of the material included in Chapters 4, "The Family," 5, "The Position of Women and Sex Mores," and 10, "The Middle Eastern Town," was previously published in my book *The Kingdom of Jordan* (Princeton University Press, 1958).

A brief summary of the results of Chapter 7, "Dual Organization," was presented on December 29, 1952, at the Annual Meeting of the American Anthropological Association in Philadelphia. Chapter 10 also incorporates part of a paper presented at the Colloquium on Islamic Culture at Princeton University in September, 1953, and subsequently published in the Bombay magazine *United Asia* (Vol. 6, No. 4, 1954) under the title "Culture Change in the Muslim Town: A Challenge for Research," and in the Arabic volume *Al-Thaqāfa al-Islāmiyya wal-Hayāt al-Mu'āṣira*, edited by Muhammad Khalafallah, Cairo, 1956; as well as parts of the chapters entitled "The Town," written by me jointly with Fahim I. Qubain, and published in the three handbooks, *The Kingdom of Jordan*, *The Republic of Lebanon*, and *The Republic of Syria* (Human Relations Area Files Subcontractor's Monographs, New Haven, 1956) edited by me. Chapter 6, "Cousin Marriage," includes a portion dealing with a man's right to marry his cousin, a shorter version of which was published in the Winter 1955 issue of the *Southwestern Journal of Anthropology* under the title "Cousin-Right in Middle Eastern Marriage." Most of Chapter 13, "The Dynamics of Westernization," was printed in the Winter 1955 issue of *The Middle East Journal*. Only one single chapter, Chapter 11, "Religion in Middle Eastern, Far Eastern, and Western Culture," is the unaltered reprint of an article originally published in the Autumn 1954 issue of the *Southwestern Journal of Anthropology*. Chapter 12, "Social and Cultural Determinants of Middle Eastern Nationalism," was presented to the Institute on Nationalism in the Middle East held at the University of Chicago in November, 1959. I gratefully acknowledge the permission given to me by the Princeton University Press, the *Southwestern Journal of Anthropology*, *The Middle East Journal*, and the magazine *United Asia* to reprint or to utilize in an altered form these chapters and articles.

New York, September, 1961 RAPHAEL PATAI

For the second edition I wrote a new chapter, entitled "The Village and Its Culture." This now is Chapter 9 of the book, while the old chapters 9 to 13 have become Chapters 10 to 14.

The third edition contains two new chapters (15 and 16). Chapter 15, entitled "The Endogamous Unilineal Descent Group," was published originally in a different form in the Winter 1965 issue of the *Southwestern Journal of Anthropology*, whose editors are herewith thanked for their permission to include it in a revised version in the present edition. Chapter 16, entitled "Women in a Man's World," was written explicitly for the present edition in order to offer a fuller picture of the life of the female half of the traditional Middle Eastern world. Also new is the Statistical Appendix, which contains basic demographic data in the form of twelve tables. The table appearing on pages 14–15 has again been updated and minor errors corrected.

New York, May, 1969 RAPHAEL PATAI

Contents

Maps and Tables

Maps

Tables

I. The Middle East as a Culture Continent

ACROSS THE middle of the three continents of the Old World stretches a vast desert-and-steppe zone, reaching from the West African littoral to Mongolia and separating the great northern zone of agriculture extending from Spain to Siberia from the southern zone of agriculture comprising Central Africa and Southern and Southeastern Asia.[1] This central zone can be divided roughly into two distinct halves: a southwestern half, reaching across North Africa and Arabia and lying largely to the south of latitude 38° N.; and a northeastern half, extending across Central Asia, to the north of the same parallel. The two halves are joined in the middle by a relatively narrow isthmus, bounded by the Persian Gulf to the south and the Caspian Sea to the north.

Students of culture have repeatedly dealt with the problem of the cultural identification of the peoples inhabiting these areas, within the context of classifying the cultures of the two continents, Asia and Africa.[2] The present discussion is confined to the cultural characteristics of the western half of the desert-and-steppe zone of the Old World, together with the more fertile regions immediately contiguous with it or contained islandlike within it.

To delimit it geographically, the entire northern part of Africa from the Mediterranean down approximately to latitude 15° N. as well as the whole of west Asia is considered. On the northwest and southeast, this area is bounded by the natural limits of great bodies of water: the Atlantic, the Mediterranean, the Black Sea, the Caspian Sea, and the Arabian Sea, with the Persian Gulf and the Red Sea as great inland divides. To the south lies the humid tropical zone of Central Africa with the intervening steppe and savanna belt clearly marking the transition not only between two distinct geographical regions, but also between two different types of cultures. To the north, between the Black and the Caspian seas, the Caucasus forms a limit almost as definite as that of the seas themselves. To the northeast, the transition is more gradual, though here the northern and eastern limits of the Iranian Plateau and the sudden drop toward the Turkestan and Indian lowlands (separated by the narrow range of the Hindu-Kush mountains) can be taken as the marginal area. It is suggested that the entire area as here described be designated by the name *Middle East.*[3] In the following pages the cultures of the peoples inhabiting this area will be investigated, as far as this is possible within the confines of a short chapter in order to determine the justification of regarding it as a cultural entity distinct from contiguous cultural entities and at the same time sufficiently homogeneous within itself.

It has to be stated preliminarily that in such an enormous land mass, many times larger than any of the culture areas determined in the Americas by Wissler[4] or in Africa by Herskovits or Murdock, one will necessarily find a considerable range of internal variation

Areas and Populations of the Political Units

Political Unit	*Area Sq. Miles*	*Population midyear 1966 (estimated)*
I. *North Africa* (from west to east)		
Mauritania, Islamic Republic of	397,683	1,070,000
Spanish Sahara (Rio de Oro and Saguia el-Hamra)	102,703	48,000
Morocco (constitutional monarchy)	174,471	13,725,000
Ifni (Spanish Overseas Province)	579	53,000
Ceuta and Melilla (Spanish)	82	160,000
Mali (republic; northern part only)†	200,000	1,850,000
Algeria (republic)	919,591	12,150,000
Niger (republic)	459,073	3,433,000
Tunisia (republic)	63,378	4,460,000
Libya (kingdom)	679,536	1,677,000
Chad (republic)	490,733	3,361,000
Egypt (United Arab Republic)	386,872	30,147,000
Sudan (republic; Northern and Central only)‡	716,205	7,200,000
II. *Asia Minor and the Fertile Crescent*		
Turkey (republic)	298,104	31,910,000
Syria (republic)	71,498	5,400,000
Lebanon (republic)	4,015	2,460,000
Israel (republic)	7,993	2,629,000
Jordan (constituional monarchy)	37,737	2,059,000
Iraq (republic)	167,568	8,388,000
Cyprus (republic)	3,572	603,000

III. *The Arabian Peninsula*		
Saudi Arabia (kingdom)	872,722	6,870,000
Yemen (republic)	75,290	5,000,000
Southern Yemen	112,075	1,146,000
Muscat and Oman (British-protected sultanate)	82,000	565,000
Trucial Oman (seven sheikhdoms under British protection)	32,278	130,000
Qatar (British-protected sheikhdom)	4,000	71,000
Bahrein (British-protected sheikhdom)	231	193,000
Kuwait (sheikhdom)	5,800	491,000
IV. *The Eastern Wing*		
Iran (kingdom)	636,367	25,283,000
Afghanistan (constitutional monarchy)	251,000	15,397,000
Balujistan (part of the republic of Pakistan)§	134,000	1,300,000
Total	7,324,815	189,229,000

*Source: United Nations *Statistical Yearbook, 1967*, New York, 1968.
†Total area, square miles 463,947; total population: 4,654,000
‡ " " " " 967,491; " " 13,940,000
§ " " " " 365,529; " " 105,044,000

as one proceeds from one area to another. If, nevertheless, in the following pages *the culture* of the Middle East is discussed, this does not mean that the significance of these variations is overlooked, or that an attempt is made at unwarranted generalization and artificial schematization. The culture of the Middle East is in fact in the sense employed here not of the same order as that of any single culture area of America or Africa. The geographic locus of this culture, as delimited above, is of such magnitude and it contains so many internal variations that the term "culture area," coined for the native cultures of America, is too narrow to be meaningfully applied to it. It is therefore suggested that the world area inhabited by the carriers of Middle Eastern culture be termed a "culture continent," a designation that both indicates the huge size of the geographical area concerned and allows for the internal variation among its constituent regions.

The concept "Middle Eastern culture continent" can be compared to the long familiar concept of modern Western culture whose geographical locus could be termed "Western culture continent." Both culture continents are characterized by a certain cultural homogeneity that demarcates them against contiguous culture continents, and, at the same time, by considerable internal variations as between one and another of their constituent cultures.

It will be shown later that one of the basic features of Middle Eastern culture is the interaction between the population groups inhabiting the desert and people living in the cultivated regions. Utilizing this point of view, the Middle East can be subdivided into four major geographical regions, each with a desert-and-steppe area in its center and with a more fertile, cultivated perimeter encircling it. These four regions are: North Africa, the Arabian Peninsula, the Iranian Plateau, and Asia Minor. By far the largest, and characterized by the least favorable desert-sown ratio, is North Africa; second in both respects is the Arabian Peninsula; third is the Iranian Plateau; and fourth, Asia Minor. Somewhere in the general area of the grazing steppe between the desert and the sown[5] are located, as a rule, the typical old Middle Eastern towns which (in addition to the coastal towns) are the cultural centers of their respective areas.

If, in a general overview of the Middle East, the relative extent of the desert and the sown is taken as a basic consideration, the impression gained is one of an arid land mass more than overwhelmingly desert, only a very small percentage of which is utilized for agricultural pursuits. Exact data are lacking, but it is estimated that not more than 5 to 10 per cent of the total area of the Middle East is utilized for cultivation with either hoe or plough, and that the lands actually under cultivation at any given time are considerably less even than this small figure. With regard to surface area, therefore, the Middle East as a whole is an overwhelmingly desert-and-steppe area, and the ways of human adaptation to life in the desert and the steppe through pastoral economies seem to be its most significant characteristics.

A very different picture is, however, obtained if the percentage of the population supporting itself by animal husbandry and agricultural pursuits respectively is taken as the basis of estimate. In this case, it is found that the Middle East as a whole is a predominantly agricultural area. Between 65 and 75 per cent of the total working population is engaged directly in agriculture. An additional percentage either lives in villages rendering services to agriculturists, as artisans, teachers, religious personnel, barbers, watchmen, etc., or engages in supplementary or irregular agriculture. Some 12 to 14 per cent of the total population of the Middle East lives in towns and cities. This leaves roughly 10 to 15 per cent only for the nomadic and seminomadic peoples who eke out a living on the noncultivable steppes and deserts of the area.

Just as each area of the Middle East comprises both desert and sown and transitional zones between these two extremes, so also the demographic picture of each country is composed of at least three types of population elements that constitute a recurrent configuration in every part of the area. The desert is the habitat of the camel nomad, the steppe belt the domain of the sheep and goat nomad, and the sown the home of the agriculturist. Transitional stages and localized variations of these population types make for additional diversification.

The camel nomads rely on their camels for sustenance to a degree unparalleled by the exploitation of any other animal species in any other culture.[6] The camel nomads spend their life in seasonal wandering over fairly extensive tribal territories in constant search of pasture for their camels.

The nomads of the steppes breed sheep and goats or occasionally cattle in place of the camels of the true nomads. This difference in itself determines the total gamut of divergences in the ways of life of these two groups. Sheep and goats are less hardy than the camels, they cannot stay away from water for days, they need better and softer pasture, and thus their mobility is much more limited. Consequently, the sheep and goat nomads stay within the grazing steppe belt or, more precisely, in that part of the steppe belt which represents the transition between it and the sown. The annual cycle of seasonal wandering is the rule also for them, but their wandering territory is much smaller and their movements are much slower than those of the camel nomads. In the Sudan, south of latitude 13° N., cattle-grazing seminomads (the so called Baqqāra) take the place of the sheep and goat nomads of the northern outskirts of the desert. Cattle gain in importance also in Southern Arabia.

A special kind of nomadism is practiced by the peoples of the mountainous regions of the Middle East, especially around the Iranian Plateau, but also in Morocco. In this type of wandering, called "transhumance," the characteristic annual cycle of movement takes the tribal groups high up into the mountains in the summer, and again down to the warmer and milder valleys or the lower levels of the plateau in the winter. Transhumance is therefore the vertical variant of the horizontal nomadism discussed hitherto.

Characteristic of all the true and seminomads, whether of the horizontal or of the vertical variety, is the black hair tent, the only shelter used by them. The basic identity of the black hair tent all over the Middle East is one of the indications that the entire territory is truly one single culture area. The only place outside the Middle East where the black hair tent is used is Tibet, and its presence there must be accounted for by diffusion.[7]

Another characteristic shared by all the wandering peoples of the Middle East, as well as by some of the settled population of the area, is the tribal structure. Each tribe is a homogeneous social unit whose native members are social equals. This definition excludes people who joined the tribe from the outside, and slaves. The tribe as such has little actual significance since tribal affinity constitutes a rather vague tie. The actual functioning unit is the wandering group, which varies greatly in size as well as in standing within the tribal structure. The number of unit-levels or of successively larger groupings of which the tribe consists also varies, so that in one place one may find a small wandering unit that is an independent and unaffiliated tribe in itself, while elsewhere a much bigger wandering unit may be merely a subdivision of a subgroup of a subtribe.

In contrast to the classless structure of each tribe in itself, the totality of wandering tribes shows a considerable range of variation with regard to degree of social standing, or "nobility." Distinction is being made between noble and client tribes such as, for example, the Sa'adī and Marabṭīn tribes of Cyrenaica of whom more will be said in Chapter 8. In general it can be stated that the camel nomads are in most cases regarded as noble tribes, while the artisan groups (the so-called *ṣunnā'*), attached to them temporarily, count as low-status people or even as vassals. Between the two rank the sheep and goat nomads and the semistationary inhabitants of the Iraqi marshes. Despised by all as standing beneath the tribal hierarchy are the settled cultivators, the slaves of the soil.

Tribal structure is such an unmistakable hallmark of nomadism that wherever it exists among settled villagers it can be taken as definitely indicating that they are the descendants of nomads who, in the not very remote past, settled down to sedentary agricultural life. Examples can be found all across the Middle East, but the most typical are the Kurds who, though settled in village strongholds, have retained not only the tribal structure but also several other characteristics that distinguish the roaming nomads from the settled cultivators.

The interrelationship between one wandering unit and another is governed by certain principles validated by tradition, enjoying unquestioned authority, and constituting everywhere the basis of tribal ethos. Among these can be mentioned the principle of collective responsibility expressed in such institutions as the blood feud, raiding, and the inviolate laws of hospitality and sanctuary, as well as in such concepts as honor, *wajh* ("face"), and nobility. All these ideas and ideals appear in their most intensive form among the camel nomads, and they successively lose their power and significance as one proceeds across the range from them to the sheep and goat nomads, to the almost sedentary groups, and finally to the completely sedentary cultivators.

The main areas of cultivation in the Middle East are those that either receive sufficient rain to make cultivation of field crops possible or can be irrigated from rivers or wells for a more intensive utilization of the land. One or both of these types of cultivated lands are present in every part of the Middle East, the typical example of the former being found in the more northerly or mountainous countries (Turkey, Iran, Syria, Morocco), while the latter is best exemplified by the riverine agricultures of the Nile and the Tigris-Euphrates valleys or the oases of the Sahara and the Arabian Desert.

Material equipment, which has to be closely adapted to the nomadic and sedentary modes of life respectively, shows considerable differences between the two sectors of the Middle Eastern peoples. Moreover, since material equipment under the technologically backward conditions still prevailing in many parts of the Middle East has to depend on the locally available raw materials, this aspect of culture reveals marked differences not only between nomads and cultivators, but also among the settled villagers themselves from one area to another. The nomadic camp is largely the same all over the Middle East: black hair tents pitched at a comfortable distance from one another, and in a definite orderly pattern. The village, on the other hand, shows a highly nucleated, closely packed structure, in which house leans against house, with narrow winding paths leading between them, without any plan or design, and in which the limiting influence of the available raw materials is strongly felt. The building material of the Middle Eastern village is stone in the mountains, mud or adobe on the plains, reed in the marshes, and palm leaves and fronds in the far south. Despite this diversity of building material, the floor plan of the houses shows an almost identical range in most parts of the Middle East. The simplest structure everywhere is the square one-room building (an exception being the so-called beehive houses in some villages in the Alawite region of Syria), which can be increased by a simple budding process into two, three, four, five, or even more stories and a correspondingly larger number of rooms. The common feature of all these houses is that they are inhabited by only one single extended family. In fact, family and house are so closely associated that in ancient as well as in modern Semitic languages the same word is used to denote both.

Comparable variations could be shown to exist with regard to clothing, furnishings, utensils, household articles, and the like; again, however, with the reservation that these differences seem significant only when material objects from different areas of the Middle East are compared with one another; when, on the other hand, they are compared with articles hailing from adjacent culture continents (Negro Africa, Europe, India, or Central Asia), the local differences all but disappear and melt into an over-all Middle Eastern type.

Notwithstanding the more obvious variations between the cultures of the Middle Eastern nomads and of the settled agriculturists, conditioned by the difference between a nomadic pastoral mode of life and a settled agricultural existence, a considerable number of basically similar or almost identical cultural features can be shown to exist between these two archetypes of Middle Eastern life. The most important of these is undoubtedly *the family*, which occupies a focal position in Middle Eastern culture and whose structure and functioning are practically identical not only among nomadic breeders and settled cultivators, but also among them as compared with urban populations.

The family in traditional Middle Eastern society—that is, in every place where Westernization has not yet made appreciable inroads—is patrilocal, patrilineal, patriarchal, endogamous, and occasionally polygynous. It is usually headed by an elderly male, and its membership comprises all his sons with their wives and children, and the unmarried daughters and granddaughters (sons' daughters). The entire family, which may consist of several dozen members, resides together, in a cluster of neighboring tents in the nomadic camp, in a single house, or in several buildings clustered around a common courtyard in the villages and towns. When the grandfather dies, the extended family breaks up into as many new units as there are sons, each of whom will then become the head of a new and separate extended family.

Marriage customs, sex mores, the position of women and the division of labor between men and women are completely analogous and in many cases identical in the nomadic camp, the agricultural village, and the town (with the exception of the upper class and the still relatively thin but growing middle class in the town). Marriage is highly endogamous, the preferred mating being between children of two brothers. Polygyny is permissive and sporadic and certainly less than 5 to 10 per cent of the married men have more than one wife simultaneously. The relationship between the sexes is governed by rigid sex mores that place special emphasis on female purity and chastity, both premarital and marital, though veiling and total seclusion of women is practiced mainly in the tradition-directed middle and upper class society of the towns. Men still claim the ancient right to kill their daughters and sisters (but not their wives) if caught in illicit sex relations. A man can easily divorce his wife at will or whim; a woman has no legal way of obtaining a divorce; she can only run away and take refuge with her own consanguineous family.

Economically, too, the extended family is the basic unit. In the nomadic tribe, the extended family holds all property—that is, camels and other livestock—in common; in the village, the extended family owns jointly the lands from whose cultivation it derives its livelihood; while in the towns it owns and manages jointly the enterprise from which its members make a living. Earnings are pooled as a rule and the expenses of the household are defrayed from the common purse controlled by the *pater familias*. The women may help in the field, if their husbands work land that they own or rent; otherwise, their place is at home and their main task is to make the meager earnings of the men go as far as possible by working hard and economizing tightly, sharing the household chores or taking turns in performing them.

The Middle Eastern birthrate is among the highest in the world; but it is counterbalanced by a very high rate of infant and child mortality as a consequence of which general life expectancy is cut down to appallingly low averages. Institutionalized schooling in its traditional form means religious education; it is, however, the privilege of the few only, and is rudimentary. Social conditioning is usually achieved informally, and takes place within the family circle. The children begin at a tender age to participate in the work of their parents, whereby an early differentiation between the sexes appears, the boys being introduced into male occupations by their father or elder brothers, and the girls into those of women by their mother or elder sisters. Girls, when they marry at or frequently before puberty, are whisked away from the parental home, and their relationship with their parents then becomes loose and remote, except in the case of cousin marriage. Otherwise, the Middle Eastern bride becomes absorbed into the household of her husband's family. The tutelage of her own mother is supplanted by the more rigid one of her mother-in-law, and only many years later, after she has given birth to children, and especially to sons, and these are on their way to manhood, can she begin to assert herself as a *mater familias* in her own right.

The achievement of independent status comes as tardily to the son as to the daughter. He takes a wife when his father can spare the bride-price. After marriage he continues to live within the extended family of which his father is either the head or a member. Age is an asset in Middle Eastern outlook, so that the older a man becomes, the smaller the number of the males in the extended family older than himself and the greater the number of those younger than he, the more he grows in esteem, the greater the weight of his opinion, and the more easily he can live according to his own inclinations.

The family is beyond doubt one of the most important institutions in Middle Eastern culture. It may therefore serve as an example to illustrate, briefly at least, the marked differences between the Middle East and each one of the contiguous culture continents.[8]

To the northwest of the Middle East, in Europe, the typical family is the small biological family in which descent is reckoned bilaterally; as a rule it is neither patrilocal nor matrilocal, but neolocal; in it the role and the status of husband and wife are balanced to a much greater extent than in the Middle East. There is a great variety in the way of choosing spouses; endogamy, in the sense of marriage between close relatives, is comparatively rare, while the marriage of relations as close as first cousins is not countenanced by the Christian religion. Only monogamy is lawful. However, the relationship between the sexes is much freer than in the Middle East; premarital and to a lesser extent also extramarital sexual relationships are tolerated. Divorce proceedings can be instituted by either husband or wife.

To the south of the Middle East, in Negro Africa, the typical family is the extended one: either patrilineal, headed by the oldest surviving brother in a given generation or matrilineal, headed by the mother's oldest brother. After the death of the original head of the family it does not break up, as it does in the Middle East, but continues to function as a unit under the new headship of the next oldest brother. Marriage is exogamous, the totemic or rarely nontotemic clan being the exogamous unit. Sexual mores show a wide range of variety. Divorce can be initiated by either the husband or the wife.

To the southeast of the Middle East in the subcontinent of India, the rule is the patrilineal, patrilocal, and patriarchal extended family, though matrilineal descent also occurs. Upon the father's death the oldest son becomes the head of the family; in this respect the Indian family stands nearer to the African than to the Middle Eastern counterpart. The extended family or larger kinship group (*gotra*) is exogamous; the endogamous unit is the subcaste. Monogamy is the rule among the Hindus, though polygyny occurs, as well as some localized polyandry. Sex mores show a wide range of variation, with the prevalence of purdah or seclusion of women, and sati, the burning alive of widows (now prohibited by law) in direct ratio to caste status. Divorce is not allowed by Hindu tradition.

To the northeast of the Middle East, in the Central Asian culture area, the family is patrilineal, patrilocal, extended, and exogamous. Upon the death of the family head, his eldest surviving brother takes his place. Polygyny is permitted, as in the Middle East. Sex mores are lax; there is no emphasis on female purity, no veiling, and no seclusion of women. Women can have no legal recourse to divorce.

With respect to marriage and the family the Middle East is thus clearly set off against the four adjoining world areas; while the similarity of traits within it serves as an additional indication of its character as a distinct culture continent.

Also with regard to social units larger than the extended family, the three main sectors of Middle Eastern society show a number of basic correspondences. The Middle Eastern towns, however, have been for several decades centers of foreign (Western) cultural influences, as a consequence of which much of the original Middle Eastern tradition in social organization has been obliterated in them (especially in the middle and upper classes) and can be found only in the villages and the nomadic tribes.

Nomadic camp and agricultural village, however, must not be conceived as two opposite forms of local aggregates. The existence of a continuous range of transitional forms between the two clearly shows that camp and village are merely the two extreme forms of a variety of possible mixtures of elements taken from both. The presence of these "mixed" forms of local aggregates is due not only to the continued processes of sedentarization; the reverse process is also known to have taken place repeatedly: settled villagers have taken up nomadism, either completely or partially.

The cultivation of the soil and animal husbandry can, moreover, mutually complement each other. When the observer is confronted with the habitat of a human group making a living in both ways, he may not be able to decide whether it should be counted as a village or as a nomadic encampment.

The nomadic wandering unit often consists of not just one, but two or even more groups of extended families, each one of which is sometimes called *ḥamūla*; similarly, also, the settled village may contain two or more groups, each with a great inner cohesion, and varying degrees of mutual tension. The nomadic *ḥamūla*, as a rule, pitches its tents together in one part of the camp; the village group (also called *ḥamūla* in some parts of the Middle East) inhabits one quarter of the village. The *ḥamūla*, whether in village or camp, is definitely a kinship group, and as such commands the loyalty of its member families.

The place of the individual within his society is determined, first, by his membership in an extended family, and secondly, by the membership of his extended family in a *ḥamūla*. This means that in traditional Middle Eastern society participation in social groups larger than the family is a family affair and not an individual concern. Adherence to larger groups can never cut across family ties. On the contrary, the fact that the family belongs to a larger social group only strengthens the family unity, for the stronger the family as a whole the greater its weight within the larger unit.

The largest traditional social grouping to be found all over the Middle East is a loose, informal twofold faction which, at the same time, is powerful in its hold over the population, whether nomadic or sedentary. This social grouping resembles in several respects the kind usually referred to by the term "moiety" or "dual organization." In some parts of the Middle East (e.g., in Arabia and the Levant coast) entire tribes and villages belong to one or the other of such dual factions known by name pairs such as Qaḥṭān and 'Adnān, Yafa' and Ḥamdān, Hināwī and Ghāfirī, Qays and Yaman. In other places, the individual villages are split into two sections or moieties. One of the two moieties in a village may be bound by ties of friendship or allegiance to corresponding moieties in other villages, while the other moieties of the same villages form another confederation. Whether the villages as a whole or only one half of each of them belong to a moiety, there is usually much competition and rivalry, and frequently even bloody fights between the two sides. In many cases political initiative has made use of the existing dual organization with the result that the moieties today often have political significance, though differences in descent and custom are by no means forgotten. A detailed examination of Middle Eastern dual organization will be found in Chapter 7.

With regard to social control, distinction must be made between the local and the higher level. On the local level, the social control of the typical and traditional Middle Eastern village resembled until recently (roughly up to the end of World War I) that of the nomadic tribe to a considerable degree. It was the same kind of semiautocratic and semidemocratic, highly variable and informal social control characteristic of the nomadic tribe, which makes difficult a description in concrete terms. The village headman (called *mukhtār* in the Fertile Crescent countries, *muhtar* in Turkey, *ʻomda* in Egypt, *aga* in Kurdistan, *amīn* in North Africa) corresponds to the tribal *shaykh*; he is usually the head of the most influential family or group of families in the village. The office of headmanship is inherited from a man by a son or another near relative, but succession also requires the approval of the elders of the village. These elders make up the informally (and recently more frequently formally) constituted village council, the *majlis* (*jemaʻa* in North Africa).

The balance of power between the headman and the council depends upon the personality of the headman. The authority of the tribal *shaykh* rests not on force, which as a rule does not stand at his disposal, but on the esteem, renown, and prestige he enjoys. The same is true to a more limited extent of the village headman, though the latter usually wields more influence over his council, and his power over the simple villagers is also correspondingly greater. One of the reasons for this difference may be seen in the lack of mobility of the cultivators inhabiting the villages as compared to the much greater freedom of movement of the nomadic tribesmen. A dissatisfied tribesman can, if worst comes to worst, leave his tribe and join with his family and flocks another tribe, even though such a move may mean loss of status; an agriculturist villager who has been antagonized or even oppressed by his headman has no such way out. Another reason is the frequent indebtedness of the villagers to the headman or to a wealthy absentee landowner whose representative he is; such a situation can easily be exploited by the headman to make the debtor subservient to him.

In the heyday of Turkish rule over the Middle East the village could and would rely as little on any central governmental authority as the nomadic tribe. The only difference between the two was that the volatile nomadic tribe was never successfully bent under the yoke of taxation, while the lot of the villagers was to bear a heavy yoke of oppressive taxes. The official political or administrative contact between the village and the higher (district or central) authorities was largely confined to conscription and tax collection. The taxes were (and are) a heavy burden on the villagers, in return for which they received nothing: no services, no help, no protection. As long as the village headman delivered the taxes, he and his village were left alone and could continue undisturbed in their traditional ways of life.

In recent decades, this pattern has been undergoing considerable change. The nomadic tribe occupies today more or less the position held by the village half a century ago; it has to pay taxes to the central government as the village does, although there is a marked difference even here: many nomadic tribes receive, in the person of their *shaykhs*, considerable governmental subventions that sometimes equal the sums collected in taxes. One of the results of this development is that the position of the *shaykh* has become stronger vis-à-vis his council and tribesmen, and that he can assume a more autocratic attitude.

The village, on the other hand, has become a more and more integral part of the state, politically, economically, educationally, and in several other respects. The old, traditional village institutions such as the mosque, the *kuttāb* (Koran school), the guest house, the communal threshing floor, and the like survive; but recent decades have witnessed the great innovation that, for the first time in thousands of years, the villagers receive something from the state in return for their taxes: schools, sanitation, economic aid, police and military protection. These services, however, are still in their infancy.

In general, the socioeconomic conditions characteristic of the Middle Eastern cultivators today can be summed up in a few somber lines. Most of the cultivators are subsistence farmers living on their produce, with a predominantly cereal diet which, though perhaps barely adequate in caloric value, is lacking in protein and protective foods. As a consequence of this and the generally low standards of hygiene, the incidence of disease is high, in some areas appallingly so. Adequate water supplies are rare; because of the perennial irrigation method practiced in some riverain tracts and the presence of stagnant waters elsewhere, malaria is the most prevalent single disease in many regions. The vast majority of the cultivators in the Middle East are either dwarfholders, sharecropper tenants, or landless laborers. A small number of wealthy, often extremely rich landowning families concentrate in their hands a substantial proportion of the cultivated land, a situation in which land reforms have only recently begun to make a dent. Lands owned by smallholders in villages were until recently often held under the ancient system of communal ownership.[9]

It is very difficult to reach valid generalizations with regard to governmental and political forms in the Middle East. At present, the tendency prevails in most Middle Eastern states to follow Western patterns of government—which is consistent with the readiness of urban upper-class Middle Easterners to adopt Western techniques. Thus we find republics and kingdoms with houses of representatives, ministers of state, and the like. However, these are rarely more than new façades behind which still stand the old structures of autocratic rule exercised by small, wealthy, and powerful feudal groups. Several Middle Eastern countries passed from traditional despotism, through a brief period of experimentation with parliamentary democracy, to modern dictatorship. In some Middle Eastern states, even of the external forms of Western governmental techniques only a few have been adopted: no distinction, for instance, is being made to this day between state income and expenditure on the one hand and the ruler's privy purse on the other. This is part of the age-old Middle Eastern governmental tradition, which also includes the feudal rule of the few based on the power of a mercenary army, often of foreign extraction. Under such circumstances, dynastic constancy is rare; the throne or the power is more often usurped than inherited. While on the local level (in tribes and villages) the rule of persons other than of the blood would be unimaginable, on the highest level foreigners can succeed in attaining positions of sovereignty.

The relationship of the cities to the countryside in the Middle East today is reminiscent of that between town and country in medieval Europe. The Middle Eastern towns, of which more will be said in Chapter 9, are the undisputed industrial, commercial, financial, political, judicial, educational, literary, recreational, artistic, intellectual, medical, and religious centers of their respective hinterlands. Externally the *sūq*, or bazaar, is undoubtedly the most characteristic as well as the most fascinating part of the towns, with its narrow alleys, covered with vaulted stone arches or with matting or awning, and with each trade occupying a separate street. Organizationally, the *sūq* is the most tangible expression of the existence and activities of the craft guilds (now largely defunct) such as those of tailors, outfitters, slipper and sandal makers, saddlers, embroiderers, goldsmiths, etc. Each of these guilds has its head, its provost, its council, its grades of apprentices, journeymen, and masters, its constitution, rules, and other organizational trappings.[10] In most cases artisanship, and with it membership in a guild, are hereditary; sometimes, as in Tunis, guild membership as well as the position of guild chief has to be passed on from father to son.

The presence of social classes is characteristic of the Middle Eastern towns, in contrast to villages and nomadic tribes. The urban class structure shows great vertical mobility. The great majority of the townspeople belong to the lower class, and make their living as craftsmen, shopkeepers, itinerant vendors, unskilled laborers, porters, workers employed in services, fishermen (in coastal towns), beggars, etc. The thin but growing middle class is made up of master craftsmen, merchants, teachers, other professional people who do not belong to the "great" families, minor officials, small house-owners, and others of moderate means. The very small but extremely powerful upper class consists in each

chambers or tents, and caravan serais always surprises the Western observer with its rapidity, efficiency, and penetration.

Poetry is so much part of everyday living that the ambulant vendors in the streets of Oriental towns praise their wares in rhymed ditties recited to special tunes. Schoolchildren in the old-fashioned Koran schools compete with one another in composing poems by way of a pastime, and in many lands versification is indulged in by people in all walks of life, rich and poor, literate and illiterate.

Inseparable from poetry is music, which is perhaps the most individualistic of arts in the Middle East. Not only will two performers never give the same interpretation of a traditional musical piece, but the same musician will only rarely play or sing the same song twice in exactly the same manner. The performer is usually also his own composer, and even when playing a well-known tune he will inevitably introduce variations and additions of his own, under the spur of the moment's mood. Moreover, the Middle Eastern musician, as a rule, also builds his own musical instrument; his musical training as an apprentice to a master begins by learning how to make for himself an instrument of his own.[12] In the shadow theater, a favorite though at present rapidly declining pastime, the master of the theater makes his own figures, writes his own plays, directs the performance, and plays the main roles.[13] Similarly, the storytellers who can be heard in cafés during the festive nights of the fast month Ramadan, although bound by certain general traditional lines, nevertheless combine the arts of the novelist, the poet, and the actor, and often those of the composer and instrumental performer as well. The distinction sharply drawn in the West between creative artist and performer simply does not exist in the Middle East, where every performance involves the creation of at least a new, individual variation on the original theme.

Tradition also determines the framework of the visual arts; but here too the frame can be filled in in varying ways, according to the talents and inclinations of the individual artist or artisan. What is, however, even more significant for the cultural picture as a whole is the fact that in traditional Middle Eastern culture almost all branches of everyday work are permeated with aesthetic qualities; the beauty of objects everywhere complements their utility. Art is called upon to embellish everything. The richer a man the more time he spends in practicing and enjoying the arts, but the poor as well, the great masses of the simple people, live a life enriched by aesthetic values.

No definite line can be drawn between the arts and crafts in Middle Eastern culture. Articles of clothing such as headgear, mantles, belts, and sandals are in style, color, and decoration closely dependent upon custom fixed by age-old tradition which allows individual talent and taste to express themselves only in relatively minor variations. At the same time, the absence of mass production and the factory system and the corresponding prevalence of handcrafts, mean a greater reliance on trained skill and dexterity, on the ability of the individual artisan to design and execute an article according to the discriminating taste of individual customers. The execution of a piece of work, whether it be a shoe, chair, water pipe, brass tray, rug, lamp, camel litter, basket, or earthenware jug, from its inception to its completion, gives the artisan a deep sense of satisfaction and a keen interest in his work. Most artisans are actually artists whose aesthetic judgment plays an important role in their work. Thus aesthetics is an integral part of artisanship.

Aesthetic tradition is closely linked to religious tradition in the Middle East. Although religious rituals may in principle be performed everywhere, they have always been preferably localized at temples and shrines that are highly aesthetic foci of visual and vocal arts all over the Middle East. Annual religious festivals, which are great events in the life of Middle Eastern peoples, are aesthetic-religious-emotional affairs rich in artistic pageantry.

Although officially the vast majority (about 95 per cent) of the Middle Eastern peoples belong to one of several sects of Islam, actually their religious life contains many elements going back to pre-Islamic and even to pre-Christian and pre-Hebrew times. The belief in and propitiation of various spirits, ghosts, and demons (*ghūls*, *jinns*, *'afrīts*, *zārs* etc.), many of them connected with natural objects; divination and interpretation of dreams and omens; belief in the evil eye; the use of charms and amulets; the practice of making vows and sacrifices; these are in the main the more ancient elements of belief and ritual that are often overlaid with only a thin veneer of Islamic doctrine and practice. This is true of both nomads and sedentary peoples, though the latter are generally more inclined to venerate saints at annual pilgrimages to their tombs and to observe the Five Pillars of the Faith,[14] which are almost entirely ignored by the nomads. The absence of ancestor worship from this quasi-animistic religious complex is remarkable.

It is a sign of the complexity of Middle Eastern religious culture that, side by side with the persistence of such early manifestations of religion, one finds such developments as theological schools and colleges, and religious doctrines spiritually and ethically equal to those of Judaism and Western Christianity. Significant in this connection are the religious orders and brotherhoods whose members dedicate their lives to the service of God by voluntarily denying themselves worldly goods to varying degrees, and by following special "paths" and rituals of their own, often for the purpose of inducing ecstasy. These confraternities, one of the most important of which is that of the Senussi in Cyrenaica, sprang primarily from Sufism (Islamic mysticism), but they often became, very soon after their initial success, strongly political and practical in character.

More significant, however, than the varieties of religious doctrine and practice, is the basically religious orientation of the Middle Eastern peoples. The totality of life is permeated with religion, which holds supreme sway over the great majority of the population, and especially in the nomadic camp and the agricultural village that have been the strongholds of religious traditionalism. Religion is thus the fundamental motivating force behind most aspects of culture, and has its say in practically every act and moment in life. Observance of traditional forms and rites, whether of the official or the popular kind, is an integral part of everyday life. Religion not expressed in formal observance is inconceivable. Morality, too, always appears in the guise of religion and is merely one of its manifestations; moral law dissociated from religion does not exist for people steeped in Middle Eastern culture.

The connection between religion and art has been touched

upon already, but it goes further than the stimulus given by religion to the arts or the service rendered by them to religion. The scope of Middle Eastern art is itself closely circumscribed by religion, to the extent that certain fields are excluded and others concentrated upon intensively. The decorative arts and architecture in which the Middle Eastern artistic genius most fully expresses itself are the fields most closely associated with religion. But religion claims its due even in the secular uses of art, as exemplified by the ever recurring use of the name of Allah and of Koranic passages as decorative devices on a multitude of objects including tiles and trays, lamps and daggers, vases and plates, etc., made of such divers materials as glass, clay, china, wood, and various precious or common metals.

All custom and tradition are basically religious; for whatever is old and customary and traditional is hallowed by religion that itself is mainly tradition and custom, and only to a small extent doctrine and law. Thus the entire field of custom, wide and infinitely ramified in its permeation of everyday life, is incapable of being divorced from religion either in theory or in practice. Whatever man does in his waking or sleeping hours during his entire lifespan on this earth, and also what is done to him in his prenatal and post-mortem existence, always conform to custom, tradition, and religion. These three, then, religion, tradition, and custom, form an inseparable three-in-one constellation that rule the skies of Middle Eastern life.

Another characteristic trait of religion in the Middle East is its distinctly dual aspect of materialism on the one hand and spiritualism on the other. The two neatly balanced main concerns of Middle Eastern religion are physical well-being in this world and spiritual welfare after death. God is expected to dispense material blessings to his people in this life, and to compensate the unfortunate but deserving with his blessings in the afterlife. Hence the accent of righteousness, on the purity of the soul, as the only real achievement of man, in contradistinction to worldly goods that are viewed as worthless encumbrances. The supreme good man can acquire is of a moral quality, but moralism always involves ritualism. For the great masses of the poor, many of whom live in poverty unknown in our Western world, religion with its moralistic and spiritualist tenets and with its great promise of future reward is an asset of inestimable psychological value. Owing to the sway religion holds over performance, and the grooves it cuts into thinking and feeling, life with its vicissitudes and disappointments is appraised from a wider angle, from a long-range perspective, in which sojourn on this earth with all its possible gains and losses appears as a mere lower and lesser half of a great totality of existence whose essentials and ultimates lie in the Beyond. Spiritual outlook thus moves on a higher plane, beyond the reaches of discomfort, pain, anguish, and privation. Hence that composure, that peace of mind, preserved even in the face of great adversity, which ever and again astonish Western observers. The other side of the picture is that religious systems able to give *this* to their followers almost inevitably exercise a powerful hold on them and create a state of mind conducive to intolerance, fanaticism, and cleavage to narrow sectarian lines.

To sum up, the following features characterize traditional Middle Eastern culture: (1) A basic ecologic dichotomy: on the one hand, camel-breeding nomadic tribes living on animal husbandry and, on the other, settled villagers living on agricultural cultivation, corresponding to the desert and the sown regions. (2) The presence of transitional or intermediary types of human societies ranging from sheep and goat or cattle herders practicing a limited nomadism, through seminomadic tribes in various stages of sedentarization, to almost completely settled tribes. (3) The nomadic and seminomadic groups exhibit a tribal structure that is practically identical everywhere. (4) The village is usually divided along kinship lines, but is fairly homogeneous as far as occupational structure is concerned, practically all its inhabitants engaging in agricultural pursuits. (5) Constant commercial exchange takes place between the settled and the nomadic population in each area, with the local town as its focus. (6) Until a few decades ago, however, the nomadic tribes often raided the weaker villagers, regarding them as their legitimate prey. (7) The urban population, and more precisely its middle and upper class, though numerically insignificant, takes in every respect the leadership (in religion, education, art, politics, business, etc.).

(8) The triple class structure is pronounced in the towns, rudimentary in the villages, and almost nonexistent in the nomadic camp. (9) Westernization is centered in the towns and, within the towns, is strongest among the upper class, less advanced in the middle class, and incipient in the lower class. (10) The extended, patrilineal, patrilocal, patriarchal, endogamous, and polygynous family is the basic social and economic unit in camp, village, and town, the individual being subordinated to the family. (11) Strongly marked double standards of sexual morality prevail, with great emphasis on premarital virginity and female purity. (12) Veiling of women is practiced sporadically, being most prevelant in the conservative middle and upper classes of urban society. (13) In the nomadic camps and the villages, the social units larger than the family are based on kinship lines. (14) In the towns such associations as the guilds are based on occupation but membership is often inherited. (15) The individual participates in social groupings larger than the family not on an individual basis but through his family membership. (16) Indications of a dual organization can be found everywhere. (17) On the local level (in camps and villages) social control and political leadership are based on family ties and influences, with the powers divided between headman and council. (18) On the higher level, in the capitals and other centrally located towns, the feudalistic, oligarchic, and at times despotic rule is slowly being mitigated by newly introduced Western forms of government, respectively transformed into dictatorship with capitalistic control and a disproportionate accumulation of wealth in the hands of a few "great" families. (19) Poverty, subsistence-level life, with extremely high incidence of disease, high birth rate, high death rate, and low life expectancy are general, with the situation somewhat better in the towns than in the villages and camps. (20) Very high rates of illiteracy all over the Middle East stamp it with the character of an illiterate culture. (21) There is a great preoccupation with folklore: folk poetry, folk song, folk tales, folk music, riddles, proverbs. (22) There is also an intensive permeation of everyday life by the aesthetic element, with the fields and the overall forms of aesthetic expression being determined by tradition. (23) One of the most outstanding characteristics is an all-pervasive

religiosity, consisting of elements of belief, ritual, custom, and morality, and embracing a wide range of variation regarding concrete content. (24) The belief in God and His will is intense and general, but is accompanied by the belief in spirits, demons, and ghosts and by saint worship in the villages ; ancestor worship, on the other hand, is absent. (25) Finally, a broad outlook on human existence can be found everywhere, including the firm belief in a reward and punishment in an after life and accompanied by detachment from material values and indifference to adversity.

II. Some Problems of the Middle Eastern Culture Continent

Characteristics of the Culture Area

Observations on the culture of the Middle East may be made in the light of four characteristics that are generally taken to indicate a culture area type of spatial distribution.

The first of these four characteristics is the existence of a certain correlation between a culture area and the geographical area that is its locus. Culture areas roughly correspond to ecologic areas. Certain elements in the culture evince a dependence on geographic and ecologic factors. There is thus a definite relationship between the culture and its geographic environment.

The second characteristic derives from the observation that there are cultures in which traits group themselves geographically, and others in which they do not.[1] This observation was made by Ruth Benedict and, in accordance with it, Herskovits has stated some fifteen years later than "Experience has shown . . . that it [the idea of culture areas] is not adapted to use where the distribution of geographical differences between peoples is overridden by class stratification resulting from a high degree of specialization that . . . characterizes larger population aggregates" such as the literate societies of Europe and America. "The typical behavior of social class or occupational group is important here. Categories derived from distinctions drawn empirically on the basis of local differences are obviously inapplicable to such cases, and should be replaced by those that are functionally relevant."[2] Translated into quantitative terms, the second characteristic of the culture area could, therefore, be expressed as follows: the less the social and occupational stratification in a geographical area, the greater the theoretical applicability of the culture area concept.

The third characteristic of the culture area is that its center is well defined but its margins are rarely, if ever, clearcut. Boas has pointed out that the areal distribution of different aspects of culture, such as technology, beliefs, social forms, religion, art, and music, may be nonconcordant.[3]

This means that the usefulness of the culture area concept as a classificatory tool is limited, since it frequently leaves doubt as to the borderline that divides two contiguous culture areas from each other. This criticism has been met only partially by stressing the fact that, as Kroeber put it, "the culmination of these [different] aspects [of culture] tend actually to coincide in the same centers" which therefore "are to be construed as foci of radiation."[4] Wissler has accordingly mapped his areas in America only schematically, emphasizing their centers in which the culture is most typical and intensive.[5] Implicit in this discussion about the clear-cut center and dubious borders is the quantitative assumption that the greater the cultural homogeneity within an area and the clearer its limits, the less doubtful its culture area character.

The fourth characteristic of the culture area refers to the time aspect. Wissler stated that "a distribution of narrow range may be suspected of being an innovation, whereas one of wide range would be of respectable age."[6] Kroeber, further generalizing, emphasized that the culture area "is primarily classificatory and descriptive, therefore static; but like every sound 'natural' classification it implies a genetic one."[7] A culture area is thus assumed to be the result of historical processes. One could tentatively formulate a quantitative relationship between age and area: the larger the spatial extent of the culture area, the longer the historical processes that went into its making.

The "Culture Continent" Character of the Middle East

Let us now examine the Middle East in the light of these four characteristics. With regard to the first characteristic, the dependence of culture on habitat, it can be stated categorically that there are few world areas in which there is such a close correlation as in the Middle East between the geographic pattern of the natural environment and the cultural pattern of the peoples. Between 90 and 95 per cent of the entire area is desert or desert-like steppe, interspersed everywhere, however, as well as surrounded by fertile regions of cultivated or cultivable land. This alternation of desert and sown with a transition either sudden or gradual from the one into the other is the basic ecologic pattern of the Middle East. To the south this area is bounded by the humid forest region of central Africa; to the north by the Mediterranean and the Black Seas; and to the southeast by the Arabian Sea and the humid forest region of the Indian subcontinent. To the northeast, in Central Asia, is found the only contiguous area that to some extent is comparable geographically to the Middle East. However, the Middle East with its true deserts lies south of latitude 38° N., whereas the Central Asian steppes lie to the north of the same latitude. Differences in elevation, water resources, and climatic conditions further set off the two regions, and make different cultural adaptations necessary. The limits of the natural area of the Middle East are thus drawn clearly enough and, as we shall see instantly, are closely concordant with the limits of the Middle Eastern culture continent.

When we examine the cultural correspondences to this geographic area and pattern, we are actually shifting our attention from the first to the second characteristic of the culture area, according to which a geographic patterning of cultures within a larger region is a criterium of the applicability of the culture area concept.

The Middle East lies in this respect, just as it does geographically, in the middle between Negro Africa and Europe. Negro Africa is characterized by chiefly geographic groupings of cultures almost as suitable for classification on an areal basis as are the native cultures of America. In the Middle East no area shows a cultural homogeneity comparable to that of a typical culture area in Negro Africa. On the other hand, neither does the Middle East partake of the European pattern with its accent on social classes and occupational groupings.

The specifically Middle Eastern sociocultural pattern is characterized by the presence in every part of the area of two main population categories, each with a typical ecologic adjustment of its own: nomadic tribes inhabiting the deserts and steppes on the one hand, and settled groups concentrated in those regions capable of agricultural cultivation on the other. This schematic dichotomy into nomadic and settled aggregates reveals, of course, under closer inspection a much more complicated picture of social structure. With the exception of the townspeople, these further subdivisions show a close correspondence to finer distinctions within subtypes of geographic environment, and thus further corroborate the first characteristic of the culture area, according to which a definite correlation exists between a culture area and the geographic area it occupies.

Between the true desert and the sown there is in most parts of the Middle East a transitional semidesert belt, barely suited for agricultural purposes but offering much better pastures than the true desert. This semidesert belt is the home of the sheep- and goat-breeding nomads whose wandering territory is much more restricted than that of the true or camel nomads. Again, in the mountainous sections of the Middle East, is found yet another type of seminomads: the mountain nomads who practice transhumance. In the cultivable areas, for example, along the Mediterranean littoral and the great riverbeds of the Nile, the Tigris, and the Euphrates, in the oases and the mountain tracts, are found agricultural villages with a population in many respects different from any of the nomadic varieties. These sedentary peoples who form more than 85 per cent of the total population of the Middle East are mostly villagers but, in addition, they range from small-townpeople to big-city folk with a display of occupational specialization increasing in proportion to the size of the urban aggregates they inhabit.

Starting out from a big city such as Damascus in Syria, Cairo in Egypt, Tripoli in Libya, or Casablanca in Morocco, one can find first a number of agricultural villages situated in the midst of cultivated territory, then a steppe region utilized by goat and sheep herders practicing a limited nomadism, and finally the desert where are encamped the camel-breeding Bedouin tribes, all within a radius of fifty miles or less. Were one to apply the culture area concept to such a narrowly delimited tract alone, one would find that four separate culture areas can be distinguished in it: urban, agricultural, seminomadic, and true nomadic. However, as one proceeds from one country to another, from one region to another, one finds this same spatial sequence repeated again and again, so that the fourfold division appears as a single unit showing a definite configurational patterning. The entire Middle Eastern culture continent thus appears as a tissue consisting of a number of cells, each one of which has an identical or very similar inner structure.

Such a cell pattern in itself is not a uniquely Middle Eastern phenomenon. It is known to exist to a smaller or larger extent in most human societies. In the modern Western world one finds it represented by the ubiquitous range from city to village or farm. But unique for the Middle East is the specific structure of the cell with its four components, the urban, agricultural, seminomadic, and nomadic population elements. In fact, this pattern of social structure with its local heterogeneity that recurs consistently all over the area is so typical for the Middle East that it must be regarded as one of the most important criteria when an attempt is being made to determine its limits.

In turning now to the third characteristic, the one that can be reformulated as stating that a culture area is only as good as its boundaries, let us attempt to draw the borderline of the Middle East with both the geographic and the cultural angles in mind. This task is made relatively easy because in no geographic area contiguous to the Middle East is either the typical Middle Eastern desert-sown pattern or the equally typical Middle Eastern sociocultural configuration duplicated.

Even if we disregard for a moment the nomadic-and-settled pattern and concentrate on the nomadic element alone, no contiguous geographic area is found to contain a nomadic population sufficiently similar to the Middle Eastern nomads to raise serious doubts as to the delimitation of the Middle Eastern culture continent.

The only comparable nomadic culture in any world area contiguous to the Middle East is found in Central Asia. However, in addition to the environmental factors referred to above, cultural factors that can be isolated by a careful perusal of documentation available from both areas show that Central Asial nomadism and Middle Eastern nomadism constitute two very distinct cultures, different enough to preclude their inclusion under one cultural entity.[8] It is sufficient to refer to one complex only that can serve both as a characteristic of the nomadic element in all parts of the Middle East and as a clearly marked distinguishing feature between it and the Central Asian nomads. This is the type of shelter used all over the Middle East by the nomads and semi-nomads: the black hair tent, which essentially consists of a single large rectangular piece of tent cloth made of camel's and goat's hair, spread upon a number of poles and held in place by long outstretched ropes pegged to the ground. This black hair tent is practically the only type of shelter used by the nomads and semi-nomads of the Middle East, its form and construction showing only minor and insignificant variations from Morocco and Río de Oro in the west to Afghanistan and Balujistan in the east. In the Indus Valley the nomadic camp is replaced by settled agricultural villages that are the westernmost outposts of the cultures of the Indian subcontinent.

In the Plain of Turkestan the place of the Middle Eastern black tent is taken by the *yurt*, the round dome-capped tent built around a complex and solid frame of latticelike rods of willow or beech-wood, tied together with rawhide, and covered with white or gray sheep's felt. The boundary line between the black hair tent and the *yurt* is sharply drawn. To its northeastern edge the Iranian Plateau is the domain of the Iranian tribes with their black hair tents; down in the plains, beginning with the Gorgan Valley within the political boundaries of Iran and Afghanistan, and to the northeast for thousands of miles is the territory of the Turkoman, Kirgiz, Kazak, and Mongol *yurt*-dwelling tribes. Wherever *yurts* appear further to the west, that is, within the Middle East, they belong to isolated Turkoman tribes who in the course of their wanderings reached these western lands. On the other hand, a variety of the black hair tent reappears to the east in Tibet, after a break of several hundreds of miles. What is, however, more significant for a delimitation of the Middle East is the fact that no intermediary or transitional forms exist between the black hair tent and the *yurt*, and that consequently the spatial distribution of each is even more clearly marked off against the other.

The black hair tent is, of course, much more than a single item in the material equipment of nomadic tribes. It is the symbol and the tangible expression of a highly coordinated, complex, and specific way of life: Middle Eastern pastoral nomadism. The hair tent means a special set of material equipment; it indicates animal husbandry concentrating on camels and/or sheep and goats; it is an evidence of seasonal wandering, tribal organization, and of a definite system of values and social attitudes. Wherever it is found it thus testifies to the presence of the nomadic or seminomadic component of the Middle Eastern sociocultural configuration.

The nomads and seminomads, however, are only part of the Middle Eastern sociocultural pattern. They have, in every section of the Middle East, clearly patterned contacts with the settled population. That is, the interaction among the different parts of the local cells is largely the same all over the area. In fact, this specific dynamism and functional interdependence among the different population elements is everywhere the inevitable concomitant of the structural patterning referred to earlier.

Equally significant for a study of the Middle East from the culture area point of view is the fact that in all those aspects of culture not contingent upon ecologic adjustment a surprising homogeneity can be observed among the population elements inhabiting the area, however different the economic bases of their existence.

More about the definiteness of the boundaries of the Middle Eastern culture area can be said within the context of its time aspect. The correlation between time and space was stated to be the fourth characteristic of the culture area. The problem of Americanists such as Wissler was to reconstruct probable historical processes from a study of geographic distribution. Their age-area concept began with observed data in a geographic area and aimed at reaching an understanding of otherwise unknown occurrences in past ages.

In the Middle East, we are faced with a reversed situation. Owing to the specific trends of interests, first religious and later scientific, an enormous amount of attention has been focused on the history and archaeology of the Middle East, to the relative neglect of its present-day cultures. The result is that we know more about several phases of life in ancient Egypt or in ancient

Mesopotamia than in modern Egypt or Iraq. Compared to what we know about cultural interchange and influences among the great cultures of ancient Near Eastern civilization, our knowledge of the distribution and formation of modern cultures in the area is meager. In such a situation, the quest from the known to the unknown must, obviously, proceed in the opposite direction from the one familiar to Americanists and to anthropologists in general. Our rich historical knowledge of the area must be brought to bear upon the problems of the spatial distribution and interrelation of the present-day cultures in the area.

If Wissler's dictum that a wide distributional range indicates respectable age is true also in the reverse, the unparalleled age of documented cultures in the core area of the Middle East will lead us to expect an extremely wide spatial distribution of the modern culture that is the end result of this long cultural history. In other words, we will expect to find widely diffused over an uncommonly extensive geographic region cultures or cultural complexes going back ultimately to ancient Near Eastern origins.

Yet another consideration will strengthen us in this expectation. The culture areas in America were found roughly to correspond to ecologic or natural areas. As against the relatively small size of these areas in America, and especially in North America, one encounters in the Middle East a huge area characterized by a more or less uniform overriding geographic pattern, to which a similarly large area of cultural diffusion can be expected to correspond. The two factors, historical and geographic, represent an exceptional set of circumstances that facilitated the spread of Middle Eastern culture from the old core area until it reached the present-day dimensions of the Middle Eastern culture continent.

In a rough diachronic scheme, three major elements can be distinguished in the cultural configuration of each part of the Middle East: two making for homogeneity and a third for diversity. The two homogenizing influences are those of Islam and of the ancient Near Eastern civilizations, while the diversifying factor is the local tradition of greatly varying age.

Islamic culture started out from Arabia in the seventh century and spread over the entire Middle East within a century after the death of Mohammed (632). Islam, it may be reiterated here, is more than a religion in the sense in which this concept is known to us from the Western world. It is rather comparable to Hinduism, notwithstanding the basic differences between the two with regard to concrete content, insofar as both Hinduism and Islam are *total ways of life*. Islam as a total way of life is founded on a tradition that goes back to Mohammed, either actually or fictitiously, or to his companions and first disciples. It incorporates religious, cultic, and doctrinal elements, and was in its very beginnings a mixture of Mohammedan innovation and local Ḥijāzī tradition and folk custom, which it disseminated in the course of its conquests from Sind to Spain, from the Golden River to the Golden Road.

However, the distribution of Islam is considerably wider than that of Middle Eastern culture. There is, moreover, a marked difference between the cultures of the Middle Eastern Muslim peoples and those of the large Muslim ethnic aggregates residing beyond the boundaries of the Middle East. This brings us to the older, pre-Islamic processes of cultural diffusion that took place in the area. For some four thousand years preceding Alexander the Great, the ancient Near East was the primary center of cultural development and dissemination over a major part of the three continents of the Old World. Influences from this core area emanated in a sequence of waves. It would be extremely fascinating and instructive to collate the available information as to the differences in the spatial spread of ancient Near Eastern cultural influences on the one hand and of Islamic cultural influences on the other, all around the margins of the Middle East. This, however, cannot be done at the present time. Only from one contiguous area, that of African cultures, can a few data be adduced illustrating the problem and at the same time helping to reach a clearer understanding of the relationship between age and area in the Middle East.

The Boundaries

Historical data as to the spread of ancient Near Eastern culture into Negro Africa are meager, but a study of the spatial distribution of certain cultural elements points the way. There are several cultural traits or complexes that originated in antiquity somewhere in the general area of the ancient Near East, and which today are no longer found in the Middle East but have survived in Negro Africa.

One of these is the extremely significant complex of *sacred kingship*, which occupied a focal position in ancient Near Eastern

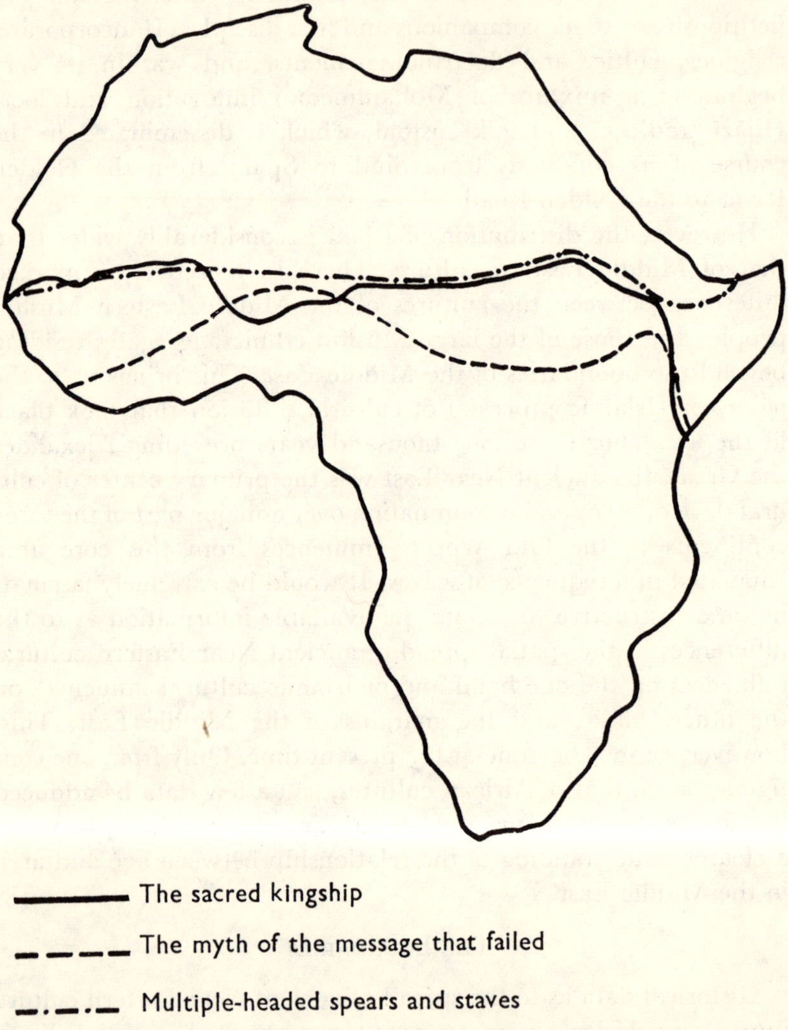

Map 1. The northern boundary lines of the present-day distribution of three ancient Near Eastern cultural features in Africa

cultures, and spread far beyond the present boundaries of Islam in Africa. Within the Middle East itself, sacred kingship has been obliterated by Islam with the result that sacred kingship and Islam form two mutually exclusive complexes sharply delimited against each other.[9]

Although the socioreligious complexes of Islam and sacred kingship respectively are of outstanding importance in the life of the peoples concerned, they in themselves would not be sufficient to delimit the southern boundary line of the Middle Eastern culture area. However, we find that this boundary line is roughly the same as that of several material traits that too originated in the ancient Near East and were subsequently superseded in the Middle East by more recent developments, to survive in the ancient form only in Negro Africa. *Multiple-headed spears* are a case in point. Bidents or two-headed spears were ritual objects in ancient Egypt and adjoining Libya in prehistoric as well as historic times. In ancient South Arabian (Sabaean and Minaean) inscriptions bidents, together with tridents, appear as symbols of lightning. The trident as a symbol of lightning and as a royal or divine attribute is known from the Hittites, the Assyrians, the Babylonians, and later the Greeks. Actual tridents survive from ancient Persia and countries to the southeast.

In the modern Middle East multiple-headed spears do not exist. In one place, Morocco, their ceremonial use disappeared about a hundred years ago. In Negro Africa, however, the multiple-pointed spear is very much in evidence to this day, as a badge of office, a ceremonial weapon, a royal emblem, or a cult object. The northern boundary line of its present-day distribution is practically identical with that of sacred kingship.

The distribution of the multiple-headed spears to the east of the Middle Eastern area is not as clear as one would like to have it. But it seems that the further away one moves from the Middle East, the more recent are the specimens found, until one reaches the East Indies, South East Asia, and China, where bidents and tridents have been in use as ceremonial or actual weapons down to the present time.[10]

The disappearance of multiple-headed spears from secular use can be explained by its suppression by Islam as an emblem of sacred kings, and a subsequent extension of this suppression also to its secular use. That sacred kingship itself could not be tolerated by a strictly monotheistic and in its origins highly puritanistic faith such as Islam is easily understandable.

The monotheistic-puritanistic origins of Islam are responsible for the suppression and complete elimination of yet another important ancient Near Eastern culture complex from most of the Middle Eastern area. The *plastic representation* and portraiture of living beings, animal, human, and divine, was of such significance in the ancient Near East that without them ancient Near Eastern religions (with the exception of the religion of the Hebrews from the sixth century B.C. onward) would have been inconceivable. And since religion was in its earliest Near Eastern manifestations as much a total way of life as it is today in the Middle East, everyday life in the ancient Near East would also have been unthinkable without the esthetoreligious satisfactions offered by plastic arts, and secondarily also by graphic arts. Masterpieces of ancient Egyptian, Syrian, Mesopotamian, Anatolian, and Iranian plastic art survive to this day as splendid witnesses to highly developed cultures with definite artistic orientations. Islam, continuing the late-Hebrew tradition of aversion against plastic (as well as graphic) representations, put an end to this great artistic efflorescence, and forced the artistic genius of the peoples converted to its creed into such limited expressions as afforded by decorative arts. The Middle East has thus become artistically an essentially sculptureless area, to such an extent that even the Coptic church, the largest, oldest, and most Middle Eastern of all the Eastern Christian churches, foregoes any plastic representation of Jesus, Mary, and the saints.

Only to the northeast of the Middle Eastern culture area do we encounter another culture that is likewise devoid of representative art. In Central Asia, Islam has had the same effect in this respect as in the Middle East: it eliminated any plastic art that may have existed previously. To the north, in the Mediterranean area of Christian Europe, sculpture is a significant element in religious life in the Catholic as well as the Orthodox churches. To the south, the borderline that marks the limits of the distribution of the sacred kingship and the multiple-headed spear also marks the borders of the vigorous Negro sculpture zone. To the southeast, in India, sculpture occupies in Hindu as well as in Buddhist cults a position similar to the one it has in Southern Europe.

With regard to *music*, it is the contention of musicologists who studied the Middle East that it is an area with definite musical characteristics of its own. It is pointed out that the same musical instruments are used and the same types of music are produced all over the area. Some of these musical instruments are old in the area, and certainly antedate Islam. Other ancient Near Eastern instruments disappeared from the area itself and survive in Negro Africa. A concrete example of the latter is the peculiar ancient Egyptian harp, known from its pictorial representation on ancient monuments, which does not exist any longer in any part of the Middle East but survives in unchanged form among the Azande and the Baganda in East Africa, and among the Jukun, Busawa, Igbira, Chamba, Verre, and others in West Africa.[11] All these tribes are grouped along the southern borders of the Middle Eastern culture continent, and just outside its limits.

Our last example to illustrate the same type of spatial distribution and the same position of the borderline is taken from the world of *myth*. In the literatures of the ancient Near East there is a type of story or myth known as "The Perverted Message" or "The Message That Failed." Frazer has shown that the Biblical story of the fall of man and the loss of his immortality is one version of this story.[12] In the modern Middle East no traces of this story are known to have survived. But the story of the message that failed reappears in a well-documented distribution in Negro Africa, again just south of the limits of the Middle Eastern culture area.[13]

If these examples could be sufficiently multiplied, they would show the Middle Eastern culture as occupying that centrally located geographic area in which the Islamic culture has superseded ancient Near Eastern culture complexes. Just outside its limits, however, many ancient Near Eastern culture complexes survive. This marginal survival is best documented in Negro Africa. In other contiguous areas more research is needed to demonstrate the same phenomenon, although hypothetically its presence seems most probable. The Middle Eastern culture continent would thus be found to comprise those regions which are Islamic at present and which in the past were under the cultural sway of the great ancient Near Eastern cultures. Regions that were reached by only one of these two great cultural waves are marginal to the Middle Eastern culture continent, and lie outside its boundaries proper. The area thus defined historically is coextensive with the geographically determined desert and sown area, as well as with the ethnographically delimited distribution of the nomadic and settled configuration.

The proposed southern delimitation of the Middle East in Africa has recently received important corroboration by the work of George Peter Murdock. After a careful examination of the culture groups of Africa, Murdock compiled three distribution maps of its culture provinces (all the three south of what is suggested above as the southern boundary of the Middle East) as well as a distribution map of East African pastoralists.[14] The northern boundary line, resulting from a superimposition of these four maps on one another, coincides generally with the southern boundary line proposed above. This line can thus be considered fairly well established.

To the northeast, the limits of the Middle East run roughly along the Caucasus and the northern borders of Iran and Afghanistan. Elsewhere the writer has adduced evidence to show that Middle Eastern nomadism can be clearly distinguished from Central Asian nomadism and that, strictly speaking, the limits of the Middle East should be drawn where the typical Middle Eastern black hair tent is replaced by the yurt, the round, dome-shaped felt tent, equally typical of Central Asian nomadism.[15] This delimitation excludes a corner of Iran (the Gorgan valley to the southeast of the Caspian Sea) and part of northern Afghanistan from the Middle Eastern culture continent. We shall, nevertheless, discuss briefly this marginal area at the end of our listing of the culture areas of the Middle East.

To the east, the boundary line of the Middle East runs roughly north to south across the middle of Western Pakistan. To the west of this line live the nomadic Balujis who are a definitely Middle Eastern people by all criteria. To the east of it live the Sinds, in every respect a South Asian (Indian) population.

The Problem of Subdivision

The problem of how to subdivide the vast land area of the Middle East into cultural subareas has received only scant attention. Especially its Asian part has remained neglected in this respect. Those who put forward suggestions as to the mapping of culture areas in the African part of the Middle East were without exception Africanists, interested more in the "black" two thirds than in the "white" northern one third of Africa.

The first attempt to map the major regions of Africa was made by an ingenious Frenchman, A. de Préville, in 1894.[16] Taking the main animal species bred by the pastoral peoples as the basis of classification, he generalized broadly and divided North Africa into four roughly horizontal strips, which he then extended over into the Asian part of the Middle East, giving them an upward slant. As the map opposite page 14 in his book shows at a glance, he regarded the entire north coast of Africa as far south as approximately the 30th parallel as the region of horsemen (*cavaliers*). In southwest Asia he assigned to this region a broad belt north of a line drawn from the southern tip of the Sinai Peninsula to the northern end of the Persian Gulf and thence continuing in a northeasterly direction. South of this lay his second zone, the region of camelmen (*chameliers*), which comprised most of the Sahara, Central Arabia, and southern Iran. The third one was the much thinner region of goatmen (*chevriers*), stretching from the Atlantic coast of Africa south of Río de Oro, across the Red Sea and the southern part of the Persian Gulf, to southern Iran. His southernmost zone within our area was the region of cattlemen (*vachers*), corresponding roughly to the area between the 12th and the 16th parallels all through the width of Africa, turning south to include most of Ethiopia and Somalia, then across the Bab el-Mandeb along the South Arabian coast, and finally across the Gulf of Oman into the southeastern corner of Iran.

Although there is little in this attempt that can stand the test of time, credit must be given to Préville for the idea of the geographic plotting of regions in the Middle East on the basis of types of animal husbandry.

The next attempt, made by Jerome Dowd in 1907, constitutes

what was in fact a step backward as compared to the work of Préville. Quite apart from the numerous untenable hypotheses contained in Dowd's book, he divided the entire northern third of Africa into two zones only: a northern "camel zone" and a southern "cattle zone." His dividing line between the two regions was drawn from west to east somewhere in the middle of Préville's region of goatmen.[17]

Completely different from these early amateurish attempts was the one made in 1924 by an outstanding Africanist, Melville J. Herskovits. Although Herskovits titled his first published paper on the subject "A Preliminary Consideration of the Culture Areas of Africa,"[18] he retained the general outline in two subsequent revisions with a few changes confined to Negro Africa. In this revised form he reprinted his map of the "Culture Areas of Africa" in his *Man and His Works*.[19]

As an Africanist, Herskovits' main interest as well as field experience lay in Negro Africa. In the discussion accompanying his map he described at some detail the culture area he named "Western Sudan," which comprises the southwestern corner of the African part of the Middle East (as delimited above, p. 13), as well as the northwestern areas of Negro African cultures; but he dismissed in a few lines the areas he termed "Eastern Sudan," "Desert Area," and "Egypt."[20] As to the north coast of Africa, down to a distance of over three hundred miles from the Mediterranean coastline of Tunisia, Algeria, and Morocco, he excluded it entirely from his scheme on the ground of "its close affinity to Europe."[21]

To any student of the Middle East it is beyond doubt that the North African coastal area constitutes one of the most characteristic varieties of typical Middle Eastern culture, and that its affinity to Europe, although closer than that of most of the rest of Africa, about equals in degree that of Lower Egypt and the Levant coastal area.

The east-west dividing line Herskovits draws between the "Desert Area" and the "Western Sudan" runs directly through the very middle of the Tuareg area and cannot, therefore, be regarded as meaningful. Similarly, his north-to-south dividing line between "Western Sudan" and "Eastern Sudan" runs through the Kanuric-speaking East-Saharan area, and should therefore be moved some three hundred miles to the west.

In 1929, the German Africanist, Richard Thurnwald, published a study on the "Social Systems of Africa."[22] Thurnwald did not attempt to map culture areas, but he classified African social systems into nine types, of which, however, only two have representatives in the Middle Eastern part of Africa as well. Conversely, the great majority of the social systems found in this part do not fit into any of Thurnwald's nine categories. Evidently, this prominent Africanist has also paid but scant attention to the northern one third of the continent of his specialization.

In 1937, Wilfrid D. Hambly in his *Source Book for African Anthropology*[23] mapped the culture areas of Africa. The Middle Eastern part of Africa was divided by him as follows: (1) The Nile Valley; (2) "A region of migration of northern Hamites," occupying the entire north coast of Africa, from Mauretania in the west to close to the Nile delta in the east, and extending approximately 440 miles southward from the Tunisian-Algerian-Moroccan coast line; (3) "The Saharan region of camel-keeping cultures," subdivided into (3*A*) Tuareg (west-central Sahara), (3*B*) Tebu, Tibbu and Teda of Tibesti, and (3*C*) Arabs of the Libyan oases. This No. 3 covers the entire Sahara, and borders in the south on the narrow east-west beltlike area (4), termed "A region of pastoral nomads possessing cattle, sheep, goats, horses, and perhaps camels also." Hambly included in this area most of the region between the Nile and the Red Sea. To the south of (4), again beltlike in its east-west stretch, lies (5), the dividing line between the two running in a roughly straight line touching the Senegal River, the northern bend of the Niger, and Lake Chad. This is stated to be a "parkland area" and a pastoral region with seasonal migrations.

The main advance of this scheme as against the earlier one of Herskovits is in the adumbration of a threefold subdivision of the Sahara area (No. 3). Apart from this, the criticism leveled against Herskovits applies also to Hambly.

The most recent mapping of the culture provinces in Middle Eastern Africa has been made by George Peter Murdock in his volume *Africa: Its Peoples and Their Culture History.*[24] While the writer found himself in agreement with Murdock with regard to the delimitation of the southern boundary of Middle Eastern cultures in Africa, he must disagree with him as to his classifications.

Murdock treats the entire Middle Eastern Africa in three of the eleven parts of this book. In Part 4, entitled "North African Agricultural Civilizations," he discusses the Berbers (Chap. 15) and the Saharan Negroes (Chap. 16); in Part 9, "East African Pastoralism," one chapter deals with the "Beja" (Chap. 40); while Part 11, "North and West African Pastoralism," comprises four chapters, "Bedouin Arabs" (Chap. 52); "Tuareg" (Chap. 53); "Baggara" (Chap. 54), and "Fulani" (Chap. 55).

The over-all classificatory point of view, therefore, is ecologic: the population is grouped into an agricultural and a pastoral category. This in itself is perfectly sound, and in agreement with the present writer's own elaboration of the basic dichotomy of all the Middle Eastern peoples into nomads and cultivators.[25] However, this ecologic classification is of little use when the purpose is to isolate criteria with whose help the Middle East can be divided into culture areas, since, as is pointed out repeatedly in the present volume, both nomads and cultivators are found in every part of the Middle East. Moreover, for the same reason, the breakdown into agricultural and pastoral peoples is not coterminous with linguistic, religious, racial, or ethnic classification, nor with over-all geographic subdivisions. Under the general ecologic classification indicated in his titles of parts 4, 9, and 11, Murdock nevertheless treats ethnic or linguistic groups inhabiting certain geographic areas. He therefore involves himself in numerous difficulties and contradictions.

The first chapter in the book that deals with a Middle Eastern group is Chapter 15, entitled "Berbers." This is one of the chapters contained in Part 4, "North African Agricultural Civilizations" (pp. 111 ff.). Murdock adopts "a strictly linguistic classification in segregating the Berbers from the Arabs in North Africa" (p. 111); in other words, he regards as Berbers only those groups who still speak Berber. These, he finds, fall into 29 groups (totaling four and a half million people), practically all of whom are located in northwestern Africa, i.e. north of latitude 15° N.

and west of longitude 15° E. Of them, 17 groups (or 3,271,000) are stated to be sedentary cultivators; four groups, numbering 733,000, are semisedentary or practice transhumance; three, numbering 450,000, are nomads. As to the remaining three groups, no data are supplied. Geographically, however, the largest part of the Berber language area is inhabited by nomadic groups, the Tuareg. In fact, the Tuareg are treated again, and in greater detail, in Part 11 under "North and West African Pastoralism." A classification which thus places the same population group into two different categories cannot be regarded as satisfactory. Murdock's explanation, that the Tuareg have adapted to a desert environment involving "so many innovations as well as borrowings from the indigenous Negroes and the Bedouin Arabs, that we shall treat them separately in Chapter 53" (p.115), does not eliminate the inconsistency. If his Chapter 15, "Berbers," treats of a population group belonging to "North African Agricultural Civilizations," it is impermissible to include in it Berber-speaking groups which for nearly a thousand years have not been agricultural but nomadic pastoral, and which in addition not only differ from but in fact contrast with the agricultural Berbers in descent rules, social organization, sex mores, material culture, etc. It is obvious that in this case the inconsistency was caused by the attempt to utilize simultaneously an ecologic and a linguistic classification. This cannot work, simply because not all Berbers are agriculturalists.

The inconsistency resulting from the application of these two conflicting classificatory criteria is even more pronounced in Part 11. Here, as the first group of "North and West African Pastoralists," the "Bedouin Arabs" (Chap. 52, pp. 392 ff.) are discussed. "Bedouin Arabs" are, of course, the prototype of desert-dwelling, animal-herding nomads. But the criterion applied by Murdock in listing groups under this heading was, as in the case of his "Berbers," the linguistic one. He lists here *all* the Arabic-speaking groups of North and West Africa, 42 in number, with a total of 32 to 33 million people. Of these, however, only 12 groups numbering close to two million are nomadic pastoralists; three more, numbering a few hundred thousand, are seminomadic or consist of mixed nomadic and sedentary subgroups; and 21 groups, numbering about 30 million, are sedentary cultivators. The ecologic character of the five remaining groups is not stated. Again Murdock tries to smooth over the inconsistency by stating that among the 42 groups listed by him as "Bedouin Arabs" "a number of Arabic-speaking peoples who are descended from the coastal populations that participated fully in the earlier Greco-Roman civilization" should "be segregated." These he terms "Littoral peoples" (Algerians, Cyrenaicans, Egyptians, Jebala, Moroccans, Sahel, Tripolitanians, and Tunisians), and describes as "sedentary and partially urbanized," who, although Islamized and Arabized in the first period of Arab political conquest, "remained to a considerable extent aloof from the Hilalian Bedouins" who invaded North Africa in the eleventh century and established in it the prototype of Bedouin culture (pp. 396 f.). Their economy is based primarily on cereal agriculture with auxiliary arboriculture, animal husbandry, urban handicraft, and trade. They thus contrast with the Bedouin Arabs who "retained, wherever possible, the nomadic pastoral economy they brought with them from Arabia" (p. 397). It is puzzling, to say the least, why a language group of 33 million should be named after its smallest component element, which constitutes about 6 per cent of the total, when over 90 per cent is not Bedouin but sedentary, not pastoral but agricultural, and not even Arab, as far as descent is concerned, but merely "Arabized." If the Berber nomadic Tuareg are classed among "North African agricultural civilizations" because prior to the Hilalian invasion their ancestors were cultivators, then certainly the 30 million "littoral peoples," who were cultivators for centuries prior to the Hilalian invasion and remained agriculturalists to this day, should also be classified under the same "North African agricultural civilizations."

The first conclusion from the foregoing critical consideration of previous attempts at classifying the cultures in North Africa is that in trying to solve the problem of the subdivision of the Middle East into culture areas one must, first of all, liberate the culture area concept from its close association with the geographic area that characterized it in its original application to native American cultures and still haunts those who are engaged in studies of spatial distribution of non-Western cultures. Culture is, of course, carried by human groups, and these, in turn, must have geographic loci as their habitat. In this sense, clusterings of cultures are correlated to geographic areas in the Middle East as well as in any other part of the globe. But, a mapping of cultural similarities and differences in the Middle East does not result in contiguous and clear-cut geographic areas. Instead of regarding the Middle East with its constituent cultures as a patchwork quilt, one has to regard it as a "Kelim" rug, that famous woven variety of Persian carpetry in which the patterning is achieved by the skillful way in which once the warp and once the woof is allowed to emerge to the surface. The basic material consists, throughout the entire area of the carpet, of the same two types of yarn; yet the patterns can nevertheless show considerable variation when one corner of the carpet is compared to another.

This is exactly the case with the specific configuration the component cultures evince in all parts of the Middle East. Unless one were to delimit a culture area extremely narrowly, such as a single oasis cluster or a single nomadic tribal territory, one encounters everywhere both the warp and the woof of the cultural texture, both the nomadic breeders and the settled cultivators. Any attempt at a subdivision of the Middle East into culture areas must find a place in its scheme for both. The proportion in which the two are represented in an area or province and the question of cultural predominance that undoubtedly is correlated with it—these are criteria that can and must be used for purposes of subdivision and classification. The predominance of the Bedouin element in Central Arabia, for instance, stamps that area with a character greatly differing from that of the Nile Valley with its exclusively sedentary population of fellahin.

A phenomenon similar to the one pointed out here has, in fact, been recognized in connection with the mapping of the culture areas of South America. Apart from the coastal area to the north and the west, the entire land mass was divided in 1922 by Wissler into a larger northern area called Amazon and a smaller southern area called Guanaco. Kroeber, a year later, retained Wissler's areas, but renamed them Tropical Forest and Patagonia, respectively.[26] In the great *Handbook of the South American Indians* of the Smithsonian Institution these areas were drastically revised, on the basis of a huge amount of additional information gathered in the intervening years. The neat, straight lines and clearcut, contiguous, almost geometric simplicity of the two areas completely disappeared. Instead, a considerable amount of mutual interpenetration of two major culture types is shown. The area still called the Tropical Forest is found to extend far down the west coast, but contains several major and many minor pockets inhabited by peoples who belong to what is called Marginal culture type, as well as a smaller number of pockets formed by the Circum-Caribbean culture type. The Marginal cultures occupy the entire southern tip of the continent, but their northernmost pocket appears as far north as Venezuela.

This pattern, though complex when compared with the earlier attempts, is simplicity itself in relation to the much more involved interlacings found in the Middle East. Carriers of nomadic and settled cultures are present everywhere, and in many places the picture is further complicated by the presence of towns that dot the area with partly Westernized population islands and thereby obscure the differences between their hinterlands.

Next, the cultural variations evinced by one or both of the constituent ecologic groups in each geographic area must be considered. Both the bedouins of Arabia and the Tuareg of the Sahara are, for example, camel-herding nomads with all the cultural characteristics that this entails in material equipment, in food habits, in the adaptation to desert conditions, and even in social organization and values. Yet, at the same time, a number of significant traits set the two groups sharply off against each other. There are, for instance, marked differences in clothing, language, descent rules, and sex mores.

Or, take the differences between two fellah groups: the Syrian and the Egyptian. Here the clothing, language, descent rules, and sex mores are, although by no means identical, at least very similar. But there are clear differences in methods of work and in the availability of leisure, as well as in temperament and character. Such are the criteria that can with advantage be utilized for classificatory purposes.

The available data, meager as they are, indicate that we have in the Middle East a continuum of nomadic culture and a parallel continuum of settled culture. Starting out from the North Arabian desert as the presumable center of the Middle Eastern nomadic complex, one finds, upon moving up into Jordan and Syria, certain new traits giving nomadic culture there a somewhat different character. Progressing eastward into Iraq, again a new set of traits is added and upon crossing into Iran, yet another one. A similar progression of change can be observed when moving westward across the Red Sea and along the expanses of North Africa. As a concrete example the black hair tent can again be mentioned with its slight variations from tribe to tribe and more marked ones from area to area.

As to the settled cultures, they change in a like manner and even more pronouncedly. Sailing up the Nile from Cairo towards the Sudan frontier and across it, one has a fine opportunity for observing this gradual change. From one village to the next the difference is unnoticeable; having passed twenty or thirty villages and recalling the first one, it becomes discernible; at the hundredth, apparent; south of the Sudan borderline, striking. Thorough studies, including compilations of lists of such progressively increasing differences, will make it possible to plot the Middle Eastern culture areas with a solid factual basis to rely on, instead of conjecture and informed guesswork.

To them have to be added the observations made by old and new local authors and students of Middle Eastern history and society with regard to differences in value culture between one part of the area and another. To mention only one example of such general characterizations, Maqrizi, the fourteenth century Arab historian, quotes Ka'b al-Aḥbār, one of the companions of the Prophet Mohammed, to the effect that when Allah created all things, He gave them each a companion. "I am going to Syria," said Reason; "I will go with you," said Rebellion. "I am going to the Desert," said Poverty; "I am going with you," said Health. "I am going to Egypt," said Abundance; "I shall accompany you," said Resignation.[27] Translated into our terminology, this means that the Syrians were regarded as clever but rebellious; the nomads of the Arabian Desert as poor but healthy; and the Egyptians as wealthy and submissive. Another version of this tradition substitutes for the Syrians bravery in the place of cleverness; and adds that the Iraqis are proud and hypocritical, and that the Yemenis are characterized by faith and modesty.

Nor must one overlook the interaction between the indigenous local cultures and the cultural influences that spread in successive waves from the core area toward the boundaries of the present-day Middle East. In spite of the power of these waves, and especially the last one, Islam, vestiges of the old local cultures have survived in many places, primarily among the settled rural populations of the regions remote from the core area. Even where no distinct "archaic" traits can be recognized, and where a thorough blending of the old and the new has taken place, the persistent effect of the old local cultures can be discerned in the resultant somewhat different local hue of the over-all color of Middle Eastern culture.

Yet another factor that has strengthened the differences among these local entities has been the absence of communications, especially on the folk level, between one localized society and the next. Isolation has not only enabled the old cultural differences to survive; it also favored the development of new differences in the shape of local variants of the superimposed imported cultures. These differences assume significance as soon as we shift our attention from the culture continent as a whole to its component parts. A study of local cultural histories is therefore indispensable for classificatory purposes.

These then are the main avenues of research that will have to be followed for a definitive classification of the Middle Eastern culture continent into culture areas: more descriptive ethnographic material is needed from practically every area; this has to be supplemented by anthropological analyses of the historical material, much of which is available to this day only in the Arabic or Persian or Turkish original. The task will be an arduous one, but the results will be richly rewarding: a fuller understanding of the present-day mosaic of the Middle East, and of the longest recorded cultural development that went into its making.

The Culture Areas of the Middle East

For the time being, a preliminary and tentative mapping of the culture areas in the Middle East can be attempted on the basis of the presently available data. Let us begin with the North African

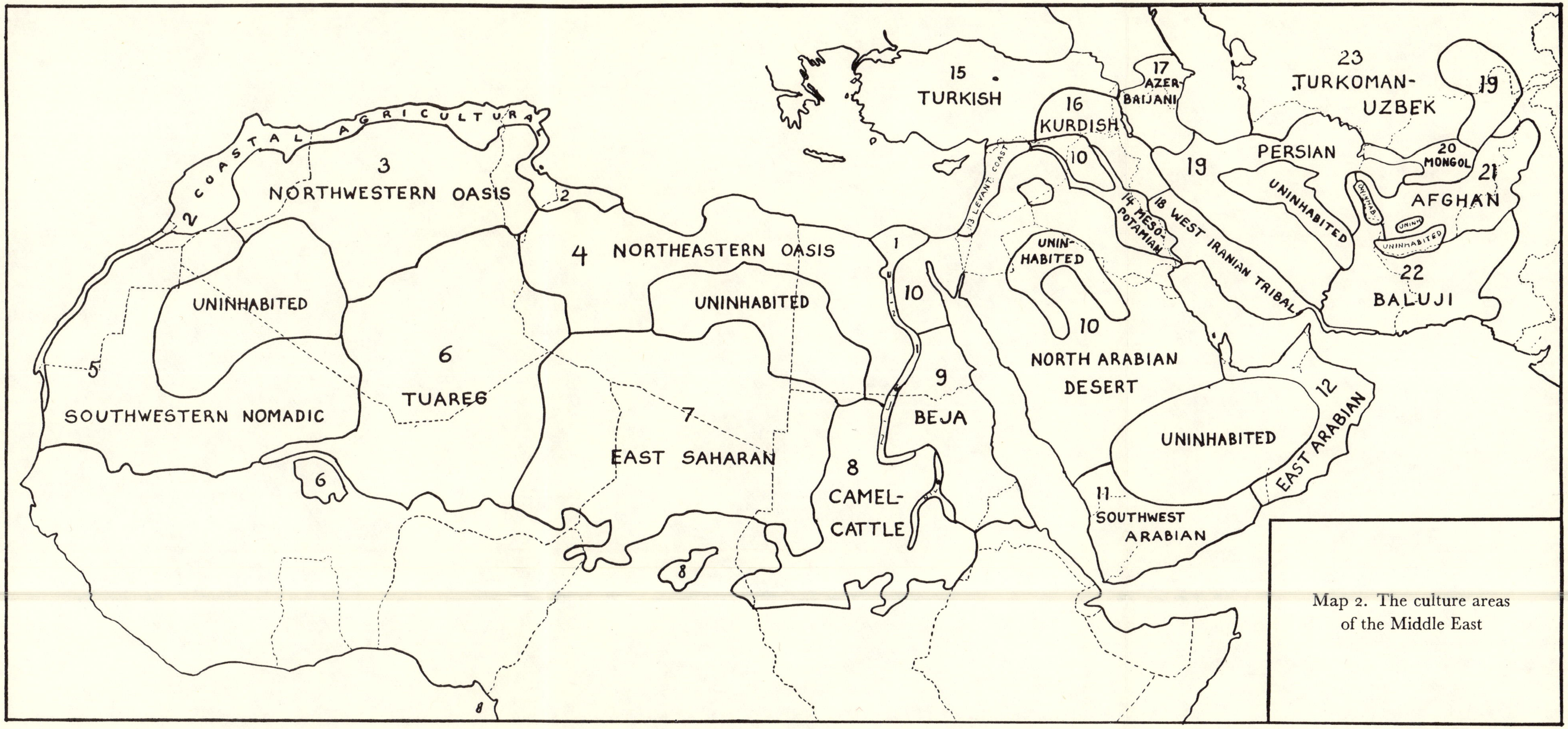

Map 2. The culture areas of the Middle East

part of the Middle East, and state at the very outset that the following outline could not have been arrived at without the huge amount of material assembled by Murdock in his *Africa: Its Peoples and their Culture History*, and the excellent detailed "Tribal Map of Africa" appended to that volume. While the author was constrained above to criticize the classifications adopted by Murdock, he wishes to acknowledge fully his indebtedness to Murdock's tribal map and his brief characterizations of the hundreds of tribes plotted on it. Only in a few instances did the author find it necessary to alter the boundary lines of groups drawn by Murdock, as for example in the case of some riverain and oasis groups to whom Murdock assigned unduly large territories.

No such careful listing or mapping of tribes was available for the Asian part of the Middle East. The lists and maps of the Arabian Bedouin tribes prepared by Baron Oppenheim[28] were of little help because all the tribes described by him had to be included in one single culture area (No. 10). Of greater usefulness was the ethnic and linguistic map of the Near East published in 1944 in *Petermans Geographische Mitteilungen*. In most cases, however, the writer had to draw upon his own familiarity with the area in deciding where to draw the boundary lines between what appeared to him as contiguous but different culture areas.

An added difficulty was presented by the ethnic complexities of major parts of the Asian Middle East. Especially rugged mountain areas, such as those inhabited by the Kurds and the Lur and Turkic-speaking tribes in western Iran, do not easily lend themselves to a mapping of culture areas. While the natural conditions tend to impose a definite way of life on all the inhabitants, the isolation resulting from lack of communications and from the frequent difficulty of establishing contact even across a single mountain range makes for the retention of cultural traits that may have been brought into the area many centuries ago by the remote ancestors of the present-day population. Thus, the typical picture in these regions is that of simultaneous existence side by side of representatives of two or more cultures, more often than not in overt or quiescent enmity. In western Iran, for example one finds side by side Sunni Muslim Kurdish tribes, Armenian-speaking Christians, Shīʿite Muslim Azerbaijani Turks, Aramaic-

less, in general, the family and social organization is of the over-all Middle Eastern pattern.

6. *The Tuareg Area.* Inhabited by Berber-speaking nomadic tribes, the Tuareg area has a scattering of oases in which cultivation is carried out by servile classes for their nomadic overlords. Family and social organization differ considerably from the general Middle Eastern pattern: Descent is matrilineal; the society is structured into distinct layers of status groups, which almost amount to castes; women have great freedom (it is the noble men and not the women who wear the veil); marriage is monogamous but sex mores are reported to be lax. Adherence to Islam is lukewarm. More women than men can read and write the old Tuareg script. In place of the usual Middle Eastern black hair tent, the Tuareg use hide tents dyed red or yellow—another archaic trait.[30]

7. *The East Saharan Area.* Separated from Area 4 by a large expanse of uninhabited desert, this area is again richer in oases and, although still a predominantly pastoral area, its southern part receives from 4 to 20 inches of rain annually, and consequently is savanna rather than desert with the importance of cultivation increasing as one proceeds southward. The area is inhabited by Saharan Negroes, many of whom have become converted to Islam as late as the eighteenth century. They speak a number of related languages called "Kanuric" by Murdock and "Central Saharan" by Greenberg.[31]

Most of the area is inhabited by nomadic tribes whose herds consist not only of camels and sheep and goats as in Areas 3 to 6, but in the southeast of cattle in addition: an influence of the adjoining camel-cattle area (see Area 8). Oases are scattered all over the area, but only in its eastern and western extremes do people engage in agriculture in large numbers.

8. *The Camel-Cattle Area.* This area is inhabited by Nubian tribes of mixed Arab-Negro ancestry whose main intermingling occurred following the Arab conquest of the region in the beginning of the sixteenth century. Most of them are nomadic or seminomadic with the camel as the main animal in the north, cattle in the south. The southern cattle herding tribes are often referred to collectively as *Baqqāra*, Arabic for "cattle herders." Among the

latter, agriculture plays a considerable role. Family and social organization resemble the general Middle Eastern type; however, a higher incidence of polygyny and an initial matrilocal residence are noted. Also, the Middle Eastern black hair tent is in this area frequently replaced by other types of temporary shelter. This detail illustrates the marginal character of this area in relation to the Middle East. The Baqqāra are warlike and fanatical Muslims.

9. *The Beja Area.* This lies between the Upper Nile and the Red Sea. Most Beja tribes have retained their own Hamitic language, called *tu-Bedawiye*, although one of them has adopted Arabic, and sections of another speak Tigre. Racially they are Caucasoid, their economy is pastoral nomadic with camels, cattle, sheep, and goats as the main livestock. Owing to poor grazing conditions, they must move in very small groups. Family and social organization conform to the general Middle Eastern pattern. South Arabian influences can be seen in their grass- and leaf-covered huts.

10. *The North Arabian Desert Area.* Moving across into Asia, we designate as Area 10 the large land mass that is the original home base of the Arabs who, during and following the lifetime of Mohammed, conquered the entire Middle East. It is the birthplace of much of the Muslim way of life that is still followed by the conservative population sectors all over the Middle East. The area includes the entire northern part of the Arabian Peninsula, as well as the Syrian Desert, the Negev Desert of Israel, the Sinai Peninsula and the Eastern Desert of Egypt. Although the majority of the population is settled in villages and towns and the sedentarization of the remaining nomads progresses apace, this is still a Bedouin area in two senses: geographically, the vast majority of its surface is utilized only by the nomadic herders, and psychologically it is their ethos and ideals that are still upheld by the entire population. The dominant religion in central Arabia is the puritanistic Wahhābī sect of Islam. The core of this area, together with Area 11 is the least Westernized of all parts of the Middle East. In it are found the typical Middle Eastern forms of family life and social organization at their fullest, with the retention of such elements, outmoded elsewhere, as slavery, large harems, eunuchs, despotic monarchy, bodily mutilation as punishment, and the like.

18. *The West Iranian Tribal Area.* This is one of the most mixed areas in the entire Middle East as far as ethnic composition is concerned. It is however, precisely this mosaiclike appearance that stamps it with the character of a separate culture area, in addition to the fact that the majority of the population groups, whatever their provenance, language, religious affiliation, and physical appearance, practice transhumant sheep and goat nomadism. The northern half of the area is dominated by the Lurs, a huge tribal confederation of the Shīʿite faith and speaking Lur, which is an Iranian dialect. The southern part is the home of two large tribal confederations, the Bakhtiyārīs, another powerful Shīʿite tribal confederation, who speak another Iranian dialect and whose unveiled women enjoy greater freedom than is usual among tribal populations; and the Qashqais, a Turkic-speaking Sunnite Muslim tribal confederation, living to the east of the former.

19. *The Persian Area.* This area comprises most of Iran, as well as a detached smaller area in the northeastern corner of Afghanistan where the Persian-speaking inhabitants are known as Tajiks. The great majority of the population of this area consists of Persian-speaking Shīʿite Muslim villagers, practicing, as a rule, extensive rain-fed agriculture. In contrast to the rest of the Muslim Middle East, in this area pictorial representation of human beings and wine drinking is practiced. Love of physical exercises, gymnastics, and hot baths seems to be a survival of old Hellenistic influence, while nineteenth-century Russian influences are also discernible, especially in the towns. One of the characteristic local features of religion is the performance of annual passion plays provoking great emotional response in the audience. The area has developed a high urban civilization with great local refinements in the visual and musical arts.

20. *The Mongol Area.* Located entirely in the central and western parts of Afghanistan, the Mongol Area is inhabited by several groups that exhibit either a clear-cut Mongoloid physical type or a mixture of Mongoloid and Iranian features. The Hazara Mongols in central Afghanistan are Shīʿite Muslims, live in villages, cultivate the land, and speak an Iranian dialect, described by some students as "archaic." Hazara splinter groups are found

also in western Afghanistan and across the Iranian border, where they are Sunni Muslims, and were until recently nomadic. Another group belonging to this area is that of the Chahar Aymak (literally: Four Tribes), tribes of a mixed physical type, who live in yurts that indicate their Central Asian origin.

21. *The Afghan Area.* Southeastern Afghanistan as well as the adjoining area of West Pakistan comprise this area. The language is Pushtu (or Pakhtun), related to Persian; religion Sunnī Islam. The Afghans are the dominant element in Afghanistan, and comprise both nomadic and settled components, as well as townspeople. In the southeast, near the former Indian (now Pakistani) border, where the inhospitable mountains offered no adequate living even when stock breeding and agriculture were combined, the tribes traditionally supplemented their income by raiding caravans or selling them their protection.

22. *The Baluji Area.* The southeastern corner of Iran and the southwestern corner of Pakistan make up this area. Its inhabitants are Balujis, with the Brahuis forming an island in the middle of the area. Both the Balujis and the Brahuis are pastoral nomads, dwelling in the well-known Middle Eastern type of black hair tent, and practice transhumance, but their main livestock is not sheep and goats, as in the case of most other transhumants, but camels. Along the borders, the Balujis used to raid the Persian villages, and to give "protection" to those who paid for it. The Balujis speak an Iranian language, while the Brahuis speak a Dravidic tongue.

23. *The Turkoman-Uzbek Area.* This is marginal to the Middle East and extends far into Central Asia. Some Turkoman tribes live in Iran, near the southwestern shores of the Caspian Sea, others in northwestern Afghanistan, while the Middle Eastern Uzbeks are found in northeastern Afghanistan. The Turkomans, relative newcomers in this area, live in the typical Central Asian yurt and practice stock breeding, but supplement it with agriculture. They are Sunni Muslims, speak a Turkic language, and are Mongoloid in physical type. The Uzbeks, also of Central Asian origin, are similar to the Turkomans in every respect, but have become more sedentarized and more assimilated linguistically to their Tajik neighbors, with whom they often intermarry.

the spontaneously thriving vegetation diminishes little by little or that the cultivated patches become rarer, while the alternating unutilized and fallow stretches become larger and more numerous, until the cultivated areas disappear altogether and the only remaining plant life is the typical desert vegetation of scanty shrubs and thorns. In mountainous territories, as in central Anatolia in the north or Yemen in the south, the hills are almost entirely bare, except where patient terracing has transformed the barren slopes into gardens. In such regions, neglect of cultivation for even a single season means immediate reversion of the land to a state of wilderness.

In these mountain zones, where ground water usually lies too deep so that the only source of utilizable water is the seasonal rainfall, ingenious devices have been developed to catch every drop of rain and prevent its running off into a deep-lying and stony *wādī*-bed. But since rainwater can be caught and preserved only where it falls, the crests of mountain ranges often mark the boundary line between an arid region one side that remains dry and desolate and a region on the other side that receives precipitation during the rainy season owing to the prevailing winds.

The ratio between the desert and the sown varies from place to place in the lands of the Middle East. In general, the entire area is overwhelmingly desert: approximately 90 per cent. The least desertlike countries, Turkey and Lebanon, are in the north and on the North African shore, with the exception of Libya. The greatest expanse of desert lies in the countries among which are divided politically the Sahara and the Great Arabian Desert. But even in the countries with the most favorable desert-sown balance the presence of the desert is felt everywhere: precipitation is generally poor; humidity low, except on the seashore; the wind, though it has a steady prevailing trend, turns occasionally to bring a fine, powderlike dust from the desert across the sown lands; from time to time locusts invade the sown from their desert breeding grounds; and from practically every high mountain one can discern during the summer season the low black tents of the nomadic desert people, pitched on the borderline between the desert and the sown.

Not only is the boundary between the desert and the sown not sharply delineated in most cases; it also shifts considerably. The borders of the two different land types are constantly advancing and receding. A few years with insufficient rain may force the villagers to give up previously cultivated plots of land, which are then swallowed up by the desert. Conversely, a succession of rainy seasons with abundant precipitation may enable the agriculturalists to bring under plough or hoe some acreage that was formerly barren desert. In the case of irrigated lands, best exemplified by Egypt and, to a lesser extent, by Iraq, careful regulation of the great life-sustaining rivers means the conquest of valuable *feddans* or *dunams* from the desert, while neglect of the waterworks, either because of local mismanagement or lack of a strong central government, results in floods and waste or a silting up of river beds, with a consequent catastrophic curtailment of arable land.

A third factor affecting the fluctuation between the desert and the sown, in addition to water supply and labor, is *war*. Throughout all history, desert people waged wars against the settled sons of the sown, and if they prevailed the settlers had to retreat and abandon the outskirts of the sown, which were rapidly incorporated into the desert.

People of the Western World have, as a rule, some familiarity with the more common varieties of cultivated land, such as fields and gardens. Firsthand knowledge of the desert is much rarer. To many, the very word "desert" means endless, softly rolling sand dunes absolutely devoid of animal or vegetable life, a concept popularized by many motion pictures. There are, to be sure, such deserts in the Middle East, in North Africa, in the Arabian Peninsula, as well as in Iran; but they have throughout history remained uninhabited. Traditionally, they have been crossed by camel caravans traveling along long-established routes and, in recent years, also by motor vehicles. But the barren, empty deserts cannot provide a home base for even the most rugged nomads.

The desert in which the nomads make their home, and which represents for them the "wide-open spaces" with freedom of life and movement, is of a different character. Admittedly, it is a very unfriendly place, forbidding and frightening in its desolation. But, barren though it may be, it does enjoy some scanty rain and can

but their means of livelihood was cattle, sheep, and goat husbandry and their beast of burden was the ass, whereas both these functions are fulfilled by the camel among the "grand" nomads, as the French call the camel herders. In the absence of the camel, the Amorites of four thousand years ago could not utilize the arid open spaces of the desert in which only the camel can survive; they had to remain closer to the cultivable land and their mobility was limited. For nomads, limited mobility means small tribal groups; any undue increase forces them to split up and seek separate pastures, as happened in the case of Abraham and Lot whose combined flocks were too "heavy" for the land to bear.[2] The Amorites also lacked horses, which made them a much less formidable enemy than the Bedouins of later times. Some idea of the outward appearance of the Amorites can be gained from the murals of Beni Hasan, which show a nomadic chieftain, Absha, accompanied by his tribesmen and their families. In these murals, dating from about 1900 B.C., both men and women are dressed in elaborately woven, multicolored woolen tunics; the men wear sandals, the women shoes. The arms, carried by the men, are composite bows, heavy throwing sticks, and spears. An eight-stringed lyre held by one of the men shows that these people were familiar with instrumental music.[3]

Tribes of steppe Bedouins, that is, nomads without camels or with only a few, whose mode of life is similar to that of the Amorites, are found to this day all over the Middle East. They are shepherds and goatherds, with limited mobility and a much smaller wandering territory than that of the camel Bedouins. Their life is tied to the outskirts of the sown, which they never can leave far behind. They are the enemies of the cultivators for whose fields a grazing flock means ruin. They must keep to the steppe belt between the desert and the sown, and in many cases they buy protection from the more powerful camel-herding tribes to whom otherwise they would fall easy prey. Their limited mobility, their closer contact with agriculturalists, the very difference between tending camel herds and sheep or goat flocks, all these result in their occupying an intermediate position between the settled population and the camel nomads.

The more significant characteristics of the culture of the camel nomads all over the Middle East can be summarized as follows: animal husbandry with reliance mainly on the camel as a means of transportation, source of food (milk and milk products as well as meat occasionally), supply of raw materials for tent and clothing from its hair, for leather utensils, containers, and trappings from its skin, and for fuel from its dung; seasonal wandering with the herd within a certain tribal territory, reaching in the rainy season deep into the heart of the desert, and in the dry summers near the steppe and the richer settled land; tribal organization based on real or imagined common origin and family groupings, headed by chieftains; collective responsibility expressed in such institutions as the blood feud, raiding, and the inviolate laws of hospitality and sanctuary, as well as in such concepts as honor, "face," and nobility; great familiarity with the natural features of the desert, and a remarkable degree of physical and mental adaptation to the unparalleled harshness of desert life.

It is more difficult to find a common denominator underlying the more diversified life forms of the Middle Eastern cultivators. The common elements characteristic of this group are relatively fewer, with a greater preponderance of regional or local traits. Geographic and climatic conditions as well as religious and ethnic differentiation make for greater variety. A village in the mountains of Kurdistan is necessarily very different from one on the banks of the Nile which, in turn, cannot resemble too closely one along the Moroccan coast. Likewise, a Maronite Christian village in Lebanon, a Shī'ite Muslim village in Iran, and a Druze village in the Jebel Druze each has its own peculiar characteristics.

In a Bedouin tribe each and every family subsists on animal husbandry; but a village has, in addition to its bulk of agriculturalists, also a few artisans such as cobblers, blacksmiths, weavers, or masons, as well as such other specialists as teachers, imams, watchmen, barbers, and the like. Social stratification parallels occupational specialization, so that in most villages landowners, tenant farmers, and day laborers occupy a definite place in the social hierarchy.

In the nomadic tribe, whose families traditionally trace their descent either to a real or, more often, to an eponymous or

took to dwelling in tents, "so that they may live many days on the face of the land."[8] This "return to the desert," which was motivated by purely religious considerations, was an exceptional phenomenon in the history of ancient Israel, though the remembrance of the nomadic days of old, clad in legendary colors, was kept alive in the consciousness of the people as the days when Israel "went with God in the desert, in a land that is not sown."[9] Several centuries later, in a similar situation, when the downfall of the Second Commonwealth and the Second Temple of Jerusalem was felt to be impending, a group of religious extremists again took to the desert, though this time it was not a tribal group like the Rechabites, but a sect, the Essenes, and instead of pitching tents for dwellings they built themselves houses or sought shelter in caves. It is among these groups who returned to the desert that the famous Dead Sea Scrolls originated.

In modern times, both groups and individuals have taken to the desert in flight rather than as an act of religious devotion. Oppressive governmental measures, threats by too powerful adversaries, feuds in which the weaker party could not hope to hold its own—these are some of the circumstances that have caused people seek out the lesser dangers of the desert.

According to J. Braslawski, who made a special study of the composition of the Bedouin tribes of the Negev (today part of Israel), the names of several of these tribes or tribal groups bear witness to their descent from non-Bedouin or sedentary peoples. The Zaghārne families of the Tiyāha tribe came from the town of Zughr at the southeastern end of the Dead Sea; the Sa'idiyyīn in Jordan have a tradition that they came from the village of Jebal near Kerak.[10] Some Bedouin tribes trace their descent to the Crusaders;[11] while others, though claiming the noblest descent among the Arabs, that of the prophet Mohammed, are actually of Albanian ancestry.[12]

In spite of these movements from the sown into the desert and the much more significant countermovements from the desert to the sown, both the settled cultivator and the nomadic herdsman remain to this day the two basic polar types in the Middle East. Future developments are difficult to foresee. Certain signs indicate that the sown is about to make significant encroachments upon the desert. In Egypt and in Iraq plans are being made to increase the irrigated areas. In Israel, successful beginnings have been made to bring water and agriculture to the Negev desert. The most valuable pasture land of the fringes of the desert will thus gradually slip out of the hands of the nomads. Moreover, the processes of sedentarization, sporadic and haphazard in the past, seem to be gaining momentum at present, a trend that will probably continue and may even increase in the future.

Yet all this means neither the vanishing of the desert nor the disappearance of the nomad in the Middle East. The greatest engineering efforts will in the foreseeable future not achieve more than an increase of the cultivated area by 10, 20, or perhaps 30 per cent, which corresponds to a decrease of the desert area by a mere 1, 2, or perhaps 3 per cent. The desert people will likewise remain. Most desert tribes live at subsistence level; this means that the numbers of their ranks lost through sedentarization are immediately replenished by a greater natural increase that is also aided by the rudiments of sanitation and hygiene beginning to reach the more accessible tribes now for the first time.

Only the nomads with their unique adaptation to the rigors of the wasteland and wilderness can live in the desert. Because of their presence in the desert over many centuries, a fine ecologic balance has evolved between the flora, the fauna, and humankind—a balance that would be gravely disturbed if the human inhabitants were to depart. A different and perhaps more cogent consideration is the right of every human group to the way of life it has developed for itself and the intrinsic value of each particular culture for its carriers. From the long-range point of view of cultural history, the passing of the desert people would be regrettable, for it would mean the preclusion of even that slight chance still existing today that these people might again in the future, as they did in the past, contribute something unique, original, and valuable to the totality of human cultures in the world.

Idirh in the High Atlas that the entire population of the village, about 200 persons, lived in about twenty houses. In other words, the average number of persons per family was about ten.[5]

2. The Middle Eastern family is *patrilineal*, that is, a person is regarded as belonging to the family to which his father belongs, and not the family of his mother. An Arabic proverb current in many countries expresses this succinctly: "The people rely in descent on the father and not on the mother; the mother is like a vessel of oil that is emptied." Inasmuch as social groupings larger than the extended family are practically always composed of extended families and not of individuals, every person automatically becomes and remains a member of that larger social group (such as clan, tribe, and to some extent even political party) to which his father's extended family belongs.

This is the general rule everywhere in the Middle East irrespective of religious affiliation: in other words, this rule prevails not only among the various Muslim sects but also among the Christians and Jews. The only major exception to the rule of patrilineal descent is that of the Tuareg in the Sahara. Among them descent is matrilineal, and therefore a man's status is determined by the social group to which his mother belongs. If a woman marries outside her own tribe, the children belong to her tribe, and, although the parental couple resides with the husband's tribe, the children eventually return to live with their mother's tribe. A noblewoman's children are nobles, irrespective of the father's status; and vice versa: a nobleman's children are noble only if their mother too is noble. In recent decades, however, it has become more and more evident that this ancient matrilineal rule tends to break down. Noble fathers, powerful enough to assert themselves, have often succeeded in passing off as nobles their children born to them of servile wives.[6]

Since the preferred marriage in the Middle East in general is between children of two brothers (cf. below, Chapter 6) or failing this, between children of other near relatives, or of families belonging to the same local or tribal group, patrilineal descent often does not alienate the children from their mother. Difficulties in the patrilineal family arise when the mother comes from a different group, and especially when hostilities break out between the father's family and the family of the mother's father. In such cases the children are expected to side with their father and to show no hesitancy in actively aiding their father's family in its fight or feud against their mother's family. While such situations may occasionally result in tragedies, or at least in grave psychological conflicts, especially in the case of women who stand between their fathers and their husbands, as a rule the marriage between the son of one family (or tribe or local aggregate) and the daughter of another is regarded as a bond of alliance between the two groups. The children issuing from such unions, although by tradition and mores belonging only to the father's group, are regarded with affection by the mother's family as well, and are therefore to some extent a guarantee of mutual friendship and good will for both sides. It has been a policy of long standing in the Middle East, practiced to this day especially by the ruling houses of the Arabian Peninsula, for princes and rulers to marry women of different tribes and peoples and thus to cement their allegiance to them.

Another outcome of the patrilineal mode of reckoning descent, combined with the institution of concubinage and the legal recognition of the children of concubines, was the occasional replacement of "white" by "black" heirs and successors. In various parts of the Middle East, and especially along the West coast of the Arabian peninsula and in North Africa, Somali, Abyssinian, Sudanese, or Negro slave girls have been incorporated into "white" households, and the offspring of these mixed unions have counted as full and equal members of the father's family and social group. If, as it at times happened, the only son of a man in ruling position was by such a dark-skinned concubine, there was nothing in the social or cultural traditions to prevent his becoming the heir to his father's position. The recently deceased Sultan of Morocco, for example, was as fair-skinned as any northerner, but his children are rather dark complexioned.[7] Discrimination on the basis of skin color is largely absent in the Middle East, and from the earliest days of Islam to the present Negroes and half-Negroes have always been able to rise to the highest positions, such as generals of the army, governors of provinces, and independent rulers.[8]

of Lower Iraq, noticed that his only daughter was harboring tender feelings towards one of the youths of a marsh tribe. And although the two young people never met face to face, and the youth asked for the girl's hand in marriage, the old shaykh preferred to kill his only daughter rather than let her marry into a low-status tribe.[15]

The so-called noble (*aṣīlīn*) Bedouin tribes of the Syrian and Arabian Desert (see Chapter 8) guard most jealously their purity of blood, and do not permit either their men or their women to marry members of an inferior tribe. In choosing a marriage partner for either a son or a daughter satisfactory descent is an indispensable prerequisite.[16] Members of the noble Rwala, one of the leading tribes of the Syrian desert, cannot marry persons belonging to the Ṣleyb, Hawāzim, Fheyjāt, Shararāt, or ʿĀzim tribes which, although camel-breeders like the Rwala themselves, are low-status groups since they are unable to defend themselves, and pay *khuwwa*, protection-money, to the more vigorous tribes. The Rwala hold themselves aloof even from other free Arab tribes and discourage, though do not absolutely forbid, intermarriage with them. As to marriages with male slaves or slave girls, such occurrences are a legitimate reason for putting the offender to death. A Rweylī marrying a slave girl would be killed by his own kin, *ahl*, whom he defiled by his act. Intermarriage is forbidden for the Rwala also with the *ṣāni*ʿ (pl. *ṣunnā*ʿ) groups, those blacksmiths and tinkers who from time to time attach themselves to Rwala (and other Bedouin) camps, and of whom it is known to the Rwala that they have no marriage restrictions.[17]

The same restrictions exist also among the powerful Shammar tribes of Iraq and the Syrian Desert. No son of a Shammar tribe can marry a slave girl or a girl from an inferior tribe such as those mentioned above. If he did, his own people would kill him. If a noble tribesman takes up such trades as blacksmithing, salt-making, or salt-carrying, lime-burning, charcoal-burning, skinning animals and curing the skins, he makes himself dishonorable and the Shammar and other noble tribes will refrain from intermarrying with him and his.[18]

Similar limitations prevail in Southern Arabia where, for

instance, the Qara mountain tribesmen do not intermarry with the Shahara whom they regard as no better than slaves. The Shahara, again, do not marry outside their own people.[19]

Where different ethnic groups meet, even though all of them are Muslims, marriage limitations often restrict the choice of a mate to one's own group. In Afghanistan, for example, it seems that it is unlawful for a down-country man, that is, one from India, even though he be a Muslim, to marry an Afghan. Jewett reports a case where such a marriage was concluded, and the Afghan authorities kept the offender, a Muslim Pathan from India, in jail for about a year.[20] At the other or western end of the Middle East, in the town of Timbuctoo, which is inhabited by three distinct ethnic elements of differing statuses, men of high status groups can acquire wives or concubines from any status group, but the men of low status are limited by the fact that the high status women do not marry inferiors.[21]

An additional limitation in the choice of marriage partners stems from the socioeconomic stratification present to some extent everywhere in the Middle East. The three main ecologic groups of the nomads, villagers and townspeople from three distinct social classes among whom intermarriage is discountenanced in theory and rare in practice. As a South-Arabian proverb expresses it: "*Qūl bū'i Nūḥ: al-hegrī luh hegrah, al-'askarī luh 'askarīyah, wal-'abd luh gārīyah.*" "Said Father Noah: the ploughman to the plough-woman, the retainer to the retainer-woman, and the slave to the slave-woman."[22]

Yet another endogamous limitation is imposed upon the people by their preference for finding marriage partners within their own local group. A study carried out in the 1920's in Arṭās, a South-Palestinian Muslim Arab village, showed that the great majority of marriages were contracted by young men and women both of whom resided in the village or in its immediate vicinity.[23] This is not an isolated instance but typical for conditions in the Middle East in general. Among the fellahin of Egypt, for example, ". . . a woman or girl in this country will seldom consent, or her parents allow her, to marry a man who will not promise to reside with her in her native town or village."[24] Since a village is often inhabited by members of one or two (rarely more than two)

In a social survey carried out recently in Beirut among a representative sample of almost two thousand families only two plural marriages were found. In the one case the man had two wives, in the other three. The author of the report comments: "The economics of subsistence militates against plural marriages."[36] Data from other places seem to indicate that cultural influences must also be taken into consideration.

As against the rights of a man to marry more than one wife, he has certain obligations toward his wives that occasionally may make life difficult for him. Among several tribes of the Syrian-Arabian Desert a man has to divide his marital attentions equally between his two wives. He must alternately spend one night with one and one with the other. Each of the wives cooks for him a day in turn, and on that day it is the woman's right to have the husband spend the night with her, whether he cohabits with her or not. If the husband spends the night with one wife out of turn, he must compensate the other with a sheep or a goat as the price for her night. Sometimes the two wives strike a bargain and one of them buys a night from the other whose turn it is.[37]

"Be Fruitful and Multiply"

One of the motivations for large numbers of children is the emphasis on family coherence and family strength. Only a family with many children, and preferably boys, can be a strong family. The greater the number of children the greater also the prestige of the father and, through him, of the family as a whole. It is therefore the duty of every man in the family to beget as many children as possible. Even among the Christians this is found to be true. In Lebanon, for instance, ". . . a large family is desired . . . and a childless home is regarded as under a heavenly curse. Since the husband cannot divorce [his wife] (being Catholic) he loses all the hope of propagating himself. Children are wanted as a source of riches, comfort in old age, power against enemies, and, after death, to help into heaven. Therefore a bride who is robust, healthy and from a big family herself, is wanted."[38] The same attitude prevails among the Copts of Egypt.

The average number of children born to a married couple in

the Middle East is very high, resulting in sizable families in spite of the effects of the high infant and child mortality. Unfortunately, no adequate statistical studies are available on the rate of reproduction of women in most Middle Eastern countries. Some indication as to the results one may expect should such studies be made can be found in data from Palestine, where, according to 1945 figures, the average number of children born to Muslim women during their lifetime was between 9 and 10, of whom about 6 reached adulthood. Both the general conditions and the specific motives believed to foster attitudes that make for large families are found in the Middle Eastern countries in a rarely complete combination. The general conditions are: illiteracy, great dependence on agriculture, isolation, a generally low standard of life, and a fatalistic outlook; the specific motives comprise religious injunctions to be fruitful and multiply, the specific form of family organization (the extended family), the widespread desire for heirs and especially for male heirs, the high infant mortality as a result of which relatively few children survive even if many are born; also the absence of any economic motivation to limit the number of children since the cost of satisfying the needs of the children is small, and they begin to contribute to the family income at an early age.[39] All these factors together constitute an interlocking system of social and family organization resulting in a strong pressure to reproduce. Only in the urban sector, and especially in its middle and upper classes, are the families smaller.

In view of the great emphasis placed on having many children, and the growth of the prestige of both man and wife with the increase of the number of their (male) children, it will be understandable that a correlate of these attitudes is a resultant dim view of sterility. A childless woman is regarded with contempt mixed with commiseration, and is often believed to be cursed by God who is the closer and opener of wombs. Such a woman will search desperately for a remedy and will fall victim to quacks and medicine men or women who still abound among the nomadic tribes, the remoter villages, and even in the slums of the towns. Should this search bring no result, the woman must resign herself to being divorced, or to sharing her husband with a second wife who, if fertile, will hold dominance over her. Although this traditional attitude toward childlessness is being gradually mitigated under the impact of Westernization, traces of it are still present even in the urban middle and upper classes.

Since all the motivations of the traditional Middle Eastern family are directed towards having many children, birth control is something to which a woman would as a rule resort only in great secrecy, and only after she has given birth to a great number of children. If a woman has three or four sons and she feels that the frequent and continuing childbearing is too great a burden, she may try one or more of the traditionally available contraceptive methods, such as prolonged lactation (in the belief that this prevents new conception), or one of the magical means offered by the same medicine men or women whose help is invoked also in the case of childlessness. Needless to say, these means are inadequate, and one cannot speak of any effective traditional method of family planning. As to the introduction of modern family planning, the general atmosphere of the Middle Eastern family and society is, for the time being, highly unfavorable to it in spite of official pronouncements made recently by leading religious authorities of the *el-Azhar* (the highest Muslim institute of religious learning in Cairo, Egypt) to the effect that there is no religious injunction in Islam against birth control.

"Familism" and Socialization

The influence of the family on the life of the individual in the Middle East is very great, much greater than usual in the modern urban society of the Western world. In fact, the entire culture of the Middle East is so permeated with family loyalty and influence that the terms "familism" and "kinship culture" have properly been applied to it. The individual is much more the product of his family and much less that of other socializing factors than is true in the West. Well beyond the onset of adulthood and deep into his middle age, his life is joined to his extended family. Subservience to family authority and reliance on the advice of elders remain characteristic traits of men in their thirties and forties.[40] Ingrained habits of family loyalty are so strong that even in public and official positions it is extremely difficult for the individual to divest himself of a protective attitude towards his kinsmen, who as a matter of course expect him to render special services and favors to them.

A most fundamental difference between the Western family and the Middle Eastern family can be found in the educational field: In the Western family efforts are made to educate the child from a very early age for independence. The parents take pride in a child who can do things for himself, who can find his way alone, and who therefore in their opinion is well prepared to take his place independently in a competitive society.

In traditional Middle Eastern society, on the other hand, the basic educational aim pursued by the family, whether consciously or not, is to mold the child into an obedient member of the family group, able to integrate into the working of his immediate social environment. Only very slowly and gradually, in most cases at a relatively advanced age, is he expected to act independently. The growing child, the adolescent boy has to learn to subordinate his wishes to those of his father and possibly to those of his elder brothers. He has to learn that the interests of the family come first and has to govern his actions with the family point of view in mind. Great stress is laid on coherence in the family because a divided family cannot hold its own in collective competition with the interests of other possibly stronger and more powerful families.

There is a considerable difference between the early socialization of a boy and of a girl and in this difference can be found one of the basic factors that make for the specific Middle Eastern flavor of the relationship between man and woman in adulthood. In the villages, both boys and girls are still swaddled, although in the cities modern women fight against it.[41] The period of lactation lasts one to two years in the case of a girl and two to three years in the case of a boy, which means that a boy is breast fed for almost twice as long as a girl. During the period of lactation, the mother as a matter of course is constantly at the disposal of the child, picking him up and giving him her breast. During the midday hour, when she takes a hot lunch to her husband and menfolk working in the field, she carries the baby along with her on her hip, shoulder, head, or back. With weaning, there is a sudden break in this close intimate relationship between mother and child; thereafter, the mother no longer picks him up when he cries, no longer stands at his beck and call. When the mother leaves the house for the field or brings water from the well, she now leaves the child at home either in the care of an older sibling or completely alone to play in the dust of the small courtyard of the house. The child now cries unheeded, his customarily solicitous mother nowhere in sight. It is no exaggeration to say that weaning in the life of the Middle Eastern child is something of a traumatic experience.

This experience comes in the life of a girl at a very early age, when she is between one and two years old, and the formation of mental habits has not yet reached as advanced a stage as in the case of the boy who is weaned at twice her age. The impressions of the relatively short period during which the girl child is the object of maternal solicitude are very early overlaid by the new and lasting experience of finding herself neglected, of crying without being listened to, of being paid no attention. In later life, this experience is intensified and before long the girl learns that she is a rather unimportant member of the family, that her function is to serve her brothers, her elder sisters, her mother and father. When she is four or five, she is given some simple duties in the household and begins to help her mother in tending her smaller siblings. At about this time the mother very consciously begins to prepare the girl for her marriage, explaining to her whenever occasion arises that soon she will move into the house of her husband's parents and there will serve not only her husband but, primarily, her husband's mother. In this way the girl is conditioned for the subordinate role she will play in the home of her husband where for all practical purposes she will become a servant of her mother-in-law.

As to formal schooling of girls, this is still objected to by many Muslim villagers. In the villages studied in connection with the Kasmie Rural Improvement Project in Lebanon in 1952 it was found that 234 boys but only 13 girls attended elementary school. With regard to the Shī'ites in particular it was observed that they "do not encourage their daughters to attend schools. They feel that it is a hindrance to a happy marriage and often encourages disobedience to one's elders."[42]

The subordinate position of a girl, first in the house of her own parents, then in the house of her husband and his parents, serves as an additional motive for making a woman want to have as many children as possible and as soon as possible. The servile situation of a young wife changes only when children are born to her. She will still have to serve her mother-in-law, but her prestige increases with the birth of each child and especially with the birth of male children. It is when her sons grow up and marry that the woman reaches a period of life when the burden of everyday work is lightened by her daughters-in-law who now take over her chores. Just as the young girl learns in her parents' home how to behave in the home of her future parents-in-law, so the young wife is taught by her mother-in-law how to behave when she herself becomes a mother-in-law. In this manner both the mother-daughter relationship and the mother-in-law–daughter-in-law relationship is perpetuated from generation to generation.

Among the Christians this emphasis upon the desirability of bearing a boy is also present. "When the midwife announces a boy, there is much joy, firing of rifles, dancing, arak drinking. But she does not move if it is a girl, and later receives a small remuneration; everyone goes quietly after his daily task."[43]

To return now to the first years of a boy child's life. The lactation period lasts, as stated, from two to three years. During this time, certain definite expectations begin to form in the boy's mind. A two- to three-year-old boy who already can speak, walk, run, play, is still the master of his mother in the sense that whenever he wishes he may ask for her breast. As a result of this long period of lactation the boy child becomes imbued with the idea that his mother is there to serve him, that she must heed all his whims and wishes, and as he grows older, that the other womenfolk in the home also are there for the same purpose. The experience of weaning is of course a shock to the boy child as well, but, coming so much later than it comes for the girl, it does not eradicate the first impression he gained concerning his own relationship with the female world, namely that females are meant to serve him. Although corporal punishment is frequent, the boy may roam at will with older children and without the supervision of his parents. When the boy grows older his socialization and education are shifted from the hands of his mother to those of his father. He is taken by his father to the fields and allowed to help with the agricultural work. At the same time the boy notices that his mother or sisters serve him in more or less the same manner in which they serve his father: they bring food for him as well, also make his clothes, and so on. In this manner the impression that females are subservient creatures is reinforced in the male child's mind during the first decade of his existence. When he reaches adolescence and consciously observes the relationship between men and women, this impression is of course reinforced further and with it comes the recognition of the male role of leadership in the family and society at large. Naturally, this is translated into the expectation that, when he marries, his wife will be not so much his equal companion as a subservient fulfiller of his needs. When marriage actually occurs and the young bride is installed in the home that the boy shares with his parents and siblings, this expectation is fulfilled inasmuch as his own mother makes it clear what role his young wife must play in the household.

At the same time the boy, now a young husband, remains in an inferior position vis-à-vis his own father. He may accompany his father to his work in the fields and also to the deliberations of the village council, but he will have to take a back seat and is expected to listen quietly to his elders, discouraged from uttering any premature ill-considered opinion. Only when he himself becomes a father does his prestige slowly increase, and with each addition to his family, he is regarded as more of an authority in his own house.

Early Marriage

Under traditional circumstances, which prevail to this day among practically all the nomads and villagers of the Middle East and many of the townspeople, marriages are arranged by the parents of the young people. A son or daughter is expected to carry out the decision of his or her parents in this, just as in other matters of greater or lesser importance. In view of the very early average age of marriage for girls, there seems to be some justification for the traditionally held view that parents are better judges of the suitability of a match for their daughter than the girl herself. The average age of marriage for men is higher, but in this case the fact that the family property is controlled by his father, who alone can make all decisions in connection with the bride price, serves as a powerful factor in making a son submit to parental choice. Moreover, in the extended patrilocal family set-up, for a son to bring into the house of his parents a bride to whom his parents object would be all but impossible.

In conservative villages and in the tradition-bound sectors of the urban population, very early marriages are still the rule. This is indicated by demographic studies which, unfortunately, are still sporadic. A study carried out in 1944 in five Palestinian Arab villages showed that 12 per cent of the women aged thirteen to seventeen and 89 per cent of the women aged eighteen to twenty-two were married. Among all Palestinian Muslims the average age at marriage for women was 20.2 in 1931 and 19.1 in 1938–39; for men 25.8 in 1931 and 26.6 in 1938–39.[44]

Taking twenty as the age limit, we find that in the United States, of all the women who were married in 1956, about 37 per cent were under twenty years of age; in England and Wales, about 20 per cent; in Egypt (1955), almost 50 per cent; in Jordan (1957), over 60 per cent; in the provincial and district capitals of Turkey, (1955), undoubtedly under the influence of Westernization, only 33 per cent.

In the age of the bridegrooms at marriage, the differences between the Western rates and those of the Middle East are in the reverse. In the United States in 1956, about 10 per cent of the men who married were under twenty years of age; in England and Wales, about 4 per cent; in Egypt, about 4 per cent; in Jordan, a little over 10 per cent; in the provincial and district capitals of Turkey, between 5 and 6 per cent.

In other words, fewer young men can afford to marry in Egypt, for example, than in the United States; but many more girls are married very young in the Middle East than in the West.[45]

Such early marriages for girls represent an age-old Middle Eastern tradition. The stated reasons often voiced to this day by conservative parents are: fear of unchastity and of losing the money expected in the form of the bride price (which is paid by the bridegroom or his father to the father of the bride who can use it as he deems fit, although as a rule all or part of it is invested into the trousseau of the bride); preference for educating the girl in the house of her mother-in-law; preference for a young wife, motivated by the relatively early aging of women; the often present opportunity to exchange women, that is to give in marriage the daughter (or sister) of one to another in exchange for the latter's daughter (or sister); the desire of the groom's mother to have household help.

Another result of these factors is that the percentage of people remaining unmarried is very small, though somewhat higher among the males than among the females. In Egypt (in 1937), for instance, 99 per cent of the women in the forty to forty-nine age group were married or widowed or divorced, while the corresponding figure for males was 97 per cent.[46] In Turkey (1935), the corresponding percentages were 97.5 per cent and 96 per cent.[47]

In recent decades several Middle Eastern countries have passed laws fixing the minimum age of marriage. Article 4 of the Syrian law on the status of the family stipulates that the fiancé must have completed his eighteenth and the fiancée her seventeenth year of age for the marriage to be valid; and Article 88 of the Turkish civil code prescribes the same ages as a condition of marriage. In Egypt, legislation in 1923 fixed the minimum age of marriage for girls at sixteen and for boys at eighteen. However, the translation of such laws into practice is a difficult matter in view of the persistence of the traditional preferences among the people and the difficulty in enforcement. Thus, as a rule, there is only a negligible difference between the average age of marriage before the enactment of such laws as compared with that several years after it.[48]

Such increase as has occurred in the average age of marriage is largely confined to the middle and upper classes of the urban population. In a representative sample of 1,665 male heads of household in Beirut studied in 1952–53 it was found that 0.30 per cent had married at the age of fifteen or under; 11.23 per cent between the ages of sixteen and twenty; and 27.33 per cent between the ages of twenty-one and twenty-five, or a total of 38.86 per cent had married up to the age of twenty-five. Among the fathers of these heads of household, that is, men one generation older, the corresponding figures were as follows: married at the age of fifteen and under, 8 per cent; sixteen to twenty, 24.0 per cent; twenty-one to twenty-five, 20.0 per cent; or a total of 52 per cent married up to the age of twenty-five. In other words, within one generation the percentage of men married up to the age of twenty-five, decreased from 52 per cent to 38.86 per cent, and the percentage of men married up to the age of twenty decreased from 32 per cent to 11.52 per cent.

PERCENTAGES OF AGE AT MARRIAGE IN BEIRUT, 1952–53[49]

Males	*Former generation*	*Present generation*
15 and under	8.0	0.30
16–20	24.0	11.23
21–25	20.0	27.33
25 and under	52.0	38.86
Over 25	48.0	61.14
TOTAL	100.0	100.00
Females		
15 and under	28.88	18.22
16–20	43.97	44.81
20 and under	72.85	63.03
Over 20	27.15	36.97
TOTAL	100.00	100.00

Among the mothers of the heads of household, 28.88 per cent had married at the age of fifteen or under, and 43.97 per cent at the age of sixteen to twenty. Among the female heads of household and the wives of male heads of household, the corresponding percentages were 18.22 and 44.81. There was thus a very considerable decrease within one generation in marriages of women at the age of fifteen and under, but no decrease, in fact a slight increase, in marriages at the ages from sixteen to twenty.

The same trend of later marriages seems to continue among the next generation (that is, the children of the heads of household studied), but the presentation of the data is such that no definite conclusions can be drawn from them.

Among the factors making for a higher average age at marriage can be mentioned the spread of education, as a result of which more and more girls are at school at an age when their mothers were married, and the increasingly longer period required of young men for establishing themselves in positions. Of course, these factors are present to an appreciable degree only in the urban upper and middle classes. Among the working class and the rural population early marriages are still the rule. In fact, in these latter circles a girl over twenty-four or twenty-five who has not yet married is regarded as having something wrong with her.

Again, only in the middle and upper classes of the urban population has the traditional family and marriage pattern undergone significant modifications in recent years. Children, both sons and daughters, who have had high school or even college education have increasingly emancipated themselves from the traditional type of paternal control with the result that not only paternal authority but also the traditional extended family experiences a definite decline (or if one prefers: modification) in these circles.

Since marriage is the most important event in the life of the family, a brief description of the attendant rites seems in place. These rites exhibit a wide range of local variations. The following summary refers to the Eastern Mediterranean area, where in the villages and in conservative urban circles two ceremonies precede marriage. The first is called *khuṭbeh* or unofficial engagement; the second, *katb el-ketāb* or signing of the contract. In the *khuṭbeh* a few relatives and friends are invited to the bride's house, where the parents of the bridegroom and bride announce to the guests the intended marriage. Some time later, the ceremony of *katb el-ketāb* is held. This ceremony is attended by an official of the Sharī'a Muslim Court and a large gathering of villagers. The official registers in the contract the consent of the couple to marry and the amount of dowry paid by the bridegroom. The dowry consists of two parts: one paid on date of contract, and the second deferred and paid in case of divorce. The dowry paid on date of contract may be wholly in money or partly in money and partly in land. The money is paid for the purchase of clothing for the bride, since custom dictates that the bride should take with her a bridal trousseau when she marries. The remainder of the money is used for the purchase of jewelry for the bride. In general, whenever the father can afford it, he furnishes the expensive clothing and all the dowry is used for the purchase of jewelry or land for the bride.

The actual marriage may take place immediately after this ceremony or more frequently, several months later. In towns, this period is usually longer and may extend to a year or even two. During the three days or the week that precede the actual marriage ceremony, the women villagers gather and dance in the bride's home. On the evening of the wedding a lavish feast is served in the bridegroom's house, attended by most of the villagers and also by guests from outside. Guests usually bring with them presents in money and in food such as rice, sugar, or sheep.[50]

Divorce

Divorce in Muslim society is extremely simple. The husband can divorce his wife at will by pronouncing the traditional formula, "I divorce you," in the presence of two witnesses. The wife does not have the right either to oppose such a divorce or to initiate it on her own behalf. Once the fateful sentence has been uttered, she must go back to her father's (or brother's) family, and can claim that portion of the bride price which is retained by the husband and paid to her only upon divorce. If a wife leaves her husband (by returning to her own family) and her husband agrees to divorce her, she forfeits this part of the bride price. After a divorce a man may remarry at once, but a woman must wait for three months to make sure she is not pregnant. Should she find herself pregnant, she cannot remarry until she gives birth to the child and weans it. During this time her former husband (the father of the child), must support her and the baby. According to Muslim law all the children of divorced parents belong to the father, and the mother must deliver them up to him, usually at the age of seven. It is important to note that among Muslim peoples no stigma attaches to divorce, and divorced women remarry, as a rule, soon after they are premitted by law to do so. In fact, among the Bedouins it is not at all rare that a woman marries several men in succession. A girl of the 'Ajmān, one of the nobles tribes of Arabia, by the name of al-Jāzī bint Muḥammed al-Hazām al-Hithlayn, who in her youth was a famous beauty, was married to King Ibn Sa'ūd; then to his brother, the Amir Muḥammad; then to the king's brother-in-law, the Amir Sa'ūd al-'Arafa; then to the paramount chief of the Muṭayr tribe, Shaykh Bandar al-Duwīsh; then to a relative of the latter, Shaykh Mutluq al-Jaba'a of the Qaḥṭān tribe; then to the chief of the 'Ajmān, Shaykh Rakān ibn Dhaydān al-Hithlayn. In between the above marriages, she was married two more times to King Ibn Sa'ūd who was able, on both occasions, to persuade her then husband to divorce her because "I have not got over my love for her." Al-Jāzī was thus married no less than eight times within the relatively short period during which Bedouin women enjoy the youthful attributes and attractions of beauty.[51]

No statistical data are available from most Middle Eastern countries as to the frequencies of divorce and subsequent remarriage, but that these frequencies must be high can be gauged from the observation made in Mandatory Palestine where among the women of five Muslim Arab villages aged thirty-eight or more no less than 30.8 per cent have been married twice or more.[53]

A glance at the frequency of divorces is also instructive. This can be measured by the number of annual divorces per 1,000 married couples, which in the United States was 8.9 in 1939–41 and 10.4 in 1949–51, the highest rates in the Western world. In the Middle East, however, these rates are higher still. In Egypt, the only country from which relatively reliable data are available, they were 13.6 in 1936–38 and 16.9 in 1946–48.[52]

These figures show that in the Middle East relatively more married women get divorced than in America. Nevertheless, there is considerable dissatisfaction in feminist circles in the Middle East with the divorce laws. The Arab Women's Congress in Cairo in 1944 resolved to demand reforms of the divorce law in two directions:

"The right to divorce is to be granted to women as well as men, and no divorce is to come into effect without the decision of the court." No unqualified condemnation of polygyny was resolved, since allowance for it was made in cases of sterility and incurable sickness, a fact that demonstrates how far custom and tradition still influence the Muslim women even of the educated class.[54]

Family and Society

The family in the Middle East is the traditional economic unit. That is to say, in the nomadic tribes the family jointly owns the herds and flocks; in the villages, the family jointly owns and works the land; and in the towns, unless Westernization has changed the situation, the family jointly owns and works in a craft, or trade, or business. Hand in hand with this goes the tradition of passing on occupations in inheritance from father to son or, failing a son, to a nephew or other relative. Where modern influences are prevalent this system suffers a breakdown and, with the disintegration of the traditional extended family, its young male members strike out more and more frequently into new and individual directions.

Inheritance of property is regulated in the Middle Eastern countries, with the exception of Turkey, by the religious laws of the community to which the family belongs. As far as the Muslims are concerned, there is a Koranic prescription (Sura 4), according to which, if a man dies, first his debts are paid from his estate, then his wife and other members of his family besides his children get certain shares, then the residual estate is equally divided among his sons (each of whom gets a full share), and his daughters (each of whom gets half a share). This rule is observed primarily among traditional townspeople and villagers. Among the nomads, ancient pre-Islamic usages and customary laws (*'urf*) still persist, and the rules of inheritance contained in them are followed. Among the Bedouins of Jordan and Syria, for example, daughters do not inherit, and the Turkish government attempted in vain to enforce the *sharī'a* (canon) law.[55] In addition to the exclusion of daughters from inheritance, traditional law as followed by the nomads permits a man to dispose of his entire property before death as he chooses, while according to Muslim canon law he has the right to give away at will only one third of it.

Adoption is recognized and practiced by the nomads, whereas canon law rejects it (based on Koran 33 : 4 f., 37).

The main differences between the attitudes of the rural and the urban families can be subsumed under the point of view of conservatism *versus* modernism. The typical rural family is conservative, tradition-bound, and averse to change. It is suspicious of innovations, and values the *status quo*. It emphasizes the importance of the family and its collective interests as against those of its individual members. It expects subordination of individuals, and especially of the younger generation, to the interests and wishes of the family as a whole as expressed by its head and its older members. It has great cohesion, which continues even when the family branches out into several subdivisions located in different places of residence. It protects its individual members and helps them economically, socially, and with "string pulling" whenever necessary.

When a rural family moves into the city many of these traditional features are lost. The individual often becomes separated from his family or the nuclear family deprived of the protective framework of the extended family. As a result, the old values represented and upheld by the family tend to disappear. Only rarely can the family in the city retain its tradition-directed tenor. Traditionalism and modernism compete with each other even within the family, causing not infrequently deep rifts between the conservative older and the modern younger generations. The transition from traditional familism to modern urban living and the preservation of family mores, with which the problem of the attitude toward religion is intrinsically interwoven, are regarded by thoughtful people as basic difficulties in the path of Westernization. As Hourani put it,

> . . . the patriarchal family system remains in existence, but its days are probably numbered. The claims of the family are still prior to those of the individual member of it; but its solidarity is gradually being undermined by the ways of modern urban life

and by the emergence for large sections of the population of alternatives to the cultivation of inherited land in the ancestral village.

The structure of the family is being radically transformed by the change in the status of women. The change is particularly great among the urban middle class. Girls' schools have been opened, and it is possible for women to enter an ever-increasing number of occupations, including the liberal professions. But so far only the edge has been touched of the great problem, which like all great problems in this country is closely bound up with religion: how far is it possible in a modern society to retain the traditional Islamic view of women's status—seclusion and the veil, the theory and in a minority of cases the practice of polygamy, the divorce laws and so on? Of all the difficult questions which the process of Westernization raises, this is perhaps the most difficult; and its difficulty and urgency are likely to increase. The process of change is being speeded by one manifestation of Western civilization above all: the film which expresses a way of feminine life, and a conception of the relations between men and women, which are far from those prevalent in the Islamic world.[56]

Demographic Data

To supplement the foregoing analysis of the Middle Eastern family some demographic data might be useful. Such data, however, are very scanty in most Middle Eastern countries, and it is consequently necessary to extrapolate when generalizations are called for.

Even the most basic of all demographic data, the birth and death rates, are lacking in most Middle Eastern countries.

Only from two Muslim Arab populations (Egyptians and Palestinian Muslims) do we possess series of data extending over a number of years. These figures show that the typical crude birth rate ranges between 40 and 50, placing these countries into the top brackets of the so-called "high fertility countries." No general trend of either decrease or increase is observable, although the war years were accompanied by a definite drop in crude birth rates, the low having been reached in both countries in 1942.

The birth rates of the Christian population groups in the Middle East (Palestinian Christian Arabs; Cyprus, with its 80 per cent of Greek Christians; and also Lebanon with its slight Christian Arab majority) are lower. They range from 25 to 35.

High birth rate is usually accompanied by high death rate, and this is what we find in the Middle East. The Egyptian crude death rate ranged, in the course of the two decades of 1930 to 1950 between 25 and 29, reaching the low of 19.2 in 1950–52. The death rate of the Palestinian Muslims decreased from over 26 in 1932 to less than 20 by 1942. The Christian populations, characterized by a lower birth rate, show a correspondingly lower death rate, as well as a hesitant but noticeable trend for the decrease of the latter (from 16 in 1932 to less than 10 in 1945 in Palestine, and to 6.7 in 1953–55 in Cyprus).

The differential between crude birth rate and crude death rate gives the crude rate of natural increase, which shows an increasing trend in those populations of the Middle East that evince a decreasing trend in death rate.

As to the probable future trends of population movement in the Middle East only a few very general observations can be made. The most immediate demographic effect of industrialization, Westernization, and urbanization is a gradual improvement in the rate of infant mortality that can be noticed in several Middle Eastern countries already today. This is followed by a slower but no less definite decrease in general mortality, as a consequence of which the number of births increases over the number of deaths, and the total population embarks upon a more and more pronounced natural increase.

After a while, industrialization is followed by a fall in birth rate, as was shown not only in Europe but also in Japan. However, the decrease in birth rate in the Middle East may not become significant enough to be felt in the national or regional population movements for many more years to come. This means that for the next few years—possibly up to two decades or more—the increase in the number of children who once born will survive will not be counterbalanced or offset by a decrease in the number of children born. After the lapse of this transitional period, however, the onset of a decreasing tendency in the natural increase can be expected. The outlook and values of an ever-growing proportion of the population will undergo a slow and gradual change. The present deeply embedded values, powerful in their hold, safeguarded by social sanctions, will slowly and gradually give way under the impact of Westernization, of changing and improving economic and social conditions. The end result can well be a changed set of demographic traits approximating those of the Western world.

A very important figure in vital statistics is the rate of infant mortality, calculated as either the number of children dying under one year of age per every thousand live births during the year or the number of children dying under one year of age per every thousand children under one year of age at the middle of the year. The difference between the two methods is considerable, the second yielding a higher figure than the first.

The importance of the rates of infant mortality for drawing a demographic picture of any community lies in the fact that the higher the infant mortality rate the greater the waste of human lives, energy, emotional stress, and economic effort expended by the population in relation to every child who is successfully brought up to the age of maturity. Moreover, high general mortality rates usually go hand in hand with high infant mortality rates as well as with high birth rates; so that the end result (that is, the natural increase) of these three high rates together can be the same or only slightly higher than the end result of low birth rates coupled with low infant and general mortality rates. High birth rate and high infant mortality rate (as well as high child mortality up to five years of age) are conducive to a low standard of living because the earning capacity of the adult members of the family is divided among a large number of small children, many of whom do not reach the age of economic productivity.

Only scattered returns are available from a few Middle Eastern countries as to infant mortality, and even those are not reliable because of the probability of incomplete registration. Nevertheless, the figures indicate that infant mortality is on the decrease, as shown by the accompanying data (rates based on live births during the year):[57]

People	*Year*	*Mortality*	*Year*	*Mortality*
Aden Colony	1948	171.3	1958	137.7
Egypt	1944	152.3	1954	140.4
Cyprus	1948	66.9	1958	30.0
Palestine Muslims	1935	148.1	1945	93.9
Palestine Christians	1935	125.8	1945	89.0
Palestine Jews	1935	64.2	1945	35.8

See Statistical Appendix, Table 3, for infant mortality rates 1963–67.

The main single cause for the decrease in infant mortality which can be assumed to be characteristic for the major parts of the Middle East area, is undoubtedly the greater care, both medical and social, enjoyed by the newborn. The beneficial results of infant care can be demonstrated by referring to the extremely great difference in infant mortality rates in Egypt between children under the care of health centers and those not under the care of such centers. In 1945, the infant mortality rate per thousand among children under the care of health centers was 181, among those not under the care of centers, 323; by 1948 the rate of the first group was reduced to 80, while those in the second group showed a decrease to 241 only.

It is a remarkable fact that the male infant mortality is in every case higher, in some cases considerably higher, than the female infant mortality, even in Muslim populations who traditionally value their male children more than their female children, and who, therefore, presumably pay more attention to the health and well-being of a male infant than of a female.

Child mortality rate is the number of children per thousand live births who die before they reach their fifth birthday. The data for child mortality are even scantier than those of infant mortality, but we know, for instance, that in Egypt the rate is 340,[58] and it can be assumed not to be much different in other Middle Eastern countries in which conditions are similar to those of Egypt.

To put the above figures in the proper perspective, they should be compared not only with corresponding figures from the Western world, but also with those of Negro Africa.

In the tribal population of southern Sudan, which culturally has close affinities to Negro Africa, infant mortality seems to be several times higher than in the Middle East. Limited studies carried out among the Nuba mountain tribes resulted in the following infant mortality rates per 1,000 live births:

Tribe	*Mortality*
Heiban	423
Otoro	361
Tira	323

In the same three tribes it was found that the number of children born per mother was low (when compared with the Middle Eastern average), and that the number of children remaining alive per mother was scarcely sufficient to replace the present generation.[59]

Tribe	*Number of women*	*Children born per mother*	*Children alive per mother*
Heiban	100	4.2	2.3
Otoro	77	5	2.7
Tira	112	2.8	1.7
Koalib	33	3.2	1.7

These figures, when taken in conjunction with the estimated infant mortality of 600 in Mukalla in the Aden Protectorate,[60] indicate that the infant mortality rates of the more advanced regions of the Middle East, high though they are, represent a definite advance over the largely uncontrolled situation prevailing in most of Negro Africa and Southern Arabia.

Terminology

The importance of the family and of family life is expressed, among other manifestations, in the extremely rich terminology centering around the family and used in the everyday colloquial in Arab countries. There is, for instance, a considerable number of nouns denoting the *family*, and used sometimes interchangeably, sometimes with fine gradations of meaning. The family consisting of father, mother, and children is called *'ayle* (variant: *'ēle*, or *'īāl*; in plural *'iyāl*, *'ayāl*, or *'ailāt*). Another term for the same concept is *bēt*, which, however, may also mean the extended family living in one house. The extended family is called *āl*, or *ahl*, or *finde* (variants: *fendi*, *fende*), or *feriq* (also pronounced *ferich*).

Since one's relationship to a cousin who is one's father's brother's son or daughter is very different from one's relationship to other types of cousins, it is necessary to distinguish between different types of cousins. In fact, the single English word "cousin," when translated into Arabic, must be reproduced by one of eight terms which are listed below:

ibn 'amm (*'ammī*) (my) father's brother's son	*ibn khāl* (*khālī*) (my) mother's brother's son
bint 'amm (*'ammī*) (my) father's brother's daughter	*bint khāl* (*khālī*) (my) mother's brother's daughter
ibn 'amme (*'ammtī*) (my) father's sister's son	*ibn khāle* (*khāltī*) (my) mother's sister's son
bint 'amme (*'ammtī*) (my) father's sister's daughter	*bint khāle* (*khāltī*) (my) mother's sister's daughter

Terms for first-degree relatives are as follows:[61]

abī, abū'ī	my	father	*bintī*	my	daughter
bābā		daddy	*waladī*	,,	child (m.)
ummī, immī	,,	mother	*ulādī*	,,	children
māma		mummy	*'amm*, (*'ammī*)	,,	father's brother
akhi, akhū'ī	,,	brother			
ukhtī	,,	sister	*'amme* (*'ammtī*)	,,	father's sister
zūjī, jūzī	,,	husband			
bint 'ammī, martī	,,	wife	*khāl* (*khālī*)	,,	mother's brother
maddāmtī	,,	,, (in the cities)	*khāle* (*khāltī*)	,,	mother's sister
ibnī, bnayyī	,,	son			

V. *The Position of Women and Sex Mores*

MIDDLE EASTERN society is complex and mosaiclike. It is intricately structured both vertically and horizontally. In many parts of the huge land area of the Middle East lack of communications has favored the emergence of local differences beneath the over-all but often rather thinly spread veneer of Islamic culture. The strong traditionalism characteristic of the area has tended to perpetuate local variants. These conditions have resulted in the presence of a wide variety of sex mores ranging from the extreme of great strictness on the one hand to that of considerable laxity on the other.

The picture painted by travelogues and even by more serious studies of the area or of a region within it is often one-sided and distorted. Some writers emphasize the restrictions sexual morality places on women, others include titillating details as to socially sanctioned immorality of which they succeeded in getting a glimpse. Generalizations often follow, and the area as a whole is said to conform to one stereotyped pattern.

Islam has, of course, been the most important single factor in determining the traditional position assigned to women all over the Middle East. To this day, the foremost manifestation of the inequality of the sexes can be seen in the different moral standards applied by Islam to men and women. Official Islam countenances a considerable sexual laxity in men while imposing a rigid code of sex mores on women. In a traditional Muslim social environment men and women form two distinct and separate societies that do not mix or mingle. Only in the family circle can closely related men and women meet. Social life in the sense of several unrelated families or couples periodically meeting in a private home or in a public place (such as a café) does not exist, with a few exceptions confined to the thin upper layer of urban society in the countries close to the Mediterranean littoral. The Muslim Middle East has been a man's world and its society a man's society, and these they remained to a large extent to this very day.

Veiling and Seclusion

The official Muslim attitude toward sex is expressed in such institutions as the veiling and segregation of women (often referred to by the Indian term *purdah*). The two are usually thrown together, although in fact they are two different and often unconnected expressions of the position of women. A woman may wear the veil without being secluded, or she may live in such extreme seclusion that she rarely if ever has opportunity to use the veil. Veiling is general or, more precisely, has been general until the impact of Westernization, among townswomen only. As recently as the beginning of the twentieth century, Muslim townswomen wore the veil when leaving their homes for shopping expeditions or for the purpose of paying a visit, and would rarely if ever talk or show their faces to any man except their own husbands and close male relatives.

"The outdoor costume of the Persian women—is made up of three pieces: the big voluminous trousers which slip over the feet and cling closely to the shape of the foot but above the ankle fall full and baggy; over these are worn the large black chuddar, the poor wearing black calico and the rich silk; and then, covering the face, is the veil. This veil is a long strip of white calico with open work for the part covering the eyes, and fastened together at the back of the head by brass, silver, or gold and jewelled clasps, according to the rank of the wearer. Through the open work part of the veil the woman is able to find her way about, and see all that there is to be seen, while no one can see the face behind the veil."[1]

In traditional Turkey the townswoman, when leaving her house, was bundled in her *çarşaf* and veiled beyond recognition. The *çarşaf* was a loose, usually black, wrap that covered her figure from head to foot, and one corner of which used to be drawn over the head and across the face, revealing only the eyes.[2]

In Afghanistan the *burqa* is worn, a covering that envelops the head, is gathered around the line of the forehead and falls to the feet, with two holes covered with netting for the eyes.[3]

The higher the social class to which the urban woman belonged, the greater was the strictness with which she observed the rules of veiling. Actually, veiling was a mark of class distinction rather than a mere Muslim religious tradition, as attested by the fact that the practice was observed by Christians and Jews as well as by Muslims.[4]

Also, the degree of seclusion to which a woman is (or was) subjected depends, within the general traditions of the locality in which she lives, on the social class to which she belongs. Among the women of the upper class, as recently as one or two generations ago, there were such who from puberty to death never left their quarters. As a result of this extreme form of seclusion it was found, in certain Muslim societies, that the incidence of tuberculosis was greater among the women who were never exposed to sunshine than among the men.

In a less stringent form of seclusion among the upper class, women were never supposed to go out to the street in the company of any man, not even in that of their own husbands, but only in the company of one or more elderly women, all of them, of course, heavily veiled.[5]

Nowadays, women of the middle class and to an even greater extent of the lower or working classes are free to go out on shopping expeditions, to visit friends, to go to the *ḥammām* (bath), and the like, veiled but alone. Since the great majority of townswomen belong to these classes, one can generalize and state that in most cases veiling is practiced even when the rules of seclusion are considerably relaxed.

Among the Jews of the Middle East, female seclusion is observed, as a rule, less strictly than among the Muslims.[6]

Among the fellahin of Syria, Jordan, Israel, and Iraq, in several of the oases of Northwestern Arabia, as well as in the smaller towns of these areas, the veiling of women is not practiced. Also, in many places in southern and eastern Arabia, including the small towns, the veil is absent. Only in the larger cities, for example, in Ṣan'a, capital of Yemen, is veiling practiced. In southern Palestine it also was practiced, probably under Egyptian influence.[7]

Occasionally it is found among both Bedouins and fellahin that brides are veiled on the day of their wedding but otherwise veiling is not practiced, or that unmarried women go unveiled, but married women have to veil their faces.[8]

Among the nomads of northern Arabia, in Iraq, among the fellahin in Israel, and the seminomadic tribes of Jordan, women who wear no veil nevertheless frequently cover the lower part of the face with a sleeve or corner of the headkerchief when encountering or speaking to a stranger.[9] Sometimes they merely take a corner of the headkerchief in the mouth.[10] It also happens that, upon encountering a stranger, the unveiled woman turns away and talks to him with her face averted.[11]

In Egypt too, village women are always ready at a moment's notice to draw the edge of the headkerchief across the lower part of the face or at least to take a corner of it into the mouth, while in some places they cover the face with a long black veil, glossy or dull, when they go out. In the Qena district this veil is dark brown, while in the Sharqiyya province it is white.[12] No veiling of women is practiced among the Tuareg who regard the veil (*lithām*) as the prerogative of the free men.[13]

As we adduce more and more examples, it becomes increasingly clear that no hard and fast rules can be found as to the presence or absence of veiling in a certain region or group. The Rwala, one of the noblest tribes of the Syrian-Arabian Desert, practice no veiling, and girls are even free to let their tresses be seen.[14] Among several other tribes of the Arabian Northwest, such as the Benī Ṣakhr, Ḥwēṭāt, Benī 'Aṭiyya, veiling is absent.[15] In some of the other tribes north of the 'Aqaba-Kuwait line the women cover the lower part of the face up to the nose with a thin black veil (*milfa*), while several tribes south of this line, such as the Muṭayr, Ḥarb, Sba'a, Reshayda, Benī Hajir, 'Awāzim, 'Ajmān, but not the Shammar and some of the Ḥijāz tribes) wear a longer or shorter black face mask (the so-called *burqa*) hanging down from the forehead and covering the entire face with the exception of the eyes visible through two eyeholes. The Ṣolubba and other low-status groups share with the noble Rwala the absence of veils.[16] In some of the oases of Arabia, such as Teyma, the women go about unveiled.[17] In southern Arabia, while veiling is practiced in most of the towns,[18] occasionally with a *burqa*-like black face cloth with a silver line stitched down the nose and two eye slits,[19] among village women, the veil is rarer[20] and in some areas completely absent.[21] Among a few tribes such as the ʻAbida in Hadhramaut, a *milfa*-type half veil is worn.[22] In the Bāṭina district of Oman in some of the villages the women are unveiled, in others they are veiled. In the interior of Oman veiling is more general.[23] The generalization of Thomas,[24] "All the women of the sands in Southern Arabia are veiled," is therefore questionable. All that one can venture to say is that up to the twentieth century veiling was the accepted practice in the middle and upper classes of urban society; that among the lower class townspeople it was largely absent; and that among the villagers and nomads it was (and is) only sporadically practiced.

This being the case, the laws and other efforts to abolish veiling affect only a limited sector of Middle Eastern society; although it has to be recognized that as a symbol of the emancipation of women the discarding of the veil is of great moment for the area as a whole. The task the male and female reformers set themselves is still far from being accomplished as the 1960's lead us toward the end of the second third of the twentieth century. In the Arabian Peninsula veiling and seclusion still survive in practically unchanged form. In Iraq, Syria, Jordan, and Lebanon, with the leading families showing the example, these old traditions begin to give way. In these countries, "the real veil that covers completely the whole figure is still carried either by a particularly conservative class of people, or by the ignorant masses in the cities; among the educated middle and upper class it is either totally removed, or else symbolically represented by a scarf to protect the hair, or by a thin veil on the face or on the hair. Yet it should be admitted that the recent removal of the veil in certain circles has not brought about the free association of men and women. This is why marriage is still a family concern. It has to be arranged by parents and to follow certain conditions and formalities, although a certain acquaintance could be made between the two parties in strictly liberal circles. Women are still treated with the utmost reserve, and the traditional respect of women and their chivalrous treatment have not been affected by their emancipation."[25]

In Egypt, the gradual and hesitant discarding of the veil, first by the upper class, then by the middle class Muslim women, serves as an example also for the Christian women of the same classes. The women of the lower class, who constitute the great majority of the female population, show themselves more reticent in this respect.[26] In Iran, the veil was largely discarded in 1936 by the Muslim townswomen;[27] but, following the abdication of Riza Shah in 1941, there was a certain resurgence of conservatism. Only in one country, Turkey, has the abolition of veiling been successfully carried out, at least in the towns;[28] in the villages in which veiling used to be practiced, the familiar female movement of pulling the edge of the headkerchief across the face was observed by this writer as recently as in the summer of 1959.

Social Intercourse

Just as the seclusion and veiling of townswomen goes back to pre-Islamic times and even to ancient Near Eastern origins, so also the unveiled status and greater freedom of movement enjoyed by village and nomadic women are ancient traditions in the area. Veiling inhibits women in doing their chores and, accordingly, in societies where the women's outdoor work is an economic necessity they go about unveiled. This is the case in most agricultural villages in the Middle East where women help their husbands or fathers in tilling the fields and in the performance of other agricultural work, as well as among the nomadic tribes where the putting up and pulling down of the tents and the tending of the flocks is the women's task.

The absence of the veil and of seclusion makes for a freer demeanor of the women in their occasional encounters with nonrelated men. In ancient Arabia the women of the desert tribes went unveiled and associated freely with men. Much of this freedom of manners has been preserved to this day among the nomadic tribes primarily, but also among some of the village folk. Especially among the goat and sheep-breeding tribes of the Arabian Peninsula, where the flocks are entrusted to the care of women and young girls, the shepherdesses feel free to enter into friendly conversation with any wayfarer passing by, whether friend or stranger. Such chance encounters are often the occasion of some good-natured banter between man and maiden.[29] The same open and unrestrained friendliness is manifested by women of the oases[30] as well as of the villages of southern Arabia.[31]

At home, in the tent, in the absence of her husband, the wife is supposed to show hospitality to guests, to invite them to the part of the tent reserved for men, and to supply them with the utensils and wherewithal for preparing coffee. If she is acquainted with the guests, she joins them after supper, drinks coffee with them, and amuses herself in their company till midnight.[32] Occasionally, some bantering takes place in the tent as well, even in the presence of the husband, between a male guest and the wife of the host; the host takes no offense at such playful courting of his wife.[33] This actually is the same custom that Ibn Battuta found in the fourteenth century among the Berbers of North Africa and which he reported with considerable indignation.[34]

Among the Arabian nomads, girls have much premarital freedom in their relations with men. Although virginity is (with certain exceptions, about which later) as highly prized among them as among the villagers and townsfolk, Bedouin girls have many opportunities for meeting their lovers outside the camp, either during the day while the girl grazes her flock, or at night. On such occasions, although the traditional mores require of the girl to guard her virginity, flirting and petting take place, and incautious girls may even become pregnant. An unmarried pregnant girl must either try abortion, in which her female relatives help her, or persuade her lover to marry her at once, or run away from her tribe and seek refuge in the settled territory, or commit suicide. Should she be found out by her menfolk, they will be in honor bound to kill her. If she was raped, she may be spared, but her child will be killed.[35]

While among the Arabian nomads secrecy and decorum must be maintained, in nineteenth century Egypt it was "not uncommon to see females of the lower orders flirting and jesting with men in public, and men laying their hands upon them very freely."[36] Especially on the occasion of certain popular religious festivals, such as the 'Ashūra, the tenth day of the month of Muḥarram, men and women used to mingle freely in the mosques, and it was said by the people of Cairo that "no man goes to the mosque of the Hasanein on the day of Ashoora but for the sake of the women; that is to be justled among them . . . ."[37]

To the west of Egypt, among the nomads of the Libyan desert, seclusion exists only among the noble tribes. In the other groups, young men and girls mix freely, boys are allowed openly to court the girls, to visit them in their camps, and to sing to them of their love in verses of their own composition, as a preliminary to marriage.[38]

Only in isolated places does one find a definite relaxation of the strict rules of sexual morality. As an outstanding example, one may cite the Siwa Oasis on the western fringes of Egypt where, according to observers, extramarital relations, prostitution, and sodomy are rampant.[39]

Sharp distinction must be drawn between this kind of sexual liberty, which is regarded as immoral by the society itself in which it is practiced, and the traditionally regulated and accepted premarital freedom accorded to women in several places in the Middle East. Apart from a number of extreme cases in which exaggerated notions of hospitality resulted in the sexual accommodation of visiting strangers,[40] where premarital freedom is accorded to women the behavior pattern established shows a certain similarity to the modern Western habit of "dating and mating." Among the westerly neighbors of the Siwans, the Tuareg of the Sahara, ". . . Before marriage, which for oriental women occurs comparatively late in life, Tuareg girls enjoy a measure of freedom which would shock even the modern respectable folk of Southern Europe . . . it is common for a girl who is in love with a man to take a camel and ride all night to see him and then return to her own place, or for a suitor to make expeditions of superhuman endurance to see his lady . . . . Illicit love affairs inevitably occur: if they have unfortunate consequences the man is called upon to marry the woman, but infanticide is not unknown. Once married, the woman is expected to behave with decorum and modesty. Public opinion on these matters is strong. The married state, however, does not prevent a woman admitting men friends to an intimacy similar to that existing, perhaps, only among the Anglo-Saxon peoples."[41] It is easily recognizable that this Tuareg custom differs only in degree but not in kind from that of the Rwala and other noble Arab tribes of the Syrian-Arabian desert referred to above.

Among the Tuareg of Ahaggar in the Central Sahara, the premarital sex relations are given a more or less institutionalized form and are supposed to lead ultimately to marriage. Around the age of sixteen, both the young men and the girls of the tribes are admitted to the *ahals*, periodic meetings, taking place late in the evening outside the camp, and usually accompanied by *asri*, that is a considerable relaxation of the mores (literally: running with loosened bridles). The *ahal*, which attracts young men from neighboring camps, starts with playing the *amzad*, a one-string instrument played with a round bow, and group singing, but soon the young men and girls start rubbing noses, which is the particular Targui form of kissing. Late at night, when the *ahal* ends, everyone is supposed to return to his or her own camp, but in actuality private trysts follow, either during the night or on later occasions. As a result of this institution, pre-Islamic in its origin, both girls and young men begin their sex life as soon as they reach maturity, and no value whatsoever is placed on virginity. Love affairs leading to marriages usually start at such *ahal* meetings. After marriage, however, the wife is supposed to remain faithful to her husband, who is expected to show no jealousy if old *ahal*-friends of his wife continue to court her in a Platonic fashion. The question whether marital fidelity of wives is merely an ideal or is actually adhered to is answered differently by different observers.[42]

At the extreme west of the Middle East, the Ouled Tidrarin, a nomadic Moorish tribe in the western central part of the Spanish Sahara, are reported "to celebrate exceptionally good harvests with a curious sort of strip-tease dance, a thoroughly pagan performance which begins with the young men and women lining up in two ranks facing one another. First a boy steps forward, places a present of sugar and tea or trinkets on the ground, and retires to his place. Then a girl steps out between the lines, lets her clothes fall to the ground, picks up the present, and goes back naked to her place. After this has been going on for a while, to the accompaniment of much whooping and yelling, self-restraint begins to crumble and eventually nature takes its course. Such doings make one wonder just what the day-to-day premarital relations between the sexes may be like, but so far no one who knows the Moors well—and there are few who do—has even mentioned the subject."[42a]

To the southwest of the Tuareg area, in the city of Timbuctoo, virginity, although valued in the eyes of Muslim law, is found upon marriage only among Arab girls, and is rare in the other ethnic groups.[43]

Also in the northeastern parts of the Middle East, tribal societies have preserved much of that ancient freedom of women that prevailed in pre-Islamic Arabia. Among the Kurdish and Lur tribes of western Iran, "young men and girls meet freely, they join in the old folk dances, and the courting of the marriageable girls goes on in the old forms, in which quick wit and repartee are combined with spontaneous or traditional poetical expression of feelings."[44]

In general, among both the villagers and the nomads the women's activities are largely confined to the home or the family circle. However, women help their husbands in certain types of work outside the home as well, such as gathering brushwood and dung, tending the flocks, fetching water, among the nomads; taking food to the menfolk working in the fields, helping them in field work, especially at harvest time, etc., among the villagers. They fatten sheep and dry the meat; pick lentils and spread them to dry; prepare crushed wheat, and bake their "handkerchief bread" in the courtyard oven fired with wood gathered by them. They make jams and tomato paste for use in stews during the winter. They carry water from the fountain, are busy with the harvesting and winnowing, and in the winter months spin with old-fashioned wooden spindles. To these activities must be added the participation of women in the traditional forms of hospitality in tent and house. All this has resulted in a considerable amount of traditionally sanctioned social contact between nonrelated men and women among the nomads and the villagers, and in the participation of both sexes in joint activities such as annual and family feasts. Nevertheless, it is a fact that men and women form two distinct and separate societies, with the family circle as the only locus for meeting on a day-to-day basis. It has been noted by one observer, for example, that three quarters of an hour before the sunset the young men of the village patrol up and down in front of the fountain, but when the girls approach to draw water, retire so as not to stand around ogling the women.[45]

This feeling of embarrassment in the presence of the opposite sex is characteristic of both men and women in many parts of the Middle East. Matters of sex, though discussed by men among themselves or by women among themselves, can never constitute a subject for public enjoyment or entertainment; sexual and physical modesty are the psychological concomitants of the strict moral code.

Aside from the exceptions referred to above, the standard for the Middle East is to regard premarital and extramarital sex relations of women with the utmost severity. In most nomadic tribes such a woman, if discovered, is put to death by her father or brothers (but not by her husband). No information as to the actual administration of such extreme punishment in villages is available, but the severity of the attitude toward female sexual laxity persists in them as well. Urban society is in a state of transition in this respect as in many other aspects of social intercourse. For lack of information all that can be said is a rough generalization to the effect that the higher the social class and the more advanced its Westernization, the less attention is paid by it to the traditional sexual code.

This being the situation, the majority of men and women have no opportunity for premarital or extramarital sexual activity, because this would immediately bring them into collision with the traditional guardians of female chastity: the women's fathers and brothers. There is an opinion, or suspicion, that this situation is favorable to the development of homosexual practices as well as sodomy, but for lack of data no statement can be ventured on this subject. In the towns, and especially in the port cities, prostitution exists, in places in legalized form. During an Arab Women's Congress in Cairo in 1944, a stand was taken against this legalized prostitution, as well as against the white slave traffic.[46]

As to sexual relations in marriage, tradition allows complete freedom to husband and wife, with the exception of the days during and immediately after the menses and a longer period after childbirth when relations are tabooed. To what extent these prohibitions are actually observed by the various ecologic and ethnoreligious groups in the Middle East is hard to say, because, again, no data are available. Where a man has two wives, he is traditionally expected to devote his attentions equally and alternatingly to each of them.

The spread of education among the young men creates a demand for the education of girls as well. The number of girls receiving primary or secondary education is still much lower in every Middle Eastern country than that of boys. One of the results of this inequality is that a class of educated young men is growing up which does not find equally educated women among whom it could choose spouses. As can be expected, therefore, the demand of the feminists for equal educational opportunities for girls is seconded by the young educated males.

Typical of the change taking place at present in the Middle Eastern urban society is the increasing freedom accorded to women. Up to recent times, women in town as well as in country were regarded as inferior to men. In the past, it was considered a disgrace for a girl to work outside her home, but in recent years girls have begun to seek employment in government offices, schools, medical clinics, hospitals, and even in business. Nevertheless, even the educated urbanites, although consciously aware of the equality of the educated woman, have not yet overcome the feeling that she is weaker than man and that she requires help, provision, and protection. Social life in the Western sense of mixed public parties, etc., is only beginning to emerge. The girl is always guarded by her family and chaperoned by her brothers, sisters, or friends. She must always be at home before dark and is never allowed to go home alone at night. A sign of the times is that nowadays an engaged couple is occasionally allowed to walk and talk together as long as they stay within the bounds of morality, while not so long ago a fiancé was not supposed to see his betrothed until the wedding night.

A certain amount of separation between the sexes exists also among the conservative Christians in the Middle East. While the Maronites in Lebanon "do not segregate their women as do Muslims, and one may ask a man after his wife's health, a reserve is maintained in public or private, and one does not talk to a woman alone. Husband does not give his wife his arm when walking or talk familiarly with her in public. Men go with men, e.g. on Sunday to feasts, the women follow in a group. Even in church they sit separated by a wooden grill."[47]

Term and Trial Marriage

Special forms of connubium that were practiced in pre-Islamic days and survived in certain parts of the Middle East down to the present time are the term marriage, usually referred to as *muṭ'ah*, or "enjoyment," and the trial marriage.

The first reports about term marriage in the Middle East are contained in Talmudic and Roman sources. The Talmud states unequivocally that among the Jews of Babylonia in the third century A.D. it was legal to marry a woman for a term as short as one day. After the expiration of the specified term the marriage was automatically terminated. In fact, even sages and rabbis when visiting in another town used to practice this custom. Of Rabh (third century A.D.) it is reported that when he visited the town of Dardashir (variant: Darshish) he used to have it announced: "Who wants to become my wife for one day?" Rabh Nahman (early fourth century A.D.) is reported to have done the same on his periodic visits to Shekansibh.[48]

Contemporary with the above is the report of the Roman historian, Ammianus Marcellinus (325–398 A.D.), who states (in Book XIV, Chap. 4, of his history of the Roman empire) that the Saracens of Arabia Felix (that is, Southern Arabia) "spend their lives in constant wanderings. They hire their women for money for a certain period according to agreement, and in order to make it a kind of marriage, the future wife offers the husband, under the name of a dowry (*dos*), a spear and a tent, so as to go away from him after the fixed day . . . ."

Term marriage seems to have been widely practiced all over Arabia in pre-Islamic days, and Mohammed therefore felt constrained to sanction it. The Koran (4 : 28) states, "such women as ye want to enjoy, give them their hire as a lawful due; for there is no crime in you about what ye agree between you after such lawful due." Nevertheless, term marriages were regarded as a lesser commitment than regular marriages and were, consequently, countenanced even with partners who were unfit for the latter. The story is told of a Ḥimyarite Sayyid who met a woman on the road and she offered him marriage then and there. However, when she found out from him that he was a Yemeni of the heretical Rāfiḍī sect, while she was of the rival Tamīmī tribe and of the Khārijite persuasion, she quickly withdrew her offer. But the Sayyid, who evidently got in the meantime keen on the idea, begged her: "Be of good sense and let your soul be generous toward me and let neither of us remember our ancestry or religion." She retorted: "When a marriage is made public, are not private concerns revealed?" The Sayyid then put forward a new idea: "I have a different suggestion to make to you . . . namely *mutʻah*, of which no one need know anything." When the woman replied that term marriage is the sister of harlotry, the Sayyid reminded her that it was allowed according to the Koran, and the woman finally consented to this form of marriage.[49]

As to the payment a man had to render in order to enjoy term marriage with a woman, a piece of clothing was sufficient. Sabra, one of the companions of Mohammed, reminisced about such an experience he had shortly after the conquest of Mecca by the Prophet. "I went with one of my friends to a woman of the Bani ʻAmir, and we inquired whether she would be willing to contract *mutʻah*. She thereupon asked what we intended to give her, and we offered her our mantles. The mantle of my friend was finer than mine, but I was more handsome than he. When the woman looked at my friend's mantle, she was visibly inclined toward it; but when she saw me, I evoked her admiration. Thereupon she stated that she chose me, and that my mantle was sufficient payment. I remained with her for three days, and then the Prophet commanded all those who had women in *mutʻah* to send them away . . . ."

According to the same source, Mohammed's companions missed their wives during a military campaign to such an extent that they wanted to castrate themselves. This the Prophet forbade them to do, but he permitted them to contract term marriages.[50] Term marriage was regarded as a safeguard against immorality, and solicitous fathers ordered their sons to contract *muṭʿah* while on pilgrimage to Mecca—at least according to one account describing such an event in the first half of the eighth century.[51]

Sunnī Islam nevertheless soon outlawed term marriages.[52] All the stringency of Sunnite jurisprudence remained, however, powerless to eradicate another variety of marriage closely related to, although not identical with, *muṭʿah.* Many Muslim jurists agreed that only if a time limit is an expressly stated condition in the marriage contract is the marriage *muṭʿah*, and thus forbidden; if a marriage is merely contracted with *the intention* that it should last only a definite period, it is valid and permitted. This type of marriage, in which both parties were fully aware that it was a temporary affair, was also widespread in pre-Islamic Arabia and has remained legal to this day.

The most famous of women practicing such provisional or trial marriages in the days of Mohammed was Umm Khārija. She was reputed to have had forty husbands from twenty different tribes. If a suitor came to her and said, "Will you marry me?" she answered, "It's a marriage," and the marriage could be consummated without any further formality or delay. It was the custom of the women who practiced these trial marriages that if they were satisfied with their new husbands they prepared for them food the morning after the wedding night; if not, they gave them no food, but sent them away. The mother of Mohammed's grandfather, it is said, was one of these oft-marrying women.[53]

In Arabia, including the holiest city of Islam, Mecca, these customs survived almost to the present time. In Ha'il and its environs in the Arabian Desert, temporary marriages little better than prostitution were common down to the 1860's. From other parts of the Peninsula their occurrence is reported as late as the beginning of the twentieth century. In many cases the temporary marriages were a concomitant of the pilgrimage to a holy city in which no hotels were available, but the pilgrim could find accommodation in the house of a local woman provided he went through the formality of marrying her. The same situation obtained in connection with any other type of travel as well. As long as the man remained in the foreign city he thus had both a home and a wife. Before leaving, he pronounced the divorce formula, thereby ending all mutual obligations.[54]

In Egypt, a prohibition of prostitution (and of public female dancing) in 1834, with bastinado as the mandatory punishment for both culprits if caught, resulted in an increase in legal marriages of extremely short duration. The man would ask the woman, "Will you marry me?" and she would answer, "Yes." His next question would be, "For how much?" and she would name the sum. The man would give her the money and she would therewith become his lawfully wedded wife. Next morning he would pronounce the formula of divorce and go his way.[55]

Trial marriages of a usually somewhat longer duration are practiced to this day among certain tribes in Southern Arabia. The Say'ars told Ingrams "that they gave their girls to anyone who wanted them. After about a couple of months' trial the man might marry the girl, otherwise she would be returned with thanks and without ill-feelings."[56]

In contrast to Sunnī Islam, the Shī'ites retained term marriage as a legal institution to this day. Most of the reports term these *muṭ'ah* marriages—a form of legalized prostitution. It is especially in the holy cities of Shī'ite Islam that the *muṭ'ah* flourishes. Reliable travelers have observed in the course of the last hundred years that in the shadow of the Shī'ite sanctuaries many women contract this type of short-term union several times a day.[57]

However, the term marriage can serve also the opposite purpose: to make sure that a marriage does not end prematurely in divorce. To ensure this, some people contract *muṭ'ah* marriage for ninety-nine years. Since such a term marriage contract can be terminated prior to its specified expiration only with the consent of both contracting parties, it gives the wife a security she can never enjoy under a regular Muslim marriage. On the other hand, in a term marriage the husband has the right to refuse marital union which in ordinary marriage would give the woman the right to divorce. Children born of *muṭ'ah* marriage have all the right of the offspring of ordinary marriages, but the term wife (called *ṣigha*), does not inherit from her husband, nor does he from her.[58]

Female Occupations

With regard to the occupations of women, the traditional situation all over the Middle East has been for them to be employed in the home and on the fields only. However, even the share of the women in agricultural work is but rarely reflected in statistical returns which, as a rule, do not count women as separate gainfully employed, or economically active, persons in case they merely help the male members of their families in the fields. It is for this reason that in the statistical returns of Egypt in 1937, only 896,950 women appeared as engaged in agriculture as against 5,198,032 men; or that among the Muslims in Palestine in 1931, only 8,451 women figured as engaged in "primary production" (mainly agriculture) as against 107,462 men.[59]

A true picture of the situation emerges from the Turkish census only, which in 1935 listed 2,734,025 women as against 2,843,752 men, as engaged in agriculture, and 3,096,799 women as against 3,383,269 men as engaged in "primary production."[60] The average Middle Eastern rural housewife undoubtedly takes her place in agricultural work at the side of her husband.

In addition to housework and fieldwork, the third traditional occupation of women in the Middle East is in the so-called "old industries," a term denoting the traditional and largely old-fashioned home industries, handicraft, rugmaking, and the like. In rural areas, the occasionally and sporadically practiced "old industries" are usually as much family undertakings as the tilling of the fields; they are taken up especially in the agricultural low seasons for the sake of augmenting the meager income of the family. In the towns, they are often carried out in small workshops in an employee capacity on a piece basis. The ratio of female to male labor employed in these "old industries" is exemplified by the results of an inquiry undertaken in 1937 in Syria and Lebanon which showed that 58,413 women were engaged in them as against 90,065 men (as well as 22,300 children).[61]

As to the so-called "new industries," that is, the recently established modern industrial undertakings, women have been much slower to take to them than men. The number of women employed in Syria and Lebanon in "new industries" in 1937 was 6,379 as against 24,007 men. The number of women employed in industry in Turkey (1935) was one fifth of the number of men, while in Egypt (1937) and among the Palestinian Muslims (1931) it was only one tenth.

The participation of women in commerce is even slighter. In Turkey 5 per cent, in Egypt 3 per cent of the total number of workers employed in commerce were women. It is only in domestic service that women are represented in some countries, for example in Turkey, by higher figures than men.

The meager participation of women in industrial work as well as in commerce as against their intensive participation in agricultural work means that the urban laborer, if he is a married man, has to earn enough to support his entire family, while the agricultural worker in the village is, as a rule, helped by his wife to make a living. The village-to-town migration and the exchange of agricultural work in favor of urban industrial labor therefore improves the economic conditions of a worker's family much less than would appear from the average income figures of family heads.

Another factor to consider in this connection is the difference between the ratio of female and male earnings in village and in town. While in the village the earnings of the women (as expressed in produce) can be as high as those of men, depending on the number of hours spent by each in the field, in urban industrial labor the wages of the women are in most cases much lower than those of men. In Syria and Lebanon in 1937, men earned in the old industries 10.50 francs, while women in similar types of work earned only 4.93 francs, that is, less than half. In new industries, men earned 13.40 fr., women 5.05 fr. In Iraq (1933), men earned 50 to 300 fils, women 25 to 50.[62] Similar differences between the wages of men and women exist in other countries.

The Emancipation of Women

Within the last forty-odd years Middle Eastern women of the leisure and educated class have been working actively toward raising the status of woman by studying her condition and agitating for reform. In Syria, "after World War I when the country became independent of Ottoman Turkey, women were still veiled but not inactive. However, the threats of traditionalists restricted them to rescue work and first-aid. Secondary schools for girls were opened by the Syrian government; some were sent to Europe for further study. The University of Damascus finally graduated two lady doctors from 'very good families' and two more as bachelors of law." A periodical, *Al Arousse* (*The Bride*), was launched and dedicated to women by a woman author. A school for the daughters of Syrian war victims was opened by a woman, and patriotic and national associations for women were organized, among them the "Society of the Tree of Literature," led by a lady of the family of Prince Abd-el-Kader; the "Society of the Drop of Milk," which provides infants with milk; the "Society of the Red Crescent" (emulating the Red Cross), which has branches operated by women, and others.[63]

In Lebanon similar efforts were made by the Federation of Arab Women's Clubs (founded in 1921), an organization comprising 28 member societies with more than 2,000 members and representing the various creeds and institutions in that country.[64] In Turkey, the law of 1934 accorded political rights to women. In Iran, where the emancipation of women was proclaimed in 1938, the reform measures lost much of their vigor after the abdication of Riza Shah Pehlevi in 1941. In Egypt, feminist movements led by the Egyptian Feminist Association, have been organized for the purpose of obtaining general suffrage. In 1944, an Arab Women's Congress was held in Cairo. Delegations from several Arab countries participated and important resolutions concerning the status of women in the Arab world were passed.[65]

Among the things for which modern Middle Eastern women have been fighting has been the right to enter the professions, for while some women have gained entrance into medicine, dentistry, nursing, law, and education, most of them are still governed by tradition and custom. However, "the new generation is overcoming the old prejudice which 20 years ago thrust the woman doctor down to the level of a midwife and nothing else. Journalism has been attempted by one or two women. The difficulty there is that a woman is somewhat restricted in going about in search of copy. . . . Girls who wished to learn typing and shorthand and go into offices were warned by their parents and guardians that they would probably lose their character if they did anything 'so fast.' However, some more far-sighted people said that if they went to English or American offices they would be quite safe."[66]

A discussion of several aspects of the traditional man-woman relationship is found in Chapter 16, "Women in a Man's World," of this volume.

VI. Cousin Marriage

THE MIDDLE Eastern family has been characterized above as patrilineal, patrilocal, patriarchal, extended, occasionally polygynous, and emphatically endogamous. The first five of these six basic traits are found also in one or more of the culture areas contiguous to the Middle East. The sixth, endogamy, and especially its most conspicuous Middle Eastern form, which is marriage between a man and his father's brother's daughter (*bint 'amm* in Arabic), is practically nonexistent outside the Middle Eastern culture continent.

Cousin Marriage Outside the Middle East

Outside the Middle East the practice of marriage between children of two brothers is extremely rare. With the spread of Islam it was introduced into India where the Muslims have a definite preference for all types of cousin marriages, with marriage between the children of two brothers being the most common. The verbalized motivation is the one usual in the Middle East: cousin marriage keeps the family free from foreign blood and retains property within the family.[1]

In Madagascar marriage between the children of two brothers also is very common, and is looked upon as the most suitable marriage since it keeps the property in the family. Since descent is matrilineal, however, a man marrying his father's brother's daughter is not considered marrying a blood relative. Children of two siblings of opposite sex are allowed to marry after the performance of a rite whose purpose is to remove the impediment of consanguinity; but marriage between the children of two uterine sisters is regarded with horror as incest.[2] Although there is a strong Arabic element in the language of Madagascar,[3] which is a clear evidence of the presence of Arab influences on the island, this marriage preference pattern is very different from the Middle Eastern one, in spite of the frequency of marriage between children of two brothers.

According to one authority, among the Bantu tribes of South Africa the natives of the mountains "of the interior" almost as a rule married the daughter of their father's brother, in order to keep property from being lost to the family.[4] For lack of more detailed information it is not possible to state whether this Bantu marriage pattern resembles the Middle Eastern or the Madagascan type.

In other parts of the world, cousin marriage means cross-cousin marriage; marriage between the children of two brothers is usually prohibited, or, in rare instances, grudgingly tolerated.[5]

Half-Sibling and Cousin Marriage in Antiquity

In the Middle East itself the practice of cousin marriage and even of half-sibling marriage goes back to antiquity.

In ancient Egypt, the Pharaohs married their sisters or half-sisters, a practice continued by the Ptolemies.[6] In Roman Egypt, marriage between full siblings and half-siblings occurred frequently in the families of agriculturists and artisans.[7] According to Diodorus (i, 27), sibling marriage was a duty for Egyptians. However, it has to be taken into consideration that in ancient Egypt the wife was called "sister," and lovers called each other "brother" and "sister," even when they were not siblings.[8]

Whether there was brother-sister marriage in ancient Iran[9] is open to serious doubts in view of objections raised by both Parsi scholars[10] and Western students. According to these authorities, what the early Iranians practiced was marriage between first cousins, which is certainly the meaning of the modern Persian equivalent of the contested ancient term. In the Pehlevi texts, which in their present form date from the sixth to the ninth century, marriages between parents and children as well as between siblings are defended and advocated, as they are in the later period of the Sassanian dynasty and in subsequent centuries.

However, from the fifteenth century on, in the Persian writings called "Rivayat," references are found to marriage of first cousins only, with obscure allusions to marriage between closer blood relations as being long extinct.[11] The ancient Persians seem to have used the terms "sister," "mother," and "daughter" both in their proper sense and in a wider sense as did the ancient Egyptians, and great care is required to avoid confusion in interpreting them.[12] Similarly, among the ancient Hebrews, and the ancient and modern Arabs, these and other kinship terms were and respectively are used in a wider sense as well. Among the Phoenicians, King Tabnith married his father's daughter (by another mother), Am'ashtoreth, and at Tyre a man was allowed to marry his father's daughter down to the time of Achilles Tatius. The same thing occurred at Mecca; and a trace of this kind of marriage has survived to modern times at Mirbāṭ.[13]

Paternal half-sibling marriage occurred, and cousin marriage was the prevalent practice among the Hebrews in the patriarchal period.[14] Abraham himself married his half-sister Sarah (from the same father but from another mother; cf. Gen. 20 : 12). Isaac married his father's brother's son's daughter (Gen. 22 : 23; 24 : 47, 48). Nahor married a daughter of his brother, Haran (Gen. 11 : 27, 29). Esau married his father's brother's two daughters, Mahalath and Basemath (Gen. 28 : 9; 36 : 3). Jacob married his mother's brother's two daughters, Leah and Rachel (Gen. 29), who were also his father's father's brother's son's son's daughters.

Close in-family marriage was practiced by the Hebrews in later times as well. Amram married Jochebed, his father's sister (Ex. 6 : 20; Num. 26 : 59). Amram's son Aaron married his father's father's father's brother's son's son's son's son's daughter Elisheba (I Chron. 2 : 10; Ex. 6 : 23). Hezron (a grandson of Judah) married his father's father's brother's son's son's daughter (I Chron. 2 : 4, 21; Gen. 50 : 23). The sons of Kish married the daughters of his brother Eleazar (I Chron. 23 : 21–22). In the days of King David marriage between paternal half-siblings was still legal (II Sam. 13). Marriage between brother and sister was still practiced in Judah at the time of Ezekiel (sixth century B.C.), although the prophet strongly condemned it as an abomination (Ezek. 22 : 11).

The hero of the Book of Tobit marries his father's brother's daughter, and according to the angel who accompanies Tobit, it would have been a mortal sin for Reuel (Tobit's uncle) to give his daughter to anybody else but to Tobit who had the right to inherit from his sonless uncle (cf. Book of Tobit 6; 1 ff. and 7 : 2, 10–12).

In the Arab world itself, while the right of a man to the hand of his *bint 'amm* goes back to pre-Islamic times,[15] marriage between half-siblings has disappeared following the spread of Islam. The only Muslim population that has countenanced it until recently seems to be the Mohammadan South Slavs.[16]

Extent and Frequency

The custom of cousin marriage has been confirmed and perpetuated by Muslim tradition and has remained alive down to the present day in all parts of the Middle East. According to the Hanafite school of legists, a man may give his daughter in marriage to his brother's son without her consent, and a young man may decide for himself whether he wants or does not want to marry his *bint 'amm*.[17] The fact that marriage between children of two brothers is regarded as the ideal marriage and is preferred in practice to all other unions is reflected in everyday linguistic usage. The common term a man employs in addressing his wife in Arabic is *bint 'ammī*, meaning "daughter of my father's brother"; while the wife addresses her husband as *ibn 'ammī*, son of my father's brother, whether the two actually stand in this relationship to each other or not.

The preference for cousin marriage is reflected in numerous proverbs and stories current among the Bedouins of Arabia and in the lands of the Fertile Crescent.[18] Marriage between the *ibn 'amm* and *bint 'amm* is well attested from all parts of the Middle East, and in several places the two are the usual marriage partners. In Turkey also marriages are arranged inside a large family circle.[19] In Iraq and all over the Arabian Peninsula, with few exceptions, marriage between children of two brothers is customary and preferred.[20]

The same custom exists in Iran as well. Ella C. Sykes reports that "if a girl is wedded to a cousin, which is constantly done to keep the property of a family together, she will never have exchanged a word with him since childhood, save in the family circle . . . ."[21] Although the author does not state whether the cousin in question is the girl's father's brother's son, this seems to be indicated by the reference to the contact between the two young people in childhood, which would be possible only in case they are the children of two brothers living in one household as members of the same extended, patrilineal, and patrilocal family. Also, the purpose of keeping the family property together is achieved only if the bride and groom are the children of two brothers, in which case the payment of the bride price is actually nothing more than a financial transaction between two brothers within the frame of one and the same extended family.

In fact, a Persian proverb states clearly: "The marriage of the daughter of the father's brother with the son of the father's brother is tied (i.e. decided upon) in heaven."[22]

This being the general view, "marriages between cousins are very much sought after, and the children of such marriages are if anything superior in physique to others."[23] The practice used to be followed from the lowest to the highest ranks of Persian society. In October 1867 the Crown Prince of Persia was married to his cousin, both being sixteen years of age.[24]

Among the nomadic tribes of the Upper Helmand River in Afghanistan "when a boy wants his first wife his mother selects a girl for him, usually one from the same band."[25] The reference here is probably to cousin marriage.

In Egypt, marriage between *ibn 'amm* and *bint 'amm* seems to be even more prevalent than in Arabia. Lane observed in the 1830's that "It is very common among the Arabs of Egypt and of other countries, but less so in Cairo than in other parts of Egypt, for a man to marry his first cousin. In this case, the husband and wife continue to call each other "cousin"; because the tie of blood is indissoluble, but that of matrimony very precarious . . . . A union of this kind is generally lasting, on account of this tie of blood; and because mutual intercourse may have formed an attachment between the parties in tender age; though if they be of higher or middle classes, the young man is seldom allowed to see the face of his female cousin, or even to meet and converse with her, after she has arrived at or near the age of puberty, until she has become his wife."[26] To this day, in Egypt, "marriages between children of *'amm* and *khāl* are most common; others are concluded within the wider circle of the family."[27]

In Upper Egypt also the father's brother's daughter is the favorite marriage partner.[28] Similarly, among the Kabābīsh, a Sudan Arab tribe, the first choice is the father's brother's daughter, second choice the mother's brother's daughter, and third choice the mother's sister's daughter.[29]

Among the Copts of Egypt marriage between a man and his father's brother's daughter is as customary as among the Muslims.[30]

In the Oasis of Siwa also, close to the western border of Egypt, the Middle Eastern pattern of cousin-marriage is often followed.[31]

Only in a very few cases do we have any knowledge of the actual frequency of *bint 'amm* marriages in any period or any locality. In most reports in which mention is made of *bint 'amm* marriage, it is stated that these are "common" or "frequent" or "usual," but no precise data as to the percentage of *bint 'amm* marriages in relation to all the marriages is given. The more valuable are the rare studies that do contain such figures, although not in every case can one put equal reliance on them.

Remarkably enough, the first numerical evaluation of the frequency of in-family marriages refers not to cousin marriage but to brother-sister marriage. According to Erman and Ranke, under the Emperor Commodus (161–192 A.D.) two thirds of all the citizens of the township of Arsinoë in Roman Egypt had a sister as wife.[31]

Cousin marriage in the late pre-Islamic period in the Ḥijāz was much less frequent than the above figure. In Medina, in the days of Mohammed, and within one or two generations preceding him, marriage with *bint 'amm* was practiced but was not too frequent. Of 21 marriages reported by Muḥammad ibn Sa'd (167/8–230 A.H.) as having been contracted by men belonging to the clan of Banī 'Āmir ibn Zurayq, four were with daughters of their father's brothers. In the same period at Mecca, out of a total of 71 marriages contracted by Mohammed's own clan, 9 were *bint 'amm* marriages, 23 were within the clan, 21 were with other clans of the Quraysh tribe to which Mohammed's clan belonged, and only 18 were with other tribes. In another clan of the Quraysh, the Makhzum, out of 25 marriages two were with the *bint 'amm*, one was within the clan, 16 were with other clans of the Quraysh, and six men (and no women) married into other tribes. In late pre-Islamic Ḥijāz therefore of the 113 marriages recorded only 15 were between the children of two brothers, or 13.3 per cent of the total. This relatively low incidence seems to be contingent on the absence of one of the main motivations of such marriages, namely the inheritance of property by daughters that was introduced by Mohammed. It has to be considered also that in the period in question, the term *bint 'amm* was not confined to father's brother's daughter, but was used loosely with reference to second, third, etc., cousins, as long as the relationship could be traced to two brothers.[33]

In modern Egypt, according to Father Ayrouth, a lifelong student of the Egyptian fellahin, 80 per cent of all the marriages contracted by the fellahin take place between first cousins.[34] Another authority who in the 1870's lived for many years in Upper Egypt states that "in two thirds of the cases it has been previously settled that the young man is to marry his female cousin, and if he has none, more distant relations are applied to, and lastly strangers.[35]

In one Upper Egyptian Coptic family studied by Legrain, there were five brothers who among them had six married sons and seven married daughters. All the six married sons had a *bint 'amm* for wife, and only one of the seven married daughters had not an *ibn 'amm* but an outsider for husband.[36]

Barth, in his study of social organization of Southern Kurdistan, found that in tribal villages 57 per cent of all the marriages were cousin marriages (48 per cent *bint 'amm* marriages) while in a nontribal village (made up of recent immigrant families) only 17 per cent were cousin marriages (13 per cent *bint 'amm* marriages). The frequency of family endogamy in the tribal villages was 71 per cent, in the nontribal village 37 per cent, while that of village endogamy was in the tribal villages 80 per cent, in the nontribal villages 78 per cent.[37] In two normal-sized tribal villages in the Hamawand area Barth found that out of a total of 21 marriages nine were contracted between paternal parallel cousins.[38]

In the South Palestinian Arab village of Arṭās in the 1920's, of 264 marriages 35, or 13.3 per cent, were *bint 'amm* marriages; 69, or 26.1 per cent, were marriages with *bint 'amm* plus marriages with second cousin or first cousin once removed; 89, or 33.7 per cent, were all the marriages within the *ḥamūla* (clan); and 151 or 57.2 per cent was the number of all the in-village marriages.[39]

The Middle Eastern cousin marriage pattern extends from Egypt and the Sudan all across the northern one third of Africa. In the oasis-village of Sīdī Khāled, some 170 miles south of the port of Algiers, the ideal marriage is between children of two brothers. Further to the south, among the Mzabites, the preferred form of marriage is between children of brothers, among both the Muslims and the Jews. The same preference obtains also among the Chaamba, an Arab nomad tribe, and among the Moors of the extreme western Sahara.[39a]

In the town of Timbuctoo, a field investigator found that among the Arabs one third of the marriages are between cousins. "Half of these are with father's brother's daughters. Slightly fewer marriages are with mother's brother's daughters. The two other kinds of first cousins are taken to wife only rarely. . . . It is possible that the frequent marriage with mother's brother's daughter is the result of Songhoi influence."[40] Since the Arabs in Timbuctoo are immigrants from North Africa and their descendants, they must have brought along with them the Middle Eastern preference for *bint 'amm* marriage. The Songhoi consist of two groups, both speaking Songhoi only. One is the Gabibi, a group indigenous to the Sudan, among whom a preference for marriage with mother's brother's daughter and a definite dislike for marriage with father's brother's daughter is found. The other Songhoi group is the Arma, who are the descendants of sixteenth-century Moroccan Arab invaders and their Sudanese wives. Among these there is a preference for marriage with both father's brother's daughter and mother's sister's daughter. The third ethnic group inhabiting Timbuctoo is the Bela, who are Tuareg slaves, and among whom marriage between cross cousins is preferred in principle, while children of two brothers are considered "prime enemies." However, in spite of the stated preference for cross-cousin marriage, marriages between the children of two brothers were found to be as numerous as marriages with mother's brother's daughter. Marriage with father's sister's daughter did not occur and distaste for it was apparent. While Miner may be right in seeing Songhoi influence in the frequency of marriage with mother's brother's daughter among the Arabs of Timbuctoo, the data from Egypt, Palestine, etc., seem rather to indicate that it may ultimately go back to a general Middle Eastern pattern in which the right of the *ibn khāl* to marry a girl is second only to the right of the *ibn 'amm*. On the other hand, there can be little doubt that the greater frequency of marriages between children of two brothers "in spite of the stated preference for cross-cousin marriage"[41] must be the result of Arab Middle Eastern influence.

The Bride Price

The preference of Middle Eastern society for cousin marriage is expressed in financial arrangements as well. All over the area it is customary for the bridegroom to pay a dowry or bride price to his bride. In effect, the bride price is as a rule paid by the father of the bridegroom to the father of the bride, and the latter is supposed to spend all or most or part of it, depending on the economic status of the family, on the outfitting of his daughter.[42] An additional provision is that the bride price agreed upon between the two fathers is not paid in full at the time or before the wedding. Part of it (in many cases one third) has to be paid only in case the husband divorces his wife, thus serving both as a deterrent against divorce (which can be effected any time and instantly by the husband) and as a trust fund for the divorced wife to draw upon.

The amount of the bride price varies greatly in different parts of the Middle East, as well as in different economic strata within the same locality. It may also depend on a number of additional factors, such as the beauty and age of the bride and, in exceptional cases, differences in status and prestige between the two intermarrying families. But, these other factors apart, the bride price is usually about twice as high if the bride is not a relative of the bridegroom as in the case of marriage between cousins or other close relatives. Among the better-off fellahin of Egypt, for instance, in the 1950's, the bride price of a cousin or other close relative varied from £E100 to £E150, while in the case of nonrelatives it ranged from £E200 to £E300.[43] Among poor fellahin (the overwhelming majority) the bride price paid for a cousin bride varied from £E15 to £E50.[44]

The custom of giving away the girl to her *ibn 'amm* for a reduced bride price is widespread in the Middle East.[45] Among the Rwala and other nomadic tribes of the Syrian Desert, the *ibn 'amm* may insist on paying a greatly reduced bride price for his cousin.[46]

Reduced bride price in the case of cousin marriage is the rule also among the fellahin of the Fertile Crescent.[47] Among the Kurds also "It is an agreed privilege for paternal cousins, to less extent also other near kin, to receive the girl at a reduced bride price. The normal bride price for village girls ranges between £30 and £100. Paternal cousins generally pay only wedding expenses."[48]

The considerable saving made possible by cousin marriage is a powerful factor in the eyes of the groom's family in favor of such marriages. Middle Eastern families in overwhelming majority are very poor, and cash expenditure is extremely difficult. Although the family of which the father is the head acquires, in return for the payment of the bride price, a new pair of working hands as well as a hopeful source of future sons, still the outlay requires an exceptional effort. This is the case not only in the settled sector of the population among whom the bride price is usually paid in cash, but also among the nomads who pay the bride price in valuables and especially in camels. And since under traditional circumstances the choice of the bride lies in the hands of the groom's father who is also expected to pay the bride price, it is easy to understand that the economic consideration of being able to save half of the bride price weighs heavily with him when making his choice. Thus it is in the economic interest of the father and of the bridegroom's family in general to choose his cousin for him as his bride.

As to the bride's family, they are expected to spend all or part of the bride price on the outfitting of the bride, or to give her the entire bride price or a considerable part of it.[49] Therefore, the purely economic interest of the bride's father in a higher bride price is not as primary as is the economic interest of the bridegroom's father in a lower bride price. Consequently, there is not as strong a financial motivation in the case of the bride's father against cousin marriage as there is in the case of the bridegroom's father for it.

In the following sections we shall deal in greater detail with what is probably the most significant aspect of Middle Eastern cousin marriage: the compulsory nature of *bint 'amm* marriage as manifested in the unwritten law that a man has the right to marry his *bint 'amm* and that nobody else is allowed to marry a girl until and unless her *ibn 'amm* (that is her father's brother's son) gives his consent.

Central Arabia

Let us begin our survey with the historical core of Middle Eastern culture, the Arabian Peninsula. In all parts of the Peninsula (with a very few exceptions, of which later) a man's right to his father's brother's daughter is upheld. This right is not voided even by a great discrepancy in age. The force of this traditional right is so strong that when it is infringed and then avenged by the offended male cousin by bloodshed, this meets public approbation.[50]

In the reports on the cousin's right, no difference in emphasis can be discovered between the accounts of travelers and explorers of the nineteenth century and of the twentieth century, which seems to indicate that no relaxation of this traditional law has taken place in the last one hundred or one hundred and fifty years. One of the early nineteenth-century accounts is that of J. L. Burckhardt. According to him, "All Arabian Bedouins acknowledge the first cousin's prior right to a girl; whose father cannot refuse to bestow her upon him in marriage. . . . A man has an exclusive right to the hand of his cousin; he is not obliged to marry her, but she cannot, without his consent, become the wife of another person. If a man permits his cousin to marry her lover, or if a husband divorces a runaway wife, he usually says, 'She was my slipper, I have cast her off.' "[51] Similarly Burton reports that "Every Badawi has a right to marry his father's brother's daughter before she is given to a stranger; hence 'cousin' (*Bint Amm*) in polite phrase signifies a 'wife'. "[52]

Doughty, on his way down to Medina, was told that marriage "betwixt brothers' children" was the most lawful. On one occasion he was asked by a petty shaykh whose wife, Hirfa, had run away, to persuade her to return to him. Upon undertaking this mission, Doughty was received by Hirfa's kinfolk, and her young cousin said to him: "I am her father (meaning, 'I have the *patria potestas* over her') and Hirfa is mine, Khalil; no! we will not give her more to Zeyd."[53] Wilfrid Blunt had a similar experience when he went to ask for the hand of a girl on behalf of a friend of his in the Nejd. While the negotiations over the bride price were in progress, a cousin "appeared on the scene and claimed his right to Muttra or an equivalent for her in coin."[54] William Robertson Smith, speaking of the township of Taif in Ḥijāz to the east of Mecca, states that "It must be understood that the preference for marriage between cousins, which exists also in Egypt, has here the character of a binding custom. A father cannot refuse his daughter to his brother's son, although another suitor offers a much higher dowry, unless the cousin is of weak intellect or notoriously of bad character. The cousin, if rejected for a rich suitor, can step in even at the last moment and stop the wedding."[55]

Southern Arabia

The same rule holds good generally in Southern Arabia.[56] However, in the Qara Mountains (in the hinterland of the Ẓufar coast in Southern Arabia), the right of the *ibn 'amm* to marry his father's brother's daughter is insisted upon only among the Mahra, a seminomadic cattle-breeding tribe. Among the other tribes of these mountains the sole right of disposal vests in the father of the girl.[57] The probable explanation of this exception is that these relatively isolated mountain tribes have not been sufficiently exposed to Muslim-Middle Eastern cultural influences and therefore have retained different (and probably older) customs.

Also among the Jews of Yemen cousin marriages are frequently practiced and occasionally insisted upon by the *ibn 'amm.* Several cases are known in which the consent of the *ibn 'amm* to the marriage of his *bint 'amm* with another man had to be bought.[58] In the village of al-Gades in Lower Yemen, studied and described by Goitein, "the predilection for marriages among cousins had the actual effect of endogamy; the general tendency was to marry close relatives. . . . It has been noted as early as the eighteenth century that Ṣan'a Jews regarded it a special blessing if a man had a great-grandchild from his own grandson and granddaughter."[59]

Northern Arabia

The nomadic tribes of Northern Arabia represent in this respect (as in many others) true Arabian traditions. The foremost tribe occupying a large wandering territory in the western section of this area is that of the Rwala. Among them, the *ibn 'amm* has the right to marry his *bint 'amm.* His position in relation to her is so strong that if any other man wants to marry the girl, he has to come to the *ibn 'amm,* ask his permission, and pay him what he wants. Curiously, Musil makes the statement that the "eben el-'amm is generally a son of her (the girl's) father's *cousin,*" whereas all that is known of this custom makes us expect the *ibn 'amm* to be among the Rwala as well the girl's father's *brother's son.* It would seem that the otherwise meticulous and accurate Musil made a mistake here. This becomes more likely if we read what Musil says in the same context, namely that if the girl has no *ibn 'amm,* she falls to the next nearest kinsman in the male line. This makes it the more probable that the *ibn 'amm* must be the nearest male relative with whom marriage is possible, that is the father's brother's son. If the *ibn 'amm* does not give his consent to the marriage of his *bint 'amm* to another man, the girl may be doomed to become an old maid. If the girl refuses to marry her *ibn 'amm* he may kill her without becoming liable to compensation. Only if the father of the girl gives her in exchange for a woman whom he himself wants to marry does this exchange marriage void the rights of the *ibn 'amm.*[60] Among other tribes also in the same area, if a man marries his daughter to another man without the consent of her *ibn 'amm* he risks his life, and there are many instances of blood revenge provoked by such acts.[61]

If the girl is in love with another man and the cousin gives her up, that is, foregoes exercising his right to marry her, this is regarded as a noble deed, worthy of praise and of being commemorated in song and story.[62]

Fed'ān Case Histories

The right of the *ibn 'amm* to the hand of his *bint 'amm* is so strong that even a most powerful shaykh cannot prevail against it. Several case histories reported from the Bedouins of the Syrian Desert bear this out.

"Aisheh was passionately loved by two men, the brilliant chief shaykh Jed'ān [of the Fed'ān] and her cousin Shanteri for whom she had only contempt and aversion. This state of affairs continued for several years, and if Aisheh did not become the wife of Jed'ān this was not because of lack of consent on the part of her parents, but because Shanteri obstinately refused to give his consent, which was indispensable. A very rigorous law of the desert confers on the first cousin of a girl a right of preference to her hand, an exclusive right which he is free to use or not to use. His female cousin is not forced to marry him, but she cannot marry anybody else until he consents to renounce his right. . . .

"Shanteri was a fine young man but he was lazy and idle. He never wanted to participate in an act of war, not even in a raid (*ghazzu*). He was effeminate, afraid of danger and exertion. He loved to adorn himself with fine clothes and to strut in the shade in idleness, without any sense of shame; and all these are faults which make a man despised by our women. . . . His rival, on the contrary, had all the qualities which are esteemed in our nomadic society. The aversion Aisheh felt for the one and her passion for the other thus can be explained easily: these sentiments earned for her the honor and sympathy of all, but there was the law which had to be respected and obeyed in spite of all other considerations.

"Jed'ān made many efforts to make Shanteri give up his right. Persuasion, flatterings, menaces, rich presents, seductive promises, nothing succeeded. Shanteri knew well that he was despised and detested. But spite, jealousy, and hatred kept his passion alive and gained the upper hand over his greed, love of gain, luxury and idleness. . . .

"[Jed'ān could do nothing to force the issue, because there is in the desert] a sanction which is based on public opinion and on the solidarity of honor and interest among all without exception, and which is the foundation of nomadic life and its safeguard, and without which a terrible anarchy would reign in the desert. A man who does not respect the laws and customs and does not fulfil the duties imposed by them commits a dishonorable and contemptible act, the scandal and the consequences of which would spread from the individual to his family which accepts only rarely the solidarity [with a dishonest act], and from the family to the tribe which does never accept it. Hence there is a double pressure on the individual, a pressure to which he most often submits, or else he is forced to go to live with another tribe. . . . Jed'ān and Aisheh did not want to be in such a situation at any price. Also, an elopement does not lead to marriage. The consent of the cousin in this case is even more necessary for the validity of the marriage than that of the parents. Shanteri would have refused it without pity; he would have found his vengeance and Aisheh would have become merely the concubine of Jed'ān, a dishonor to which every noble 'Aneze girl prefers death. And for her family this would have been an opprobrium which it could not have left unpunished, even if this had resulted in bloody conflicts.

"Too proud and too superior ever to give herself to her odious and miserable cousin, the beautiful Aisheh, innocent and hopeless victim of an inflexible law, will probably remain an old maid."[63]

This story was recorded in 1866. Twelve years later Jed'ān again underwent a very similar experience. In the meantime he not only strengthened his chieftainship over the Fed'ān, but became the military leader (*'aqīd*) of the Sba'a, another 'Aneze tribe, as well. He was now a powerful leader of two of the greatest 'Aneze tribes. In 1878, when he was fifty-five years old, he contracted a marriage (his fifteenth) with a thirty-year-old girl from the Sirḥān, a small 'Aneze tribe to which also his mother belonged. Thirty years is, of course, quite an old age for a Bedouin girl. The reason for this particular pretty girl having remained unmarried until so late an age was that her cousin had claimed her for himself in marriage and then had kept her waiting year after year without either marrying her or setting her free. But since Jed'ān was a powerful shayh, the girl's father was persuaded to disregard the cousin's right, and his daughter's wedding with Jed'ān was duly cerebrated. However, from the very outset there was some doubt as to whether the marriage was legal, since it was contracted without obtaining the cousin's consent.

Soon after the wedding, the girl's cousin, a twenty-three-year-old man, brought action against Jed'ān for the recovery of his cousin, on the plea that he had not consented to her marriage. This case was of considerable interest, because the two adversaries were a powerful shaykh and a young man of no consequence, who was regarded by everybody as a hotheaded youth and who, in addition, was generally known to have behaved ill to the girl having put her off from year to year until the girl's father grew tired of waiting. Moreover, since he was twenty-three and the girl thirty, it was assumed that his only interest in the matter was a financial one. Jed'ān, on the other hand, seems to have had no knowledge of the existence of this cousin until after the marriage, and even then he thought that it would be merely a case of damages. But the cousin demanded the girl herself, or four other daughters in her stead: a claim which according to the local custom could be considered legitimate. The father of the girl offered him his only remaining daughter in place of the one married to Jed'ān, but the cousin did not want to hear of this, and, in order to show his anger and insistence, he ran one of the old man's camels through with his spear.

Thus the matter had to be referred for arbitration to Muḥammed Dukhi ibn Smeyr, shaykh of the Weld 'Alī (another 'Aneze tribe, friendly to the Sba'a), a man of about fifty, of considerable importance and influence. The deliberations started with a preliminary argument as to whether the case should be tried according to the Bedouin *'urf* (i.e., local traditional) law, or by the Muslim *sharī'a* law. According to the *'urf*, either the marriage of the girl with Jed'ān would have to be annulled or the entire dowry received by the girl's father from Jed'ān (the actual amount was 2,000 piasters) would have to be given to the cousin.

The cousin, of course, argued that the Bedouin law must apply. The argument for the other side was that the Muslim *sharī'a* law should apply; this would have held the offer of another daughter as a sufficient compensation for the cousin, on the principle that "an injured man, if replaced in the position held before injury, ceases to be injured." This idea, that the *sharī'a* law be applied, stemmed from a jurist from Aleppo who happened to be a guest of Jed'ān and his tribe. The attempt was doomed to failure, as everybody knew that the Bedouin *'urf* law must prevail.

While these preliminaries were in progress, Beteyen ibn Mershid, shaykh of the Gomussa section of the Sba'a, arrived in the camp in order to be present at the decision of this important suit. However, Muḥammed Dukhi shirked the responsibility of deciding such a weighty lawsuit himself, and the case was referred to three arbitrators chosen by the two parties. One of the three was objected to by one side. The second was objected to by the other side. The third, remaining alone and afraid of the responsibility, declared that he would be unable to bring a decision without reference to the shaykh of the Sirḥān, the tribe to which the girl and her cousin belonged. It was agreed to adjourn the case until the arrival of the Sirḥān who were encamped at a distance of several hundreds of miles in the Jauf, in the Lower Ḥamad in the desert, from where they came up north only rarely. When the Sirḥān finally arrived, the cousin of the girl brought his complaint to the shaykh of the Sirḥān. His decision was that since the girl had taken no steps prior to her marriage to Jed'ān to oblige her cousin to keep his promise and marry her, the cousin's rights remained valid. When this decision was announced to Jed'ān, he at once put his new wife on a camel and sent her to the shaykh of the Sirḥān. Thereupon a great wedding was solemnized between the girl and her cousin, Jed'ān being among the guests attending, "and no ill-will on either side marred the cordial enjoyment of festivities for three whole days."[64]

Rwala Case Histories

Even if a man is not in a position to marry his *bint 'amm* forthwith, for lack of funds to pay the bride price or for any other reason, he may "reserve" the girl for himself by making a public and formal declaration of his intentions to marry her at a future date. Although ordinarily such a reservation of the *bint 'amm* would not seem to be necessary, if it is done it clinches the cousin's claim, so to speak, and has the character of a formal engagement. Ṭalāl and Saṭṭām were brothers, members of the princely family of the Rwala, the Sha'lān. Ṭalāl's son, 'Abdallah, reserved a daughter of Saṭṭām for himself, and "would not permit her to marry anyone else, asserting that as her nearest relative he had the first right to her."[65]

It can also happen that a man who is not the *ibn 'amm* of a girl, but a more remote relative, reserves her for himself soon after her birth, and in this case he acquires priority. Sa'ūd, son of Nūrī b. Sha'lān, emir of the Rwala, loved the sister of his mother, and she loved him, but he could not marry her because a more distant relative of her, 'Abdallah eben Ṭalāl (Nūrī's brother's son) had reserved her for himself a few days after her birth. Ever since then the girl belonged to him, and no one could marry her without his consent. To make the matter more involved, the brothers of the girls (her father seems to have died, and therefore her brothers had the *patria potestas* over her) did not permit her to marry 'Abdallah, but declared their readiness to give her to Sa'ūd eben Nūrī. Thus the girl was able to marry neither the man whom she loved nor the man who had the sole right to marry her. Prince Nūrī b. Sha'lān, when he told the story to Musil, remarked: "We could compel him ['Abdallah] to release her, but we do not wish to alienate him. . . ."[66]

A third case reported from the same princely family throws additional light on the rights and involvements of cousin marriage. Prince Nūrī had a brother, Fahad, with whose approval a certain Ṭrad al-'Arafa who posed as Fahad's son but who in reality was the son of Khalaf eben Iden, forced one of Nūrī's daughters into his tent intending to marry her. The girl, however, was able to jerk herself loose from him, and she fled into the desert where she was found by her brother Nawwāf. Nawwāf was greatly incensed at the injury done to his sister and persuaded Nūrī not to tolerate such a disgrace. Nūrī, although he was the paramount shaykh of the Rwala, felt it necessary to be assisted by three chiefs, and together with them went to Fahad to talk the matter over peaceably. After a long conference it was agreed that Ṭrad should not have Nūrī's daughter for a wife.[67]

Jordan

The example quoted above (p. 150) shows that the *ibn ʿamm* can lodge his complaint and obtain redress even after the consummation of the marriage of his *bint ʿamm* with an outsider. Among the tribes inhabiting the area east of the Jordan and the Dead Sea (which in the past was variously called Arabia Petraea or Moab and most of which today forms part of the Kingdom of Jordan) the *ibn ʿamm* enjoys similar rights. "In Arabia Petraea the *ibn ʿamm* can interfere at the last moment with the marriage of his *bint ʿamm* to another man. In order to circumvent the claim of the *ibn ʿamm*, a man will carry off a girl and place her under the protection of another tribe, and then return to her father and enter into negotiations for the marriage."[68]

According to another observer, a man not only has the right to, but *must* claim for himself, to the exclusion of every other suitor, the hand of the daughter of his paternal or maternal uncle. It happens but rarely that a man renounces this right of his own free will. Even if the girl and her father do not want him, he as a rule insists, and they have to conform with the custom. If a man has any reason to suspect that his uncle wants to give his daughter to somebody else, he resorts to the following rite: He takes five camels and leads them to the tent of the tribal shaykh. There, in the presence of witnesses, he says: "Here are camels for my cousin; I claim her." The father of the girl answers: "Take them away; we do not want it [namely the marriage]." The suitor goes, but returns five days later with four camels, and says: "Here are my four camels for the girl; I want her." Again the father answers, "Take back your camels, we do not want it." After another five days the suitor presents himself at the tent of the shaykh or of the father with three camels, only to receive the same answer. The same encounter is repeated two more times, and then finally the youth brings a sheep or a goat to the shaykh's tent or to the father's tent, slaughters the animal and says: "This is the sacrifice of the girl." This act gives him the definitive right to take his cousin to wife, and he may even carry her away with him then and there. In particular, this right to the cousin's hand exists and is exercised among the following tribes: the Benī Ṣakhr, the Ḥwēṭāt, the Hajāya, the Catholic bedouins in the vicinity of Madaba (with the dispensation of the Church), and the Fuqarā. Differences in age, or the wishes of the girl are thereby completely disregarded.[69]

The actual working of the law can be illustrated by a number of examples taken from this area. A father arranged for the marriage of his daughter with an outsider, without obtaining the consent of her *ibn 'amm*. When the marriage procession progressed with the bride toward the house of the bridegroom, the *ibn 'amm* rushed forward, snatched away the girl, and forced her into his own house. This was regarded by all as a lawful marriage, and the father who originally objected to his nephew because the outsider agreed to pay a high bride price for his daughter now received no bride price at all.[70]

In some cases one and the same bride price acquires a girl not only for the *ibn 'amm* who actually marries her in the first place, but, should he divorce her, for his brothers as well. Jaussen reports such a case in which a man paid a she-ass as the *mahr* for his *bint 'amm*, married her, then divorced her, whereupon his brother took her in marriage by virtue of the same she-ass, then he divorced her too, and she was married in succession to the third and fourth brothers, and finally remarried the first brother, all for the one bride price of a single she-ass.[71]

In general, at the beginning of the twentieth century the situation with respect to the rights of the *ibn 'amm* among the tribes of the North Arabian and Syrian deserts was as follows: If a young man desired the hand of a girl who had cousins, one of the cousins who wanted to have the girl would caution the stranger to withdraw. If the latter persisted even after this admonition, it was his task to win, or rather to buy, the consent of the cousin who was the legal suitor of the girl. Otherwise, the stranger would have exposed himself to the enmity of the cousins and to mortal danger.[72]

A Christian Case History

Jaussen reports a case of which he heard among the Catholic bedouins of Madaba in Transjordan. One of them, Soleymān Shuweyḥāt, had a daughter, Ḥaḍra. In accordance with the cousin's right, his brother's son, Khalaf Shuweyḥāt, should have married the girl. But at the time when young Khalaf reached the age of marriage, Ḥaḍra fell ill: a pimple developed on her cheek, and she appeared to be attacked by a serious illness. Khalaf thereupon took another wife without either making any demand on the father of Ḥaḍra or informing him that he renounced his rights to her. Ḥaḍra remained in her father's house until the age of twenty-two. She recovered completely, and was demanded in marriage by another member of the tribe. Khalaf, hearing of this event, made immediate use of his cousin's right and claimed the girl for his younger brother. This was the Arab right. But Soleymān summarily rejected this demand saying that Khalaf had dishonored his daughter by refusing to marry her. His daughter was now promised to another man and would not be given to Khalaf's brother. Khalaf then made an appeal of protection to Shaykh Ya'qub, asking him to help him to make the cousin's right prevail. The shaykh could not refuse such a request. But being a relative of Soleymān Shuweyḥāt he used circumspection, lest Soleymān turn to another more powerful chief and he find himself involved in a serious conflict. After a series of discussions, Ḥaḍra was married to her suitor toward whom she inclined, and who was twenty-two years old, while Khalaf's brother was merely fifteen.[73]

Palestine

Among the Arabs of Palestine "a cousin is by custom the most eligible bride, and a youth has prior claim over all other suitors and their pretensions, if he chooses to demand her in marriage."[74] This right is alluded to in a number of proverbs. "Ibn al-'amm bitayyih 'an el-faras"—"the *ibn 'amm* may take down from the mare" (in another version: from the camel), that is he can take the bride down from the animal that carries her in the marriage procession to the house of the bridegroom, thus preventing her from marrying an outsider, and marry her himself.[75] Another proverb current among the Bedouins of Southern Palestine as well as among the Rwala has it: "Her (i.e. the girl's) binding and her release are in the hands of her *ibn 'amm.*" Still another proverb warns: "The girl who is desired by her *ibn 'amm* is forbidden to a stranger." In the same sense it is also said: "The oil which is wanted by its owner is forbidden to be given to the mosque."[76]

If a girl has no *ibn 'amm*, or if the *ibn 'amm* renounces his right to her, the second in line for her hand is the *ibn khāl*, her mother's brother's son, who, in turn, is followed by the others in the family and the brother of her sister's husband, each having a right of priority in proportion to the degree of his relationship.[77]

Jaussen reports that among the inhabitants of Nablus in central Palestine the right of a man to marry his *bint 'amm* "is religiously respected" and "has an immutable value."[78] The same is true elsewhere in Palestine in tradition-abiding circles.[79]

The present writer's observations among middle-class Muslim Arabs in Palestine, and especially in Jerusalem, up to 1947, showed the cousin's right in decline. There was no longer any question of a suitor having to obtain the consent of the girl's *ibn 'amm.* Only a vague sense of preference for *bint 'amm* marriage was still noticeable here and there, but even this was disappearing under the impact of the idea that cousin marriage may result in sickly offspring.

The rural population, with its greater conservatism, evinced no such change. The persistence of the cousin's right among the Palestinian fellahin is reported by observers two generations apart.[80] In the village of Arṭās, south of Bethlehem, the cousin's right is verbalized in song and proverb. The songs often praise the *ibn 'amm* as the ideal husband. If, however, he does not marry his *bint 'amm*, but allows a stranger to take her away, he is blamed and called a "heap of dirt." The obligation of an outsider to compensate the *ibn 'amm* in money, in order to obtain his consent, is a living custom in Arṭās. Among the proverbs alluding to the cousin's right are found such statements as "The *ibn 'amm* comes first," or "The *ibn 'amm* comes first in the eyes of the government and of the fellahin."[81]

In an account of marriage preliminaries in the villages around Jerusalem, the father of the groom discusses the bride price with the father of the bride, and once this is settled the father of the bride says to him: "Now go and get the consent of her paternal uncle and cousins (" *'ammhā w'ulād 'ammhā*), buy clothes for her maternal uncle (*khālhā*). . . ." Thereupon the father of the groom goes to the paternal uncle of the bride and says to him: "How much do you want to let us get the girl?" The uncle thinks and then says: "I want 20 pieces of gold." Thereupon they discuss the amount until they settle on a sum. "The father of the groom can get the bride only if he has the consent of her *'amm* and his sons, and if he buys a robe for her *khāl* and shoes for his sons." After this, the father of the groom "makes efforts to get the consent of the girl's paternal cousins, but he has much trouble with them until he [finally] obtains their consent. . . ."[82]

Arṭās Case Histories

We have seen (pp. 150, 154) a few examples showing the complications that may arise when a father wishes to prefer an outsider as a son-in-law in order to secure a larger bride price than he would receive from his brother's son. The motivation of financial gain has caused conflicts between the father of a marriageable girl and his brother's son on several occasions in Arṭās.

Musṭafa Salem of Arṭās found a bride in Bethlehem for his son. They celebrated the betrothal feast, and he gave the girl's father about £P100 including presents. A year and a half passed, and they were about to go to the shaykh to conclude the marriage contract, when the bride's cousin appeared saying: "I come first." The girl herself said: "I want to have my cousin; he comes first." When the bridegroom's father heard this, he threatened saying: "There are judges" (i.e. there are fellah judges who will set the matter right). However, the betrothal was voided, and the bride's family had to compensate the groom's father for all he had spent on the girl.

Another case reported from Arṭās is even more instructive as to the rights of the *ibn 'amm*. Sma'īn Aḥmed, originally from Arṭās but living in Eḥbēle, had a daughter whom his cousin (his father's brother's son) 'Abdallah wanted to marry. However, an outsider offered £P150 as bride price for the girl, and thereupon Sma'īn refused to give his daughter to 'Abdallah who as a cousin would have had to pay a much smaller amount as bride price. Now Sma'īn's father and 'Abdallah's father (who were brothers) had another brother Mḥammad, and he arranged a *nidr*, or vow feast, to which he invited his brother from Eḥbēle, so that the relatives should be able to influence Sma'īn in favor of his cousin. "Far away . . . in . . . Eḥbēle, it was easy for him to refuse, but not so if he must do it before the whole group of relatives and villagers. . . ." When the evening meal was ready and about to be eaten, up rose Sma'īn's father, the oldest and most influential member of the extended family, and said: "I will not eat unless I know whether this is a betrothal feast or a vow feast." His son, the father of the girl, tried to hold his own by mentioning the high bride price offered to him by the stranger, but his father cut him short: "Nothing will come of that. We are relatives." An aunt of Sma'īn and 'Abdallah (their father's sister) also joined in the discussion and said to 'Abdallah: "I will not eat unless I know whether thou wilt give me a wedding garment." The resistance of the girl's father was thus broken down, he gave his consent, a Fātiḥa (the first chapter of the Koran) was read, and the meal began, it being understood that it was a betrothal feast. Next morning it was said: "This night Aḥmed Sma'īn [the girl's father's father] has instituted a new rule, that for a clan daughter only £P35 shall be given. So dear as it is now will not do."

In yet another case in the same village a girl's parents wanted to give her to her mother's brother's son (*ibn khāl*). But her father's brother's son (*ibn 'amm*) insisted on his rights, and finally got the girl.[83]

Syria

Moving up from Palestine into Syria, we find the same cousin right. Here too the girl's father's brother's son has the first right to her, followed by the right of more remote relatives in the male line. And here too the right can be renounced by the *ibn 'amm* for a compensation paid to him by the suitor of the girl who thus is a source of revenue for him. In Syria the right of receiving a compensation belongs to the *ibn 'amm* alone, and not to the *ibn khāl* who has no special rights in his *bint 'amme*. The proverb that refers to the cousin right and, as we have seen (p. 155) is current in Palestine, is also current in Syria in a somewhat different version: "*Inazzelhā min 'ala ḍahr el-faras*." "He (the *ibn 'amm*) can take her down from the back of the mare." Another proverb in the same sense is: "*Yakhtefhā min el-jalweh*," "He can snatch her from the wedding ceremony."[84] Among the fellahin of the Hama, Homs, Aleppo, and Deir ez-Zor regions of Syria the *ibn 'amm* asserts his right by referring to the traditional saying: "*Bent 'ammī, mā etla' men ṭarīqhā*," "She is my *bint 'amm*, I shall not move out of her way." Among the Syrian bedouins they say: "*Bent 'ammī, mā futḥa*," "She is my *bint 'amm*, I shall not release her."[85]

In the entire Hawran district, as well as among the Syrian bedouins, and especially the tribes of Sulūṭ, Benī Khāled, and el-Weld, the custom of reserving the bride for himself is practiced by the *ibn 'amm*. From the time a man reserves his *bint 'amm* for himself and until such time as he actually marries her, she becomes "protected" (*majyūra*) by him, and nobody else has the right to marry her. But even if the *ibn 'amm* has not expressly reserved the girl for himself, he has to be consulted before the girl can be given in marriage to someone else. This custom is followed not only in the rural areas and the smaller towns such as Homs, Hama, Deir ez-Zor, but, occasionally at least, even in the big cities of Syria, Damascus, and Aleppo.[86]

In the Syrian towns cousin marriage seems to be most frequent among the lower classes consisting of workers, artisans, and small employees. Here too the proverbs faithfully reflect the views of the people with regard to the rights of the *ibn 'amm* and of the desirability of cousin marriage. "A tree is found near me; who has more right to it, my neighbor or myself?" asks one of these proverbs. Folk songs also assert the rights of the *ibn 'amm*: "My *bint 'amm* is for me, is for me. . . ."[87]

As in Arab Palestine, in Syria too the urban environment is not favorable to the preservation of folk traditions. In recent decades, especially in the big cities, a man could give his daughter in marriage to a stranger even if the girl had several patrilateral parallel cousins who demanded her hand, and concurrently compensation of the *ibn 'amm* has also fallen into disuse. This development seems to be characteristic especially of the middle-class townspeople among whom cousin marriage has become much less frequent than among the lower classes. In the upper class, among the leading families, marriage between cousins is again frequent, and the *ibn 'amm* has the right of preference, here motivated by the wish to preserve the property in the family and by a feeling of superiority to other families. For these reasons, marriage between maternal cousins is less frequent in these classes than marriage between paternal cousins; and more stress is laid on marrying a girl to a cousin than on finding an in-family match for a young man.[87]

Actually, as late as the 1930's there were still a number of leading families, especially in the small towns of Syria, among whom the old tradition of in-family marriage was faithfully preserved. In Homs and Hama, for instance, there were still certain families who would not give their daughters in marriage to an outsider, but insisted on their marrying members of the family itself. No such restrictions, however, existed with regard to their male members who were free to find wives for themselves outside their own family circle. In this respect too the Syrian town closely resembled the Palestinian Arab town. Recently, however, this rule has become weakened in many places. For instance, the rule of the K. family in Hama, according to which a K. girl was allowed to marry only a K. man, has been repeatedly infringed upon as early as the 1920's.

This rule was not confined to families of high standing, but could be found also among some fellah families. The 'Abdallah family in Palmyra, for example, and several other families in the Hawran and Deir ez-Zor regions, adhered to it down to the 1930's. In the 'Atasī family also husband and wife were almost always from the same family and this was the typical situation as far as the leading families were concerned.[89]

Syrian Minorities

The right of the *ibn 'amm* is upheld also among the Syrian Turkomans, among whom also the payment of compensation to the *ibn ʿamm* has been practiced. A story concerning the rivalry between two paternal cousins for the hand of their *bint ʿamm*, who was the most beautiful Turkoman girl in Syria, was often heard a number of years ago. Both youths demanded the girl from her father, Ḥajj ʿAlī, who, in order to suppress all rivalry between the two (since this would have weakened the family), refused her to both. However, knowing that two cousins had demanded her in marriage, nobody else dared to ask for the hand of the girl. She remained an old maid, and died unmarried.

The same customs are in force among the Syrian Kurds, both those of the Damascus area and those of Kurd Dagh. Among them, too, the *ibn ʿamm* must be asked for his consent, if the girl is to marry somebody else, and has to be given compensation. The story is told of a certain ʿAbdo, a Kurd of the village of Shikhut in the Kurd Dagh region, who has not received his *khulʿa* (price of renunciation), and thereupon avenged himself by first killing the parents of his *bint ʿamm* and later the girl herself. He was apprehended, condemned to death, and executed.

The cousin right does not exist among the Circassians in Syria. They hold marriages between a man and his *bint ʿamm* or *bint khāl* absolutely forbidden, because these cousins are regarded by them as siblings. The same type of family exogamy is practiced also among the Circassians in the Caucasus, the original home of the Syrian Circassians.[90]

Iraq

In Iraq as well as in northeastern Arabia, "first cousin marriage is the rule invariably. A girl belongs of right to the son of her father's brother (*ibn ʿamm*) unless he expressly renounces his right to marry her. Even in this case she may not marry without his permission. If the girl breaks this rule or her parents prevail on her to marry someone else, her rightful lord will murder her if he can. This is the cause of most of the tribal killings of women, especially in Iraq."[91]

This custom is frequently reflected in Iraqi folk stories. In one of these, Harun al-Rashid's brother's son does not let Harun marry his daughter to anybody else, until finally Harun gives her to him in marriage. In another story, a father from the country of

Waq-waq does not want his daughter to marry her *ibn 'amm*, and therefore flees with her to Iraq. Later, however, the father returns with his daughter to Waq-waq land, whereupon the marriage feast of his daughter with his brother's son is begun. However, the girl's lover arrives in the last minute, kills the *ibn 'amm*, and then flees with the girl back to Iraq.[92]

Among the Jews of Iraq, if a man wants to give his daughter in marriage to somebody, he must first persuade the girl's cousin to renounce his right to her. If the cousin does not listen to persuasion, the girl's father pays him a sum of money to buy his consent. This is done in order to prevent enmity and tension within the family.[93]

In Northern Iraq also the *ibn 'amm* has the right to marry his *bint 'amm*. This is "the principal rule of marriage. . . . If they do not care for each other, however, the man will usually accept a present from the outside suitor, and in return will forego his right to his cousin."[94]

An Iraqi Case History

The following account, which contains all the elements of the cousin's right, is given by H. R. P. Dickson. The heroine is Binniyah, a sixteen-year-old girl of the al-Gharri tribe, headed by Shaykh Manshad al-Habayib. "Her people lived at Batha, a village on the Euphrates, some twenty miles from Nasiríyah, and she lived happily with her father and mother in their black tent until a short time previously, when they had told her that she was to marry her *ibn 'am* (first cousin) and that the wedding was to be solemnized on the new moon. The news had come as a terrible blow to her, for she loved another boy of the tribe and he loved her, and had told her of his love for her. In great distress she had told him that her father proposed giving her to her cousin on the new moon, and begged his advice and help. She would die, she had told him, rather than be the wife of anyone but him. The youth had received this calmly, but had been deeply angered, with murder in his heart. He had told Binniyah that he must have time to think out a plan, and would return on the third day and tell her what this was. They had arranged to meet on the river bank where she was accustomed to fetch water at midday, and he would find an opportunity of talking to her.

"Binniyah had passed three long days in misery and despondency. What chance had her lover, and what hope had she of getting out of the marriage arranged by her powerful father? Moreover, by Arab custom, her cousin has the right to marry her, and she could take no one else in this world unless he waived that right. She knew also that if, in spite of everyone, she married someone other than her cousin, her life would be forfeit and her cousin would be the one to kill her. Her only chance—and it was a very, very slender one—was to run away with her lover, but then she would have to flee far from her home and people and abandon all hope of ever seeing them again. If they ran away there would be an immediate pursuit, and woe betide her and her boy if the pursuers came up with them. Tribal law never forgave in such matters.

"Three days later she had been at the rendezvous by the riverside. Other women had been drawing water also, but her lover had managed to get private word with her as he had walked part of the way home. He had only one plan to offer: to run away, and on that very night. He would appear behind her tent at midnight with a fast mare and, on his giving the cry of a jackal three times, she was to slip out from under the tent curtain, join him at the back, and together they would fly away to Suq ash Shuyúkh and take refuge with the Mujarrah tribes. There they would get married, and if they could not find safety they would flee farther to distant Basra. . . .

"Midnight had arrived, and Binniyah had crept out quietly to the rear of the tent on hearing the jackal cry. Silently they had got through the sleeping camp unnoticed and then, mounting one behind the other, had sped away into the open country, their objective the palm belt opposite Nasiríyah town. Alas, someone or some dog must have given the alarm. Binniyah could not tell me how it had happened. Suffice to say, when dawn had broken the fleeing pair had seen in the distance behind them a party of horsemen, obviously following hard on their trail. . . . They had thrown off their pursuers for a moment, and Binniyah had been almost happy. Then what disillusionment! The young man had apparently decided that, handicapped by Binniyah, he would never escape, but that he might get away alone. He had suddenly told her he was leaving her. It was useless, he had said, for them both to get killed, when he could escape to Suq and reach Basra by way of the Hamár Lake. He had not given Binniyah time to argue or even plead. He had just disappeared into the darkness. Life was sweet, so why throw it away on a *bint*?"

Thereupon Binniyah fled into Dickson's house. Somewhat later Shaykh Manshad too arrived and demanded that Dickson hand the girl over to him. But Binniyah pleaded for her life: "He is only concerned with getting me out of your hands and the *hakúma's* protection. Afterwards he will hand me over to my *ibn 'am* and tribal justice."

Turning to Manshad she said: "I cannot, I dare not go back with you, Yá Manshad," she sobbed in a way that touched the heart. "You know the tribal law; it is utterly unforgiving in the case of erring girls like me, and you know full well that you must hand me over to my father and brethren, since they will demand me of you. I am afraid to die, for I am young."

So Binniyah remained for a while with the Dicksons: "In my predicament as to what to do with her, I sought the help and guidance of Dhári Beg al Fahad Al Sa'dún. I told him the whole story, and he advised me that the only hope for the girl was to have her married to some worthy citizen of Nasiríyah town. According to Dhári, if she were once properly married and settled down in the town, her tribe would no longer attempt to molest her, and in due course her *ibn 'am* and parents might forgive her, especially if her husband were to pay over a sum of money by way of compensation to the *ibn 'am* who fancied himself injured. Binniyah herself approved this step, so I acted on Dhári's advice and, after some days, found a very respectable man who ran a coffee-shop a few doors away from my house, and he agreed to marry Binniyah. The wedding was a quiet one and turned out very happily. As my contribution to the happy event I gave the bridegroom six hundred rupees to be paid over to Binniyah's cousin."[95]

Kurdistan

The same rule prevails in the Kurdish area of Northern Iraq as well. It is the tribal law among the Kurds that the cousin "has the first refusal of a lady's hand,"[96] in other words it is he who can either take her for himself or dispose of her if he so wishes. In the sedentary Hamawand tribe (in the Kirkuk Liwa of Iraq) "paternal cousins have first rights to a girl, and where the father of the girl contemplates giving her in marriage to anyone else, the paternal cousin must first release her by renouncing his claim." In the southern Kurdish feudally organized territory, neighboring on the Hamawand area, the "first rights of paternal cousins are not as strongly emphasized." Barth, who made a special study of this problem among the Kurds, recorded in the course of his field work cases of violence resulting from a breach of the father's obligation to obtain his brother's son's consent to the marriage of his daughter to somebody else. In one case, an outsider who asked for the hand of a girl was refused by her father on the grounds that (as he said), "I am afraid my brother's sons will kill me if I give her to you."[97]

One Kurdish case history should suffice to show that murder can actually result from the refusal to let a girl marry her *ibn ʿamm* (or *amoaza* in Kurdish). In 1920, in a village called Kapanak Resh, on the eastern slope of the Qara Choq Dag in the Arbil region of Iraqi Kurdistan, under the protection of the village headman, named Khālbekr, lived his widowed sister, Amīna Khanum, and her beautiful daughter, Fāṭima. In a village on the other side of the hill lived Fāṭima's cousins, Farhān the Lame and Raḥmān Agha. Farhān sent his brother several times to ask Khālbekr for the hand of his niece, but was each time refused. Finally, one of the three big Dizai chiefs, Ḥajji Pīr Daoud Agha, secretly approached Khālbekr and offered him a large bride price for his niece whom he asked in marriage for his son Maʿruf. Khālbekr gave his consent and the preparations for the marriage started but with utmost secrecy. So as to prevent the occurrence of any legal hitch, even the consent of the Muslim judge of Arbil was obtained. However, as was to be expected, these plans could not for long remain secret, and Raḥmān Agha planned revenge. One night Fāṭima was sleeping with her mother and her maid in a booth of branches just outside their house, when suddenly two men appeared and stabbed the girl and her maid to death, the mother narrowly escaping with her life. The bloody deed horrified the whole tribe, because the traditionally correct thing would have been to carry off the girl by force, or to kill her bridegroom. Since the girl herself had nothing to say in the matter of her marriage, to kill her was a crime by tribal standards. Raḥmān Agha was imprisoned, but no proof of his guilt could be found, and he was finally released.[98]

Iran

In Persian Azerbaijan the same right is accorded to a man with regard to the hand of his *ämün gyzi*, father's brother's daughter. In an account of Azerbaijani marriage customs reported by an informant from Tabriz, the fourteen-year-old boy says to his mother that he wants to marry, whereupon the mother answers: "Wait until your cousin (*ämün gyzi*) Aliye grows up, I shall take her for you as wife . . . she is your property. . . ."[99]

If among the Papis of Iran, a Lur tribe, a girl is married to a stranger, he has to compensate her cousins by giving each one of them a goat.[100]

Sinai and Egypt

The Sinai Peninsula forms the connecting link between the Asian and the African halves of the Middle East. Ethnologically, the nomads of the Peninsula are the connecting link between the peoples of the Arabian and Syrian deserts on the one hand and the tribes of Egypt and North Africa on the other. Two firsthand reports a hundred and twenty years apart attest to the prevalence of the cousin's right in Sinai. John Lewis Burckhardt, traveling in the Sinai Peninsula prior to 1816, observed that "The Arabs of Sinai . . . sometimes marry their daughters to strangers in the absence of the cousins. This happened to a guide whom I had taken from Suez. When we arrived at his encampment, one day's journey from the convent of Sinai, he expected to marry a cousin of his own, and during the whole journey he had extolled to me the festivities which I should witness on that occasion. He, too, had brought with him some new clothes for his intended bride; and was therefore exceedingly disappointed and chagrined on his arrival, when he learned that three days before the girl had been married to another. It appeared that her mother was secretly his enemy; and had contrived matters in such a manner as to render him ridiculous in the eyes of his companions. He bore his misfortune, however, like a man; and, instead of evincing any signs of displeasure, soon turned the tide of ridicule upon the mother herself, and her son-in-law. To prevent similar occurrences, a cousin, if he be determined to marry his relation, pays down the price of her as a deposit into the hands of some respectable member of the encampment, and places the girl under the protection of four men belonging to his own tribe. In this case she cannot marry another without his permission, whether he be absent or present; and he may then marry her at his leisure, whenever he pleases. If, however, he himself break off the match, the money that had been deposited is paid into the hands of the girl's master. This kind of betrothing takes place sometimes long before the girl has attained the age of puberty."[101]

The nonchalant manner in which Burckhardt's guide reacted to the marriage of his cousin to another man, as well as the institutionalized method of preventing "similar occurrences," which is different from the mere reservation of the girl practiced elsewhere (p. 152), seem to indicate that no great emphasis was placed on cousin right in those days. In the course of the subsequent century the attitude to the cousin's right must have become considerably more rigorous, since Murray in the 1930's reports that this right is generally respected among the Bedouins of Sinai as well as among those inhabiting the desert of Egypt stretching between the Nile and the Red Sea. Among the Egyptian Bedouin "every youth has the right to marry his *bint 'amm*. . . . The right is absolute, and if her father wishes to dispose of the girl otherwise, he must first obtain (and pay for) his nephew's consent. The vast majority of first marriages (every Bedouin marries several times) are of this nature, and consequently a high proportion of the population are the offspring of first cousins. So also an 'Abadi or Bishari usually marries his *bint 'amm*, but the Hadendowa are not so patrilineal and when choosing a bride give no special preference to that lady."[102]

As to the Bisharin, C. G. Seligman reports that among those in the neighborhood of Aswan in Upper Egypt whom he studied, the *bint 'amm* "is the best [wife] and a man would consider that he had prior right to the hand of his *bint 'amm*."[103]

Sudan

Moving down south into Sudan, we find that among the Kababish, an Arab tribe, marriage with the *bint 'amm* predominates. The Seligmans found that "it was clear that no other alliance for a girl would be considered if there were an *ibn 'amm* available for her. Further, if a lad were betrothed to his *bint 'amm* who was considerably younger than himself, he could not take another wife while waiting for her to grow up. A *bint 'amm* could not be second to any other woman unless she, too, were *bint 'amm* to the husband. This rule was demonstrated in the case of the shaykh of the Kababish himself: he married his *bint 'amm*, then later he married a second wife who was not his *bint 'amm*. Then he wanted to marry another *bint 'amm* of his, but before being able to do so he had first to divorce his second wife, so that he should have no wife preceding a *bint 'amm*.[104]

North Africa

Thanks to the researches of Westermarck and of a number of French scholars we have ample information as to the prevalence of *bint 'amm* marriage in Morocco, the westernmost outpost of Middle Eastern culture. Both among Arabs and Berbers, marriages between children of two brothers are not only common, but a man is held to have the right to marry his father's brother's daughter.

In Andjra, Westermarck was told that the cousin has to be asked before a girl can be given away to another man, and that if this step is omitted, the cousin is entitled to prevent the marriage even on the very day of the wedding by forcibly removing her from the bridal box. Among the Uled Bu'Aziz, a man who has contracted marriage with another man's *bint 'amm* can be compelled to give her up, if he is compensated for his expenses and if he has not yet settled down with her. In the Rif instances are known in which a man who has married his daughter to an outsider has been killed by his brother's son.[105]

Also "A Mohammedan Hausa has the right to marry the daughter of his father's brother," but he has no such right to the hand of any of the other cousins, whom he can marry only if her father agrees.[106]

Positive Motivations

Several cogent reasons have been advanced for the marriage of paternal cousins by the peoples practicing it. One of the earliest of these was given by the Persian king Ardeshir who advised his lawyers, secretaries, officers, and husbandmen to "marry near relatives for the sympathy of kinship is kept alive thereby."[107] Although the meaning of marriage between "close relatives" is not defined more fully, it must have referred to brother-sister and/or cousin marriages.

The same motivation, namely the strengthening of the kinship ties, is given in ancient Arabic sources referring to the practice of marriage between paternal cousins prevalent in pre-Islamic Arabia.[108]

We read in the *Kitāb al-Aghānī* that Qays ibn Dhariḥ, of the stock of Kinānā, fell in love with Labna, a beautiful maiden of the Quḍā'a tribe, and when he implored his father for permission to marry her, the father objected saying that he (the father, Dhariḥ) was indeed a rich and wealthy man and he did not want his son to take the side of a stranger.[109]

A related consideration in favor of paternal cousin marriage is the assumption that a man who grows up together with his *bint 'amm* within the intimate framework of one extended family knows her and develops a liking and a love for her, which in turn augur well for the happiness and stability of the marriage.

In the Middle Ages in Arab lands, a cousin (father's brother's daughter) was "often chosen as a wife, on account of the tie of blood which is likely to attach her more strongly to her husband, or on account of an affection conceived in early years."[110] Speaking of Egypt of the early nineteenth century, Lane remarks that "a union of this kind is generally lasting, on account of this tie of blood; and because mutual intercourse may have formed an attachment between the parties in tender age."[111] In Syria also in middle-class urban society, although "marriages between cousins are less frequent than in the families of high society," if they occur, "they are dictated more often by feelings of affection which develops easily between male and female cousins who in the town can see each other and talk to each other."[112] According to a Syrian proverb, "Ill luck which you know is better than good luck with which you get acquainted,"[113] that is, it is preferable to marry a cousin whose faults you know rather than a strange girl who seems to be better but with whose true qualities you will get acquainted only later. A Palestinian Arab proverb expresses the same feeling: "Follow the circular (that is, normal, or regular) path, even if it is long, and marry your *bint 'amm* even if she is a miserable [match]."[114]

A Meccan proverb encourages the young man not to be ashamed of his *bint 'amm*: "He who is ashamed of his *bint 'amm*, will get no boy from her."[115]

Several Moroccan Arabic proverbs likewise emphasize the desirability of marrying a *bint 'amm* because of the advantages of familiarity with her: "He who marries his *bint 'amm* celebrates his feast with a sheep from his own flock"; or "Marrying a stranger is like drinking water from an earthenware bottle, but marriage with a *bint 'amm* is like drinking water from a dish": that is, you can see what you drink.

The Persian proverb quoted above (p. 139) expresses the view that marriages between paternal cousins are made in heaven, that is, are preordained by God.

Another important motivation of marriage between paternal cousins is the endeavor to preserve the property in the family. This motivation comes into play as a result of the traditional Middle Eastern system of inheritance, which conflicts to some extent with the rule of patrilineal descent. Under this rule, a woman's children belong to the family (and larger kin-group) of her husband only. Whatever property a woman inherits from her father, and, in turn, leaves to her children, thus passes from her father's family into that of her husband. The marriage of a daughter with an outsider therefore ultimately results in the alienation of part of the family's property. On the other hand, if paternal cousins marry, their children are the offspring of the same grandfather through both their father and their mother, and thus whatever a daughter inherits from a man is passed on by her to her children who are also the patrilineal grandchildren of the same man. In this case, therefore, even that part of the family property that is inherited by the daughters remains in the family.

In fact, in one of the earliest Middle Eastern documents relating to this subject the inheritance of daughters is made contingent upon their marrying members of the in-group, and, as it eventually transpired, all the five female heirs in question married their father's brothers' sons (Numbers 36 : 1–12).

Although *bint 'amm* marriage was practiced in Mecca and Medina in pre-Islamic days, it can be assumed that when Mohammed reformed the laws of inheritance, allowing the daughters a share in the father's estate, this resulted in an increased frequency of *bint 'amm* marriages.[116] The basic Koranic legislation in this respect is found in Surah iv : 11, where it is said: "Allah chargeth you concerning your children: to the male the equivalent of the portion of two females, and if there be women (only), more than two, then theirs is two thirds of the inheritance, and if there be one (only), then the half."

This Islamic law is by no means adhered to by all Middle Eastern tribal and village societies, who in many cases still follow their old, pre-Islamic customary local law. In general it can nevertheless be said that some portion at least of the father's estate is inherited, as a rule, by his daughter, and thus passes on from her to her children. Therefore, the preservation of the property in the family becomes an important motivation for the preference for paternal cousin marriage, and is stated to be one of its purposes in many parts of the Middle East.[117]

In many Middle Eastern societies people are conscious of several of the motivations for cousin marriage. In Kurdistan, for instance, "Giving one's daughter to a brother's son is . . . considered thoughtful and proper. The father knows his daughter's spouse well, and will also be able to exert some control over his actions toward her after marriage; marriage should be between equals, and no one is closer in status and sentiment than a paternal cousin. The small child is pleasantly embarrassed when teased for being "in love" with a paternal cousin. The importance of endogamy in maintaining family property is also recognized, though the problem only arises with any degree of gravity where Koranic laws of inheritance, giving stipulated fractions of the estate to female descendants, are strictly followed, and this does not generally seem to be the case. . . . Such a pattern of father's brother's daughter marriage plays a prominent role in solidifying the minimal lineage as a corporate group in factional struggle. Marriages of this type thus serve to reinforce the political implications of the lineage system. . . . relative to the first potential lines of fission and segmentation within the minimal lineage itself."[118]

To sum up, in the Middle Eastern patrilineal kinship system it is of extremely great importance for the head of the family to be assured of the unwavering support of his brothers and their sons. The greater the number of the male kin on whose unquestioning loyalty he can count, the greater his influence, power, security, and prestige. One of the time-proved methods of strengthening the ties of kinship and of common interests between the head of a family and his patrilineal kinsmen is to give them his daughters in marriage. These considerations in most cases outweigh by far the loss of money resulting from the reduced bride price paid by a brother's son. The same considerations hold good also from the point of view of the young man about to choose a wife. If the wife is from a different family, and even more so if she is from a different village or tribe, the husband cannot be sure that the interests of his father-in-law will always harmonize with his own. Contrary interests, especially if they lead to mutual raiding or warfare, put the wife in a difficult and at times tragic situation whereby the inner coherence in the nuclear family of the husband and also in the extended family of which he is a member may be weakened. If on the other hand his wife is a *bint 'amm*, a daughter of his father's brother, the likelihood of the occurrence of such a conflict of interests is greatly reduced, and in general the harmonious community of interests between a man and his father-in-law is enhanced.

Close in-group or in-family endogamy is to this day the prevalent practice in all social strata of the Middle East with the exception of those exposed to modern Western influences. Endogamy still seems to satisfy most young men and women, because young people who grow up in the large and protective environment of the extended family seem to be conditioned by their upbringing to have a preference for continuing their lives in the same environment and atmosphere; given this preference, such close in-group marriages as between a man and his father's brother's daughter have all the advantages as against marrying a nonrelated outsider. Two young people who grow up in the same extended family (or at least in two closely related extended families) have in general a pre-existing community of interests and a similarity in outlook and personality determinants, and can therefore look forward to a much smoother adaptation to each other, adjustment to the larger frame of the extended family, and further growth within it, than can be the case in an out-group marriage.

Opposition to Cousin Marriage

Occasionally opposition to cousin marriage arose among those who practiced it, and was expressed in the form of good advice or proverbs. al-Maydānī (ii : 250) makes the following exhortation: "Marry the distant, but not the near [in relationship]." The reason given for the advisability of avoiding cousin marriages is most frequently the belief that the offspring of such marriages will be feeble. In Jauharī's Arabic Dictionary a *Ḥadīth* (an oral tradition going back to the Prophet Mohammed) is quoted to the effect that by marrying strangers one will not have feeble posterity. Another early Arab author, Ibn 'Abd Rabbihi, in his *Kitāb al-'iqd al-farīd* (iii : 290) says in praise of a hero: "He is a hero not borne by the cousin (of his father), he is not weakly; for the seed of relations brings forth feeble fruit."[119]

The weakness of such offspring may be manifested in their small stature. It is said of Omar that when he once asked why were the Qurayshites so small of stature, he was told that this was the result of their frequent cousin marriages. Thereupon Omar is said to have prohibited the continuation of this practice. The same idea is expressed in a verse quoted in Bajuri's Commentary to Ibn Qasim (ii : 153): "If you want nobility of descent (i.e., physical excellence) marry a stranger and do not enter into a tie with relatives." According to Bajuri, a man's desire for a closely related woman such as his *bint 'amm* is weak, and therefore the child born of such a union will also be weak.[120]

Abu Hamid al-Ghazali (1059–1111) in his principal ethical work, the *Iḥyā 'ulūm al-dīn* ("The revivification of the religious sciences"), devotes a section to the properties and characteristics required of a wife. One of these is that "the woman should not be a near relative of the husband, because near relationship diminishes the sensuous desire. 'Marry not near relations,' says the Blessed One (Mohammed), 'otherwise one must expect a weak (*ḍāwī*) progeny.' *Ḍāwī* means *naḥīf* (thin, weakly). The reason for this is that this circumstance results in a weakening effect on the sensuous desire. This latter, namely, is aroused through sensations of sight and touch, and these are especially strong in the case of a new and strange object. If, however, the object in question is familiar, and has been in front of one's eyes for a long time, then the sense becomes dulled so that it can no longer completely perceive it and be impressed by it. Therefore also the libido will not be excited by it."[121] The same feeling was expressed in modern Morocco as well as by a Berber informant of Westermarck's: "How can a man love a woman with whom he has grown up from childhood?"[122]

Another stated reason for the dislike of cousin marriages was that they might lead to quarreling and disharmony. The ancient Arabic poet, 'Amr b. Kulthūm, said: "Do not marry in your own family, for domestic enmity arises therefrom."[123] This fear too is expressed in modern Moroccan proverbs. One of these says: "Your father's brother will make you blind, and your mother's brother will make you destitute, and keep away from your blood that it shall not visit you with misfortunes." Girls in Fez when wishing to get married go to ask help at the shrine of the saint Sīdī Mbārak ben Abābū, and address him: "O Sīdī Mbārak, give me a husband who has no friends." This they do in order to avoid being given in marriage to a cousin, since cousin marriages are supposed to lead to quarrels between the husband's and the wife's families, both of whom want to interfere in the married life of the couple.[124]

In Syria also there is a proverb that speaks about the inconveniences of cousin marriage, which may lead to quarrels between the two families: "Do not approach your relatives, their scorpions will bite you."[125]

Conclusion

A comparison of the distribution data of the cousin's right with those of preference for *bint 'amm* marriage shows that there are ethnic groups in considerable numbers within the limits of the Middle Eastern culture continent whose marriage pattern includes preference for *bint 'amm* marriage without, however, according to a man the *right* to marry his *bint 'amm*. The cousin's right to marry his *bint 'amm* does not and cannot exist without preference for *bint 'amm* marriage; while preference can and does exist without the right, having apparently a wider distribution. The fullest form of *bint 'amm* marriage appears to be the one in which a man has the right to marry his *bint 'amm*. On the other hand, the existence of the preference for cousin marriage without this right can be taken as an indication of an incomplete, partial form of the institution of cousin marriage. The incomplete variety of cousin marriage (preference without right) may be contingent upon one or more of the following factors and circumstances:

a. The geographic location of the ethnic group in question may be marginal to the Middle Eastern culture continent and the pattern of cousin marriage may therefore not exist in it in the full form developed in the Middle Eastern core culture (example: the Timbuctoo area, or the Fulani in Nupe). This assumption is predicated on the known existence of cousin marriage among the Biblical Hebrews and pre-Islamic Arabs; on the known increase in incidence of cousin marriage in Arabia after Mohammed; and on its incorporation into Muslim tradition, which secured its acceptance by all (or nearly all) Islamized peoples. It also implies that the cousin's right was a later development in the Middle Eastern core culture, and that therefore it has not yet reached marginally located ethnic groups that have already absorbed the earlier form of Middle Eastern preference for cousin marriage.

b. Ethnic groups located geographically well within the central sector of the Middle Eastern culture continent may yet occupy a position of cultural marginality. Such a group may be influenced by the older and less stringent preference for cousin marriage and may have subsequently resisted or remained unaffected by the later specific and strict Middle Eastern formulation of the cousin's right (example: the Copts in Egypt).

c. As a result of modernization and Westernization, a distance may develop between the actual culture of a sector of the population in a locality and the traditional culture of the ethnic group of which the local aggregate is part. In such cases, which can be observed, for example, in the middle-class population of many Middle Eastern cities, the most stringent feature of the traditional cousin marriage complex, namely the man's right to marry his *bint 'amm*, may be discarded because it is felt that it contravenes Western ideas that are being consciously absorbed. The preference for cousin marriage may at the same time persist, insofar as both parties, now allowed their free choice of marriage partners, may still feel that cousin marriage has, after all, some of those advantages that tradition ascribes to it. In this transitional stage, the frequency of cousin marriage may still testify to a continued preference for it, while the cousin's right may be ridiculed as obsolete.

d. An external circumstance must also be taken into consideration. This is the specific nature of the sources from which the data concerning the Middle Eastern marriage pattern (and Middle Eastern culture as a whole) are derived. Work in Middle Eastern anthropology on an over-all area basis, and especially attempts at distribution studies, still have to rely to a considerable extent on accounts of travelers, officials, residents, and other nonanthropologists. These writings, while often containing valuable firsthand observations, often fall short as far as detail and completeness are concerned. The absence of any reference to the cousin's right in a given ethnic group may therefore mean not only that the cousin's right did actually not exist, but also that the author of the account failed to notice it or was not even aware of its possible existence. At least part of the distributional discrepancy between the cousin's right and the preference for cousin marriage is probably due to this circumstance.

VII. Dual Organization

STUDENTS OF culture in general and of certain world areas in particular have repeatedly devoted their attention to the form of social structure commonly referred to in anthropological literature as *dual organization*. The definitions of what constitutes dual organization vary.[1] One of the most comprehensive analyses of the characteristics of dual organization throughout the world is that of Josef Haekel, published in the 1950 volume of *Anthropos*.[2] These can be subsumed as follows:

A Sociological Dichotomy. A division of local aggregates, tribes, or clans into two; an extension of the dual division to larger territories; a dichotomy of the men's clubs, the ceremonial houses, the age groups, classes, or ceremonial groups. The existence of the two groups (usually referred to as "moieties") can be overtly manifest or present only in the consciousness of the people, or expressed in certain modes of behavior. It can be either permanent or temporary.

Occasionally there is also a tendency to *further dual subdivisions* within the moieties. In these subgroups a combination with totem clans is frequent. On the other hand, the dual system can be present without any further subdivision of the moieties.

Regulation of Marriage. The dual organization either is or is not accompanied by moiety exogamy. When there are two marriage classes they are, as a rule, the moieties of villages or tribes. Secondarily, exogamy may be lost.

Descent. Descent is counted within the moiety in general most frequently in the maternal line, but patrilineal descent occurs also in connection with dual organization.

Ideology and Symbolism. Pairs of opposites, often expressed in names, figure in the *ideology and symbolism* of the moieties, such as the symbolic division of natural objects into two groups. There are also associations with districts and directions, or with opposites such as sky—earth, above—below, male—female; or with opposites of colors; with war—peace, with contraposited animal pairs (totemistic or totemizing dual systems); with heavenly bodies such as light and dark moon or sun—moon. Often a competitive brotherly pair or some other ancestral pair figures in the moiety.

Naming. The two moieties are called by opposite names.

Antagonism and Rivalry. Symbolic or fictional enmity usually obtains between the two moieties, sometimes degenerating into serious strife. Jealousy, mutual ridiculing, joking designations, competitive fights and games are common.

Reciprocity. This is expressed in mutual services at feasts and funerals.

Evaluation and Status. There is a higher evaluation of one moiety, which is partly a practical utilization of existing ethnic stratification.

The presence of all or most of these characteristics, with differing emphases, is attested by data from the following world areas: India, the Ugric peoples of Central Asia, Indonesia, Oceania, North America, and Negro Africa.[3] Woelfel, Jeffreys, and Haekel also refer to the presence of the dual system in North Africa among certain Berber groups.[4] As far as could be verified, no attempt has been made hitherto to establish the presence of the system in the Middle East in general.

In the course of the author's researches in Middle Eastern social structure it has become apparent not only that dual organization is present in many parts of the Middle East but that, up to its present decline as a consequence of the impact of modern Western sociopolitical forms, it was a highly significant factor in the traditional social organization as well as in the political life of the area as a whole. Specifically, among the following Middle Eastern peoples were traces of dual organization observed: The nomadic and the settled population of the Arabian Peninsula from pre-Islamic days to the present, including the major tribes and tribal federations of Southern and Central Arabia as well as of the Syrian Desert. The tribes of Iran and Afghanistan. The tribal elements and the settled peoples of Iraq, Syria, Lebanon, Palestine, and Transjordan, including the urban population, and Muslims as well as Christians. The Druzes of Syria and Lebanon. The urban population as well as the villagers of Egypt. The settled and nomadic, Arab and Berber, groups of Libya, Tunisia, Algeria, and Morocco. The peoples inhabiting the oases of the Sahara, down to the deep south.

Data indicating the presence of the dual organization in the Middle East are so abundant that one may be justified in assuming that this form of social structure is one of the general characteristics of Middle Eastern culture.

General Characteristics

Pride in descent forms one of the most significant traits in the ethos of Middle Eastern peoples. Emphasis on noble ancestry is greatest among the nomadic elements, while in the settled population, both villagers and townspeople, it appears to be weakening in recent decades.

The nomads, among whom ancient traditions have survived in greater force than among other segments of Middle Eastern society, accord the highest prestige not to the richest or most warlike families or tribes, but to those who have the oldest and most noble genealogy and the most famous men among their ancestry.[5] "To know this pedigree is of practical value to any one who has to deal with Arab nomads, owing to the value which they themselves attach to genealogy, the social distinctions which they base upon it, and the estimation in which they hold those expert in its intricacies."[6]

Since among the Arabian nomadic and seminomadic tribes a knowledge of tribal genealogy has remained to this day such a highly prized accomplishment, every older tribesman has, as a rule, at least some rudimentary idea as to his tribal ancestry and can give some account of his genealogy. Folk memory, however, tends to simplify the complex family trees of both individuals and tribes, with the result that several links, representing a generation each, are often omitted and several centuries of tribal history telescoped into a few brief generations.[7] This reduction in depth is paralleled by a reduction in breadth, that is, by a simplification of the complicated structure of tribal relationships, and notably by a parallel arrangement of tribal groups into coequal elements, although originally the actual relationship may have been that of subordination of the one to the other. In this manner a complicated vertical structure is transformed by popular tradition into a relatively simple horizontal one.[8]

In addition to this simplified tribal genealogy, the more complete and probably more faithful tradition of the origins and relationship of the tribe is also as a rule preserved by one or two individuals in each tribe who are specialists in tribal lore. Since genealogic knowledge is of special importance for the families of shaykhs, whose main claim for chieftainship rests in many cases solely on their descent, these genealogical specialists, called *nassāba*, usually are members of shaykhly families.[9]

A recurrent feature of these genealogic traditions, whether popular or learned, is that in all parts of the Middle East they group the tribes, and in many cases the settled population as well, into two factions or moieties. Both the specialists and the laymen in every tribe know to which of the two locally prevailing groups their tribe belongs. An additional characteristic of this genealogic dichotomy is that frequently it has developed into a political bisection and that often tribes or tribal groups belonging genealogically to one moiety have become politically attached to and incorporated into the other. A third, even more remarkable characteristic is that in spite of the all-pervading importance of religion in Middle Eastern culture as a divisive force, groups belonging to different religious sects or even to altogether different religions are often parts of the same moiety, and conversely, that members of the same sect or faith belong to both moieties. Finally, moiety adherence also cuts across the omnipresent threefold division of Middle Eastern populations into nomadic, agricultural, and urban aggregates. The political-genealogic dichotomy of Middle Eastern society must therefore be regarded as a social phenomenon independent of and at cross purposes with all the other classificatory developments of the area.

A further general characteristic of this dichotomy is its reappearance on various levels of traditional Middle Eastern social structure, beginning with the largest social units produced by Middle Eastern society and down to the *ḥamūla*, the genetic kinship group or lineage. The prevalent pattern is that of continued bifurcation, dividing the largest unit into two, and so forth, until the smallest group comprising only a few extended families is reached.

With regard to the nomadic and seminomadic tribes of the Arabian Peninsula (including the Syrian Desert), a preliminary count showed that this type of dual tribal structure is at least twice as frequent as all the other nondual (unal or plural) tribal structures together, or that at least two thirds of all the Arabian tribes possess a dual organization.

The dual system itself is at least several centuries older than Islam. The sixth-century Byzantine historian Procopius mentions that the Homeritae (Himyarites, a subdivision of Qaḥṭān) were the overlords of the Maddeni (i.e., the Ma'addites), a northern people.[10] The Arab tradition therefore has a solid historical basis in speaking of the early wars in which the Ma'add strove to throw off the Ḥimyarite yoke.[11] As to the other Islam-dominated countries, one cannot at this stage answer satisfactorily the question of whether the dual organization was introduced into them by the spread of Islam or whether it had existed before and was ultimately derived from an ancient Near Eastern, possibly Egyptian prototype. The fact, however, remains that local dual organizations exist all over the Middle East, from the Golden River to the Golden Road, and that the Arab genealogists of the Middle Ages unhesitantly assigned every Arab, Arabicized, or Islamicized tribe to one of the two Arab ancestral stocks.

Genealogic Traditions

As to the Arabian tribes themselves, the efforts of the Arab genealogists of the first Islamic century were directed toward two goals: first, to assign every Arabian tribe to either of two ancestral lines converging ultimately in two eponymous ancestors; and, secondly, to identify these two ancestors as sons or descendants of early heroes mentioned in the Bible, in the Book of Genesis. Although much of the resulting genealogic structure must be regarded as an artificial device resorted to in order to carry through consistently a preconceived rigid genealogic scheme, there can be no doubt as to the actual division of the early Arabian population into two great stocks, nor as to the persistence in later Arabian popular thought of the tradition of the dual descent.[12]

Orientalists and Islamists have devoted much attention to the question of whether the present patrilineal descent, whose prevalence is well attested since the beginnings of Islam in the seventh century, was preceded by an older matrilineal system. This problem, however, has no direct bearing upon the subject dealt with here, for by the time the popular Arab genealogies became crystallized, there was an overwhelming consensus that every tribe was composed of the descendants in the male line of one single man: the eponymous tribal ancestor. Two related tribes were (and are to this day) generally regarded as the patrilineal descendants of two brothers, whose father, in turn, was the brother of another eponymous hero, the progenitor of one or more additional tribes, not quite as closely related to the first one. The logical conclusion of this speculative genealogic penetration farther and farther back into early legendary history was to arrive at two individuals, the first ancestors of the two all-Arabian moieties. The first of these was Qaḥṭān, ancestor of all the South Arabian tribes, and the second ʿAdnān, ancestor of all the North Arabian tribes.

Qaḥṭān was identified with the Biblical Yoqṭan (Gen. 10 : 25), son of ʿĒbher (in Arabic ʿAbar), son of Shelaḥ (Shalakh), son of Arpakhshad (Arfakhshad), son of Shēm (Sām), son of Noaḥ (Nūḥ) (Gen. 10 : 1, 21–25). Although there is no further correspondence between the sons of Yoqṭan as enumerated in Genesis and as appearing in the traditional genealogy of the South Arabian tribes, it is interesting to note that Biblical exegesis identifies several of the Yoqṭanides with South Arabian tribal or regional names.[13]

A tribal federation, called Qaḥṭān or Yaman (meaning south) actually existed in pre-Islamic times, and still occupies a considerable area southeast of Mecca. Early in the Muslim period,

Qaḥṭān was divided into two parts: the one, called Kahlān, was the larger group, comprising mostly nomadic and seminomadic tribes, while the other, called Ḥimyar, was a smaller group, consisting mostly of settled peoples.[14]

'Adnān, the father of all the North Arabian tribes, is regarded by Arab genealogists as the son of Ishmael (Ismā'īl), son of Abraham. Of the ten sons of 'Adnān,[15] Ma'add, through his son Nizār, became the progenitor of the North Arabians. Two of Nizār's sons, Rabī'a and Muḍar, are regarded as the ancestors of most northern tribes, that is, the tribes who inhabited in pre-Islamic days the northern half of the Arabian peninsula as far south as the 22nd or the 21st parallel N. Probably the most famous and noble of the northern tribes were those known collectively as Qays, after the name of their eponymous ancestor varyingly called Qays 'Aylān, son of Muḍar, or Qays son of 'Aylān, son of Muḍar.[16] The totality of northern tribes is called either 'Adnān, in which case the southern group as a whole is referred to as Qaḥṭān, or Qays, in which case the opposite moiety is called Yaman (Yemen). The northern tribes, in addition, are also referred to as Ma'add, or Nizār, or Muḍar tribes.

Since Qaḥṭān belonged, according to the Bible, to the fifth generation after Noah, while 'Adnān lived in the 12th generation after Noah, the Qaḥṭān or southern tribes were regarded as constituting the older or true aboriginal Arab stock (al-'Arab al-*'āriba*), while the northern 'Adnānis were considered as the younger group, as merely Arabicized (al-'Arab al-*musta'riba*) peoples.[17]

Ethnic Movements and Political Dualism

Whatever the historical kernel of this tradition of dual descent, it seems certain that 'Adnān (northern) and Qaḥṭān (southern) tribal groups were "separated even in pre-Islamic times by racial hatred, perhaps originally mainly based on the opposition between the desert and the sown."[18] The original home of the southern tribes was Southern Arabia, and more specifically its south-western corner, roughly corresponding to the area occupied today by the Kingdom of Yemen. Emigrations of southern tribes from this corner of the Arabian peninsula took place at an early date. Toward the end of the third century A.D., when the famous dam of Ma'rib was destroyed, a Yamani tribe fled the country and settled in the Hawran and al-Balqa districts of Syria. Even earlier than these, several other Yamanī tribes settled in the fertile region west of the Euphrates (modern Iraq), and some of these later moved on to southern Lebanon where their descendants profess to this day the Druze religion.[19]

While these examples illustrate the pre-Islamic establishment of southern tribes in the very midst of northern regions, the ethnic movements of the northern tribes can also be followed back to almost as remote a period. Arab tradition has it that the Qays tribe itself, the main prototype and protagonist of the northern division, originally inhabited the low parts of the Tihāma district in southwestern Arabia and was thus a close neighbor of the Yamanī tribes. In the sixth century, however, Qays tribes were already found spread over vast areas in northern and central Arabia. Mohammed (570–632) himself belonged, with his tribe, the Quraysh, to the northern group, although not to the Qays, but to its el-Yās branch. The people of Medina (north of Mecca), however, who were the first supporters (Anṣār) of Mohammed after his flight from Mecca (the so-called Hijra, in 622), were of Qaḥṭānī southern origin whose readiness to rally behind Mohammed may well have been motivated by the traditional rivalry between them and the northern Qurayshites of Mecca who originally opposed Mohammed. This historical accident undoubtedly played a significant role in sharpening the conflict between the two groups, for each felt that it had a valid claim to superiority: the northerners on account of their genealogic relationship to the Prophet, and the southerners on account of the incontestable merit of having been his first supporters.

Although Islam brought in many places a tremendous superiority to the 'Adnān (northern) faction, tribal rivalry became more pointed as a result of political developments in the first few decades after the death of Mohammed; and after the battle of Marj Rāhiṭ (in 65/685) the tendency to form tribal federations became even more intensified. This was a period of calculated re-alignments. The powerful tribal groups of Tamīm (in Khurasan,

Iran), Qays, and Muḍar joined forces and constituted the northern faction, while the Azd, the Yamanīs, and later the Syrian Quḍā'a (or Kalb) lined up against them as the southern moiety. The effects of this dual grouping of the most powerful tribal federations was to bisect the entire Arab world, and to wipe out, temporarily at least, other local antagonisms.[20]

The spread of Islam and the great social and political upheavals that accompanied it resulted in the uprooting of many tribes and in forced or voluntary migrations. These ethnic movements effected a further throwing together and mixing up of northern and southern tribes. Under the early Caliphs, considerable numbers of southern groups were found throughout Syria, in Mesopotamia (including large factions of the population of al-Kūfa and al-Baṣra), in Bahrein, in Isfahan. From Baṣra they penetrated even distant Khurasan where the Azdites and the Rabī'a (Bakr) were included among them.[21]

Hand in hand with actual dislocations and ethnic movements went the fictitious assignment of northern or southern genealogy to newly conquered or converted populations. In general, all the native peoples of the northern provinces, such as the Nabateans of Idumea, as well as the inhabitants of the northernmost oasis outposts such as Palmyra, came to be regarded as sons of 'Adnān, that is, as belonging to the northern stock.

While geographically the distinction between southern and northern tribes lost its meaning as a result of such ethnic movements and countermovements, the traditional Arab emphasis on nobility of descent kept the memory of the dual origin alive down to the present time. As late as the end of the nineteenth century all the noble Arab tribes regarded themselves as the descendants of either Qaḥṭān or Ishmael,[22] that is, as either southerners or northerners.

Under the Umayyad Caliphs, who took wives from both factions, the hostilities between the two led to intermittent and often extremely bloody strife. The reigning Caliph was constrained to rely alternatingly on either the Qays or the Kalb (Yaman) for support. In the latter part of the Umayyad period especially, the Caliph appeared to be "rather the head of a particular party than the sovereign of a united empire."[23] Between 719 and 745, that is, within 26 years, the actual control of the government passed five times from one faction to the other.[24]

The repeated alliances of the Qaysite Umayyad dynasty with the Yamanīs shows the diminishing importance of the genealogic as against the political factor in the constitution of the two parties. Moreover, it repeatedly happened that individuals and groups, and even the reigning monarch himself, changed party allegiance for material or political reasons. Thus the Caliph Hisham was at the beginning of his rule a Yamanī but later declared himself to be a Qaysite for what seemed to be purely pecuniary reasons. In 734, he appointed a Qaysite governor of Africa, who, upon finding only two small Qaysite tribes in Egypt, promptly imported 1,300 poor Qaysī families, thus to strengthen his popular support.[25]

In general, however, party allegiance was a serious matter that often led to hostilities and bloodshed in all parts of the expanding domains of Islam. The district of Damascus became the scene of relentless warfare for two years because a Ma'addite (northerner) had stolen a melon from a Yamanite's (southerner's) garden. In Murcia in Spain blood is said to have flowed for several years because a Muḍarite (northerner) picked a vine leaf from the yard of a Yamanite. The beginning of the ninth century saw a seven-year war fought between the Yamanites and the Ma'addites. Toward the end of the same century, in the province of Elvira in Spain, the rivalry between the two parties almost cost the Arabs their rule of the entire province.[26] "Everywhere, in the capital as well as in the provinces, on the banks of the Indus, the shores of Sicily and the borders of the Sahara, the ancestral feud, transformed into an alignment of two political parties, one against the other, made itself felt. It proved a potent factor in ultimately arresting the progress of Moslem arms in France and in the decline of the Andalusian caliphate."[27]

Oman and the East Coast of Arabia

The preponderance of the political over the genealogic factor characterizes the dual organization of the 118 tribes of Oman, in the southeastern part of the Arabian peninsula, at the present time. The Oman tribes belong to either of two factions, called

Hināwī after the powerful Benī Hinā tribe, and Ghāfirī, after the strong Benī Ghāfir tribe, respectively. These names have been current in Oman for at least two hundred years. Prior to that time, the Hināwīs used to be known for centuries as Yamanīs, and were identified as southerners, while the Ghāfirīs were known as Nizārīs and northerners. The Hināwī faction, which is the more powerful of the two, comprises, generally speaking, tribes of southern or Qaḥṭānī genealogy; while the majority of the Ghāfirī tribes are of 'Adnānī or northern origin. Of the 111 Oman tribes whose party affiliation and traditional origin are known, 61 belong today to the Hināwī party. Of these, however, only 53 are of traditionally southern (Qaḥṭānī) origin while the remaining eight tribes, although at present belonging to the Hināwī faction, are known to be of northern ('Adnānī) descent. Conversely, of the 50 tribes making up the present strength of the Ghāfirī party, only 44 are of northern origin, while the remaining six are of southern origin. These figures show that in the case of a considerable percentage of the tribes political considerations have overridden traditional ties of descent and resulted in a switch of allegiance.

The following particulars will contribute to our understanding of these relatively frequent changes of factional allegiance in Oman. The larger and more powerful tribes of the same faction are mostly in alliance or in league with one another in each district. The purpose of these alliances, called in Arabic *ṣuff*, is primarily political: they are defense alliances with mutual commitments to come to the aid of one another if attacked. The weaker tribes living in the proximity of these powerful allied tribes have no choice but to place themselves under their protection in a client-master relationship known also from other regions of the Middle East. Whatever the original descent of such weaker tribes, they must ally themselves politically with the powerful *ṣuff* in whose shadow they dwell, and ultimately affiliate themselves with their political faction. In other cases the reason for affiliating oneself with the opposite faction lies in internal quarrels between two sections of a tribe, as a result of which the weaker section is constrained to seek the help of its traditional enemies against its brother tribe.

The district alliances of tribes belonging to the same faction constitute a country-wide coalition of the Hināwī and Ghāfirī factions respectively. In spite of the obviously political coloring of these two factions, in the popular thinking of the tribes themselves they are held together by the ties of kinship.

The relationship between the two factions is that of traditional hostility and undisguised antagonism, "keeping the country in perpetual turmoil and disruption through their jealous feuds and hatreds, and this undying enmity is the key to the internal history of the land."[28]

The enmity between the two factions is so keen that a stranger wishing to travel among the tribes must take along both a Hināwī and a Ghāfirī guide to serve as guarantors of his safety.

There is no clear-cut geographic division between the two factions, although the Hināwī predominate in the southeast including the Bāṭina coast, and the Ghāfirī in the northwest, as well as in the central tribal block. The intermingling of the two factions throughout the country usually takes the form of groups of villages belonging to one of them and maintaining a constant state of feud with a neighboring group of villages belonging to the other. Often a single town or village is split into two by allegiance to the two factions, and the tension and hostility between the two are intensified when, owing to its location, one of the two moieties is able to control the water supply of the whole settlement.

The town of Nizwa, for example, which formerly was the capital of Oman, was torn for a long time by the strife between the Benī Hinā who inhabited the lower town and the Benī Riyām who occupied the upper town and were able to cut off the water supply from the lower town.[29]

The religion of the majority in both factions is the Ibāḍī sect of Islam. But among the Hināwī almost three quarters of the tribes are Ibāḍī and only one quarter Sunni Muslim, while among the Ghāfirī some 60 per cent are Ibāḍī and 40 per cent Sunni. A few Ghāfirī tribes (notably the Benī Rasib and Benī Bū 'Alī) follow the puritanistic Wahhābī creed of Central Arabia.

The Hināwī and Ghāfirī division cuts also across Trucial Oman, where, however, the Hināwī are Mālikī Sunnīs, and the Ghāfirī virtually Wahhābīs.[30]

In the eighteenth century there was a civil war and a dynastic squabble over succession in Oman between the Hināwī and the Ghāfirī factions, but the existence of the dual division and the tension still characterizing the relationship between the two, cannot be attributed to this cause alone.

Interesting are the instances in which traditions contrary to the generally prevalent belief in the tribal origin of the dual organization of Oman have remained alive in certain tribes. The Daru' and the Manāhil, for instance, although belonging to opposite moieties, maintain a tradition of common origin.[31]

The South Coast of Arabia

While the eastern section of the south of Arabia forms part of Oman, the central and western regions constitute the Eastern and Western Aden Protectorates respectively. This entire region is inhabited by both settled agriculturist and nomadic pastoral populations, both organized on a tribal basis. The typical South Arabian social organization is a tribal confederation, headed by a sultan, and consisting of nomadic tribes, agricultural villages, as well as a few towns. Very often these tribal confederations have a dual character.

The two over-all parties to either of which the individual confederations belong are called in the Hadhramaut (Ḥaḍramawt; the central part of the South Arabian coastal region) Yafa' and Ḥamdān. All the free tribes boast of belonging to one of these two factions, and only the lower classes of society such as the low-caste inhabitants of Shihr and other nontribesmen are not directly involved in this dichotomy.[32]

Both the Yafa' and the Ḥamdān belong to the southern division, that is, regard themselves as the descendants of Qaḥṭān. Saba (who was the son of Yashjub son of Ya'rub son of Qaḥṭān) had two sons, Ḥimyar and Kahlān by name.[33] These two are claimed to be the ancestors of the Yafa' and Ḥamdān respectively. The ultimately common origin of the two sections does not, of course, prevent them from continuing in a state of unceasing rivalry, enmity, and open hostility.

The most powerful group of the Ḥimyarī Yafa' confederation

is the section that has retained the original name of Yafa'. The powerful and warlike Yafa' confederation, comprising more than one hundred thousand souls, occupies a considerable tract of land to the northeast of Aden town, just south of the frontier of the Aden Protectorate. It consists of two sections: the Upper Yafa' in the north, and the Lower Yafa' in the south. The chief tribes of the Upper Yafa' are the Mausata, Dhūbī, Maflaḥī, Bo'sī and Da'ūdi; those of the Lower Yafa' are the Kaladī, Yaharī, Sa'dī, Yazīdī and Banī 'Afīf. Other tribes belonging to the Yafa' group include the Ahl Arḍī.[34]

Schematic Genealogical Table of the *Tribes of Hadhramaut*

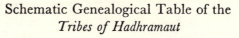

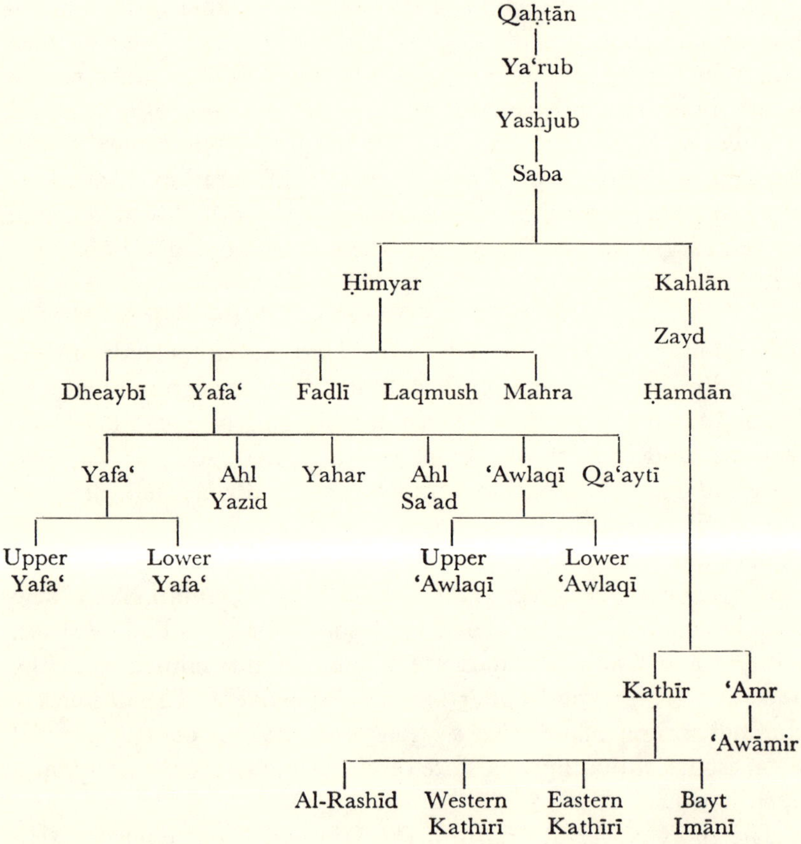

To the northeast of Aden town lies the port of Shaqra or Sughrah, which is the center of another confederation of tribes of Ḥimyarī descent constituting the Sultanate of Faḍlī. The Faḍlī are divided into numerous sections, one of the largest of which, the Merākash (sing. Merkāshī) was known for the loose morality of its women and the survival of several matriarchal or matrilineal traits.[35]

To the north of the Faḍlī is the 'Awdhalī Sultanate, named after the 'Awdhilla tribe. It includes the Dathīna district, inhabited by two great tribal confederations, the Ahl al-Sa'īdī and the 'Olah ('ölah, 'Ulah). The 'Olah again are divided into two groups: the 'Olah al-Kōr, inhabiting the Kōr (Kawr) Mountain, and the 'Olah al-Baḥr, or Sea-'Olah. The former comprises five, the latter eight tribes. According to the genealogic traditions of the 'Olah, they all are the descendants of 'Olah who was the grandson of Madḥij, and who had two sons, Sa'īd el-Buqeyrāt, from whom three of the 'Olah tribes are descended, and 'Alī el-Buqeyrāt, who became the ancestor of all the other 'Olah tribes.[36]

To the north of the 'Awdhalī Sultanate, and separated from it by an eastern tongue of Yemen, is the independent territory of Bayḥān in the Western Aden Protectorate. This territory comprises two parts: Bayḥān al-Asfal (with four districts), and Bayḥān al-Qaṣāb, inhabited by the tribe of al-Muṣ'abayn. As the name indicates ("the two Muṣ'abs"), this tribe consists of two moieties, descended from the two sons of the original progenitor, Mus'ab: Aḥmed, vulgarly called Ḥomeyd, became the ancestor of the Āl Aḥmed, and 'Arīf the father of the Āl 'Arīf. Each of the two sons, in turn, had four sons, to whom the eight subtribes trace their descent.[37] The accompanying diagram shows the structure of the Muṣ'abayn.

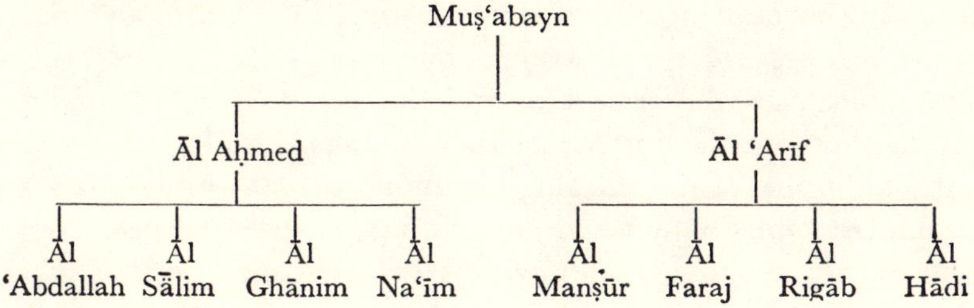

To the northeast of the Faḍli is the ʻAwlaqī tribal confederation consisting of Yafaʻi Himyarite tribes. It is divided into two sultanates: to the north is that of the Upper ʻAwlaqī, called ʻAwlaqī el-Niṣāb or ʻAwlaqī al-ʻAliyu, and to the south, on the coast, that of the Lower ʻAwlaqī, called ʻAwlaqī ʻAli Nasir or ʻAwlaqī Bā Kāzim. The Upper ʻAwlaqī are again subdivided into two parts, the Benī Maʻan (or Maʻam; comprising 18 tribes) in the southeast, and the Maḥājir (23 tribes) in the north, each with a separate ruler of its own, but both claiming Yafaʻī descent. The Lower ʻAwlaqī also fall into two sections, each with many subdivisions, called Bā Kāzim and Laqmush (or Qumūsh) respectively.[38] The Ḥammām of the Wādī Ḥammām and Wādī Markha are an ʻAwlaqī tribe who do not acknowledge the suzerainty of the ʻAwlaqī Sultan of Anṣāb (Niṣāb). The ruling family of Niṣāb claims descent from a Jaufi ancestry.[39]

To the east of the ʻAwlaqī on the coast is another Himyarite confederation, the Dheaybī (or Dhiaybī, Dhiēbī), or Ḥimyar; they used the word "ḥimyar" as their war-cry. This tribal confederation, which regards itself as kin to the Laqmush (Qumūsh), is divided into two factions: the Great Ḥimyar (*Ḥimyar al-kubra*), whose territory touches upon the Yafaʻ to the west, and the Little Ḥimyar (*Ḥimyar al-ṣughra*) who inhabit the Wādī Ḥalbān and its vicinity, and who, in turn, are subdivided into five tribes.[40]

The eastern neighbor of the Dheaybī or Ḥimyar is one of the most powerful Yafaʻī tribes, the Qaʻaytī, which occupies the seashore around the towns of Mukallā and Shiheir (Shihr), as well as the hinterland as far north as Shibam and Haurah. All these townships, as well as the towns of Hojarein and Qatan and the entire intervening territory belongs to the Qaʻaytī and constitutes the Qaʻaytī sultanate of Mukallā.[41]

East of the Qaʻaytī, on the coast, the Mahra, a large tribe numbering several thousands, occupies an extensive steppe area. This tribe does not speak Arabic, but retains its ancient Ḥimyarite dialect, as well as several archaic customs (such as taking their mothers' names instead of their fathers'), and prides itself on the antiquity of its genealogy claiming descent from ʻĀd ibn Aws ibn Irem ibn Shām (Shem) ibn Nūḥ (Noah).[42] This genealogy is, of course, a strongly abbreviated or telescoped version of a fuller tribal family tree that has been reconstructed as follows: Mahra b. Heydan b. ʿAmr b. el-Hafi b. Quḍāʿa b. Mālik b. ʿAmr b. Murra b. Zeyd b. Mālik b. Ḥimyar.[43] The Mahra tribal confederation consists of four divisions called *ʿuṣebāt*: Bin Gesūs, Shehshihī, Bin Sār, and Bin Boqi bin Aḥmed, each one of whom comprises numerous tribes. The Mahra confederation is ruled by the Bin Afrar family (claiming relationship with the Benī Alif of the Lower Yafaʿ) which is divided into two branches: the senior branch, called Saʿd bin Towar, residing in Soqotra, and the junior branch, ʿĀmr bin Towar, ruling for the sultan in Mahraland itself.[44]

While the western part of South Arabia, including the Western Aden Protectorate, is thus found to belong traditionally to the Ḥimyar moiety of Qaḥṭān (with a few exceptions to be noted later), the predominant element in the central and eastern parts of the Eastern Aden Protectorate is the Kahlān moiety of Qaḥṭān, or more precisely, the Ḥamdān elements of Kahlān. According to the traditional genealogy, Ḥamdān, who was a sixth generation descendant of Kahlān,[45] had two sons, Kathīr and ʿAmr.[46] The descendants of Kathīr are the Kathīrī, the powerful eastern neighbors of the Himyarite Qaʿaytī in the Hadhramaut,[47] who occupy not only the greater part of Central Hadhramaut including the Hadhramī towns of Seyyūn (or Saiūn), Terim, and Ghurfa, but also the entire coastal district of Ẓufar. The boundary between the two groups runs in a southeasterly direction between the Qaʿaytī town of Shibam and the Kathīrī town of Seyyūn, the seat of the Kathīrī sultan. These two towns are located at a distance of a mere ten miles from each other. These two tribes "are extremely hostile to each other."[48]

The Kathīrī themselves fall into two sections, the western of which, inhabiting Central Hadhramaut, is headed by the Kathīrī Sultan of Seyyūn (whose traditional rival is the Qaʿaytī sultan of Mukallā), while the eastern section, located around the Ẓufar coast, is ruled by the governor of Ẓufar who is a representative of the Sultan of Oman.[49] The Kathīrī Sultanate of Seyyūn consists, in addition to the towns and villages of Seyyūn, Tarim, Taris, al-Ghurfa, Mariama, and Al Gheil, also of a confederation of a considerable number of tribal groups, the Kathīrī, the

'Awāmir, the Jabirī, and the Bajrī.[50] The Eastern Kathīrī are again subdivided into two divisions, both of whom are represented in seven villages of the Ẓufar coast and are called 'Omar bin Kathīr or al-'Umar and 'Amr bin Kathīr or Āl 'Amr, respectively. The same two tribes inhabit also al-Ghurfa and Ahl Fās (two villages between Shibam and Seyyūn) and are constantly at feud with each other.[51]

The traditional rivals of the Kathīrī are the Qara who are wedged in between them and the al-Rashīd, an independent section of the Kathīrī. Al-Rashīd occupies a territory contiguous to the central portion of the Kathīrī country. The traditional enemies of al-Rashīd are the Sa'ar (or Say'ar) in the northern Hadhramaut, to the west of al-Rashīd and to the northeast of the town of Seyyūn. Another independent section of the Kathīrī is the Bayt Imānī.[52] So much for the Kathīr moiety of Hamdān.

The 'Amr moiety of Hamdān claims descent from 'Amr ibn Hamdān. The main representative of this moiety is the 'Awāmir confederation located in three separate areas: (1) al-Qaff, from the Wādī Hadhramaut as far north as the southern edge of the Rub' al-Khālī; (2) al-Ẓafra between Qaṭar and al-Buraymī; and (3) Oman. Although the three parts of the tribe have little contact with one another, a twofold division into Āl Badr and Āl Lazz runs through all of them.[53]

The genealogic affiliation of the other Hadhramī tribes is not clear, but one can assume that they too belong to the Ḥimyar or Kahlān moieties of Qaḥṭān. This country lies close to the Oman border and the typical Oman dichotomy into Hināwī and Ghāfirī is found in it as well. Thus the Harasī, Afar, Manāhil, and the 'Awāmir and al-Kathīr themselves are said to belong to the Hināwī, while the Daru', the Ālbū Shamis, and even the more distantly western Say'ar are regarded as Ghāfirī, their avowedly Qaḥṭānī descent notwithstanding. Here, however, as distinct from Oman proper, these labels have no political significance, and instead of the factional solidarity that is supreme in Oman, allegiance follows genealogic lines.[54]

The Say'ar, probably identical with the Ausaretae mentioned by Pliny, claim to be ultimately descended from the Qaḥṭān tribe through an ancestor named Mighdad al-Aswad, who is said to have been a Companion of the Prophet. One of the Say'ar tribes is the al-Junaybir which moved from the Hadhramaut to the Najrān area within Saudi Arabia. The main tribal area of the Say'ar lies to the east of that of the Dahm and to the north of the Hadhramaut valley. The Hadhramaut Say'ar are divided into two sections, a semisettled element (of which the Āl 'Abdullah bin 'Aun are a constituent tribe) called Ahl Ḥātim, centering around a scattered group of hamlets called Raydat Ahl Ḥātim, and ruled by two leading chieftains; and a purely nomadic section called Ahl bil-Layth whose chieftain has his semipermanent headquarters, called Raydat Ahl bil-Layth, at wells located some 25 to 30 miles east of Raydat Ahl Ḥātim. The two village groups together are known as Raydat al-Say'ar in the Wādī Makhya. Another Say'ar tribe is the Al Baqī Msellem one of whose two chiefs resides in Ba Rumeydan due north of Wādī Hadhramaut.[55]

To the east of the Say'ar stretches the territory of yet another dual confederation, that of the Mishqas. The southern Mishqas confederation embraces all non-Kathīrī elements south of the eastern section of the Hadhramaut valley. The Humūmī are one of these tribes, with the Bā-Aḥsan as one of its clans. The northern Mishqas comprise the Manāhil, 'Awāmir, and Tamīm tribes.[56]

Yemen

The available information on the tribal organization in the Kingdom of Yemen is very fragmentary. *The Handbook of Arabia* enumerates 74 tribes or tribal confederations in Yemen, but it states only occasionally how these units are structured, that is how many and what kind of subdivisions they comprise. As to the tribal genealogy—this is mentioned in two or three cases only. Nor is information available as to the presence or absence of the dual organization.

Among the tribes claiming a definitely southern origin are the following: Bekīl, Ḥamdān, Ḥāshid, Khaulān, Benī Murra. As against these, the following seem to be of northern extraction: Al 'Absī or 'Absiyah, 'Anaza, Benī Ismā'īl, Benī Qays.

Dual division within each of the two moieties is found among several tribes. The most important of these is that of Ḥāshid and

Bekīl. According to tribal traditions, Ḥamdān begot Jusham who begot Ḥāshid el-Akbar who begot Bekīl. Another version of the tradition has it that Ḥāshid and Bekīl were the two sons of Babroshām and his wife, the princess Nejema, who came from Anatolia to Yemen. The Ḥāshid tribes counted 22,000 armed men in the first quarter of the twentieth century, while the Bekīl at the same time counted 80,000. Both the Ḥāshid and the Bekīl follow the Zaydī sect. They live in the area called Balad Ḥamdān (to the north of the capital, Ṣan'a), the eastern part of which belongs to the Bekīl and the western to the Ḥāshid. In spite of the traditional close relationship between the two groups, their attitude toward each other has been that of enmity which occasionally erupted into fighting, as, for example, in 1885, when there was a bloody war between the two.[57]

It is interesting to note that among the Ḥāshid a threefold division is found, instead of the more common dual one. The whole of the Ḥāshid is divided into three groups: al-Khārif, Benī Ṣuraym, and al-'Usaymāt. Al-Khārif again is subdivided into three subgroups, the tribes of Jubar, Kalbīyīn, and al-Ṣayad. The Benī Ṣuraym is subdivided into nine (three times three) groups, called *tsī'e* or ninth; and the 'Usaymāt are subdivided again into three groups. These threefold divisions are called *thulth*, third.[58]

Among several other Yemenite tribes the usual dual division is found. The Ahl 'Ammar, the 'Anaza, the Ḥamdān, the Khaulan, and the Benī Sa'fan are each subdivided into two groups. In two cases at least this subdivision has a geographic connotation: the two subdivisions of the Ḥamdān are called Ḥamdān esh-Shām (Ḥamdān of the North) and Ḥamdān el-Yemen (Ḥamdān of the South), respectively. The two subdivisions of the Khaulān are called Khaulān el-Ṭawal (Long Khaulān), and Khaulān esh-Shām (Khaulān of the North) respectively.[59]

'Asīr

North of Yemen on the west coast of the Arabian peninsula lies the province of 'Asīr. In the southern part of 'Asīr the main tribal elements are comprised in a tribal confederation that falls into two main groups: 'Asīr al-Ḥijāz and 'Asīr al-Tihāma, the former occupying the main range, the latter the transverse ranges and valleys between it and the coastal plain (Tihāma). According to information obtained by Philby from the elders of the village Suda in the highlands of 'Asīr, the 'Asīr al-Ḥijāz comprise the following four tribes: 1. Banī Mughayd; 2. 'Alkam; 3. Rabī'a wa-Rufayda; 4. Banī Mālik. The 'Asīr al-Tihāma comprise seven tribes: 1. Banī Zayd; 2. Ahl Tha'lab; 3. Banī Juna; 4. Al-Qays; 5. Banī Qutba; 6. al-Shaba; and 7. Banī Dhalim. Each of these eleven tribes has a shaykh of its own and comprises several subdivisions.[60] Although Philby does not specify the genealogic claims of these tribes, we know that the Banī Mālik are of Qaḥṭān stock as are the Rabī'a wa-Rufayda.[61]

The Bani Mālik Tribes

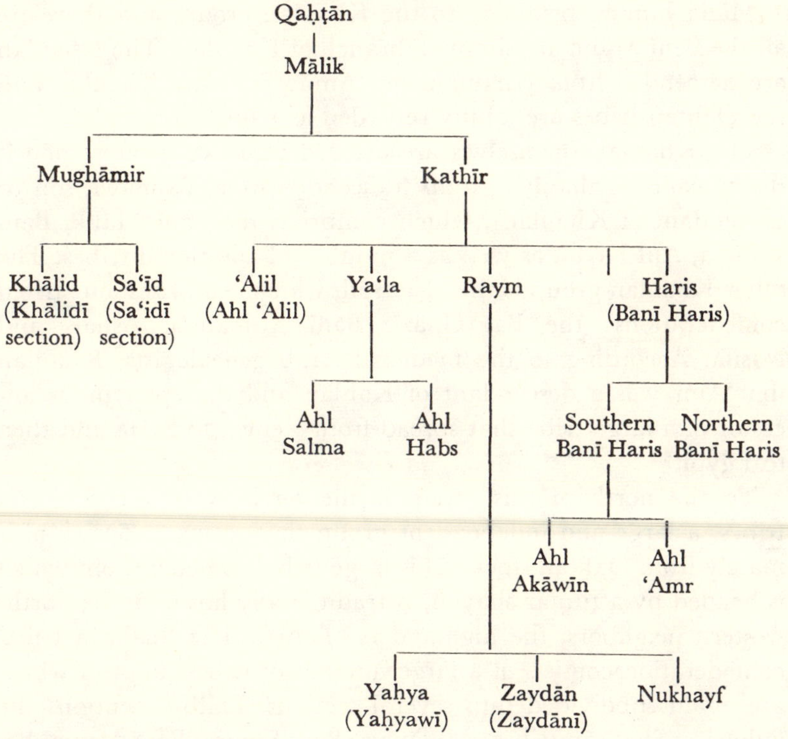

According to popular tradition, the Banī Mālik are the descendants of an eponymous ancestor called Mālik. This Mālik is said to have had two sons, Mughāmir and Kathīr, who became the progenitors of the two main branches of the present Banī Mālik. Mughāmir again had two sons: Khālid, father of the present Khālidī, and Sa'īd, father of the present Sa'īdī sections of the Banī Mālik. The other son of Mālik, Kathīr, had four sons, 'Alil (father of the present Ahl 'Alil), Ya'la, father of the present Ahl Salma and Ahl Habs), Haris (father of the present Benī Haris) and Raym. Raym again had three sons, of whom Yaḥya became the ancestor of the present Yaḥyawī section, Zaydān that of the present Zaydānī section, while the third, Nukhayf, seems to have had no descendants. The Benī Haris are divided into a southern and a northern branch, called Haris al-Yamanī and Haris am-Hashr, respectively. The southern Benī Haris have two main sections: Akāwīn and Ahl 'Amr.

Mālik himself belonged to the Khaulan group, and therefore all the Benī Mālik are simply a branch of Khaulan. The Khaulan are descended from Khaulan ibn 'Amir. Both the Khaulan and the Qaḥṭān tribes are jointly regarded as Banī 'Amir.

The Khaulan themselves are divided into two groups: one is the so called Yahanīya group (descended from Yahnawī, son or descendant of Khaulan), which comprises the Banī Mālik, Banī Juma'a, Ahl Fayfā, as well as a number of additional tribes. The other Khaulan group is the al-Furūd, which comprises four tribal confederations: the Bal Ghāzī, Banī Munabba, Ashar, and Nasīfa. According to the medieval Arab genealogists, Khaulan ibn 'Amr was a descendant of Kahlān and the eponymous ancestor of a large tribe that spread from Yemen to Syria and then to Egypt.[62]

To the north of this group is the territory of the Shahrān tribes, a large and independent group that seems to derive ultimately from Qaḥṭān stock. This large tribal confederation, which is headed by a titular shaykh, is traditionally hostile to its northwestern neighbors, the highlanders of 'Asīr. The Shahrān tribal confederation consists of a large number of tribes, most of which are again subdivided into several sections. Philby mentions the following Shahrān tribes: Mu'āwya, Banī Sulum, Banī Munabba, Wahib, Kud, Nahas, Rushayd, Banī Bijad, Banī Hamudh, Ahl Tindaha, Ahl al-Shām (comprising the Ma'raj, Ma'jūr,

'Askar, Wayla, and other subsections), 'Abs, as well as a related Banī Shihr tribe.[63] The Shahrān have both settled and nomadic sections.

Although no mention of a bisection of the Shahrān group is made by Philby, there are certain indications that seem to point in this direction. First of all, one group of the Shahrān are called Ahl al-Shām, that is, people of the north, and said to be the offshoot of the Banī Shihr of northern 'Asīr. This would indicate that other Shahrān tribes may be regarded as belonging to a southern section of the confederation. Secondly, several Shahrān tribal names (for example, Banī Sulum, 'Abs) reappear farther to the east as tribes of the Qaḥṭān confederation, which is definitely divided into a southern and a northern moiety. The partial affiliation of one and the same tribe with two larger units is a familiar phenomenon also in other parts of Arabia. Thirdly, dual division is the basic form of social organization among all the tribal units of the area (Murra, Qaḥṭān, 'Asīr, and others) and it seems therefore probable that it also existed or still exists among the Shahrān.

Another descendant of Kahlān, Ḥamdān, who, as we have seen, is regarded as the eponymous ancestor of one of the two moieties of the south Arabian tribes, reappears in the genealogic traditions of the tribes of 'Asīr and the contiguous section of the Rub' al-Khālī to the east. Ḥamdān was the son of Mālik who was the son of Zayd, but in popular 'Asīrī tradition he is known as Ḥamdān ibn Zayd.[64] In the Jauf area near the Yemen-Saudi Arabian border are the Dahm tribes, while the Wada' hold the Dhahran district just north of the Yemen-'Asīr frontier. Both these groups are large independent tribal confederations belonging to the Ḥamdān stock.[65]

Another and very widely dispersed branch of the Ḥamdān stock is that of the Yām. According to 'Asīrī tradition, Yām was the son of Yusba' who was the son of Hamdān. Yām himself had two sons, Jusham (popularly pronounced Chām), and Madhkar, who were the progenitors of the two great branches into which the Yām tribes at present are divided. To the Chām (Jusham) group belong the Rizq, Sulum, Ahl al-Ḥārith, and Ahl al-Hindī groups, as well as the very widespread Murra group of eastern

Rub' al-Khālī. The Madhkar group falls into two parts, the Mawājid, of which the Beni Nusayd are a subsection, and the Ahl Fāṭima, comprising the descendants of Fāṭima, the second wife of Madhkar. The Ahl Fāṭima again are subdivided into two groups, called Hisham and Wasil. No information seems to be available of the Wasil, but Hisham is again subdivided into two groups, called 'Ajaym and Wu'ayl. Nothing is known of the 'Ajaym, but the Wu'ayl comprise the following tribes: al-'Arja, al-Rashīd, al-Fahhād, al-Muṭliq, al-Futayḥ, al-Ḥasan, Ibn 'Īsa, al-Zayid, al-Wa'la, Ahl Ḥamad ibn Fāḍil, as well as the large and important 'Ajmān tribal federation.[66] The Ahl Fāṭima also comprise the Nisiyīn, Dhayban, and Ahl Hushaysh sections whose nearer affiliation is not known.

The Yām Tribes

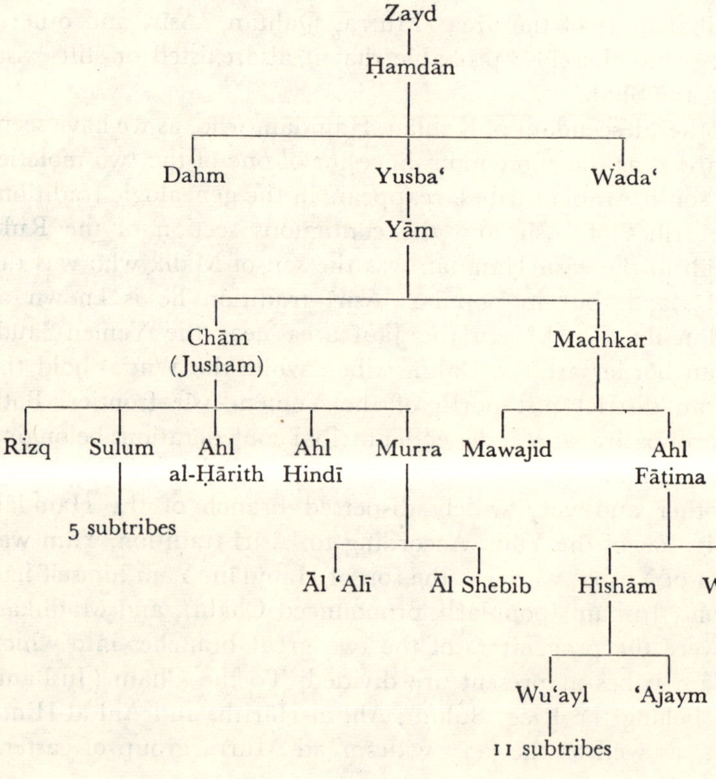

With regard to the 'Ajmān (or 'Ujmān) it should be noted that since the eighteenth century they have lived in the Ḥasa region near the central part of the east coast of Arabia,[67] at a distance of some 500 miles from Najrān, and yet the tradition of their Najrān home and Yām descent has been preserved to this day not only in 'Asīr but also among the 'Ajmān themselves in Ḥasa. According to 'Ajmān tradition the Yām tribes comprise in addition to themselves also the Murra, Manāsir, Manāhir, 'Awāmir, Rashīd, Say'ar and Karab.[68] Such recurrences of basically identical tribal traditions in widely separated areas, and going back to several generations, are calculated to increase our trust in the existence of a historical kernel underlying them. The al-'Arja and the al-Rashīd, who according to Philby's 'Asīrī informant belong to the Ahl Fāṭima,[69] appear as two actual tribal groups related to the 'Ajmān, living in southern Tuweyq, and still preserving the memory of the Najrānī origin.[70] Other 'Asīr tribes subdivided into two moieties are the following:

'Air (or Bal-'Air), divided into the nomadic Āl 'Amr, and the sedentary al-Nawāshirah sections, a total of about 35,000 persons.

'Alkam (or 'Alkam al-Haul), north of Abha, divided into 'Alkam al-Sāḥil and 'Alkam al-A'lūn, a total of about 20,000 persons.

Ghāmid, between Abha and Taif, subdivided into the settled al-Ḥadr and the nomadic Āl Ṣiyāḥ sections, at odds with each other.

Hilāl, divided into a western part along the coast and an eastern part along Halī, a total of about 35,000.

Qarn (or Bal-Qarn), from southwest of the Bishah valley to the mountain slopes, divided into a settled coastal group and a partly nomadic mountain group, a total of about 40,000.[71]

Before leaving the 'Asīr district for a glance at the interior of Southern Arabia, which is the present home of the large Murra division of the Yām, of the Qaḥṭān, and of the tribes that retained the name Yām itself, a word must be said about Zayd, the father (or grandfather) of Ḥamdān, ancestor of this large tribal group. According to Philby, this Zayd was identical with Zayd al-Hilālī, the most famous legendary hero (also called Abū Zayd al-Hilālī)[72] of the Benī Hilāl, about whom many colorful legends are still told in Southern Arabia.[73] From Philby's wording it does not become clear whether this identification is his own or was done by his 'Asīrī informants, in which case it would be a good example of that merging of different historical or legendary figures into one that is characteristics of the working of popular fancy and tradition.

The Benī Hilāl, who in the early Middle Ages left the Yemen-'Asīr region, invaded Egypt, and spread all over North Africa, were a northern, Qaysī, tribal confederation.[74] Their tribal genealogy is still remembered in Arabia in the usual abridged form as Hilāl b. Hawāzin b. Qays,[75] while the fuller form according to the medieval Arab genealogists is Hilāl b. 'Amir b. Ṣa'ṣa'a b. Mu'āwiya b. Bekr b. Hawāzin b. Manṣūr b. 'Ikrima b. Khaṣafa b. Qays.[76] Obviously therefore Zayd, the progenitor of the important Ḥamdān section of the Qaḥṭān, cannot be identical with Zayd, leader of the Benī Hilāl, an important Qaysī tribal confederation.

The Rub' al-Khālī

Under this heading will be treated briefly the tribes inhabiting the entire southern half of the interior of the Arabian Peninsula. In contrast to the large number of small groups with their intricate interrelationship, characterizing the social structure of the coastal sections of Southern Arabia, the interior, most of which is taken up by the Rub' al-Khālī, the Empty Quarter, the great South Arabian Desert, is but sparsely peopled by a few tribes (with several subdivisions, of course), each one of which is undisputed master of a very large if inhospitable tribal area.

The entire southern part of the Rub' al-Khālī, from Yemen in the west to Oman in the east, a territory of roughly 150,000 square miles of sandy desert, is held, as far as one can judge from the scarce data available, by the Murra confederation of tribes who trace their descent to 'Alī al-Murra.[77]

As to the genealogic connections of the Murra, we have already seen that they are one of the Jusham groups. According to a native authority quoted by Fu'ād Ḥamza, the Jusham comprise four groups: Āl Dimnān, Āl Hetēle, Āl Murra, and Āl Hindī.[78] Of these four we have already met the Al Hindī of the Najrān district. The Āl Dimnān and Āl Hetēle, although in the traditional genealogy offered by the native informant they appear as brothers of the Murra, that is, non-Murra tribes who have a common ancestor with the Murra, are today two small subgroups of the Murra, still headed each by a shaykh of its own, but numbering only 60 and 50 tents respectively.[79]

This change of status of a tribe or subtribe in relation to the larger unit of which it forms a part is characteristic of the vertical mobility of tribal organization. Popular memory retains the older order of several generations ago with which the actual situation may be at wide variance. In connection with the Murra, the shifting of the position of individual groups within the entire tribal structure can be shown clearly in several cases.

The accompanying illustration shows the traditional tribal organization of the Murra with its characteristic preponderance of the dual divisions and subdivisions.[80]

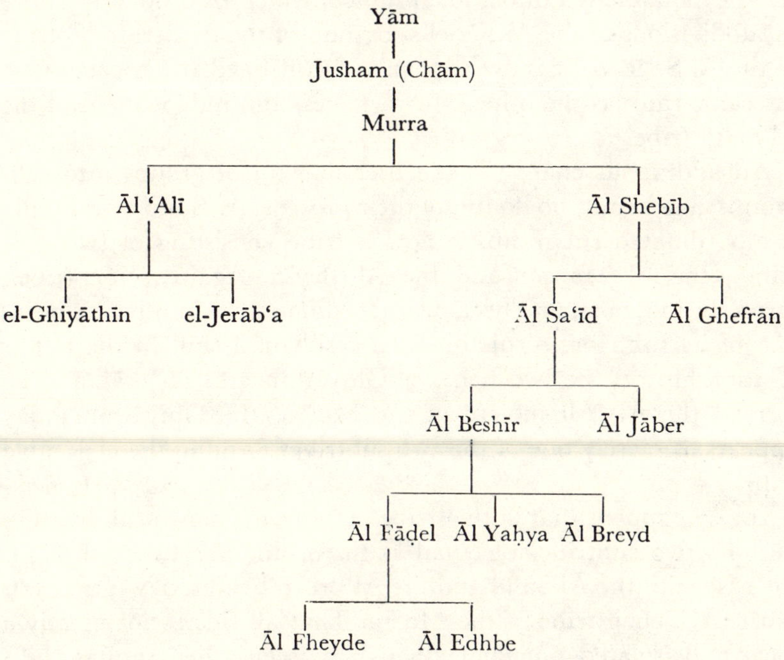

Let us compare with this the actual organization of the Murra as found by Philby:[81]

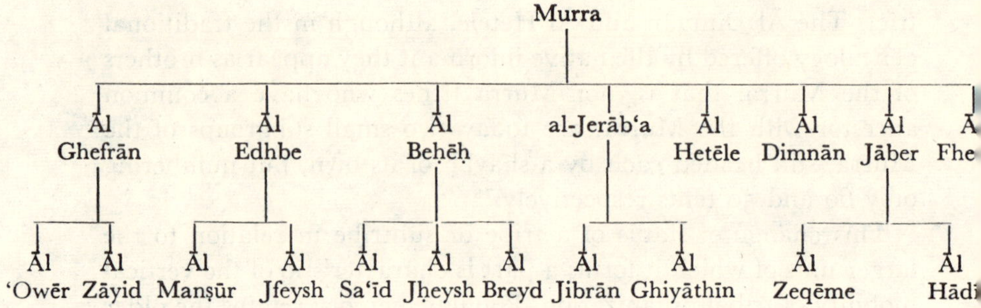

A comparison of the two genealogies enables us to make several observations with regard to the changes that took place in the structure of the Murra in the course of the last few generations. First of all the over-all division into two groups (Āl 'Alī and Āl Shebīb in the first table) disappeared. Secondly, the vertical structure has been changed into a horizontal one: the Āl Fheyde and Āl Edhbe, for instance, which traditionally figure as subdivisions of the Āl Fāḍel subgroup of the Āl Beshīr subtribe of the Āl Sa'īd tribe, now appear as full-fledged tribes occupying the same rank as the other Murra tribes, and independent of the Āl Sa'īd tribe.

An additional change is the breaking up of groups into subgroups, as a result, no doubt, of their growth: Āl Edhbe, originally a subordinated subgroup, is now a tribe consisting of two subtribes, the Āl Manṣūr and the Āl Jfeysh. Again, some tribes, formerly independent, became subordinated to another tribe as one of its subtribes, probably as a result of a shift in the power relationship: of the two tribes el-Ghiyāthīn and el-Jerāb'a, who formed the Āl 'Alī moiety of the Murra, the Ghiyāthīn today appears as merely one of the two subtribes forming the el-Jerāb'a tribe.

It also happens that both a tribe and one of its own subdivisions become two subtribes of equal status of another tribe; this was the case with the Āl Sa'īd and the Āl Breyd, who today form parts of the Āl Beḥēḥ tribe of the Murra. That all this is not merely a local and isolated phenomenon will be seen when similar shifts in the North Arabian 'Aneze confederation of tribes will be considered.

The western neighbors of the Murra are the Qaḥṭān, occupying the somewhat less unfriendly region between ʻAsīr (Shahrān) and Riyād. These tribes retained the proud ancient name of Qaḥṭān, although their actual genealogic connection with the pre-Islamic Qaḥṭān is, to say the least, doubtful.[82] Qaḥṭān today is one of the strongest confederations of tribes in Central Arabia, and as to its prestige in the desert, according to Doughty it is "the noblest blood of the South Arabians," while Philby remarks that it is "the most famous and still possibly the greatest of all the Arab tribes—the Joktan of Genesis" and is "the very cream of Arab tribal chivalry."[83]

No satisfactory information on the Qaḥṭān is available. In Oppenheim's *Die Beduinen*, basing on an older list made by J. J. Hess, the Qaḥṭān are divided into three groups: the first, ʻAbide, comprising 14 tribes; the second, Āl Muḥammed, comprising seven tribal confederations (with the number of individual tribes in each varying from three to eight), and two single tribes; the third, Āl el-Jimel, comprising three tribal confederations (with three, two, and two tribes) and two single tribes.[84]

A more detailed picture of the western Qaḥṭān can be pieced together from many scattered remarks contained in Philby's *Arabian Highlands*. First of all, it appears that the Qaḥṭān of the ʻAsīr district and its eastern outskirts (merging into the Rubʻ al-Khālī), are divided into two great groups, the *Southern Qaḥṭān* with a paramount chief of its own, residing in the village of Qauz, and the *Northern Qaḥṭān* with their paramount chief residing in the Kharj district. As the chief tribal confederations belonging to the southern Qaḥṭān Philby mentions the ʻAbida and the Sanḥān, the latter comprising the Zahra, Ahl Hirran, al-Jabara, and possibly also the Shurayf tribes. Another group of the Qaḥṭān, the Jaub, claims to be the parent stock of the ʻAbida, Shurayf, and Banī Bishr, so we can also take the Jaub and the Banī Bishr as belonging to the southern Qaḥṭān. To the Jaub belongs a subsection, Ahl Ḥasan. The general name of the northern Qaḥṭān is Jahādir. Philby refers to a number of additional important, Qaḥṭān tribal confederations such as the Benī Kalb or Uklab, the Saʻd, the Benī Sulum, the Rufayda, the Juhādil, the al-Sariʻ, and others, each with a number of tribes and subtribes, but unfortunately he fails to mention whether these belong to the northern or southern Qaḥṭān.[85] Although the information is far from being satisfactory, the by now familiar picture of a bisected tribal organization emerges, with each moiety further subdivided into two or more sections.[86]

South of the Qaḥṭān, in the southernmost part of Saudi Arabia, is the territory of a tribal confederation that has retained the ancient name of *Yām*. The Yām tribes of the Wadi Dawāsir and the Western Rub' al-Khālī offer one of the few examples of a tribal confederation bifurcated along religious sectarian lines. At present this division is no longer clear, but until recently the Yām tribes were divided into a Biyādhiyya and a Rufadha half. The Biyādhiyya persuasion is a schism that has something in common with the Wahhabi doctrines, and is of Omani origin. The various sections of the Mahshil, including the al-Rashīd and al-Fahhād, belong or have belonged until their recent conversion to Wahhabism to the Biyādiyya, which apparently dispenses with the *adhān* and congregational prayer. The Rufadha, a variety of the Ismā'īlī sect of the Shī'a, is the persuasion of the Fāṭima and Madhkar groups of the Yām, including the Rizq and the Sulum section of the Madhkar.[87]

Northern Arabia and the Syrian Desert

Under this heading will be discussed the tribes of the northern half of Saudi Arabia, as well as those tribes whose wandering territories lie wholly or partly in Jordan, Syria, or Iraq. In this area, too, the dual division is the prevailing form of tribal structure on various levels.

All the tribes, in general, relate themselves either to Qays or to Yaman. In the Syrian Desert and as far south as the Ḥijāz, in addition, the name-pair *Ahl el-Shemāl* ('People of the North') and *Ahl el-Qeblī* ('People of the South') also are in vogue.[88]

The dual division can also be found in each locality or tribal group.

Let us begin with the Ḥijāz area. One of the most powerful tribes between Mecca and Medina is the Ḥarb, who are of southern origin; they came in Islamic times from Yemen to Ḥijāz.[89]

The Ḥarb tribes fall into two groups: an eastern group, ranging about ʻAyn Ibn Fuhayd and the Jaʻla plain, Asyah, and the Dahna to the east of Qasim; and a western group ranging west of Qasim in the western Nejd around Nafi, Haid, and Dahna. The eastern group comprises three tribes, each headed by a chief shaykh: I. Banī ʻAlī (subdivided into five subtribes); II. Āl Wuhub (six subtribes); III. Āl Farda (or Frida, Froda, six subtribes). The western group comprises two tribes, neither of which is headed by a chief shaykh: Benī Salim and Benī ʻAmr. The Benī Salim again comprise two subgroups, the Mēmūn and el-Merāweha.[90]

Another Ḥijāzī group, that of the Jehēne, or Juhayna, is composed of two moieties: the Benī Mālek with fourteen tribes, and the Awlād Mūsā with nine tribes.[91]

The Hudhayl, an important Ḥijāzī tribe numbering about 50,000, is divided into a northern group located east and south of Mecca, and a southern group.

The Quraysh, descendants of the tribe of Mohammed, consists today of two weak branches, one around ʻArafāt, the other near Ṭaif. They are shepherds, numbering about 9,000.

The ʻUtaybah is a powerful nomadic tribe east of central Ḥijāz and west of central Nejd, divided into al-Rūqah (12,000) and Barqah (18,000) sections.[92]

Turning now to the Syrian desert, we find that the dual alignment of the nomadic tribes along the Qays and Yemen division is characteristic also of this area.

In the past, since the Benī Kalb was the leading tribe among the Yemenī moiety in Syria, the two parties were known by the names Kelbites and Qaysites.[93]

In the Syrian Desert, politically divided among several states, the Qays-Yaman rivalry is as alive today as it was in past centuries. Of the two most powerful tribal confederations of true or camel nomads, the ʻAneze (18,000 tents or 72,000 persons) and the Shammar, the first belongs to the Maʻadd (Qays) and the second to the Yaman or Qaḥṭān.[94] Up to the consolidation of governmental power in the Syrian Desert, which took place only in recent years, these two great tribal confederations were constantly feuding with one another as behooves traditional enemies. Since

World War II, however, raiding has become increasingly difficult, and the tribes have become used to living without this activity, which was both a source of income and a pastime.

In addition to the over-all division into Qaysī and Yamanī tribal confederations, most of the tribal confederations are in themselves divided into two moieties, which in their turn fall into successively smaller subdivisions, with a diminishing amount of intergroup hostility down the scale.

The 'Aneze themselves fall into two mutually hostile groups, the Ḍanā Bishr and the Ḍanā Muslim, the last flare-up between whom was quelled by the French in 1929.[95] According to the traditional tribal genealogy as elicited by Oppenheim from old members of the tribes, the Bishr comprise four tribes, the Sba'a, Fed'ān, el-Jebel, and el-Dehāmeshe, the first two forming the 'Obēd group and the latter two the 'Ammār or 'Amarāt group. In addition to these four, a fifth tribe, the Weld Suleymān, is now traditionally held to belong to the Bishr group, although originally, in the Nejd, the Weld Suleymān did not belong to the 'Aneze but to the Ja'āfera. Small parts of the tribe merely attached themselves to the 'Aneze and became politically dependent on these more powerful tribal groups in the course of their wanderings, which led them from the Nejd up into the Syrian Desert in the eighteenth century. To the other 'Aneze moiety, the Ḍanā Muslim, traditional tribal genealogy attributes eight tribes whose names are as follows: Weld 'Alī, el-Ḥesene, el-Mesālikh, el-Ḥajjāj (these four together forming the Benī Wahhāb section of the Muslim moiety); el-Sewāleme, el-Ashāje'a, 'Abdelle, and el-Rwala (these latter four forming the Mejlas of Jelas section of the Muslim moiety). In the actual tribal organization as observed by Oppenheim in the early part of the twentieth century, both moieties of the 'Aneze lost from their original number of tribes, leaving the Bishr with three and the Muslim with six tribes.[96]

The dual organization is evident on the subtribal level as well. Of the nine actual tribes (*qabā'il*, sing. *qabīla*) of the 'Aneze, four are subdivided into two subtribes (*'ashā'ir*, sing. *'ashīra*) each. The Fed'ān (approximately 5,000 tents) comprise the Weld and el-Khreṣe (or Khro a) subtribes; the Sba'a (approximately 2,200 tents) the Qemeṣa (or Gmoṣa) and the 'Ebede subtribes; the 'Amarāt (approximately 5,000 tents), the Jebel and Dehāmeshe subtribes; the Weld 'Alī (approximately 650 tents), the Ibn Sumēr and el-Ṭayyār subtribes. Of the remaining five tribes four are very small (150 to 700 tents each), and the last, the powerful Rwala (variously estimated at 4,000 to 5,000 tents), is divided into five subtribes.

The Dual Organization of the
'Aneze Confederacy

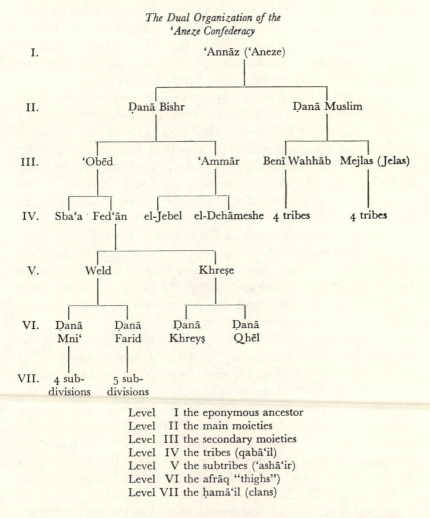

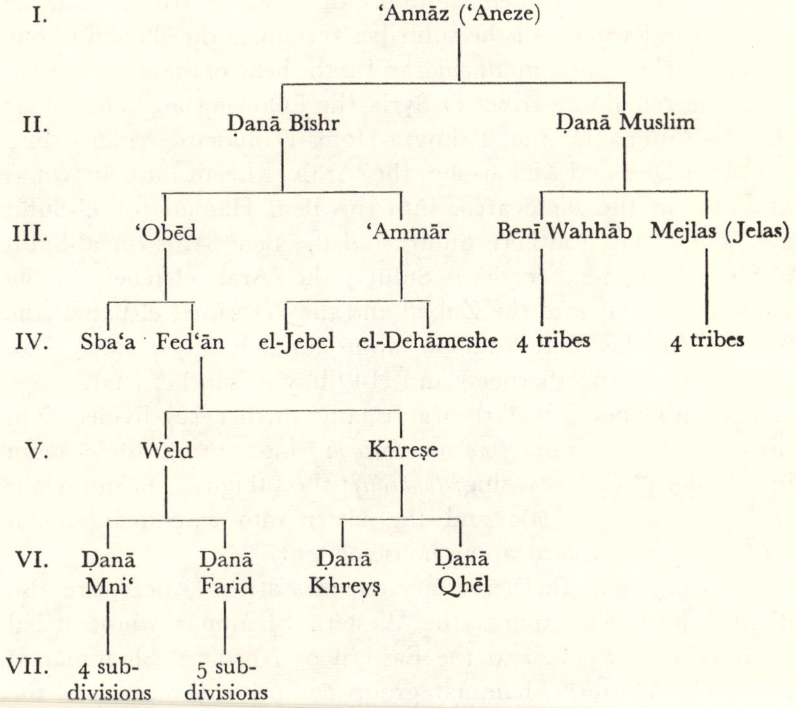

Level I the eponymous ancestor
Level II the main moieties
Level III the secondary moieties
Level IV the tribes (qabā'il)
Level V the subtribes ('ashā'ir)
Level VI the afrāq "thighs")
Level VII the ḥamā'il (clans)

A word may be said here as to the relationship of chieftainship to the dual organization, which can be illustrated by examples drawn from the ʿAneze confederacy. The confederacy as a whole recognizes no paramount chief, nor do the two moieties. On the tribal level, the bifurcated tribe may either recognize the shaykh of one of the two subtribes as the head of the entire tribe (in which case the shaykh of the other subtribe is subordinated to him, as in the ʿAmarāt tribe); or each of the two subtribes may have an independent shaykh of its own, in which case the tribe has no paramount chief (as in the Fedʿān, Sbaʿa, and Weld ʿAlī tribes). When the tribe is divided into more than two subtribes (as in the case of the Rwala), all the subtribes recognize the shaykh of one of them as their paramount chief and as the head of the entire tribe.

In the remaining tribes of Syria the following are bifurcated: the el-ʿAmūr (in the Palmyra-Homs-Damascus region) into ʿAmūr el-Dīre and Mehāreshe; the ʿArab el-Lejāh (also known as al-Sulūṭ, in the same area, into the Benī Ḥamad (or al-Sulūṭ al-Qibliyīn, i.e., southern Sulūṭ) and the Benī ʿAmr (or al-Sulūṭ al-Shimāliyīn, i.e., northern Sulūṭ); the ʿArab el-Jebel (in the Hawran region) into the Zubēd and the Wessāmet el-Bāhel; the Mawālī (in the Aleppo region, approximately 2,000 tents), into el-Shemaliyīn (northerners) and el-Qibliyīn (southerners).

The subtribes (*ʿashāʾir*) are usually further subdivided into subsubtribes (*firaq* or *afrāq* or *afāriqah*, sing. *firqah*); these again into "thighs" (*afkhādh*, sing. *fakhedh*); the "thighs" fall into clans (*ḥamāʾil*, sing. *ḥamūla*); and the latter into extended families (*ahāl*, sing. *ahl*, also meaning house or tent).[97]

The Shammar, the hereditary enemies of the ʿAneze, are also divided into two groups: the Western Shammar whose tribal territory is in Syria, and the Eastern or Northern Shammar of Iraq. The Western Shammar group comprises three tribes: the Thābet (with 1,600 tents, consisting of six subtribes); the Feddāgha (with 1,500 tents, eight subtribes); and the el-ʿAmūd (800 tents, three subtribes). The Iraqi Shammar also are divided into three tribes: the Khreṣe (1,650 tents, five subtribes); the Sāyih (3,500 tents, two subtribes); and the ʿAbdeh (3,000 tents, five subtribes).

Among the Northern Shammar of the Northern Jazīrah in Iraq dual division is in evidence in several of the Jarbah tribes:

The Dughayrāt are divided into D. al-Badwa (or Desert D.) and D. al-Ḥaḍar (or settled D.).

The Āl ʻUlayyāh are divided into Āl ʻIkāb and Āl Subayyah. The Haḍabah are divided into Āl Jadʻān and Āl Funayfin. The Āl Burayj are divided into al-Aḥāsinah and Āl Buhaymān. The Ṭauqah division is as illustrated.

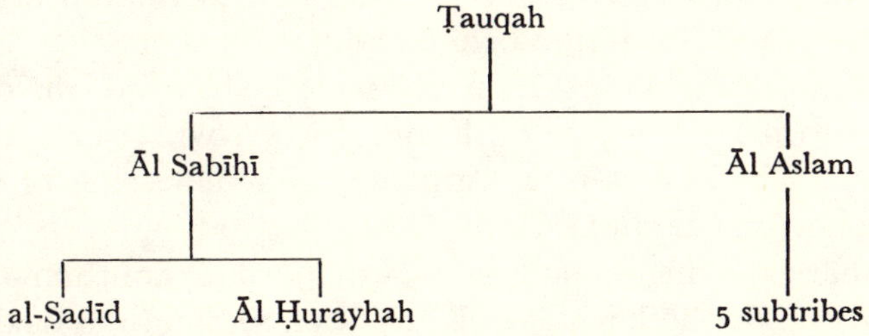

The following Kurdish tribes in Iraq also are subdivided into two sections: Bacelhan, Zengene, Hewramy (into H. Teḥt and H. Lihon), Shiwan, Pijderiy, Berwariy (into B. Bala and B. Zer).[98]

The Ṭayy confederation, located east of Niṣibin in northern Syria, also consists of two tribal groups: the Ṭayy of Niṣibin (with one paramount shaykh with eleven tribes) and the Ṭayy of Shemāmik (under another paramount shaykh with four tribes). In the past, the Ṭayy were divided into el-Ghauth and Jadila, who were constantly fighting one another.[99] The Ḥadediyyīn (2,000 tents) of Syria are divided into two sections, each with a chief of its own: the al-Kwame (four clans), and the al-Ghanātṣe (six clans).[100]

The Baqqāra, between Aleppo, Dēr, and Mosul, fall into two groups: The Baqqārat el-Zōr (with a paramount shaykh, six tribes, divided into numerous subdivisions); and the Baqqārat el-Jebel (with another paramount shaykh, eleven tribes, also divided into many subdivisions).

The Nuʻēm are divided into the Nuʻēm of Iraq and the Nuʻēm of Syria. The Nuʻēm of Iraq again are subdivided into two groups, the Nu'ēm of the Jazīrah (four tribes) and the Nu'ēm of Jebel Ḥamrīn (one tribe). The Nu'ēm of Syria are divided into three groups: the Nu'ēm of Homs (one paramount shaykh, five tribes); the Nuʻēm of Ghūṭa (no paramount shaykh, four tribes); and the Nuʻēm of Jōlān (one paramount shaykh, three tribes).

The Benī Jirius and Benī Zaydān in the Jebel ʿAjlūn Nāḥīya in Jordan claim descent from two brothers, Jirius and Zaydān. They are Christians (Greek Orthodox and Latin Catholics).

The Beni Saʿīd of Irjan (in the Jebel ʿAjlūn Nāḥīya) claim descent from Saʿīd, whose brother, Saʿad, went to Hebron where he became the ancestor of the Benī Saʿad.

The Maqātīsh and Oweysāt in the same Nāḥīya are the descendants of two brothers, Miqtish and Oweys, who came from Wādī Mūsā. They are Greek Catholics, although some of the Oweysāt follow the Latin faith.

The Bashātwa, living on both sides of the Jordan, are composed of two sections: the Shiheymāt of Kurdish origin, and the Bakkār of Nuʿēmāt extraction.

The Abābna in the Benī Juhma Nāḥīya are divided into two sections.

The Bsūl and Kawāfha in the same nāḥīya claim descent from two brothers: the Bsūl from Ḥuseyn, and the Kawāfha from Shihādeh. The father of the two brothers, Ibrāhīm, came from the al-Khazāla section of the Benī Ḥasan tribe.

The Benī Ḥamd and Benī Irshēyd clans in the Kura Nāḥīya are said to be descendants of two brothers, Ḥamd and Rashīd, who came from Khanzīra in the Kerak District.

The Falaḥāt and Lawāḥma are two clans in the Marad Nāḥīya of the Ajlun District of Transjordan; both claim descent from Ibrāhīm, a man who came to their village, Nebī Hūd, more than two hundred years ago.

The Benī Ḥasan, one of the largest tribes of Jordan, derive their descent from Mishqib ibn Ḥasan who is said to have come from Turba in the Ḥijāz. His two sons, Amsh and Mishqib, became the ancestors of the original two divisions of the tribe, the Imūsh and the Mashāqba. At present, the Benī Ḥasan are still divided into two large groups, called Hulēl (or Benī Hilayil) and Thebte (or al-Sabta). Each of the two has a paramount shaykh of its own and is subdivided into three tribes.

The Shuyāb and the Atāmna are two small tribes in the Benī ʿObeyd Nāḥīya of the Ajlūn District in Transjordan who claim descent from a common ancestor who originally lived at Hebron.

The Saqarāt of the Remtha Nāḥīya in the same district are

divided into two: the Saqarāt proper, and the Diyābāt; both live in al-Remtha.

The 'Abbād, a confederation of tribes in the Belqa District having no common ancestor, is divided into two great divisions: the Jbūriyya, and the Jrūmiyya, also known as al-Qdēriyye.

The Akrād, thus named after the Wādī al-Akrād quarter in al-Salṭ in which they live, are divided into two large sections: al-Akrād (three tribes) and al-Basābsa (eight tribes).

The Qawāqsha of al-Salṭ, a Greek Orthodox tribe that traces its descent to an ancestor who came from Salkhad in the Jebel Druze, are divided into two sections: al-Nuweysir and al-Ya'qūb.

The Ghawārna in the Kerak District are divided into those living in Ghōr al-Mazra'a and those of Ghōr al-Sāfī. The former are again divided into two: al-Aḥlāf (six sections) and al-Khanāzra (three sections). The inhabitants of Ghōr al-Sāfī are also divided into two sections: al-Awāysa (six subtribes) and al-Miḥlaf (six subtribes).

The Akasha and the Ḥijāziyyīn are two sections united to form one tribe in the Kerak District.

The Maayta in the same district are also divided into two large sections: al-Rashayda and al-Zaqayla. The former is again divided into two: al-Sahir (composed of two subtribes: al-Jubrān and al-Rashīd) and al-Ṭālib (composed of two subtribes: Awlād Id and Awlād Khalīl). The Zaqayla are also divided into two: al-Ibrāhīm and al-Salīm (the latter again composed of two subtribes, the Awlād Ayād and Awlād Muṭlaq).

The Majālī, the largest tribe in Kerak, are divided into two: the Suleymān (three sections) and the Yūsef (eight sections).

The Mdānāt, in the Kerak District, are divided into the Dabana of al-Salṭ and the Amāmira or Amayra of Ḥusn.

The Benī Hamīda in the same district are divided into al-Da'ājna and al-Matārfa. Another Benī Hamī dagroup lives in the Belqa to the north.

The Nu'ēmāt of the Kerak District, probably related to the Nu'ēm of Iraq and Syria, are divided into two subtribes: the 'Abābda (divided into al-Awasa and al-Ja'āfra) and el-Aḥāmda (divided into four subgroups).

The Qatāwna of the Kerak District, said to have come originally from Qatia in Sinai, are divided into two sections: the Awlād 'Alī and Awlād Salameh.

The Sarāyra, in the same district, are divided into Āl 'Alī and Āl Da'ud.

The Tarāwna in the same district, who came from Wādī Mūsā, are divided into 'Ayāl Jibrīn and 'Ayāl Jubrān.

The Town of Ma'ạn in the district of the same name in southern Jordan is composed of two quarters: Ma'an al-Shāmiyya (Northern Ma'an) inhabited by the 'Ayāl Maḥmūd, and Ma'an al-Ḥijāziyya (Southern Ma'an), inhabited by the 'Ayāl Aḥmed. The 'Ayāl Maḥmūd and 'Ayāl Aḥmed are said to be the descendants of two brothers, Maḥmūd and Aḥmed, who lived in the sixteenth century and quarreled over the possession of the fort of Ma'an. The 'Ayāl Maḥmūd are composed of three tribes, while the 'Ayāl Aḥmed comprise four tribes.

The 'Obeydiyyīn, one of the tribes of Wādī Mūsā in the south of Jordan, are composed of two tribes, the Hilālāt who claim to be true Layāthna, that is indigenous to Wādī Mūsā; and the Ḥasanāt who claim descent from the Billī of Ḥijāz.

The Sa'idiyyīn of the Wādī 'Araba (the boundary between Jordan and the Negev district of Israel), fall into two main groups: the Eastern Sa'idiyyīn who live in Jordan, and the Western Sa'idiyyīn who used to live west of the Wādī 'Araba, in the Negev. The Eastern Sa'idiyyīn are composed of two groups: the Srūriyyīn and the Onāt. The Western Sa'idiyyīn comprise four tribes.

The Nu'ēmāt of the Shera Mountains in southern Jordan are divided into two large groups: the Manājda and the Sleymāt. The Manājda claim descent from Manṣūr and their further dual subdivisions are shown in the accompanying chart.

The Sleymāt are divided into al-Arāqda and al-Sbu. The ancestor of the Arāqda is said to have been a slave by the name of Ireyqed, and because of their base descent the Manājda do not intermarry with them.

The Benī Ṣakhr, the largest camel nomad tribe in Jordan, are divided into two groups: al-Ṭūqa or Ṭwāqa (four tribes) and el-Ka'ābene or al-Ka'ābna (pronounced Cha'ābna; two tribes). All the six Ṣukhūr tribes recognize one single paramount shaykh.

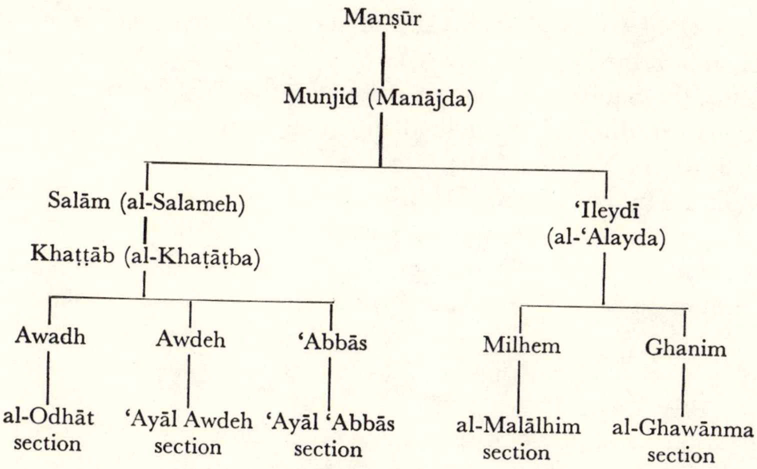

Before leaving the tribes of Jordan a word may be said about a supertribal confederation that played an important role in the history of the area. About 1650 the Sirḥān tribe moved down from the Hawran and occupied the area on the present borderline between Jordan and Saudi Arabia called after them Wādī Sirḥān. Shortly thereafter, however, the great movement of the 'Aneze tribes from the Ḥijāz up to the North Arabian Desert took place. The 'Aneze forced the Sirḥān and their allies, the Benī Ṣakhr, to move up into the Belqa. The 'Aneze pressed after them and came in conflict with the Muḥāfuẓ, as the paramount shaykh of the Sardīya was called whose followers were known collectively as Ahl al-Shamāl (People of the North). The 'Aneze defeated them too, but soon the Ahl al-Shamāl confederation was reconstituted under the leadership of the Benī Ṣakhr and with the participation of the Sardīya, 'Īsā, Fheyli, and Sirḥān tribes. By the beginning of the nineteenth century the Ahl al-Shemāl were strong enough to engage the 'Aneze and forced them successively eastward until at the end of the nineteenth century the Wādī Sirḥān area was held alternatingly by the Ahl al-Shamāl in the winter and the 'Aneze during their annual wanderings to and from their summer grazing grounds in Syria.[101]

There are two tribal groups divided between the Negev and the Sinai: The Terābīn and the Tiyāha. The Terābīn of the Sinai Peninsula comprise three tribes, while the Terābīn of the Negev have eight tribes. The Tiyāha of the Sinai have five tribes, the Tiyāha of the Negev twelve.

On the Saudi-Iraqi border is located the al-Ẓafīr tribe, a large camel-breeding tribe, divided into two sections: the Wahhābite al-Buṭūn in Nejd, and the Ṣumudah, mostly in Iraq.[102]

The Muṭayr of the Kuwait—el-Ḥasa region are subdivided into three major groups, called al-Dushān, al-ʿIlwah, and al-Burayh. The last two of these comprise each three tribes. The Dushān show a definite tendency toward a bifurcated structure.[103]

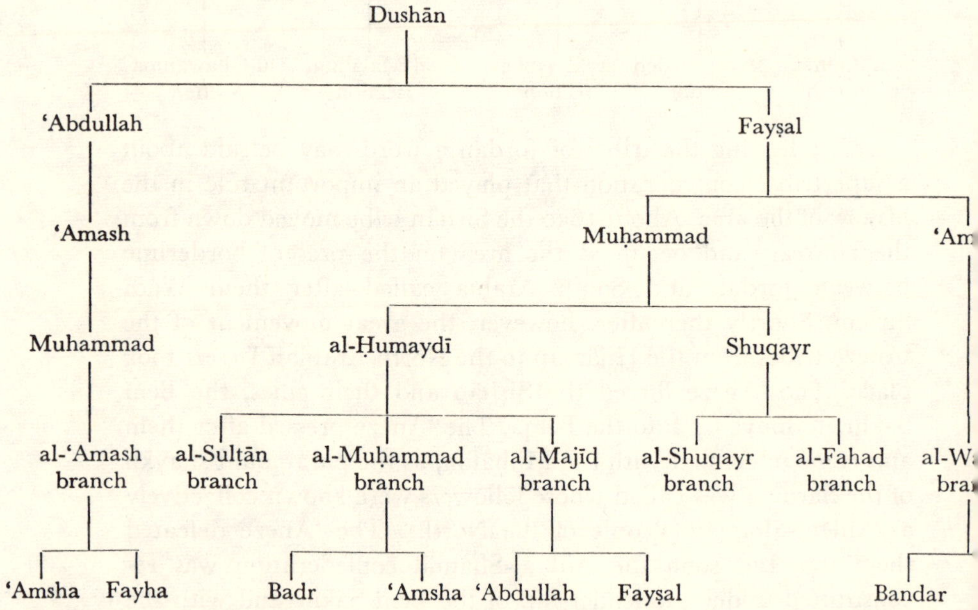

The Zubēd of Iraq are divided into three groups. The first of these is called el-Jebūr and is divided into two groups: the Jebūr of Khābūr (with one paramount shaykh and sixteen tribes) and the Jebūr of the Tigris (with fourteen tribes). The second group is that of el-Dulēm with one paramount shaykh at its head. The main group of el-Dulēm is that of the Ālbū Rudēnī, consisting of thirteen tribes and several attached subgroups. In addition, five more small tribal groups belong to the Dulēm (and owe allegiance to its paramount shaykh), counting from 200 to 800 tents each. Finally, the third group belonging to the Zubēd is el-'Obēd, under whose paramount shaykh are six tribes.

A similar threefold division is shown by the Ālbū Sha'bān group. These live in the upper Euphrates valley, and are divided into three divisions: the Welde, consisting of three subgroups, each with a paramount shaykh of its own: (1) Welde of Bāb-Menbij, six tribes; (2) Welde of Shāmīye, two tribes; and (3) Welde of the Jazīrah, eight tribes. The second group is that of the 'Afāḍele under whose paramount shaykh are seven tribes; and the third is el-Sabkha whose paramount shaykh commands a single tribe.[104]

The above listing exhausts the major tribes of the Syrian Desert. Of the tribal confederations enumerated the great majority is found to have the dual system as the basis of their tribal organization, with only two showing a threefold division. As to smaller groups, these generally are not subdivided into two main groups, but fall directly into three to twelve (or more) tribes, with or without a paramount shaykh to head the tribes that make up one larger unit. The dual division is thus found to be, if not the exclusive, the dominant and characteristic structural form of the nomadic tribes of the Arabian and Syrian deserts.

The Negev of Palestine on the fringes of the Syrian Desert also was the home of nomadic tribes aligned into two moieties. Toward the end of the eighteenth century the Qays moiety was here headed by Emir Ḥasan el-Waḥaydī, surnamed el-Daymī, who was followed by the Jabārāt, Qalāzīn, Sowāreke, and 'Amadīn tribes. Interestingly, the rival Yamanī moiety also was headed by a Waḥaydī, a close relative of Emir Ḥasan: Emir Ayash el-Waḥaydī. This moiety consisted of the Tiyāha, Terābīn, Ḥwēṭāt, and Billī tribes. Tradition has it that in one of the battles between the two Waḥaydī chieftains and their followers, 2,800 men were killed. After Napoleon left Palestine in 1798, the feuding between the two factions increased in intensity. In the first quarter of the nineteenth century, the son of Ḥasan, Salīm el-Daymī, who inherited the chieftainship of the Qays faction from his father, repeatedly attacked the Tiyāha and Terābīn tribes.

It is remarkable that the followers of the two chieftains saw no contradiction between their own traditions, according to which membership in the Qays and Yaman factions was genealogically determined, and the fact that two scions of one and the same family headed both factions. The same eighteenth-century source that tells of the feuds between the two factions also contains a brief account of the traditions concerning the origin of the two factions. According to the Negev tribes of the times, the two factions were the descendents of two brothers called Qays and Yemen, both of whom had large families.[105] Can it be that this tradition, which is at variance with the tradition about the origin of Qays and Yemen prevalent in Arabia itself, was influenced by the actual situation in which two kinsmen (in popular parlance two "brothers") headed the two factions?

In the nineteenth century the tribal line-up in the Negev and Transjordan was as follows: Qaysī tribes: Benī Ṣakhr, Shararāt, Benī 'Aṭiyye, Benī Ḥumeyda; Yamanī tribes: Tiyāha, Terābīn, 'Azāzme, Ḥanājra, Wḥeydāt, 'Adwān, Mjallī.[106]

Syria, Lebanon, Palestine

In Lebanon and Palestine the Qays-Yaman rivalry remained a living issue until modern times. Pitched battles were fought between the two parties as late as the early part of the eighteenth century,[107] and sporadic fighting continued well into the twentieth.

In this area an entire town or village may belong to one faction while a neighboring town or village may belong to the opposite faction; or else, one and the same locality may be split up between both factions. The village of Bīr in the vicinity of Jerusalem was the scene of a fight between the two factions inhabiting it, as late as a short time before World War I. Each faction tried to offend the flag of the other. A Yamanī woman took a red cock and beat it within the sight of Qaysīs (red being the Qaysī color). Thereupon Qaysī women did the same thing with a white cock (white being the Yamanī color).

Bethlehem (today in Jordan) is a Yamanī town, while Hebron (in Jordan), a mere twelve miles to the south of it, is Qaysī. A tree on a hilltop used to mark the boundary between the territories under the sway of each.[108] The factionalism was so strong that these inimical towns had to keep considerable contingents of armed men in constant readiness for defense and retaliation. Hebron had in the eighteenth century 800 to 900 armed men, and bloody fights between them and Bethlehem were common occurrences.[109]

Jerusalem, as the largest town in the neighborhood, was divided between Qaysīs and Yamanīs. In 1838, Robinson found that the majority in the Jerusalem district were Yamanīs.[110] The two foremost families in Jerusalem, who competed for leadership not only in the city but also in the whole of Arab Palestine down to the very end of the days of the British Mandate (1948), were the Yamanī Ḥusaynīs and the Qaysī Khālidīs.[111]

The village population in this area of the Judean hills and as far north as Ramallah is also divided between Qays and Yaman. Bitter wars between the two continued here as late as the nineteenth century. The enmity between the two factions was so keen that the Qaysī headman of the 'Āmar family, the shaykh of Durrah village, had all strangers who came into his village questioned: "For whom are you? For Qays or for Yaman?" If he answered, "Qays," he was honored; if "Yaman," he was put to death.[112]

Just as in the days of the Umayyads, the dual organization of the population in the eighteenth and nineteenth centuries was a factor to be reckoned with by administrative officers and military leaders as well. The military expeditions and punitive actions of governors were more than once frustrated because local levies would not fight against rebels of their own factions. An outstanding example was the experience of Othman Pasha el-Sadiq at his attack on the township of Nablus in Palestine in 1764.[113]

In Ramleh in the Palestinian coastal plain, fellahin of rival factions used to destroy each other's valuable olive groves, and in general it became a point of honor to ruin the rival town's crops, to injure its fruit trees, and, on the other hand, to guide, support and, in case of threatened retaliation, to protect the Bedouin raiding parties of one's own faction. As Volney remarked, "This discord which has prevailed throughout the country, from the earliest times of the Arabs causes a perpetual civil war. The peasants are incessantly making inroads on each other's lands, destroying their corn, dourra, sesamum and olive trees, and carrying off their sheep, goats, and camels. The Turks, who are everywhere negligent in repressing similar disorders, are the less attentive to them here, since their authority is very precarious; the Bedouins, whose camps occupy the level country, are continually at open hostilities with them, of which the peasants avail themselves to resist their authority, or to do mischief to each other, according to the blind caprice of their ignorance, or the interests of the moment. Hence arises an anarchy, which is still more dreadful than the despotism which prevails elsewhere, while the mutual devastations of the contending parties render the appearance of this part of Syria more wrecked than that of any other."[114]

During the last few decades of Turkish rule in Palestine much was done to subdue the rival elements or, at least, not to let the antagonisms emerge into the open. While as late as the second half of the nineteenth century the Qays and Yaman factions, headed by shaykhs and aided by Bedouins, waged feuds and rendered commerce and travel precarious or impossible, by the end of the century this state of affairs was a thing of the past. The squabbles, while they lasted, were not confined to Qays *versus* Yaman strife; they broke out, frequently enough, even between groups belonging to one and the same moiety. In the second half of the nineteenth century, for instance, a feud of some seriousness arose between the Christian Arab villagers of Ramallah and the Christian Arab villagers of neighboring el-Bire. The Ramallah Christians were helped by the Ramallah Muslims, while the el-Bire Christians were supported by the el-Bire Muslims. All the inhabitants of both places belonged to the Qays faction, and normally the relationship between them was amicable enough.[115]

In addition to the Qays and Yaman factions there were in Arab Palestine a number of other village organizations, more localized in their character, the common feature of all of which was their duality. The villages around Jerusalem, for instance, were divided into a group of Benī Ḥasan villages, and into a rival group of Benī Mālek villages. In the Ramallah district there were Benī Ḥārith villages (with the village of Bir Zeyt as their center), and Benī Zayd villages (with Deyr Ghassāneh as their center). Information on this subject is far from being adequate, and it is impossible to tell whether these village groupings appeared only in the dual form, or whether single and triple groupings also existed.[116] Neither is it clear in most cases what, if any, was the connection between these local groupings and the wider Qays and Yaman factions.

In the town of Ramallah itself, however, the connection is clear. The entire population of Ramallah has remained split into two opposing factions down to the present time. One is called Ḥaddādeh or Sharaqa (Eastern), the other Ḥamāyel. Each is subdivided into four clans (*ḥamūla-s*). The story goes that a shaykh or emir of a Christian Bedouin tribe, named Sabra el-Ḥaddādīn, a Qaysite who lived in the Shobak Karak district of Transjordan, was the original ancestor of all the ḥamūlas of Ramallah. His eldest son was Rashīd whose first wife bore him a son Ḥaddād, and died. He married a second wife, a widow who had a son by her first husband, a Yamani. Rashīd adopted this boy, Shukayr and had three more sons by his second wife. These four sons of Rashīd's second wife became the ancestors of the four ḥamūlas of the Ḥamāyel moiety in Ramallah; while Ḥaddād, his son by his first wife, became the ancestor of the four Ḥaddādeh ḥamūlas of the town, through his four sons. Thus the peculiar situation obtains in Ramallah that all the four ḥamūlas of the Ḥaddādeh moiety and three ḥamūlas of the Ḥamāyel moiety are Qaysites, while the fourth ḥamūla of the Ḥamāyel moiety is Yamanite, and is still referred to as "Yaman." They display the white color and the white flag at weddings and on all formal occasions, in contrast to the red of the Qays ḥamūlas.[117]

Among the Druzes in Lebanon, the Qays-Yaman duality completely overshadowed all other divisions. They were caught by the feuds between the two factions to such an extent that their entire history was modified by it. In the course of several centuries the constant feuding between the two factions depleted the manhood not only of the Druzes, but of the Lebanon as a whole. In 1698, the Shīʿite Mutawālīs, who inhabited the mountainous country between the Sea of Galilee and Sidon (Arabic: Ṣayda), revolted under the leadership of a Yamanī shaykh. The Druze Emir Bashir I of the Qays party, in alliance with the Pashas of Sidon and Tripoli, put down the revolt and installed the head of an influential local Qaysī family as shaykh of Safed.[118] In 1711 a decisive battle took place between the Qaysīs and the Yamanīs at 'Ayn-Darah, which resulted in the utter defeat of the Yamanī faction. Many Druzes who belonged to this faction thereupon emigrated to the Hawran region and laid the foundation of a new Druze concentration in that south Syrian district.[119] Among the Druzes, the Qaysī faction used to carry a red flag and is known to the present day under the name Reds, while the Yamanī faction had a white flag and is still known as Whites.[120]

Forthwith, however, two new competing factions emerged in the Lebanon and continued the feuds of the old Qaysī and Yamanī moieties. These were in Yesbek and Jumblat factions which, as heirs to Qays and Yaman, rallied the support of the population of these regions in the elections during the mandatory period of the country (1921–1936).[121]

In Palestine, many if not most Arab villages were divided into two ḥamūlas, although small villages had often only one ḥamūla, while large ones had three or even more. The ḥamūla is a group of families tied together by actual or assumed genetic relationship. A ḥamūla usually inhabits a special quarter in the village, called ḥāra, so that a typical two-ḥamūla village consists of two ḥāras. Each ḥamūla is headed by an unofficial head whose office is hereditary within the leading family of the ḥamūla, though it does not necessarily pass from father to son, and can also be acquired by a powerful member of another family belonging to the ḥamūla. In villages whose lands belong to absentee landlords or which are in a status of economic dependence on outside moneylenders, merchants, or others, the headship of the ḥamūla is usually occupied by men who have the confidence of the landowner or the economic potentate. The usual relationship between the two ḥamūlas is one of strife, squabble, and enmity. Every individual difference that is bound to arise from time to time in the course of the social and economic relations between two individuals belonging to two different ḥamūlas becomes immediately a concern of the ḥamūlas in their entirety, and thus a cause for renewed fighting. Most of the ḥamūlas are endogamous, and marriages between two ḥamūlas of the same village are much less frequent than those contracted within one and the same ḥamūla.

The ḥamūlas are in most cases subdivided into sub-ḥamūlas which fall into a number of extended families. Most of the ḥamūlas preserve a tradition according to which their ancestors came and settled in the village as a compact group of immigrants. In villages inhabited by members of more than one sect, such as Muslims, Druzes, Greek Orthodox, etc., the religious community takes the place of the usual ḥamūla-structure.[122]

Iran and Afghanistan

Several volumes exist in Persian on the tribes of various provinces in Iran. However, of the books available to the author only one contained information on the internal structure of the tribes. This was a volume on the tribes of Kūh-Gīlūyē, a small district in the province of Kuzistan, at the northern tip of the Persian Gulf.[123]

It appears that bifurcation is the rule among the Kūh-Gīlūyē tribes. Almost half the entire district is the domain of the Bovīr-Aḥmad tribe, which is divided into Bovīr-Aḥmad Garmsīri and Bovīr-Aḥmad Sardsīri. This name pair, Garmsīri and Sardsīri (meaning "of the warm place" and "of the cold place" respectively) occurs repeatedly in Kūh-Gīlūyē as well as in its vicinity, as a designation of two moieties. The Bovīr-Aḥmad Sardsīri is again subdivided into two, the Bovīr-Aḥmad S. Bālā (Bovīr-Aḥmad of the upper cold place) and the Bovīr-Aḥmad S. Pā'in (Bovīr-Aḥmad of the lower cold place).

The central part of Kūh-Gīlūyē is the home of the Ṭayyibī tribe, subdivided into T. Garmsīri (warm Ṭayyibī) and T. Sardsīri (cold Ṭayyibī). Just to the north of the Kūh-Gīlūyē district is the tribal area of the Jānekī tribe, subdivided into J. Garmsīri (to the northwest of Kūh-Gīlūyē) and J. Sardsīri (to the northeast).

Yet another name pair, in addition to warm—cold, upper—lower, is "of the mountain" and "of the plain." The Līrāvī tribe is subdivided into Līrāvī Kūh (mountain Līrāvī) and L. Dasht (plains Līrāvī). The entire Līrāvī tribe forms one of the two moieties of the Jākī tribe, the other being the Chahār Benīche, which, in accordance with its name ("Four B.") falls into four tribes.

groups. One of these, the Kand, is bifurcated into two tribes, the Ghori or Ghura, and the Khakhay or Khashay. One part of the latter is the Yūsufzay tribe, which is subdivided into five subtribes. One of these, the Akōzays, are again subdivided into several sections, including the Rānīzays. The Rānīzays comprise five clans; one of the latter is again subdivided into four subclans. One of these, the Ghaybī Khēl, comprises two subgroups, one of which, the Nūr Muḥammed Khēls, are again subdivided into Gharīb Khēl and Dwar Khēl.

In the eighteenth and nineteenth centuries the two foremost rival groups were the Bārakzay and the Sadōzay tribes, both of whom supplied the country with dynasties of rulers, and whose feuding kept Afghanistan in a constant state of turmoil for most of the past two centuries.

The Kāfirs of Afghanistan (now called the Nūristānīs or Jadīdīs that is, new converts to Islam) are divided into two groups: the Siyāh-pūsh or black-clad, and the Safīd-pūsh or white-clad.

The Tājīks, as the Persian-speaking population of Afghanistan is called, fall into two principal groups: the mountain Tājīks (in the high mountain valleys of Badakhshān and in Wakhan, the east tongue of Afghanistan); and plain-dwelling Tājīks, also known as Pārsiwāns.[127]

The Brahuis who inhabit the central area of Balujistan are organized into two main groups, the Sarāwān and the Jahlāwān.[128]

EGYPT AND SUDAN

Egypt was the classical example of dual organization in antiquity. In the fourth millennium B.C., the king of Upper Egypt conquered Lower Egypt, and since that time the country is always referred to as Upper and Lower Egypt. The ancient Biblical name of Egypt, *Miṣrayim*, has the dual ending " . . .*ayim*," thereby indicating the duality of the kingdom. The Crown of Upper Egypt was white and that of Lower Egypt red, the two colors that symbolize to this day the two moieties in some Middle Eastern lands. The white and red crown together formed the characteristic double crown of the Pharaohs, well known from innumerable pictorial and plastic representations.

We may begin the tracing of the presence of the dual organization in Muslim Egypt with the Mamluks who ruled Egypt from 1250 to 1517. During the later Mamluk rivalries the population of Egypt, and especially the artisan guilds, were divided into two competing factions, called Sa'd and Ḥaram. The rivalry was so keen and so general that even the 'ulamā', the learned religious leaders and authorized expositors of Muslim law, took sides for and against Sa'd and Ḥaram. The division between the two factions continued after the conquest of Egypt by the Ottomans (1517) and even spread into the Egyptian army, which became divided into two rival camps, the Fikarites and the Kassemites.

Jabarti (1754–1822), to whom we are indebted for this information goes on to describe the original popular tradition attributed to this dual division of the Egyptian army. There was, he says, an old Circassian Emir by the name of Sudun, who lived at the time Turkish Sultan Selim conquered Egypt, and he had two sons, named Kassem and Zulfikar, both of them great heroes. At the command of the Sultan, the two brothers engaged in a bout, and after a wonderful fight the Sultan divided his army between the two, giving to Zulfikar the greatest part of the Turkish cavalry, while to Kassem he gave most of the brave Egyptian warriors. Furthermore, he gave the Fikarites the white color as their emblem, and to the Kassemites the red color. The two groups engaged again in a fight, but this time the bout degenerated into a real combat, until finally the Sultan gave the signal for retreat. Ever since that day these two parties continued to exist in the Egyptian army, each of them preserving the color that its chief received as their emblem, showing repugnance toward the color of the rival party, down to table ware and kitchen utensils.

Soon the Fikarites declared themselves for the Sa'dite party and the Kassemites for the Ḥaramites. The division grew in significance from day to day. It passed from masters to slaves, from fathers to sons, and became the cause of many crimes, massacres, pillages, rapes, and arsons.

Another tradition as to the origin of this dual division in the Egyptian army is also recorded by Jabarti. According to this second version, the Kassemites were the partisans of Kassem Bey el-Daftardar, and the Fikarites were the followers of Zulfikar Bey

under the names of Sa'd and Ḥaram, who constantly harm each other by all possible means.

> When asked about the origin of this division, they tell ridiculous stories, or admit that they are ignorant of it. Moreover, this origin interests them the least; the hostilities are never suspended, and each party has always recent injuries to avenge.
>
> Although the existence of these two parties is generally known, the shaykhs of Cairo, who are regarded as knowing best the history of their country, are not in agreement as to the circumstances which gave birth to them. The opinion which I hold to be the most reasonable boils down to the following:
>
> During the civil wars which ruined Arabia under the Calif Yezid ibn Hayweh, about the year 65 of the Hegira (685 A.D.), the two armies took as rallying cries in one nocturnal combat the names of Sa'd and Ḥaram, by which their respective chiefs' families were known. These names the fighters and subsequently their descendants applied to themselves. In this manner the discord was perpetuated and became an insurmountable obstacle to their reconciliation. The Arabs who in various ages came to establish themselves in Egypt brought along, together with the name of the faction to which their ancestors belonged, their inveterate hatred against the opposite faction, and this hatred has perpetuated itself down to the present from generation to generation.
>
> It is to this internal division that one must attribute the influence of the Bedouin Arabs and the terror they inspired in the interior of the Delta: a small number of horsemen could carry off ordinarily without resistance the flocks of a considerable population . . . .
>
> These Arabs, always sure of being welcomed and saved by the villages of the party opposing the one they despoiled, and not preserving the liaison with one party longer than dictated by the exigencies of their momentary interests, exercise their brigandage with impunity in the whole province.[132]

The Sa'd-Ḥaram feuding remained notorious well into the nineteenth century, when Edward William Lane, making his firsthand observations of Egyptian life in the 1820's and 30's, wrote: "In many instances, the blood-revenge is taken a century or more after the commission of the act which has occasioned it; when the feud, for that time, has lain dormant, and perhaps is remembered by scarcely more than one individual. Two tribes in Lower Egypt, which are called 'Saad' and 'Həram,' are most notorious for these petty wars and feuds, (like the 'Keys' and

'Yemen' of Syria), and hence their names are commonly applied to any two persons or parties at enmity with each other."[133]

The Egyptian Bedouins are divided into two great groups, Se'ādī and Salāleme, who trace their descent to Sa'de and Dhīb respectively. Most of these became sedentarized in 1898 and some of them migrated to Syria.[134]

As examples of tribes with a dual division among the Bedouins of the Sinai Peninsula the Muzayna and Suwārka can be mentioned. The Muzayna, one of the Towara tribes who inhabit the southern tip of Sinai, claim a certain 'Alwān as their original ancestor. His two sons, 'Alī and Ghanim, became the progénitors of the two moieties of the tribe. The Suwārka, the largest tribe in Sinai (approximately 4,000 persons) claim to be the descendants of two brothers, Nuṣayr and Manṣūr, whose original ancestor was Okasha. The progeny of Nuṣayr are the 'Aradāt, also called Ghōz el-'Arab, who have the reputation of exceptional cleanliness in food and dress. Manṣūr's progeny, twelve sections, are nicknamed Awlād el-Tharwa, "children of the gray-haired woman," because Manṣūr is supposed to have married a gray-haired woman and she became the mother of his children.[135]

The dichotomy into two opposing factions was a characteristic feature of society in Upper Egypt as well. Here, just as in Lower Egypt, a number of villages belonged (and do belong to this day) to one faction, while a similar number belonged to the opposing faction. In the urban sector, on the other hand, and again as in Lower Egypt, members of the two opposing factions lived in one and the same town. The earliest mention of the dichotomy of towns in Muslim times in Upper Egypt is contained in the famous travel accounts written by Ibn Battuta (1304–1368/9), who visited the town of Aydhāb in the summer of 1326. Today the town of Aydhāb is merely a site of ruins, 12 miles north of the town of Halayb on the shores of the Red Sea, just south of the Egyptian border. But in the fourteenth century it was a populous town, inhabited by Beja camel-breeders. The town was divided into two parts: one part, comprising one third of the town, belonged to the Sultan of Egypt, while the other part, comprising two thirds of the town, belonged to the Beja king, al-Ḥudrubi. Just at the time of Ibn Battuta's visit the two factions were

official head of the village whose office is both elective and hereditary as well as appointive, form the village leadership whose task is to settle disputes that arise in the village.

The participation of the villages in the wider political life of the country is channeled entirely by the dual division into G'āfra and 'Abābda. The G'āfra villages traditionally vote for a candidate who belongs to their group. The 'Abābda, of course, have their own candidate. On one recent occasion, the 'Abābda encouraged a second G'āfra candidate to run against his own clansman, and as a result of the splitting of the G'āfra vote between the two G'āfra candidates, the election was lost by them. Political views have little if anything to do with the elections.[140]

The Bishārīn, a Beja tribe in northeastern Sudan, are divided into two main classes: the Umm 'Alī and the Umm Nājī. They seem to have a genealogic connection with the Awlād Kāhil (or Kawāhla), an Arab tribe that lived near 'Aydhāb in the fourteenth century.[141]

North Africa

The main problem in connection with the dual organization in North Africa is whether its prevalence among the Berber tribes is due to Arab influence or goes back to pre-Islamic times. No satisfactory answer can be given to this question, which has received much too scanty attention on the part of historians.

The dual organization of the *Arab tribes* in North Africa, so much seems to be certain, was brought along by them from the east. Of the two main tribal groups, the Benī Sulaym and the Benī Hilāl, the former is the senior branch. Both came from the Nejd and are of Muḍarī (Qaysī) stock. According to tradition, Sulaym, who lived in the third century A.D. and Hilāl in the 5th had as their common ancestor Manṣūr who was the grandson of Qays. The Sulaym tribes are spread today from Egypt to Tunisia and are divided in Cyrenaica into two main branches, the Jibārna and the Harabī. The Benī Hilāl settled in the western part of the same territory; tribes claiming Hilālī descent are found today mainly in Tripolitania and Tunisia. Client or vassal tribes as well as noble or free tribes are grouped under the same dual genealogy. The secondary tribes have attached themselves to the dominant tribes and by a process well known also from the tribal life of the Syrian Desert have grafted their branch of descent onto the family tree of the noble tribes. The term used by the Bedouins of Libya to describe this process is *laf* (to connect, to wrap).[142]

It is not intended to discuss here the extremely intricate problem of the origin of the North African *Berber tribes.* For our present purposes it will be sufficient to summarize briefly the popular traditions which, just as in Arabia proper, assign a dual origin to the Berber tribes.

These popular traditions are reflected in the genealogic speculations contained in the writings of medieval Arab historians and summarized by Ibn Ḳhaldun (1332–1406). The traditions are contradictory and confusing, as popular traditions often are, but they all agree on one basic point: that, namely, all the non-Arab North African tribes belong to either of two groups, called *Beranes* and *Botr*, respectively. According to information obtained by Ibn Hazm from the son of Abu Yezid, chief of the Zenāta (one of the Botr tribes), and reported by Ibn Khaldun, the descendants of Madghis el-Abter, that is the Botr tribes, "did not belong to the Berber race."[143]

A number of other genealogists of the Berber people (Sabeq ibn Soleyman el-Matmati, Hani ibn Masdur (or Isdur) el-Kumi, Kahlān ibn abi Lua) quoted elsewhere by Ibn Khaldun (i : 168) projected further back the fictitious ancestry of the Berbers and connected them with Biblical figures. According to them, the Beranes were the children of Berr, who was the son (or descendant) of Mazigh, the son of Canaan, the son of Ham, the son of Noah. The Beranes tribes, therefore, are represented as laterally related to the South Arabian Yamani tribes, whose ancestor, Qaḥṭān, was the great-great-grandson of Shem, brother of Ham. According to the same genealogists, the Botr tribes were the descendants of Berr (not identical with the first Berr) who was the son of Qays, a descendant of Ishmael. In this manner the Arabian theory of dual descent was deftly applied to the Berbers.

The appearance of the name Berr in the traditional lineage of both North African groups of tribes is explained by other traditions as referring to one and the same person. Ibn Hazm, while

Ṣanhāja, first with the Ghomara and then with the Zenāta. Those who were familiar mainly or only with the Ṣanhāja-Zenāta wars, the bulk of which took place only a few centuries before the times of Ibn Khaldun, were inclined to assign a Beranes status to the traditional enemies of a Botr tribe. Those, however, who remembered also the much earlier Ṣanhāja-Ghomara fights, excluded the Ṣanhāja from the Beranes stock and attributed them a Yamanī (or Qaḥṭānī) descent.

In modern times, the social organization in North Africa still reflects the historical and traditional forces that molded it for the past fifteen hundred years. The dichotomy of tribes into two mutually hostile groups still characterizes the area, although under European (French) influence the importance of these traditional rivalries is today definitely on the decline.

An alliance of tribes is called in North Africa *leff*, while a smaller alliance, composed of related families, is called *ṣoff*.[149] As a rule, two competing *leffs* are lined up against each other in any larger area of North Africa. In Northern Morocco the two *leffs* are still called by the traditional name pair, Ṣenhāja and Ghomara.[150] The political tension between the two notwithstanding, in both of these groups of tribes as well as in the Ktama (Ketama) group (all the three of whom belong according to "most genealogists" quoted by Ibn Khaldun to the Beranes group), Senhajan and Jebalan cultural traits predominate; while in the eastern part of Morocco and especially among the Benī Bu Yaḥyī (let us recall that Yaḥya figures as an ancestral name in the genealogy of the Zenāta) and the Metalsa tribes, Zenātan nomadic cultural traits predominate. In between the two areas there is a territory in which both the Zenatan and the Senhajan traits are absent and which has been designated as the center of a Central Riffian culture.

The Ṣenhāja and the Ghomara are distinguished from each other by certain differences reminiscent of the differences in custom between the Qays and the Yaman villages in Palestine. The Ṣenhāja leave food in the bowl, for shame of taking the last bit, and also in order to keep the *baraka*, the blessing of plenty, in the house; the Ghomara leave none. The Ṣenhāja are hospitable to strangers, the Ghomara are cold to them.[151]

In Ibala and the Rif the dual groups of tribes who are constantly at war with each other have curious totemistic relations to animals and food prohibitions: the Ṣanhāja are connected with quadrupeds, the Ghomara with birds.[152]

The claim of ancestry is, of course, not an infallible guide to the actual descent of North African tribes. Some of the Rifian tribes, for instance, claim Ṣanhāja, others Zenāta ancestry; still others claim that their ancestors were the indigenous heathens of North Africa; and yet others claim foreign, western ancestry. It is interesting that in one and the same tribe various subdivisions sometimes claim different ancestries.[153]

But to return to the dual division of North African tribes. In the Anti-Atlas region of Southern Morocco the two *leffs* are called Igezzulen (in the west) and Isuktan or Ahoggwa (in the east); in the Western Atlas Ait Atman and Ait Iraten; in the Atlantic plains of Morocco Sofian and Benī Mālek; in the Jurjura Kabylia up to the end of the eighteenth century there were two *ṣoffs*, which however were organizationally similar to the *leffs* in other places, named Ṣoff Ufella and Ṣoff Bu-Adda.[154] Among the Masmuda, sedentary Berbers of the Moroccan High Atlas, there are, in addition to strong alliances in the form of *leffs*, also larger local organizations grouped into *tagbilt*-s or cantons, each with a name of its own, engaged pair-wise in keen rivalry with each other and playing an important part in political life. A similar situation prevails in the Aures Mountains.[155]

When neighboring villages are lined up against each other in two competing and hostile moieties, these groupings may be called either *leff* or *ṣoff*. When a village is internally divided into two parties these are usually called *ṣoffs*. Whatever the name, the two parties are usually about equal in strength, and in case of intermoiety hostilities the moiety solidarity overrides everything else, the entire *ṣoff* (or *leff*) rallying to the support of a menaced member. Only when the interests of the village or of the tribe as a whole are menaced by a common danger is the partisan spirit of the *ṣoff* or of the *leff* attenuated for a while In some places a group may be broken up into three *ṣoffs*. Generally, however, there are two *ṣoffs* in a village, although *ṣoff*-allegiance of individual families is often changed[156]—a situation resembling the one met with in Oman.

two mosques, belonging respectively to the two, gives concrete expression to the dichotomy.

In the town of El Oued (or El Wed), some seventy miles to the east of Touggourt, and among the Hassaouna of the Fezzan, the main dividing line between the two parties is ethnic, with the Arabs forming the one, and the Berbers the other group.

A characteristic of the Saharan dual organization is that it is generally based on the socially predominant groups, with the exclusion of the lowest rungs of society. Some minority groups, however, reproduce, on a small scale, the dichotomy characterizing the ruling classes. The Jews of Ghardaia (some 300 miles south of Algiers), for instance, although numbering only 1,200 souls, are split into two bitterly opposed factions that disagree violently on nearly all questions of general policy. In their relations with Muslims or Christians they are united, but in internal matters, social or economic, the two parties have as little as possible to do with each other.

The dual organization seems to be most highly developed in the commercial centers of the northern Sahara, and apparently fades out gradually toward the south as the commercial function of sedentary settlements in general becomes more attenuated. Membership in the moieties is, like other social affiliation, hereditary, but members can, and sometimes do, change sides with bewildering suddenness—a phenomenon which, as will be remembered, is not confined to this part of the Middle East.[160a]

Among the tribes of Cyrenaica the al-Ḥasa can serve as an example of dual organization, as is shown. In fact, the structure of this tribe closely resembles that of the 'Aneze, insofar as the tribe is divided into two subtribes, each of whom is again subdivided into two groups.[161]

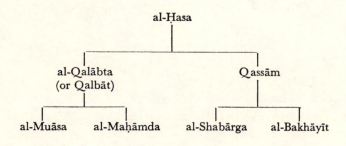

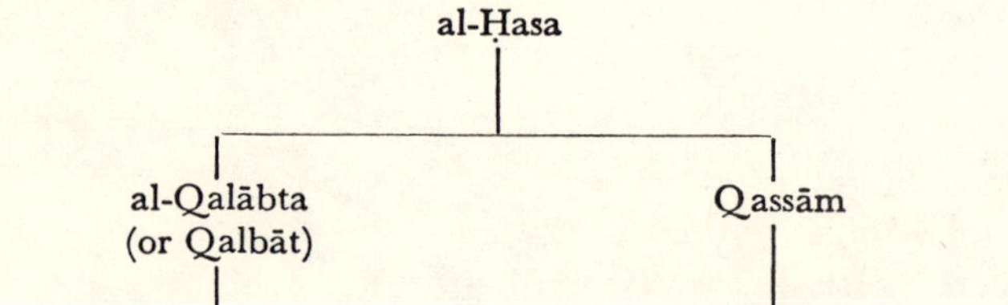

Occasionally the dichotomy of a village or the traditional hostility of two neighboring villages survive today only in ceremonial fights in which two halves of the population are lined up against each other and which at times have prognostic significance. The Berber Shlöh tribe of the Imejjat in the southwestern corner of Morocco celebrate in October the feast of Sīdī Ḥamad u-Mūsā. After a ceremonial meal "all the people divide into two parties, a northern representing the Gharb and a southern representing Sus, and a fight with slings ensues, which, though only a game, is often attended with serious accidents. It is believed that if Sus wins in this contest the year will be good, and if the Gharb wins, bad."[162]

Dual division is a characteristic feature of the social organization of the Arab nomads of the Sahara of whom the Chaamba (Shaamba) can be taken as an example. The Chaamba area lies in central Algeria, north of the Tuareg territory. They used to have a well developed *sof*-like dual system which has by now lost much of its former force but clear traces of which still persist. The tents of a single camp, for instance, are usually pitched in two more or less distinct clusters; the two groups are known as Sheraga (easterners) and Gharba (westerners). The Sheraga are traditionally progressive in all things; the Gharba, conservative. The two still retain a spirit of profound rivalry. The men form two distinct groups in the traditional ceremonial *fantasiyas* (gymkhanas). The boys form two opposing teams in their informal hockey games. Combat teams of warriors usually include men of one party only.

As to descent traditions, we find the familiar picture of origin from two brothers. The Berazga division of the Chaamba, for instance, are divided intwo two tribes based on Metlili, the Ouled Allouch (Wled Allush) and the Ouled (Wled) Abd-el-Kader. The first, numbering about 4,000, is divided into seven clans, of which the most noble is the Ouled Touameur (Wled Twamr), the supposed descendants of Twamr, the mythical founder of Metlili. Hanich (Hanish), Twamr's younger brother, is believed to be the ancestor of the Ouled Hanich, the leading clan of the Ouled Abd-el-Kader which number about 3,300 and is divided into five clans. The Wled Allush tribe belongs to the

groupings of the Tuareg, they all can be reduced to two original groups, the Tademaket and the Ahaggar.

Evidence of Tuareg dual organization can be found also in the following details: The noble Kel Rela were also called Kel Ahem Mellen (People of White Tents), in contrast to another tribe, the Issetafenin, the ancestors of the present-day Aulimmiden, who were called Kel Ahen Settefet (People of Black Tents). At the present time, the Kel Rela are also called the "upper people" because they inhabit the elevated center part of the Ahaggar; while their cousin tribe, the Taitok, are also called the "lower people," because they inhabit the lower western part of the Ahaggar. These two, the Kel Rela and the Taitok, had prolonged fights over the *tobol*, the large drum that is the symbol of paramount chieftainship of the Ahaggar Tuareg. Although today there is a third noble tribe in the Ahaggar, the Tēgēhē Mellet, who also claim descent from a daughter of Ti-n-Hinan, there are conflicting traditions as to the origin of this tribe, and if one gives credit to the one that attributes Shamba extraction to it, the Ahaggar nobility is left with a clear-cut dual division.

The over-all organization of all the Tuareg thus gives the following picture:

- I. Northern Tuareg
    - 1. Ihaggaren
        - a. Kel Rela
        - b. Taitok
    - 2. Kel Ajjer
- II. Southern Tuareg
    - 1. Aulimmiden
    - 2. Tengeregif
- III. Kel Air or Kel Azben or Southeastern Tuareg
    - 1. Kel Geres
    - 2. Kel Owi[172]

Conclusion

To sum up, the main characteristics of Middle Eastern dual organization along the lines indicated by Haekel's study appear to be as follows:

1. Middle Eastern dual organization is characterized by a dual division of tribal federations and of settled populations inhabiting extensive territories, as well as of single tribes and villages. The dual division is present in

a. Overtly manifest groupings, as well as in

b. The consciousness of the people;

c. Expressed occasionally in differences in mode of behavior and attributed character traits; and is

d. A permanent phenomenon.

An additional ethnologic characteristic of Middle Eastern dual organization is that it does not as a rule contraposit one major ethnic group as against the other, even where the ethnic stratification would be favorable to such a development. In North Africa, for example, it is not the Berbers on the one hand and the Arabs on the other who form two moieties. The Berbers among themselves are divided into two moieties, as are the Arabs among themselves. Within one and the same ethnic group, however, the dual division transcends other social, cultural, and religious groupings. In Lebanon and Palestine, for example, each of the two moieties, here called Qays and Yaman, is composed of nomads, villagers, and townspeople, as well as of Muslims, Christians, and Druzes.

2. Middle Eastern dual organization is characterized by a very frequent subdivision of each of the moieties into secondary and tertiary groupings. Of the two most powerful tribal confederations of the Syrian Desert, one, the ʻAneze, belongs to the Qays moiety, while the other, the Shammar, belongs to the Yaman or Qaḥṭān moiety. Both the ʻAneze and the Shammar are divided into two submoieties: the ʻAneze into Ḍanā Bishr and Ḍanā Muslim; and the Shammar into the Eastern (or Northern) Shammar and the Western Shammar. Again, the Ḍanā Bishr is divided into four (today only three) tribes. Each of these tribes is further subdivided into subtribes, and each of the subtribes into still smaller groups.

3. In the emphatically endogamous Middle Eastern society, the dual organization cannot play a significant role with regard to the regulation of marriage. A man's preferred wife is his father's brother's daughter, or failing this, another next of kin in the male

No noble Arab tribe, for instance, would stoop to fight another tribe that is inferior to it in status. How the distinction between noble and vassal tribes fits into the dual organization pattern is not quite clear at present. But it seems certain that it never happens that a noble tribe, or noble tribes, should form one moiety, with a vassal tribe or tribes forming the other. The inferior tribes in general are vassals of a noble tribe that belongs to one of the two moieties but they do not as a rule participate in the intermoiety fighting, which is a strictly noble affair.

VIII. *Noble and Vassal Tribes*

A CHARACTERISTIC OF Middle Eastern social organization is the presence among the nomadic population of superior or noble tribes on the one hand and of inferior or vassal or client tribes on the other. As far as geographic location is concerned, this distinction between noble and vassal tribes is also found in practically every part of the Middle East inhabited by nomadic tribes. The noble tribes generally show a much greater organizational coherence than the vassal tribes. A noble tribe, though subdivided into several divisions and wandering units, will generally be found to inhabit a definite geographic area that is regarded as its tribal territory, and under normal circumstances its movements will be confined to the boundaries of this area. The typical vassal tribe, on the other hand, is broken up into many splinter groups, widely scattered over large areas, without cohesion and often without contact among them.

One of the best-known and -studied vassal tribes, the Ṣolubba (variants: Ṣulubba, Ṣleyb, Ṣalib, Ṣulaba, Ṣoliba, etc.) are dispersed all over the northern half of the Arabian Peninsula, and further to the north in the Syrian Desert and the adjoining territories, while according to some observers they can be found as far south as Yemen.[1] Ṣolubba splinter groups are attached to practically every tribe within this wide area, and while they all go under the name of Ṣolubba, they can be identified more closely by the name of the tribe of which they are the clients. Thus there are in the Syrian Desert Shammar Ṣolubba, 'Amārāt Ṣolubba, Rwala Ṣolubba, Muṭayr Ṣolubba, etc.[2] The Muṭayr, in addition, have two serf tribes, the Rashayda and their cousins, the Hirshān [3]

more than two generations later (in the beginning of the twentieth century) the Rwala still regarded the Ḥwēṭāt and the Benī 'Aṭiyye as inferior tribes and refused to intermarry with them.[15] Similarly, the Hteym between Medina and Hail used to pay *khuwwa* some generations ago, and although of recent years they fight like any Bedouin tribe, they cannot change their inferior social status.[16]

Conditions imposed by a victorious tribe upon another tribe defeated by it in war also can stamp the latter with an inferior status. About the same time when part of the Ḥwētāt tribe paid *khuwwa* to the Shararāt, another part of the Ḥwētāt defeated the Beni 'Uqba in battle and imposed upon them the following six conditions: (1) The Beni 'Uqba, having lost their rights to the land, become *khwān*. (2) They give up the privilege of escorting the Ḥajj-caravan to Mecca. (3) If a Ḥwētī were proved to have plundered a pilgrim, his tribe was to make good the loss, but if the thief escaped detection, the Beni 'Uqba have to pay the value of the stolen property in cash or kind. (4) The Beni 'Uqba are not allowed to receive as guests any tribe at enmity with the Ḥwētāt. (5) If a sheikh of the Ḥwētāt fancied a camel belonging to one of the Beni 'Uqba, the latter must sell it to him under cost price. (6) The Beni 'Uqba are not allowed to wear the '*abā*, the cloak of the Bedouin.[17]

The Ḥwētāt occupy an exceptional position insofar as they are superior with regard to one tribe and inferior in relation to another. The general pattern is that a vassal tribe is inferior in relation to all noble tribes, and the only groups inferior to them are gypsylike splinter tribes and small scattered groupings of the ṣunnā', the tinkers and blacksmiths.

Some of the noble tribes hold themselves to be superior to other noble tribes and frown upon intermarriage with them, for example, the Rwala and the 'Aneze in general, or the Shammar.[18] Even the Hwētāt regard themselves as superior not only to the fellahin, but also to all the nomadic, tent-dwelling Bedouin Arabs.[19] This can be explained by the generally prevailing ethnocentrism that is narrowly localized among the nomadic people within the tribe or, occasionally, within a subsection of the tribe.

A more remarkable feature is the consensus of opinion among both the noble and the vassal tribes with regard to the general dichotomy of the tribal population into these two over-all groupings. The attitude of the noble to the vassal tribes is expressed in certain phrases of institutionalized conduct. In addition to the prohibition of intermarrying with them, which has been referred to above, they are regarded as weak and unwarlike and therefore not a suitable object of attack or raid according to the unwritten code of Bedouin chivalry. "Paying to all men a petty tribute, they are molested by none of them. No Beduwy, they say, will rob a Solubby, although he met him alone, in the deep of the wilderness, and with the skin of an ostrich in his hand, that is worth a *thelul* (a good riding camel)."[20] "By the unwritten Bedouin laws, they [the Ṣleyb] are outside the pale but inviolate. . . . They have no allies and no other Bedouin tribe is permitted to raid or attack them. . . ."[21] For this inviolateness the Ṣleyb have to pay with suffering insults and contempt: "They have never taken part in the wars and feuds which have occupied the greater part of the Bedouins' lives for centuries. A Sulubbi, like a woman, was a creature with whom it was too inferior to fight. . . . Beduin travelers or raiders invariably called at Sulubba tents if they could find them and demanded food and hospitality. The Beduin, who is normally a model of sedateness and reserved decorum among strangers, exhibited the worst aspects of his character in a Sulubba camp. He shouted, bullied, cursed, and swaggered in a manner sometimes shameful. He demanded the best of food, cursed his host, complained of everything, ate all he could and then demanded more food to take with him as supplies for his journey. . . ."[22]

According to another observer, "When raiding tribes pass through their territory and chance to stop where their tents are pitched, they can demand water of the Salib, and coffee, but not food."[23]

On the other hand, if the Ṣolubba come to the camp of a noble tribe, they are not received hospitably. One of the features in the stereotype of the Ṣolubba is that they will shamelessly beg for food.[24] Doughty records that if a Ṣolubbi asks for sour milk at the tent of a noble Bedouin, "the housewife will pour out leban from her semila [skin], but it is in their own bowl, to the poor Ṣolubba: for Beduins, otherwise little nice, will not willingly drink after Ṣolubbies. . . ."[25] More liberal-minded noble tribesmen may invite the Ṣolubba to take water and coffee in their tents, but they will sit apart from the rest of the guests, and for the night they will pitch their own little tent where they will prepare their own meal and spend the night.[26]

It is in accordance with this general attitude toward the inferior tribes that the penalty for injuring or killing one of them is especially severe: "In Southern Sinai, the penalty for hitting or killing a Hiteimi used to be greater than that for a man, i.e. they were put in the category of women, slaves and the like."[27]

Although the vassal tribes are thus held in general contempt, members of the noble tribes usually admit that the inferior tribes surpass them in certain accomplishments that are very useful in the desert. According to the Bedouins of northern Arabia, the Ṣolubba are excellent hunters who can at will choose the wild game that they wish to fell on a certain day, or that they will keep in reserve for themselves to be hunted in the future.[28] It is also acknowledged by the noble tribes that the Ṣolubba know the desert better than they, and members of noble tribes therefore often employ the Ṣolubba as guides in the desert or consult them regarding routes and grazing or camping grounds.[29] Also the Hteym are regarded as the best hunters in the Ḥijāz, as well as excellent camel-breeders,[30] and the Shararāt as expert guides.[31]

The attitude of the inferior tribes toward themselves and toward the superior tribes clearly reflects their low social position. The name Hteymī has been used as an insult by superior tribes to such an extent that even the Hteym themselves came to regard it as such. "To call a man a Hiteimi is an insult even if he is one; and if he is not, it is a serious slander to be expiated by a fine and the building of white cairns."[32]

In their approach to members of superior tribes the Ṣolubba exhibit an exaggerated humility. "Sulubba men are in general a miserable, fawning lot, affecting endearing and diminutive Arab terms of address, and are cringing in their manner."[33] Other authors us even stronger terms in describing their behavior.

Glubb describes an encounter he witnessed: the "Sulubba cowered and whined. Long oppression has indeed made them very low class. The ingratiating whine in which they address the Beduin as 'Ya Amaimi,' 'Oh my little uncle,' makes one ashamed of human nature."[34]

The same attitude can be observed among the Hteym in their relations to members of other tribes: ". . . when the Fellahs say, *Tatahattim* (=*tatamaskin* or *tatazalli*), they mean, "Thou cringest, thou makest thyself contemptible as a Hutaymi." Moreover, they must pay the dishonoring *Akhâwat* or 'brother-tax' to all the Bedouin amongst whom they settle."[35]

Just as a noble tribe can lose its superior status by being forced into payment of *khuwwa* to a more powerful tribe, an inferior, *khuwwa*-paying tribe can move up on the social scale and can become independent if its increased strength enables it to throw off the overlordship of the tribe of which it is a client. This upward social mobility is illustrated by the recent history of the 'Awāzim tribe whose strength is approximately 4,000 fighting men, excluding those who live in Kuwait and environs, and which possesses some 100,000 camels and 250,000 sheep. This tribe, which ranges from the northeastern corner of Arabia (Kuwait town) as far south as Ras Bidiya in the Ḥasa district, is divided into some 20 sections, each with 40 to 150 tents. The 'Awāzim (sing. 'Āzimī) were looked upon as the vassals of the powerful and noble 'Ajmān tribe whose tribal territory is to the south of that of the 'Awāzim. In order to weaken the 'Ajmān who were unfriendly to him, King Ibn Saud of Saudi Arabia honored the 'Awāzim with the title of an independent tribe, armed them with modern weapons, and distributed much ammunition amongst them. During 1929–30, the years of the Ikhwān rebellion, over 1,500 new British rifles were thus distributed among the 'Awāzim. Today the 'Awāzim are nominally independent, apart, that is, from the allegiance they owe to Ibn Saud, and they regard their former overlords, the 'Ajmān, as their hereditary enemies.[36]

In a similar manner other tribes, too, succeeded in shaking off the yoke of *khuwwa* payment and in establishing themselves as free fighting tribes; for example, some of the Ṣolubba in 1919–22 and the Hteym.[37] Total equality with the old noble (*aṣīlīn*) tribes, however, could not be achieved by them. While the noble tribe was not powerful enough to prevent its former vassal from attaining independence, it still had one means left at its disposal of which it could not be deprived and by which it continued to assert its superiority over its newly liberated vassal. This means was the prohibition of intermarriage, which has already been referred to earlier.

Bedouin society is most sensitive with regard to sex mores in general and marriage regulations and restrictions in particular. Among the settled peoples of the Middle East, and especially the townspeople, marriage restrictions are stringent only as far as women are concerned; while no special stigma is attached to a man marrying lower than his class, the marriage of a woman to a man of lower status would not only be resented but would be a cause justifying forced intervention. This difference does not exist in nomadic society in which neither the marriage of a man with a girl from a lower tribe nor the giving of a girl in wedlock to a man from an inferior group is tolerated. Consequently, the continuation of the marriage prohibition against any tribe on the part of a superior tribe is a much more effective social barrier than it could ever be in a settled community.

Thus, although the ʿAwāzim with the help of Ibn Saud have emancipated themselves completely from the ʿAjmān, the latter will still not intermarry with them, which means that the social distance has not appreciably diminished between the two. The Ḥwēṭāt and the Benī ʿAṭiyye are still regarded as inferior by the Rwala, who will not intermarry with them. Marriage between a noble tribe and a Ṣolubba tribe is quite out of the question. "No Arab can marry a Ṣolubba girl. He would be killed by his people if he did, and she also." If a young man from a noble tribe nevertheless loses his head over a Ṣolubba girl, the two have to flee their tribes and seek safety in distance. When the Emir Fawāz of the Rwala took a pretty Ṣolubba maiden into the desert and kept her there as a mistress (without formally marrying her, which would have been impossible even for a prince or chief shaykh of the powerful tribe), he was "roundly cursed by all good Badawin."[38] A Rweylī or any other noble Bedouin cannot marry a girl from the Hteym or Ṣunnāʿ tribe just as he cannot marry a slave. If he were to disregard these prohibitions he would be killed by his own next of kin.[39]

In fact, the prohibition of intermarriage with an inferior tribe is so general among all the Arab tribes that it can be taken as one of the chief criteria of tribal inferiority. This tradition is so strong that it is carried over from the desert into the town, as illustrated by the following occurrence: In 1931 'Abdullah Beg al-Ṣana' who, though of Ṣāni' origin, attained the high position of Director General of the Ministry of Interior in Iraq, married in Baghdad a girl from the noble Sa'dūn tribe. Both the girl and her mother had agreed to the marriage. Shortly thereafter 'Abdullah was killed by the girl's kin because he was admittedly of servile origin. At the subsequent trial several ministers of the state were called in by the defense to show that the murder was no crime according to the traditional Arab standards. When the murderer, a shaykh, was nevertheless condemned to death by an Iraqi court, his sentence was commuted to 15 years of imprisonment, and after only 19 months King Fayṣal pardoned him.[40]

Details of the marriage restrictions make one aware of differences in status within the vassal groups themselves. The Ṣolubba, Hteym, and other vassal tribes, although despised, are still regarded as free Arabs (*ḥorr*). As such, they stand higher in the social scale than the slaves who are as a rule black (*'abd*), and even than the *ṣunnā'*, the blacksmiths who, although white, are not independent, and therefore inferior to the other vassal tribes. Consequently, no intermarriage is countenanced by the vassal tribes with the slaves and the blacksmiths. Freed slaves marry among the freedmen groups in the towns, or the daughter of a blacksmith.[41]

In this connection it may be mentioned that the women of vassal tribes generally enjoy more freedom than the women of the noble tribes. Among the noble tribes there are several who veil their women. The women of the vassal tribes, however, do not wear any veil, and therefore, especially in places where the noble women are veiled, are easily recognizable. The Ṣolubba women, for instance, never veil and rarely wear a *milfa* (a face or head veil as opposed to the *burqa*, face mask). Among the Ṣolubba, who are very fond of dancing, it is moreover customary for men and women to dance together—in itself a highly disgraceful and unseemly thing in the eyes of the noble tribes—and, what is even more shocking for them, in the course of the dance the men occasionally kiss their partners on the mouth before the audience. Also, some Ṣolubba husbands tolerate that their wives prostitute themselves.[42] The Hteym, "inhabiting the seaboard about Yambu', are taxed by other Badawin as low and vile of origin. The unchastity of the women is connived at by the men; who, however, are brave and celebrated as marksmen. . . ."[43]

Vassal tribes usually but by no means always engage in occupations different from those of the noble tribes. Sometimes, as in the case of the 'Awāzim, the Hazim, the Sulaylāt, they pursue the same occupations as the noble tribes, breeding camels and sheep.[44] In most cases, however, members of vassal tribes or splinter groups engage in all kinds of works and tasks that the noble tribes disdain. The Ṣolubba, for instance, are hunters, tinkers, trackers, guides, coppersmiths, leatherworkers, woodworkers, cattle surgeons, doctors for men, women, and beasts; while their women are washerwomen, preparers of poisons and love potions, casters of the evil eye, versed in witchcraft, and even engage in prostitution.[45] Some Shararāt live with members of noble tribes, perform the menial tasks of servants and herdsmen, and are excellent guides.[46] The Ṣunnā' are ironworkers, farriers, swordsmiths, gunsmiths, they shoe the horses, beat out the tent stakes of their hosts, etc.[47] The Zatut in Southern Arabia are circumcisers, barbers, bloodletters, auctioneers, ironworkers. The Shahara in Southern Arabia hew wood and draw water for their Qara overlords.[48] The 'Aqeyl are merchants controlling the camel trade between Kassala and Egypt, and agents among the tribes of wholesale merchants who have their establishments in the larger towns on the borders of Arabia, as well as in Egypt and India.[49] The Jebeliya in the Sinai Peninsula engage in gardening and some of them are employed as servants of the monastery of Sinai.[50] The Kauliyah or gypsies in Iraq are fortune tellers, palmists, and thieves, while their women perform the female circumcision practiced in Southern Iraq, and among the Muntafiq tribes of the Euphrates and Banī Tamīm Arabs.[51] The Hteym in Arabia "make, eat, and sell cheese, for which reason that food is despised by the Ḥarb. . . . The Khalawiyah (pl. of Khalawī) are equally despised; they are generally blacksmiths, have a fine breed of greyhounds, and give asses as a dowry, which secures them the derision of their fellows."[52]

The following traits are thus found to distinguish the vassal tribes from the noble ones:

1. The noble tribes exhibit a coherent tribal structure; the vassal tribes are fragmentized and scattered.

2. The noble tribes are strong enough to protect themselves against enemies; the vassal tribes are unable to do this and pay *khuwwa*, brotherhood money, to a noble tribe whose clients they thus become, or to an individual member of such a noble tribe who is then in honor bound to protect them.

3. The noble tribes do not intermarry with the vassal tribes on account of the latters' inferiority.

4. The only occupation befitting a member of a noble tribe is tending the herds. The noblest of the noble tribes are camel-herders, the second-class noble tribes have mostly sheep and goats. The vassal tribes, though they too may possess these animals, engage mainly in handicraft, as well as in hunting.

5. A favorite pastime (under traditional conditions) of a noble tribe is raiding and warfare, undertaken either for the sake of booty or as a point of "honor." The vassal tribes, as a rule, do not fight, not only because they are weak, but also because they have no comparable "honor" to defend.

6. The women of the noble tribes conform, in general, to a more stringent code of sex mores than the women of vassal tribes. Women of vassal tribes go unveiled.

At the present stage of our knowledge of Middle Eastern social structure it is impossible to answer the question concerning the origin of this division of the nomadic peoples into noble and vassal tribes. All that can be done at present is to adduce some data as to the ideas current among the tribes themselves with regard to this social dichotomy. Since Middle Eastern tribes in Southwest Asia as well as in North Africa are extremely conscious of origin and descent, it will come as no surprise that the noble or vassal status of a tribe is, as a rule, attributed to a noble and a servile descent respectively.

The Ṣolubba, whose name resembles the Arabic word for cross, are regarded by many tribes, as well as by several European students of the Middle East, as descendants of Crusaders, or Crusaders' mercenaries, or their camp followers.[53] The theory of the non-Arab ancestry of the Ṣolubba is supported by the non-Arab language that they use among themselves (with non-Ṣolubba they speak of course Arabic), and in which some observers thought to have recognized traces of French or Latin roots.[54] Others regard this explanation of the descent of the Ṣolubba and of the frequency of a blond type in their midst as "a modern European fantasia,"[55] and believe that they are the "oldest inhabitants of the desert."[56]

Equally little is known of the actual descent of the Hteym, concerning whom there is not even such a plausible theory current as about the origin of the Ṣolubba.[57]

As to the Ṣunnāʿ, according to some they are of Negro origin[58] while in other tribes they are regarded as of white blood, but nevertheless not independent or free. Still others maintain that the Ṣunnāʿ are of inferior descent simply because nothing is known of their genealogy, and because they themselves have no pride of descent, and marry any newcomer, whether from town or tribe, whether free, vassal, or slave.[59]

Of the ʿAwāzim it is stated that "they are not of pure descent." The Sulaylāt are said to be descended from an ʿAneze man who married a Ṣolubba woman. According to another version of this explanation of their inferior status, it was Ibn Ghafil, the grandfather of the present chief of the Sulaylāt, who married a Ṣolubba gipsy woman, and therefore his entire tribe lost status.[60]

Nothing derogatory is known or circulated about the descent of the ʿAqeyl. The Jebeliya are believed to be descendants of Bosnian and Wallachian serfs who were given by Justinian to the Monastery of St. Catherine in the Sinai Peninsula in the sixth century and who were, of course, originally Christian.[61] The Shahara, the most ancient tribe in the Qara mountain district of Southern Arabia, were vanquished and subjugated by the Qara.[62]

The Marsh Arabs of Southern Iraq are regarded as inferior by the surrounding desert tribes not on account of inferior descent but simply because of their settling down and becoming marsh dwellers.[63] Similarly, the still seminomadic riverain Ajwān on the Euphrates around Nasiriyah are regarded with contempt by the true Bedouin.[64]

In Cyrenaica, the Marabṭīn (or Murābiṭīn) tribes, although nominally vassals of the Sa'adī tribes, maintain in actuality a much higher status than the typical vassal groups in the Asiatic part of the Middle East. They constitute larger tribal units, that is, they approximate even in this respect the Sa'adī tribes. These larger groups live, in fact, independently and pay no *khuwwa* or any other dues to the Sa'adī tribes who are the nominal owners of the land. According to a Senussi leader, the Marabṭīn tribes are the descendants of the Yemeni (South Arabian) tribes who colonized North Africa after the first invasion of the continent by the Arabs. In the eleventh century they were subjugated by the Benī Sulaym who conquered the country and continued in it their nomadic mode of life.[65]

A division into noble and vassal tribes is characteristic of the social organization of the Tuareg. According to the traditions of the Ihaggaren, the Tuareg of Ahaggar, some two or three hundred years ago two Berber women came from Morocco to the Sīlet oasis. One was noble, Ti-n-Hinan by name, and the other was her serving-woman, Takama (or, according to others, Temālek). Ti-n-Hinan settled in Abalessa and gave birth to three daughters: about the father or fathers of these daughters the Targui legend has nothing to say. From the first daughter, Kella, descended all the Kel Rela; the second daughter became the ancestress of the Taitok, and the third, named Tahenkot, became the progenitress of the Tēgēhē Mellet. These three are the noble tribes of Ahaggar, whose chiefs have *tobol*-s, large drums that are the symbol of chieftainship.

The servant girl, Takama, also gave birth to two daughters, one of whom became the ancestress of the Ihadanaren, a second-rank tribe; while the other became the mother of the two vassal tribes, Dag Rāli and Ait Loaien. Ti-n-Hinan gave the oases of Sīlet and Ennedid to the two daughters of Takama, and their descendants still own them to this day.

The Ti-n-Hinan legend is an interesting illustration of the

Middle Eastern tendency to "telescope" history. Excavations carried out at Abalessa unearthed the tomb of the Tuareg queen whom tradition regards as the ancestress of the tribes and calls Ti-n-Hinan. But the archaeological evidence shows beyond doubt that the tomb was pre-Islamic, and that the real Ti-n-Hinan must have therefore lived in a much more remote period than attributed to her by popular tradition.[66]

However that may be, descent from Ti-n-Hinan is as much a part of living tradition among the Tuareg as is their division into noble and vassal groups. The Tuareg themselves commonly speak of "noble clans" and "vassal clans." When the warriors of a noble clan go raiding, they often take along the fighting men of one or more of their vassal class, who subsequently receive a substantial share of the plunder. It is said that vassals also have an obligation to fight at the side of their noble masters in intertribal wars. If this be true, it would constitute an interesting deviation from the general Middle Eastern custom, which keeps vassal groups out of any fighting.

The vassals of the Tuareg pay annual tribute to their tribal chiefs or to the Amenokal, the paramount chief of the Ahaggar confederation, or to both. These payments consist, as a rule, of dates, millet, melted butter, young camels, sheep and goats, as well as all kinds of manufactured articles. Also shares are paid from profits the vassal groups make on imported articles and on their caravan commerce. If they go out independently of their masters on raiding expeditions, about one half of the booty is paid over to the nobles. In addition, each vassal family used to contribute toward the upkeep of a particular noble family. A peculiar development of this relationship was that the noble men and women used to go begging from their vassals who could hardly afford to refuse them. "But if this systematic begging became unbearable, as it often did, the vassals would simply pull up stakes and move quietly out of reach of their noble parasites." In recent years, however, the Amenokal and his whole camp has been supported by the French Government, so that these higher nobles are no longer in need of support by their vassals.

Traditions and environment combined have evolved a division of labor and responsibilities between the noble and vassal Tuareg.

"The nobles of a tribe, together with the headmen of the vassal clans, ride out in search of new pastures and at the same time act as military scouts, always on the watch for enemy raiders as well as for potential victims, alien camps or caravans which they can raid themselves. The vassals in their turn are responsible for the daily management and immediate protection of the flocks and herds, most of which belong to them anyway; and they contribute an armed reserve that can be called up quickly in case a battle becomes imminent or a good opportunity for a quick raid presents itself."[67]

A somewhat similar situation prevails among the Teda, to the east of the Tuareg, in the Tibesti massif of the southeastern Sahara. They are divided into some forty clans, headed by the noble clan of the Tomaghera (or Tomagra), the Gunda and the Arna. Beneath them rank the commoners and the vassals, between whom there is little if any status difference. The lowest ranks comprise, in descending order, the Azza (hunters, smiths, and artisans), the negroid serfs (*Ḥarrāthīn*), and the Negro slaves. Many vassal clans are divided into two or more fractions, each attached to a different noble clan. The tribal chiefs of the noble clans are chosen usually by a council of clan leaders, but, "curiously enough, it is said that they are named sometimes by the council of family headmen of the vassal clan supposed to have been longest resident in the tribal territory."[68]

Among the nomadic Arab Chaamba (or Shaamba) tribes in central Algeria, each tribe contains noble clans and vassal clans. One of the noble clans in each tribe is usually considered as more noble than the rest, its rank being based on its assumed descent from an early and famous or holy ancestor, but clan rank can be changed rapidly if a group is outstandingly successful or the reverse. Below the nobles are the tributary vassal clans which, however, are relatively few in numbers.[69]

The Moors, the pastoral nomadic tribes of the Spanish Sahara and of the adjoining, formerly French, Saharan territory, too, comprise both noble and vassal clans. Vertical mobility is considerable here, too, but sheer numbers and consequent group strength are not always decisive factors in determining rank; in some of the most powerful tribes one finds vassal clans that are twice as big as the noble ones. Wealth in livestock does not seem to be the deciding factor either, for some vassal tribes are far richer than their noble masters. As Briggs has observed, "it looks as though an efficient fighting organization, together with the strong leadership and rigid discipline which this implies, is the only thing that can surely raise a nomadic Moorish community above others of its kind."

Rank status is greatly influenced by tribute payment. The rule is that the receiver of tribute ranks higher than the payer. But the situation is complicated by the variety of reasons for which tribute is paid. Thus not only do weaker groups pay tribute to stronger ones for armed protection or for economic assistance in times of hardship; also, rich groups pay tribute to poorer ones if the latter are more warlike and therefore useful as mercenaries. Even some Maraboutic clans, whose holiness is, as a rule, sufficient to protect them, pay for protection; these are known as "Marabouts of the shade" in distinction from the independent "Marabouts of the sun."

The tribute payment is usually rendered by the headman of a vassal family to the headman of a noble family; in other words, the client-patron relationship is established between families rather than entire clans. The right to such tribute can be sold by the headman of the noble family to the head of another noble family, but this is done only in extreme and sudden emergency. Otherwise, the nobles prefer to go begging to their vassals in a manner similar to the one usual among the Tuareg.[70]

IX. *The Village and Its Culture*

About ten thousand years ago, man learned how to produce food by domesticating certain plants and animals. This development, whose importance for human history cannot be overemphasized, took place in the ancient Near East and led to the establishment of the oldest villages in the world inhabited by farming people. Stone implements, such as sickles, hand mills, querns, mortars, pestles, grinding stones, axes, and hoes, found in Natufian sites in Palestine, in M'leyfat and Jarmo in northern Iraq, in post-Natufian Jericho, and elsewhere, indicate that the people who lived in these villages had well-developed agricultural techniques, while other finds show that they grew wheat and barley and kept domesticated animals such as goats, dogs, and cats. It took some 3,000 years for Near Eastern farming to reach India and the Sudan, and about another thousand years to spread into Europe. The oldest farm village in England dates from about 2500 B.C.

As they settled in permanent villages, the Neolithic Near Eastern farmers developed pottery (this proved invaluable for archaeologists in their efforts to date excavated layers on ancient sites), learned to use animals for pulling the plow, developed techniques for spinning and weaving, relied increasingly on milk instead of meat to supplement their vegetable diet, evolved, for the first time, a social organization larger and more complex than the family and the kinship-based band, and created religious rituals whose primary purpose was to ensure the growing of crops and the increase of flocks. All these cultural features remained basic and essential to Middle Eastern village life down to the twentieth century. And, since some two-thirds to three-fourths of all the people of the Middle East are villagers, it appears that ways of life developed in the area ten thousand years ago continued to hold sway over the majority of the population throughout this period unmatched in its length in human history.

The Origin of Villages and Sedentarization

Although many villages in the Middle East have thus occupied for thousands of years the site on which they are located today, there are numerous villages in the area which are quite new and whose foundation took place within the lifetime of their oldest inhabitants. Still others were established several generations ago, but the historical event of their founding has been retained in the memory of the people in a folkloristic or quasimythological version. In such places there is usually a tradition about the foundation of the village by one individual or by several brothers, whom the villagers consider as their ancestor or ancestors.

Nor does the village as a permanent settlement, form everywhere a sharp contrast to the mobile nomadic camp. Between camps and village there are transitional forms resulting from the process of sedentarization (the settling down of nomads in a permanent location) which has been going on in the Middle East wherever the nomadic pastoral and the settled agricultural areas abut on each other. Most typically, the process of sedentarization was, and still is, characteristic of the North Arabian Desert Area (cf. above, p. 67) and is either spontaneous, as in Syria and Jordan, or government sponsored, as in Saudi Arabia (cf. above, p. 81). If sedentarization is spontaneous, it may take several generations before the process is completed. A tribe, or a part of it, may be forced by a more powerful adversary to leave its traditional wandering territory and to confine itself to the fringes of the desert. Or, it may be forced to move out of its old pastures when the latter are being put under cultivation by fellahin who enjoy the protection of the government. Or, the tribe may feel attracted to sedentary life, in spite of age-old prejudices against it, by the greater security and the more constant food supply available to settled cultivators. Or, finally, a tribe may be driven by economic necessity to supplement its livelihood by cultivating that part of its traditional wandering territory which is capable of yielding some harvest. In the case of camel-nomads, this phase may be preceded by a gradual replacement of their camels by sheep and goats with a corresponding reduction in the size of the wandering territory. Once crops are being planted, the tribe finds that it has to guard them against the encroachment of others. It is often not feasible to break up a tribal unit into one group that continues to wander with the animals, and another that remains behind to guard the fields, because such a split-up of tribal strength exposes each of the half-units to enemy attacks. Thus the tribe decides to remain encamped on the fields it cultivates from the time of sowing to that of reaping, and then, in the summer, to resume its wandering existence. However, the summer is precisely the time when the desert is most inhospitable and when even in the traditional circumstances of full nomadism the tribe's movements would be restricted to a relatively small area close to the cultivated lands better provided with water and hence with vegetation. Next, a stage is reached in which the tents of the tribe remain pitched on the same spot year after year, which, in turn, gradually leads to the addition of permanent structural features to the tents and around them. Permanent storage facilities for the grain are erected, fences built to prevent the animals from straying, rain water cisterns are dug, and mud walls are built under the tent cloth, resulting in a habitation that is half house and half tent. Before long the tent itself is replaced by a permanent house. Once this step is taken, the nomadic camp has completed its transformation into a village.

What is preserved of the nomadic traditions in such a new village, often for many generations, is the tribal structure and consciousness. The people in such villages still consider themselves a tribe, their head the tribal chief (*shaykh*), and their status as higher than that of the long-settled fellahin. They pride themselves on their Bedouin descent, and uphold, with great emphasis, the Bedouin ethos, comprising such features as "face" (honor), hospitality, blood revenge, generosity, and disdain for the veneration of saints, of which we still have more to say later. In the Kingdom of Jordan there are numerous well-documented cases of the settling of nomadic tribes in this manner, and it can be assumed that the majority of the villages on the east bank of the Jordan developed from such tribal settlements.[1]

Not each time, however, do Bedouins who give up nomadic life become villagers. Occasionally, they move to a city, where they swell the ranks of the unemployed or under-employed, live in slum sections on the outskirts, or, at best, become part of the growing urban lower class. This development has been observed, for instance, in Saudi Arabia.[2] The difference between this type of sedentarization and the one which results in the foundation of new villages is that the tribe-to-town movement is always an individual affair involving unattached and impecunious male members of the tribes, and of the tribes of lower status at that (see above, pp. 251 ff.), while the tribe-to-village process is a group movement in which a tribe or a tribal sub-group in its entirety is involved, and which therefore, does not entail social disorganization.

In order to encourage sedentarization, the King of Saudi Arabia had wells dug around Riyād, his capital, and food distributed among the tribesmen who converged to water their herds or flocks. Also in other parts of the country, along the oil pipelines, wells were dug with the same end in view. As a result of these measures, as well as other factors, many tribal units have settled down, and tribal villages, in a stage of semi-sedentarization or complete sedentarization, have become numerous in the Nejd, Hijāz, and 'Asīr districts of Saudi Arabia.[3] Employment of tribesmen by Aramcó (the Arabian-American Oil Company) has also contributed to the same tribe-to-village movement.

King Ibn Saud (the founder of Saudi Arabia who died in 1953) inaugurated in the early years of his career the policy of sedentarization, partly for political and partly for economic reasons. By 1927 there were more than a hundred agricultural settlements in the country, established and inhabited by the *Ikhwan* (literally, Brothers), a Wahhabi confraternity which he encouraged and headed. The settlers were given land, seed, and money. Wells were dug for them, and they were given other advantages as well. Some of these Ikhwan villages still exist at the present time. All in all, however, in spite of these efforts, only about 12 per cent of the Saudi Arabian population consists of settled cultivators.[4]

Saudi Arabia is thus the least sedentarized country in the Middle East, contrasting in this respect with the rest of the area where the majority of the population is in villages.

Location and Size

The typical Middle Eastern village consists of a tightly packed cluster of houses among which wind narrow alleys, and around which lie the lands cultivated by the villagers.

In principle, the site on which the village is located has to satisfy three basic needs: protection against the forces of nature and attacks by man, water, and good soil. As to the first, because of the dangers of flooding during the often heavy winter rains, villages are as a rule not built in low-lying valleys, but rather on hilltops. Such an elevated location also affords some protection against enemies. Although security is an important consideration in building the village in the form of a nucleated aggregate, it is remarkable how rarely did Middle Eastern villages take the next logical step, namely to protect themselves from enemy attack by the building of a wall around the village or by fortifying it in some other way. In the plains, the village is always open: armed resistance is precluded by this one feature alone. In the mountains, even if the village is located on a peak, it is rarely fortified. An exception is constituted by the villages in Iran and Afghanistan which have old fortification walls, now crumbling,[5] and by the new Wahhabi villages in the Nejd district of Saudi Arabia which are provided with defensive towers.[6]

As the absence of fortifications indicates, the typical Middle Eastern village is not a politically separate entity which must be ready to repel its enemies; it is rather dependent, as far as armed protection is concerned, on the force available to the city-based area chieftain (and, in modern times, the central government), to whom it pays taxes in exchange for this single benefit: protection against outside attacks. Only in rugged mountain areas, such as Kurdistan, are (or were) the villages politically independent units, ready and able to defend themselves. Villages located on the fringes of the settled area used to be beholden to one of the major nomadic tribes who protected them in exchange for annual dues, which in most cases amounted to as much as, or even more than, the government taxes.

As far as the availability of water and the fertility of the soil are concerned, these are rarely present to a completely satisfactory degree, except on the banks of great rivers, such as the Nile or the Tigris-Euphrates system, and in oases rich in wells or springs. In areas of extensive rainfed agriculture, the crop yield depends primarily on the amount of annual rainfall which can vary considerably from year to year. Lean years are an always-present threat which the peasant does not know how to counter except by laying aside as much of his harvest as possible from one year to the next. This expedient, however, is available only to the few well-to-do cultivators; the great majority even in a normal year gathers barely enough to survive until the next harvest. Even drinking water is not always easily available within the village. Especially in the hilly and mountainous areas the village well is often located outside and far below the village so that the fetching of water for household purposes becomes a major time- and strength-consuming task for the village women.

Other things being equal, there is a direct correlation between the fertility of the land and the size of the village. Since the cultivator, as a rule, has to be able to return home for his night's rest, his land must be within such a distance from his house that he can make the round trip daily with his draught animals, with enough time to spare for his work in the field and his sleep at home. If the land is fertile and produces much, a peasant needs, and in most cases actually works, only a small parcel to meet his annual food requirements. In Egypt, for instance, the great majority of the fellahin (72 per cent) own and work less than one *feddan* (or 1.038 acre) of land.[7] Thus, a large number of people, living in one village, can daily walk to their small parcels. Consequently, one finds in Egypt large villages inhabited by as many as 15,000 persons.[8] Fifteen thousand individuals make about 3,000 families, and the total land worked by such a village (at half an acre per family) woulb be 1,500 acres, or an area a little more than two square miles in extent. Any part of such an area can easily be reached from a centrally, or even peripherally, located village.

As against this, in East Jordan, the average size of the individual agricultural holdings varies from ten acres in the highlands to 27.5 acres in lands bordering upon the desert. Correspondingly, the average size of a settlement is 400 persons per village.[9] Four hundred individuals make about 80 families. Taking twenty acres as the average size of a holding, the 80 families would have to cultivate 1,600 acres, an area somewhat larger than that providing livelihood to 15,000 (or 38 times as many) Egyptians.

One can thus formulate a law as to the size of villages in the Middle East: the greater the fertility of the land, the greater the size of the village, because the smaller the average land holdings.

This law is graphically illustrated not only by the contrast between the Egyptian and the Jordanian villages, but also by the closely settled oases which are found in many parts of the Middle East. In the oases, the fertility of the land, irrigated by wells and springs, in many cases enables several villages to exist in close proximity, each surrounded by its fields. This is the case with the oases in Saudi Arabia,[10] and even more so in the Sahara Desert, where the oasis of Siwa (just inside the western border of Egypt), for example, contains several villages with a total cultivated area of some 35 square miles and a total population of some 4,000.

The Houses

While the size of the village is thus related to soil fertility (or to the amount of food produced per acre), the physical appearance of the village depends on the building materials available in its immediate vicinity. One therefore finds that in the mountainous areas the village houses are built of stone (ranging from unhewn rocks to hewn blocs), and have in many cases two floors. On the plains, the houses are built of mud or adobe (sun-dried) bricks, and mostly have only one storey. In the marshes of southern Iraq, the Marsh-Arabs live in reed-huts, some of which are quite large and boast elaborate decoration. Also in the ʻAsīr province of Saudi Arabia reeds are used for the construction of beehive huts, here under African influence.[11] In the southern reaches of the Middle East, e.g. in Southern Arabia, palm leaves and fronds are used as building material. In the north, e.g. the Caucasus and Turkey, occasionally wood is used. Some primitive village communities in the mountains of North Africa still live in caves, with partly built-up fronts. In the very hot parts of Iraq, Iran, and Afghanistan, some houses have underground cellars in which the temperature remains cooler than in the rooms whose walls and ceilings are exposed to the sun, and where the family lives on hot summer days and also keeps the perishable foods. More frequently, however, the flat roofs provide a cool place for the family to sleep in the summer.

In some villages one finds a variety of building materials, especially where the influence of nearby cities makes itself felt. Thus, in a Sudanese village-suburb of Khartoum it was found that while most houses were made of a combination of mud and manure, several were of fired red brick, and there was a tendency to tear down mud houses and replace them by red brick structures.[12]

As to the floor plan of the house, this ranges from the simplest one-room structure to elaborate multi-room dwellings. In its basic form the four walls of the house enclose a single, rectangular, small room. The house of the poor Alawite fellah in Syria, for example, is a ten by fourteen-foot rectangle, about seven feet high, with a single narrow and low door leading into it; it has no windows, and has a mud floor. The left side of the room contains the fireplace with a hole over it through the ceiling. The left rear corner is the place for the sheep and goats. The right side of the floor forms a platform of raised earth about 2½ feet higher than the left: this is the family room, with the provisions in one corner, and the mats and bedding in another next to the cradle. In the center, a stone column supports the roof. "Everything is blackened by smoke, without air, without light, without space . . ."[13]

The better houses, owned by wealthier villagers, have two rooms: one to receive guests, and the second, the combined family and bedroom. Such a house will also have a separate stable or shed for the animals, as a rule across the courtyard. In Iran the village houses have more frequently three or four rooms, lined up on one side of a courtyard. Rugs, often made by the village women, cover the floors.[14] As one moves higher on the economic scale, the number and quality of the furniture increases. Affluence in many villages all over the Middle East, nowadays, usually means the purchase and display of some European-style furniture, such as chairs, sofas, tables, beds.

We cannot enter into a discussion of the numerous local variations of the basic quadrangular floor-plan of the Middle Eastern village house, but one peculiar development, that of the so-called bee-hive houses in the Aleppo region of Syria, should not be left unmentioned. Remarkable also are the watchtowers adjoining the better houses in Afghan villages, once important for protection, now only for prestige.[15]

Extended families often occupy a compound within the village, consisting of several adjoining houses all opening onto one courtyard which in turn has one main gate leading into it from the street. Many times, of course, each of the "houses" within such a compound is nothing more than a single room with a separate entrance from the courtyard and with no door between it and the adjoining rooms. Occasionally, a larger compound has a separate guest-room, which is put at the disposal of guests visiting with any member of the extended family.[16]

Economy and Work Routine

On the most elementary level, the village is economically self-sufficient. Its fields and flocks provide all the food it needs; the women use the sheep's wool and the goat's hair to make clothes and other textiles; the animal's skins are used for sandals and other leather trappings. The local potter makes pots using the available clay, the carpenter makes plows, harrows, threshing sledges, beams, etc., in exchange for payment in kind. Even the local barber is paid in kind, as is the keeper of the mosque and shrine, if the village has these religious institutions. As conditions improve and the villages produce more food than they consume, they sell the surplus and use the money to buy what is considered most important beyond the most basic needs: coffee, sugar, salt, tobacco, kerosene, metal pots and pans, steel implements, etc.

In whatever stage of economic development, the mainstay of

village life is the land, and the villagers' dependence on their land is complete.* The land has its periodic demands which must be met on time, for any neglect must be paid for dearly in reduced or ruined crops. It is this servitude to the land, noted by the nomadic Bedouins, which made them term the fellahin "the slaves of the soil" and which acts as the chief impediment to attempts at sedentarization.

Yet the male villagers enjoy slack seasons which alternate regularly with those of intensive work in the fields. Not so the women, whose routine consists of daily repetition of the same chores: fetching water, grinding corn, baking bread, preparing meals, kneading the dung for fuel, taking care of the children, spinning, weaving, embroidering, and so forth.

Sharecropping was in the past the most common form of farming in the Middle East, and it has remained so, although to a somewhat reduced extent as a result of land reforms initiated in several countries following World War II. The traditional situation in the area was that as against the many who owned little or no land, there were a few who owned exceedingly large tracts cultivated for them, as a rule, by sharecroppers. An outstanding example of such landlordism was that of Iran, where it was estimated that of the 41,000 villages of the country, 40,000 were owned outright by landlords.[17] The division of the crops varied (and varies) greatly, but in most cases the sharecropper receives no more than one-fifth to one-third of the harvest. In Iran, the prevalent system of crop allocation is the so-called *khamseh* ("five"), under which the landlord gets one-fifth of the crop for the land, one-fifth for the water, one-fifth for the seed, and one-fifth for the draught animals. The sharecropper receives the last one-fifth for his labor.[18]

A similar five-fold division of the crops is practiced in North Africa where the system is called by the same name, *khammes*.

In Syria the most widespread division of the harvest between the sharecropper and the landlord follows the *muraba'a* system whereby the sharecropper receives one quarter (hence the name),

*It is not possible in the present context to discuss the various types of land tenure (*miri*, *mulk*, *musha'*, *matruka*, *waqf*, *mawat-mubah*, etc.) found in the Middle East, although, to some extent, these have a bearing on the life of the fellahin.

and the landlord, who supplies also the seeds and farm animals, three-quarters of the crops.[19]

In West Pakistan, more than 50 per cent of the cultivated land is worked by sharecroppers, and according to the 1960 census there were 1.9 million landless agricultural laborers. The sharecropper has to give half of the crop to the landlord, in addition to which he must also defray the cost of collecting it, and has to present gifts to the landlord's family for weddings, births, and funerals, so that the whole share of the landlord often amounts to as much as 70 per cent of the harvest. The tenant also has to provide services for the landlord, such as carrying a bride in the landlord's family to the bridegroom's house in a kind of sedan chair, or to send one member of his family to become a servant in the landlord's house for little or no pay.[20]

The conditions are much better in Turkey where 73 per cent of the rural population own the land they cultivate totally, and 21 per cent partially (the remaining 6 per cent of the rural population do not farm but are engaged in other occupations). The average holding in Turkey is 7.7 hectares (or about 19 acres), the same as in Jordan.[21]

In addition to sharecropping, indebtedness is a great scourge of Middle Eastern village life. Apart from the fact that even in normal years the sharecropper's share is in many cases barely sufficient for him and his family, there is the inevitable occurrence of lean years, which can be disastrous for the sharecropper. In such years he runs short of food before the next harvest, and is forced to borrow either from a moneylender or from the landlord at exorbitant rates of interest which make it well-nigh impossible for him to get rid of his debt. The same circumstances compel many a small landowner to sell his land and to continue working it thereafter as the sharecropper of the new landlord. This is one factor that explains how and why the holdings of the great landlords tended in the past to become larger, while the precentage of land owned by smallholders became smaller.

Considering the unrelenting economic pressure under which most Middle Eastern villagers spend their entire lives, it is remarkable indeed that they have always been and remain to this day the carriers of a popular culture, very much alive, and affording great aesthetic satisfaction. Folk music, folk stories, folk poetry, folk dances, and various types of visual arts and crafts such as basketry, embroidery, and rug making have been engaged in by the villagers in every place and at all times, and never fail to astound the visitor with their variety, richness and beauty. Even in those villages where dire poverty prevents most people from purchasing or producing objects of visual arts or crafts, life is made richer by reciting and listening to a great variety of oral literature, telling of the wondrous exploits of heroes of old, and keeping alive a glimmer of a world beyond the drab routine of everyday existence. It is largely due to these popular traditions that life in a Middle Eastern village, with all its poverty, disease and hard work offers more than meets the eye, and affords satisfactions unsuspected by the casual observer.

Food and Health

In spite of the fact that Middle Eastern villagers spend practically their entire working life in an unceasing effort to produce food for themselves, the diet of a considerable percentage of the population is unbalanced, and occasionally insufficient. A comparison between the food eaten by the fellahin and that consumed by the townspeople indicates that the former have a much smaller variety, and that practically all of their foodstuffs are of vegetable origin (see below, p. 279). The staples are cereals and legumes, less frequently vegetables. Meat, fish and animal products (such as milk, eggs, or animal fats) are very rarely eaten, in most cases only on the occasion of a family feast.

As far as nutritional sufficiency is concerned, it is the concensus of observers that the daily diet is inadequate and unsatisfactory,[22] and that considerable sectors of the village population suffer from malnutrition. The Egyptian fellahin's diet, for instance, consists of bread and millet with the addition of a little onion and cheese, and minute quantities of sugar and fruit. Meat is eaten only rarely, milk is drunk only during illness. The food intake is below minimum requirements. The average rations decreased from 1900 to 1930; thereafter they increased, but not to a significant extent.[23]

The conditions are not much different in the countries of the so-called Fertile Crescent. In Iraq, for example, "malnutrition contributes perhaps the major health problem. . . . Actual starvation is rare, but for the bulk of the population resistance to disease is lowered by a diet which is deficient in quantity, caloric content, and balance."[24]

It is interesting to note that the Marsh Arabs in Lower Iraq are, on the whole, better fed than their neighbors: in addition to rice, which is the staple food, they eat milk, butter, cheese, fish and wildfowl. However, periodic hunger is not a stranger to them, especially in the early summer, when the previous year's rice crop has been consumed, and the flooding waters curtail fishing.[25]

Malnutrition is the term applied by physicians and students of social conditions to most Syrians as well. In Syria the staple diet consists of the traditional flat, round bead (the so-called *pita*), olives, some garden vegetables such as peppers, and sour milk (*leben*). Meat, while highly appreciated, remains out of reach for the average fellah.[26]

In Iran, the staple food is bread or rice, sour milk, cheese, and clarified butter, occasionally supplemented with eggs, chickens, rarely mutton, onions, cucumber, radishes, melons, tree-fruits, nuts, and tea.[27]

In sum, the Middle Eastern villagers derive a much higher percentage of their daily calorie intake from cereals and starches and a much smaller one from protein (especially the animal protein and fat consumption are minimal) than is the case in Western countries. However, as this author had occasion to observe elsewhere, "despite the obvious insufficiencies which must not be minimized, it has to be borne in mind that a population that has lived for many generations in a certain natural environment on a certain type of diet can derive greater nutritional benefits from this diet than a population not used to it."[28]

Observers coming from the technologically advanced countries of the West, with their stress on hygiene, preventive medicine and other public health measures, are often appalled when confronted with life in the Middle Eastern villages. One of these Western students of the Middle East had this to say about the peasants in Iran:

"The peasant lives, for the most part, in conditions of grinding poverty; the landowner, although he enjoys comparative affluence, is in constant fear of being despoiled of his wealth by intrigue, or of being cheated of it by a discontented peasantry. . . ."[29]

Even more depressing to the Western visitor are the health conditions in the Middle Eastern village. The following observations, made in Iraq, can apply to other parts of the area as well, and especially to those in which irrigated agriculture is practiced:

"It is not exaggerating to state that the average agricultural worker (*fellah*) is a living pathological specimen, as he is probably a victim of ankylostomiasis [hookworm, leading to abdominal pain, intermittent fever, progressive anemia, and emaciation], ascariasis [an intestinal parasite causing diarrhea], malaria, bilharzia [blood flukes producing urinal discharge of blood and dystentery], trachoma [an infectious disease of the eye], bejel [a non-venereal form of syphilis] and possibly tuberculosis also."[30] It has been estimated that in the south of Iraq as many as 30 per cent of the total population has bilharzia, with even higher incidences in certain provinces. Malaria is common in all the irrigated areas of Iraq, with the highest incidence reported in the Mosul province, where it contributes to an infant mortality rate as high as 500 per 1,000 live births. As to trachoma, the highest incidence (80 per cent) is found in the Dujaylah settlement, a community development project 25 miles south of the Al Kut Barrage, on the Tigris, and just north of the large marsh area, where otherwise the settlers enjoy a higher income and a better diet than do the ordinary tenants.[31] In Syria, in some rural areas 10 per cent of the population suffered from tuberculosis in 1955; 7 per cent of the total population of the country are registered each year as new cases of malaria; in the Jazīrah—Deir ez-Zor (northeastern) region, in 1954, a 100 per cent incidence of bilharzia was indicated; in villages of the Homs district 57 per cent of the inhabitants had malaria and the infant mortality was 300 per

1,000 of live births; mycosis (a scalp infection due to fungus) in some areas reached 50 per cent; bejel afflicted 25 per cent of the children in rural areas of northern Syria.[32]

Health conditions are particularly bad in the Egyptian villages, where the introduction of perennial irrigation caused an increase in water-borne diseases. Foremost among these is bilharzia whose incidence is 45 to 75 per cent in the Delta, where perennial irrigation is practiced, but only 5 per cent in Upper Egypt where there is no perennial irrigation. In five typical villages within 30 miles of Cairo, a Rockefeller Foundation study found that 92 per cent of the villagers had bilharzia, 100 per cent amoebic dysentery, 64 per cent intestinal worms, 6.5 per cent syphilis and 5 per cent pellagra. In addition, 2 per cent of the population annually had typhoid, 6 per cent were typhoid carriers, 2 per cent had active tuberculosis, 6 per cent acute eye infection, 89 per cent trachoma, 6.4 per cent were blind in one eye, and 1 per cent totally blind.[33]

In an oasis-village in Algeria (Sidi Khaled) a United Nations team of clinicians tested the entire population for tuberculosis in 1950 and found 70 to 80 per cent to be infected.[34]

However unsatisfactory the health conditions are at present, in comparison with the recent past there has been a marked improvement. Up to the 1940's periodic epidemics took their toll in many countries. In Egypt, a typhoid epidemic killed 16,706 persons in 1942; a malaria outbreak affected a quarter of a million in Upper Egypt (number of dead unknown) in 1942-44; relapsing fever killed several thousand in 1944; and over 10,000 (half of those who contracted the disease) died of cholera in 1947. However, even these numbers of victims are small compared to those who used to succumb to epidemics in earlier decades (for instance, in 1835 more than 80,000, or one-third of the total population, died in Cairo alone of cholera).[35] By the very nature of the population composition, these epidemics found most of their victims in the villages, causing large fluctuations in the numbers of inhabitants; however, the decrease in the wake of an epidemic was, as a rule, quickly made up again by the natural increase.

These conditions are now a thing of the past, and epidemics no longer occur in the Middle East except in its most tradition-bound parts, in the Arabian Peninsula. In most of the area the remaining problem is the control of, not epidemics, but endemic diseases such as those touched upon above.

The Village Family

Not much has to be added on this subject to what is said above (in chapter 4), since in giving a generalized picture of the Middle Eastern family the village families, which outnumber by far all the other types of families, had to receive primary consideration. One question, however, requires some attention: if a considerable percentage of village houses consists of one single room only, how can the typical Middle Eastern extended family find room in them? The answer lies in the following considerations: under traditional circumstances, the exceedingly high infant mortality, referred to in the preceding section, effectively counterbalanced the high birth rate, with the result that the population in most parts of the Middle East remained constant until the onset of Westernization and the public health measures introduced with it. This meant that, on the average, a married couple had only one daughter who reached adulthood, at which time, or even earlier, she was married to another villager and had moved in with his parents; and one son, who, when he married, brought his wife into his parents' house. In this manner, there was a period in the latter part of the parents' lives, when they had to share their house with their son and his wife, as well as the latters' children, whether the house consisted of one or more rooms. Where most people live under such crowded conditions (aggravated in many cases by the animals which are taken into the same one room for the night), while they may not be exactly comfortable, neither do they suffer from a sense of as acute a discomfort as would individual families whose crowded accommodations contrast with more spacious living quarters enjoyed by their neighbors.

An important result of this close symbiosis of the generations is that a child would feel about as close to his paternal grandparents as to his own father and mother. This circumstance, in turn, explains to some extent the extremely strong cohesion characterizing the Middle Eastern family. The work, of course, is shared by and divided among all the members of the extended family who live under one roof: father and son take care of the agricultural tasks, occasionally helped by the mother and the daughter-in-law.

The life of the village woman revolves entirely within and around her family. She takes care of the children, cooks, fetches water, prepares fuel, grinds the corn and bakes the bread, manages the household, and discharges family obligations at the time of marriages, circumcisions, births, and deaths, which are also her main occasions for entertainment. More frequently, women amuse themselves by visiting one another, gossiping at the village well or while washing the clothes on the riverbank, and by visiting the local or nearby shrine of a saint. The woman's status is determined by that of her husband, and, in later life, by the position achieved by her sons. Much of the honor of the family is in the hands of its women: a single misstep by a wife or a daughter can blacken the "face," i.e. honor, of her family and lead to her doom.

Social Groupings

As in the nomadic tribes, so in the villages, several related extended families form a larger social unit, a lineage or clan, called *ḥamūla* (or *qabīla*) in Arabic-speaking countries. A village may have one or more ḥamūlas. When a village is inhabited by members of two or more religio-ethnic groups (e.g. Muslims and Christians, or Muslims and Druzes), each of these groups forms separate ḥamūlas. The relationship among the ḥamūlas is often tense, especially when the village is divided between two hamūlas, in which case the competition between the two may have its traditionally formalized manifestations (see above, pp. 177ff.).

Social stratification in the village is, as a rule, rudimentary. Since the village is divided into ḥamūlas of generally equal status, and the members of each ḥamūla are related to one another (often being able actually to trace their patrilineal descent to one single ancestor), there should be, in principle, no class differences among them. In practice, however, economic status differences divide the villagers into clearly recognizable classes. At the top of this socio-economic stratification are the few families who own more land than the average villager and cultivate it with the help of sharecroppers or hired hands. The houses of these wealthy villagers are larger, and better built and furnished than those of the others; they themselves eat better, dress better, have a higher percentage of polygynous marriages, give more education to their children (sending them to the city for supplementary schooling), and maintain closer ties with the outside world. Whatever inroads Westernization is making in a village is usually expressed first in features found in this class.

The second class is that of the average landowning families whose crops are just sufficient to enable them to live modestly but satisfactorily by village standards, working their land with the help of members of their extended family only. The third class is that of the tenant farmers who own no land, and who consequently have to work harder and be satisfied with less, since a major part of the crops they harvest must be paid over as rent to their landowners. The next lower class is that of the sharecroppers who work for others in return for a small share of the crops. If a small landowner needs a hired hand and cannot pay him, one way of obtaining his labor is to give him his daughter to wife in exchange for a specified number of years' labor, in a manner similar to the agreement reached between Laban and Jacob.[36]

Even lower on the socio-economic scale than the sharecropper (who at least has a permanent home and works year-in year-out the same land) is the landless seasonal worker, who, in a bad year, remains completely without any livelihood. Starvation is a menace that he and his family may have to face any year. It is primarily from among these people that famines take their toll, as was the case, for instance, in 1942-43 in Pakistan, when most of the 1,700,000 people who starved to death were landless farm workers.

In considering the social structure of the Middle Eastern village, and, in particular, what it means for the individual to be a member of the village society, one of the most important features is the highly personal character of all interpersonal relationship. In a village of average size (say 500 individuals) everybody knows everybody else personally, and the life of each individual is lived in constant contact with others: members of one's own nuclear family in the first place, then, in descending order, members of one's extended family, one's ḥamūla, and lastly of the village. Especially the great stations of the human life cycle—birth, circumcision, marriage and death—are reached and passed with the fullest participation of numerous kinsmen and kinswomen. A sick person is visited by many, if a man is building a house for himself he is helped by his neighbors or clansmen, if misfortune befalls one the many are there to comfort him and help him out. It is literally true that in a village one is never alone, never lonely, never lost.

The village kinship structure also serves as a basis for settling quarrels or mediating disputes, either in informal discussion with one or more elders, or by resorting to more formalized arbitration.

The members of one ḥamūla usually live together in one quarter in the village. The ḥamūlas may also have their fields in one block, and each may have a separate guest house, threshing floor, oven, etc. The ḥamūla is the preferred endogamous unit, and its members are tied to one another by obligations of collective responsibility, such as prevail in the nomadic tribes (see above, pp. 19, 79).

In many villages one finds clearly marked indications of dual organization, with its typical mutual antagonism, competition, and tensions. Since this form of social organization has been described above (pp. 177–250) in some detail, there is no need to go into it here. One example may perhaps be added in order to show that dual division exists even where it lacks any formal structuring. In the Anatolian village of Sakaltutan, Stirling found that the upper and lower quarters into which the village was divided "were sharply contrasted and expressed their rivalry in ceaseless jokes, in quasi-serious running down of each other to me, in the hiring of separate shepherds; they even spoke of fighting, though fighting between quarters is in fact fighting between lineages under another name."[38]

In most villages only a very few persons are found who engage in non-agricultural pursuits on a full or part time basis. The village *imam-khatib*-teacher (or *mulla*) is one (in villages which have a mosque), the barber-bath keeper another; a watchman (or watchmen), carpenter, smith, tinker, store keeper, and keeper of the saint's tomb, may or may not be found in a village depending on its size and economic status. The religious functionaries may enjoy considerable prestige; the other specialists are less regarded, although in each case their actual status depends largely on the economic position they are able to achieve. The general rule all over the Middle East is that the more land a villager owns the more he is respected and looked up to. Two examples may illustrate this.

In Moroccan villages the social elite is comprised of the wealthy class, those who own relatively large tracts of land and considerable livestock, as well as some of the two luxury animals, the horse and the camel. However, families which trace their descent from the Prophet Mohammed or from local saints (*marabout*) also enjoy high ascribed status. Certain families have the traditional prerogative of supplying the village chieftain (*qaid*) or the village religious judge (*qadi*), and this too, means considerable prestige.[39] A similar pattern is found at the other end of the Middle East, in West Pakistan. At the top of the social scale are the landlords, one or two among whom are recognized as village headmen, and as such are expected to provide protection, settle disputes, and give advice to the others in the village.[40]

The socio-economic stratification of the village can be illustrated by referring to Iraq. In a typical Iraqi village, on the top of the scale is the absentee landlord (*mallak*) who may own the entire village or even several villages, but never lives in any of them. He usually has a representative (*sargal*) in the village, who, although an outsider, is accepted by the villagers as a member of the landowning class because of his power. Small landowners rank highest on the socio-economic scale among the resident villagers. In many cases they can and do employ tenant farmers and sharecroppers. The prestige of the small *mallak* is derived not so much from his economic status as from the fact of his land ownership, indicating to what extent it is the land that determines status. Next come the independent smallholders who own just enough land to make ends meet, working the land themselves with the help of their families. A tenant farmer or sharecropper may work more land and make a living from his share on a level with that of the independent smallholder, but the very fact that he does not own land places him in a lower prestige category. In northern Iraq many fellahin own a very small plot of land, and work, in addition, a larger piece as tenant farmers or sharecroppers in order to earn a minimal living. In the Shīʿite south, most fellahin are entirely landless. If a village has craftsmen or merchants, these are considered quite high on the social scale, because, although they do not own land, they usually make a better living than the independent farmers, and are thus able to obtain and display the indicators of wealth which are symbols of power in the village: education for their children, veiling and hair covering for their women, horses for themselves, and impressive family feasts (weddings, circumcisions). In addition to the veiling of the women, the practice of polygyny is also a distinctive mark of status and prestige, and is, in fact, most prevalent in the small *mallak* class.[41]

Village Institutions

Under this heading we shall discuss briefly those institutions which from time to time bring together the Middle Eastern villagers and thus enable them to enjoy a modicum of social life and conviviality, which cannot take place in the private homes because of the traditional segregation between the sexes. For it is a remarkable and paradoxical situation that in a society which upholds hospitality as one of the greatest male virtues, visits in private homes take place almost exclusively among women. In contrast to women, who visit one another quite frequently,[42] it is quite rare for a male villager to visit the home of another. Such male visitors as appear from time to time in private homes are, in general, persons from outside the village who have come on some errand. It is these outsiders on whom one is supposed to lavish hospitality.

The kind of social life which is most typical of the Western world, namely the get-together of several married couples and/or unmarried men and women in the home of one of their ranks for the purpose of partaking together of a meal or refreshments, chatting, and perhaps dancing, cannot and does not exist in the Middle Eastern village, and even in the cities is only now being hesitatingly introduced among the Westernized elements. Only at important family feasts, such as a wedding, does a family play host to a large number of fellow villagers, with the men and the women forming strictly segregated groups.

Where "the bulk of evening sociability takes place in private houses" and in "small gatherings of close friends the two sexes intermingle freely and equally," as was observed by Gulick in the Lebanese Christian village of Munsif,[43] this exceptional departure from the traditional Middle Eastern pattern is due primarily to the inroads Westernization has made in the life of rural Lebanon, and especially of the Christian villagers, and their close contact with the largely Westernized city of Beirut. In general, the absence of social intercourse among male villagers in the home of one of them is compensated for to some degree by the village institutions where they can get together as frequently as they wish to enjoy social contacts. Of these, the village square is perhaps the most important. This is usually an open place, located either in the middle of the village or just outside its complex of houses, which serves a great variety of purposes. In some villages the square is the threshing floor, used in turn by all the peasants as they gather in their crops. The same square serves as dance floor for the occasion when a group of young men or of girls feels like dancing a *dabke*[44] or another traditional folk dance, such as the Turkish "punching dance" performed by the men in connection with weddings,[45] or the Afghan *attan* danced by the village men around a fire in the evening to the accompaniment of guns and drums.[46] In many villages the square functions also as the market place with all that this entails in meeting friends and exchanging small talk.

In the men's life the guest-house (Arabic: *madyafa* in Egypt, *madafa* in Jordan, *mudif* in Iraq; *misafir odasi* in Turkey) is the most important meeting place. Most villages have such a guest house which is used for the reception of important guests visiting the village and for putting them up for the night, as well as for the meetings of the village council, and simply for gatherings of men many an evening, especially during the slack winter season. In some villages, notably in Egypt, the guest house is maintained by the 'omda (the village headman) and is a state-authorized institution. In others, each hamūla maintains its own guest house, in which case the adult males of the hamūla take their communal meals in it during the nights of the fast-month Ramadan. The size, quality and furnishing of these hamūla guest houses often manifest the competitive spirit that exists between the hamūlas. In yet other villages, the larger and wealthier extended families each have their own guest house. In the village of Sakaltutan, for instance, in central Anatolia, which had 105 households, Stirling counted in 1950 sixteen guest houses (he calls them "guest rooms"), twelve of which were in actual use most of the time, primarily as clubrooms for the village men in which they gathered after the evening meal, that is shortly after sundown, and remained for about one hour and a half. In January and February, however, they often sat in the guest room all day. Most of the men attended the same guest room regularly, and did it primarily for warmth, company, and information, and in order to escape the discomfort and indignity of spending the evening with one's wife and children at home where no male kin or neighbor would pay a visit. Several of the guest rooms in Sakaltutan were used as household living space where the male members of the owner's family ate, and the old men and unmarried boys slept. Four of the guest rooms were either communally owned by an entire lineage (the largest of which consisted of twenty households), or at least used by most men of the lineage even if owned by one of its members.[47]

Another institution which serves as a gathering place for the male villager is the mosque. However, far from all Middle Eastern villages have mosques (or churches), and most villagers go to the mosque to pray only on Friday, and even on that day (the traditional *yawm al-Jum'a*, Day of Gathering), not all of them do so. Nevertheless, many villagers do meet in the mosque quite frequently, and thus have an occasion to chat before and after the prayers. The religious leader of the village is the mosque's *imam* (prayer-leader) who also functions as the *khatib* (preacher) and the *shaykh* (master) of the *kuttab* (religious school) usually attached to the mosque.

The bath-house (*hammām*) is yet another village institution which is a focus of social life, and this one for both men and women. However, even fewer villages have a hammām than have a place of worship. Where there is a bath, its keeper usually also shaves the men.[48] Again, as in several other respects, an exception is presented by Iran where every village has its bath, built, as a rule, at the expense of the local landowner and consisting of several rooms, in most cases built below ground level. The attendant in charge receives payment in kind (wheat, fruit, straw, fuel) from the villagers who can use the bath as often as they wish, with certain days or hours set apart for the men, others for the women.[49]

Larger villages usually have a coffee-house (in Iran and Afghanistan a tea-house) which is the exclusive gathering place of men, and among them, too, only of those who have achieved an income level at least a line above the barest minimum. Time is whiled away at the coffee house drinking the small cups of Turkish coffee, smoking the *narghile* (water pipe), playing card games or shash-bash (a kind of backgammon), listening to the radio, or, on Ramadan nights, to a visiting *kassās* (story-teller) who recites old, familiar, but always fascinating pieces of folklore, and, above all, conversing with relatives, friends and neighbors.

Such large villages usually have also one or more stores, or even a row of stores which constitutes a rudimentary *sūq*. Since the purchasing of merchandise in a store is a typically male task in the Middle East, the village store has developed into a kind of socializing center for the men.[50]

As far as the women are concerned, their favorite place of meeting and gossiping is the village well. Every village must have access to water for drinking and household purposes, and except for villages located on river banks or on canals, and a few which must rely on rainwater gathered in cisterns, all villages have a well. The fetching of water from the well (or the river) is everywhere one of the daily chores of the women, and the well is, therefore, the place where the women meet and talk. The short time they spend there, exchanging news and gossip, is for most village women the only rest period they enjoy in the busy routine of their dawn-to-dusk working day, and often the only entertainment available for them.

While in most villages the women grind their own corn and bake their own bread, in the larger and more progressive villages there is a baker, in which case the daily visit to his establishment is an additional occasion for the women to meet, chat and relax for a while. As Gulick observed in the Lebanese Christian village of Munsif, the two bakeries "are intensively used as loci of social interaction on the part of women . . . here the women meet regularly and for protracted lengths of time."[51]

Yet another place where the women meet is the cemetery. On a special day (or days) of the year the women go to the cemetery to mourn the dead, and on such occasions they take along some food and sit around among the graves for quite a long time, shedding tears for the departed dear ones, but also enjoying the outing as a social occasion.

The shrine, housing the grave of a saint and located either in the village or nearby, is primarily frequented by women. They bring along a small gift, in many cases some foodstuff, which they give to the keeper of the shrine, or place next to the tomb of the *wali* (holy man), then pray to him and pour out their hearts in supplication. The usual troubles besetting people everywhere in the world, such as illness, childlessness, affairs of the heart, and the like, form the subject of their prayers, as well as such more specifically Middle Eastern issues as the intention of the husband to take a second wife, or the reluctance of a cousin to give up his right to the hand of a girl who wants to marry someone else. Each saint has an annual feast, usually on the traditional anniversary of his birth (*mawlid*), on which occasion a veritable folk-celebration takes place, occasionally together with popular amusements, markets, competitive games, and dances. A characteristic of many of these shrines is that they are venerated by Christians and Jews as well as Muslims.

Political Organization

Strictly speaking, no distinction can be made in Middle Eastern villages between social and political organizations. Kinship groups (hamūlas, lineages) are the basic aggregates on a super-familial level, and they determine the residential arrangements as well as whatever rudimentary political structuring exists in the village.

As a general rule it can be stated that each hamūla tends to occupy a separate section or quarter in the village. While this has already been stated above, we must repeat it in order that it may lead on to a connected and significant feature: the head of each hamūla (who is usually the head of the most important extended family in the hamūla) acts, to all intents and purposes, as the head of a quarter of the village, a kind of district chief. He represents the interests of his section (not only of the hamūla-members but also of individuals outside the kinship structure who may reside there) vis-à-vis other quarters of the village.

The oasis village of Sidi Khaled in Algeria can serve as an example. This large village, which numbered 5,300 persons in 1950, is divided into four quarters, each inhabited by one or more lineages. Each of these is headed by a *kebir* (literally "Big One"), whose prime function is to settle differences within his own lineage, to deal with other kebirs, and to officiate at weddings. All the kebirs together form the *jemʿa* or village council, an informal body in which, in the past, other men of importance also participated. Under the French rule the council was transformed into an elected body of twelve, which in practice meant that each lineage nominated its leader (the same who had been its kebir), and then the entire slate was voted in by the population. In this manner, what was originally a feature of the traditional *social* organization of the village became transformed into a *political* body with little or no difference in its functions.[52]

Such village councils, informally organized, composed of hamūla-heads and other elders, and functioning as a deliberating and consultative body, but nevertheless important enough to influence or even determine action by the village head, exist in the villages all over the Middle East. In the Arab countries they are called *majlis* (which, incidentally, is also the name of the parliament in Iran and elsewhere); in Turkey *ihtiyar heyeti* (council of elders).

The most influential hamūla in a village usually has the right to appoint one of its members to serve as village headman. In practice, the office is often hereditary within an extended family, although, upon the death of a headman, the hamūla council convenes and decides on his successor.

The functions of the headman include the maintenance of public order and security (for which purpose he may have a few village policemen under his command), the registration of marriages, births and deaths, the collection of taxes, the mediation of disputes, and the representation of the village before the higher governmental authorities. He also entertains official guests. The headman receives no remuneration, but he is amply compensated by the prestige of his office, and certain privileges he enjoys.

As the political organization of the Middle Eastern states develops, the village headman's function is gradually being transformed: originally the spokesman of the kingroups inhabiting the village, he becomes more and more the representative of the government. In the Sudanese village of Burri al-Lamāb, for instance, the *'omda* (headman) is responsible for obtaining the tax money, which is gathered by his five assistants, called *shaykhs*, each of whom lives in one of the five settlements (called a *hilla*) of which the *'umudiyya* (district) is composed. The 'omda transmits the tax money to the central government, settles minor disputes, calls in the police when necessary, sits on the local district court and acts as advisor to the judge, submits requests to the Khartoum North Rural Council, participates in the distribution of lands for developing the New Quarter of the village, etc.[53]

This new development often leads to the refusal of the wealthy and influential villagers to accept the position of headman, which now falls more often to younger and less important men, with the result that the headmanship continues to lose prestige. As Stirling aptly put it on the basis of his observations in Turkish villages: "The headman was no longer the top of the village but the bottom of the official State hierarchy. It was not a pleasant position to hold."[54]

Religion

Religion in the villages all over the Middle East consists of an Islamic element* and the local survivals of pre-Islamic forms. In some places the Islamization of village religion has been accomplished with great thoroughness, the non-Islamic features having been almost totally eliminated; in others, Islam is no more than skin-deep and beneath it the pre-Islamic doctrines and practices throb with great vitality. Almost nowhere, however, are the people actually aware of this dichotomy.

Take a village like Burri al-Lamāb near Khartoum in the Sudan. Officially its inhabitants profess Sunni Islam of the Māliki legal school. The Muslim doctrine of the Oneness of God is upheld, Mohammed is venerated as the Messenger of God; the Muslim prayers are said, although many men, especially the younger ones, do not pray regularly; most of the women do not know how to pray at all. Almsgiving is observed rather irregularly, but the fasting during the month of Ramadan is observed by nearly everyone. Only a few make the pilgrimage to Mecca in observance of the fifth of the Five Pillars of the Faith in Islam. Many drink alcoholic beverages, although this is forbidden by Islam. While the official Muslim position is that infibulation of females is forbidden, this pre-Islamic practice persists. Also certain pre-Islamic practices connected with death and burial continue. The Islamic prohibition of gambling is ignored. There is a strong cult of saints (tolerated by Islam everywhere except in Saudi Arabia), and numerous cults of curing and divination, with a pronounced belief in the evil eye (which is generally Middle Eastern). In spite of disapproval by the official Muslim hierarchy, the zār-cult (the exorcism of evil spirits by a female priestess or *shaykha*) flourishes. This cult penetrated the Sudan from Abyssinia in the nineteenth century and is still spreading.[55]

In sharp contrast to the above are the religious doctrines and practices of a typical Muslim village in, say, Jordan, where even folk-religion has become so thoroughly Islamized that one finds barely a trace of non-Islamic influences. Perhaps the strong veneration of saints (this is even stronger in Iraq and North

*In this general statement about the role of religion in the life of the Middle Eastern villages it is not possible to dwell on the minority religions. It can be stated in passing, however, that the role of Jewish, Christian, Druze, and other religions closely parallels that of Islam.

Africa) could be mentioned as a survival of pre-Islamic cults, but then the cult of these *walis* has been so completely incorporated into Islam that its pre-Islamic origin is forgotten and of no significance.

In general, it can be stated that the villagers constitute a conservative element as far as religious observance is concerned, certainly more so than most nomadic tribes and the semi-Westernized townspeople.

An important manifestation of religious life in Middle Eastern villages is the brotherhood (Arabic *tarīqah,* literally "way"), which is in many villages the only non-kinship-based association. In Iraqi villages, for instance, all classes may join a tarīqah, and within it, at least theoretically, no class differences exist; however, this does not carry over into other aspects of life, and even in the tarīqah it is usually the village leaders who wield control.[56] In one Sudanese village no less than five brotherhoods were reported with a total membership amounting to 14 per cent of the males over puberty.[57] In some places, these brotherhoods are quite powerful countrywide organizations with special fortress-homes, such as that of the Tijani brotherhood at Ain Madhi, some fifty miles west of Laghuat in Algeria.[58]

In Egyptian villages many boys, when they reach adolescence, join the mystic order of Nakhshabandiya, whereupon they are called "boys of the Path" (*awlād attarīq*), and participate in night prayers and the mystic rituals of the *zikr* in which a main feature is the repetitive and ecstatic utterance of God's names and attributes. The visit of boys of one village to their confreres in another is a joyous and festive occasion.[59]

Until quite recently, formal education in traditional Middle Eastern villages was a purely religious matter. Quite often the local religious specialist, associated with the village mosque, would be in charge of the school, gathering the boys for a few hours daily to the mosque court and teaching them reading (primarily reading the Koran), as well as some writing and arithmetic. For these services, the children's families would give the teacher some wheat or barley at harvest time or other products they could afford.

In recent decades the governments of most Middle Eastern countries have begun to build a network of elementary schools in the villages. In some (Lebanon, for instance), this has by now become quite extensive; in others it is still rudimentary. In Iran, for example, there is only one such *maktab* for every twenty-five or thirty villages.[60]

In large villages there may be several traditional Koran schools which continue to function even after the government establishes an official elementary school. Thus, for instance, in the Upper Egyptian province of Aswan, in a group of villages around Silwa there are five kuttabs and one recognized maktab. All the kuttabs are attached to or adjacent to mosques and run by their sheikhs, who keep discipline by administering bastinado to the offender.[61]

The Winds of Change

The winds of change, blowing from the West with unabating intensity ever since the days of World War II, are beginning today to penetrate even the most remote Middle Eastern villages in Morocco and Mauritania in the west, Afghanistan and Balujistan in the east, the Caucasus in the north and the Aden-Oman coast in the south. Distance, of course, is an obstacle which even powerful blasts have difficulty in overcoming. In general, the degree of Westernization exhibited by a village seems to depend on two factors: the distance of the village from the nearest urban center, and the extent of Western influence found in that urban center itself. The closer the village to the urban center and the greater the Western influence in the latter, the stronger the Westernization in the village.

In accordance with this rule one finds that in Lebanon, whose small size makes for a proximity of all its villages to the capital, Beirut, which itself is considerably Westernized, all villages bear the stamp of marked Western influence. The contrary is true for a country like Afghanistan, where some villages are so remote and self-sufficient that their inhabitants have never been to town, and where even the two biggest cities, Kabul and Herat, are far behind Beirut or Alexandria in Westernization. Nevertheless, even in Afghan villages, second-hand Western clothes, those shabby forerunners of Westernization, have already made their appearance.[62]

As against this, a village near Alexandria in Egypt was found in 1960 to contain the following modern Western features: a kindergarten, attended by 156 boys and 30 girls; a primary school with 350 boys, and another with 230 girls (note the proportion!); an average of seven children per family (the survival of so many children is a sign of relatively advanced health measures without as yet having reached the stage where the parents would use contraception); a governmental medical unit for internal diseases; a constable with thirty armed watchmen; the constable and the 'omda (the mayor) read newspapers; a loudspeaker installed in the middle of the village over which any villager can make public announcements; numerous radios (battery operated). And the mayor, in thoroughly Western fashion, wanted the canal, on which the village utterly depended, enlarged and the village provided with a resident doctor and a veterinarian and electricity and running water in every house.[63]

In another group of five villages in Lower Egypt (with populations ranging from 700 to 5,000) it was found that about one half of a random sample interviewed in 1958 listened to the radio, and about one fifth read newspapers, their favorite topic being political news. This study took place only a few years after Nasser had become president of Egypt, and yet 80 per cent of the males and 50 per cent of the females knew that he was president, that the monarchy had been terminated and a republic established.[64] It is surprising, indeed, that the Egyptian villagers, who for millennia had never known what was going on beyond the next village (with which they had reciprocal ties), should within the last few years have become aware to such an extent of the larger world around them.

Perhaps the most immediate reaction shown by the villagers, and especially those of the younger generation, to contact with the more or less Westernized city is the emergence of dissatisfaction. The young villager, made aware, as a result of visits to the city, of his low subsistence standards, tends to regard village life as unrewarding and to feel attracted by the urban environment. At the same time, objectively, too, his position in the village becomes more difficult as more of his siblings remain alive than used to, which means that—to put it in the most elementary terms—less food is available per capita. All this results in a village-to-town migration of young men which, in turn, tends to restore, to some extent at least, the balance between land and people disturbed by the reduced infant mortality.

The very fact that one son removes himself from the home environment and thereby weakens the ties between himself and his parental family, tends to also effect a loosening of these ties between the son who remains at home and his parents. The very example of the brother who went away makes the brother who remained at home, as well as their parents, aware of the possibility of secession, and this in turn weakens both paternal authority and filial self-subordination to it. A village family with one son in the city has some interest in what goes on in the city, is open toward the outer world, and less resistant to external influences and innovations.

In villages close to a city the change can come with traumatic suddenness. Take the village of Balgat, located six miles from Ankara, the capital of Turkey. In 1950 it took two hours to reach it over a dirt road. Everything was full of dust, including the furniture in the houses. All the villagers were farmers. The single store stocked cheap clothes, cigarettes, and drinks, and barely anything else. The only radio belonged to the village headman. Yet all the villagers were satisfied with their lot, and felt that they would kill themselves rather than go to live in another place.

By 1954 a paved road had been built over which the village was reached from Ankara in twenty minutes in a regularly scheduled bus. More than a hundred families had radios, seven had refrigerators, there were four tractors, three trucks and one passenger car. Few remained on the farm, many having taken jobs in the city. The villagers were much better dressed. The people exhibited "a hopeful eagerness for better days, an exuberant faith in change, an urge to advance toward tomorrow."[65]

Ethos and Attitudes

Among many villagers all over the Middle East there is a tradition to the effect that their ancestors were nomadic tribesmen who, because of varying causes and circumstances, settled down and founded the village in which they themselves still live. Consequently, many of these villages still consider themselves as tribes, no longer nomadic, but tribes nevertheless, with all that tribal organization entails in kinships structure and ethos.

In outlying mountain areas, such as Kurdistan and Afghanistan, and on the fringes between the Desert and the Sown in Jordan, Syria, and Iraq, this tribal ethos is still strong in the villages. While land represents no less a value among these villagers than it does among others, the tribal ethos is expressed in a stronger emphasis on kinship, descent, hospitality, honor, revenge—all typically Bedouin values (cf. above, p. 19).

The one feature of the nomadic ethos which, above all, survives in most villages is hospitality, and this in spite of the fact that with their extremely meager resources, the reception of even a single guest entails considerable sacrifice for most villages. In honoring a guest arriving from outside the village, the villager honors himself and his family, and he will at all times choose to go hungry for several days if that is the price he must pay for feeding his guests as lavishly as possible in his circumstances.

Much of the honor concept in village life (as among the nomads) is focused on the women. ". . . honour, *namus* . . . was directly related to the women of the lineage households. To show interest in a woman other than by formally seeking her hand in marriage was a deadly insult to her menfolk. Most killings, or attempted killings . . . were directly or indirectly the result of the alleged 'insulting' of a woman."

Closely connected with a man's honor viewed in these terms is his virility, "mainly measured by procreative success." A woman's honor, on the other hand, "is very largely a matter of sexual modesty."[66]

While hospitality and honor can be considered village values directly derived from the Bedouin ethos, the village value system contains a strong religious element which is lacking in most nomadic tribes. In fact, the village code of behavior is basically a religious-traditional one, which means that the observance of purely moral precepts and ritual duties are not kept strictly apart. A good man is decent, compassionate, kind, neighborly, forgiving, patient, honest, and respects the rights of others; but he is also ritually observant, says his prayers, performs his ablutions, observes the fast of Ramadan and the feasts of Islam.[67]

Religion continues to command the loyalty of Middle Eastern villagers in spite of the weakening of its hold upon them which has been noted by numerous students of the area. As a very broad generalization it can be stated that traditional religious beliefs and observances are still extremely potent in the Middle Eastern village, while they have undergone a noticeable decline in the urban centers (with the exception of those in the Arabian Peninsula). Of course, even in the villages, where Western influences penetrate, religion inevitably must retrench to a certain degree, as exemplified by the disrepute into which traditional religious methods of curing the sick fall when modern medicine becomes available.

What the village itself means to its inhabitants can best be described by referring to what the villagers themselves have to say about it. In Turkish villages Stirling found that "every village has the best drinking water, and the best climate." And as to the character of its people, "every village is more hospitable, more honorable, more virile, more peaceable, gives better weddings, than any of its neighbors. Other villages are savage, mean, dishonorable, lying, lazy, cowardly."[68] Also Gulick noted in the Lebanese Christian village he studied that "there are strong suggestions that to the average Munsifi, the village as a whole is more meaningful as a unit than his particular minimal lineage [i.e. kingroups three to seven generations in depth], and this is unquestionably true as far as the maximal lineage [one of the three large genealogical groups in the village reckoning descent from one of the three sons of the founder of the village] is concerned."[69] Thus "the village as an institution is a significant focus of loyalty and identification for everyone in it regardless of age."[70]

In spite of the above assertion it would seem that the typical villager is bound by stronger ties of emotion and loyalty to his kingroup than to his village. Thousands of Middle Eastern villagers have abandoned their villages and settled overseas, but continue to send regular remittances to their kinfolk who remained behind in the village. Or, if one still doubts the validity of this statement about the primacy of kinship ties, one has only to look at the frequent intra-village fights or tensions, in which members of one kingroup are always solidly lined up against members of another. In fact, Gulick himself reached this conclusion when discussing changes in values that modern conditions introduced into the life of Munsif: "The family and lineage maintain their function as serving as a link between the individual and the village as a whole, a kingroup toward which feelings of utmost loyalty and unity are directed."[71]

Next to religion and kin, the third traditional village value is the land. However, as a result of modern developments, many villagers must recognize that the cultivation of land is not the only possible way of life. Where infant mortality is being reduced, the larger number of surviving children compels some of them to leave the village and seek livelihood elsewhere—in the nearby town, the capital city, the oil installations, or overseas. As a result, while attachment to the land among those who remain behind is as strong as ever, the knowledge that there are other ways of life makes the village's emotional dependence on the land less strong than it used to be. In Westernized villages, especially in those near a big city, many of the young generation begin to question the desirability of village life as a whole.

Before leaving this subject of the village ethos a few words seem in place about fatalism and passivity, two terms that crop up quite frequently in books and articles dealing with the Middle Eastern peasants. Why have we not witnessed, it is asked, one single peasant uprising in any Middle Eastern country for several decades, in spite of the fact that the lot of the villagers has become not better, but worse, compared to the improvements that have taken place in the city? The oft-voiced answer that the fellah is fatalistic and passive is certainly not satisfactory.

It would be closer to the truth to say that the poverty and disease, which is the shared fate of most Middle Eastern villagers, do not necessarily seem to them as oppressive and as painful as they appear to the Western observer. For one thing, it is the commonly experienced mode of existence, and, as is well known, a shared ill is easier to bear. For another, they know that their parents, grandparents and more remote ancestors—all highly venerated figures in the traditional Middle Eastern value system—lived in the same conditions, suffered the same fate, and this knowledge makes the present hardships more tolerable. We must consider it horrible and tragic that about half the children born to Egyptian fellahin die before they reach their fifth birthday, but if this is the norm in a society, and has been for countless generations, the people living within it do not find their infant mortality quite as tragic. This is, actually, neither fatalism nor passivity nor even resignation, but an attitude adjusted to a given frame of existence which for uncounted generations has circumscribed life in the village. To call the fellahin fatalistic because they do not rebel against the circumstances of their lives makes about as much sense as to call the population of England or the United States fatalistic because they do not rebel against the inevitability of work, taxes, or death.

X. *The Middle Eastern Town*

In the Middle East are located the most ancient towns of the world. Sites occupied continuously or intermittently for four thousand years or even longer are nothing exceptional in this world area. Throughout this long period the towns were of central importance to their respective hinterlands, a position they hold to this very day, and therefore the primary goals of all conquerors. A change of hands in them often meant a considerable shift of population, the elimination of the leaders and of the articulate or otherwise important elements either by ruthless liquidation or by exile, and their replacement by new settlers with a view to political reliability and loyalty.

The fate of the towns was thus always characterized by more frequent and incisive changes than that of the villages. The villages, among which too there are many with a history of millennia, have remained largely the same throughout their history, with basically the same way of life carried on largely by the same ethnic group, generation after generation. The towns, on the other hand, have often experienced catastrophic ups and downs, they changed rulers, were destroyed and rebuilt, or evacuated and resettled. Their importance increased in one period and decreased in another, depending on their position within the empire to which they happened to be annexed. These great political, social, and cultural upheavals notwithstanding, the towns remained the undisputed centers of every cultural achievement in their areas of influence.

Town and Village

The concentration of all cultural and civilizational achievements in the towns means that in the Middle East there is a considerable contrast between the rural and the urban varieties of culture. Without attempting to probe into the historical origins of this situation, it can be stated briefly that whatever differences had existed between town and country in the Middle East in pre-Islamic times were greatly accentuated by Islam, itself a religion of townspeople[1]—that turned town and country into veritable opposites.

> The contrast which exists between the rural community and the city in every society was rarely more striking than in the medieval Islamic world. Here it was not merely a contrast between isolation and congregation, between the dispersed economy of the village and the concentrated economy of the town, between oppressed poverty and relative freedom and wealth, between producer and consumer. It was a contrast of civilizations. The medieval Moslem culture was above all an urban culture. While Islam but lightly touched the secular life of the countryside, it rebuilt and refashioned the cities from their foundations, and stamped them with an individual impress which has persisted even to the present day. Between the Egyptian or Syrian city and its country districts there was little or no tie but the economic one—indeed, the possibility of any stronger tie was all but ruled out by the contempt with which the townsman regarded the peasant—while the cities of widely distant countries shared a common culture, a common order of life, a common disposition of mind, and a sense of unity fostered by these joint possessions and traditions, even when physical intercourse between them was relatively limited. There is a marked change of spiritual atmosphere in the cities; though they share in the general decline of the eighteenth century, there is something of independence in the bearing of the townsmen, a conviction of their dignity as citizens of Islam, and a readiness to assert their rights, even though it might degenerate into mere rioting and mob demonstrations.[2]

The contrast between the town and the country outlined in this passage persists to this day. In fact, the first outcome of Westernization was an augmentation of the disparateness between the city that showed a relative readiness to absorb Western influences and the village that was not reached by this outside force. Although this initial stage has now been largely left behind, inasmuch as urban influences, and with them Western cultural traits, tend nowadays to spread more and more into the rural areas, resulting in a diminishing of the age-old gap between city and village, the very persistence of this gap for hundreds of years is a noteworthy fact that has to be understood and appreciated in trying to evaluate the role of the town in Middle Eastern culture.

For it is remarkable indeed that in the Middle East as a whole, where more than three fourths of the population lives in rural areas, the village should have contributed so little to the culture of the country. Broadly speaking, the role of the rural population has been confined to providing food and taxes, and some raw materials and folklore. Everything else originated in the towns.

Only on the lowest economic level is the rural population self-sufficient in the sense that it satisfies all its needs in producing simple utensils, apparel, and housing in accordance with age-old methods of home craft. As soon as a village raises itself over the barest subsistence level, it becomes dependent on wares and merchandise produced in the towns. The higher the standard of living of villagers, the more they rely on the town even for the satisfaction of primary needs such as food, clothing, housing, utensils, and all kinds of consumer goods. In exchange for this the country has only its agricultural products to offer, bought up by the town through a series of middlemen at advantageous prices.

In addition to being the economic, trading, manufacturing (and more recently industrial), commercial and financial center, the typical Middle Eastern town is also the seat of all the administrative, political, judicial, religious, and educational institutions, and concentrates within its confines all those elements who devote themselves wholly or partly to occupations pursued in these institutions, or to literary, journalistic, or artistic work, or, in fact, to any other field outside food production. During the last few decades, as a result of Westernization, such institutions as modern universities, hospitals, libraries, academies, scientific and other societies, as well as amusement centers and the like, have been added to the cultural features that are all concentrated in the towns.

A particular feature of Middle Eastern social structure has facilitated this development. This feature has been (and is to this day) the preference for urban residence (and, in particular, residence in the capital city) by the owners of landed estates. The actual supervision of these estates has traditionally been entrusted to managers, while the landlord and his family lived in the city and had no direct contact whatsoever with the people whose work made it possible for him to indulge in leisure and luxury. The residence of these landed proprietors in the towns meant a concentration in them of all those trades, crafts, and arts that depended on the existence of a class of wealthy connoisseurs. In this manner the congregation of absentee landlords in the towns became a powerful factor in the development of a specific, refined, and sophisticated urban culture, separated by a wide gulf from the simple folk culture of the villages.

A more recent outcome of the concentration of the wealthy landlord class in the towns was that this same class began to utilize some of its accumulated capital for investment into new economic enterprises such as commercial, financial, and industrial undertakings. Furthermore, when in the wake of continuing Westernization Western forms of government were adopted, it was again this same class whose presence and availability in the capital and district centers enabled it to become the foremost element in the formation of governments, ministerial and other administrative offices, and representative bodies. Thus, while a visitor to the capital at the turn of the century would have found the upper class comprising chiefly great landowning families, half a century later he would have found the upper class still consisting largely of the same families but this time also as leaders in many economic, administrative, and political fields.

The outcome of this deep cleavage between town and country has been that the town has been regarded by all those who knew about its existence and had some knowledge of it even though only from hearsay, as the place where one can live a good life, attain status, prestige, satisfaction, and enjoyment, in short, as the seat of everything desirable. The village, in contrast, and especially in the eyes of the townspeople, has become the symbol of backwardness. The attraction the town exerted on the villagers in the past explains at least partly the constant flow of migrants from village to town, a process that has become greatly accelerated as a result of Westernization and the greater employment opportunities offered by the industrial plants established in the towns. A result of this internal migration from village to town has been a faster increase of the urban than of the rural population. The village-to-town movement has gathered additional speed during the Second World War as a result of war conditions. In some places it was easier to obtain supplies in the towns than in the rural areas; in others, industrial development spurred by wartime demands attracted unemployed or underemployed agricultural workers; and again elsewhere the villagers were attracted by work provided by the Allied forces. These developments reinforced the general tendency to prefer urban life and employment with its higher prestige to agricultural activities in the rural districts. After the war, there was in some cases a movement back to the countryside, but this was merely a temporary reversal of the general trend which by and large continued.

One of the results of Westernization and industrialization is the rapid growth of cities. The largest city of the entire Middle East, Cairo, had only 240,000 inhabitants in the 1830's, according to Lane's estimate.[3] In a century their number increased tenfold, and by 1947 it was more than two and a half millions. Three more cities passed the million mark in recent years: Teheran, capital of Iran (1,500,000 in 1956), Istanbul, former capital of Turkey (1,215,000 in 1955), and Alexandria, the second largest city in Egypt (1,157,000 in 1947). Two more cities were in the half million to million range: Baghdad, capital of Iraq (730,000), and Casablanca, the most important port city of Morocco (700,000). Eleven additional cities had inhabitants whose numbers ranged from one quarter to a half million: Ankara, the new capital of Turkey (453,000); Beirut, capital of Lebanon (450,000); Tunis, capital of Tunisia (410,000); Tel Aviv-Jaffa in Israel (400,000); Damascus, capital of Syria, and Aleppo in northern Syria (400,000 each); Algiers, capital of Algeria (361,000); Oran in Algeria (299,000); Izmir in Turkey (286,000); and the Iranian cities of Tabriz (290,000) and Isfahan (254,000). Another thirty cities had populations ranging from one hundred thousand to a quarter of a million. Thus, of the 156 million people living in the Middle East, only about 15 million or 10 per cent, lived in the middle of the twentieth century in cities of more than 100,000.

Nevertheless, the influence of urban civilization in the Middle East as a whole is considerable. Especially in the vicinity of the cities and towns is their presence strongly felt. The inhabitants of villages within walking distance and, where good transportation is available, within easy traveling distance, are frequent visitors to the town. There they transact business or spend their leisure time sitting in coffeehouses, attending a motion picture performance, or listening to the litigations in the law courts. They familiarize themselves with the ways of the townspeople, become influenced by their clothing habits, their speech forms, their outlook. Some of them will spend some time working in the town or even find permanent employment there and either take up residence in the town or become commuters.

The urbanizing influence of the town radiating into its environs is manifested, among other things, in such external changes as the adoption of urban styles of architecture, the installation oj street lights, the introduction of water supply, the erection of a bus station, a coffeehouse, etc. The proximity of the town also brings about certain economic advantages for nearby villagse, such as easier marketing of their products, additional income derived from urban employment, etc. All these effects of the town make a village situated close by very different from a remote village, the urban influences diminishing with the increasing distance. Cultural standards of the town also affect the villages in its vicinity. Schools are built, or children are sent for schooling to town. Interest in political events taking place in the town begins to engross the villagers, and so forth.

Until now we spoke of village and town as though they were two clearly distinguishable disparate entities. In fact, however, it is not always easy to distinguish between village and town in the Middle East because the size of the local aggregate does not always provide a reliable criterion.

A careful scrutiny of the constant and most outstanding differences between village and town discloses that they boil down ultimately to distinctions in occupational structure. The village is characterized by a largely homogeneous occupational structure: most of the people in the village are engaged in agriculture, with merely a sprinkling of individuals engaged in service occupations, such as a shoemaker, tailor, carpenter, watchman, barber, religious functionary, etc. In the town, on the other hand, one finds a heterogeneous occupational structure, with the majority, moreover, engaged as a rule in nonfarming occupations.

The heterogeneous occupational structure of the Middle Eastern town is contingent on a number of factors. The concentration in the town of the landed proprietors, already referred to above, attracts a considerable number of specialists in trades, crafts, arts, and professions to cater to the needs of this wealthy upper crust of society. Since antiquity the town has been a place of exchange, a *sūq* or bazaar, where the villager and the nomad come to sell their surplus products and to buy the town-produced goods. This position of the town as the central place of commerce enables a sizable merchant class to make a living here. The town is usually the administrative center of a province or district or a subdistrict seat, depending on its size and importance. It has a mayor and a municipal council, a district governor or a district officer, law courts of first or second appeal, a police force, some military post, a telegraph and post office, and other paraphernalia of government; consequently in it live numerous government employees, officials, clerks, soldiers (if it is a garrison town), and similar personnel. These, in turn, give work and employment to many more people engaged in service occupations. In contradistinction, the village may or may not have a small police force; otherwise, the only symbol of government is the headman who acts as a representative of both the government and the people.

As to the public institutions found in Middle Eastern cities, it is difficult to generalize. The number and character of these institutions seem to show a direct correlation to the size of the city and a reversed correlation with its distance from the Mediterranean littoral. In other words, the larger the city and the closer to the Mediterranean it is located, the more public institutions are found in it and the more Western the character of these institutions. This observation would seem to hold good with reference to such institutions as hospitals, clinics, secondary public or private schools, colleges, museums, newspapers, societies, men's clubs, literary and sports clubs, motion picture theaters, cafés and restaurants, dance halls, night clubs. The same holds good with regard to the availability of electric current and piped water. The general rule is that the larger the town the more Westernized it is, and probably the higher the percentage in its population of the Westernized and semi-Westernized elements. In the largest towns there are whole sections that have a completely Western character; no comparable quarters can be found in the small towns.

Under traditional circumstances town life was the culminating refinement of which the local subcultures of the Middle East were capable. One of the most typical examples of this was Damascus with its bazaars filled with the finest products of Syrian craftsmanship, with its great concentration of wealth and luxuries on the one hand and of intellectual, artistic, and literary activity on the other. The tenor of life in a city such as Damascus, although surpassing by far that of the countryside, was nevertheless part and parcel of one and the same cultural *genus*. With the impact of Westernization, urban culture in the large Middle Eastern cities has begun to absorb more and more of the traits introduced from a very different cultural *genus*, that of the modern Western world, and consequently an increasing distance began to develop between urban and rural culture. In fact, increasingly large proportions of the urban population, especially in the coastal towns of North Africa and in the largest cities of Egypt and the Levant, are adopting a way of life which in its external forms consciously copies the West. A villager from the remote hinterland feels almost as lost in the modern sections of Casablanca, Algiers, Alexandria, or Beirut as he would in Rome or Paris. Only in the most recent years, as indicated above, has this distance begun to diminish again, owing to the fact that the influence of the new Westernized urban culture radiates more and more powerfully into the surrounding countryside, gradually drawing closer to itself the still largely tradition-bound culture of the rural communities.

Townsman and Peasant

Whatever will be the outcome of this most recent trend, for the time being the situation is that the disparate cultures of town and country endow the townsman and the peasant with two greatly differing social personalities. To be a true townsman means not only to live in a town, but also to adhere to a definite way of life, to enjoy a certain social status, and to engage only in certain types of occupations, to the definite exclusion, in the first place, of agriculture. An urbanite may own land and make a living from income derived from the land, but under no condition will he personally engage in agriculture. On the other hand, it is not an indispensable prerequisite for the maintenance of an urban status to reside in a town or city. A townsman may move to a village, spend decades there, acquire property, conduct his business, raise his children there, contribute to the welfare of the village, and even participate in its social life, yet he will still remain regarded as a townsman both by the villagers and by himself, a man distinct from the villagers (fellahin) and, in a certain sense, an outsider.

In Middle Eastern society one of the surest manifestations of status differences is the marriage barrier. Consequently, there has always been a strong tendency for the children of townsmen and of villagers not to intermarry, even though they may be next-door neighbors, play together every day, and grow up together. Only recently, with the general changes in traditional mores, are these restrictions somewhat relaxed. Another characteristic feature distinguishing the townsman from the villager even after a lifetime spent in a village, is that when the townsman retires from active life, he moves back to the town rather than live out his last years in the village.

The fellah, although secretly he may be envious of urban life, dislikes certain qualities that he believes characterize the townsman. He regards the urbanite as soft, pampered, and dissipated. Conversely, the latter despises the fellah and regards him as ignorant, backward, primitive, and uncouth.

Among the traits that have traditionally differentiated the townsman from the fellah, in addition to occupation, are his clothes, his food, his house, and his social life. The townsman may or may not wear European clothes; the fellah, never. Once he does so, he has ceased, strictly speaking, to be a fellah. (This statement does not apply to some minority groups such as the Circassians who do wear European clothes, and have their own special village and social organization.) The difference in dress is even more pronounced among the women. Fellah women, as has been pointed out, do not wear the veil; whereas many urban Muslim women traditionally do. The *fellāḥa* (peasant woman) wears a simple black garment of durable cotton material, in some areas with an embroidered front. Urban women wear a conglomeration of European clothes, and the Muslim among them, when leaving the house, were usually covered by a black overdress.

The fellah's food is generally very simple. It consists mostly of bread, ground wheat (burghul), lentils, olives and olive oil (depending on the region), some rice, sour milk (leben), some butter, and rarely meat. Very few vegetables are eaten with the exception of onions. Milk is used generally for babies only, although a pudding is made of it sometimes. Goat meat is generally preferred to mutton.

A townsman's food is much more varied and more luxurious. Vegetables and fruits are fairly extensively used. Mutton is preferred to goat meat, but beef is also consumed. Some of the well-known Middle Eastern dishes, such as stuffed grape leaves, stuffed chicken, stuffed squash, kibbeh, various broiled meats, ḥummuṣ, etc., are strictly urban foods seldom indulged in by the fellah. While pastries are fairly common among the townsmen, the fellahin seldom have them.

Traditionally, the house of the fellah is a one-room structure that shelters his family and sometimes his animals. It is generally devoid of even the simplest amenities. The urban house is a stone structure of two or more rooms constructed, until recently, with the seclusion of women in mind. It may be surrounded by a high-walled courtyard. Today, it may have running water, electricity, and a kitchen and bathroom inside the house.

As far as social life is concerned, contact between men and women is less restricted among the villagers than among the townspeople. Urban women until fairly recently were completely secluded, restricted to taking care of the home and the children. Village women, in addition to doing their household chores, work side by side with their menfolk in the fields; they are freer, and have a limited amount of social intercourse with men.

The relative inactivity of townswomen often results in a tendency to become fat and flabby. The village woman, on the other hand, is active, works hard, and walks gracefully, being able to carry a heavy water jar on her head without holding it.

The ageing process in village women is often accompanied by loss of weight.

The differences in style of living between the fellah and the townsman amount to almost a class difference. The lines, however, are not rigid, and the fellah can and frequently does pass into the urban group. Furthermore, education, village to town migration, and Westernization are closing the gap at an increasing rate.

Social Organization

With regard to social organization, a distinction has to be made between old and new towns respectively, between the indigenous established population of a town and the newcomers. Little can be said here about the social organization of the newly settled groups or elements: these, to some extent and for a certain length of time, tend to retain the social organization that they brought along from their home locality. In many cases, however, under the impact of the changed conditions, their social organization, and even their family organization, disintegrate to the extent that they appear as an amorphous population aggregate.

The old sections of the towns are characterized by a tendency toward a mosaiclike clustering of population elements. The tangible manifestation of this age-old tendency is the quarter. The most important basis of the formation of these quarters may be the *ḥamūla* (lineage or clan), or else the religious or ethnic group. Thus the typical east-Mediterranean town has a Christian (for example, Greek Orthodox) quarter, an Armenian quarter, a Jewish quarter, a Kurdish quarter, etc., and, of course, several Muslim quarters inhabited by Sunni Muslim Arabs who form the majority of the population.[4]

This structure of the Middle Eastern town is an inevitable outcome of a number of factors characteristic of society. Among these can be mentioned the religious-community basis of social organization, recognized and stabilized by the Turkish millet system and the great coherence of minority groups living in the midst of an unsympathetic majority, feeling secure only among themselves and suspicious of every outgroup.

The result of this quarter system in traditional circumstances has been to confine social contact within each town largely to the inhabitants of one and the same quarter. This in turn greatly facilitated the preservation of the social identity of the ethnic or religious group as a separate minority. In recent decades considerable changes have begun to manifest themselves in this respect. With the penetration of Westernization, modernization, and industrialization, the separateness and socioeconomic self-reliance of the quarters is gradually giving way to a greater and greater interdependence of the various sections and their inhabitants.

While the minorities thus are being brought closer to the dominant majority of the town they inhabit, one must not lose sight of the fact that, compared with the percentage of the minorities in the country as a whole, they constitute a much higher proportion among the urban population. Statistical data are not available, but the concentration of minorities in the towns is apparent to every visitor. In most cases, moreover, the urban minority groups surpass the Muslim Arab or Muslim Persian or Muslim Turkish majority in economic standing, literacy, skills, professional accomplishments, etc. Occasionally the minorities engage in occupations not practiced by the Muslim majority, and conversely, there are occupations engaged in only by the Muslims but not by members of the minority groups. In Damascus, for example, only Christians are engaged in meat-drying and the manufacture of alcoholic beverages.[5]

Up to the end of the First World War the Middle Eastern towns were characterized by a two-class system. A small number of rich people on the one hand and a large number of artisans, small shopkeepers, workers (including many agriculturists who lived in the smaller towns) on the other—this was the prevalent social structure of the towns. The life of the first or upper class was a life of opulence, ease, and luxury, while the second or working class exerted itself laboring many hours a day, seven days a week, hardly earning enough to make the barest living on the most meager subsistence level.

In spite of this great inequality in standard of living between the few rich and the many poor, and in spite of the spatial proximity of the two groups, there was a certain balance between the two and an acquiescence manifested by the poor with regard to their own position. Two factors were mainly responsible for the existence of this attitude among the working classes: first, tradition and religious influence; all situations in which a person finds himself are predestined by Allah, and it is the duty of man to submit himself to the will of God. Only God knows what is best for man, and by submitting to His will in this world man acquires merits that will be rewarded by Him in the Beyond. The second factor was the informal, almost egalitarian character of all contacts between people of different social classes. The forms of relationship between superior and inferior (such as between employer and employee, master and servant, ruler and subject, etc.) were patterned after those of father and son in the traditional Middle Eastern patriarchal family. The equation of all superior statuses with the paternal status and of all inferior statuses with the filial status made it easier for people in inferior positions to subordinate themselves to those in superior positions; the situation presented itself merely as an extension of the family situation in which the individual developed and in which his personality received its first and most decisive molding influences.

Many of these attitudes still persist to this day, although, of course, with the emergence of large cities interpersonal contact between the upper and the working classes tends to shift more and more from the personal to the impersonal level. Wealth and leadership still show a high correlation: ownership of landed property, of commercial, industrial, and financial enterprise on the one hand, and political, social, and cultural leadership on the other are still frequently concentrated in the hands of single individuals or of members of one family. The power and influence of the great families, however, have been severely challenged and are on the decline.

As a result of incipient industrialization in the Middle Eastern towns the urban working class is undergoing a considerable transformation not only with regard to the objective conditions and circumstances in which it performs its tasks, but also with reference to its attitudes toward the employer-owner class. The paternal-filial relationship between these two classes is rapidly becoming a thing of the past, to be replaced by an impersonal relationship in which the regulative influence of laws and rules becomes more and more necessary. The improvement of the working conditions and the impersonalization of the employer-employee relationship are probably the two most important changes that characterize the transformation of the Middle Eastern working class.

The middle class is the most recent accretion to the Middle Eastern urban class structure. It is still relatively small in numbers, although not insignificant in weight. The emergence of a middle class is a direct outcome of Westernization, in the sense that most individuals who belong to this class and are conscious of it are engaged in occupations that emerged as a result of Westernization. Other persons or families who on the basis of their economic level would have to be counted with the middle class (such as merchants, house owners, workshop owners, lower officials of the traditional type, etc.), are actually people not identified with the middle class but aspiring to rise into the ranks of the upper class. The true or new middle class therefore comprises in the main members of the professions (doctors, lawyers, teachers, social workers, writers, journalists, etc.). In this connection it must be remembered that much of the traditional urban upper-class attitude of disdain toward manual labor still survives even in the modern town, and that consequently there is a hesitancy in engaging in occupations such as mechanics or engineering. There are fewer persons engaged in these specialties than needed by the country and those who are engaged in them are counted by public opinion as members of the working class rather than of the middle class.

An interesting question of more than theoretical significance is, from where are the members of this new urban middle class recruited? A satisfactory reply to this question would have to be based on statistical studies concerning the occupations of the fathers of those individuals who today form this new class. In the absence of such studies all one can do is make a cautious surmise as follows: seemingly the members of the new middle class come from three main sources: the rural areas, from relatively well-to-do fellah families who have the means to educate their sons, enabling the more ambitious and more talented to continue in high school in the town and ultimately to become professional workers; the urban working class, as a result of a similar process; the urban upper class, most of whose scions have the opportunity for high school education that leads some of them into the professions. According to the prevailing social values, however, these professional individuals who belong to the "great" families are counted as members of the upper class.

Culture Change

Innovations and resultant cultural changes emanate as a rule from the urban centers toward the peripheries. In the cultural exchange between a country and the world at large, it is the centrally located urban aggregates that first receive the impact of new cultural traits introduced from abroad in the technological, organizational, or ideational fields. The rural sector receives these changes in a secondhand form, as it were, after their adaptation by the city to the requirements of the urban variety of the local culture.

While the above holds good in a general way for the world at large, it is doubly true in the Middle Eastern culture continent. In world areas contiguous to the Middle East the rural sector has played a relatively larger role in the cultural interchange between town and country than in the Middle East itself. In the Middle East, even in most ancient times, the urban centers were practically the sole carriers and advancers of culture. Even in our present day the Middle Eastern village is a more or less passive recipient of cultural changes, improvements, and modernizations, all of which radiate from the town.

With the possible exception of Ottoman soldiers in Turkey's imperial days and of a few isolated instances of recruitment of rural labor for modern industrial work (as in the case of Aramco), only the town population of Middle Eastern countries has had the opportunity for firsthand acquaintance with Western culture, or at least with some of its more conspicuous traits. Within the town itself, more than a fleeting and superficial familiarity with what the West has to offer is limited to the members of the upper and middle classes.

Western culture penetrates the Middle Eastern town in a great many ways: through the offices, business and industrial premises, educational and other institutions, and the homes of the upper and middle classes. Members of these classes therefore function as the sieve through which must pass all Western influence before reaching the working classes in the towns and the people in the rural areas.

Since foreign influence, in most cases Western, reaches the town first, and only later emanates from it to the rural areas, there is as a rule a considerable time lag between a stage reached in the process of culture change in the town and the corresponding stage in the rural areas. There is, moreover, also a definite differential in intensity: in the town, and especially in the upper and middle classes of its population, culture change reaches a peak not found in rural areas. Furthermore, corresponding to the heterogeneous social and cultural structuring of the town (in contrast to the much more homogeneous village), the degree and extent of culture change show a much greater diversity; in other words, in the town the different sectors and classes of the population manifest a wide difference with regard to culture change, ranging from the almost completely Westernized element on the one hand to sectors very little touched by Westernization on the other.

One more factor must be mentioned: Since the town is the locus of the almost exclusive concentration of Middle Eastern intellectual life, it is only in the town that we expect to find, and actually do find, a variety of consciously formulated attitudes toward specific and concrete manifestations of culture change, toward the total trend of Westernization as a whole, and toward traditional Middle Eastern culture. The average villager is more inclined to follow the lead of those whom he respects and holds in authority. Therefore, the village aggregate as a rule will be found to be characterized by one typical attitude, or at the utmost by a very narrow range of attitudes, toward the problems of culture change. In the town, on the other hand, the heterogeneity of the consciously propounded and advocated attitudes may become a dividing factor and the basis for headlong clashes.

Another problem has now to be touched upon, albeit briefly.

It has repeatedly been observed that culture change, that is, the adoption of Western culture traits, is inevitably accompanied by a rejection or disappearance of traditional Middle Eastern culture traits. In some cases we understand *a priori* that this must be so. If somebody desires to have his house furnished in the Western manner, he can carry out his decision only after he has discarded the old furniture to make place for the new. But here the question arises: why must one make the complete switch to Western furniture? Instead, why does one not introduce only some pieces of Western furnishing, primarily those of undoubted utility, while at the same time retaining some pieces of the traditional Middle Eastern furnishings, primarily those of undoubted beauty, thus accomplishing in the house a combination of the good and desirable features of this facet of both cultures? This simple example conveys some idea as to the problems of culture change in such varied fields as architecture, clothing, food consumption and cuisine, family life, social organization, manners and morals, aesthetics, religious outlook, and *Weltanschauung*.

The extent to which Western influence has changed the life of the upper and middle classes in the Muslim towns, and especially in the big cities, can best be gauged by comparing the present-day life of these social groups in a large urban center such as Cairo with the detailed and admirable account given of the same city by Edward William Lane some three generations ago.[6] Living in Cairo in the twenties and thirties of the past century, Lane felt, and with a masterly pen conveyed the feeling to his readers, that he was moving in a world essentially different from his own English background both in basic mentality and the minutest manifestations. Cairo of today—or at least large sections of it—is much more similar culturally to London than Lane would ever have dreamt was possible.

This cultural change in the town itself affects directly the town-country relationship. Even in traditional circumstances, the Middle Eastern town always attracted the country population and its growth was partly contingent upon a slow but steady village-to-town migration. This influx has become immensely augmented as a result of the Westernization of the town itself with its concomitant industrialization and rapidly increasing employment opportunities. Although the natural increase of the Middle Eastern town population is smaller than that of the villagers, the village-to-town movement results in a proportionately much greater increase of the urban than of the rural sectors. A country-wide result, therefore, of the technologic aspect of culture change in the towns is a definite gradual shift from the traditional Middle Eastern pattern of rural-urban population distribution toward the Western pattern with its typical half-and-half division between rural and urban population.

The accelerated processes of culture change that the Middle Eastern town undergoes today confront it with a large number of taxing problems. Leaving aside for the moment the administrative, educational, medical, sanitational, economic and technological aspects of these problems, I wish briefly to dwell only on that aspect that touches upon social psychology in its relation to the changing cultural background.

The over-all effect of the cultural innovations introduced from the West into the towns of the Middle East is one of a general rise in the urban standard of living. The almost proverbial scourges of the Middle East: disease, poverty, and ignorance are slowly being forced to loosen their deadly grip. But these highly desirable developments are all too often accompanied by evils that all but cancel out their intrinsic value. Freya Stark, one of the few Westerners who has acquired true insight into the Arab psyche, has stated: "Discontent with their standards is the first step in the degradation of the East. Surrounded by our mechanical glamour, the virtues wrung out of the hardness of their lives easily come to appear poor and useless in their eyes; their spirit loses its dignity in this world, its belief in the next."[7]

It must be assumed that there exists a causal connection between the penetration of Westernization, and especially of Western technology, on the one hand, and the deterioration of the satisfactions derived from traditional culture on the other. This is borne out by a number of disquieting social phenomena, including the lure of Communism for certain elements. The why and the how of these undesirable and potentially dangerous concomitants of Westernization have not yet been satisfactorily studied and understood. Nor have the processes of Westernization in the

Muslim town in general been sufficiently investigated. To mention only a few of the problems falling under this general heading: What are the processes of adjustment of Middle Eastern villagers to urban life? What are the cultural effects of industrialization on the working classes in the Middle East? What is the correlation between the adoption of Western culture traits and rejection or disappearance of traditional Middle Eastern culture traits? The great practical significance of research into these and similar problems for the cultural future of the Middle East needs no elaboration.

XI. *Religion in Middle Eastern, Far Eastern and Western Culture*[1]

In this chapter an attempt will be made to examine the role of religion in the three cultural archetypes of the Middle East, the Far East and the modern West. Geographically, the Middle East will be taken as delimited in Chapter One;[2] the Far East as composed of the Indian subcontinent, Southeast Asia, China, and Japan; and the modern West as including all the countries in which Western civilization has reached its typical development, notably Western Europe and America north of the Rio Grande.

In trying to outline within the confines of a brief chapter the differential roles religion plays in the cultures of these three major world areas, generalization and disregard of detail will be inevitable. Only an attempt at a rough and over-all preliminary typology can be essayed to the neglect of extramodal variants. Nor will particular doctrines and practices be emphasized. Whether divinity is conceived in polytheistic, trinitarian, dualistic, or unitarian terms would appear irrelevant in relation to such a more basic question as: Is the religion centered around a personal deity or not? Similarly, rules of religious ritual must seem unimportant when interest is focused primarily on the degree of influence religious ritual as a whole exerts upon everyday life.

The role religion plays and the position it holds in a culture can be discerned by examining various aspects of religion in their relationship to the total context of culture.

In the first place, religion functions as a normative force regulating customary behavior, inasmuch as it has both positive and negative commandments with which the individual is expected to comply. The extent to which religious rules and teachings influence human activities and modes of thought varies from one culture to another. *The normative function* of religion can therefore be recognized as one of the variables in the relationship of religion and culture.

Another aspect of the relationship between religion and culture is reflected in *the psychological effect* of religion on emotional life. The quality as well as the intensity of this psychological effect of religion can vary from culture to culture and thus supply us with a second variable.

A third variable can be seen in the character of the general orientation of the teachings of religion concerning supernatural beings, forces, or things. As a rule religions deal to some extent with the supernatural and possess certain theologies and metaphysics. An examination of the general character of the religious teachings concerning *the supernatural component* yields the third variable.

Each religion also has a definite outlook on its own value in relation to that of other religions. Its relationship to other religions may range from complete toleration to the complete lack of it, with a corresponding range of self-evaluation. This variable, best called *religiocentrism* (on the analogy of ethnocentrism), can serve as an additional avenue of approach to the study of our subject.

Lastly, religions channel human ambitions towards different goals, and especially in adversity and suffering hold out to man comforts of varying types. This *teleologic or purposive orientation* of religion will serve then as the fifth and last variable in examining the role of religion in Middle Eastern, Far Eastern, and modern Western cultures.

The Normative Function

In a study dealing with the general cultural characteristics of the Middle East, the religious component of Middle Eastern culture has been characterized as permeating the totality of life and as holding supreme sway over performance, thinking, and feeling: in brief, over life as a whole. Religion is the fundamental motivating force in most phases and aspects of culture, and is in evidence in practically every act and moment of existence. The observance of the traditional forms and rites, whether of the "official" or of the popular kind, is an integral part of everyday life.

A close connection exists between religion and other aspects of culture in the Middle East. Art in its entire scope is closely circumscribed by religion, and all the arts serve primarily religious purposes.

All custom and tradition are basically religious; for whatever is old and customary and traditional is hallowed by religion. Religious practice itself is mainly tradition and custom, so that practically every act and every activity is either in conformity with or contrary to religion.[3] These observations hold equally good for Islam, which is the religion of about 90 per cent of the population of the Middle East, for the Eastern Christian churches, and for Judaism in its Middle Eastern form. In brief, religion in the Middle East is the main normative force.

In these traits Middle Eastern religion closely approximates Far Eastern religions.

Hinduism, the closest major eastern neighbor of Islam, "deals directly with the Hindu's total life, including morals, economics, politics, and even music, medicine, military science, architecture, phonetics, grammar, astronomy and ceremonial. Hindus may include all these in what they call religion."[4] "Correct caste behavior is enforced largely by the weight of religious sanction. . . . Religion enters into all phases of Hindu life. Washing oneself in the morning, preparing and eating meals, sowing the fields take on sacramental quality when performed with the appropriate ritual. Religious merit is acquired as much by simple adherence to one's caste conventions and family obligations as by any special act of worship. . . . The cultural life of the village is almost completely bound up with religious observances and religious holidays. . . . Hinduism and Islam . . . provide the sanction which gives each individual his place in society, his code of social relations, and his guide to personal behavior. . . ."[5]

Similarly Buddhism, the dominant religion of southeast Asia, Ceylon, and Tibet, which is highly influential also in India, China, Korea and Japan, is "a pervasive influence shaping men's attitudes towards life and their ultimate aspirations and hopes far more than appears on the surface of things." The Buddhist teachings extend into such fields as the relationship of parents and children, teachers and disciples, husbands and wives, friend and friend, masters and servants, laymen and monks, and include such details as for example the recreations and luxuries a master should provide for his servant.[6]

In China in general, "religion and conduct belong together. . . . Religion in China is connected with politics. It expresses the emotional and esthetic aspects of life while conduct and politics express the active aspects."[7]

Taoism, the Chinese philosophical religion, contains, in addition to its mystical element, a set of political principles, a philsosophy of government, a number of economic principles and moral precepts, and gave rise to a large number of societies or brotherhoods that were a powerful ethical force elevating the moral tone of the community, ministering to the wounded, the refugees, and the needy, and often robbing the rich to help the poor.[8]

Confucianism, several centuries older in China than Taoism, has ethical teachings close to those of Buddhism. Its relationship to the arts can be gauged from the following saying contained in the Confucianist Book of Rites: "Poetry is what gives the first stimulus to character; ceremonial is what gives it stability; music is what brings it to full development."[9] Confucian doctrines are replete with detailed rules (in the form of good advice or "wisdom") with regard to conduct, the attainment of happiness, and the ordering of life.[10] The "New Life Movement" established by Chiang Kai-Shek at Nanchang in 1934, which has a close kinship with Confucianism, advocates that "life should be artistic"; that "the people are to be trained to take a new attitude toward nature as revealed in modern science"; that "tidiness and truthfulness should be emulated" and the like.[11]

These few instances suffice to show that basically common features characterize the normative function of religion within the totality of culture in the Middle East and in the Far East. In both areas religion is a major factor, if not the major factor, in directing and regulating life.

Religion in the Western world differs from both Middle Eastern and Far Eastern religion insofar as since the onset of the industrial revolution it has been on the retreat. The dominating religion of the West, Christianity, although originally born in the same region that was the cradle of Judaism and Islam, the central part of the Middle East, and partaking of the same general characteristics that these two creeds have or had in common with the religions of the Far East, has profoundly changed its character since the emergence of modern Western civilization. The function of religion, as it can be observed today in the modern Western world, is restricted to a rather narrowly delimited field of its own. Its ritual and its practical precepts have little to do with the everyday pursuits of Western life, and its credos and tenets are equally divorced from the essentially secular goals and values of modern Western culture. Even in the lives of those religiously observant, an hour or two a week set aside for the satisfaction of the traditionally persisting religious needs are deemed sufficient.

Furthermore, while both in the Middle East and in the Far East the great majority of the people are religious, and with the exception of those regions where the impact of Westernization has considerably altered the situation, persons whose lives are not dominated by religion are few and exceptional, in the modern West (and especially in the highly urbanized areas) the majority of the population does no longer possess deep religious attachment but is religiously either lukewarm or indifferent.[12]

Religion in the Middle East and the Far East thus appears as the dominant normative force, while in the modern West it has largely ceased to be a significant normative factor.

The Psychological Effect

In the Middle East, religion is an asset the psychological value of which cannot be overestimated. It is a psychological factor of first-class magnitude, lending unfailing spiritual sustenance to all true believers, that is to the overwhelming majority of the population. The religious Middle Easterner appraises life with all its adversities and vicissitudes from a wider angle, from a long-range perspective as it were, in which sojourn on this earth with all its possible gains and losses appears as merely the lower and lesser half of the great totality of existence, the essentials and ultimates of which lie in the Beyond. Spiritual outlook thus moves along a higher plane, beyond the reaches of discomfort, pain, anguish, and privation. Hence that composure, that peace of mind even in the face of great adversity which in the Middle East ever and again gives rise to wonderment in the Western observer.[13]

Rebecca West noted this phenomenon as far west as among the Muslims of Bosnia. Comparing her Christian Bosnian guide with his Muslim neighbors, she observed: "The lad was worse off for being a Christian; he had not that air of being sustained in his poverty by secret spiritual funds that is so noticeable in the poverty-stricken Moslem."[14]

In the Middle East proper, no such distinction between Islam and other faiths is apparent with respect to what can be termed the spiritual sustaining power of religion. The different rites of Islam, the semi-Muslim sects (such as the Druzes, the Nusairis, etc.), the various Christian churches, and the Oriental Jewish communities all share this basic characteristic of being able to generate a psychological certainty of possessing the Truth, of following the Right Path, and of wielding the Perfect Key to the gates of the Great Beyond. Among them is the feeling that one does what is right because one observes the commandments of one's religion, and that one is inwardly protected from serious harm because God in whom one trusts keeps an eye on each individual and ultimately metes out just retribution. These convictions give the true believers of every faith, creed, and sect an extraordinary sense of security, an ability to preserve their calm and dignity and detachment, without depriving them of the ability to seek and enjoy whatever pleasures can be wrung from this world.

The same psychological effect of religion can be observed in the Far East.

In India, where as we have seen religion pervades all aspects of life, it constitutes, just as in the Middle East, a sustaining force of matchless effectiveness. Religion functions as a sort of protecting caul that envelopes the human on his way from birth to death, leaving him psychologically unscathed by the poverty, ill-health, misery, and suffering that are the inevitable concomitants of life for the great majority of Indians. No matter what his religious group, his total life is a religious life, and in its pursuit he attains security and self-confidence.

The "liberated living man" who has attained spiritual perfection is characterized in the *Yogavisistha* as follows: "Pleasures do not delight him; pains do not distress. There is no feeling of like or dislike produced in his mind even towards serious, violent, and continued states of pleasure or pain. . . . He rests unagitated in the Supreme Bliss. . . . He is full of mercy and magnanimity even when surrounded by enemies. . . ."[15]

Farther to the east, the same religious mentality characterizes the followers of Buddhism, Taoism, and Confucianism. Younghill Kang, describing his native Korean village, says: ". . . my family did not seem to mind their helpless poverty, since most of them were indulging in the mystical doctrine of Buddhism, or in the classics of Confucius, who always advocated that a man should not be ashamed of coarse food, humble clothing, and modest dwelling. . . . The sage said: "Living on coarse rice and water, with bent arm for pillow, mirth may yet be mine. . . ." My grandmother . . . was a true Oriental woman. The quietism of Buddha, the mysterious calm of Taoism, the ethical insight of Confucianism all helped to make her an unusually refined personality. . . ."[16]

Speaking of Asia in general, Kurt Singer remarks: "Oriental harmony . . . is a mood in which Oriental man accepts both peace and strife as he accepts the change from light to darkness, summer and autumn, life and death. . . ." Therefore, ". . . life in the Orient is happier and more harmonious than in the West. . . ."[17] Similarly, Northrop notes "the equanimity, the poise, the steady, sure peace of mind, and all-embracing calmness and joy of the Oriental. . . ."[18]

Compared with this gift bestowed by religion upon Middle Eastern and Far Eastern man, Western religion must indeed seem pallid and impotent. The Bosnian observation of Rebecca West can be generalized, for the impression that religion in the West has remained a sustaining force only in rare cases thrusts itself even upon the most casual observer. In a society in which religion is detached from the chief interests and pursuits of everyday life, in which the principle of separation of church and state is upheld, and where the desire to attain purely secular aims is the main incentive in human life, religion evidently must have lost any spiritual sustaining power it may have had in the past. Toynbee speaks of "the spiritual vacuum which has been hollowed in our Western hearts by the progressive decay of religious belief that has been going on for some two-and-a-half centuries."[19]

Minor undulations in the psychological influence of religion can, it is true, be observed. In times of stress and strain there is a certain religious resurgence. But these waves even when at their peak remain far below the high and steady level maintained by the powerful outpour of psychological sustenance emanating from religion in the Middle East and the Far East.

The Supernatural Component

The supernatural component of religion has to be dealt with on two levels: the doctrinary or official level and the popular level.

The official doctrines about the supernatural are contained, in all the three world areas examined here, in voluminous religious literatures the composition of which was effected in the course of several centuries, and the older layers of which have acquired a character of sanctity. The degree of conformity evinced by the actually maintained beliefs as to the supernatural depends as a rule on the extent of the individual's absorption of the traditional literature of his religion. On the popular level, that is among the great masses of the people, where the familiarity with the traditional literature is minimal, the conformity of the concept of the supernatural with that of the official doctrine is very slight.

Middle Eastern religions in their supernatural aspect occupy an intermediary position between the religions of the Far East and of the modern West, inasmuch as on the popular level their typological affinities definitely lie with the Far Eastern religions while on the official doctrinary level they and the Western religions belong to one group.

That the popular religious beliefs and practices of Judaism, Christianity, and Islam in the Middle East are practically identical did not escape the keen eye of Lane well over a hundred years ago. "It is a very remarkable trait," he wrote in the 1830's, "in the character of the people of Egypt and other countries of the East, that Muslims, Christians and Jews adopt each other's superstitions, while they abhor the leading doctrines of each other's faiths."[20] Likewise, a more general similarity can be observed, not in the concrete details, but in the over-all type of popular religious beliefs and practices of the Middle East as a whole on the one hand and of the Far East as a whole on the other.

Popular religious belief in both world areas can best be described as polytheodemonistic, with complementary practices carried out at innumerable shrines, temples, and sanctuaries. A large plurality of gods, godlings, heroes, demons, ancestors, and patron saints are believed in, sculpturally or symbolically represented, and served in a great variety of rites in Japan, China, Indonesia, Indo-china, and India. In China, ancestor worship added considerably to the number of the available deities, while in India to the hosts of gods and goddesses are added sacred animals, rivers, and the like. In the Middle East, the worship of holy or merely haunted spots marked by springs, trees, and stones, or of shrines supposed to be the tombs of saints, is the popular institutionalized and formalized expression of a polydemonistic belief in spirits, ghouls, afrits, jinns, and other demons whose numbers are legion and who constantly interfere with the lives of men. Formless powers and forces such as the much-sought-after *baraka* or holiness or the greatly feared evil eye round up the picture of popular Middle Eastern religion.

Little of this type of popular religiosity has survived in the modern West. To be sure, in countries or regions where old local folk cultures still linger on, as for instance amid the agricultural peasantry of Europe, the popular veneration and worship of saints as well as the belief in demons and spirits, in the evil eye, and other supernatural powers, are the truly forceful elements of religious life. The spiritual distance between this type of religion and that of the official exponents of the faith can be visualized if one thinks of the Christianity of an Italian fishing village in comparison with that of the Vatican. In the urban population of industrialized Western Europe or in America north of the Rio Grande, however, this type of popular religion is practically extinct or is on its way to becoming so, and the chief difference between the religion of the people and that of the official religious leadership is one of degree rather than one of kind. It is only the religious leadership whose life is mainly concerned with religion, while in the life of the simple people religion plays, as has been pointed out above, a negligible role. The average individual, even if he is a member of a church or a religious community, will know very little of the officially sanctioned religious doctrines of his faith; but he will as a rule not hold beliefs or practice religious rites contrary to those of his church (as this is the case in the Middle East). He will simply neglect out of ignorance or indifference the rites of his church, and will have little knowledge of and even less interest in the doctrines of his church concerning the supernatural.

While with regard to the popular side of the relationship to the supernatural in the three world areas the line of demarcation thus clearly runs between the West and the Middle East, the official doctrine concerning the supernatural shows a basic typological homogeneity in the West and the Middle East setting both apart from the religions of the Far East.

Far Eastern religions, with the exception of Japanese Shintoism which, however, need not concern us in this context, are basically *nontheistic* in their original unadulterated doctrines, while Middle Eastern and Western religions in the official formulation of their tenets are *theistic*, or more precisely *monotheistic*. Theism in religion, as defined by Northrop, "is the thesis that the divine is identified with an immortal, non-transistory factor in the nature of things, which is determinate in character. A theistic God is one whose character can be conveyed positively by a determinate thesis. His nature is describable in terms of specific attributes."[21]

Monotheism, therefore, is the doctrine of *one* theistic God whose nature is describable in terms of specific attributes. The belief in such a God, as characterized by his determinate attributes, is the basic creed of the theistic religions.

Students of Far Eastern religions (again with the exception of Shinto) are unanimous in describing them not merely as nontheistic but also as noncreedal. John Clark Archer has commented upon the noticeable absence from Hinduism of formalized creed and characterized it as "theologically non-creedal."[22] Of the six recognized Hindu religiophilosophical systems only one, the Vedanta, is concerned with the concept of the divine. According to the Vedanta doctrine, however, Brahman (God) is indefinable, since every predicate, even the most general and indefinite, implies a contrary, an opposite, and besides Brahman there is non-else; he is all-pervading, all-comprising. In Shankara's formulation of the Vedanta there seems to be no place left for "faith" as a positive experience,[23] or a positive belief in some eternal that is determinate in character.[24]

It is difficult to reduce to a common denominator the teachings of the numerous schools of thought of Buddhism in the several countries in which they developed. Reischauer states that "there are a good many of the better educated and liberal leaders [of Buddhism] who claim that the very essence of true Buddhism is not a fixed or unchanging doctrine but rather a certain attitude of mind, a spirit of free inquiry and passion for truth."[25] This noncreedal character of modern Buddhism is completely in keeping with the original noncreedal and nontheistic formulation of Buddha's teachings. As a Japanese authority on Buddhism put it, "Buddhism teaches that there is no personal creator or ruler of the world."[26]

Confucianism, although it enjoins the worship of Heaven and Earth, of Confucius himself, of imperial and other ancestors and heroes, has never attained a theistic quality, and does not concern itself with the supernatural. It recognizes the divine, but as the divine is not determinate, it cannot have a concept of it, only a name for it. Moreover, it can realize it in experience but not say what it is in terms of determinate qualities.[24] Taoism centers around "the physical concept of the way of the heavens in relation to earth, transfigured and deepened by the mystic trance. The Tao is universal but not transcendent.[27] It produces all and yet is not above all. It is not a person or an individual. It is the basic, cosmic energy which informs all."[28]

The numerous religious societies that spring up in China to meet critical situations, "have no creed but they have a ritual."[29]

Hinduism, Buddhism, Confucianism, and Taoism are thus in their uncorrupted form nontheistic and noncreedal, all of them holding that the divine is indeterminate and that no specific attributes can be ascribed to it. In contrast to them the religions of the Middle East and the West are both theistic and creedal.

The chief source of Muslim religious doctrine, the Koran, as well as later theological writings, is replete with divine appellatives and attributes the study of which developed into a formidable science at a relatively early date in the history of Islam. The determinate attributes of Allah are grouped under the seven headings of Life, Knowledge, Power, Will, Hearing, Seeing, and Speech,[30] in addition to which he is described as merciful, gracious, the guardian over all, the reviver, the deliverer, and other such terms totaling ninety-nine in number.

Similarly in Christian theology God is described as a supreme being whose attributes include, to mention only a few, infinite power, wisdom, goodness, who has an inscrutable will and holds sovereign dominion over the world.[31]

Much of both the Muslim and the Christian doctrines of God goes ultimately back to the Hebrew Bible in which God is described by a rich variety of moral excellencies, including power, wisdom, foresight, righteousness, love, mercy, and loving-kindness. Post-Biblical Jewish literature repeatedly contains lengthy enumerations of these and other divine attributes.

With regard to the supernatural aspect, Far Eastern religions are thus found to be polytheodemonistic on the popular level and nontheistic on the higher doctrinary level; Middle Eastern religions, polytheodemonistic on the popular level and monotheistic on the higher doctrinary level; Western religions, polytheodemonistic on the folk-culture level, indifferently monotheistic on the modern popular level, and exclusively monotheistic on the official religious level.

The Religiocentric Aspect

One of the significant characteristics of the Far Eastern nontheistic religions is the high degree of toleration they display toward other religions. This trait is usually accompanied by a merging or fusion of different religions. Religious jealousy or exclusiveness, the conviction that one's own religion is the only valid and true one and that all other faiths are necessarily erroneous, is rare and is frowned upon.

While Europe (and the West as a whole) is predominantly Christian, and the Middle East is equally predominantly Muslim, no such exclusive and homogeneous religious characteristic exists in the Far East. Religious pluralism is the rule, however narrowly one tries to define the geographic unit subjected to scrutiny. Members of the same family, or even single individuals, often belong to two or more religions simultaneously, or, in other cases, alternatingly. Not only is there no stigma attached (as there is in the West and the Middle East) to such religious changeovers; they are taken as manifestations of a commendably sincere quest for the Truth.

Seekers for truth are likened in an ancient Oriental parable to people setting out from different starting points to climb a high mountain. The peak is too steep for the climbers to aim directly upward, so each of them begins spiraling the slopes in different directions. When two of the climbers meet somewhere, both may be convinced that the other is on a false track since he is going in an opposite direction. But actually, of course, though following different paths, both and all aim toward the same truth symbolized by one and the same lofty summit.

Just as Far Eastern religions are noncreedal and nontheistic, they are also nonaggressive, tolerant, and nonproselytizing. They do not require of their adherents, as Western and Middle Eastern religions do, to believe that their own teachings are the embodiment of the only true and perfect faith and that all other religions are bogged down in ignorance and error. They freely borrow from one another, and incorporate even substantial teachings taken from different schools.

In India, "Hinduism . . . is as much Buddhist as it is Brahman. The Tantric doctrines . . . appear as much in the Buddhism of Tibet as they do in the Hinduism of India. Recently, Surendranath Dasgupta, the leader of the contemporary Indian philosophical and religious thought, has proposed an actual practical unification of Buddhism and Hinduism."[32]

As a modern Indian philosopher has put it, "Every seeker of truth and perfection is allowed in Hindu society to pursue his own method freely, and nobody is expected to interfere or meddle with it. . . . This tolerance of differences of opinion and creed within its own fold and even outside itself is an essential characteristic of Indian culture."[33]

The same open-minded receptiveness characterizes the Hindu approach to Western religions. As Max Weber already has pointed out, a Hindu could accept the most specifically Christian sectarian doctrines without ceasing to be a Hindu. In fact the extreme religious "tolerance" characteristic of Hinduism appeared to Weber to have reached such a level as to make him conclude that "Hinduism is something different from 'religion' in our sense of the word."[34]

In Indo-China, in Annam, Cochin China, and Tonkin, "a peculiar combination of Confucianism, Taoism and Buddhism prevails. . . ." The official religion of the Annamese empire included Confucianist, Buddhist, and Taoist elements all intermixed, yet it remained essentially a combination of magic, animism, and ancestor worship.[35]

Passing on to China, we again find that "religion in China does not follow the pattern of interreligious exclusiveness of the West. . . . The temples are dedicated to a variety of gods. . . . There is one temple in this region which houses Confucius, Lao-tze (Founder of Taoism), and Buddha. This mixture is seen everywhere in China. . . .[36] Individual Chinese or Korean families are often composed of Confucians, Taoists, and Buddhists . . . and even single individuals accept all three religions at once."[37]

Some of the numerous religious societies the emergence of which in times of crisis is characteristic of China "placed above their old gods the God of all religions. Christianity, Islam, Buddhism, Confucianism and Taoism were viewed as ways of salvation under the direction of the God of all Religions."[38]

The same is reported of Japan. "Japanese . . . rarely accept one religious sect to the exclusion of others; almost everyone considers himself at once a Buddhist, a Shintoist, and a Confucian. Individuals worship any deity regardless of cult affiliation. . . ."[39] Or, as observed by another student of Far Eastern religions: ". . . in countries like China and Japan many of the adherents of Buddhism at the same time give allegience to the original national faiths. . . ."[40]

All this sounds as alien to anyone brought up in one of the three monotheistic religions that originated in the Middle East as the monotheistic religious exclusiveness and aggressiveness appears "narrow, intolerant and provincial"[41] to Far Easterners reared in one or more of their nontheistic religions. As Krishnalal Shridharani wrote, "It is forgivable to insist on *one* God, but to insist upon *The* Prophet and *The* Law is intellectually wrong. The assertion of Louis XIV that 'I am The State' is quite innocent compared to anyone's assertion that 'I am The Law.' . . . This exclusiveness is antispiritual inasmuch as it is overweening in the light of the limitations of human perception."[42]

Western observers as well noted the "enormity of intolerance and persecution [which] has shown its hideous countenance, almost without fail, whenever and wherever a higher religion has been preached,"[43] such as Biblical Judaism and its daughter religions, Christianity and Islam. In Christian Europe, religious conformity was a matter upon which the local secular power felt called upon to rule, if necessary by armed force. "In Central Europe . . . the secular princes did successfully use their power to force down the throats of their subjects whichever of the competing varieties of Western Christianity the local potentate happened to favour."[44]

Speaking of the theistic religions of the Middle East and the West, Northrop observes: "All the theistic religions are aggressive, all except recent Judaism are dominated by a missionary zeal, and all tend to regard religious views other than their own as heathen, erroneous, or inferior. Each tends to have a provincial self-righteousness which assumes that its doctrine is completely perfect, and consequently that its adherents are divinely commissioned and by duty bound to replace all other religions with 'the one perfect religion.' "[45]

The basically different self-evaluation of theistic religions in relation to other religions from that of nontheistic religions explains the significant difference in geographic distribution between the two types of religions. Since theistic religions are by their very nature doctrinary, creedal, aggressive, intolerant, and proselytizing, each one of them as occasion arose tended to establish itself as the only religion in the territory or region in which it won for itself a majority position or in which it attained the physical ability of doing so. Adherents of other religions were either expelled, or forcibly converted, or, in exceptional cases, allowed to remain as "tolerated" and "protected" peoples, in residentially and socially segregated, despised and disliked groups. As a result of this, Europe and America became compactly Christian continents, all the natives of the former (with the exception of a small Muslim island in the Balkans) and practically all the latter having been converted to one or another variety of Christianity. The fate of the Jews in Europe, as a group stubbornly adhering to an alien religion, at times persecuted and at times tolerated, is too well known to need more than passing mention.

To the south and the east of Christian Europe, Islam established itself in a similarly compact and definite block. The Islamization of the entire Middle East from Morocco and Río de Oro in the west to Turkestan, Afghanistan, and what is today Pakistan in the east was a rapid process accomplished in a phenomenally short time. In close analogy to the Christian *Ecclesia militans*, the spread of Islam by force was made a principle: *Dīn Muḥammad bissayf*—the religion of Mohammed with the sword. The result was a geographic region as exclusively Muslim as Europe became Christian. Where the two met, they fought, until one of them was completely defeated and had to retreat, as best exemplified by medieval Spain, or the flow and ebb of Turkish power in Hungary in the sixteenth to eighteenth centuries. After the Muslim retreat from those European countries no trace was allowed to remain of its long rule: no Muslim community or group was left behind; the population as a whole reverted to Christianity or was replaced by Christians. In the south and the east, on the other hand, Islam was more successful than Christianity in its proselytizing activities. In the twentieth century its boundaries are still pushing southward across the Sudan belt into Negro Africa, and are being strengthened in Indonesia and other parts of the Far East. What is happening to Islam's Central Asian outpost is little known; the Iron Curtain guards its secrets well.

While the traditional adherent of Judaism, Christianity, and Islam remains to this day convinced that only his religion or, more narrowly, only his own particular sect is the sole holder of the truth, including the only true ritual, the general attitude towards religious and sectarian differences, at least as far as

Christianity is concerned, underwent a decisive change since the second half of the seventeenth century. "In this half century the Catholic and Protestant factions . . . seem to have become aware that they no longer cared sufficiently for the theological issues at stake to relish making any further sacrifices for their sake. They repudiated the traditional virtue of "enthusiasm" (which by derivation means being filled with the spirit of God) and henceforth regarded it as a vice."[46]

This toleration of religions in Christian Europe, however, was based on "disillusionment, apprehension and cynicism. It was not an arduous achievement of religious fervour but a facile by-product of its abatement."[47]

We thus recognize that in the Far East religious toleration is a result of the deep religiosity characteristic of its cultures, while in the West, and to some extent in the Middle East as well, religious tolerance emerged as a result of a general and successive liberation of the cultures from the grip of religion. In the Far East, the more religious a person is the more tolerant he is of other religions, the more ready he is to concede that other religions also have their values, their truths, and their "paths." In the Middle East and the West, tolerance of other religions stands as a rule in reverse ratio to the fervor with which an individual follows the precepts of his own religion.

The Teleologic Orientation

The last aspect of religion to be considered here is its teleological or purposive orientation, with respect to which it again is found that Middle Eastern religion has close affinities with Western religion, while both differ greatly from Far Eastern religions.

The ultimate aim of religion is to satisfy certain spiritual needs of which man is aware at varying frequencies, and to help him in the crises and other difficulties that he inevitably meets as he makes his way from cradle to grave. In the three world areas under scrutiny we find that this basic purpose is served either by supplying psychological satisfaction to this-worldly aspirations of man, or by giving his ambitions an other-worldly orientation, or by a combination of both.

Confucianism exemplifies the first of these three ways. Although in every other respect it belongs closely together with the other Far Eastern noncreedal and nontheistic religions, "it has almost no other-worldly content, confining itself to practical maxims on the sensible conduct of life in this world."[48] Confucianism offers its followers a satisfactory cosmology, and detailed ethical doctrines, concentrating especially on the duties and obligations of people standing in certain social or familial relationship to one another. A worship of Heaven and Earth, of imperial ancestors and heroes with appropriate and well ordered ritual rounds out the picture.[49] This is a religion eminently suited to human needs as channeled by Chinese culture: as long as things are more or less in good order. Chinese observers themselves noted, however, that when confronted with tragedy and death, their compatriots tend to become Buddhists[50] or Taoists. In funeral processions, for example, Confucianist families often employ a group of Taoist and/or Buddhist monks.[51] Moreover, it can be stated that Confucianism pure and undiluted is a relatively rare phenomenon; in most cases it is merely one of the threads that go into the texture of religious life in China.

With the exception of Confucianism (and Shintoism, which on account of its theistic content and aggressive character is not considered in this paper among the Far Eastern religions), Far Eastern religions typically satisfy human psychological needs by giving them an other-wordly orientation. This world is regarded as a vale of tears into which man is born against his will. The ultimate goal that man can obtain and that he therefore should try to achieve lies in the Beyond, in a remote state of peace that man can reach either directly upon his death, or, in accordance with most teachings, after a series of rebirths and reincarnations in various human or other forms.

This other-wordly orientation given to life by religion goes in the case of Hinduism hand in hand with a basically pessimistic attitude toward this world. According to Shankara, only the spiritual has reality, all else is sheer illusion, or *maya*. Life goes on by karmic repetition; deeds and rebirth are causally related. Man has to accept his lot, and "live at best within it in the distant hope that the round would eventually be broken and his spirit would escape to another, agreeable portion of the fixed universe, whence he would not come back again to birth."[52] Only if one is able to find the true self can one escape karma and yet remain in the world bringing spiritual equanimity into it.[24]

The same idea is further developed in Buddhism. Buddha is told to have said: "I have obtained emancipation by the destruction of desire. . . . I have obtained coolness (by extinction of passions) and have obtained *Nirvana*. . . ."[53] Human life is predominantly an existence of suffering. Conditions of individual existence are painful; whatever pleasures and satisfactions may exist in life are overshadowed by pain and sorrow. The best in life is fleeting and impermanent. This is the first of the "Four Noble Truths" of Buddha. The second is that the cause of human suffering is human desire and cravings. The third and the fourth truths state that man can conquer his craving thirst by following the "Noble Eightfold Path," which includes the renunciation of the life of pleasure, the nurturing of the spirit, moral conduct, peaceful occupations, the suppression of evil states of mind, strict self-discipline, a concentration of mind and meditation, until an understanding of the nature of the self is achieved, with a complete freedom from all passions and fetters binding one to this life. Thus prepared, the enlightened self can enter a state of peace, or *Nirvana*, and thus "gain release from 'rounds of existence' in this evil world." *Nirvana*, however, remains a distant hope. In the meantime, man's efforts should be directed toward attaining a more favorable rebirth into this world. This can be effected by following certain ideals of conduct, namely the "five precepts" forbidding the destruction of life, theft, unchastity, falsehoods, and strong drink.[54]

Also according to Taoist doctrine, the sensuous world is a mere appearance. "Long life was not in the tradition of Taoism. The ancient Taoists regarded the body as not worth preserving. . . ." Under the influence of Buddhism, also in Taoism a "moral relation was established between this life and the condition of the soul beyond this life by the theory of karma, the equivalence of deed and reward. This proved a great boon in easing the tensions of life. Poverty and wealth, sickness and health, happiness and misfortune were not only explained by this formula, but were made endurable."

The northern school of Taoism in modern China "emphasizes meditation, and metaphysical speculation, and practices breathing."[55]

For all these religions Kurt Singer's generalization holds good: "It is a basic tendency of the Asiatic mind to keep aloof from every thought that hinders him in his great movement of withdrawal from the world, an illusory veil to be cast off by him who is awakened, a tiny shore which must be left in order to reach the infinite expanses of the Great Void."[56]

No such other-worldliness, no such exclusive concentration on spiritual or meditational detachment characterizes the three theistic religions of Judaism, Christianity and Islam. These three Middle Eastern and Western religions emphasize more or less equally the material well-being of the individual in this world, and the spiritual well-being or salvation of his individual soul after the death of the body. They therefore represent a combination of this-worldly and other-worldly orientations. While spiritual and moral values are stressed, these are underlined or reinforced by concretely formulated and tangible promises of rewards in the future life for good conduct, or alternatively, punishments for rebelliousness and disobedience. The amount of stress put in Judaism, Christianity, and Islam, as well as in the different sects of the latter two, on the belief in Paradise or Heaven for the good and on Purgatory or Hell for the evil, varies; but common to all is the accent on divine justice tempered with mercy that measures out reward and punishment to each individual according to his deeds which after death are carefully weighed and evaluated. It is, therefore, in the well-conceived self-interest of every individual (inasmuch as he is a believer) to pay as much attention as he can to the salvation of his soul. This can be achieved by following the precepts of one's church or religion or sect with regard to one's duties toward fellow-men and toward the deity. The duties toward one's fellow-men are mainly deedal, that is, consist of do's and don't's, while the duties toward God are both creedal and deedal in varying combinations.

Simultaneously, however, both deed and creed aim at a second, and often more important, end: to assure and secure the material well-being of the individual and his society in this world. One must believe in the particular credos of one's religion or sect and fulfill the various do's and don't's in relation to both God and fellow-men in order to be blessed as a reward by God with all the material benefits that are valued in this life and are striven for also in other, more direct ways. This is expressed succinctly in the Christian supplication for the daily bread contained in the "Lord's Prayer" (Matthew 6 : 11). It is dwelt upon in greater detail in the Jewish "Shema" in which material blessings are made directly contingent upon the observation of God's commandments (Deut. 11 : 13–25), and in the "Eighteen Benedictions," the main portion of every Jewish service, in which God is asked, among other blessings, for forgiveness, redemption, health, good crops, the rebuilding of Jerusalem, the coming of the Messiah, etc. This prayer is repeated by observant Jews three times every weekday and four times on Saturdays and holidays.

The Koran, too, is explicit with regard to Allah's reward of those who pray to him:

O ye who have believed when proclamation is made for the prayer on the day of the assembly [Friday] endeavor to come to the remembrance of Allah, and leave off bargaining; that is better for you, if he have knowledge. Then when the prayer is finished scatter abroad in the land and seek the bounty of Allah, but call Allah frequently to mind; mayhap ye will prosper (Koran 62 : 9–10).

In the popular religion in the Middle East manifested in saint worship and the institution of the *Ziyāra* (visitation of shrines), the quest for material blessings is even more predominant.

These three theistic religions, therefore, are oriented toward two goals: to secure immediate material blessings in this world and to hold out the promise of the Beyond, the happy life after death.

With regard to teleologic orientation, religion in the Far East is other-worldly, while in the Middle East and in the West it is equally concerned with this world and with the Beyond. One of the factors that militate against religion retaining its influence in the modern West is the definite this-worldly orientation of modern Western culture in which religion with its promise of a life in the Beyond seems out of tune. But as far as religion is still alive or again comes alive in the Western world, it displays the same orientation toward the same two foci of well-being in this world and rewards in the other world that is the common heritage of all religions that originated in the ancient Middle East.

In summary, the function of religion within the total cultural context of each of the three world areas considered can be characterized as follows:

1. In the Far East and in the Middle East religion is the dominant normative force regulating behavior; in the West it has largely lost its normative function.

2. Psychologically, in the Far East and in the Middle East religion is a powerful sustaining influence; in the West it has also largely lost this function.

3. On the popular level of the supernatural aspect, in the Far East and in the Middle East religion is polytheodemonistic; in the West this character of religion is on the wane with the decline of folk cultures.

3a. On the higher doctrinary level of the supernatural aspect, in the Far East religion is nontheistic and noncreedal; in the Middle East and in the West it is both theistic and creedal.

4. Religion in the Far East is characterized by the absence of religiocentrism: there is a marked toleration of other religions and a mutual borrowing and influencing; in the Middle East and in the West there is a high degree of religiocentrism, with intolerance and scorn of other religions: each religion is exclusive and regards itself as the "one and only" true faith.

5. As to teleologic orientation, in the Far East religion has a distinctly other-worldly orientation often accompanied by a definitely negative attitude toward this world; in the Middle East and in the West religion is characterized by a dual orientation toward both this world and the other world.

The place of Middle Eastern religion in this scheme is intermediary. Religion is the dominant normative force in Middle Eastern culture as it is in the Far East. It has a powerful psychologic influence as it has in the Far East. On the popular level its supernatural component is polytheodemonistic as in the Far East. On the other hand, on the higher doctrinary level, it is theistic and creedal as is religion in the West. It displays a high degree of religiocentrism as does religion in the West. And it shares with the West a dual, this-worldly and other-worldly teleologic orientation.

XII. Social and Cultural Determinants of Middle Eastern Nationalism

Western and Middle Eastern Nationalism

THE STORY of the penetration of the Western-born idea of nationalism into the Middle East has attracted considerable attention on the part of European and American scholars. Following the pioneering study of Hans Kohn, *A History of Nationalism in the East*, originally published in German in 1928 and in English in 1929, the history of Middle Eastern nationalism has been studied from various angles. Its origins, going back to the Napoleonic occupation of Egypt in 1798, have been unraveled, and its place within the context of the general process of Westernization duly noted. Attention was given also to the way in which nationalism transformed communal and political life in the major and even minor states witin the area. Similarly, the historical sequence of nationalistic developments in the Middle East, from the first emergence of parliamentary governments in emulation of the West to their decline in certain countries and replacement by dictatorial rule, has been investigated.

On the other hand, certain important aspects of Middle Eastern nationalism have received lamentably scanty attention. The writer, for instance, knows of no exhaustive or detailed study of the specific traits that characterize Middle Eastern nationalism, nor of a probing into the question of which of these features can be found also in the Western world and which of them are specific to the Middle East or to some countries in it. When we come to the problem of the causes, the motivating factors that gave Middle Eastern nationalism its specific flavor, we find not only no answers but, in most cases, not even questions raised. The present chapter will attempt to deal with at least part of these issues. It will try to isolate some of the social and cultural determinants that went into the making of modern Middle Eastern nationalism and gave it its special character.

To begin with, it should be stated that even within the immediate geographic vicinity of its European birthplace, nationalism has manifested a wide range of variations in orientation, emphasis, and general character. It is, of course, possible to give a generally valid definition of nationalism, such as "a state or condition of mind characteristic of certain peoples with a homogeneous culture, living together in close association on a given territory, and sharing a belief in a distinctive existence and a common destiny."[1] However, to any such general definition one must unfailingly append, as was in fact done by the author of the one quoted, the caution that nationalism "varies all the way from the healthy patriotism of the Swiss nation to the fanatical intolerance of Nazi Germany."[2]

Nationalism is generally regarded as a "healthy patriotism" when the positive, affirmative elements predominate in it, and when it is coupled with democracy and liberalism. It is branded as "fanatical intolerance" when it appears in the company of exclusivism, racism, fascism, or any form of totalitarian dictatorship, and when its emphasis is largely negative, expressed in *anti*, rather than *pro*, policies, aims, and slogans, directed primarily against other peoples, ideas, and endeavors. In Europe, generally speaking, liberal nationalisms emerged in the nineteenth century; fascist or totalitarian nationalisms were the product of the twentieth century, following World War I. This observation leads directly to the formulation of the first problem that arises in a consideration of the characteristics of Middle Eastern nationalism.

The Middle East was reached by the nationalist tide well before the onset of its second period in Europe, that of fascist or totalitarian nationalisms. One would, therefore, have expected that, when emulating the Western example, the Middle Eastern peoples would develop their own brand of nationalism in keeping with the general trend of "healthy patriotism" of the period.

Yet this was not the case. Quite on the contrary, the Middle Eastern nationalist movements started out with a strong *anti*-emphasis. This is what happened with early Turkish nationalism, which had a clear-cut aim in opposing the rule of the Sultan but a much hazier idea as to what it was to strive for. As for the Arabs, Hazem Zaki Nuseibeh, a keen analyst of Arab nationalism, and himself an Arab, pointed out "how predominant the negative element was" in the early phases of their nationalism, which lasted roughly until the eve of World War I; "the impelling force," according to Nuseibeh, "was either fear of an advancing European imperialism and the inability of the state to withstand it, or distrust of the Turkish intentions and designs."[3]

Following the above observation, one could go on to isolating additional important specific characteristics of Middle Eastern nationalism until one felt that one had a more or less complete portrait of it, and then reviewing the factors in traditional Middle Eastern culture that would seem to explain these characteristics. Such a procedure, however, would be too cumbersome and complicated, since it would have to deal with two sets of extremely complex phenomena, and attempt to establish a correlation between them.

Let us, instead, switch our attention at this point to those aspects of traditional Middle Eastern culture and society that can be assumed to have had an influence on the development of the first trait of Middle Eastern nationalism discussed above. After having dealt, albeit briefly, with these aspects, we can go on to a discussion of the traditional determinants of a second, and then a third, special feature of modern Middle Eastern nationalism. In this manner we shall deal with only one trait at a time, a procedure that should prove both simpler and clearer. In sum we shall nevertheless arrive at an over-all view of Middle Eastern nationalism *in toto* with its manifold determinants anchored in traditional Middle Eastern society and culture.

Such a national trait as xenophobic dislike and distrust of foreigners must evidently be a resultant, among possible other factors, of those forces which in the past molded traditional ingroup-outgroup attitudes among the peoples of the area.

There are, in particular, two ruling institutions in traditional Middle Eastern culture that not only shaped the traditional ingroup-outgroup attitudes but, more than that, were of basic importance in the very process of group formation itself. Both are heavily value-laden, closely interrelated, and mutually support and reinforce each other. Both are, in fact, more than institutions; they are ideologies, powerful motivations, and ends in themselves. They are phenomena nonexistent in modern Western culture whose designation requires the coining of new terms: religionism and familism.

"Religionism" and Nationalism

Religionism can be defined as the domination by religion of life as a whole, on all levels, individual, familial, social, cultural, and even national and political.

To what extent politics were dominated by religion down to the last years of the Ottoman Empire can be shown by adducing as an example an event that took place as late as 1913. In that year a revolt broke out in Macedonia against the Sultan, who wanted to dispatch troops to suppress it. But this would have amounted to a war of Muslims against Muslims, which is forbidden by religion, and can be undertaken only if a special *fetwa*, religious decision, is issued by the Shaykh ul-Islam, the chief religious authority in the Empire. The Sultan, Abdul Hamid, could not obtain the *fetwa*, and thus was unable to order his troops to Macedonia. Once the impotence of the Sultan became thereby manifest, his ministers were able to pressure him into granting a constitution. This was the effective end of the Sultan's rule in Turkey.[4]

A concomitant of the religion-centered outlook is the conviction that only one's own religion, that is to say the religion of one's own family, tribe, or larger social aggregate is the right one, while other faiths are, with equal sincerity, regarded as inferior, mistaken, and wrong. As far as Islam is concerned, it teaches that Mohammed was the last and greatest of prophets, that the Koran is the ultimate revelation of God's will, and that not to accept Islam is a sinful shortsightedness, for which idolators have to be punished by death and the *ahl al-kitāb*, the monotheistic People of the Book, by subjugation and reduction to the quasi-vassal status of *dhimmis*.

For centuries Islam almost unfailingly helped the true believers to victory after victory over the infidels in the three continents of the old world. The march of history appeared to the Muslims to fall into a clear pattern: infidels were defeated by the Sword of Islam and converted to the true faith. Thereupon, having become Muslims, they in turn achieved victories over other infidels. In this way the *Dār al-Islām*, the pacified House of Islam, continued to expand, and the *Dār al-Ḥarb*, the House of War, to recede. These circumstances engendered in the Muslims a feeling of contempt for the unbelievers which, with the passage of generations, became an ingrained and organic part of Muslim religionism.

Of the many facets of the Muslim outlook on the infidels the one that most directly influenced the formation of the antiforeign component in Middle Eastern nationalism was their attitude to the *dhimmis*, the subject People of the Book. The Muslim, to put it succinctly, viewed the *dhimmi* dimly. The less able the Muslims became, from the seventeenth century on, to withstand the onslaught of the Christian world, the more unkind their attitude became to the *dhimmis* who continued to live in their midst. Since the traditional conviction that the infidel was inferior could no longer feed on new victories over him, it had to be maintained instead by a constant reassertion of Muslim superiority over the *dhimmis*. If this was the case among the Turks and the Persians who, in spite of the rising tide of Christian power, remained independent and masters of their own destiny, it had to be even more so among the Arabs who themselves had become the subjects of the Ottoman Turks and were treated by them as *ra'īya*, flocks, as human cattle, to be shepherded for the benefit of the conqueror, to be milked, fleeced, and allowed to live their own lives so long as they gave no trouble.[5] For these Arabs it was a psychological necessity for the maintenance of their self-esteem and for at least a partial fulfilment of the expectations of their traditional religionism to have, near at hand, another human group to look down upon, to pity, to distrust.

Religionism had yet another important effect on Middle Eastern nationalisms. In spite of certain superficial resemblances between the *Fuhrer*-centered nationalism in several Arab countries and the European Fascist-type nationalisms, there is one significant difference between the two: Fascism, Nazism, and Communism all felt constrained to turn against religion and to try to break or at least to weaken the hold of the church on the people. The new nationalist ideology, with its own brand of *ethos* and *mythos*, was supposed to supplant the Christian teachings and ethics. Not so Middle Eastern nationalism which, in spite of its alien origin and nonautochthonous nature, knew how to build on the old religious foundation of Middle Eastern culture, and to appear as the genuine offspring of the local, indigenous tradition.[6] In this manner the simple, average Middle Easterner was spared the dilemma into which the totalitarian nationalist movements forced the European Christian who had to choose between Catholicism and Fascism, between Lutheranism and Nazism, between Pravoslavism and Communism. Instead, the new nationalism sought to convince the Middle Easterner that the more enthusiastically he followed his particular national leader, the better a Muslim he would be; or, if he happened to be a Christian Arab, the better a Christian Arab he would be. Thus, under the quasi-charismatic leadership of a military *Führer*, Middle Eastern nationalism has become a new religious creed, a new stage in the development of the faith, imbued with all the attributes of a religiocentrism of which there is more today in the Middle East than in any Western, Westernized, or semi-Westernized world area.

Familism and Nationalism

Closely related to Middle Eastern religion is familism. Familism can be defined as the centrality of the family in social organization, its primacy in the loyalty scale, and its supremacy over individual life. All the six basic characteristics of the Middle Eastern family have a close correlation to familism: a family that is patriarchal, patrilineal, patrilocal, endogamous, polygynous, and extended must needs be central, primary, and supreme in both social and individual life.[7] Negative and in the larger sense disruptive correlates of this type of familism are interfamilial tension, competition, and enmity which, in the centuries of Arab and Muslim history, have repeatedly caused protracted and far-flung blood feuds, and have occasionally developed or, if you will, degenerated, into large-scale bloody internecine wars sapping the strength of the people in many a part of the Middle East.

One of the numerous proverbs that express with admirable succinctness basic features in the Arab self-stereotype reflects on both sides of the old Arab coin of familism. Variants of this proverb are current in the non-Arabic speaking areas of the Middle East as well, and it has more than once been quoted by Western writers as a Kurdish, Persian, or Afghan saying. It states: "I and my cousins against the world, I and my brothers against my cousins, I against my brothers." Translated into sociologese, this proverb verbalizes the existence of a clearly marked hierarchy of loyalties in which the closer kin group takes precedence over wider kin groups.

The principle of familism has been so strongly embedded in the Middle Eastern consciousness that social aggregates larger than the family have traditionally been conceived of as mere extensions of families. The actually functioning family has for uncounted generations consisted of the descendants in the male line of one common grandfather who occupied the position of family head. The tribe or the village in an un-Westernized Middle Eastern district is regarded by its members to this day as consisting of several such extended families related to one another and descended from one common ancestor. Villages located in one area or tribes wandering in one another's proximity are, again, considered to be the progeny of a more remote but still common ancestor.[8] This popular tendency has received the stamp of scholarly approval when learned medieval Arab genealogists, building upon popular traditions, set up a highly speculative but everywhere readily accepted genealogic scheme, tracing back all the Arabs to a single pair of forefathers and, through them, ultimately to one original ancestral progenitor.[9] We have only to think of the stories of the Book of Genesis to realize that this tendency has not been one peculiar to the Arabs, but had its prototype in the ancient Near East as well.[10]

Another important feature shared by the ancient Hebrews and the more recent peoples of the Middle East and having a direct bearing on the centrality of familism in the formation of *any* ingroup-outgroup dichotomy is the attribution of a kin-group character to groups of patently nonrelated individuals who happened to engage in one and the same occupation. In Biblical times all the harp and pipe players were regarded as the descendants of one single common ancestor, and so were the forgers of brass and iron and the tent-dwelling cattle owners (Gen. 4: 20–22). Josephus Flavius, in the first century A.D., using undoubtedly expressions based on popular views still current in his days, speaks of "the tribe of prophets." And Evliya Chelebi, the famous Turkish traveler, writing less than three centuries ago, reports of several of the numerous guilds into which the artisans, tradesmen, and professional people of Constantinople were organized in his day that they venerate certain historical or mythical individuals as the original progenitors of all the members of their particular guilds.[11]

The effects of this concept complex were significant and far-reaching with regard to Muslim state organization, to prenationalistic attitudes to the non-Muslim world, and, most recently, to the specific forms assumed by nationalism in the Arab and other Middle Eastern states.

The effect of familism on Muslim state organization was, as could be expected, that the state was from the very outset of its development considered a mere extension of the family, enlarged this time not tenfold to a hundredfold as in the case of a tribe or the village, but a thousandfold to ten thousandfold. The entire Muslim realm was, from its very inception, regarded as a familial grouping, gigantically enlarged but in its essence nevertheless a social body similar to the family. Therefore, the same loyalty scale that was the guiding principle in the familial and social organization and demanded diminishing loyalty with increase of group size was applied also to the state. Loyalty to the state could thus never approximate the level of intensity characterizing close in-group loyalties. The tenuous ties that thus existed between the subject tribes, villages, and urban aggregates on the one hand and the Caliph, the remote "father" enthroned in his faraway capital on the other, could never supersede the more immediate pull that direct loyalties to locally present "fathers" such as the actual family head, the tribal chieftain, the village headman, the landlord, etc., continued to exert. In fact, the limited imagination of the simple peasant, for instance, could not even conceive of a greater or higher power position than that of the highest local official with whom he had direct personal contact, such as the *mudir*, the district officer, in Egypt. The story is told of such a peasant that when for the first time in his life he had an opportunity to prostrate himself in front of the Khedive (viceroy), he pronounced a blessing over him, saying, "May Allah make you as powerful as our *Mudir*!"

The same family-patterned relationship between sovereign and subjects made it necessary for the Caliph and other rulers in the Muslim realm to rely in the first place on that group among their subjects on whose loyalty they could count in their capacity of immediate chieftain rather than as the Caliph, king, or overlord. Similar situations are known to have existed in other empires, outside the Middle Eastern culture continent, but they reached a comparable extent only when based on a similar intensity of familism. Be this as it may, the fact remains that the Caliph ruled through his kinsmen: his immediate and more remote relatives, his tribesmen, and last but not least, his slaves, who were indoctrinated to see in him their *pater familias*, and who, in turn, were regarded as family members. This was the method by which the Ottoman Turks were able for centuries to hold sway over a far-flung empire peopled by Arabs, Kurds, Greeks, Armenians, Copts, Berbers, Druzes, and dozens of other minority groups. The entire population of the Ottoman Empire was thus divided into two sectors: there were the ruled groups who constituted the vast majority, and then there was the ruling minority of the Ottoman Turks, organized and considered, by the ruled peoples as well as by themselves, as one family with the Caliph at its head.

Tyranny and despotism too appear in a different light when viewed against the background of a familistic society. What son dare question the commands and exactions of his father? It is not for him to weigh and consider but to obey and be judged. The duty of the son is to serve the father. The father in return protects the son. Without the father's protection the son is lost; he could never hold his own against inimical outsiders. Similarly, the duty of the subjects was to serve the Caliph by paying taxes, by indented labor, by conscription. In exchange, they received protection against enemies who otherwise could have destroyed them.

Bribery, the pattern of both giving and accepting gratuities either for services rendered by a superior to an inferior or simply for receiving from a superior what is one's due by tradition-sanctioned custom, can also be explained as an extension of the familial relationship between the mighty father and the dependent sons. You want something from your father? The way to getting it is to perform a special service for him, to become a favorite, for the occasion at least. This is how Isaac's two sons competed for the blessing of their blind old father, and this is how the simple subject of a ruler attempts to gain his ear. In the family situation, after all, there is rarely a clear-cut right or wrong, independently of the will of the father. Whatever the competing sons feel and opine, the father's decision is the final factor that makes the point of view of one right while rendering the argument of the other wrong. And both sons, the one toward whose present the father did not turn as well as his more fortunate brother, know that soon a conflict may arise between them and an outsider, and in that case they will have the unquestioning support of the father.

This is the family situation in which are rooted all types of interaction between subject and ruler in the traditional House of Islam.

Group Attitudes and Nationalism

Some general features of the prenationalistic attitudes toward the non-Muslim world can also be considered as extensions of traditional attitudes that developed in and around Middle Eastern familism. In a familistic situation the attitude of a given group, whether an actual extended family or a larger aggregate molded after its pattern, to an equivalent out-group can be twofold. As long as the out-group is independent of the in-group, the two are rivals, competitors, actual or at least potential enemies. In the interests of self-preservation, the in-group feels impelled to attack the out-group, to reduce its strength, and to make it subservient to itself. Once this is achieved, a new attitude tends to replace the first: that of benevolent toleration, mixed with condescension or even contempt.

The best example of the working of this interaction on a level broader than that of the extended family can be found among the tribes of the Syrian Desert. The more powerful among these tribes were able to reduce the weaker tribes to a status of vassaldom and to exact the payment of *khuwwa* or protection money from them.[12] A free or noble tribe will not intermarry with a vassal tribe, this would be beneath its dignity. Nor will it attack or engage in fighting with a vassal tribe, whether its own or that of another free tribe; this again would be beneath its dignity. If the vassal tribe is attacked by an outsider, its protector tribe will rise up and defend or avenge it.

It would be an interesting task to work out in detail the analogies between this intertribal situation and the conditions in which interfamilial rivalries were utilized by energetic and fortunate family heads to advance themselves, to strengthen their own family by extending their protection to poor and weak relatives, by inviting nonrelated families to become their clients, and by acquiring many slaves and interbreeding with them, and in this manner to assure their own ascendancy over other families. While such a procedure lies beyond the scope of the present subject, it is well within it to point out certain parallels between the attitudes, arrangements, and institutions developed around the intertribal situations on the one hand and those characterizing traditional Muslim conduct in international situations on the other.[13]

An international situation—and the following remarks will largely be confined to international situations and interactions between the Muslim and the Christian worlds—used to be encountered by the Muslims with attitudes and reactions predetermined by the intertribal experience. That is to say, the outside world, the Christian world, was approached by the Muslim world as a whole as one tribe would be by another: it was an encounter with a potential or actual enemy. From the earliest days of the foundation of the new faith, when Muslim Arab conquerors swept with astounding rapidity over the entire Middle East, they viewed the world as being divided into two parts: the *Dār al-Islām*, the House of Islam, containing that part of the world pacified by the sword of Mohammed's religion on the one hand and, on the other, the *Dār al-Ḥarb*, or House of War that lay outside the former realm and against which to engage in Holy War was regarded as a sacred religious duty, invoked as late as the years of World War I. Mohammed himself enjoined upon his followers to fight both idolaters and monotheistic peoples "who believe not in Allah" (Koran 9 : 29). However, while the former had either to be exterminated or converted to Islam, the latter, "those who have been given the Scripture," had to be fought only "until they pay the tribute readily, being brought low" (*ibid.*). These "people of the Book" came very soon to be known as people under protection, or *dhimmi*-s, in Arabic. In a very ancient Muslim document, said to be the testament of the Caliph Omar II (who died in 720, that is, merely 88 years after the death of Mohammed), the duties of the Muslims toward the *dhimmis* are spelled out: ". . . and I commend to your favor the people under 'protection.' Do battle to guard them and put no burden on them greater than they can bear, provided they pay what is due from them to the Muslims, willingly, or under subjection, being humbled. . . ."

This of course is the application of the same principle that governed in pre-Islamic days, and has continued to govern down to the present the relationship between a strong, free noble tribe and its subjected, protection-money-paying, vassal tribe.

When the idea of nationalism became the ruling doctrine in a modern Middle Eastern country, the people of that country were required or at least expected to expand the familistic attitude so as to include the entire population of their country. A good Egyptian Muslim, for instance, was now supposed to regard not only the Egyptian Muslims but also the Copts and the other religioethnic minorities as members of his national family. As a result of this changed situation the nearby close-at-hand traditional objects of the out-group hostility suddenly disappeared. There were now no more *dhimmis* to look down upon and thereby to strengthen one's own feeling of superiority. The attitude of contempt and suspicion of outsiders that was an age-old complement of familism had to look for new objects. The foreigner, the intruder, in all his variegated appearances, was the new peg on which the old hostilities could most conveniently be hung.

While these processes took place inside several Middle Eastern countries, the latter simultaneously found themselves confronted with the irresistible ascendancy of a Christian Europe. In the earlier encounters, during the Crusades, and in the centuries of Ottoman expansion in Europe, the feeling of Muslim cultural superiority was repeatedly reaffirmed and strengthened. In the nineteenth century for the first time Christian Europe appeared to the Muslim world not only as a superior opponent in armed clashes but also as a possessor of cultural attainments superior to those had by the House of Islam.

It was an unfortunate coincidence as far as the Arab countries were concerned that, before they had time truly to integrate Western culture into their traditional cultural configuration, they were brought under the control of the same Western powers which up to that period were the chief profferors of Western cultural imports.[14] A result of this coincidence was the emergence of a tense ambivalent attitude: on the one hand, Western culture continued to exert its magic pull, and even increased it; on the other, the carriers of these cultural enticements came to be regarded as hated oppressors. Thus the two main facets in Western culture that were unquestioningly accepted by the Arab countries—technology in the realm of reality culture and nationalism in that of value culture—were both utilized for the end of ridding themselves of the bearers of these gifts. The nationalistic aim of independence became paramount and it was subserved by everything that could be learned from the West. In fact, the feeling of many was that the more Westernized they became the greater the likelihood of their liberation from Western dominance.

However, in order to understand the roots of Middle Eastern and particularly Arab anti-Westernism, it is not enough to refer to the coincidence of Westernization and Western domination. One has only to mention the case of India to realize that the simultaneous occurrence of these two phenomena in itself does not automatically result in a violent anti-Western attitude. The outcropping of the anti-Western xenophobia in the Arab countries had to draw on a third root as well. This can be found in the Arab cultural complexes of religionism and familism discussed above. For a people whose national personality was conditioned by this type of value syndrome it was much more intolerable to be dominated by a Christian government than for a people such as the Indians whose religions are nontheistic and tolerant, and whose family dynamics are suffused by the *laisser faire* engendered by a general other-worldly orientation.[15] In contrast, the Arab ethos with its imperative emphasis on in-group cohesion, on out-group enmity, and on the exclusive values and undoubted superiority of Islam was a fertile soil for the luxuriant growth of a nationalistic xenophobia once the seeds of Western dominance were sown in it.

Foreign domination, for the same reasons, was resented by the Arabs even when it was exercised by the Ottoman Turks. Yet, while the Turkish yoke weighed heavily on Arab necks and the desire to throw it off was always present, to carry it was not felt an indignity. It was, after all, merely the domination of one Muslim group by another. On the other hand, to be subjected and ruled by Christians was regarded as shameful in particular because it made them into bad Muslims who did not fulfil one of the basic commandments of their religion: to fight the People of the Book and turn them into submissive *dhimmis*. When the new ideas of nationalism are added over and above all this, there stands before us the full complement of the main factors making xenophobia one of the pivotal facets in Arab nationalism.

The *Führer* Image and Nationalism

Another feature of Middle Eastern nationalism is its tendency to embody itself symbolically in an autocratic father image. Middle Eastern autocracy appears in two typical forms, of which the older is clearly a heritage of the past, of the local Middle Eastern millennial sociopolitical development, while the younger is a focusing on a father-image reshaped after modern Western *Führer*-type leaders.

The old Middle Eastern father image is, of course, that of the paternalistic absolute monarch, the theocratic ruler, who still functions in more or less the same sociocultural context as he used to for many centuries in the past. From the head of the extended family to the shaykh of the tribe, to the Caliph of all the Muslims, to the Sultan or Emir of a given population aggregate, and finally to the king of a twentieth-century Muslim theocratic state, there leads an unbroken line of inner historical sequence. The last representatives of this old type of father-ruler image can be found in Yemen and Saudi Arabia and in the smaller Sultanates and shaykhdoms ringing the Arabian Peninsula.

There is little reliable information on nationalism in the Arabian Peninsula in general. However, it so happens that there, more than in any other Middle Eastern country, the inhabitants of each political entity largely share the same religion, the same language, the same descent traditions, the same racial characteristics, the same attitudes and values, thus forming homogeneous population aggregates which, even in their prenationalistic phase, had come very close to resembling the typical nation-states in the Western world such as, say, Italy or Sweden. What the rulers of these states try to achieve is the consolidation of their power over areas within their political boundaries that lie outside the traditional domain of the tribes proper, which used to be headed by them or their fathers. In those territories they have to overcome the traditional in-group loyalty and out-group enmity that for centuries kept Arabia in a state of utter political fragmentation. They are trying to attain this aim by the use of both old Middle Eastern and modern Western methods. The former include the handing out of "purses" to the chiefs of the tribes whose loyalty must be secured, of marrying their daughters for longer or shorter periods, and of inviting them to sit in council. The latter consist mainly of acquiring superior Western arms such as airplanes and tanks, which prevent uprisings by making them utterly hopeless; of utilizing Western means of mass communication, especially the radio (the press only to a negligible extent since most of the people in the peninsula are still illiterate), for the inculcation of a feeling of solidarity with the ruler and his house. The moment the delicate balance of loyalties is tipped definitely in favor of the ruler rather than of the local chieftain, the kingdom or principality has crossed the boundary from traditional Middle Eastern tribal organization to modern nationalism.

As far as the new *Führer*-type father image is concerned, it is interesting to note that in no Middle Eastern country has he directly taken the place of or evolved from the old type of paternalistic monarch. Everywhere a longer or shorter period of experimentation with parliamentary government intervened. At first, the power of the paternalistic ruler was curtailed, and the leaders of political parties gained predominance. (This is the stage that Afghanistan has only just entered, while Iran and Jordan are well advanced in it.) Then the king was altogether eliminated, and a period of republican parliamentarianism began in which, however, the old upper class, the same that used to support the king and was in turn favored by him, continued to occupy a powerful position. The next phase was the emergence of the new leader, who was not a member of the upper ruling class but an army officer of middle-class background. Egypt, Syria, and Iraq have all reached this stage after having passed through the previous one, while Turkey has left it behind and introduced a democratic parliamentary two-party system.

In the dictatorship stage, the *Führer*-figure, of course, symbolizes the nationalistic aspirations of the people. All these aspirations and ideas are purposely fostered, disseminated, and by unceasing reiteration made part of the people's consciousness. Up to this point Middle Eastern totalitarian nationalism closely follows German Nazism, Italian fascism, and the Communist nationalisms. Where the original Middle Eastern elements enter this picture is at the level of contact with religious tradition. Just as the nationalist idea cannot come in conflict with religion, so its leader must remain a religious figure. The modern Egyptian or Iraqi leader, although a Westernized man by education and inclination, bent on the speedy introduction of reforms in the social and economic life of his people, bends his knee and touches his forehead to the prayer rug in the mosque together with all the true believers, in strict accordance with old religious tradition just as the early Arab and Turkish kings and sultans did for thirteen hundred years. Europen nationalist leaders may have been regarded as anti-Christs in the secret hearts of a fearful but faithful minority in the totalitarian countries in the 1920's, 30's, and 40's. No Middle Eastern nationalist leader in the 1950's gave cause to be regarded as an anti-Mohammed, be his teachings and acts as modern and as nontraditional as they may.

Pan-Arab Nationalism

A third factor that distinguishes Arab nationalism from Western nationalism is its superstate character. There are, to be sure, inter-Arab rivalries and hostilities, and there are particularistic trends in Arab nationalism, and these can be strong under certain conditions.[16] The baiting Jordanian King Hussein and his country suffered at the hands of President Nasser of Egypt resulted in a strengthening of Jordanian particularistic nationalism in not insignificant sectors of the Jordanian population. But apart from such special reactions, the general trend of Arab nationalism runs in the direction of Pan-Arabism, that is to say, its ultimate aim is to achieve the unification of all the Arabic-speaking peoples in one Arab superstate. This trend is clearly noticeable not only in those Arab countries that have achieved a predominant position in the Arab world and strive to establish their hegemony by uniting all the other Arab countries under them. This in itself would be consonant with the more extreme forms nationalism has occasionally taken in the Western world, of which the Nazi German nationalistic drive to rule Europe can be cited as the most blatant example.

What is not readily understandable without reference to the specific Arab sociocultural background, is the endeavor of true Arab nationalists in the smaller and weaker Arab countries to unite their countries with a larger and stronger Arab state which, as they only too well know, means in practice the submergence of their own countries in the larger Arab body politic in question. In view of the world-wide trend of nationalism to seek its fulfillment in the breaking up of large political entities into smaller ones peopled by ethnically, linguistically, and culturally homogeneous populations, one must look for very specific factors powerful enough to counter this trend. The only explanation that suggests itself is the still forceful cultural and genealogic tradition that managed to survive and become incorporated into the modern ideologies of Arab nationalism. The Arabs or, to put it more cautiously, many Arabs in every Arab country, small or large, still hold that all the Arabs are the descendants of one or two common ancestors and therefore form but a widely furcated family of tribes. The application of nationalistic ideas to such a situation must inevitably result in the conviction that the *summum bonum* of any Arab state, shaykhdom, territory, or unit of whatsoever description lies in the unification of all Arabs in one Pan-Arab state.[17]

Considering that as recently as until the end of World War I, that is, well within the memory of many persons still alive, all the Arab states were merely administrative provinces within the Ottoman Empire, it is not at all difficult to understand the attraction of the Pan-Arab idea. Those who have deeper historical knowledge look back beyond the inception of the Ottoman rule when there were Arab empires administered from a centrally located seat of government such as Damascus, or Baghdad, or Cairo. The aim of Pan-Arabism is thus regarded as a mere reunification of territories cut up into separate political entities by European power machinations. The old cultural ties have continued to reach across the newly established international boundaries and have, in fact, been intensified by the use of Western methods of mass communication such as the newspapers, the radio, and the motion pictures.

Nonracial Nationalism

We can touch only briefly upon one additional specific characteristic of Middle Eastern nationalism. This is the remarkable *absence of racism* even in the midst of the most excessive culminations of nationalistic fervor. With the Nazi example close at hand, and with the tendency to imitate nationalistic European dictatorships in many other respects, it is truly significant that racial intolerance has been added by no Arab dictatorship to its methods of whipping up popular enthusiasm. The explanation lies in the absence of racial intolerance, of even racial consciousness, in Arab and Muslim history. In the traditional Middle East, religion was the thing in judging an individual or a group, not racial antecedents, and thus the application of race as a criterion of distinction between man and man has remained foreign to the Middle East to this very day.

The sum total of these observations concerning the social and cultural determinants in Middle Eastern nationalism seems to add up to the following:

The Middle Eastern peoples have received nationalism from the Western world, because they saw in this idea a tool they were able to put to good use in the cause of their own advancement as they understood it. But in shaping the precise forms of nationalism for home consumption they were directed by ideas and values anchored in their own sociocultural past and still constituting powerful motivating forces at the present time.

XIII. *The Dynamics of Westernization*

The Nature of Westernization

A discussion of the dynamics of Westernization in the Middle East can best be opened by stating that Westernization is a specific variety of culture change. Since culture change is the process by which the material equipment, the techniques, the organization, the attitudes, the concepts, the points of view, and the values of a culture are transformed as a result of contact between its carriers and those of a different culture, Westernization is the culture change that takes place in any non-Western society under the impact of contact with Western groups or individuals. It is, therefore, a cultural process in the course of which a society or part of it adopts Western culture either totally or partially. It involves the discarding of elements and complexes of the traditional culture in order to replace them with Western cultural elements and complexes.

In theory, when two groups of individuals with different cultures come in contact, changes can result in the cultural patterns of either or both groups.[1] In practice, however, when carriers of Western culture establish contact with non-Western societies the chances are heavily weighted in favor of the acculturation of the non-Western group to Western culture. Of the large number of factors that bring this about, the following seem to be among the most important:

Western people often arrive on the non-Western scene as conquerors or occupy positions of power and leadership, and form a ruling class. This is what happened in the Middle East in the former and present colonial areas (Pakistan, Southern Arabia, Cyprus, North Africa) and in the former mandated territories

(Iraq, Syria, Lebanon, Palestine, Transjordan). Elsewhere (Afghanistan, Iran, Turkey, Saudi Arabia) Western penetration has been mainly economic, but even this was sufficient to secure for the Westerners high positions as employers and as possessors of superior techniques and technical equipment. In addition, their financial situation was incomparably better than that of the average native, and they formed a closed society from which the natives were excluded. The prestige that these foreigners thus acquired among the natives was transferred to the culture they represented, and especially to the overt manifestations of their civilization, that is, their technology, their material equipment, and all the other external trappings with which they surrounded themselves. Especially among members of the urban upper class who had official business, and more rarely, social contact with the Westerners, and also had the requisite financial means, the desire was thus engendered to emulate the Westerners by acquiring their paraphernalia and learning how to use it. Incidentally, the traits adopted in this manner were in many cases of practical usefulness in addition to their prestige value, a circumstance which, of course, added to their attractiveness.

For the last two or three decades the manifestations of Westernization in the Middle East have literally forced themselves upon the attention of students of the area. At least scattered references to them can be found in nearly every book or article dealing with any aspect of Middle Eastern life. As a result, the phenomenology of Westernization is sufficiently well attested, and it would be a simple task to draw up a long list showing what traditional features in Middle Eastern culture have been replaced in the course of the past 100 or 150 years by what new features introduced from the West.

The situation is different with regard to the dynamics of Westernization. What is the nature of the forces which, in many contact situations, caused Western culture to prevail and traditional Middle Eastern culture to succumb? Why and how did the Westerners attempt to make Middle Easterners accept their culture, and what were the motivations of the Middle Easterners in welcoming and often seeking out these changes? Why were certain facets of Western culture more readily accepted than others, while some were rejected altogether? What were the effects of the acceptance of certain specific Western cultural elements on the total context of Middle Eastern culture? To these and many other related questions no satisfactory answers can be found in the available literature.

In the present chapter an attempt is made to outline very briefly some of the main features, forces, and processes the interplay of which resulted in the Westernization observable today, especially in urban aggregates in many Middle Eastern countries. A discussion of the resistance and opposition that are also incident to Westernization in the Middle East will be left to the subsequent chapter.

Cultural Affinity

When attention is focused on a comparison of traditional Middle Eastern with modern Western culture as typified by their most characteristic representatives (for example, the United States and England with their urbanized majority as prototypes of modern Western culture, and Iraq, Iran, or the Arabian Peninsula with their agricultural and seminomadic majority as those of traditional Middle Eastern culture), they appear as significantly different and even contrasting in many respects.[2] In such a purview basic affinities can receive little notice. But as soon as the horizon is widened so as to include, for instance, the Far East as well, certain similarities become apparent against the more markedly different textures of those remoter culture areas.[3] The culture of the West then appears as more closely related to that of the Middle East than to the cultures of either central and southern Asia or Negro Africa.

The cultural affinity between the West and the Middle East has historical roots. Disregarding the prehistoric and earliest historical connections between the two world areas, the Middle East was in ancient times for several centuries under Greek and Roman domination and thus absorbed much of those cultural influences that so decisively molded the culture of Europe. Soon after, the West was subjected to powerful religious influences emanating from the Middle East in the form of the young faith of Christianity. At a later age, Islamic culture penetrated deeply into the West through the Iberian Peninsula and the Danube Basin, resulting in cultural exchange, another phase of which was a concomitant of the Crusades. As a result of these interchanges, at about the end of the Middle Ages the cultures of the two adjoining areas evinced considerable similarities of a general nature.

It was only with the advent of the Industrial Revolution and the subsequent technologic, economic, and social development in Europe that these similarities began rapidly to diminish. In the eighteenth and nineteenth centuries, the distance between the two cultures increased as a result of the relative cultural stability of the Middle East throughout this period and the cumulative and accelerating changes that were taking place in the culture of the West. Thus, when toward the middle of the nineteenth century the two cultures entered a new phase of their more than two-thousand-year-old intermittent contact, the situation was somewhat as follows:

The Europeans, as they became familiar with the culture of the Middle East, recognized in it similarities with certain aspects of the medieval phase of European culture, and noticed the absence of practically all those developments to which they were wont to point proudly in their own culture as significant accretions. From this discernment it was but one step to the formulation of the reproach of backwardness, and only one more step to the endeavor to fill in with their own Western achievements those facets of Middle Eastern culture which, they felt, were lacking or lagging.

The Middle Easterners, on the other hand, were in the possession of a culture still sufficiently similar in several basic aspects to the one brought to them by the Westerners to be able to recognize without too much difficulty that in certain fields the West was definitely ahead of them. Having for centuries used water for irrigation, clay for vessels, iron for utensils, wool and cotton for clothing, stone and bricks for building, ships for water transport, etc., it was much easier for them to appreciate the Western improvements in these and other such activities than for the carriers of a culture completely lacking these elements.

Channels of Western Influence

Broadly speaking, the channels of Western influences on Middle Eastern culture fall into two main categories: impersonal or mechanical influences and personal contacts. In the case of impersonal influences, the group or the individual exposed to Westernization has no direct contact with personal exponents of any aspect of Western culture. Such persons, to be sure, are present somewhere in the background, but they are unseen and unfelt. These impersonal or mechanical influences are: (1) equipment, supplies, and consumers' goods; (2) newspapers, magazines, and books; (3) the radio; (4) motion pictures; and (5) phonograph records.

As to personal contacts, these can be subdivided into three groups that can be called respectively primary, secondary, and tertiary sources of Westernization. Primary sources of Westernization in personal contacts are represented by those individuals who come to the Middle East from the Western world and are, therefore, fully saturated with their specific brand of Western culture. Such persons either purposely or involuntarily impart something of their culture to the people with whom they come in contact. To this category belong the members of diplomatic corps stationed in the Middle Eastern countries; members of religious, medical, educational, technical, economic, and other missions; members of Western philanthropic institutions; also, Westerners who have settled in the Middle East for business purposes or who are sent there temporarily to represent or to work for Western firms; and finally, tourists. Secondary sources of Westernization by personal contact are provided by natives of Middle Eastern countries who have spent some time in the Western world and who, after their return to their native land, become (again either intentionally or unintentionally) Westernizing agents. To this group belong emigrants returning from overseas countries; returning students; returning diplomatic personnel and, to some extent at least, religious pilgrims who make for a certain amount of cultural interchange between various Middle Eastern and neighboring countries. As tertiary sources of personal Westernization must be regarded all those Middle Eastern individuals or groups who, having themselves absorbed a certain amount of Western cultural traits in the course of their contact with primary and/or secondary sources, become disseminators of Western influences in their social environment.

Apart from the returning emigrants and the members of various missions and philanthropic institutions, whose personal contacts include the native peasant and working classes, all the other primary and secondary personal Westernizing agents affect directly only the members of the urban upper class. The great majority of the Middle Eastern populations, the nomads, the cultivators, and the workers (unless they happen to be employed by a Western concern such as Aramco or the defunct Anglo-Iranian Oil Company) are exposed to the Westernizing influences of tertiary personal sources and of impersonal or mechanical sources only.

It is almost impossible to make any statement as to the differential degrees of Westernization in the various countries of the Middle East and within each country in the various social classes or occupational or other social groupings without courting the danger of undue generalization and schematization. Illustrative rather than generalizing statements will therefore have to serve the purpose. The differences in the extent of Westernization between country and country can best be illustrated by referring to Turkey on the one hand and Yemen on the other, the former having gone a relatively long way, while the latter is still poised hesitantly on the crossroads. Again, the differences within a single country can be made comprehensible by stating that the ruling class in a country like Egypt is well advanced in Westernization, while her peasant majority has barely budged from the traditional mode of life followed by their grandfathers. These two observations, by the way, also indicate how difficult it is to speak of Westernization in the Middle East *in general.*

The Impact of the West

A complete analysis of the diverse ways in which the Western impact has made itself felt on the Middle Eastern scene would have to include a discussion of the roles of several Western institutions in the contact situations between the two cultures. Western institutions, for instance, played an important part in shaping the reforms introduced in the Tanzimat period in the Ottoman Empire and by Muḥammad 'Ali in Egypt. Also, certain Western political concepts, notably that of nationalism, as well as several principles characteristic of Western democracy (for example, the right of self-determination, sovereignty of the people, social obligations of the state) found their way to the Middle East through educational and philanthropic channels, and were echoed in Middle Eastern ideologic developments. It is proposed, however, to limit the present discussion to two other major but hitherto largely neglected aspects of Western influence on the Middle East, namely the aspects of technology and prestige, and to an analysis of the widening range of changes resulting from these primary points of impact.

Westerners, having once set themselves up in the midst of the Middle East, began to display their technology and to spread, both purposely and incidentally, certain elements of it among the natives of the area. The technologic aspect of culture is the one that can most easily be loaned and borrowed. This generalization, of course, holds good only with regard to the *use* of technologic equipment, not its production. It may not be easy to learn how to make a motor-driven pump, but in a few minutes one can learn how to use it and recognize its advantages over the old method of lifting water with the *shaduf*.

In addition to its high degree of transmissibility and its function as an apparent index of advancement, the acceptance of the products of Western technology by the natives of the Middle East was facilitated by the fact that in their own culture technology did not occupy a focal position. Therefore, the Middle Easterners, like the carriers of many other cultures, initially regarded the switch to the use of Western equipment as a change of minor importance only, which would not affect their focal values. Only later, in fact when it was too late, did it dawn upon them that the admittance of even a single Western culture element inevitably brought in its wake more and more new elements with more and more changes, resulting in serious disturbances in the vital texture of their traditional culture.

While the technological beginnings of Westernization explain much of the success of this worldwide cultural process, other factors significantly supported and bolstered it. Among these must be mentioned in the first place the new prestige order that developed after the appearance of the Westerners on the native Middle Eastern scene. Having in many cases achieved ruling and controlling or at least leading and dominant positions in the Middle Eastern countries they penetrated, the Westerners superimposed themselves upon the native social order and became something like a topmost or upper-upper class.

It is not easy to analyze the various components that go into the making of Western prestige. The power element must have been the most important in the earlier, "imperialistic" days, to be replaced, as time went by, by varying combinations of such components as wealth, the possession of strange gadgets and awe-inspiring equipment, specialized knowledge in new fields of increasing importance (such as medicine and agriculture), positions of trust and influence given to Westerners by the local government, and entrance to and free association as equals with the highest elite of native leadership. The aura of prestige surrounding the Westerner soon enveloped his culture as well, with the result that the acquisition of Western culture became a matter of social desirability over and above its recognized utility.

Whatever the specific context of the social stratification in an area, the rich native upper class had the most opportunity for firsthand and close contact with Westerners, had the amplest financial means necessary to acquire the trappings of Western civilization, and was the first to succumb to the lure of the West. Once this movement was on the way, the other native social classes that were ranked beneath the native upper class had an additional incentive for the adoption of a Western style of life so far as this was possible within their limited means: the desire to climb up the native social ladder by acquiring at least some of the same characteristics that the upper class itself had only recently acquired from the Westerners. For instance, in the native garb there were well-defined class differences: the urban effendi, the member of the urban lower class, the fellah, or the Bedouin each had his own distinctive garb that "placed" him as soon as his figure was discerned at a distance. Now, however, the effendi had adopted the Western suit; if the urban worker was able to follow his example, he achieved two aims at once; he demonstrated his advanced social status vis-à-vis his more backward countrymen by dressing like a European, and he also assimilated to the new-style effendi, thus achieving an approximation, in outward appearance at least, of the coveted upper class status. In this manner the acquisition of Western cultural trappings became a symbol of identification with the foreign ruling group for the native upper class and of social advancement for all other classes.

Social Cleavage

Generally speaking, however, Westernization in its impact upon the traditional Middle Eastern social structure resulted in a widening of the distance between the top and the bottom layers of society. Prior to its inception, the style of life of the native upper class represented the highest culmination of which the local culture was capable. Having concentrated in its hands most of the wealth of the area, the upper class was able to make use of the best cultural forces available in Islamic lands. The best Muslim architects built their palaces, mosques, and madrasahs; the best tailors sewed their clothes; the best sandalmakers made their shoes; the best swordsmiths forged their blades; the best artists and craftsmen provided them with decoration of body, lodging, and furnishing, and with exquisite *objets d'art*; the best poets, storytellers, musicians, dancers, and mimes entertained them; in brief, while greatly surpassing in quality and refinement anything that was within the reach of the lower classes, the culture of the upper class was identical with the culture of the masses. Thus, there existed what can be termed a lower-class–upper-class cultural continuum.

This continuum was disrupted with the impact of Westernization, which hit first and foremost the upper class. Members of this class, to the extent to which they were attracted to Western culture, ceased to be creators, inspirers, and consumers of native cultural products. The local culture became to all practical purposes nonexistent for them, and they became avid consumers in all fields of importations from the countries of the West.

A general decline in native arts and crafts was one of the consequences of this situation. Since the number of customers who insisted on and could pay for high quality rapidly diminished, quality itself declined. There was a vulgarization and deterioration of the traditional arts and crafts, soon to be followed by an adaptation of the native skills to patterns and styles imported from the West in an effort to compete with the imported products themselves, which constantly gained in popularity. This competition in turn resulted in an increased spread of the cheaper kind of Western-style consumers' goods now offered in both an imported and a locally made variety.

However, what the lower classes were able to afford by way of Western-style goods was extremely meager in comparison with the all but wholesale switch to a Western style of life effected or at least attempted by members of the upper class. Especially in the rural areas, where something like four fifths of the total population of the Middle East still lives, the generally low standard of living enabled the people to acquire only a fraction of even those limited offerings of Western-style products that reached them via the weekly markets, the itinerant pedlars, or the local stores.

Thus, while under traditional circumstances the upper class, sitting on the narrow top of the social pyramid, was connected with the lower classes forming the pyramid's broad and massive base by a cultural continuum, Westernization successively severed the vital cultural arteries running between the top and the bottom and created a cultural discrepancy between the two. The elite was now no longer the top exponent of the traditional culture of the same masses, upon the continued existence of which its upper-class status depended. It was Western-oriented, and having like its European preceptors identified Westernization with progress, it regarded the members of the lower classes who still represented the poor version of the traditional culture as backward and primitive.

In the reaction of the lower classes to the widening cultural gulf between them and the native controlling group, certain ambivalences were demonstrated. On the one hand, the traditional resentment felt by the needy at the display of wealth and waste by the idle rich increased when this display included a growing number of newfangled Western traits objectionable to the more tradition-bound outlook of the poor. On the other hand, there was the irresistible attraction exerted by the glitter of

Western cultural trappings, which, however, remained mostly unattainable for the poverty-stricken masses. The frustration thus engendered was not infrequently channeled into one of the special Middle Eastern varieties of nativistic movements of which the Muslim Brotherhood is the best known example.

Creation of an Urban Proletariat

One of the earliest outcomes of Westernization was thus to throw into disequilibrium the traditional social balance and to disturb the age-old, well settled social strata of the Middle East by culturally alienating the native upper class from the rest of the population. Two additional changes effected by the impact of Westernization on the native society were both urban developments. They were the creation of a rudimentary urban proletariat and an urban middle class.

The social class or the occupational group in traditional Middle Eastern society that came closest to what is generally understood by an urban proletariat was that of the artisans. Yet an artisan or a craftsman, even though he may have been employed for many years, first as an apprentice, then as a journeyman, counted as a person on the way to becoming a master craftsman, and this potential position, as well as membership in the corporation or guild, defined his status as something very different from that of the urban proletarian laborer. Furthermore, in many cases the apprentice who embarked on a career of artisanship was a son, nephew, cousin, or other close relative of the master craftsman under whose guidance and control he acquired the skills of his trade. This hereditary or familial character of the crafts and guilds placed the urban artisan in a definitely higher position than that of the rural agriculturist, whether the latter was a day laborer, a tenant sharecropper, or even a smallholder. The fact of the matter was that under traditional circumstances there was no urban element which in status and social position corresponded to the rural proletariat, which constituted the majority of each country's population.

Such an urban proletariat has begun to come into being as a result of Westernization. The onset of industrialization created a demand for a labor force that was recruited partly from the towns themselves and partly from the surrounding countryside. The new industrial laborers received low wages, had to put up with hard working conditions, and were crowded into suburban slums of which the North African "bidonvilles" (or "tin-can" towns) are today the worst examples. All the conditions for the emergence of a depressed and underprivileged urban proletariat are present, and the labor aspect of industrialization has been characterized by all those evils which to overcome took the modern West several decades.

Compared with the growth of Western industrialization, Middle Eastern industrialization, though limited in extent, was sudden and spurtlike. Moreover, it did not grow organically out of local conditions, but was imposed or introduced from the outside. It was therefore likely to be accompanied by grave tensions and disturbances concomitant upon an all too rapid transition from the traditional forms of social interaction characterized by familism, personal relationships, and the prevalence of a kin-oriented ascribed status, to the modern Western forms of social interaction with its impersonal relationships and preponderance of individually achieved status.

These difficulties were further aggravated by the equally sudden disappearance from the life of this new proletariat of many of those emotional, aesthetic, and spiritual satisfactions that gave it color, content, and interest as long as it ran in its old traditional channels. In the old setting there were the friendships formed in childhood, the colorful feasts of family life accompanying birth, circumcision, marriage, and death, the annual festivals of the Muslim or the agricultural calendar, the birthdays of saints, the enjoyment of story, song, dance, and other traditional forms of aesthetic entertainment, and the trust, the peace of mind, and the equanimity that were the spiritual rewards of unquestioning compliance with the simple and few rites of Islamic worship. In a culture in which the extended family was the traditional protective frame of life and the prime locale of practically all activities, these satisfactions were severely strained by the severance of the family ties and the submergence of the uprooted individual in the disillusioned crowd of slum inhabitants.

These negative features were, however, outweighed by several compulsive factors that contributed to the steady growth of the urban proletariat. One of these was the pronounced status difference between town and country. In the town (with the possible exception of Lebanon), a goodly amount of contempt was felt toward the village and the villager, as manifested in the derogatory connotation of the term "fellah" and in the invariably comic and foolish figure the fellah cut in the shadow theater and other forms of popular entertainment. In the villages, a high status was ascribed to the town and to everything and everybody connected with it. This resulted in a constant though not very sizable village-to-town migration throughout the past centuries. With the spread of Westernization this movement increased, for the town now meant greater opportunities for industrial employment, to which was added the glamor and attraction of the Western style of life.

Another change owing to Westernization that resulted in an increased migration of villagers to the cities was the slowly but perceptibly improving sanitary and hygienic conditions, especially in villages not too distant from urban centers. These improvements enabled a larger percentage of children born to survive and reach maturity, without, for the time being at least, affecting the traditionally high birthrate of the area. This resulted in a rural population pressure not experienced by previous generations. Some of the surplus population, unable to find a livelihood in the villages, had to migrate to the towns, and for lack of skills or other opportunities, swelled the numbers of the urban proletariat.

Thus a social class came into being that was characterized by a greater dissatisfaction with its own status than any population element under traditional circumstances. One of the causes of this proletarian resentment has been discerned by Toynbee: the consciousness of being disinherited from one's ancestral place in society.[4] Another is the spatial proximity to higher social classes and the familiarity with their style of life. The tension created in rootless underprivileged groups as a result of this proximity, known from many other parts of the world, is aggravated in the Middle East by the cultural gulf that separates the two elements. Moreover, luxuries and wealth in the traditional Middle East were kept indoors, to be enjoyed in the privacy of walled-in palaces and gardens, unsuspected by those who happened to pass by the simple and drab frontage facing the street. In contrast, luxurious living in the Western style means public display to be seen and envied by all. As Carleton Coon has put it, "The West has tended to widen the social gulf between rich and poor in the Middle East by dangling in the faces of the poor conveniences and luxuries of which they had never before heard and which they now cannot have, while giving the rich new and expensive tastes, and the need for more and more income."[5]

Middle-Class Development

The second urban development resulting from Westernization was the creation of a new and increasingly numerous middle class. It is true, of course, that in the traditional Middle Eastern town there was an established and highly specialized array of craftsmen, merchants, and professional people, whose position roughly corresponded to that occupied by the middle class in the modern West. What Westernization effected, therefore, was not so much the creation of a new class as a transformation of this traditional sector of the population into a middle class more and more similar to its Western equivalent.

Since the traditional Middle Eastern craft, commercial, and professional guilds comprised literally hundreds of highly specialized occupations, their transformation, or "modernization," was a complicated and ramified process characterized by great differences in speed and extent. These differences depended, first of all, on the effective causes that brought about the transformation itself. With reference to the craft guilds, it appears that their decline and partial or total disappearance was caused mainly by the impact of Western technology and/or Western fashions of consumption. The adoption of Western clothing, for instance, contributed in every part of the Middle East to the decline of local clothing industries. Occasionally it has happened that local crafts declined and disappeared not as a result of the shrinking of their markets but in consequence of the competition of goods produced in Europe in cheap imitation of the local styles.

Articles imported from the West were the products of a superior technology with which local artisanship was unable to compete. Of later origin, but today of increasing importance, is the competition of industrial undertakings established in the Middle Eastern towns themselves, first by foreigners, then by members of the indigenous minorities, and most recently by the state and rather hesitatingly also by members of the Muslim upper class. In some cases these so-called "new industries" in the Middle East were new also in the sense that they engaged in types of production not previously practiced in the area (for example, the extraction of minerals, chemicals), in which case they did not directly contribute to the decline of the traditional crafts. In other cases, however, they were new only in the sense that they introduced Western methods of production, while the products themselves or their equivalents had been both manufactured locally and consumed in the area for many generations (for example, certain foods and textiles, especially in Turkey, Iran, and Egypt), in which case they powerfully competed with and caused the decline of the old native industries.

If in the case of the craft guilds the changing fashion, which is a matter of taste and preference, was a contributing cause of their decline, in the case of commercial guilds the same fashion changes resulted not in a decline, but in a transformation of the character of many business establishments. For the craftsman it was a matter of grave importance if he had to cease producing a certain type of merchandise, and only in rare cases could he switch to the production of the same basic goods but in a modern, that is, Western style. For the merchant, on the other hand, it was a matter of relative indifference what type of wares he carried in his store as long as he knew how to handle them and was able to make his profit. For this reason, while the external appearance of stores and shops has in many cases become modernized, with the plate glass shop window replacing the old wooden shutters, and while the contents of the stores also reflect the changing times, the merchant has suffered less from Westernization and Western competition than the craftsman.

On the other hand, deep inroads were made by changes of fashion, taste, and preference in the traditional professions of the

Middle East. Gone from the urban scene are most if not all of the bloodletters, leeches, surgeons, barbers, bonesetters, healers, readers, exorcists, diviners, soothsayers, fortune tellers, astrologists, dream interpreters, and many other professionals who ministered in traditionally accepted and specialized ways to man's desire to better his physical or mental condition. Not so long ago the confidants, advisers, and companions of kings and princes, they are gone, not in the sense of having completely disappeared, but gone, as it were, underground, withdrawn to the slums, to the quarters inhabited by the villagers recently attracted to the towns, or gone altogether from the larger cities where they could no longer find clients to the more remote small towns relatively untouched by the new ideas brought in from the West.

This development surely reflects a radical change in mental attitudes dominant for centuries. But in probing for its causes, one cannot help doubting that this change was actually accomplished by a sudden conversion to more rational thinking. The clearly demonstrated "miracles" of Western medicine had of course much to do with the abandonment of the traditional methods of improving the physical condition of the body. But even this had to be preceded by some inclination to weigh rationally and unemotionally the evidence for and against both competing systems. Whence did this inclination come? And as to those specialists who administered to the mental comfort of rich and poor alike, of both educated and ignorant, their efforts were summarily dismissed by the Westerners as "sheer superstition" without, however, having anything positive to offer in their stead. Whence, therefore, the inclination to adopt this Western attitude as well, without the backing of any new empirical evidence as to the futility of occult practices, and without anything Western to take their place?

The answer seems again to lie in the prestige of the Westerners and their culture, to which reference was made earlier. The prestige enjoyed by everything Western in the eyes of the natives created in the latter a propensity to emulate all the ways of the West. In fact, it often led to a subservient desire to acquire not only Western equipment, but also Western behavior, mannerisms, and attitudes. Consequently, Western medicine was accepted not only because it was demonstrably superior to traditional Middle

Eastern medical practices, but also because it was Western; and the Western contemptuous attitude toward traditional Middle Eastern mantic and magical practices was adopted on its face value only, merely because it was vouched for by Western prestige.

The complementary aspect of the decline of the traditional Middle Eastern guilds and corporations is the emergence of new professional elements whose totality forms the new middle class. An increasing section of the urban population aspires or is compelled to join the ranks of this new and vigorous social class, the importance of which for the cultural development of the Middle East as a whole is still growing.

Among the members of the old craft guilds who were forced out of their professions by the impact of Westernization, some had no choice but to join the ranks of the urban industrial proletariat; others managed to survive the changing conditions, retain their independent positions, and take their places in the new order by adapting their products to the new consumers' demands. An even greater percentage of the members of the old commercial guilds succeeded in retaining or even improving their positions as independent owners of stores of varying sizes with varying numbers of employees. These merchants, too, are today solid members of the middle class in the larger cities of the Middle East. The professional sector of the middle class is its newest element. Only rarely were members of the old professions able to fit into the life of the Westernized city or to adapt themselves to the changed conditions. As a rule, the new professional class is recruited from among the sons of members of the other classes or sectors of the urban population, or of the better-to-do rural population.

It has been observed in many Middle Eastern countries, as well as in other parts of Asia (for example, in India and Pakistan), that the aim of the great majority of young people who can afford a college or at least a high school education is to go into law, politics, journalism, administration, or at least into clerical, religious, and teaching positions, and to practice these professions in the towns only. Education in their eyes is the open sesame to city life and to a livelihood earned *not* with one's hands. This aversion to rural life and any type of labor that they consider to be manual is a heritage of the traditional Middle Eastern urban mentality that saw in the ability to escape working with one's hands the clinching proof of social advancement. It is interesting to note that this prejudice against village life and "manual" work is retained even in circles that otherwise pride themselves with their thorough Westernization.

As a result of this attitude the new Middle Eastern middle class is lop-sided when judged by Western standards: it has a profusion of white-collar workers and intellectuals, many of whom are chronically unemployed, or underemployed and underpaid, while on the other hand it lacks a sufficient number of doctors, engineers, architects, chemists, technicians. Another consequence is the marked concentration of professional people in the cities, which greatly contributes to the growth of the cultural distance between town and country.

Dislocation of Value Judgments

In a traditional and well-settled culture such as that of the Middle East, reality (that is, tangible) ingredients and value ingredients, to use Kroeber's terminology,[6] are usually well adjusted. The two categories reinforce each other, and the extent of their mutual support lends the culture coherence, balance, and inner consistency. Take, for example, the matter of wealth and poverty. The typical situation in the Middle East was for centuries the concentration of great riches in the hands of a very few, with great poverty the share of the many. This was and in many places still is a factual reality. The ideologic counterpart of this situation was that the division of worldly goods is willed by God, that the possession of wealth is not one of those really important things for which man should strive, that there is a certain religious virtue in poverty, and that it is a religious duty of the rich to dole out alms to the poor.[7] In this manner extreme economic inequality was organically incorporated into the culture, not only by being accepted realistically but also by being underpinned ideologically.

In a contact situation such as Westernization presents, this old balance between reality culture and value culture is disturbed. As Kroeber has emphasized, the reality ingredients of a culture can be loaned and borrowed much more readily than its value ingredients. Therefore, very often there is a lag in the acceptance of value culture, while reality culture is accepted readily. One of the causes of this lag is the emotional attachment of society to its own value culture and its resistance to the introduction of new, foreign value ingredients. Since, however, reality culture and value culture are interdependent, the reality ingredients of one culture cannot be expected to fulfill the same function in another culture if the latter retains its own value ingredients.

This thesis can be illustrated by examples from almost any field in which Western influences are felt in the Middle East. Take, for instance, the factory system introduced from the West. The adoption of all the technical equipment, the learning of all the skills and tricks of the trade, will not ensure the operation of a factory with the precision, reliability, and efficiency attained in the West as long as the basically negative attitude toward manual labor persists and the value of the work and the worker is not recognized. In other words, reality ingredients alone cannot guarantee the satisfactory functioning of an institution that in its home environment comprises value ingredients as well.

All this, of course, does not mean that reality ingredients of a culture can be transplanted into another culture without causing changes in the values of the latter, or that values from one culture can be superimposed on another culture without causing changes in its reality ingredients. Quite the contrary. The close coordination and interdependence between reality culture and value culture make it impossible to introduce changes in the one without creating changes, with some delay perhaps, in the other. Thus, once the establishment of factories introduced new reality ingredients into the life of Middle Eastern towns, it became only a question of time until changes in values would follow. As a matter of fact, some signs of these changes already are visible here and there. In eastern Saudi Arabia, for instance, where the Arabian American Oil Company offers excellent working conditions to the still largely nomadic population of the peninsula, the tribesmen, until recently utterly contemptuous of all manual labor with the exception of the only noble task of breeding camels, flock in increasing numbers to the company's recruiting stations without suffering loss of prestige.

In general, the approach of the West to the Middle East, especially in recent years, has been characterized by a careful avoidance of ideologic issues and a concentration instead on a number of practical problems. Technical, economic, and related missions sent in recent years to the Middle East by the United Nations or the United States, as well as by private business enterprises working in the area, have adopted the principle of noninterference with traditional ideologies and values as a fundamental directive.

In the case of Western religious missions, the abstention from ideologic influencing was not as much a matter of free choice as a matter of prudence in view of the hostility with which Islamic society would have reacted to open attempts at conversion.[8] The result was that while religious missions healed and treated tens of thousands of Muslim sick, gave education to other tens of thousands of Muslim children, and may have influenced by precept and example the ethical outlook of many others, they converted very few natives. Religion being a focal concern in the culture of the Middle East,[9] conversion was regarded as apostasy and resulted in an open breach with family, society, and value culture. The convert to Christianity was ostracized by his peers and, what is equally important, since Islam was held with unshakable conviction to be the only true religion, to leave it was regarded as an evidence of utter folly.

More recently, to the 150-year-old impact of the Western world on the Middle East has been added a new attack coming from the Russian totalitarian subvariety of Western culture. In contrast to its West European predecessor, the Soviet impact is directed mainly at the ideologic facet of the traditional Middle East culture. Part of the Communist effort is to convince the people whom it seeks to win that the doctrines of Communism and Islam are not only compatible, but that actually Communism is the true interpretation of the original and pure form of Islam. And, as Bernard Lewis has shown, certain external resemblances can, in fact, be discerned between the traditional Islamic forms of autocratic-theocratic social structure and the Soviet totalitarian-dictatorial state form.[10] While there is no need to exaggerate the danger of a Communist revolution in any Middle Eastern country, the Communist attack on the native culture at its ideologic roots is a serious threat that can create grave disturbances in the traditional cultural and social equilibrium even short of a political overthrow.

While the direct impact of Christian missions on the religious life of the Middle East has been negligible, Westernization has indirectly resulted in an increasing coolness toward religion as a whole. It has been emphasized repeatedly that religion in the Middle East under traditional circumstances was a total way of life.[11] The craft guilds, for instance, were religious organizations; the wearing of the locally customary garb was religiously sanctioned; medicine was a religious vocation, as was teaching. Sovereignty itself was a religious office. While there was no hierarchy or priesthood in any sense comparable to those of the Catholic and Episcopalian churches, a considerable percentage of the urban population was engaged in directly religious professions. Many additional families, both in town and country, were supported by religious foundations that concentrated in their hands a considerable proportion of each country's landed property.

The most important instrument through which religion exercised its hold on the individual was the traditional Middle Eastern patrilineal, patrilocal, patriarchal, endogamous extended family. The dependence of the individual on his family and his integration into it were so intense that Middle Eastern culture was rightly termed a kinship culture.[12] And since this family system itself was a religious institution, sanctioned and supported by religion, family and religion mutually strengthened each other. As we have seen, Westernization brought about a decline of paternal authority; a break-up of the extended family; a movement from village to town; a change-over in the towns themselves from the family economy of the old-fashioned crafts to the impersonal economic system of the factory with its employment of individuals as such, irrespective of family ties, and with its considerable labor turnover; and a conscious imitation, especially in the middle and upper classes, of Western family and social forms. All this resulted not only in a crucial change in the character of family life itself, but also in a trend away from religion and toward secularism. When the individual, and as a rule the young male individual, extricated himself from the hold of his family, he left behind an intrinsically religious atmosphere, the rejection of which thenceforward became a part of his negation of the old, tightly knit family system itself.

Another point to make is that under traditional circumstances leadership, wealth, position, power, and control belonged, with very few exceptions, to members of the ruling religion, Islam, who all vied with one another in the public demonstration of their orthodoxy and piety. Religiosity was thus one of the hallmarks of the traditional upper crust, and consequently no question could arise in the minds of the other classes as to the importance, value, and obligatory nature of religious observance.

On this scene appeared the prestige-laden Westerner, occupying superior positions, carrying a culture that evoked the desire to emulate it. These foreigners were not only adherents of a different faith, but their attitude toward their own Christian religion was, on the whole, lukewarm. Among those Middle Easterners whose general attitude toward Westernization was positive, the emulation of Western ways therefore meant, among other things, to display unconcern about their own religion. On the other hand, among those whose ties to their own religion-centered traditional culture proved stronger than the Westerly pull, Western irreligiosity became an additional cause to reject whatever the West had to offer and to seek refuge in "return to Islam" movements.

XIV. *Resistance to Westernization*

The Issue of Western Domination

As many Middle Easterners understand it, the basic motivation of the Western world in establishing contact with the Middle East was the endeavor to dominate it politically and exploit it economically. The Middle Eastern view is that for several decades the Western powers controlled the Middle East with the help of the Middle Eastern ruling classes who were either coerced or bribed into serving the Western interests. As a result, the peoples of the Middle East have remained poor and oppressed; in fact, their poverty and oppression have even increased. By the end of World War II however, the patience of the people became at long last exhausted; they burst forth in movements against foreign domination, against misery and poverty, and against those of their own rulers who, under the auspices and with the blessing of the foreign governments, had oppressed and exploited them. They produced strong and fearless leaders, nationalized their natural resources and the large foreign-owned industrial and commercial establishments, and declared many of the foreign residents as unwelcome. They sincerely felt, and never tired reiterating, that "We would rather die than accept British or Russian or any other domination over our fatherland."

As against this, the Western argument is as follows: Without Western initiative the natural resources of the Middle East would have remained unutilized. The Western powers were invited by the rulers of the Middle Eastern countries themselves to find and exploit their natural resources and to introduce Western technology. The Western companies that thereupon were set up shared their profits with the legal owners of the natural resources, the kings and governments of the Middle Eastern countries. These rulers, however, instead of passing on at least part of the benefits to the people themselves, pocketed all the income. They are, therefore, responsible for the poverty and degradation in which nine tenths of the Middle Eastern peoples live. They direct and foment the hatred of the West, of the "foreigners," in the hope of thus making the foreigners responsible in the eyes of the masses for the "animal-like standard of living forced on their people . . . by their own corrupt, greedy selves."[1]

In the leadlong clash of these two opposite views, the minimum measure of agreement that exists between them is apt to pass unnoticed. The fact of the matter, however, is that a major share of the direct responsibility for the poverty and misery of the people is laid by both sides at the door (or rather the luxurious portals) of the local ruling classes, whether their actions and attitudes are held to be instigated by foreigners or by their own selfish attitude.

Resentment against effendis, pashas, agas, shaykhs, beys, deys, notables, landowners, and other traditional overlords is increasingly felt by the people, is more and more overtly expressed by their educated and articulate spokesmen, and is becoming a stronger and stronger impetus for social and land reforms. Although protestations against landlord exploitation still go hand in hand with a display of antiforeign sentiments, from the view of ideologic development it has to be pointed out that the very concepts of land reform and of a more equitable sharing of material benefits were born in the West whence they have penetrated the Middle East in recent years. The traditional Middle Eastern idea, which, by the way, made poverty and misery much more easily bearable, is that the landlord or the chieftain is a sort of family head, that all his tenants or vassals are subordinate members of his quasi-family, and that therefore it is not only actually inevitable, but also right in principle for the peasants to live on the barest subsistence level while sustaining their lords in luxury. To wish for a change in this situation, to revolt against a landlord, to threaten to kill him (as actually has happened several times lately in Iran), would have been as inconceivable in the past as it would be for a son in a traditional Middle Eastern patriarchal family to take a stand against his father. A great measure of Western mentality had to be acquired before the people became receptive to reform ideas with reference to these important areas of entrenched traditionalism.

Technology, Science, and Medicine

Of all the different aspects of Western culture that are being introduced in the life of the Middle East, the acquisition and use of technical equipment and methods encounters the least resistance. There is, of course, an innate disinclination to change old techniques that were inherited from one's ancestors and knowledge of which was acquired in early youth. A peasant father whose son returns home after three years in an agricultural school will not readily discard the old methods of cultivation that enabled him to make a living (and, incidentally, to send his son to school) for the new ones fervently advocated by the youngster. His resistance to change will be based on a preference for the familiar and a distrust of everything new, unknown and untried. Experience, shows, however, that if the son succeeds in demonstrating to the father the superiority of the method or the implement he recommends, the father soon changes his mind. Readiness to give up initial distrust and to accept demonstrated improvement was observed repeatedly in various Middle Eastern countries by social workers among the rural population.[2] Demonstrated advantages in technical improvements tipped the scale in favor of acceptance of superior Western machinery and the discarding of the old traditional implements in Palestine among the Arab weavers of Majdal.[3] Once the initial resistance is overcome, the readiness to accept demonstrated improvements soon turns into eagerness to benefit by them. This explains the numerous petitions sent by peasants from remote villages in Turkey or in Syria to the central authorities clamoring for a road, a hospital, a motorized pump, and many other technical improvements.[4]

In addition to demonstrating in practice the good results of the suggested change rather than explaining them in theory, there is a second prerequisite for successful culture change in the technologic field: innovations must be introduced gradually. A change that if sprung upon the people precipitately would meet with determined resistance can become acceptable without any noticeable repercussion if protracted over a number of years. The law that forbade the Turkish people to wear the red fez, with immediate effect, resulted in much unnecessary resentment and bitterness. In several other Middle Eastern countries the old-fashioned headgear, together with the veil, is disappearing gradually; in the absence of sudden compulsion, the discarding of these traditional items of clothing spreads by the spontaneous process of voluntary imitation.

The sum of these observations is that of all aspects of Western culture it is the material equipment that meets with the least resistance in the Middle East, and that further changes in this field can best be effected by demonstrating their advantages and by introducing them gradually.

The situation with regard to the introduction of the exact sciences and the scientific method is similar. These facets of culture *ipso facto* touch directly upon the lives of the small urban upper and middle classes only, whose contacts with Western culture are close and manifold. The great Western advances in all branches of science are fully acknowledged by these groups, and with the increasing recognition of the role and function of science in the life of a modern state there is a growing readiness on the part of the young educated group to take up the study of sciences in place of the traditional academic concentration on theology and law. As a matter of fact, the endeavor to get rid of Western interference and domination is an additional factor directing many young people into those scientific and technical occupations which until recently were the exclusive domain of Westerners.

It goes without saying that the attitude toward medicine and sanitation is the same as that toward Western technology and science. The demonstrated advantages of modern medicine and sanitation meet little resistance, and in many cases, even in the most remote villages, there is a demand for more of these modern miracles of the west than the local government can supply.

Education

The changeover from traditional Middle Eastern to modern Western educational methods and aims can serve as an additional illustration of the practicability of introducing any change, even the most far-reaching one, if it is preceded by careful demonstration and is made gradually. Both these conditions were fulfilled in the course of the modest beginnings and the slow growth of modern educational institutions in the Middle East. Thus there was little organized resistance on the part of traditional forces who would have preferred to retain the outmoded *kuttābs* (Koran schools) as the only educational institutions. The first modern schools were founded by Western educators or patterned after a Western (French, British, American) model. In a short time modern Muslim schools were founded, until eventually they outnumbered the traditional Koran schools.[5]

Another effect of the introduction of modern education was the increase in the percentage of children attending school. The Koran schools could never boast an enrollment of more than a small percentage of the male school-age population. Since the establishment of modern schools this percentage has been steadily on the increase in every Middle Eastern country. Since no corresponding increase has taken place in the Koran schools, the result is that an ever-growing majority of the children attend modern schools while a decreasing percentage of them is still sent by their parents to Koran schools.[6] Although the modern educational effort of the Middle East is still far from having reached its goal, several countries have passed laws of general compulsory elementary education, and thus have officially adopted the principle that every child is duty bound to acquire a system of knowledge much of which has been adopted from the West only recently.

At the same time, however, in the curriculum of the modern Middle Eastern elementary schools (outside Turkey) great emphasis is put on the Koran, on Islam, on Islamic history, and the history of the country in which the school is situated (including its pre-Islamic phase). Expanding modern education thus creates in ever-increasing numbers of children and youths a much greater appreciation of their own culture than was ever the case under the old *kuttāb* education. The rudiments of Western learning are absorbed together with an increased religionational consciousness that potentially contains the seeds of anti-Western feelings.

Arts and Literature

In the realm of technology, it is relatively easy to demonstrate the superiority of a modern Western achievement over the traditional Middle Eastern one. It is not too hard to convince an Arab weaver that the wide fly-shuttle loom is superior to the old narrow-width hand loom, or to show a village population that if it cleans up a polluted source of water its health improves. Because of this, the introduction of Western technical improvements meets with least resistance.

In other aspects of culture, such as the arts, music, and literature, it is not possible to demonstrate the superiority of one culture over another. What an individual or a group prefers in these fields is largely a matter of taste and education, and the end result of cumulative previous experience. When therefore Middle Easterners rave about the greatness of Beethoven and Tchaikovsky while deprecating the primitivity of their own music, they clearly have allowed their judgment to be influenced by factors extraneous to the musical enjoyment itself. There can be little doubt that the ostensible enjoyment of jazz music by the urban Turkish youth[7] originates in the wish to be regarded as modern and fashionable. Eventually, of course, a few years of listening to a new musical variety may result in a genuine preference for it. The great majority of the Middle Easterners, however, still enjoy their own traditional music only, still sing their old folksongs and popular songs, and still prefer to hear familiar tunes in radio broadcasts.[8] They show interest, although without too much appreciation, when "modern-Oriental" songs sung by such famous performers (that is, famous in the cities) as Abdul Wahhab or Umm Kulthum are broadcast, but have neither interest in nor understanding for the Western music to which the Westernized musical directors of the Middle Eastern broadcasting stations devote a considerable proportion of the program time.

As with music, so with the visual arts, and especially their rich decorative varieties. On the one hand, traditional tastes still predominate among the "simple people"; and on the other, some of the more enlightened Middle Eastern governments have initiated measures to insure the survival of the fine crafts in which decorative art has traditionally found its expression. Only in the cities are foreign art forms, introduced from the West, becoming fashionable among the sophisticated groups.

It may be argued that the resistance to the penetration of Western musical and visual art forms is a rather unimportant aspect of the resistance to Westernization in the Middle East. It must, however, be remembered that it is precisely in the arts that the regional and local character of any culture most overtly and specifically manifests itself. A loss of the traditional character of the Middle Eastern arts would not only make the life of the area's peoples poorer and drabber, it would also detract from the sum total of mankind's artistic creativity.

Literature in Middle Eastern popular culture is of much smaller significance than the visual arts and music. The enjoyment of written literature is confined to a still very small educated urban class, and the active participation in it is the privilege of a very few individuals. Poetry, both in its artistic and popular forms, is still very much alive, and the old traditions of the great medieval Arab and Persian poets are still followed, although the resultant products are recognizedly inferior. But the Western literary forms of the novel and the short story are used almost exclusively by modern Middle Eastern writers of prose, and it is the consensus among Middle Eastern literati themselves that the original works of these local authors are less enjoyable than the translations of European and American prose prepared by the same writers.

The only persons in a position to put up a considered resistance to this form of Western cultural penetration are the religious functionaries and the traditionally educated and tradition-bound elements whose number is dwindling rapidly. They do not object to the perusal per se of Western literary products in the original or in translation; neither do they oppose in principle the fashionable trend among the young generation of authors to write in a style and in prose forms imitative of Western literatures. They protest these modern developments because Western literary forms are usually filled with a Western spirit; because the heroes of the novel and short story, as a rule, either are Westerners or behave, think, and feel like Westerners; and because thereby *belles lettres* as a whole serve as a propaganda instrument for Western attitudes, mores, and values. More has to be said on this very sensitive issue; but first it seems necessary to discuss the contrast between Middle Eastern and Western social control and intercourse that constitutes the background against which the clash over mores and values takes place.

Social Control

The next aspect of Western culture that encounters a more definite resistance is social control including organization, administration, and governmental forms. In traditional Middle Eastern society, social control and political organization are based on family ties, or at least are modeled after the structural pattern characterizing the family. The tribal or village headman, and even the landowner who owns entire villages, occupies a position vis-à-vis his people not unlike that of the patriarch of the family. Even King Ibn Saud kept to this tradition as long as it was physically possible for him. Western observers have often remarked at the ease with which the simplest tribesman could gain entrance to the King, and the familiarity with which he conversed with the powerful monarch of the Arabian Peninsula. In this "kinship culture"[9] the parallelism between familial and social structure goes even further. In the family, the son has no clearly defined rights of his own, for all his rights are vested in and defended by his father. In the social order, the individual lacks legally circumscribed rights apart from those which are represented by the headman of the larger social group to which he belongs. However, just as the son can always count on the love and protection of his father, the individual is in accordance with the prevailing ethos sure of the benevolence and help of his chieftain, headman, landlord, or other leading personality. This situation became somewhat complicated with the appearance on the Arab scene of Turkish, that is, foreign governors and other officials, but even the relationship between these and their Arab subjects was never as impersonal as is the case in a Western-type governmental and administrative set-up. It would therefore be shortsighted to attribute the resistance to the changeover from the traditional to modern Western organizational, administrative, and governmental forms to vested interests of the ruling classes alone. These undoubtedly constitute a powerful contributing factor; but it will take a great educational effort to accustom the governed classes to the impersonal Western organization with its insistence on equal rights and duties for everybody, instead of the personal Middle Eastern approach[10] with its emphasis on kinship, friendship, benevolence, and conveniently purchasable good will.

The great emphasis put by traditional-minded Middle Easterners on the accustomed forms of social control and intercourse is a motivation, among those of them with sufficient insight to recognize indirect causal connections, for resistance to even the most innocuous aspects of Westernization. They observe that the acceptance of such unobjectionable elements of Western culture as technology, sanitation, industrialization, and the like inevitably brings about the penetration of Western social forms and behavior patterns as well. A young man who is sent by his father to a modern school, acquires a trade or profession, and subsequently finds employment in a factory or office, earns probably more than his father and gets accustomed to moving around in a world in which his father is a complete stranger. Such a young man will rarely exhibit to the full those traits of filial obedience, of self-subordination to the joint interests of his family, as expressed and represented by his father or possibly his grandfather, which are highly prized values in the traditional mores of the Middle East. To engage in a new occupation invariably means that the individual doing so removes himself from the closed circle of joint family endeavor. Occupational change thus brings about economic separation, and this in turn results in the creation of a social distance that would have been unthinkable in the traditional set-up. The next step usually is the assertion of a certain independence by the young man in the choice of a wife, contrary to the traditional custom according to which the parents of the young people take the initiative and make the decision with regard to the marriage of their children. This is followed by the setting up of a separate household by the young people, again contrary to the custom which demands that the young couple become integrated into the household of the bridegroom's father. In this manner, educational and occupational changes, in themselves features of Western culture desirable from the Middle Eastern point of view, result in the breakdown or at least in a considerable weakening of the traditional extended family system that is one of the mainstays of Middle Eastern society. The substitution of the Western family pattern is regarded by most people (at least by those of the older generation) as highly undesirable, and is therefore resisted.

Nor is the effect of education and occupational change confined to the breakdown of the traditional extended family. In the Middle East, as we have seen, all the larger social units, whether one of the two famous moieties, an urban trade guild, or a new political party, are firmly founded upon the extended family which, as a rule, has been committed for many generations to supporting them. In the past, since the individual was a member of an extended family, and the extended family as a whole derived its strength from its membership in such a larger unit, he was, as a rule, not able to break ranks, to change affiliation or allegiance. The result was a certain stability in the entire social structuring of the population.

Up to a certain point, the changes brought about by modern times could be accommodated within this pre-existing social system owing to its inherent flexibility. When, for instance, voting and "modern" political parties were introduced, which in itself was done in emulation of Western political forms, the groups economically dependent on the great landlords and residing in their villages were transformed without much difficulty into political constituencies: instruction had only to be handed down to all those who had newly acquired the right to vote that they cast their ballot either for the landlord or for the man to whom he in turn owed allegiance.

With the increase of literacy and of the occupational, economic, and social independence of the individual from his own extended family, the political system that had retained its traditional Middle Eastern content under the newly introduced Western forms began to crumble. Once the primary bond to one's extended family was weakened, the loyalties that the family as a whole owed to a larger group and its leaders also lost much of their hold. For this reason, if for no other, the family heads and all those who under the traditional system hold positions of importance and wield influence must be opposed to the changeover from the traditional Middle Eastern social forms to newfangled ones introduced from the West.

Mores, Morals, and Values

Before entering the very sensitive area of mores, morals, and values, a general remark seems to be in place about an all too often encountered preconception that makes difficult if not impossible the understanding of any resistance to Westernization. This preconception is the conviction that Western ways of life, Western mentality and behavior are superior to their Middle Eastern counterparts. To the average Westerner who visits the Middle East or who has any dealings with the area from a distance, the situation is a clear-cut one: "native" peoples are given an opportunity to benefit by the vast storehouses of Western experience; they are presented with the end results of a long and laborious civilizatory development; they can therefore learn within a short time what it took the West several centuries to achieve, and thus are enabled to step out of the Middle Ages right into the twentieth century. If they do not want to learn, if they do not wish to be helped, if they are "choosy," rejecting this and accepting only part of that, this is but an additional manifestation of their backwardness and stubbornness.

As against this rule-of-the-thumb explanation of any opposition to Westernization, it is well to consider that Middle Eastern cultures, as the other great cultures of the Orient, "are thousands of years older than the West . . . with aesthetic, religious, and social values in many respects superior."[11] Middle Eastern opposition to Westernization can, therefore, stem from the apprehension, even if not often clearly articulated, that a wholesale adoption of Western civilization would entail the displacement and loss of many greatly cherished traditional Middle Eastern cultural values.

The issue of modern *versus* traditional mores and morals often result in conflict even within the context of one single culture between the old and the young generation. When the old generation is in addition the exponent of the traditions of one culture and the young one that of the dominant moral tenor of another very different culture, the conflict between them can become much more pronounced and embittered.

Although from Chapters 2 and 5 it became apparent that considerable variations exist between one culture area in the Middle East and another in several important facets of the traditional mores and morals, precisely those areas that have hitherto become exposed to Western influences share a certain fundamental value syndrome negated in its entirety by modern Western culture. In many cases the contrast between the two systems of mores and values is explicit and blatant; in others, it is implicit and latent, but its existence is nevertheless felt by those whom their own full awareness and appreciation of traditional Middle Eastern values sensitize even to differences in emphasis. A few areas can be indicated, albeit with sketchy brevity.

Traditional Middle Eastern mores insist on segregation between the sexes to varying degrees; the modern West has built its entire social life on the mingling of the sexes, allowing and even prescribing intimate bodily contact between members of the opposite sex barely acquainted with each other as, for example, at dances. The Middle East has developed a garb that reveals neither the feminine nor the masculine body form; in fact, the long robes traditionally worn reveal the sex of the wearer only by their color and decorative pattern, and not by outlining the shape of the physical frame. In the modern West, clothes emphasize rather than hide the difference between the physical shapes of the two sexes, and, on certain occasions, reveal almost the entire body.

In the traditional Middle East age is a value; the older a person becomes the more he is honored and the more prestige he has. In the West, age is considered a drawback and, with few exceptions, the older a person is the less his importance for society and even for his own family.

Education and socialization in the Middle East aim at making the young ones into obedient members of their families. Both during maturation and after having reached adulthood, the younger generation must follow the instructions of the elders, and subordinate its own interests to those of the family. In the West, the purpose of education is to make the youngsters independent as early as possible; it is anticipated that they will soon "fly the coop," make their own decisions, find their own way, and fight their own battles. Family cohesion is minimal and neither expected in actuality nor upheld in theory.

In the traditional Middle East, the drive for material success is mitigated and balanced by a religious outlook that stresses the need to be prepared for afterlife. In the Modern West, work for success here and now, measured primarily in income and property, completely absorbs most people.

The above items are merely examples of a long list of contrasting values whose sum total is the ethos in each of the two cultures. That people steeped in traditional Middle Eastern culture object to the abandonment of their own value system for that of the modern West should not be difficult to appreciate. Most people, and especially those who are carriers of traditional cultures, tend to regard their own values as "right," and different values as "wrong." This tendency becomes even more pronounced in a culture permeated by religion to the extent to which the Middle Eastern is. For Middle Eastern religiocentricity the adoption of Western value culture appears not merely as the exchange of a proved set of values for an inferior one, but as a fatal deviation from the "straight path" (Koran 1 : 5).

In traditional Middle Eastern society, whether rural or urban, nomadic or settled, the daughter's place is at home until such time as she is safely married off by her parents to a man as closely related to the family as possible. Formal schooling for girls is a Western innovation the acceptance of which still lags behind that of the schooling of boys.[12] But those girls who are sent to school are by this single act placed in a position largely similar to that of the educated young man in relation to their families.

Outside the family circle itself, the educational facilities granted to varying percentages of the women in Middle Eastern countries bore results that were alarming to those who clung to traditional social forms and mores. In one country only, namely in Turkey, complete political equality of women with men was made law in 1934. In other countries women are still demanding such rights with varying intensity. In Egypt, for instance, there is a strong feminist movement, but there is also strong opposition to it on the part of the *'ulamā* of el-Azhar and other orthodox Muslims who maintain that woman's place is in the home and that according to Islamic law public authority is confined to men. In Syria only literate women won the franchise (in 1949) while both literate and illiterate men are permitted to vote.

Any change in the traditional position of women in the Middle East is a step in the direction of Westernization and is advocated by feminists in their desire to secure for women a position similar to that held by them in the Western world. On the other hand, opposition to these feminist aspirations stems from the socio-religious attitude of the conservative elements who see in the feminist movement an infringement of traditional religious law and custom.

The Realm of Law

Religious conservatism is the ideological and emotional foundation also of the opposition to the introduction of new systems of laws. Law in the Middle East has been the domain proper of religion for the past five thousand years. The Islamic versions of religious law, although the youngest of indigenous legal systems in the area, are by now about a thousand years old and therefore do not cover all the contingencies of later developments. They are especially out of touch with the legal needs arising as a result of Westernization. In the more Westernized states Islamic Canon Law (*sharīʿa*) has been supplemented by a modern civil law taken over from the West, while in the more tradition-bound countries the older tribal or local (*ʿurf*, *ʿāda*, *izref*, *ittifāqāt*) law is still adhered to by the nonurban population. These three legal systems function independently and without coordination, and the observance of one of them occasionally entails a breach of the other.

The survival of the *ʿurf* after thirteen hundred years of Islamic legal domination is an eloquent testimony to the religiolegal conservatism of the Middle East. In relation to the problem of further modernization of the realm of law this conservatism is expressed by the opposition to any additional expansion of the domain of modern civil law at the expense of traditional Islamic law. In most countries the present stage of legal development is considered satisfactory, whether modern civil law has made considerable headway as in Egypt, or is still completely excluded as in Yemen. Secularization of the law is opposed in many countries not only by individuals and public bodies with vested religious interests, but also by thoughtful people who are otherwise not particularly conservatively minded.

As to the conservative element, they feel keenly that Westernization, as von Grunebaum put it, "develops what secularizing tendencies there are in the Islamic heritage, it relegates the Canon Law, in a sense the greatest achievement of traditional Islam, to the background and it assails the social basis of traditional society by changing the status of women, introducing democratic procedures, and a new kind of education."[13]

Islam and the "Infidel"

Islam, the ruling Middle Eastern religion, is thoroughly Oriental insofar as it exercises as strong a hold over the thoughts and emotions of the great majority of the population as do the great religions of southeast Asia, in sharp contrast to the modest place of religion in the modern Western world. In one fundamental aspect, however, Middle Eastern religion is basically different from the other major Oriental religions, and falls into one category with Western religion (Christianity), in keeping with the common origin of the two. The major South Asian and Southeast Asian religions (with the exception of Shinto) are nontheistic and tolerant of other faiths. Islam, like Christianity and like the parent religion of both, Judaism, is theistic, proselytizing,[14] aggressive, and often intolerant. Common to all theistic religions is the tendency to regard "religious views other than their own as heathen, erroneous, or inferior."[15] Thus while in South Asia and Southeast Asia the presence of Europeans who were of a different religious persuasion did not arouse resentment on religious grounds, the appearance of Christians in the Muslim world evoked the typical impatient reaction of a theistic religion to an encounter with members of another faith. The appellative "Christian" (like that of "Jew") has remained to this day an expression of contempt in the more isolated parts of the Middle East. The traditional attitude of Muslims to "infidels" has almost the same quality that characterized the missionary and inquisitorial zeal of the Spaniards after their arrival in the New World: the "infidel" (in the Middle East) or the "idolatrous pagan" (in New Spain) must be saved by conversion to the only true faith (Islam in the Middle East, Catholicism in New Spain) in his own interest and even against his will. This attitude explains the periodic outbreaks of violence, subsiding only when formal conversion was accomplished, perpetrated by Muslim mobs against Christians and Jews living in their midst who, in normal times, were merely treated with varying degrees of contempt as *dhimmi*, tolerated subject people. Violence against foreigners has been rare even in those countries of the Middle East that have preserved much of their isolation, but the feeling of contempt against those who are not "believers" is still present. The self-assurance of these foreigners in the superior positions they occupy, their impolite manners,[16] and even their eagerness to teach and instruct are in striking contrast to the accustomed submissive behavior pattern of the *dhimmi*, the native Christians and Jews. And not only does the foreigner do all the things from which a *dhimmi* (if he ever dreamt of presuming) would be immediately and most effectively discouraged, he cannot even be reproached for it. Here is an unbeliever who is an adherent of the same churches (regarded by the Muslim as places of semi-idolatrous worship since they are decorated with pictures and statues) as the native Christian. Yet instead of following the customary pattern of *dhimmi* submissiveness, his bearing betrays his pride; he expects all and sundry to comply with his wishes, and to follow his instructions; instead of asking for favors, he has the power to grant them. In this emotion-guided chain of reactions there is little place for such practical considerations as the actual usefulness of the foreigner or the economic advantages and material benefits his presence means for the country at large. An emotional tension is thus built up that can find no outlet (apart from rare outbreaks of violence usually discouraged by the authorities) and therefore leads to what to the Westerner appear as completely unreasonable demands aiming not at the benefit of the Middle Eastern people concerned but at the elimination of the "stone of offense," the foreigner.

Like all other phenomena connected with Westernization, the variations of this religiously grounded antiforeigner feeling constitute a scale of fine gradation from the "most intense" on the one end to the "minimal" on the other. Nor must it be forgotten that the population of no Muslim country is homogeneous, and that considerable differences can be found in the attitude to foreigners among the various classes and groups of the urban population, as well as among the urban people in general on the one hand and the inhabitants of the villages, especially the more remote ones, on the other.

Westernization and Secularization

This antiforeign feeling is a heritage of past centuries when the whole world was in Muslim eyes divided into the *Dār al-Islām* and *Dār al-Ḥarb*, the House of Islam or Peace, and the House of War. In this view, every country and individual not belonging to the *Dār al-Islām* was *eo ipso* an enemy. In modern times, increasing familiarity with people who were characterized above as primary personal sources of Westernization, and many other kinds of contact with the Western world, have rendered this view obsolete. In the meantime, however, a new motivation started to serve as fuel for the old fire.

It has been observed by Middle Eastern people in the last two generations that wherever Westerners and with them Western civilizatory attainments penetrate, traditional religiosity suffers a setback. This has proved to be the case even if nothing but the most external and mechanical phases of Western civilization were introduced. Not as if these were accompanied by a danger of conversion to Christianity (in no other culture has Christian missionary activity been crowned with less success than in the Middle East) but because the adoption of Western civilizatory trappings tended to loosen the hold religion traditionally has had over all aspects of life, and to make people negligent in the fulfillment of religious ritual. Westernized Middle Easterners will assert that they are good Muslims in their feeling and thinking even though they do not observe the Fast and the Prayers, the prohibition of drinking wine and eating pork, and other ritual injunctions of Islam. Tradition-bound Muslims, however, attach to these assertions even less value than similar statements by non-practicing Catholics have in the eyes of practicing Catholics. To the average Middle Easterner, in whose life religion is still the fundamental motivating force[17]—religion not expressed in formal observance is unthinkable. There is therefore an opposition even to the culturally "harmless" or "neutral" components of Western civilization such as technical and organizational improvement, not because these in themselves are deemed undesirable, but because it is understood that they are almost inevitably followed by a decline of religious observance. It is felt that a breakdown or even a mere cracking of the religious-spiritual-emotional edifice, a total or partial loss of the traditional mental climate, and a narrowing down of the wide outlook would be too high a price to pay for mere material betterment.

Superficial Westernization

It has been noticed by both Western and Middle Eastern observers that the first effect of Westernization is to focus the interest of those caught in it on the overt manifestations of Western culture, such as technology and organizational know-how; that a true absorption of Western cultural patterns with their implicit ideational mainsprings takes place very rarely; and that in many cases the individual nevertheless tends to abandon his own traditional cultural values, and becomes rootless and superficial.[18] Especially younger people often suffer serious personality damage because, having acquired the external trappings and mastered the overt mannerisms of the Westerners, they feel free to throw off the traditional restraints of their old culture without having first grasped and often without even suspecting the existence of the different set of restraints invisibly controlling Western behavior patterns and directing them into morally sanctioned channels. In contacts between males and females, parents and children, teachers and pupils, elders and youths, employers and employees, the rejection of the old social forms, a seemingly unavoidable concomitant of Westernization, often means the complete disappearance of any check or constraint.

It is not hard to see why thoughtful Middle Easterners should be disquieted by these developments, and why some of them should advocate a policy of cultural isolationism. It simply amounts to rejection of the honey for fear of the bee's sting.

Ambivalence

Complete rejection, however, of everything offered by Western culture is rare. It is an extreme, polar position. More frequent is an attitude that can best be described as ambivalent, as composed of both negative and positive factors. On the positive side there is the irresistible glitter of many features dangled by the West before the eyes of the Middle East. The reaction to these is a strong desire to acquire them, to imitate them, to master them, to enjoy them, and to profit by them. Hand in hand with attraction, however, goes repulsion; there is the feeling that the people who seem so ready to teach and to impart these good things are themselves not virtuous, that any or all of the following objections apply to them: they are unbelievers; they are foreigners; they wish to gain (or retain, or strengthen, or renew, as the case might be) domination over the country; their ultimate aim is exploitation; their mores and morals are undesirable. There is, in brief, the fear that if the peoples of the Middle East swallow the bait of the attractive offerings of the West, they will soon be unwittingly influenced by Western thinking, outlook, points of view, behavior, and will in the process lose their own values, individuality, ideals, concepts, which make them the true sons of their fathers and bring them honor, status, and respectability. Thus the desire to learn from the West in the material and other fields in which Western supremacy is unquestioningly acknowledged is powerfully counteracted, or at least inhibited, by the fear of being contaminated by those Western traits against whose acceptance traditional, moral, ethical, religious, emotional, and ideational scruples militate.

Few are the people in the Middle East who are consciously aware of this ambivalence in their attitude to Western values. Fewer still are those who are able to resolve the conflict created by it. In many cases one of the two contrasting attitudes gains dominance in consciousness while the other is forced back, repressed, and relegated into the subconscious where it becomes an irritating factor and a source of frustration.

Outlook

In conclusion it should be pointed out that the development of the traditional Middle East appears to have lingered for several centuries close to the beginning of that road which, according to Redfield, led precivilized human society toward its bifurcation into urban civilization and folk society.[19] Furthermore, in accordance with Redfield's generalized statement to the effect that the technical order is the destroyer of the moral order,[20] the increasing new ramifications of the technical order in the cities have made the ancient walls of the Middle Eastern moral order begin to crack and crumble. The literati of the Middle Eastern urban society have viewed this breakdown of their highly prized moral order under the impact of Westernization with understandable alarm, and have issued impassioned pleas for resistance. It is difficult to foretell what the results of these efforts will be, especially in view of the fact that the growing "intelligentsia," as Toynbee calls those members of the native community who "have learned the tricks of the intrusive civilization,"[21] exerts a powerful pull in the direction of Westernization. But certain signs indicate that the Middle Eastern developments will bear out the correctness of Redfield's observation that "the effects of the technical order (also) include the creation of new moral orders."[22] This constructive and recreative effect of the introduction of a new technical order lags behind its immediate effect, which is destructive, but its manifestations are becoming more and more evident each day, and in them lies the justification for looking with confidence towards the cultural future of the Middle East.

As to the future relationship between the Middle East and the Western world, the experience of the last two decades has shown that economical aid and technical assistance, though important and even imperative, are in themselves not sufficient to make for understanding and cooperation between peoples belonging to two different cultures. Aid offered on the basis of what is important and desirable in Western culture can meet with conditional or grudging acceptance or even forthright refusal by people sharing a different culture and having therefore a different scale of values. The air lift organized by the U.S. Air Force a few years ago to help thousands of pilgrims reach Mecca in time and thus fulfill a lifelong dream undoubtedly did more to create among the peoples of the Middle East an appreciation of the sincerity of America's attitude towards them than millions of dollars of economic aid could have done.

In order properly to evaluate what Middle Eastern culture will willingly accept from the embarrassingly rich storehouses of Western civilization, a better and sounder understanding of Middle Eastern culture must first be acquired. The same prerequisite is necessary in order to gauge the probable effects of newly introduced traits on the cultural context of tradition-directed peoples. Also, the ways and means in which new cultural offerings can be made palatable must be studied much more thoroughly than was hitherto the case. In brief the only way in which the Gordian knot of resistance to Westernization in the Middle East can be unraveled is that of studying the Middle East, of obtaining a fuller picture of its traditional culture, a better understanding of the processes of change taking place in it at present, and a deeper insight into the psychology of human groups brought up in Middle Eastern culture. The task is taxing, but the prize, harmony between the West and a neighboring world area of crucial importance, is well worth it.

XV. The Endogamous Unilineal Descent Group

A DISCUSSION of endogamous unilineal descent groups is long overdue because the very existence of such groups has hitherto been either largely overlooked or else explicitly denied in general structural studies dealing with the unilineal descent group (in the following: UDG), and because the identification of exogamous marriage patterns with the UDG has led to certain distortions in the latter's generalized portraiture.

A NEGLECTED SUBJECT

Let us begin with a few examples of the neglect of the endogamous variety of UDGs. Of general texts in anthropology, those of Herskovits and Slotkin can illustrate two approaches to the phenomenon. Herskovits, in his *Man and His Works*,[1] discusses exogamy in some detail but says absolutely nothing about endogamy, although in a chapter on "Social Organization: the Structure of Society" one would expect at least a brief reference to the fact that in some societies marriage preference is endogamous. Slotkin[2] divides hereditary kinship groups into (a) unilateral and exogamous and (b) bilateral and either open or endogamous; he does not mention the third possibility, namely, that a hereditary kinship group can be unilateral and endogamous. This omission is the more remarkable since in giving his only example of a unilateral, exogamous, patrilineal, and patrilocal kinship group, he refers to the Arabs of the South Palestinian village Arṭās,[3] who, however, are endogamous.

Of general theoretical discussions devoted to UDGs, we can take Fortes' influential paper, "The Structure of Unilineal

Descent Groups," as typifying the silence with reference to endogamous UDGs.[4] In this paper, Fortes summarizes the findings of British anthropologists (including his own) in the field of African kinship studies and gives an excellent outline of the main features of the UDG. As will be pointed out below, roughly one half of continental Africa is inhabited by peoples with endogamous UDGs. Yet while Fortes refers repeatedly to the exogamy of the African societies south of the Sahara[5] and also to the Bedouin of Cyrenaica,[6] nowhere does he even as much as hint that these Bedouin practice endogamy (in fact the term "endogamy" or "endogamous" does not appear even once), so that the reader is left with the false impression that the Cyrenaican Bedouin share the practice of exogamy with the societies south of the Sahara.

Of theoretical papers dealing with certain aspects of descent groups and overlooking the existence of endogamous UDGs there is no dearth. Two examples, both published in the 1964 volume of the *American Anthropologist*, will suffice. Coult,[7] basing himself on Firth[8] and Murdock,[9] repeats the fallacious dichotomy we already met in Slotkin: "Unilineal descent groups tend to be exogamous, whereas ambilineal descent groups tend not to be so." The somewhat flexible "tend to be" soon becomes an actual differentiating criterion: "The absence of exogamy is an important feature differentiating the two types of descent groups,"[10] namely, the unilineal and ambilineal. What is implied here is practically identical with Slotkin's proposition: descent groups are of two types: either unilineal and exogamous, or ambilineal and nonexogamous. Apart from the curious avoidance of the term "endogamous," which seems called for in a discussion of marriage patterns, it is baffling that the possibility of the existence of a third type of descent groups—one which is unilineal and endogamous—is again excluded from a theoretical classification of descent groups.

The second paper, by Moore,[11] opens with the statement: "Kinship networks involve a paradox. On the one hand marriage links exogamic kin groups . . ." creating the distinct impression that all kinship networks are "exogamic." A few pages later,[12] in commenting on Levi-Strauss' argument that animal species, which are endogamous, are nevertheless suitable symbols of exogamous groups because totemism puts its emphasis "not on the animality but on the duality," Moore says, "This part of the Levi-Strauss argument is superfluous. The endogamy of animal species makes animals not less, but more appropriate as emblems of descent groups. This is *obviously not because of any actual endogamy in descent groups*, but because descent groups are symbolically self-perpetuating" (emphasis mine, R.P.). Thus we are offered a neat distinction between animal and human groups: animal groups are endogamous, while human descent groups "obviously" are not.

The Incidence of Endogamous Societies

Is this neglect of endogamous UDGs justified on the basis of their relatively insignificant incidence in relation to the frequency of exogamous UDGs? Some students of social structure who noticed the lack of endogamous UDGs seem to be inclined to answer this question in the affirmative. Murphy and Kasdan, for example, comment that comparatively little interest has been devoted to the study of preferential patrilateral parallel cousin marriage and kin group endogamy. This is understandable when one considers that the contemporary occurrence of this practice is limited to the Arabs and their immediate Muslim neighbors, while the reverse phenomena of exogamy and cross-cousin marriage recur throughout the world.[13] Let us consider whether this alibi for the neglect of endogamy actually holds.

We may turn, to begin with, to Murdock's "World Ethnographic Sample." Of 564 or 565 societies listed by Murdock in this sample, he found cross-cousin (patrilateral, matrilateral, and symmetrical) marriage preference in 153 societies.[14] These 153 societies are the sum total of no less than twelve different types of societies and marriage preferences. On the average, therefore, one type of society with one type of cross-cousin marriage preference comprises 12.75 groups.

In the same table on which the above calculation is based, Murdock lists twelve societies with patrilineal descent with preferential marriage with a parallel cousin. This type of marriage preference is confined to societies with patrilineal descent and is absent in the three other types of descent groups, the matrilineal, the double descent, and the bilateral. Comparing equivalent units of classification, we find that, according to Murdock's evidence, preferential marriage with a parallel cousin in patrilineal descent groups has approximately the same incidence as the average of any single type of cross-cousin marriage preference in any single type of descent group.

Nor is this all. For Murdock himself can be added to the list of those students of social structure who pay little or no attention to endogamy. Although he recognizes and lists preferential parallel-cousin marriage, he establishes no category of endogamy. In columns 10 and 11 of his "World Ethnographic Sample," where he lists several categories of exogamous patrilineal and matrilineal kin groups, the category of endogamous kin groups is missing.

In the absence of such a category, let us have a closer look at Murdock's category "P" (preferential marriage with a parallel cousin) which figures in his column 10. Although in Table 3 he gives twelve as the number of societies practicing preferential parallel cousin marriage, in his Table 1 he lists thirteen such societies (Beja, Hausa, Kababish, Berabish, Egyptians, Shawiya, Ulad Nail, Kurd, Afghan, Iranians, Sindhi, Merina, and Guahibo).[15] More importantly, however, a scrutiny of the cultures listed by Murdock in his Moslem Sudan, Sahara, North Africa, and Near East areas reveals that these include at least eight additional societies which practice (or practiced) preferential parallel (patrilateral) cousin marriage and which were incorrectly assigned to other categories. They are as follows:

1. The Songhoi (Moslem Sudan) are identified by Murdock as a society in which "marriage with a parallel cousin [is] disapproved but not specifically forbidden." Miner, however, found at least one Songhoi group, the Arma of Timbuctoo, among whom there is equal preference for marriage with both father's brother's daughter and mother's sister's daughter.[16]

2. The Mzab (Sahara) are listed by Murdock as a society concerning whose marriage preference no information is avail-

able. It is known today that the Mzabites prefer patrilateral parallel cousin marriage.[17]

3. The Siwans (Sahara) are listed by Murdock as a society in which "marriage with a parallel cousin [father's brother's daughter] is allowed but not preferred." Walter Cline reported as long ago as 1936 that marriage with FaBrDa (father's brother's daughter) was the preferred pattern in Siwa.[18]

4. The Riffians (North Africa) are stated by Murdock to be a society practicing "lineage exogamy, that is, marriage [is] forbidden with any lineage mate (or with comparable relatives in the absence of lineages) but permitted with remoter unilinear kinsmen." In fact, the Riffians not only prefer marriage with FaBrDa, but ego has the right to marry her, and the infringement of this right by ego's FaBr (by giving his daughter in marriage to an outsider) results in his being killed by his brother's son. Preference for patrilateral cousin marriage is general in Morocco, among both Arabs and Berbers.[19]

5. The Bedouin (Rwala, Near East) are listed by Murdock as a society in which "marriage with a parallel cousin is forbidden, unilinear exogamy being absent." The emphatic preference for FaBrDa marriage among the Rwala, and Bedouins in general, is so well known[20] that one must assume that this particular entry is due to a printer's error, and that "p" (preferred) should be substituted for the "f" (forbidden).

6. The Hebrews (800 B.C., Near East) are listed by Murdock as a society in which "marriage with a parallel cousin (FaBrDa) was allowed but not preferred." My own studies have amply shown that among the ancient Hebrews FaBrDa marriage was strongly preferred.[21]

7. The Lebanese (Munsif, Near East) are categorized by Murdock as a society in which "marriage with a parallel cousin [is] forbidden, unilinear exogamy being absent." The true situation, much too complicated to be summarized in a brief sentence, is as follows: In the Lebanese Christian Arab village of Munsif[22] as well as in other Christian Arab communities in Lebanon, Syria, Jordan, and so forth, the church forbids all types of first-cousin marriages. Popular custom, however, prefers it. If a man wants to marry a first cousin, he merely

applies to the bishop for permission. The frequency of such marriages, which often are entered into without church dispensation, attests to the existence of the general Middle Eastern preference for marriage with a patrilateral parallel cousin among the Christian Arabs as well.[23]

8. The Turks (Anatolia) are listed by Murdock as a society in which "marriage with a parallel cousin" is "allowed but not preferred." The available evidence, however, shows that FaBrDa marriage is (or was) preferred among the Turks in the traditional order.[24]

If these eight cases are added to the thirteen listed in Murdock's table, we obtain a total of twenty-one societies with preference for FaBrDa marriage. Moreover, since this type of marriage preference is always the most emphatic expression of patrilineal endogamy, it follows that the corrected number of societies with preference for such marriage also indicates a wider incidence of patrilineal endogamy.

Obviously, the above number, which is merely the corrected figure of the societies practicing parallel cousin marriage preference among the 565 societies selected by Murdock, for his sample, does not give a complete picture of the incidence of this practice the world over. The data gathered above in Chapter 6 (pp. 135–76) indicate that this type of preference characterizes the marriage pattern in the entire Middle East. The African part of the Middle East extends over the entire northern half of the continent. It would therefore seem desirable that a trait (endogamy) characterizing this half of Africa be given the same consideration in a study of African UDGs as the alternative trait (exogamy) found in sub-Saharan Africa.

Paternal Authority: The Sons

The identification of unilineal descent with exogamy and bilateral descent with the absence of exogamy (which include endogamy), a notion that has become almost axiomatic, has led to attempts to show that the Arab kin group which is undeniably endogamous and, indeed, exhibits a strong preference for marriage with a father's brother's daughter, is not really unilineal. The fact is that the Arab kin group, as well as the typical kin group in the Middle East in general (including such non-Arab and/or non-Muslim ethnic groups as the Christian Copts of Egypt, the Christian Nestorians of Kurdistan, the Jews of every Middle Eastern country, etc.), is emphatically unilineal. One striking expression of this unilineality is the great stress on paternal authority or potestality.

At the same time, there is in Middle Eastern families and kin groups a considerable degree of informality, and especially in nomadic family and social life on all levels. It is a well known fact, surprising to Western observers, that the lowliest Bedouin was able to sit down next to mighty King ʿAbdul ʿAziz Ibn Saud in the council tent or chamber, addressing him as "Ya Saʿud (literally "O, Saud," but carrying overtones oi familiarity; a man would address a son, a servant, or a slave with the same word, "Ya"). Does this mean that the king had no authority? Certainly not.

As to paternal authority, a vast array of documentation is available to prove beyond doubt not only that it is exercised within the family but also that there is an actual subordination of a son's personal interests to those of the family as represented by the father or grandfather. Indeed, the entire system is calculated to subordinate son to father. The son's dependence on his father is hammered into him during the course of his entire education. He early learns that his position in the larger society (tribe, village, etc.) depends upon the status of his father. And even when he begins to earn money, his entire income goes to his father, who also controls all property. It is the father who decides when and whom his son should marry, and who pays for him the bride-price to the bride's father. Thus, beyond all apparent informality, there is an almost total concentration of power in the hands of the father over both his sons and daughters.

As to the actual authoritarian posture of the father in the Middle Eastern family, the available evidence is so ample that in the present context it is only possible to sample it.

The Rwala Bedouin: "If they [the young children] deserve it, they are spanked with a stick, not only by their mother or father, but by the slaves both male and female. The Rwala believe that the rod originated in Paradise . . . and that it also leads man back to it. . . . [When the son reaches the age of 14 to 16] the father would not think of punishing the disobedience of his son simply with a stick but uses a saber or a dagger instead. By cutting or stabbing them the father not merely punishes the boys but hardens them for their future life. In the opinion of the Bedouins, the son who disobeys is guilty of rebellion for which the proper punishment is the saber. . . ."[25]

The Kuwait Bedouin: "[The mother] will fly at her husband if he attempts to punish their child. . . ." A man had his own son put to death because the boy had killed his tent-neighbor in the heat of a foolish quarrel. "The rights of a Bedouin father over his children are absolute." "A son does not greet his father as he would another man. He must show proper modesty, and especially amongst strangers must take a back seat and appear to obliterate himself in the presence of his parent. . . . On the other hand, a father will greet his small sons with effusive affection, and the youngsters will always run to him to be kissed and fondled . . . girls are not so fondled. . . ."[26]

In Iraq: "The eldest male in the Bedouin clan, the village, or city household has absolute authority. He makes all decisions within the household unit, receives income, including that earned by married sons, and disburses it for the benefit of the unit. He bears the sole responsibility for discipline within the family . . ."[27] ". . . among Moslems and Christians alike the family is the paramount social unit and family authority is vested in the father. . . . Ultimate authority in the extended family generally rests with the oldest male. . . . In the rearing of the Iraqi child, strong emphasis is placed on teaching him to conform to the patterns laid down by his elders and to be an obedient member of the family group. Family solidarity is stressed and the child learns early that his wishes are subordinate to the interests of the family. Corporal punishment is employed, but more commonly among urban dwellers than in rural families. . . . the mother, in her role as the compassionate figure in the family, may temper through discreet intervention any undue severity on the part of the father. . . . In rural families sons even after marriage are expected to give obedience to their fathers."[28]

In the Arab countries of the East Mediterranean littoral

(Syria, Lebanon, Jordan, and Arab Palestine) the father is the master of his own nuclear family, while the elderly male who is the head of the extended family is the undisputed ruler of the entire group. In olden times the rule of the family head comprised jurisdiction over life and death as well as other matters within his family. The father's authority remains strong, especially in the rural family, in the nomadic tribe and the village. The prevalent mores demand that the younger members of the family obey and respect the decisions of the senior.[29]

In Egypt: "Corporal punishment is not uncommon, either by beating, striking, whipping or slapping. Such punishment is inflicted upon the child normally after he has committed a serious misdemeanour, such as talking back at his parents while being rebuked. . . . The father's authority cannot be flouted: and a change in the tone of his voice must be seriously considered. Although his punishment might be less frequent than that of the mother, yet it is more severely administered. While the former pinches the ear, or the thigh, and seldom slaps, the latter normally slaps and thrashes with a rope or a cane. It is also worth noting here that very little chance is given to the child to justify his misdemeanor . . . childhood is the most appropriate period for punishing and disciplining the child. . . . The only form of corporal punishment administered to adolescents on some rare occasions is slapping." "The absolute authority of the father over children is due to the fact that they belong to him and his family. . . ." The emphasis on paternal authority is so great that, "in order to be respected and obeyed" a man "avoids excessive intimacy" with his children and with his wife. A son must observe "many avoidances," especially in public, which manifest his subordination to his father. He must even avoid arguing face to face with his father, and has to send a messenger instead. Respect for a family head is so strong that if he publicly humiliates a younger member of, not only his own, but another family, e.g., by slapping his face, the latter is not allowed to retaliate in kind, but has to go with his complaint to his own family head.[30]

In Burri al-Lamāb near Khartoum, Sudan, the father is usually "severe and aloof" and "controls the family wealth."

"In the past, from the age of seven until the middle or late teens a boy was constantly disciplined by his father, who beat him with a stick." Today, with independent employment available to adolescent boys in Khartoum, they are less dependent on their fathers and less subservient. Nevertheless, "physical punishment such as pinching, twisting an ear, or slapping with the hand is common for younger children, while older ones, who are expected to be *mu'addab*, are sometimes whipped or beaten with a stick. . . ."[31]

In Algeria, in both oasis and city, "methods (of punishment administered by mothers) are less severe than those administered by men to boys of six or more. . . . it was initially clear that the Arabs were comparatively brutal toward children. . . . Beating [was] the preferred punishment for boys. . . . The Arabs operate on the principle that sons must be made to fear their fathers."[32]

Among the Teda of Tibesti (in the southeastern central Sahara), "children respect their parents, the father absolutely and the mother relatively. . . . The father pays all family expense, including the price of his sons' brides; but he can also beat his sons until they reach the age of fifteen and his daghters even after they are married, although he rarely does so. . . ."[33]

At the other end of the Middle East, in Afghanistan, "Some Afghan fathers are friendly with their children, some are aloof. All, however, demand complete obedience and respect. . . . boys stand in awe of their fathers. . . . The father is in charge of discipline and punishment. For this reason the mother can be more indulgent. . . ."[34]

These references, which could be multiplied at will, show clearly that paternal authority and discipline, frequently expressed in severe corporal punishment, are the unquestionable rule among the Arab Bedouin, settled Arab, and other Middle Eastern families. Authority is concentrated in the hands of the oldest male member of the family, that is, the head of the extended family; or, if the family is not extended, it is wielded by the head of whatever the actual family grouping happens to be. We can thus state categorically that internally exercised authority is normative in the Middle Eastern family; in fact, it is strong enough to make the family, whatever its actual size and structure, the fundamental building block of any and every larger social unit. As far as this point is concerned, the Arab and Middle Eastern social structure, therefore, exhibits the same features of authority which Fortes found characteristic of the African UFGs in general.

Paternal Authority: The Daughters

In making a girl the ward of her father, Middle Eastern folk custom and Muslim sharīʿa law mutually reinforce each other. Of the four Sunni schools of jurisprudence, three require that a woman be contracted in marriage by her guardian, who, in the case of young girls, is invariably the father if he is alive. Only one school, the Ḥanafī, allows a Muslim woman to enter on her own into a marriage contract, on condition that she chooses a husband who is her equal in social standing.[35]

In Southern Arabia: "In Oman . . . a girl, unmarried or married, who had willingly transgressed and was with child, would be killed by her father, brother or paternal cousin, but not her husband. . . . For a girl's first marriage it is the inviolate rule for her father to provide a husband without consulting her. This rule in Ibāḍī Oman is so rigorous among the elect that it would be shameful for a father to consult the wishes of his daughter. . . . The right of *bin ʿam*, the paternal cousin, elsewhere in Arabia universally accepted, is not insisted upon in these mountains, except by the Mahra, where the sole right of disposal vests in the father."[36]

As far as the actual extent of the *patria potestas* over marrying off a daughter is concerned even in relatively Westernized segments of Arab society, a poignant illustration is supplied by the Algerian feminist Fadela M'rabet, whose book *La Femme Algerien* was published in Paris in 1965. In it she reveals that in 1964 "no less than 175 young Algerian girls had chosen suicide rather than marry the man selected for them by their parents."[37]

That by "parents" Mme M'rabet means "fathers" becomes clear from a letter she wrote, in the same year in which her book was published, to *Le Monde*, stating among other things that "the greater number of marriages are still forced unions; fathers are still all-powerful, and can interrupt at will the studies of their daughters (in order to marry off or cloister them). . . ."[38]

The right of the girl's father's brother's son to her hand is in many cases supported by the ḥamūla elders who are interested in strengthening the cohesion within the ḥamūla by cousin marriage and other forms of endogamy. If the father has other plans for his daughter, he can, however, resort to the expedient of not allowing her to marry at all.

The illustration of this point is a case described in detail by Abner Cohen from the Arab village of Bint el-Ḥudūd in the Triangle Area in Israel. When Fatima was asked in marriage by both her cousin Ibrāhīm, an uneducated unskilled laborer, and the nonrelated Khālid, a teacher and highly educated man, her father wanted to give her to the latter. But not daring to go against the wishes of his ḥamūla, whose elders insisted on the traditional cousin marriage, all the father could do was not to give his daughter to either of the suitors. Long delays, several postponements and repeated interventions, representations, and intrigues by the notables of the ḥamūlas of the girl's father and of Khālid ensued, until the girl's father was brought to the point where he refused to give permission to his daughter to marry Khālid. The two ḥamūlas came near to large scale group fighting, and the bride's brother (who sided with Khālid) was actually severely beaten by men of his own hamūla. The police and other outside authorities, including the military officer of the area, were brought into the picture, until finally the two ḥamūlas made peace between themselves, and Fatima was married to Khālid.[39]

Another case illustrating the father's ability to deny his daughter to his brother's son if he so wishes is supplied by Emanuel Marx. "A man can do little to obtain his father's brother's daughter unless he is supported by his section. When a man of the Abu Qwēdar peasant group (Abu Rqaiq tribe) claimed his cousin's hand, her father demanded the exorbitant bride-wealth [i.e., bride-price] of IL. 12,000, over four times the average payment, and as the section did not support the suitor he had to relinquish his claim."[40]

As we see from the two cases quoted, the support of the section (ḥamūla) is a decisive factor in case there is a disagreement between the father of the girl and her *ibn ʿamm* (cousin; more precisely father's brother's son). He whom the ḥamūla, as represented by its elders, supports is likely to win out. However, the final decision still remains in the hands of the girl's father, and all the elders or the ḥamūla can do is to try to pressure him into consenting to the marriage. Thus these examples, while they afford an insight into the power relationships between the head of a family and his ḥamūla, as well as between two competing ḥamūlas, basically confirm our interpretation of the father's potestality over his daughter.

Local variations apart, the general rule is as follows: (a) A man has the right to marry his *bint ʿamm*. (b) A girl cannot marry anybody else unless her *ibn ʿamm* gives his consent which, as a rule, can be bought for a consideration, such as camels, cash, and so forth. (c) If the father of the girl objects, the *ibn ʿamm* cannot marry her against the father's will, although in such a case the girl cannot marry anybody else either. (d) Therefore, the *ibn ʿamm's* right to marry his *bint ʿamm* does not preclude the prerogative of her father either to give her to him or to withhold her from him. (e) This being the case, the father does exercise considerable *patria potestas* over his daughter in respect of her marriage. He has, in fact, three choices: (1) He either conforms to expectation and gives his daughter to her *ibn ʿamm*, receiving a greatly reduced bride-price for her but insuring the increased loyalty of his *ibn akh* (nephew) to him. (2) Or, he pays off the nephew with part of the full bride-price he receives from a more distantly related or nonrelated suitor of his daughter. (3) Or, he refuses his daughter to his nephew and lets her remain unmarried until such time as the nephew, possibly as a result of persuasion by the ḥamūla elders, declares himself ready to receive compensation for giving up his rights in his *bint ʿamm*.

Cousin Marriage and Ingroup Marriage

While a father's brother's daughter is thus the ideal choice throughout the Middle East, among Arabs and non-Arabs Muslims and non-Muslims alike, in practice only a relatively small percentage of men actually marry (or did marry in the past) a girl related to them in this manner. The available statistics, admittedly fragmentary and often unreliable, nevertheless show that nowhere do such marriages constitute even as much as one half of all marriages. The figures range from a maximum of 48 per cent (an exceptionally high figure) in certain tribal villages in Southern Kurdistan, through 17 per cent among the Arabs of Timbuctoo, down to 13.3 per cent, which happens to be the figure for both late pre-Islamic Ḥijāz and the South Palestinian Arab village of Artās in the 1920's, 12.6 per cent in the Israli Arab village of Bint el-Hudūd (in the 1960's), and to 11 per cent in the Sudan.[41]

In the great majority of cases in all Middle Eastern societies, marriages take place between a man and a woman who are either members of one and the same lineage but whose common patrilineal ancestor, if he can be traced at all, is several generations removed, or they belong to the same aggregate (tribe, village) but to different lineages comprised in it. This—that is, lineage or local endogamy, and not father's-brother's-daughter marriage—is the actual meaning of endogamy in the Middle Eastern context. Moreover, it should be clearly understood that Middle Eastern endogamy, even in this sense, is not the precise opposite of what students of social structure as a rule understand by exogamy. A society is exogamous if marriage within the same UDG is forbidden. Middle Eastern society is not endogamous in the sense that marriage outside one's own UDG is forbidden; it is endogamous merely in the sense that marriage within one's own UDG is given first preference, that second preference is given to other UDGs which form part of the same local aggregate, and that choices made outside the local aggregate are regarded with increasing disapproval as the distance from the in-group increases. The criteria for reckoning social distance differ from group to group, but as a broad generalization one can state that differences in descent traditions, religious affiliation, and the economic basis of livelihood are considered serious impedimenta. Non-Muslims are, as a general rule, beyond the pale. The extent of in-village versus out-village marriage can be gauged from the following sample figures:

In Southern Kurdistan 78 and 80 per cent of the marriages were found to be in-village marriages.[42] In Morocco it was 79 per cent.[43] In the Sudan, in a village suburb of Khartoum, where 79 per cent of the marriages were locally endogamous (with only one half of these between relatives), Barclay observed that the general principle of preferred lineage endogamy characteristic of Arab social structure is limited or reinforced according to the relative prestige of the lineage. Lineage exogamy may actually be preferred over endogamy where a marriage might establish ties to a more powerful and wealthy lineage. On the other hand, an already powerful lineage may seek to compound its power through endogamy.[44]

We thus find that Middle Eastern endogamy as it actually operates is an institution which brings together people who, in the great majority of cases, are not patrilateral parallel cousins. This means that in Middle Eastern society the officially sanctioned patrilineal reckoning of descent is the only one which can and actually does count, because any attempt to figure ego's descent matrilineally would, in most cases, lead immediately out of the patrilineage to a group of maternal biological ancestors who constitute a separate descent group to which ego does not belong.

Even in cases where a person's parents are patrilateral parallel cousins, he will, as a matter of actual fact, reckon his descent through his father only. In traditional Arab society great emphasis is placed on one's paternal geneology, that is, the line leading from ego, through his male progenitors only, to an outstanding ancestor. In such a chain of descent there will be men who married their fathers' brothers' daughter, men whose wives were more remotely related to them, men whose wives were not related to them at all, and men who begot their son (or sons) of slave-concubines. This being the case, it would be almost impossible to find a man whose patriline and matriline are identical over several generations.

Descent is important in the Middle East for establishing the ascribed status of an individual, for providing him with the basis of his claim to position, occupation, property, a girl's hand, economic help, armed support, social, legal, or religious functions, a seat in council, membership in larger social units, and so on. In all this, and in many more respects or purposes, a man's patrilineal descent counts for everything; his matriline counts for nothing.

The Lineage

How is the Middle Eastern endogamous UDG delineated? The answer to this question is simple and can easily be obtained from any lineage member anywhere in the Middle East: The lineage is the group within which there exists the knowledge, the consciousness, and the sentiment of being a distinct unit, and whose members actually cooperate in numerous institutions and undertakings. In a village comprising, for example, three lineages, all the people, including children, know very definitely to which lineage they belong, are proud of their lineage, and share a self-stereotype of their own lineage as well as stereotypes of other lineages. The interlineage demarcation is sharp; the accident of birth determines lineage membership, which cannot be changed.

In daily life, the power of the lineage to hold people together is great. In a nomadic tribe, the actual wandering unit may be composed of several patrilineages which camp, march, fight, hunt, graze their camels, sit in council, and so on, in close association with, but at the same time separately from, one another. In the village, composed of several ḥamūlas, each has its fixed land share,[45] its guest house, its threshing floor, its evening parties; at occasions such as circumcisions, weddings, or funerals, the entire patrilineage attends as a rule, members of other patrilineages only rarely. Each lineage has its own head and elders,[46] who exercise strong and effective, although informal, social control over their constituent families. The lineage has traditional forums, such as councils, which settle disputes among its constituent extended families and represent them toward the outside.[47] In some places, the intralineage cohesion is so strong that all members of a lineage are considered as one family and can enter any house of a fellow member, either through the men's or the women's door.[48]

As to the structural balance between consanguineal and affinal relationship, this is maintained in the Middle Eastern endogamous UDG by exactly the same mechanisms which maintain it in exogamous UDGs. Since in the majority of cases husband and wife are merely remote consanguineal relatives, the marital bond between them ties together two clearly distinct and separate families.

The Mother's Kin

In all Middle Eastern endogamous UDGs the mother's kin occupies a special place in ego's life. The mother's kin and the father's kin are not identical even in those few cases in which the two are patrilateral parallel cousins, because the mother has her own brothers and sisters who are directly related to ego through her and not through ego's father. It is these relatives, denoted by the special term *khwāla*, who form the kin group to which ego is tied by complementary filiation. If ego's paternal grandfather and maternal grandfather are paternal half-siblings, the process of complementary filiation can go back to the grandparental generation, to the uterine siblings of the maternal grandfather. As indicated above, however, in most cases mother's kin is a family group separate from father's kin, and there is thus no circumstantial obstacle whatsoever to complementary filiation.

In fact, complementary filiation to mother's kin assumes a particular importance precisely because of the traditionally exercised stern authoritarianism of the father. In contrast to him, the mother assumes the character of the loving, compassionate, forgiving parent figure, and these traits, by transference or extension, are attributed to the mother's entire kin group. The mother's kin thus is expected to be, and actually becomes, a group of most sympathetic relatives on whose help ego can rely in situations which require informal or psychological, rather than formal, physical, legal, or armed, support, which is always forthcoming from the patrikin. "One of the most salient features," says Ammar, "that underlies the structural relationships [in the Egyptian village] is that although the fabric forming the ideological basis for the social structure is entirely patrilineal as far as descent, inheritance and prestige are concerned, yet it is dyed in a sentimental and emotional colouring which is preponderantly matrilineal."[49]

Thus while ego fears his father more, he loves his mother more,[50] and this feeling is transferred from the mother to her relatives. This is not merely an observed fact but also felt and verbalized by the Middle Easterners themselves, as in the Sudanese Arab saying: "Everyone loves this *khaal* (mother's brother) very much because he is our mothers's relative, and everyone loves his mother most."[51] Such a situation can, of course, prevail even in a family in which the parents are patrilateral parallel cousins, and it is an example of how complementary filiation can and does work in any endogamous UDG.

Also the existence of special terms to denote ego's father's kin (e.g., '*aṣaba*; lit. "backbone") and mother's kin (e.g., *laḥma*; lit. "flesh"),[52] is indicative of the tendency to recognize complementary filiation. In sum, complementary filiation is possible in Middle Eastern unilineal and endogamous descent groups, because the mother is only in a minority of cases the patrilateral parallel cousin of the father; its function is, in most cases, to link ego, through the mother, secondarily to a kin group of which he is not a member; and its significance is recognized by being given formal expression in the existence of a separate set of kinship terms and psychological expression in a special emotional relationship to the mother's kindred.

While complementary filiation exists and plays a considerable role in Middle Eastern social structure, it is not however, the primary mechanism by which segmentation of the lineage is brought about, though Fortes[53] found this to be the case in sub-Saharan Africa. While it happens that subgroups are formed on the basis of their separate maternal descent within a patrilineage, the primary mechanism for segmentation is the division of the lineage into groups (sublineages) each of which traces its descent back to one of the sons of the founder of the lineage. Such segmentation, as a rule, is the transitional stage for the break-up of the lineage into as many new lineages as there are sublineages. Nevertheless, complementary filiation provides, in the Middle Eastern context as well, "the essential link between a sibling group and the kin of the parent who does not determine descent,"[54] that is the matrikin. The extent to which the rule of complementary filiation is used in Middle Eastern societies "to build double unilineal systems"[55] is doubtful. The fact is that, however close a consanguineal relative ego's mother may be of his father, matrilineal ancestry is considered entirely negligible. This lack of importance is best illustrated by the inability of even the best tribal genealogists to recall the names of their grandmothers or great-grandmothers, although they are able to rattle off the names of their male ancestors up to ten or more generations.

The Khamse

The unilineal character of the Middle Eastern (and, in particular, the Bedouin Arab) kin group is further emphasized through the *khamse*, the blood responsibility group. The *khamse* is always composed only of ego's patrilineal relatives. The exact composition of the *khamse* varies from tribe to tribe, but common to all is the exclusively male linkage. As the name *khamse*, meaning "five," indicates, it is composed of those male relatives of ego who are removed from him by no more than five male links. Thus, among the Bedouins of the Negev, ego's *khamse* consists of all the males who are his own descendants (sons, son's sons, etc.), and the descendants of his father, his father's father, his father's father's father, his father's father's father's father.[56] That is, in this case, the *khamse* is figured on the basis of five generations of ascendants, ego counting as one, and all their descendants. Among the Rwala, the *khamse* is reckoned differently, resulting in a considerably smaller group: it comprises all those male agnates of ego who are connected to him by not more than five links, and who, moreover, are removed from him by no more than three generations. Thus a Rweylī's *khamse* consists of his sons: son's sons; sons' sons' sons; his father; father's father; father's father's father; and the male descendants of these up to five links. In this system, second cousins (father's father's brothers' sons' sons) are the most remote collaterals who belong to ego's *khamse.*[57] Jaussen's description of the *khamse* among the nomadic tribes of southern Transjordan[58] is confused, and it is best to take no account of it.

Whatever the precise constitution of the *khamse*, the most significant feature characterizing it is that it always consists of a group of closely related men who belong to the same lineage. Each man has, within the larger group of relatives which constitutes his lineage, a smaller group of closer relatives who form his *khamse*. The men of the *khamse* form the contingent which guarantees ego's safety and to which he is responsible, because any criminal act on his part would expose his *khamse* to revenge. If a man is killed, it is his *khamse* which is in duty bound to avenge him, by hunting down and killing the murderer or a member of his *khamse*; if a man commits a murder, it is among the membership of his *khamse* that the avengers will seek a victim in accordance with the principle of "blood demands blood." If there is a possibility of arranging for the payment of blood-money, the two parties between whom the matter has to be negotiated consist of the two *khamses*: that of the victim and that of the murderer.

Since it is always in the interest of the *khamse* to arrange for a settlement rather than to allow blood revenge to take place, the very existence of the *khamse* makes for greater stability in both intralineal and interlineal relations. If the victim and the murderer belong to the same lineage, the two *khamses* go into action and, by arranging for a settlement and thereby preventing further strife which may disrupt the lineage, they actually strengthen the lineage structure. If the victim and the murderer belong to two different lineages, the sociolegal work of each *khamse* serves ultimately to strengthen the position of its lineage vis-à-vis that of the other by bargaining for as advantageous a compensation as possible under the circumstances.

As far as the internal structure of the lineage is concerned, the *khamses* contained in it act like interlinked rings in a chain mail, reinforcing the fabric of the lineage. From this point of view, the lineage appears as the sum total of interrelated *khamses*, and the total male contingent of a lineage can be arrived at by ascertaining the blood responsibility group of *any* lineage member and then taking each member of this *khamse* and establishing the membership of their respective *khamses*, and so forth. When, in this manner, one has listed all the men who are part of an interlocking *khamse* system, one has enumerated all the male members of the lineage. These males, together with their mothers, wives, sisters, and daughters, form the lineage. Since no *khamse* cuts across lineage lines, the *khamse* structure is, in fact, an aid in isolating one lineage from another. Thus, in respect of a corporate obligation which is of paramount inportance in Bedouin society (in other sectors of traditional Middle Eastern society it is of lesser, though still considerable, significance), the lineage is the bounded and stable group with which the individual is totally identified.

In this connection, the question of interchangeability must be touched upon. According to Fortes, in the lineage as a corporate group "all the members . . . are to outsiders jurally equal," and it is this feature which "underlies so-called collective responsibility in blood-vengeance and self-help."[59] Like several others of Fortes' observations on UDGs based on sub-Saharan Africa, this too must be modified somewhat in order to make it applicable to the Middle Eastern endogamous UDGs.

There is, to be sure, a certain degree of "jural" equality and hence interchangeability "to outsiders" of all members of the Middle Eastern endogamous UDG. For one thing, a lineage can occasionally be so young and small that it consists of one single *khamse* only and yet forms a discrete unit. In such a case, there will be to outsiders a complete jural equality of all the lineage members. Beyond this, however, and here is where the necessity for modification enters, the jural equality is replaced by the principle of concentric preferential degrees. The clearest expression of this principle is found in connection with mate selection. It will be recalled that cousin marriage was recognized above as the most preferred type of marriage, followed by successively less and less preferred categories as the concentric circles of more and more remote consanguineal relatives gradually widen. In an analogous manner, from the point of view of personal safety, the group upon which ego can most reliably count is that of his closest consanguineal relatives (i.e., Fa,Brs,Sos);

second, that of consanguineal relatives once and twice removed (FaFa, SosSos, BrSos, FaBrSos); third, that of the still larger and more remote patrilateral relatives comprised in the *khamse;* and fourth, that of the entire lineage. In any actual case, the duty of avenging a murder devolves on the nearest available consanguineal kin of the victim: if he has brothers, it is their duty to seek out and kill his murderer; if the nearest male patrilineal consanguine is a third cousin (i.e., a person outside the *khamse* as commonly counted), it is his obligation. The weight of responsibility does not diminish with the increase of the distance between the victim and the avenger. In the same manner, if the blood avengers cannot find the murderer, they will try to kill one of his brothers; if no relative nearer than a third cousin or even more remote kinsman is available, his killing will still be considered as the proper way of avenging the victim and of restoring the honor of his family and lineage. It is in this sense that the membership of a lineage is interchangeable, one for another: every member of the lineage may be called upon to substitute for any other member, if a more closely related, that is, more preferred, patrilineal consanguineal male is not available. By the logic of this arrangement, the more remote the closest available relatives are from ego, the larger the number of those who are interchangeable and can, consequently, become the target of the blood avengers' fury; in the same way, the more remote the closest patrilateral relatives of a girl the larger the number of young men who are considered as having preference in asking for her in marriage.

What unmistakably emerges from these considerations is the principle of concentric circles in the lineage structure. Every ego is the epicenter of his own world, and the closest concentric circles of each ego usually differ from those of others. But the larger the circles, the more they tend to be coterminous; and the largest, that of the lineage as a whole, has equal validity for all its members.

Structural Differences between the Exogamous and the Endogamous UDG

A fundamental question remains to be examined: What, if any, structural differences exist between exogamous and endogamous UDGs? Taking Fortes' analysis of the exogamous UDG and my own studies of the endogamous UDG as the basis for comparison, we can begin by recalling what Fortes noted about the incidence of the exogamous UDG. He observed that exogamous UDGs "are not of significance among peoples who live in small groups, depend on rudimentary technology, and have little durable property."[60] Many such peoples live in the Middle East, on the peripheries of the Rub' al-Khālī desert in Southern Arabia, for example, yet the available evidence shows that UDGs are of as great significance among them as among the tribes of the North Arabian and Syrian deserts who live in much larger groups, whose technology is more advanced, and who have considerably more durable property.

According to Fortes, UDGs "break down when a modern economic framework with occupational differentiation linked to a wide range of specialized skills, to productive capital and to monetary media of exchange is introduced."[61] The Middle Eastern endogamous UDGs do not break down under such conditions; they merely become weakened or modified. In the Middle East, occupational differentiation, a wide range of specialized skills, productive capital, and monetary media of exchange are not recent introductions accompanying the erection of a modern economic framework. They are parts of local traditional developments which went on for centuries in its cities and which never caused a breakdown in the UDGs. The endogamous urban extended family and the UDG of the Middle East were always the social framework within which all economic development took place. In fact, in seventeenth century Constantinople, to mention only one example, each of the hundreds of guilds into which the artisans, tradesmen, and professionals were organized considered itself as a lineage descended from the mythical or historical founder of its occupational specialization.[62]

Fortes' observations about the relationship between lineage and political structure[63] have to be modified with reference to the endogamous UDGs in the Middle East. Here, too, the lineage "is the basis of local organization and of political institutions." But the fact that the Middle East has had national governments "centered in kingship, administrative machinery and courts of law" has not resulted in a "primary emphasis . . . on the legal aspect of the lineage." On the contrary, the political systems in the Middle East either grew out of the lineage structure and retained its characteristics or, if they had no lineage basis, artificially assumed what can be called a lineage camouflage. The most typical example is the Middle Eastern variety of the dual organization which, whether or not so anchored in history, was everywhere considered an alignment of two super-lineages, each traditionally descended from a single ancestor, opposed to each other and largely political in their actual functioning.[64] Because of this, the Middle Eastern situation does not bear out the statement Fortes appends to his aforementioned observation that "the more centralized the political system the greater the tendency seems to be for the corporate strenth of descent groups to be reduced or for such corporate groups to be nonexistent." In the Middle East, where even occupational groups, in order to be able to function effectively, considered themselves, and acted as if they were, UDGs, a centralized political system was compelled to base its power on the actual or assumed UDGs. The feudal order of traditional Middle Eastern states and societies made it imperative for the central political power to base itself ultimately upon the power structure of the UDG, and hence the greater the latter's corporate strength the greater the support they were able to give to the central, most paternal, most patriarchal authority. It was precisely because of this close interrelationship between UDG and state that the Muslim state could find no room in its structure for non-Muslim groups, such as Christians or Jews, who could not belong to the quasi-familial corporate body of the state but remained indigenous foreigners, *millets*, for hundreds of years.

Nor does the Middle Eastern political community "assert [its] common interest . . . as against the private interests of the component lineages through religious institutions and sanctions."[65] The Middle Eastern church-state (of which, as indicated, the non-Muslims were not members) was the ultimate extension of the UDG system. Its institutions and sanctions, therefore, asserted nothing against the private interests of its component lineages but, on the contrary, were the sum total of the latter. Again the situation can be visualized with the help of the interlocking links of the chain mail: ego's lineage forms one link; all the lineages and quasi-lineages (such as the guilds) form the interlocking fabric of the whole which is the state.

To pass now from the position of the lineage within the general social context to its particular features, let us consider Fortes' observations that in the UDG, which "is an arrangement of persons that serves the attainment of legitimate social and personal ends," there is generally a "connection between lineage structure and the ownership of the most-valued productive property of the society" and the "control over reproductive resources and relations as is evident from the common occurrence of exogamy as a criterion of lineage differentiation."[66]

A conspectus of the Middle Eastern endogamous UDG bears out the first part of this observation. In the Middle East, the "connection between lineage structure and the ownership of the most-valued productive property of the society" finds its expression in the claim the lineage as a whole has to the ownership of the wandering territory (or a definite share in it) or, among the settled agriculturists, to a definite area within the village lands. In both types of traditional Middle Eastern society, the land is the single most important productive property; whether used as pasture for camel herds or goat flocks, or for cultivation, the land is the basis of livelihood. It is therefore significant that it is precisely this property which is held jointly by the lineage, although in villages the lineage usually assigns usufruct to its constituent families.

As to "the control over reproductive resources and relations," or, to put it simply, the regulation of marriages, this too, characterizes the Middle Eastern endogamous UDG. However, it is expressed not by "the common occurrence of exogamy as a criterion of lineage differentiation," but, on the contrary, by the emphatic preference for in-lineage endogamy. To use Fortes' terminology, the Middle Eastern UDG exercises "control over the reproductive resources and relations" by insisting that these must subserve the supreme end of the replenishment and increase of its own human contingent. In other words, the common occurrence of endogamy is as much a criterion of lineage differentiation in the Middle East as exogamy is in sub-Saharan Africa. In general, then, all UDGs endeavor to exercise control over the reproductive resources, but the problem of how to attain this in practice is solved either by exogamy or by endogamy.

Yet another observation made by Fortes points to one more difference between the exogamous UDG which he discusses and the endogamous UDG which prevails in the Middle East. "In an exogamous lineage system," he writes, it "is very conspicuous" that "a married person always has two mutually antagonistic kinship statuses, that of spouse and parent in one family context and that of child and sibling in another."[67] That this should be true in the case of a married woman is evident; it is less so in the case of a married man, who may be in patrilocal residence with his wife and children and be a member of a patrilineal extended family headed by his own father, in which case there is no reason why his two kinship statuses should be "mutually antagonistic." In the Middle Eastern endogamous lineage system, the closer the consanguineal relationship between a wife and her husband, the smaller the likelihood that even in the case of a women her two statuses, that of wife and mother and that of daughter and sister, can become "mutually antagonistic." In fact, whether or not one accepts the frequently voiced traditional Middle Eastern explanation of the preference for FaBrDa marriage that it tends to promote harmony in the family, such marriages actually tend to prevent the occurrence of the antagonism between the two female statuses which Fortes found to be conspicuous in sub-Saharan Africa.

Apart from the above differences between the exogamous and endogamous UDGs, the observations of Fortes on the former hold equally true for the latter. The emphasis may not be identical on each point, but essentially the two types of UDGs show a homogeneous visage. The lineage as a corporate group; the individual having "no legal or political status except as a member of a lineage;" the "exercise of defined rights, duties, office and social tasks vested in the lineage as a corporate unit;" the emergence of the lineage "most precisely in a complementary relationship with or in opposition to like units;" the tendency to use personal kinship "to define and sanction a field of social relations for each individual;" the continuous process of further and further segmentation; the hierarchically organized segments "by fixed steps of greater and greater inclusiveness, each step being defined by genealogical reference;" the patterning of lineage segmentation after the model of the parental family; and the spatial (or local) characteristics of the lineage[68]—all this applies to the Middle Eastern endogamous UDG as well.

We have shown above in some detail that the Middle Eastern endogamous UDG "exhibits a structure of authority" very much in the manner described by Fortes. This authority, we may now add, is formally wielded by the heads of segments whose prestige and influence is the greater the larger the groups they head, although consultation, counsel, and suasion rather than arbitrary, autocratic decision is on all levels the mechanism of leadership. This, too, has been recognized by Fortes.[69]

That the model of the lineage is the parental family[70] can be illustrated by Middle Eastern examples probably as well as by any other. In fact, the lineage, and even a tribe, and ultimately the entire Arab nation are considered as simply an enlarged family. This can best be exemplified by the process of tribal fusion. When a lineage or a larger unit (A) attaches itself to a more powerful unit such as a tribe (B), an association which is usually secured for reasons of safety, even if the two groups were originally unrelated, within two or three generations the ancestor of group A will have been incorporated into the tribal genealogy of group B as a son of group B's progenitor. Or, as another example, of two originally equal sub-tribes (A and B), conceptualized in the persons of two brothers who figure as their eponymous ancestors, one, A, becomes weakened and must subordinate itself to its brother sub-tribe. Soon thereafter this change in relative status will be reflected in the emergence of a new traditional genealogy in which the ancestor of A appears as the son of the ancestor of B.[71] Thus, not only is existing lineage structure projected "backward as pseudo-history,"[72] but this backward projection constantly changes in order to keep up with the changing structure of lineages and larger units.

Internal Autonomy

Finally, the most important difference between the exogamous and the endogamous UDGs lies in the differential effect which exogamy and endogamy have on the relationship of the UDG to its social environment and on the issue of its internal social autonomy or self-sufficiency. The exogamous UDG cannot exist without the proximity of, and interrelations with, other similar groups, or at least one such group. In theory, an isolated exogamous UDG cannot survive: within one generation it must either die out or cease to be exogamous. The relationship between two or more intermarrying exogamous UDGs need not necessarily be friendly or neighborly, but some structural relationship must exist between them. The effects of the existence of such a relationship between neighboring exogamous UDGs cannot fail to be felt in many areas of economic, social, political, moral, and religious life.

The endogamous UDG, on the other hand, is genetically self-sufficient. This means, first of all, that there is no necessity for it to maintain any social relations with outgroups, since it replenishes and augments its human contingent by inbreeding. It also provides itself with sustenance by the common effort of its membership, and it guarantees its own safety by the numbers of its adult males. On the simplest level, the endogamous UDG can actually sustain itself in complete isolation from all outside society, in a total bio-social autarchy. This situation is the background of numerous ancient Near Eastern (including biblical) myths which represent catastrophes or other events that befell a UDG as if they had affected mankind as a whole: for its members the UDG simply is all of humanity. Such isolated UDGs can still be found in some parts of the Middle East.

As far as the mechanics of cultural transmission are concerned, the endogamous UDG is the most favorable social matrix for the development and perpetuation of cultural variants. The cultural differences between UDGs living in proximity may appear minor when viewed from a perspective, but they are considered highly significant by the members of each UDG. Cases have been known of a Bedouin tribesman recognizing even from the gait of others glimpsed at a great distance whether they belonged to the same or another tribal group. Such keen discernment may be vital in a social configuration in which members of all outgroups are likely to be enemies. The perpetuation of the cultural variant of the UDG resulting from isolation and inbreeding has undoubtedly something to do with the oft-cited "immovability" of the Middle East, which in anthropological terms means that the processes of culture change in the Middle Eastern endogamous UDG were exceptionally slow until the post-World War II irruption of Westernization.

The social isolation and self-sufficiency concomitant to endogamy are responsible to a considerable degree for the hostile attitude to all outgroups frequently evinced by the UDG. In an economically inhospitable physical environment, the competition for natural resources is keen, often ruthless, and the endogamous UDG, which has no use for outgroups, tends to consider them simply as depletors. Hence the traditional Bedouin institution of raiding outgroups, that risky but rapid method of instantly replenishing the UDGs only source of livelihood, the herds.

As against these in-turned interests, which if left alone would result in complete fragmentation if not anarchy, the endogamous UDG system has certain built-in checks and balances. The most important of these is the valuation of patrilineal descent which extends beyond the UDG itself and binds together several UDGs. The UDG multiplies by fission. When it grows too large (the criteria of "too large" may be in economic, social, or other terms), it divides into two or more new UDGs which retain the knowledge (i.e., tradition) of their common origin, typically conceptualized in the form of related founder-progenitors. The same process when carried on and repeated many times results in huge pyramidal structures. Such processes of fission projected back into the past give the traditional genealogical structure of entire nations: e.g., the twelve tribes of the biblical Hebrews who believed themselves to be the descendants of twelve brothers; or the twelve tribes of the 'Aneze confederacy of the North Arabian desert who are considered the descendants of twelve individuals who were the sons of two brothers ('Obed and 'Ammār) and of the latter's FaBrSos, another pair of brothers (Wahhab and Mejlas).[73]

The effect of this comprehensive genealogical system is to counterbalance the isolationist tendencies of the UDG and tie it to similar UDGs, to assign it a place in the larger society, and to make it aware of the identity of its natural allies. The situation can, again, be made tangible by referring to the concentric circles: the fewer the generations which separate ego's UDG from the common ancestor from whom both his UDG and another UDG are traditionally descended, the smaller the circle to which both groups belong, and hence the closer the relationship between the two.

This also explains the very great emphasis placed in a system of endogamous UDGs on descent. Descent, which in Middle Eastern culture means patrilineal descent, is the only factor through which ego can relate to individuals or groups outside his own small world represented by his UDG. This provides the explanation for the kingroup-like appearance of all social, political, occupational, religious, and other groupings produced by traditional Middle Eastern society, and the justification of designating the culture of the Middle East a "kinship culture."

XVI. *Women in a Man's World*

Introduction

To begin with, let it be stated clearly and emphatically that the preoccupation of this volume (in Chapters 4 and 5 above, and in the present chapter) with the formal, tradition-determined structural and dynamic aspects of the man-woman relationship and with the place of women in family and society in the Middle East must not be taken as indicating that love between boy and girl, bride and bridegroom, husband and wife is less of a moving force or a source of inspiration there than it is in our Western world. Quite to the contrary, it could easily be shown that in the Middle East, where romantic love has to overcome formidable barriers erected by tradition between the sexes, it must be a more powerful motivation. This could be attested by marshaling the unequivocal evidence of a great love poetry from pre-Islamic times to the present, of a prose literature in which romantic love and intrigue play an important role, of true case histories in which love caused great tragedies or inspired extraordinary feats, of a record of elopements flying into the face of all tradition, of interviews with men and women of various age groups for whom love is or was the shining star on life's horizon.

Since, however, all this is not the subject of the present anthropological inquiry, we must remain content with this briefest allusion to the presence and power of romantic love in Middle Eastern society, and now turn to a discussion of its socio-cultural setting.

For an understanding of the extraordinary difficulties confronting Middle Eastern society in granting equal rights to women and in female emancipation (in the Western sense) it is necessary to become acquainted, first of all, with the traditional mores and values that have governed the position of women and man-woman relations in the past and that are operative in large sectors of the area's population to this day.

Some facets of this subject have been discussed briefly above, especially the veiling and seclusion of women, the traditional varieties of social intercourse between men and women and the changes occurring in them under the impact of modernization, the term and trial marriages, the traditional occupations of women, and the early steps taken in a few countries toward their official emancipation by law (see above, pp. 115–34). In addition to these issues, however, important though they are in themselves, there are several others which should be discussed in order to lay the proper groundwork for a fuller appreciation of the pangs of transition gripping at present many women as well as men in Middle Eastern society.

The first of these issues to be discussed will be some of the differences in the early treatment of male and female infants. We shall try to correlate these differences with those characterizing the modal adult male and female personalities and the mutual expectations and power relationships between men and women in traditional Middle Eastern society.

This will be followed by an analysis of the psychological significance of circumcision, to which all Muslim, Copt and Jewish males and a considerable proportion of Muslim and Copt females are subjected. To what extent, we shall ask, does this important event impress boys and girls with the differential roles expected of them in adult life? In seeking an answer to this question we shall have to describe in some detail the most important local variants of the ceremony, as well as the differences in the public or festive character given to the operation in the cases of boys and of girls.

Next, the issue of formal education will be taken up. The central question in this area will be: To what extent has the absence of institutionalized schooling for girls contributed to the relegation of women to a culturally separate world of their own?

Thereafter, we turn to religion, that all-pervading factor in traditional Middle Eastern culture (cf. above, pp. 33–36, 294–96, 322–44, 348–50, 383–85, 400–02), which, however, means quite different things in the lives of men and women. The central questions in this connection will be: To what extent have the women, largely excluded from participation in the official practices of Islam, found compensation for this deprivation by participation in cults, rituals, and ceremonies of their own? What beliefs are expressed in these cults? And what is the attitude of the men and their official religious leaders to this extra-Islamic religious world?

Lastly, we shall discuss the degree to which the worlds of men and women, though coexisting side by side, form two separate entities. We shall look into questions such as: What are the forces that make for this separation? What are the areas of contact between the two? How do men view women, how do women view men, and how do men and women view themselves in relation to the opposite sex? And what traces of the early socialization processes can be found in the man-woman relationship?

Early Socialization

It is by now a commonplace in psychologically oriented antropological studies that the quality of early socialization (or child-care customs) decisively molds the personality of the infant and child, and that much of what the individual absorbs in this manner in the early years remains with him throughout his life.[1]

In the last twenty years or so, several studies dealing with Arab populations have discussed in lesser or greater detail the early child-care customs and their effect on the Arab adult personality.[2] In fact, the influence of early childhood training on personality did not escape folk observation and has been expressed in numerous proverbs current among the Arabs of Palestine and other countries: "Character impressed by the mother's milk cannot be altered by anything but death."[3] Or: "Teaching the grownup is like writing in the sand; teaching the youth is like engraving on stone."[4] Or: "A child's heart is like a precious jewel without inscription; it is therefore ready to absorb whatever is engraved upon it." Or: "The tail of a dog remains curved even if it is put into a hundred pressers."[5]

Yet these studies and popular sayings, while pointing up the influence of childhood conditioning on later life, do not deal specifically with the effect the differential treatment accorded to male and female infants has on the development of the typical male versus female personality. This is the subject to which we shall now address ourselves.

To begin with, it should be pointed out that in traditional Middle Eastern society, much more so than in the modern West, both men and women are the product of an enculturative process administered exclusively by women in the early years of a child's life. The mother herself is, of course, a product of her society and culture, and in her treatment of her children she is narrowly circumscribed by the strictures and expectations of her own cultural background and actual environment. Yet whatever the sources and causes of her own behavior patterns (of which child care is one facet), the fact remains that in the early formation of the Middle Eastern personality the mother plays the central, dominant, and overwhelming role.

There can be no doubt that the differences in the male and female personality, as well as in the mutual role expectations and fulfillments, can be traced back, in part at least, to disparities in the treatment accorded boys and girls in early infancy by their mother. The unequal treatment of the two sexes does not begin at birth, but, in fact, antedates it. Father and mother, as well as uncles, aunts, grandparents, cousins and other relatives, hope the baby will be a boy. If, indeed, the baby is a boy, he is greeted with great rejoicing. His birth is the occasion for as lavish a family feast as circumstances allow. It evokes the feeling on everybody's part that the family has been enriched by the addition of an important new member. The birth of a girl, on the other hand, is regarded as one of those inevitable evils of life which cannot be helped. Whatever the mother's feelings toward her newborn daughter, institutionally her position in the family improves only if she subsequently gives birth to sons; a woman who has daughters only is not much better off than one who remains childless; the ignominy of divorce threatens her and often becomes a reality. Consequently, the emotional attitude of the mother to her offspring is inevitably influenced by the child's sex; if it is a boy, she will be much more lenient with him, will take better care of him, devote more attention to him, and be more ready to fulfill his wishes.

A basic pedagogical principle in the Arab family, applied from earliest childhood, is to pamper the boy but not the girl.[6] This is expressed, among other ways, in the difference in the duration of the period of lactation discussed above on pages 97–98.

While the prolonged lactation of a male infant as compared to a female is the general custom in most Middle Eastern societies, the opposite also occurs. In the Upper Egyptian village of Silwa (Aswan Province), Hamed Ammar observed that "a boy is usually nursed less than a girl." The shorter period of a boy's nursing is taken by Ammar to be "a clear indication of the accelerating process of boys' growth."[7] However, in Silwa, people believe that to cut short the period of lactation makes a child "obstinate and disobedient,"[8] and therein may lie the explanation. A male infant is nursed for a shorter period, since obstinacy and disobedience in a boy are personality traits viewed as positive values, since they are related to desirable male characteristics such as having a strong will, being domineering, determined, brave, and the like. In the case of a girl, all such tendencies would be considered most undesirable; consequently, she is nursed for a longer period so as to make her pliable and obedient.

Even in early infancy the process of concentrating female ministrations to the male in the sexual or erotic area begins. While nothing is done by the mother to quiet down a crying girl child who has been weaned, in many parts of the Muslim world the mother soothes her crying boy, whether before or after weaning, by playing with his penis. In the Lebanese Muslim village of Buarij, for instance, Anne H. Fuller observed that both "mothers and grandmothers handle the genitals of a boy infant in order to sooth him."[9] Similarly, in Silwa, Ammar found that not only the mother but also visitors "try to win a smile from the baby by tickling or caressing [it] . . . or in the case of a boy by playing with his genitals."[10] Although Dr. Ammar does not state that the visitors who thus stimulate the baby boy are women, the social situation in an Egyptian village makes it most unlikely that any man would engage in such acts, or even that he would pay a visit to a woman. At a later age, in preparation for circumcision, which is performed on boys at the age of three to six years, the mother will "prepare him gradually for the event by caressing his organ and playfully endeavoring to separate the foreskin from the glans. While doing this, she would hum words to the effect that what she is doing will help him become a man amongst men."[11]

In this manner erotic pleasure becomes early associated in the boys' mind with the availability of a subservient female willing to minister to his needs, and, indeed, his whims. This is the role a man grows up to expect, above all, from his wife.

In the patriarchal order of the Arab family structure, the girl-child's position (as shown above on pages 98–99) is no different from that of a handmaiden who has to serve every one else in the household—mother, father, brothers, and elder sisters, as well as the members of the extended family—grandparents, uncles, aunts. In order to accustom the girl-child to serving her husband and his family, it is considered advisable to send the little girl to live with her future in-laws as early as possible so that she get from them what is called by the Arabs a "second education," in addition to the first one she received from her own mother. Considering this difference in upbringing between boys and girls, it is small wonder that the modal male and female character is formed in such a manner that the marital relationship is one of domination on the part of the husband and submission on the part of the wife.

Childhood conditioning also explains to some extent the parent-child relationship in later years. Compared to the very close relationship between mother and child, that between the father and his offspring appears loose and remote. The father, of course, wields all the authority, and consequently is feared and respected by son and daughter alike. His word is law and his will is done. Not only in the early years, but also in youth and adulthood, there is a closer relationship with, and a more emotional attachment to, the mother than the father. This is the great reward, and in many cases the only reward, that a woman has in Arab society, and it comes very late in life.

The demonstrations of love, respect, and devotion from sons and daughters, but especially from sons, to their mother, are varied and numerous. The parental blessing—which in Arab society still retains something of its ancient holiness and efficacy—is valued much more highly if it comes from the mother than from the father. It is a well-known fact that in any unusual difficulty or predicament, a person gets support and help from the mother rather than from the father. The father is respected and obeyed, because this is the unchangeable tradition; the mother is loved because in the early years of life she was the only one to whom the child could turn.[12]

Because the Arab family is patriarchal, patrilineal, and patrilocal, only the boys maintain a continued close relationship to their parents. The daughters leave the parental home upon marriage, and, as the Arab saying has it, while they ruin their fathers' houses, they build up the houses of their husbands and their families. The parent-child relationship is thus a very brief one in the case of girls, most of whom marry at an early age. In the case of boys, on the other hand, it lasts quite long; it is, in fact, much longer and also closer than is customary in Western society. The son brings his wife into the home of his own parents in which he continues to live, and the wife is submerged by his parental family and absorbed into it.

In this situation the affectionate attachment of the son to his mother becomes an additional factor making for the subordination of the wife and her domination by the husband. Not only must the wife, especially the young wife, remain subordinate to her husband's mother in matters of prestige and authority and share her husband's esteem and affection with her mother-in-law, but also the mother actually takes precedence over the wife. Should any difference of opinion or will arise between the mother and the wife, the man will take the side of his mother. The wife, cut off from her own parents and confronted by the closely knit mother-son team, has no choice but to submit, to accept her role of a handmaiden to the entire family of her husband, and hope that her position will change for the better as the years pass and her own sons grow up.

The brother-sister relationship in the Arab family has fewer institutionalized and formalized aspects than the relationship patterns between parents and children or between husband and wife. Only rarely are there generally accepted customs regulating the duties or rights of brothers with regard to their sisters or vice versa. The jealous guardianship of the sister's honor cannot be adduced as an example, for this is the duty not only of the brother but also of any male member of the extended family. One of the few formal expressions of the brother-sister relationship is the obligation of the brothers to give presents to their sisters on certain important religious occasions, even if they live in a distant village.

The true significance of sibling affection appears only after marriage. Conflicts and even serious disturbances can occur between spouses because of their attachment to brothers or sisters. If a sister is not married, she continues to live in the parental household where her brother's wife assumes the position of female head after the mother's death. Nevertheless, when a quarrel between his wife and his sister occurs, the husband is expected to take the side of his sister, whether she is married or not. More favorably situated, with regard to the brother's affections, is the married sister who visits her brother's house only rarely. Custom entitles her to gifts of food on these occasions, making her feel that she continues to have a greater share in what was her parents' home than has the woman whom her brother brought into it.

Circumcision: Male and Female

The central event in the lives of Middle Eastern children, contributing decisively to the differential personality development of men and women, is circumcision. Male circumcision is general and obligatory for all Muslims, Jews, and Copts. Female excision, reportedly practiced widely in many parts of the Middle East among the Muslims, as well as among the Copts of Egypt, is in all probability more prevalent than would appear from its reported incidence. It is generally practiced among numerous non-Middle Eastern Muslim peoples and tribes in the Sudan belt of Africa, as well as to the south of it among non-Muslims. In many places in the Middle East the people show a certain reluctance to discuss the subject. Excision usually consists of clitoridectomy, that is, the ablation of the clitoris; often it involves the excision of the labia minora, and occasionally, of the labia majora as well.

Both male and female circumcision are pre-Islamic in origin. The earliest reports on the male operation come from ancient Egypt, Phoenicia, and Syria,[13] and from the Bible.[14] By the first century A.D. the practice was established among the Arabs, who, according to Josephus Flavius, circumcised their sons after the thirteenth year because Ishmael, the founder of the nation, was circumcised at that age.[15] Josephus also reports that the Judean rulers Hyrcanus and Aristobulos forced circumcision on the Idumaeans and the Ituraeans, respectively.[16]

While circumcision is not mentioned in the Koran, it was practiced by the pre-Islamic Arabs, and Mohammed adopted it unquestioningly. The various Sunni Muslim schools of jurisprudence differ as to whether it is indispensable (the Shāfiʿī and the Shīʿite view) or merely commendable (the Mālikī position), but the fact remains that all Muslims at all times and in all places (with a few marginal exceptions) have practiced it.[17]

The earliest reference to female circumcision, seems to be one contained in an Egyptian Hellenistic papyrus which also states that it was performed on adult women in the midst of considerable festivities.[18] The Greek geographer and historian Strabo (ca. 64 B.C.–19 A.D.), who was with Aelius Gallus in Egypt and Arabia and devoted an entire book of his great *Geography* to Egypt and Libya, repeatedly states that both the Egyptians and the Jews (whom he considered to be Egyptian in origin) practiced circumcision of males and excision of females.[19]

In view of the complete absence of any other testimony as to excision among the Jews, Strabo's reference to them in connection with this practice must be discounted. As to the prevalence of the operation among the Egyptians, on the other hand, his report is corroborated by independent evidence, some of which was assembled by the late seventeeth- early eighteenth-century Orientalist Adrian Reland.[20]

That clitoridectomy was an old Arab custom long antedating not only Islam but also the pre-Islamic Arabic literary documents is attested by the existence of a special Arabic root, *bẓr*, which in its noun form means clitoris and in its verbal form its excision.[21] The existence of such terminology indicates that the operation was performed in Arabic-speaking peoples even before its first mention in extant literary sources. The name of the woman who performed the operation on girls was *mubaẓẓirah.*[22] The operation seems to have been performed, just as it was in ancient Egypt, shortly before marriage. The instrument used was a blade or razor.[23]

In late pre-Islamic and early Islamic times, excision was considered, at least among some Arab tribes, as an indispensable prerequisite for marriage. The Hudhaylite poet Khālid ibn Wathila considered it an impossibility that he should marry and settle down among the Ḥimyarites "who do not circumcise their women."[24] It is reported, of Khālid al-Qasrī, the well-known governor of Iraq appointed by the Caliph Hishām (reigned 724–43), that he had his mother, a Christian woman, circumcised in her old age so that he should not be called "son of the uncircumcised woman."[25]

In modern times, female circumcision has been reported from various parts of the Middle East. Since our main interest is in the present-day incidence of the practice, we shall mention only briefly that it was observed, in the seventeeth century by Sir Thomas Herbert and Sir John Chardin in Persia;[26] in the eighteenth century by Adrian Reland and Carsten Niebuhr in Mecca, Oman, the shores of the Persian Gulf, Basra, Baghdad, and Egypt (both Muslims and Copts);[27] and in the nineteenth century by an increasing number of explorers and travelers. Numerous Orientalists have noted in general terms that the operation is still widespread in the twentieth century.[28]

The general trend has been to perform circumcision at a progressively earlier age in males. In ancient Egypt, according to the testimony of murals, the operation was carried out on full-grown boys. In the Bible there is an indication that circumcision was a preliminary to marriage: the term *ḥatan damim* (bridegroom of blood) was applied to boys undergoing the operation (Exodus 4:24–25). The same Semitic root from which the Hebrew nouns *ḥatan* (bridegroom) and *ḥatunah* (marriage) are derived developed in Arabic into *khtan*, *khitān*, or *khitāna* (in Morocco: *khtāna*), meaning circumcision. An alternative term for circumcision is *ṭahāra* or *ṭuhūr* (in Morocco: *ṭhāra*), literally "cleansing," which is expressive of the view that through circumcision the boy becomes clean and capable of performing the religious exercises of praying and entering the mosque.[29]

In numerous Middle Eastern ethnic groups circumcision retains its connection with marriage, and occasionally it is a direct preliminary to marriage, a kind of test of the groom's courage, with the bride looking on.[30] In other places, the operation is performed at puberty or thereafter, and the presence of marriageable girls, who often perform provocative dances at these rites, leaves no doubt that it signifies the entrance of the boy into the phase of life in which he can claim sexual access to the women of the tribe. Circumcision at the age of fourteen or later is practiced in some parts of Arabia, on the Island of Soqotra, in the Libyan Desert, and in other areas.[31]

In most parts of the Middle East, however, the circumcision of boys takes place between the ages of three and seven. Recently, the tendency has been to perform it in the first few months of the boy's life.[32] Also, modernization and the increasing availability of modern medical facilities in the larger cities of the Middle East have resulted in a preference for the performance of the operation during early infancy.

The amount of public attention accompanying the ceremony is one of the most significant features distinguishing male from female circumcision. The circumcision of boys is always a public, joyous, and festive occasion, often assuming a group character, and it is performed on several or even many boys at a time. That of girls, by contrast, is a private affair, often done furtively or secretly. It is frequently "covered with a veil of mystery; sometimes no males are allowed to assist at it."[33]

In turning now to a description of circumcision ceremonies in various parts of the Middle East today, we shall repeatedly have opportunity to illustrate this basic difference which has been observed by Niebuhr some two hundred years ago.[34] Let us begin with the central area of the Middle East, and proceed from there first to the west and then to the east.

Lebanon. Among the Lebanese Muslim Arab villagers it is the generally accepted view that circumcision makes a male socially acceptable for intercourse. The women unequivocally state that no decent woman would have intercourse with an uncircumcised Christian, for such a man is considered dirty. Muslim men, on their part, like to boast that circumcision makes a man more potent.[35] In other words, the operation enables a man to engage in socially sanctioned sexual activity, when the time for it arrives, and ensures that he will be able to function in that area with distinction.

Circumcision in the Lebanese village is a group ceremony, performed usually once a year, on boys any time after their first year of life up until adolescence.

There is no female circumcision in Lebanon. But a girl, on first menstruating, may embrace the large-bellied flour jar, a symbolic little rite witnessed only by her mother.[36]

Palestine and Transjordan. Among the Arabs of Palestine and Transjordan, most of the boys are circumcised at the Nebi Musa feast, the traditional Muslim celebration of the birthday of the "prophet" Moses. Also, the Muslim sanctuaries of Jerusalem and Hebron are favorite places for group circumcision ceremonies.[37]

Hilma Granqvist described in detail the elaborate and pompous ceremonies that accompanied circumcision in the Palestinian Arab village of Arṭās. She personally witnessed two ceremonies in each of which three brothers were involved. The boys circumcised were from eight months to five years of age. The feast was a public affair in which the entire village participated and which lasted six or seven days. There was much dancing and singing; processions marched through the village, parading the boys seated on horseback or carried by a relative. Also a pitchfork wrapped in a woman's bridal garb was carried along (ostensibly to deflect the evil eye from the boys, but actually symbolizing the original significance of the ceremony, namely to make the boys marriageable). Occasionally, at the very hour of circumcision, a betrothal was actually arranged for the boy, and as soon as the wound was healed he married the girl.[38]

As to female circumcision among the settled Muslim Arab population of Palestine to the west of the Jordan, Father Antonin Jaussen supplies some information. Among the inhabitants of the city of Nablus, whom he studied in the 1920's, he found that the operation, universal in the past, was still performed on "some girls" as well as on barren women. The increasing neglect of the operation was regretted by Shaykh Aḥmad, Jaussen's informant, and attributed by him to a general decline of religious sentiment. "According to the *sunna* (the traditional religious custom)," he said, "the circumcision of girls is as necessary as that of boys." The operation used to be performed by a woman called *khāfiḍah* or *mubẓirah*, and consisted of the ablation of the clitoris. According to Jaussen's informants, it was still performed unfailingly by the Shī'ites, as well as by the two subdivisions of the Balābshah clan in Nablus, the al-Qawsh and the al-Qamhawi. The operation was carried out on girls aged two to six, and if it was not done in childhood, it was performed prior to marriage. If a Balābshah man married a girl from another clan and she was not circumcised, she had to submit to the operation before the wedding. A female informant reported a case to Jaussen in which the head of the Balābshah clan demanded that a young woman from another clan, whom a member of his clan had married, undergo the operation. The young wife refused and escaped back to her father's house. Thereupon the husband, who loved the girl dearly, left his own clan and renounced his parentage.[39]

Among the Bedouins of the Palestine-Transjordan region the custom is well attested. Two explorers, both publishing the results of their studies in 1908, reported that they found both male and female circumcision practiced by the 'Amārīn, 'Azāzme, Hamā'ideh, Ḥwēṭāt, Terābīn, and Tiyāha tribes, whose traditional wandering territories were in southern Transjordan and the Negev Desert, as well as among most tribes of Kerak and Ma'an. The operation was performed, by a female circumciser, as the time of a girl's marriage drew near. Among the Ma'an tribes, it was called *sirr* (a hidden and mysterious thing), since it was done in secret, by the women among themselves. Among the other tribes, both the male and female operation was called *ṭaher* (purification). In no case was female circumcision an occasion for public feasting and rejoicing as that of the boys, which was accompanied by the slaughtering of an animal, the women's *zaghārīt* trilling, the singing of special songs, and so on. The boys were circumcised in a group ceremony, between the ages of one to five, once in two years.[40]

Arabia. In the Ḥijāz province of Arabia, including the holy city of Mecca, the circumcision of boys, performed at the age of three to seven years, is the occasion of a lavish and elaborate feast. The circumcision of girls, on the other hand, is done very quietly, with only women present.[41]

In some Arab tribes (such as certain divisions of the Kuraysh in the Ḥijāz, the Kabakab, the Talaha, and other tribes of the Tihāma region of the 'Asīr district), the circumcision of boys, performed at puberty or thereafter, and in the presence of the boy's betrothed, takes the form of an extremely cruel operation involving the removal of the skin of the entire male organ and of its environs on the belly and inner thighs. While this is being done, the youth must show unflinching fortitude, standing upright, shouting "with a mighty joy" and brandishing a long dagger. The bride sits before him, beats a drum, and trills the *zaghrata*, the shrill, sustained cry of joy (also called *zaghrūt* in Arabia, *zagharūta* in the Sudan, *zghārīt* in Morocco, etc.), which is produced by rapidly moving the tongue from side to side or up and down in the mouth while a high-pitched, squealing cry is emitted from the throat. Should the youth so much as whimper, she has the right to refuse to marry him.[42]

In Southern Arabia both male and female circumcision is practiced, at ages which vary from area to area. In the Qara Mountains (running parallel to the Ẓufar coast), boys are circumcised on reaching adolescence, and girls on the day they are born. In Oman, boys are circumcised at about six, and girls at ten years of age. In the Mahra tribe (which is spread over a large area to the north and west of the Qara Mountains) male circumcision used to be performed in the past on the eve of a man's marriage, that is, after puberty, but "today a decent interval is allowed." The same was the custom among the al-Rashīd and Bayt Imānī tribes, although recently they adopted the practice of circumcising their boys at the age of five or six. Male circumcision in the Qara Moutains is an elaborate group ceremony, and as soon as the operation is done, the boy promptly rises, bleeding, and runs around the assembled men and women raising and lowering a sword as if oblivious to pain, to show his manliness. The women open their upper garments "as a gesture of baring their breasts." Among the Mahra, "eight or ten of the most presentable females are paraded." Female circumcision among the Mahra and the other tribes of the central part of Southern Arabia involves clitoridectomy; among the Arabs of Oman it is merely an incision into the top of the clitoris. No "manifestations of joy, indeed no manifestations at all, accompany the clitoridectomy of the infant female, which is done in secret."[43] Nevertheless, the operation is considered of such paramount importance that it is an almost unimaginable disgrace for a woman to remain uncircumcised. The insult which, as we have heard, the govenor of Iraq tried to avoid in the eighth century, can still be heard in Southern Arabia: "Oh you misbegotten of an uncircumcised mother!"[44]

Kuwait and Iraq. Among the Bedouins of the Kuwait area circumcision is performed when the boy is between three and a half and seven years of age and is accompanied by a great family feast. Among the townspeople of Kuwait and the Nejd (the north-central part of the Arabian Peninsula) the circumcision festivities are even more elaborate and last for several hours every day for seven days.

Female circumcision is widely practiced in Southern Iraq, for example, among the Shammar, the Muntafiq shepherd tribes of the Euphrates, the gypsies (Kauliyah) of Iraq, as well as in the city of Basra among the Sunnī Muslims, who hold it to be an old tradtion of their Banī Tamīm ancestry. Among the Shammar, the circumcision of girls is done "quickly and without any fuss." No one except the female members of the family is told, even the neighbors know nothing about it.[45]

Egypt. In Egypt circumcision is often performed in connection with a *moulid*, the celebration of a saint's birthday. Well in advance of the *moulid*, big framed pictures showing circumcisers at their work are put up over the barbers' shops or circumcision booths, often with a notice that the operation will be performed free of charge.[46]

The circumcision processions often join up with a *zeffa*, the great festive procession in which the *moulid* celebrations culminate.

Both boys and girls are circumcised, and, or so it seems, both sexes are operated on by the same male practitioner. In Cairo, the operation assumes not merely a group, but a mass character, with a thousand or more performed within a few days in connection with a single *moulid*.[47]

In general terms, the circumcision of boys in Upper Egypt takes a similar turn. The boys are usually between three and six years old, and there is a great public celebration in honor of the occasion which is "the greatest experience that the child undergoes." There is a striking similarity, Dr. Ammar observes, between the public celebrations of circumcision and marriage. The boy is supposed to endure the operation without crying or showing any signs of pain: it is a true initiation into manhood.

In contrast to the public and festive character of the circumcision of boys, that of girls is accompanied only by some modest observance "confined purely to women, and no man, not even the father, is expected to participate, or to show an interest in it." Moreover, the girl is allowed, and even expected, to cry. Female circumcision is believed to remove the center of excitability from the genitals of the girl and thus "is deemed necessary to ensure premarital chastity."[48] Also in the Egyptian village of Sirs el-Layyan, it was believed that the sexual appetite of women was twenty times that of men, and that clitoridectomy, which is performed on all women, effectively reduces desire in them.[49]

Among the Copts of Egypt, whose ancestors had practiced both male and female circumcision for centuries prior to the Arab conquest and the Islamization of the country (seventh century), the survival of both customs was, of course, facilitated by the fact that they coincided with the Muslim rites. In the first half of the nineteenth century, Lane found that excision was "still universally practiced in every part of Egypt, both by the Muslims and Copts, except in Alexandria and perhaps a few other places on the shore of the Mediterranean: it is also common, if not equally prevalent, in Arabia." Subsequently Lane states that while "most of the Copts circumcise their sons," female circumcision "is observed among the Copts without exception." The boys, he says, are usually seven to eight years old when they are circumcised in a private rite. He does not state how old the girls are when the operation is performed on them.[50] In 1941, however, Marie Bonaparte found that most of the Muslim and Copt women in Egypt were usually subjected to excision between the ages of five and ten, that the operation consisted of the ablation of the glans clitoridis and of the labia minora, and that its stated purpose was to "calm down" the women, that is, to diminish their libido. At the same time it was considered a disgrace for a woman not to be circumcised, and the supreme insult hurled by Muslims at European women was "Mother of Clitoris."[51]

In various places in the Middle East, the circumcision of a boy is celebrated in combination with his wedding. Among the ʿAbābda, for instance, in the Eastern Desert of Egypt, a hut is pitched for the circumcision ceremony, where the bride and groom take up residence afterwards. Both marriage and circumcision are called *ʿirs* (literally: wedding) among the ʿAbābda.[52]

Sudan. Among the Sudanese villagers of Burri al-Lamāb, male circumcision and female infibulation are practiced. Boys are circumcised when they are three to ten years of age, and the attendant ceremonies, lasting from two to five days, are patterned after a wedding. As in a wedding, the entire village, both men and women, participate. On the first day, after the meal, there may be an entertainment in which "unmarried village girls connected with the family perform the traditional Sudanese women's dance." This highly suggestive and erotic performance seems to indicate that circumcision is the prerequisite for a youth to have a claim on the sexual services of the related girls, one of whom will within a few years become his wife.[53]

This claim on the women is expressed in a much more unrestrained manner among another Sudanese group, the Rubatāb. Here, the boy is fourteeen to sixteen at circumcision, and during the operation he is expected to show his manliness by shouting loudly "*ana bashīr*," that is, "I rejoice." After the operation, he takes his penis in his left hand and a sword in the right and approaches the women before whom he is supposed to shake the sword and smile, while they trill the *zagharūta*. Then the boy struts before the men and cracks a whip. In contrast to this public demonstration of manliness expected of a newly circumcised boy, "the girls are usually circumcised without any feast," although "they too, rarely utter any cry at the pain of the operation."[54]

But to return to Burri al-Lamāb—in that village, as in all parts of the Sudan, female circumcision takes the form of infibulation. This involves the removal of a large portion of the labia majora and mons veneris and the paring of the labia minora. Thereafter, the girl's legs are strapped together for forty days to make the wounds on the two sides grow together by contact during the healing process, except where a reed or tube has been inserted immediately after the operation to allow for the passage of urine and the menses. During the first fifteen days, the girl is treated much like a mother in childbed. However, whatever festivities are performed are less elaborate than those for a boy. The *'ulamā*, the official expositors of Muslim law, expressly forbid this operation; nevertheless most men in the village believe that Islam prescribes it for girls just as it does circumcision for boys.[55]

Consequently all, or almost all, girls are subjected to this operation, as a rule between the ages of four and ten. As a rule the girls are quite happy in anticipation of the event, because they then become centers of attention for the first time in their lives. A girl who is not circumcised in this manner is teased by other girls, and accused of being a baby.

All over the Sudan, as in other areas where female circumcision is practiced, it is believed that the operation reduces the girl's proclivity to becoming sexually excited. Many men also believe that infibulation protects the girl from being attacked sexually, that it ensures that she will remain a virgin until marriage, and that, upon marriage, intercourse with her will be more enjoyable for the husband. What in fact results from infibulation is that it may make sexual intercourse almost impossible and reduce a woman's sexual pleasure.[56]

Sahara. Group circumcision for boys aged five to seven is the rule among the Tuareg of the Sahara. Teda boys are circumcised between the ages of twelve and fourteen, and the group ceremony is held at the date harvest and accompanied by "goat sacrifices and feasts which not infrequently degenerate into drunken brawls." "Girls are not circumcised, but undergo a puberty rite which consists of shutting them up in groups for a few days, and tattooing their lips and gums blue." Among the Chaamba Arab nomads, too, boys aged six to seven or older are circumcised in a group ceremony, the boys being expected to make some ritual demonstration of their courage. Among the Moors of the Spanish Sahara (descendants of Arab invaders and nomadic Berber tribes) boys are circumcised in groups between the ages of six and seven. The ceremony marks the transition from maternal to paternal control over the boy. Sometimes Moorish girls, too, are subjected to circumcision, that is, the excision of the clitoris and the *labia minora.*[57]

Timbuctoo. In Timbuctoo, among the Songhoi, the circumcision of boys, usually before puberty, is a large-scale group ceremony held once in three to five years. The circumcision of Songhoi girls was discontinued centuries ago. Usually about 150 boys are circumcised at one time. The ceremony is called a "boy's first marriage," and indeed it includes numerous rites which occur also in weddings. At the same time, the ceremony also reflects traits reminiscent of primitive (non-Muslim) African initiation rituals, for example, the terrifying aspect of the barbers who perform the operation and whose faces are painted white (indicative of ghosts or devils) with black on the forehead and cheeks and around the eyes. Among the Bela of Timbuctoo, the ceremony is similar: it takes place when the boys are about eight years old.[58]

Morocco. In Morocco the circumcision of boys takes place between the ages of two to seven years, although in some places it is performed when the boy is but a few months old. The operation is accompanied by elaborate ceremonies and feasts, often at the shrines of saints. In Tangier, for instance, the group circumcision of boys takes place on the day following the feast of Sidi Muhammed l-Ḥajj, the patron saint of the city. It is in most cases a group occasion, and it has many features resembling marriage ceremonies. Among the Uled Bu'Azīz, for example, it is called "the wedding of the circumcision," and the boy is termed "bridegroom."[59]

Iran. The early seventeenth-century British traveler, Sir Thomas Herbert, describes circumcision in the Persia of his day as follows:

> Men, and sometimes Women, conform to it [circumcision]; the Men for Paradise, the Women for honours sake, or *Ben-sidi-Ally* Fables whose paraphrases: from nine to fifteen the Females may; and in Cairo and the adjacent parts, at this day it is frequently practised: nor is this a recent custom, for *Strabo lib. 16* in that case makes this physical observation, *Quemadmodum viri praeputium habent, mulieres habent etiam quandam glandulosam carmen quam Nympham vocant, non ineptam accipiendo characteri Circumcisionis.* The Male at *Izmael*'s age . . . are enjoined it.

In the sequence Sir Thomas describes the pomp and circumstance of the ceremony among the wealthy Persians.[60]

In the eighteenth century, Sir John Chardin found the practice of female circumcision "among a few nomad tribes" of Persia.[61] Still later, in the nineteenth century, however, Jakob Eduard Polak could not longer find any trace of the practice.[62] On the other hand, it has been reported to be still extant among the Kurds of Iran.[63]

The circumcision of boys which was performed in Persia at adolescence in the past, has gradually been advanced to early childhood. It is a group ceremony, with care being taken that the number of boys circumcised at the same time should be odd, lest misfortune befall. The feast is a public one, lasting for several days.[64]

A field study undertaken by Fredrik Barth from December, 1957, to July, 1958, among the Basseri tribe of the Khamseh confederacy in southern Iran, found that boys were generally circumcised by a village barber or physician before the age of two months and that there was no corresponding operation on girls.[65]

Conclusions. The circumcision of a boy, the greatest event in his early life, makes him the center of attention for a few days at a highly impressionable stage of his life. Even at the early age in which circumcision is nowadays performed, he is aware that this attention is due to the fact that he is a male; it is, moreover, localized with threatening precision upon his penis. In this manner the boy is definitively reinforced in the feeling, which had gradually developed in him as a result of the ministrations of his mother up to that day (including in some places the handling of his genitals for pacification as well as in preparation for circumcision), that his superiority to woman is due to the fact that he has a male organ. When puberty sets in, within a few years following the ceremony (or about the same time), this by then deep-rooted sense of superiority is joined by a powerful drive toward the sexual possession of women. In this manner, a close correlation soon develops in the male psyche between two drives, both of which are focused on the woman: the drive to dominate her—to bend her to obedience and subservience—and the drive to possess her sexually.

If male circumcision is calculated to impress the boy with his own importance as the proud possessor of a male physique, female circumcision, which, as indicated above, is probably practiced more often than it is reported, achieves a precisely opposite effect: it impresses the girl with her own inferiority in relation to boys. It is performed in secret, as if it were a shameful thing. While the male operation serves the assumed purpose of increasing the men's virility, its female equivalent is performed in order to reduce the woman's femininity in terms of her sexual desire. As Marie Bonaparte put it, it serves to "intimidate" the girls' sexuality, while from the male point of view it "feminizes to the utmost" the woman by removing that slight semblance of a rudimentary penis that she possesses in the clitoris,[66] and thus reassures the man in his sexual superiority. The girl is told that she must undergo the operation—which is much more painful than male circumcision—in order to prevent any suspicion on the part of her future bridegroom that she is not a virgin.[67] In other words, she must suffer pain, and be subjected to a diminution of her libido, for the sake of her future husband. She must, moreover, accept, and resign herself to, the implied reproach that she is a creature unable to control her sexual desires which are easily and illicitly aroused, and therefore must be deprived of that part of her body in which these illicit desires are localized. The surgery is, indeed, a painful object lesson for the girl in the imperative of molding her life, even at considerable personal sacrifice, to the desires of the man (whom she may not even have met at the time) who will soon become her husband and dominate her life.

In the Egyptian village he studied, Hamed Ammar observed that the circumcision of girls is performed in a manner reminiscent of childbirth. The girl is seated "on a chair or vessel, while three women assist her by holding the girl's legs apart as well as supporting her back, a posture very similar to that assumed at childbirth."[68] The circumcision of the girl thus assumes the form of a rehearsal of parturition: the position, the pain, the blood, the exclusion of the male– the basic ingredients are all there. It is this event, *the* central event in the women's life, for which the operation prepares the girl: for the successful fulfillment of the woman's role– to serve "as the vessel that empties."

The circumcision of boys, on the other hand, has the character of a rehearsal of marriage and is, in fact, termed in some places the boy's first marriage, while he himself is called bridegroom. Circumcision, moreover, impresses the boy with the necessity of being brave which is the price he must pay for acquiring the socially sanctioned prerogative of dominating the women. By circumcision his generative organ is given the appearance of maturity and thus establishes him as a member of the male half of his society, and as a master over the female. This significance of the operation becomes especially clear in those ethnic groups in which the boy parades his bleeding penis in front of the assembled women, brandishing a sword meanwhile.

In those parts of the Middle East where female circumcision is not practiced, the attendance of the girls at periodically performed festive male group circumcision ceremonies is sufficient to put the stamp of finality on their awareness of the men's superiority and their own subordinate status. The women's role in the male circumcision ceremony is not merely passive. They not only are present, watching the elaborate ceremony with fascination, they are not only the spectators before whom the boy parades his newly-won manhood, or objects on which he exercises his sword-brandishing threats. They engage in two types of activities calculated to make the boy (and all the men present) feel important, superior, aggressive, and, in a word, manly. One is the provocative dancing, and the other the oft-repeated, shrill, trilling sustained cries of joy. While the dances symbolize the willingness of the marriagable girls to be taken by the boy (and, by implication, by the other men in the company), the women's trilling indicates their joy over yet another member of the male sex having passed through the indispensable prerequisite of manhood. Whether it comes in early childhood or in adolescence, the great, frightening, and yet exhilarating ceremony of circumcision is thus the one central event which, more than any other single occurrence, contributes to the formation of the differential personalities of the two sexes.

Women's Education

If Westernization has created a distance between the modernized urbanites and the tradition-bound rural folk ot the Middle East (cf. above, pp. 372–74), the cleavage it has brought about between the womenfolk of the two sectors is by far more pronounced. Perhaps the best indicator of this differential effect of Westernization on the male and female halves of the population is literacy. Among pre-Westernized men, there has always been a certain percentage of literacy. The effect of Westernization in this respect was simply an increase in the literacy rate. Among pre-Westernized women, on the other hand, the traditional situation was general illiteracy. Therefore, the introduction of education for girls created a completely new phenomenon in the world of Middle Eastern women: the emergence of a class of literate women, a group whose entire orientation as a consequence of literacy had become basically different from that of their illiterate mothers and sisters.

In the traditional Middle East, since women were not expected to take an active part in the official Muslim (or Christian or Jewish) religious rituals and ceremonies or even to attend them, it was unnecessary to let them acquire the knowledge required for such participation. Therefore, in the traditional Muslim world only boys were sent to the Koran school, the *kuttab* (in Arab lands) or *maktab* (in Iran), which was the only elementary-level indigenous educational institution developed by Muslim society. Since it was considered a religious duty to enable boys to acquire at least the rudiments of education needed for praying, reading the Koran, and related religious activities, the boys of those families which could afford it were usually sent to school for at least two or three years in the towns, and to a lesser extent in the villages as well. Girls, on the other hand were sent to school only in exceptional circumstances. In traditional Muslim society there was no such thing as a girls' school, and to let girls sit in the same class with boys was considered forbidden by religion. As a result, the men (or at least some of them) were literate, while the women were illiterate. This generalization can be readily illustrated by examples from any part of the Middle Eastern culture continent.

Until 1951 no one in the Turkish village of Sakaltutan in Central Anatolia had had more than three years "of the most elementary type of elementary schooling." Only one woman in the entire village of about six hundred people was literate. The one-class school of the village, however, included a few girls.[69]

In the Upper Egyptian village of Silwa, studied by Hamed Ammar in 1950–51, all the five unsubsidized Kuttabs were attended only by boys. The sixth Kuttab, which was recognized and aided by the government, had a few girl pupils as well, who began to attend it shortly prior to the time of Ammar's field work in the village.[70] In Egypt as a whole, in 1913–14, girls constituted 14 per cent of all pupils in all schools. By 1944–45 their percentage had risen to 40 per cent, indicating the great strides forward made by the women of that country within one generation. Yet all this advancement notwithstanding, in 1947 only 12.7 per cent of all Egyptian females over the age of five could read and write as against 32.8 per cent of the males.

Similar advances have been made by women in other Muslim countries. In Iraq, in 1930, only 20 per cent of the elementary school pupils were girls; in 1955 they accounted for 25 per cent. In Transjordan in 1922–23, 10 per cent of all pupils were girls; in 1955—31.4 per cent.[71]

As to the proportion of girls attending school in relation to the total female school-age population, a 1963 report of the United Nations shows that in that year 29 per cent of the school-age girls attended school in Iraq and Syria, 37 per cent in Jordan, 39 per cent in Egypt, and 44 per cent in Lebanon.[72]

The traditional wing of the Middle Eastern spectrum registered no comparable advances in the education of girls. A typical position on female education is that of Saudi Arabia, where a governmental school system was introduced in the 1930s. Public education is free on all levels, moreover boys from needy families are given monthly allowances to enable them to go to school. Girls, however, are barred from all state primary and secondary schools, although several private girls' schools have recently been established at Mecca and Medina.[73] While no data or even estimates seem to be available on the percentage of literacy among males, female literacy is generally taken to be almost nil.

In Afghanistan, another rather tradition-bound country, most of the women are illiterate; schools for girls are a recent innovation, and only a few girls have had an opportunity to attend them. As late as 1960, of the 175,600 pupils in elementary schools only 19,900 were girls; of the 11,300 students in middle and secondary schools, 2,500 were girls.[74]

The problem of women's education in the Muslim world is rooted not merely in the traditional absence of incentives to make them literate. That alone could be overcome with relative ease by the emergence of such new interests as the increasing desire of the young male generation to find wives who can be life companions as well as sexual partners. But the education of women was actually countermotivated by old, established Muslim views on the God-given inferior nature of women which had the religious sanction of the authority of Mohammed and which happened to coincide in many places with pre-Islamic popular traditions. These views will be discussed later in this chapter, and they are mentioned here only in order to make it clear that in the traditional Muslim view the education of girls was considered not merely unnecessary and superfluous, but positively wrong, and that it is this still widely prevalent position that the political and cultural leaders of most countries must overcome (in addition to the numerous correlated economic and technical problems) before they can make elementary education universal for both boys and girls.

What has already been achieved in this area in recent years can be elicited from the United Nations *Demographic Yearbook 1967* and *Statistical Yearbook 1967* (both published in New York in 1968), which contain informative material showing the number of children enrolled in elementary schools (in 1965) in most countries of world. This table was utilized to extract the data for the Middle Eastern countries (see Table 8 in the Statistical Appendix). The figures indicate that in no country in the area (except Cyprus, Ifni, and Israel; the female school enrollment in Lebanon was not available) has the number of girl pupils approximated that of boy pupils in elementary schools. This, of course, means that even in the next generation of adults the number of illiterates will remain higher among women than among men. The United Nations statistical sources do not show what percentage of the school-age population in the countries listed is actually enrolled in schools; however, they contain a breakdown of the male and female populations into five-year age groups (including the five-to-nine and ten-to-fourteen-year age groups), and these figures were utilized to calculate the eight-year age group of six to thirteen, which is the optimum minimal period of school attendance. On this basis the percentage of children attending school in the total school-age population was calculated. As the table shows, many Middle Eastern countries are still a long way from translating into practice the ideal of general elementary education which most of them embrace in theory. The fact that, despite the deeply rooted traditional views on female education, an increasing percentage of girls is attending elementary schools is an indication of both the power of the modernizing influences and the ability of Muslim society to adapt itself to the inevitable changes brought about by the rapidly increasing interaction between the Middle East and the West.

Women's Religion

No carriers of a folk culture can live without the sustaining power of a body of religious practices and tenets. Women in Islamic lands have largely been excluded from active participation in Muslim religious practices and have traditionally been denied any institutionalized education in the officially sanctioned doctrines of Islam. This, however, does not mean that women of the traditional sectors of Muslim society have had no religious practices and tenets to observe. It means only that their religion is not identical with that of the men. In fact, women have a religion of their own, hiding under a thin veil of conformity with the requirements of official Islam, beneath which it throbs with a great vitality. This religion of the simple, illiterate, and uneducated women (who comprise the great majority of the female sex in the Middle East generally) has preserved a surprising amount of pre-Islamic or extra-Islamic beliefs and rituals. The men, if they deign at all to take notice of these beliefs and rituals, shrug them off as women's folly, not worthy of the attention, or even the censure, of men.

The women's religion in Islamic lands comprises a vast array of beliefs and ritual activities which cannot be discussed even cursorily in the present context. I have, therefore, selected one specific women's ritual for somewhat detailed consideration, that of exorcizing the *zār* (a type of evil spirit) which is probably the most outstanding example of a separate women's cult in the entire Middle East, and which is widely practiced in numerous countries of the area to this day.

Before entering into a discussion of the *zār* cult and its related belief system, I will say a few words about other differences between the men's and the women's religion. The women's world, in general, is a place much more replete than man's with magic forces, evil and good spirits, harmful and beneficial influences, haunted springs, rocks, trees, caves, and the like. As Abdulla M. Lutfiyya observed in a Jordanian village, "the villagers, especially women, hardly ever pass or enter a place that is believed to be haunted without seeking protection from these spirits by invoking the formula 'By your permission, O masters of the places.'"[75] Similarly, Anne Fuller noted in her study of Buarij, a Lebanese Muslim village:

> Women are more concerned with the world of evil spirits than men are, since their primary function is to rear the tender young whose lives are most endangered by the unseen world. . . .
>
> Women cling to the belief in evil spirits and to the body of folk and nature practices more tenaciously than men, who often mock at many of these practices. Women, through child-bearing and child-rearing, feel greater exposure to the capricious agencies of life, and since they do not attend the mosque, they must look elsewhere for support.[76]

Related to the belief in evil spirits is the faith in the power of dead saints who can counteract the baleful demonic influences and give blessings and benefits to those who venerate them. The cult of saints itself has been repeatedly referred to above (pp. 294–95, 330, 342, 375), where it has been pointed out that it is a phenomenon typical of the settled villagers and townspeople, but largely absent among the nomadic tribes (pp. 34, 38), and that pilgrimages to saints' shrines are one of the rare opportunities for village women to find entertainment outside their homes (p. 283, 291). It has, however, not been sufficiently emphasized that visits to saints' shrines, and the veneration of saints in general, is typical of the religious life of women rather than of men.[77]

A correlative of the belief in, and propitiation of, evil spirits and the veneration of saints is the belief in, and practice of, magic in its manifold and endless manifestations. It is not that Middle Eastern men, and especially their non-Westernized majority, are free of proclivities to magic, but the hold magic has over woman is infinitely greater. This may have something to do with the fact that the life of women, their happiness or unhappiness, depends to a much greater extent on elusive, uncontrollable factors than that of men.

For instance, if a couple has no children, it is unquestioningly the woman who is considered as being barren, and it is her life, not that of her husband, that is being threatened with disgrace, divorce, and ruin. Again, it is woman much more than man who is threatened by the danger of something going wrong with the marriage: it is the husband, not she, whose love may cool off, whose interest may be directed to another woman, who may legally bring a co-wife into the house, and who, in a moment of anger, may send her packing. Also, it is the mother more than the father who is closely attached to the children, whose love for the children is greater, and whose personal happiness and status in the home depends to a considerable extent upon the survival of the children. For all these reasons, and many more, it is the woman who turns to magic, to popular remedies and incantations, to potions and concoctions and the like, in the vain but unceasing attempt to control those factors of life over which neither insight, nor intelligence, nor practical measures can have any influence. Thus it is among women that age-old magical practices survive, and it is women much more fre-frequently than men who fall victim to those psychosomatic ailments which, in many countries, are believed to be manifestations of *zār* or other spirit possessions.

The *zār* cult, of African origin, has its devotees not only in Negro Africa,[78] Abyssinia,[79] and Somalia,[80] but also in the Sudan,[81] Egypt (both Lower and Upper),[82] Southern Arabia[83] including the Aden Protectorate,[84] the Ḥijāz province, including the holy city of Mecca,[85] and the ʿUtaybah Bedouins between Ḥijāz and Nejd.[86]

In contrast to all Muslim religious ceremonies, in which the leader is invariably a man and the participants are either exclusively or in their majority men, the *zār* rituals are always led by a female mistress of ceremonies, called *ʿālima* ("knowing woman") in Egypt, *umm az-zār*, (mother of *zārs*) in Southern Arabia, *shaykha* ("sheikess") in the Sudan; and their participants are only or mostly women. The essence of the ceremony is the exorcism of the *zār* who likes to enter into the body of a person, thereby causing all kinds of painful symptoms. Afflicted individuals, mostly women, but occasionally men as well, can and do seek out the "mother of *zār*," begging her to help them by driving the tormenting demon out of their bodies. Snouck

Hurgronje observed that "the fight with the *zār* constitutes both the saddest and the merriest sides of the life of the Meccan woman." When a person is afflicted, the men as a rule recommend the use of remedies or a religious ceremony to get rid of the devilish power that causes the illness. The women, however, insist on a *zār* ceremony, and they prevail. Hurgronje, moreover, found that each of the ethnic groups of the city had a special variety of *zār* ritual: thus there was a Maghrebite (Northwest African), Sudanese, Abyssinian, Turkish, and so on, *zār* exorcism. The feature common to them all was that the *shēkhet ez-zār* (mistress of *zārs*) who functioned as the exorcist was always an elderly woman. Also identical were the basic features of asking the *zār* for his identification, then inquiring what gift he wished to receive in return for leaving the body of the patient (the usual answer is a new dress or some jewelry), and the handing of the gift to the patient. In late nineteenth-century Mecca, studied by Hurgronje, *zār* possession was both an epidemic and a fad among the women.[87]

Some fifty years later Bertram Thomas described the *zār* ritual of Oman. He found that, although it was prohibited by the official religious functionaries, the cult of the *zār* flourished in all the fishing villages of Oman. The ceremony, performed in a palm-frond hut, "is presided over by a priestess or witch or medium . . . who is not infrequently an old negress" and called *umm az-zār* (mother of *zārs*). The devotees, perhaps a hundred or so, usually almost all women, assemble at night. Much incense is burned, the *zār*-possessed is brought in and laid down in the middle of the floor, the devotees sit around him in rows, while the *umm az-zār* occupies a chair. Three drums begin to beat a slow rhythm; those present gently sway their bodies and, as the rhythm quickens, so do their movements. The *umm az-zār* now chants her formula, the devotees respond, and the music and movements become more and more vigorous. "The patient himself becomes infected," sits up, and begins to nod his head in harmony with his neighbors; this is taken as a sign that the *zār* in him begins to respond and can be approached.

The *umm az-zār* now asks the *zār* whether he is male or female and what he wants; then, his name and his father's name. The *zār* replies through the mouth of the patient, usually asking first for the blood of a sacrifice. In most instances, the ceremony is not concluded in one night, but continues through a second and third night, with seven the maximum. The drumming increases in intensity, and finally the women present, one after another "fall swooning in an intoxication of voluptuous ecstasy." When such a condition finally overtakes the patient, this "is regarded as the *zār*'s final throw before leaving his body." Thereupon, immediately, the patient's body is invaded "by the spirit's opposite sexual number, for the *zār*s are male and female and work in pairs." Moreover, there are free and slave *zār*s, and each of them can possess many people simultaneously. The names of the most popular *zār*-pairs are Warar and Mug; Saif Shungar and Of Mamid (sometimes called Tulubizan); Alem Sejjed and either Mug or Ingalul. Other male *zār*s are Dumfur, Bursait, Nuray, Dira, Al Qust, Dair Sejjed, Am Bessu, Fasil; female ones, Suriq, Iskander, Dai Katu, Taizar, and Wilaj.

The exit of the first *zār* is the sign for a coffee break. "The coffee-cup goes round and the incense burners are replenished," after which a cow or a sheep (these are the animals usually demanded by the *zār*) is slaughtered, some of its blood being allowed to fill a coffee cup which the patient promptly drinks. The sex of the animal slaughtered must be the same as that of the *zār* possessing the patient. The carcass of the animal is then roasted whole, brought to the patient, who starts eating the head. "Thereafter the assembly partakes of the burnt sacrifice."[88]

Barclay characterizes the *zār* cult in the Sudan as "predominantly a woman's religious activity, having little or no relation to formal Islamic practices and being frowned upon by the official Muslim hierachy." Men may be brought to a *zār* ceremony if they are possessed, but male *zār* possession is rare. Ideally, men should not be present at the ceremony, and, in fact, few men in the Sudan have ever seen a *zār* session. The ceremony itself largely takes the form described by Thomas from Oman. It seems, however, that in the Sudan there is an even greater assortment of *zār*s of various descriptions than in Southern Arabia. The cult itself is the basis for a kind of women's association, which "may be viewed as a functional counterpart to the men's religious brotherhoods" (p. 203). Psychologically, the *zār* cult affords women an opportunity to act out unconscious stirrings, to give free rein to aggression or masochistic feelings, to indulge in a degree of nudism (in the "cannibal *zār*" ceremony), to dance in a highly erotic and suggestive fashion, and the like.[89]

It is quite clear that in the Sudan, and probably also in other countries in which it is practiced, the *zār* cult provides the women, who are completely excluded from the male Dionysian brotherhoods and largely so from the Apollonian orthodox Muslim ceremonies, with a counterpart of their own for everything they miss in the male cult varieties. As has been suggested by Barclay, women constitute a class of marginal participants in the Muslim community (p. 207), and especially so in the religious realm. For this they are compensated by the *zār* cult which is completely dominated by them and in which it is the menfolk who are, at best, marginal.

The cult of the *zār* has attracted the displeasure and censure of orthodox Muslim men as early as the turn of the century. In 1903 Muḥammed Ḥilmi Zain ed-Dīn published in Cairo a treatise entitled *Maḍarr az-zār* ("The Harmfulness of the Zār"), and about the same time a sixteen-page Arabic pamphlet was printed, likewise in Cairo, entitled *The Zār: Contains an Interesting Humorous zagal (song) Which Describes Everything Done by the Shaykhs of the Zār From the Things Which Turn the Face of the Educated People Red and Many Anecdotes and Songs of Exorcism.*[90] The pamphlet contains quotations to show the folly of the *zār* exorcisms.

Nevertheless, in the face of all opposition, reproach and prohibition, written and oral, the *zār* cult continues to flourish among the women of the southern half of the Middle East, and it can be foreseen that it will continue to do so until either one of two developments takes place: either the women will be enabled to participate with men in the official practices of Islam on a more or less equal footing, or they will become Westernized to a degree where they will no longer need the emotional experience and satisfaction they now derive from the *zār*.

"Woman Is a Vessel that Empties"

"Women is a vessel that empties"—this Arabic proverb, current in many lands and in several variants, epitomizes the traditional Muslim view on the role of the mother between the father and his children. The children belong to the father; the mother has no rights whatsoever in them. It is the father's seed out of which the child develops, although this development takes place in the mother's body. The woman's body, like a vessel, holds the child until birth, when, its task accomplished, it empties.

In accordance with this view, which is codified in old Muslim religious law, when a man divorces his wife the children remain with the father. Very small children, who are still in need of their mother's care, go with her, but only temporarily; when boys reach the age of two years (and girls the age of seven), they must return to their father. This, at least, is the practice of the Shī'ites. The schools of Sunni law allow the children to remain with the mother for longer periods.[91]

The forcible separation of mother and children at divorce or soon thereafter means that when a woman is divorced by her husband, who can effect the act in a matter of minutes (cf. above, pp. 21–22, 95, 105–07), she is deprived not only of her husband but of her children as well.

The exclusion of the mother from the legal continuum that runs from the father to his children has even wider consequences in that women in general are excluded from all corporate entities, such as the *khamse*, the ḥamūla, and so on, which are strictly patrilineal. This is the overall rule for the Middle East as a whole with the exception of the Tuareg of the Sahara, who reckon descent matrilineally (cf. above, p. 66, No. 6). In all other areas of the Middle East, the patrilineal descent means that a woman, although born into the patriline of her father, does not count as a full member in it; she bears no share of the responsibility for the conduct of each member of the patriline, which devolves only upon the males. On the other hand, if she herself becomes guilty of misconduct, especially in the ultrasensitive area of sexual modesty, all the male members of her patriline are responsible, bear the consequences, and must take remedial action. A woman does not transmit the patrilineal heritage to her children—they belong to her husband's patriline—so that from the point of view of her parental family she represents a dead end, and from that of her conjugal family she is an outsider.

This exclusion of the woman is further underlined by the disregard for the mother in assigning a place to a man in the corporate group of his father. All sons of a man are considered jurally equal in status, without regard to their mothers' status. This is why a man's sons by his legally wedded wives and by his concubines are jurally equal, and inherit from their father identical status and also identical shares in his estate.

As to inheritance, it has been pointed out above (pp. 107–08) that despite the Koranic prescription, many tradition-bound Middle Eastern social groups, especially the nomads, still follow the pre-Islamic *'urf* (customary law) which deprives daughters of all inheritance. If a daughter were to inherit, she in turn would leave her share to her children, who, however, belong not to the family of her father but to that of her husband, and in this manner a part of the family's estate would become alienated. Therefore, the principle followed is: only he who inherits status inherits property.[92]

Segregation: Modesty and Honor

These, then, are some of the major elements in the traditional man-woman relationship in the Middle East. As we have seen, their origin goes back in many cases to the ancient Near Eastern world or at least to pre-Islamic Arabia. But it was only after Islam had swept across half the world that the Muslim-Arab elaboration and crystallization of the male-female interaction became firmly embedded all over the Middle East into the matrix of folk tradition of which it has remained an integral part down to the present time. This traditional man-woman relationship is the cultural baseline from which all change in the direction of Westernization and modernization must start out.

The centuries-old enculturation of each successive generation to this tradition resulted not only in an unquestioning acceptance of its mores and values, but also in a tendency to oppose and reject any attempt to introduce alterations into it.

One way of measuring the degree to which a culture is successful is by observing the extent to which its carriers are satisfied or dissatisfied with its mores and values. As far as the Middle Eastern women are concerned, their great majority seems satisfied with the traditional framework of their lives. That this should be the case in village society (three fourths of the total population of the area) is not surprising since, in rural communities, most women are still illiterate and know very little, if anything at all, of the modern world that has begun to break into the capital and other large cities of their country. Much more remarkable is the fact that the traditional mores and values are upheld to a considerable degree even in that small and select group of young women who are in the forefront of modernization, namely, girls at coeducational colleges and universities. This has been shown to be the case by a study conducted in the late 1950's by Dr. Ibrahim Abdulla Muhyi, a professor of psychology at the University of Baghdad. He circulated a questionnaire among students of both sexes in representative colleges and secondary schools in Syria, Lebanon, Iraq, Jordan, and Egypt, all countries in which women students constitute a very small percentage within their age group. Moreover, the very fact that their parents permitted them to enroll at secondary and higher institutions of learning (in the latter in coeducational classes) indicates that their parents, too, were considerably removed from the conservative Arab position on women. This exceptional background and environment notwithstanding, a high percentage of the girl respondents exhibited a remarkably conservative attitude. For instance, 80 per cent of the Muslim and 50 per cent of the Christian girls questioned felt that dancing with boys should not be allowed.

It is interesting to note that the views of men students largely coincided with those of the girl students in all questions of freedom from traditional restraints, with the Christian boys consistently taking a more liberal attitude than the Muslim boys.

On the question of dancing, for instance, 60 per cent of the Muslim men and 30 per cent of the Christians felt that it should not be allowed. Forty-eight per cent of the Muslim men and 28 of the Christians thought that girls should not be allowed a free choice of friends; 62 per cent of the Muslim men and 25 per cent of the Christians thought that girls should not be allowed to go out with mixed groups of boys and girls; 50 per cent of the Muslim men and 45 per cent of the Christians felt girls should not be allowed to do paid work; 70 per cent of the Muslim men and 65 per cent of the Christians thought girls should not be allowed to go to the cinema alone.

Related to the question of freedom is that of sex acceptance. Here the returns showed that both the Muslim and Christian college girls were more dissatisfied with the traditional roles assigned to them by their society than their approval of the same traditional limitations on their freedom would indicate. To the question whether they sometimes felt they would be happier as boys, 53 per cent of the Muslim and 48 per cent of the Christian girls answered in the affirmative (as against 28 per cent of United States girls). On this Dr. Muhyi comments that since "Middle Eastern woman lives in what is essentially a man's world" these findings are not surprising. They "may mean that for any Middle Eastern girl who seeks higher education there are basic frustrations."[93] We may add that the results of the study indicate that while there is a general and diffuse dissatisfaction with their female status among the college girls who have had a chance to glimpse a freer world, this dissatisfaction has not yet been concretized to the extent where it would express itself in a wish to change any of the specific traditional limitations.

In order to make tangible the traditional forces which the Muslim woman confronts in her fight for emancipation, let us summarize at this point the conservative argument for keeping women in their traditionally sanctioned place as expounded and recapitulated by Hajji Shaykh Yusuf in a Persian book published in 1926. In this book the author states that "the physical and animal side in woman is stronger than in man," while "the spiritual and angelic is greater in man than in woman." Also, she is "deficient and in need of a helper, sponsor and guardian, since woman in origin, creation, body, propriety of conduct, opinion, intelligence and action is inferior to man." As the Muslim "writers on ethics have declared," woman "is overcome by fleshly desires . . . the characteristics of love for amusement, addiction to imaginations, approval of intrigue and revolutions and fickleness are more pronounced in woman than in man." Women "are great babblers, more inclined to irritation and to the following of injurious beliefs than man."

This being the condition of womenhood, the author continues, Islam has exempted woman from all kinds of religious obligations which are mandatory for men, and also deprived women of certain rights that are the prerogative of men. Thus women do not have to go to Holy War, or participate in Friday observances or perform other religious precepts that are beyond their strength; they cannot have more than one husband, they do not have the gift of prophecy, they cannot be Imams, cannot initiate divorce, must be veiled and secluded, and must not read treatises on "love and passion." They receive only half as much of the estate of their father as their brothers, and their testimony is worth only one half that ot a man.

Both men and women, however, have certain rights over the opposite sex. Man has the right to expect the woman to obey him; she must not give alms from his property and must not fast or leave the house without his permission. To these is added one more right which, however, the translator found "unprintable." Woman, on the other hand, is entitled to receive food, drink, clothing, and shelter from the man, and also a personal maid, if he can afford it. The man, moreover, must forgive the woman's sins and must be pleasant to her.

In defense of the veil, the author says that since men are "drawn by carnal desire and by nature" to beautiful women, the unattractive among them would be at a great disadvantage if women were not veiled: no man would marry them, which, in turn, would lead to a decrease of the population. Also, men unable to procure beautiful wives would be drawn to homosexuality.

If women are refractory, says Hajji Shaykh Yusuf, quoting Koran 4:38, man has the right first to admonish and then to beat them.[94]

That women are "by nature" inferior to men, that Allah preferred man over woman, and that women are consequently deprived of certain religious, legal, and social prerogatives, is an old Muslim view often expounded by jurists and expositors of religious law, commenting upon Koran 4:38, which reads in part: "Men stand superior to woman in that God hath preferred the one over the other. . . ."[95] Because, moreover, the prevalent Muslim view since the later Middle Ages was that a woman must not engage in any activity that might attract public attention toward her, women were generally excluded from seeking Islamic learning, in spite of the early *ḥadīth* which made this endeavor incumbent upon every Muslim woman as well as man.[96]

The traditional urban ideals concerning the interrelationship of men and women in the Muslim world required a complete separation of the sexes. The world outside the home belongs in its entirety to men. Women were supposed to venture out of the home only when there was a compelling reason for such an excursion. Even the purchase of food for the family meals was not considered a purpose justifying a woman's appearance in the *sūq* (bazaar). The regular and usual arrangement was that the husband, or another male member of the household, made these purchases. In the home, on the other hand, the husband, although in theory still the master, in fact often assumed the character of a guest. This was especially pronounced in the case of a man who had sufficient means to marry more than one wife; then he quite definitely assumed the character of visiting husband in relation to each of his wives.

The physical separation of the men's realm from the women's realm (*ḥarīm* in Arab lands, *harem* in Turkey, *enderun* in Iran) was parallelled by a similar dichotomy between the men's and the women's worlds of interest. The husband's main concerns and preoccupations were all directed outward: his work, his ambitions, his position in the ḥamūla or family structure, his relationship with his male friends, his entertainments, his cultural and religious pursuits. In all this the wife had no part or place.

The husband did not expect her to be his intellectual companion, nor could she, being mostly illiterate and also otherwise uneducated, expect or hope to share his interests. When a husband entered his house, and especially when he sought the company of his wife, he left outside not only a physical world which was unknown to her, but also a whole network of affairs of which she knew nothing, and which she could not understand even if he had taken the trouble to discuss them with her.[92]

Thus, the one area of life that husband and wife could and did fully share was that of sex and procreation. As a result, the sexual aspect of the husband-wife relationship assumed an inordinate importance, a development for which both sexes were thoroughly predisposed by their respective childhood and youth conditioning. Nor did the experience that awaited them in the actual marital situation contribute to a modification of this attitude. On the contrary, the typical husband-wife relationship reinforced the expectation among both men and women that the members of the opposite sex considered them primarily as sex objects.

A similar attitude, although perhaps not quite as emphatic as in the Middle East, has been observed in the Latin world, both around the Mediterranean and in Latin America. In southern Italy, for instance, it is a commonly held belief "that the woman will, of necessity, 'fall victim to temptation,'" and this belief "brings about its own realization. In a society where everyone believes that a man or woman will inevitably make love unless prevented, a man who finds himself alone with a woman is practically forced to proposition her, since otherwise her attractiveness or his virility would be questioned. In such circumstances, the southern woman, knowing that women forget moral standards when confronted with temptation, easily gives in."[97]

In the traditional Middle East, the same beliefs were reinforced by the traditional practice to segregate women, which was surrounded by a complex value system centering on the virginity and chastity of women and the virility and honor of men. In Turkey, for instance, it was found in a recent study carried out in two social classes in Ankara "that the concept of woman as the weaker sex, unable to govern itself and therefore in need of unceasing control by the men of the family, has been internalized to a very high degree. . . . The situation amounts to a veritable "virginity cult" that manifests itself in various forms but is clearly present in all strata of society. Male superiority, on the other hand, provides the basis and justification for double standards in sexual morality."[98]

Similarly, in Arab villages, Richard T. Antoun has found that there are two disparate belief patterns concerning women: one has it that "women are physically weak and legally and economically inferior to men. Their honor, their property, and their lives are, therefore, susceptible to exploitation by the arbitrary whims of males. This is particularly true since men are by nature aggressive and women are by nature vulnerable. Women must, therefore, be protected; the function of the modesty code is to offer this protection." The other belief pattern runs on a different track: "women are driven by inordinate sexuality. They are animalistic in their behavior. They manifest exaggerated aggressiveness. They are informed by evil forces. They bring discord to the body social."[99]

The foregoing analysis pointed to some of the forces and events through which such beliefs are inculcated into each successive generation. It also showed that there is no basic conflict between the two belief patterns found by Antoun. On the contrary, the two are mutually complementary, and the adherence to either of them carries with it the inner necessity to embrace the other one as well. Woman is physically smaller and weaker than man—this, to begin with, is a fact of nature. Since she is weaker, she must be protected by the men—first by the father into whose house she is born, then by the husband who acquires almost all the rights the father had in her by paying him the bride-price and making her his wife. In the traditional view, the physical weakness of the woman extends also to her mind and personality: she is weak also in her intellect, and this, in turn, has a number of weighty consequences. First of all, she is not a suitable subject for intellectual training (she is not sent to school and her illiteracy, in fact, renders her inferior to the literate male contingent). Second, she does not have to observe the laws and rules of religion (she is excluded from traditional Muslim worship). Third, she does not have the intellectual capacity to control her sexual desires (she must be subjected to infibulation or clitoridectomy, or at least, kept in seclusion and away from men).

Woman's sexuality, it then appears, is more powerful than that of man, not because it is stronger per se, but because woman is less capable than man of controlling it. This point was clearly expressed by Antoun's informant when he said: "When a man kisses a girl, her eye is broken [she loses her capacity for shame]."[100] The words in brackets are Antoun's explanation of the expression "her eye is broken." I would venture that a more accurate explanation would be: she loses her capacity to resist; her will is broken, so that thereafter the man can take advantage of her. Of course, in the popular view the inability of woman to control her sexual drives is often expressed by simply saying that woman's lust is greater than that of man.[101] Since this is the case, folk mores build a protective fence around woman's sexuality: the fence of modesty which narrowly limits woman's mobility and, indeed, visibility, and which makes even the slightest, most remote, and most innocuous contact between her and a man a grievous offense.

On the other hand, the popular view does not exempt the men either from the taint of lust. On the contrary, all the sayings of folk wisdom concerning the greater sexuality of women notwithstanding, the entire pattern of life in the Middle East bears unmistakable testimony to the solidly entrenched assumption that it is a part of man's innate proclivity to take sexual advantage of every woman if he has an opportunity to do so. The entire system of segregation between the sexes makes sense only if it serves to protect woman against man who is endowed with an aggressive and ruthless sexuality.

This view came through quite clearly in the responses to Dr. Muhyi's questionnaire referred to above: more than 75 per cent of the boys agreed "that young women should not be allowed to go to the movies alone, because, as the interviews suggest, alone, she might be molested." To which Dr. Muhyi adds that "the Middle Eastern girls have been taught that men are not to be trusted, and they are duly cautious. . . . Whereas the parent generation responded to the male threat by erecting defenses about their women, the young women of today are more frequently insisting that they themselves are capable of acting with discretion."[102]

The picture emerging from such observations is one entirely different from that given in the usual traditional explanations of the restrictions placed upon women. The true Middle Eastern male view, we now understand, is not that women are more prone to succumb to carnal desires than men and must therefore be secluded. On the contrary, it is the men who, having been brought up to emphasize their virility and sexual aggressiveness, must be prevented from taking advantage of the women. One way of achieving this is tacitly to tolerate masturbation (which boys learn in groups), homosexuality, and sodomy among boys and unmarried young men.[103] Another way is to protect women by imposing on them the duty of keeping out of the men's sight. Moreover, in order to make doubly sure that the women obey the rules of segregation, and that the men are not too eager to seek opportunities to violate the same rules, the tradition has made the chastity of women the pivot on which the honor of their menfolk turns: the slightest immodesty in a woman causes an immeasurable loss of honor to her father and brothers. Thus the preservation of female modesty is surrounded by such intensely emotional safeguards that its perpetuation is practically guaranteed.

Outlook

Every culture, in a sense, is caught in a vicious circle of its own making from which it can break out only by dint of unrelenting effort sustained at least over two generations. The foregoing discussion dealt with some of the main features of the traditional Middle Eastern male-female relationship which an increasing number of women as well as man in more and more countries of the area consider just such a vicious circle. The efforts to break out of it have been directed to numerous points of attack, such as legal equality, religious reform, economic change, occupational penetration, medical progress, and, last but not least, educational facilities for women. Wherever a feminist movement was able to emerge in the Middle East, both its female leaders and male supporters rightly felt that, in the particular cultural configuration characterizing the area, the one key that can open more doors and windows than any other is that of education.

Educational development, an almost Sisyphean task in view of the high birth rate in the Middle East, must, in the eyes of many, receive first priority. Only after an entire generation of pupils, future mothers and fathers, has gone through school where it was inculcated with a new view of the total spectrum of the man-woman relationship, can it be expected to introduce basic changes in the early processes of infant enculturation and child socialization. These changes will have to include, in the first place, a replacement of the traditional preferred treatment of male children with equality for boys and girls so as to prevent the formation of the old male and female stereotypes in the children's minds and to discourage the re-emergence of the corresponding modal male and female personalities. When this second generation grows up and enters the age of parenthood, then, and only then, can the first, crucial phase of modernization be considered accomplished, and the new view of the man-woman relationship be assumed to have been internalized.

Nor, as has been recognized by thoughtful Middle Easterners quite some time ago, are educational reforms and the contingent improvements in the women's position merely to the advantage of the female half of the population. On the contrary, the men have as much to gain from it as the women. To put it in the simplest terms, educated and emancipated women will make better wives and mothers. This new insight underlies the increasingly evident preference shown by educated young men in the Middle East for marrying educated young women, which in turn has become an important additional motivation for many girls to seek education and for their parents to permit them to do so. Although, as Table 8 in the Statistical Appendix clearly shows, the school attendance of girls in most Middle Eastern countries still lags markedly behind that of boys, there can be no doubt that as the schooling of boys becomes more general the number of girls in schools will come closer to equaling that of boys.

In fine, numerous indicators show that the process of the emancipation of women is on its way and that changes in the man-woman relationship have begun. At this point, it has become largely academic for either students of the Middle East or the area's own cultural, social, and political leaders to discuss whether these changes are desirable or not. Instead, or so it seems to this veteran student of the area, as thorough an investigation as is still possible today should be undertaken of the traditional texture of the Middle Eastern man-woman relations with a view to isolating those of its constituent features whose retention can enrich the newly emerging social and familial patterns and prevent them from becoming a carbon copy of those of the West with all their oft-lamented and too-well-known ills and woes.

Statistical Appendix

One of the numerous difficulties that confront the student of Middle Eastern society derives from the nature of its statistics. For several countries in the area, the available statistical information is most scanty. In certain cases, even when statistical data for a country are contained in the United Nations publications, they are unreliable or incomplete. Take, for instance, the data pertaining to the number of males and females in certain age groups. It is well known that in the low age brackets the number of males, though as a rule greater than that of females, does not exceed the latter by more than 5 or 6 per cent. In other words, for every 100 girls there are no more than 105 or 106 boys. Yet many Middle Eastern countries report a disproportionate numerical preponderance of boys over girls. For the five-to-fourteen-year age group this relationship is 126:100 in the Sudan, 118:100 in Niger, 116:100 in Chad, 114:100 in Jordan and Pakistan, 113:100 in Syria and Morocco, 110:100 in Libya, Turkey, and Iran, 109:100 in Mali, and 108:100 in Iraq and the United Arab Republic.

The probable explanation for this seems to be the under-registration of girls for one or more of the following reasons: the failure by fathers to report the number of their daughters because no importance is attached to them or because the presence of an unmarried daughter over the age of fifteen in the household is considered shameful; the impossibility of inquiring into the number of wives, which is considered a private matter unsuited for discussion with an outsider.[1] In Afghanistan, "in both villages and urban centers only the males could be counted, since religious feeling and an intense concern for family privacy make it impossible to inquire how many women there are in a household."[2]

In spite of these shortcomings, the statistical material compiled by the United Nations is useful. Thus Table 1 shows that the Middle East as a whole is an area of high birthrates and high deathrates (although occasional under-registration clouds the picture), as well as high natural increase and relatively low expectation of life. It also shows the wide variations that exist in each of these rates as between one country and another in the area. Table 2 shows the high annual rates of population increase, Table 3 the high infant mortality rates, again with a considerable range from country to country.

Table 4 shows the very wide range of the number of inhabitants per physician, from one doctor to every 73,330 inhabitants in Chad to one doctor to every 410 inhabitants in Israel. It appears that high infant mortality goes together with a small number of doctors and with low life expectancy. In all these respects the southern tier of the Middle East is, in general, considerably worse off than its northern countries.

Table 5 shows that the average size of households in the Middle East is between 5 and 6 persons, or about twice as large as the West European and American average. This confirms statistically our findings that the extended family is still a widely prevalent institution in the area.

Table 6 shows that, in spite of the generally very low annual per capita national income characterizing most countries in the Middle East, the area also includes the one country with the highest such income in the world: Kuwait. The explanation lies in the small population of this sheikhdom and its very sizable oil revenues which are counted in figuring the per capita national income, although in fact, only a minor portion of it filters down to the population at large.

Table 7 indicates that as far as daily calorie intake is concerned, of those countries from which data are available, it ranges from a definitely inadequate 1,720 calories (Sudan) to a more than adequate 3,110 calories (Turkey). The protein intake exceeds the daily dietary allowance of 70 grams recommended by the

Food and Nutrition Board of the United States National Research Council in 1948 in all countries except Afghanistan, Iran, Iraq, Jordan, Libya, Pakistan, and Sudan.

The sizable Table 8 shows the number of male and female teachers and of boys and girls enrolled in elementary schools in the countries of the Middle East, as well as the percentage of the latter in the total male and female school-age population. This percentage is not supplied in the United Nations *Statistical Yearbook*, which contains only the absolute figures for boys and girls enrolled in schools and, for most countries, for all the boys and girls aged five to fourteen (given in two five-year age groups, five to nine, and ten to fourteen). On this basis the estimated number of boys and girls aged six to thirteen (an eight-year age group) was calculated, and from it the percentage of those enrolled in schools within this age group. Since several Middle Eastern countries require elementary education for a period shorter than eight years, the percentages in the last three columns of Table 8 show, not what proportion of those children who by law are supposed to be in school actually go to school, but the proportion of those children who actually go to school in the total number of children aged six to thirteen, which is the period of life that, by common and practically worldwide consensus, a child should spend studying in school. Here it should be repeated that all these figures and percentages are merely very rough approximations.

Tables 9 through 12 require no individual comments. Taken together they indicate the extraordinary width of the range exhibited by the countries in the area in those cultural activities whose medium is the written word (books, pamphlets, and daily papers), oral mass communication (the radio), and the motion picture.

Table 1. Birth and Death Rates, Natural Increase and Expectation of Life at Birth*

Country	Year	Crude birth rate	Crude death rate	Natural increase (per 1,000)	Expectation of life: Date	Male	Female
Algeria	1963	44.1	10.0	34.1	1948	——35——	
Ceuta	1967	17.3†	6.7†	10.6		...	...
Chad	1963/64	45	31	14	1964	29	35
Cyprus	1967	25.6	6.5	19.1	1948–50	63.6	68.8
Ifni	1960	36.0	12.3	23.7		...	...
Iran	1965	48	24.5	...		...	...
Iraq	1966	17.8†	3.9†	13.9		...	...
Israel	1966	25.5	6.3	19.2	1965	70.52	73.19
Jordan	1959/63	47	16	31	1959–63	50.6	52.0
Kuwait	1966	51.6'	5.7†	45.9		...	...
Lebanon	1967	31.2	4.6†	26.6		...	...
Libya	1964	25.1	4.1†	21.0		...	...
Mali	1960/61	61	30	31	1957	——27——	
Mauritania	1964/65	45	28	17	1961/62	——40——	
Melilla	1967	15.7†	6.3†	9.4		...	...
Morocco	1962	46.1	18.7	27.4	1962	——47——	
Niger	1959/60	52	27	25	1959/60	——37——	
Pakistan	1965	49	18	31	1962	53.72	48.80
Spanish Sahara	1965	14.0†	4.0†	10.0		...	...
Sudan	1956	51.7	18.5	33.2	1950	——40——	
Syria	1967	32.1	4.5†	27.6		...	...
Tunisia	1959	47	26	21		...	...
Turkey	1966	43	16	27	1966	——52.7——	
United Arab Republic	1967	39.3	14.3	25.0	1960	51.6	53.8
France	1967	16.8	10.8	6.0	1965	67.8	75.0
Italy	1967	18.1	9.7	8.4	1960–62	67.24	72.27
United Kingdom	1967	17.2	11.2	6.0	1963–65	68.3	74.4
United States	1967	17.9	9.4	8.5	1966	66.7	73.8

*Source: United Nations *Demographic Yearbook 1967*, New York, 1968.
†Obviously incomplete registration.

TABLE 2. Annual Rates of Population Increase*
Estimates for 1963–67 in Percentages

Country	*Per cent*	*Country*	*Per cent*
Afghanistan	2.0	Morocco	2.8
Algeria	2.9	Niger	2.7
Bahrain	3.5	Pakistan	2.1
Ceuta	2.0	Qatar	8.1†
Chad	1.5	Saudi Arabia	1.7
Cyprus	1.0	Southern Yemen	2.2
Ifni	1.0	Sudan	2.8
Iran	3.1	Syria	2.9
Iraq	2.5	Trucial Oman	5.2
Israel	2.9	Tunisia	2.3
Jordan	4.1	Turkey	2.5
Kuwait	7.6†	United Arab Republic	2.5
Lebanon	2.5	Yemen (1963–66)	1.6
Libya	3.7	France	1.0
Mali	1.9	Italy	0.8
Mauritania	2.0	United Kingdom	0.6
Melilla	−0.3	United States	1.3

*Source: United Nations *Demographic Yearbook 1967*, New York, 1968.
†High rate due partly to immigration.

TABLE 3. Infant Mortality Rates*
(Death of Infants under 1 Year of Age per 1,000 Live Births, Excluding Foetal Deaths)

Country	*Year*	*Rate*	*Year*	*Rate*
Aden	1965	75.8		
Algeria	1963	70.1	1965	86.3
Ceuta	1966	61.4	1967	56.2
Chad	1963/64	160		
Cyprus	1965	27.6	1967	26.7
Ifni	1960	53.2		
Iraq			1966	17.9†
Israel	1965	27.4	1966	25.3
" (Jews)	1966	21.6		
Jordan	1965	42.0	1959/63	36.3
Kuwait	1966	37.0		
Lebanon			1967	13.6†
Mali	1960/61	123		
Mauritania	1964/65	185–191	1964/65	187
Melilla	1966	23.2	1967	27.1
Morocco	1962	149		
Niger	1959/60	200		
Pakistan	1963	145.6	1965	142
Southern Yemen	1966	79.9		
Sudan	1955	93.6	1956	93.6
Syria			1967	28.1
Tunisia	1960	74.3	1959	110
Turkey			1966	161
United Arab Republic	1963	118.6	1967	83.2
France	1966	21.7	1967	17.1
Italy	1966	34.3	1967	34.3
United Kingdom	1966	19.6	1967	19.0
United States	1966	23.4	1967	22.1

*Sources: United Nations *Demographic Yearbook 1966* and *1967* and *Statistical Yearbook 1967*, New York, 1968.

†Obviously incomplete registration.

TABLE 4. Number of Inhabitants per Physician*

Country	*Year*	*Number*
Afghanistan	1966	22,140
Chad	1965	73,330
Cyprus	1965	1,320
Ifni	1964	2,880
Iran	1965	3,880
Iraq	1964	4,760
Israel	1965	410
Jordan	1966	4,040
Kuwait	1965	810
Lebanon	1965	1,390
Libya	1966	3,160
Morocco	1965	12,120
Muscat and Oman	1965	23,540
Niger	1964	64,740
Pakistan	1965	6,200
Qatar	1966	1,180
Saudi Arabia	1964	13,000
Southern Yemen	1966	2,140
Sudan	1964	30,720
Syria	1963	5,110
Tunisia	1964	8,990
Turkey	1965	2,860
United Arab Republic	1964	2,380
United States	1965	670

*Source: United Nations *Statistical Yearbook 1967*, New York, 1968.

TABLE 5. Average Size of Private Households*

Country	*Year*	*Number of persons per household*
Bahrain	1965	5.9
Cyprus	1960	4.0
Iran	1966	5.0
Iraq	1966	5.0
Israel	1963	3.8
Jordan	1961	5.3
Kuwait	1965	6.7
Libya	1964	4.7
Mali	1960/61	5.3
Melilla	1962	4.9
Morocco	1960	4.8
Niger	1959/60	4.4
Pakistan	1960	5.4
Sudan	1964/65	5.5
Syria	1961/62	5.9
Turkey	1960	5.7
United Arab Republic	1960	5.0
France	1962	3.1
Italy	1961	3.6
United Kingdom	1966	2.9
United States	1960	3.3

*Source: United Nations *Statistical Yearbook 1967*, New York, 1968.

TABLE 6. Estimates of Per Capita National Income*
(In U.S. Dollars)

Country	*Year*	$
Afghanistan	1963	52
Algeria	1965	193
Chad	1965	66
Cyprus	1966	642
Iran	1965	207
Iraq	1965	217
Israel	1966	1,155
Jordan	1965	112
Kuwait	1966	3,257†
Lebanon	1965	338
Libya	1966	680
Mali	1963	66
Mauritania	1965	106
Morocco	1965	180
Muscat and Oman	1958	58
Niger	1965	82
Pakistan	1965	95
Saudi Arabia	1958	60
Southern Yemen	1963	120
Sudan	1965	88
Syria	1963	163
Tunisia	1965	161
Turkey	1966	276
United Arab Republic	1965	161
Yemen	1958	41
France	1966	1,542
Italy	1966	944
United Kingdom	1966	1,517
United States	1966	3,153

*Source: United Nations *Statistical Yearbook 1967*, New York, 1968.
†Includes oil revenues.

TABLE 7. Net Daily Food Supplies Per Capita*

Country	*Year*	*Calories*	*% Animal origin*	*Protein grams*
Afghanistan	1961–62	2,050	13	68
Iran	1960	2,050	12	60
Iraq	1960–62	2,140	14	62
Israel	1964/65	2,820	20	86
Jordan	1964	2,390	7	59
Lebanon	1965	2,700	13	74
Libya	1964	1,910	8	50
Pakistan	1965/66	2,280	11	52
Sudan	1966	1,720	22	60
Syria	1963	2,360	14	72
Turkey	1960/61	3,110	10	98
United Arab Republic	1963/64	2,930	6	84
France	1965	3,250	41	103
Italy	1965/66	2,820	18	84
United Kingdom	1965/66	3,250	42	89
United States	1965	3,140	38	92

*Source: United Nations *Statistical Yearbook 1967*, New York, 1968.

Table 8. Elementary Education in the Middle East*

Country	Year	Teaching Staff: Total	Teaching Staff: Females	Students enrolled: Total	Students enrolled: Males	Students enrolled: Females	Estimated school-age population (Aged 6–13): Total	Estimated school-age population (Aged 6–13): Males	Estimated school-age population (Aged 6–13): Females	Percentage of school enrollment in school-age population: Total	Percentage of school enrollment in school-age population: Males	Percentage of school enrollment in school-age population: Females
Afghanistan†	1965	7,852	1,344	397,155	341,632	55,523	3,080,000‡	1,600,000	1,480,000	12.89	21.35	3.75
Algeria	1965	30,672†	...	1,357,608	837,203	520,405	2,590,000	1,340,000	1,250,000	52.39	62.47	41.63
Bahrain	1965	1,215	524	31,579	19,306	12,273†	38,500	20,000	18,500	82.02	96.53	66.34
Chad	1965	1,723†	68†	163,962	132,988	30,974	672,000‡	350,000	322,000	24.39	37.99	9.61
Cyprus	1965	2,077	782	72,191	36,917	35,214	115,000	59,000	56,000	62.77	62.57	62.88
Ifni	1965	37	21	1,143	568	575	10,600	5,000	4,600	10.78	11.36	12.50
Iran	1966	...	...	2,378,082	...	...	5,775,000	...	...	41.17	...	...
Iraq	1965	42,878	14,514	964,327	678,819	285,508	1,615,000	837,000	778,000	59.71	81.10	36.69
Israel	1965	22,507	14,865	449,837	232,231	217,576	468,000	241,000	227,000	96.11	98.36	95.84
Jordan	1965	7,692	3,468	295,177	171,534	123,643	417,000	218,000	199,000	70.78	78.68	62.13
Kuwait	1965	2,316	1,041	49,562	28,118	21,444	77,000	40,000	37,000	64.36	70.29	57.95
Lebanon	1965	14,786	...	354,270	...	...	492,000‡	...	...	72.00	...	...
Libya	1964	5,937	1,304	175,591	133,481	42,110	387,000	228,000	159,000	45.37	58.54	26.48
Mali	1965	3,826	627	161,605	110,275	51,330	1,136,000	583,000	553,000	14.22	18.91	9.28
Mauritania	1964	...	...	19,103	14,708	4,395	214,000	110,000	104,000	8.92	13.37	4.22
Morocco	1965	27,621†	...	1,124,078	787,738	336,340	2,897,000	1,450,000	1,447,000	38.80	54.32	23.24
Niger	1965	1,484	...	61,948	42,448	19,500	774,000	408,000	366,000	8.00	10.40	5.32
Pakistan	1965	181,625	19,332	6,920,632	4,943,768	1,976,864	21,340,000	11,420,000	9,920,000	32.43	43.29	19.92
Qatar	1965	574	212	11,188	6,636	4,552	14,000	7,400	6,600	79.91	89.67	68.96
Saudi Arabia	1965	...	...	244,010	...	...	1,374,000	...	...	17.75		
Southern Yemen	1966	1,239	293	35,767	27,629	8,138	229,000	119,000	110,000	15.61	23.21	7.39
Spanish Sahara	1965	50	14	1,923	1,171	752	9,000	4,750	4,250	13.24	24.60	17.90
Syria	1965	19,040	6,875	688,165	470,962	217,203	1,221,000	648,000	573,000	56.36	72.67	37.90
Tunisia	1965	12,878†	1,406†	734,216	479,657	254,559	940,000§	500,000§	440,000§	78.10	95.93	57.85
Turkey	1964	79,261	20,722	3,735,512	2,227,148	1,508,364	6,625,000	3,475,000	3,150,000	56.38	64.05	47.88
United Arab Republic	1965	87,390	36,967	3,450,338	2,110,467	1,339,871	6,280,000	3,260,000	3,020,000	54.94	64.73	44.36
Yemen	1965	1,726	27	69,139	65,583	3,556	1,000,000	525,000	475,000	6.91	12.49	0.74

*Source: United Nations *Statistical Yearbook 1967*, New York, 1968. Estimates of school-age population and percentages of school enrollment calculated by author.
†Public education only. ‡Estimated at 20 per cent of total population. §Adjusted figures. ... = Data not available.

TABLE 9. Book Production*
(Total annual number of titles, including books and pamphlets, published in 1964–66)

Country	*Year*	*Number*	*Number of books published per 100,000 of population*
Afghanistan	1965	108	0.70
Algeria	1964	158†	1.30
Cyprus	1964	170	28.19
Iran	1965	985	3.89
Iraq	1964	286†	3.40
Israel	1964	1,038	39.48
Jordan	1966	27†	1.31
Kuwait	1964	158	32.17
Lebanon	1966	438	17.80
Pakistan	1965	2,027	1.92
Syria	1965	458	8.48
Tunisia	1964	107	2.39
Turkey	1965	5,442	17.05
United Arab Republic	1966	3,060	10.18
United States	1966	58,517	30.79

*Source: United Nations *Statistical Yearbook 1967*, New York, 1968. Last column calculated by author.

†First editions only.

TABLE 10. Daily Newspapers*
(Number, estimated circulation, and copies per 1,000 of population)

Country	Year	Number	Circulation: Total	Circulation: Per 1,000 population
Afghanistan	1966	18	101,000	6
Algeria	1965	5	170,000	15
Chad	1965	1	1,500	0.4
Cyprus	1966	11	82,000	136
Iran	1961	27	312,000	15
Iraq	1963	8	85,000	12
Israel	1963	24	701,000	243
Jordan	1965	7	17,000	8
Kuwait	1964	4	12,000	28
Lebanon	1965	37	...	...
Libya	1966	4	8,000	5
Mali	1966	2	3,000	0.5
Morocco	1963	10	220,000	17
Niger	1965	1	1,300	0.4
Pakistan	1965	95	1,839,000	18
Saudi Arabia	1966	7	55,000	8
Sudan	1962	7	64,000	5
Syria	1966	8	62,000	11
Tunisia	1966	5	120,000	27
Turkey	1961	472	1,299,000	45
United Arab Republic	1964	12	...	...
France	1964	128	11,872,000	245
Italy	1965	92	5,811,000	113
United Kingdom	1966	106	26,700,000	488
United States	1966	1,754	61,397,000	312

*Source: United Nations *Statistical Yearbook 1967*, New York, 1968. Last column calculated by author.

TABLE 11. Radio Broadcasting Receivers*
(Number of licenses issued, or estimated number of receivers in use, 1964–66)

Country	*Year*	*Number*	*Receivers per 100 of population*
Afghanistan	1965	200,000	1.29
Algeria	1964	1,500,000	12.34
Bahrain	1966	202,000	104.66
Chad	1966	30,000	0.89
Cyprus	1966	139.000	23.25
Iran	1966	1,700,000	6.72
Iraq	1965	2,500,000	29.80
Israel	1965	743,000	28.26
Jordan	1965	269,000	13.06
Kuwait	1964	175,000	35.64
Lebanon	1966	450,000	18.29
Libya	1966	74,000	4.41
Mali	1966	30,000	0.64
Mauritania	1964	31,000	2.89
Morocco	1966	748,000	5.44
Niger	1964	100,000	2.91
Pakistan	1964	549,000	0.52
Southern Yemen	1965	300,000	26.17
Sudan	1964	225,000	1.61
Syria	1965	1,745,000	32.31
Tunisia	1966	370,000	22.06
Turkey	1966	2,637,000	8.26
United States	1966	262,700,000	138.26

*Source: United Nations *Statistical Yearbook 1967*, New York, 1968. Last column calculated by author.

TABLE 12. Number of Cinemas and Annual Attendance*

Country	*Year*	*Number*	*Annual attendance per inhabitant*
Afghanistan	1965	19	0.4
Algeria	1965	81	4
Bahrain	1965	10	7
Chad	1966	8	0.2
Cyprus	1966	150	14
Iran	1961	238	3
Iraq	1965	84	1
Israel	1961	172	13
Jordan	1965	55	3
Kuwait	1964	7	. . .
Lebanon	1965	165	14
Mali	1963	19	0.8
Mauritania	1964	7	. . .
Morocco	1964	226	1.5
Pakistan	1964	325	. . .
Southern Yemen	1963	18	0.2
Spanish Sahara	1966	4	15
Sudan	1961	47	0.8
Syria	1966	112	4
Trucial Oman	1960	2	. . .
Tunisia	1965	128	. . .
United Arab Republic	1965	171	2
Yemen	1965	17	0.4
France	1966	7,350	5
Italy	1966	13,300	12
United Kingdom	1966	1,847	5
United States	1965	14,000	12

*Source: United Nations *Statistical Yearbook 1967* New York. 1968.

Notes

CHAPTER 1—

1. The latest and best cartographic representation of this basic trichotomy of the Old World can be found in the *Atlas International Larousse*, 1950, p. 23A.

2. M. J. Herskovits, "The Culture Areas of Africa," *Africa*, Vol. III, London, 1931; *idem.*, *Backgrounds of African Art*, Denver, 1945; *idem.*, *Man and His Works*, New York, 1948, pp. 190–93; G. P. Murdock, *Africa: Its Peoples and Their Culture History*, New York, 1959; E. Bacon and A. E. Hudson, "Asia (Ethnology)," *Encyclopaedia Britannica*, 1945, Vol. II, pp. 523–25; E. Bacon, "A Preliminary Attempt to Determine the Culture Areas of Asia," *Southwestern Journal of Anthropology*, 1946, II: 117–32; W. Schmidt and W. Koppers, *Voelker und Kulturen*, Regensburg, 1924.

3. This delimitation is at variance with the presently accepted one. Generally, only the Asiatic part of this area plus Egypt is regarded as the Middle East or the Near East. Cf., for example, R. Linton (ed.), *Most of the World*, New York, 1949, where a separate article deals with the Near East and another with North Africa. W. B. Fisher, in his recent geography of the Middle East (*The Middle East: A Physical, Social and Regional Geography*, London and New York, 1950), includes also Cyrenaica in addition to the above in the Middle East.

4. Clark Wissler, *The American Indian*, New York, 1922, pp. 217–57.

5. The expression is taken from the title of Gertrude Bell's well-known book, *Syria: the Desert and the Sown*, London, 1907.

6. R. Patai, "Nomadism: Middle Eastern and Central Asian," *Southwestern Journal of Anthropology*, 1951, Winter.

7. Feilberg, *La Tente Noire*, Copenhagen, 1944; Patai, "Nomadism."

8. A similar comparison between each significant culture trait discerned as characteristic of the Middle Eastern culture continent and the equivalent elements in the contiguous culture continents of Europe, Africa, Central Asia, and India, would be highly desirable.

9. R. Patai, "Musha'a Tenure and Cooperation in Palestine," *American Anthropologist*, 1949, Vol. 51, No. 3; Fisher, *The Middle East*, pp. 180–81.

10. R. Maunier, *The Sociology of Colonies*, London, 1949, Vol. II, 613–35.

11. This brief description could make no allowance for local variations, of which there are many.

12. Edith Gerson-Kiwi, "The Musicians of the Orient," *Edoth: A Quarterly for Folklore and Ethnology*, Jerusalem, 1946, Vol. I, pp. 227–33.

13. Jacob, M. Landau, "Shadow Plays in the Near East," *Edoth*, 1947, Vol. III, pp. xxiii–cliv; *idem.*, *Studies in the Arab Theater and Cinema*, Philadelphia, 1958, pp. 9–47.

14. In Arabic: *arkān ad-dīn*. The five pillars of the faith are: confession of the faith (*shahāda*), pilgrimage to Mecca (*ḥajj*), legal alms (*zakāt*), daily prayers (*ṣalāt*), and fasting in the month of Ramadhan (*ṣawm*).

CHAPTER 2—

1. Cf. Ruth Benedict, *Patterns of Culture*, Boston and New York, 1934, p. 230.
2. M. J. Herskovits, *Man and His Works*, New York, 1948, p. 199.
3. Franz Boas, *General Anthropology*, New York, 1938, p. 671.
4. A. L. Kroeber, in *Encyclopaedia of Social Sciences*, Vol. IV, pp. 646–47.
5. Cf. Clark Wissler, *The American Indian*, New York, 1922, pp. 217–57.
6. Clark Wissler, *The Relation of Nature to Man in Aboriginal America*, New York, 1926, p. xv.
7. Kroeber, *loc. cit.*
8. These differences are treated in greater detail in R. Patai's "Nomadism: Middle Eastern and Central Asian," *Southwestern Journal of Anthropology*, Vol. 7, No. 4, Winter 1951, pp. 401–14.
9. Cf. Tor Irstam, *The King of Ganda: Studies in the Institutions of Sacral Kingship in Africa*, The Ethnographical Museum of Sweden, Stockholm, New Series, Publ. No. 8, 1944; Raphael Patai, "Hebrew Installation Rites," *Hebrew Union College Annual*, Cincinnati, 1947 (Vol. xx), pp. 143–225; *idem.*, *Man and Temple in Ancient Jewish Myth and Ritual*, Edinburgh, 1947, p. 207.
10. Cf. K. G. Lindblom, "Spears with Two or More Heads Particularly in Africa," *Essays Presented to C. G. Seligman*, London, 1934, pp. 149–81, 175–77.
11. Cf. Robert Hartman, *Les Peuples de l'Afrique*, Paris,. 1886 (?), p. 165, with two figures on p. 164; C. G. Seligman, *Egypt and Negro Africa*, London, 1934, pp. 12, 63–65, with pictures; C. K. Meek, *A Sudanese Kingdom*, London, 1931, p. 458.
12. Cf. Sir James George Frazer, *Folk Lore in the Old Testament*, London, 1919, Vol. I, pp. 52–65.
13. Cf. Hans Abrahamsson, *The Origin of Death, Studies in African Mythology*, Uppsala, 1951.
14. G. P. Murdock, *Africa: Its Peoples and Their Culture History*, New York, 1959, pp. 71, 223, 272, 315.
15. Cf. R. Patai, "Nomadism: Middle Eastern and Central Asian," *Southwestern Journal of Anthropology*, Vol. 7, pp. 401–11.
16. Cf. A. de Préville, *Les sociétés africaines: leur origine, leur évolution—leur avenir*, Paris, 1894.
17. Cf. Jerome Dowd, *The Negro Races*, Vol. I, New York, 1907.
18. *American Anthropologist*, Vol. xxvi, pp. 50–63.
19. New York, 1948, p. 191, and subsequent editions.
20. Cf. M. J. Herskovits, *Backgrounds of African Art*, Denver, 1945, pp. 15 ff.
21. Herskovits, *Man and His Works*, *op. cit.*, p. 192.
22. Cf. *Africa: Journal of the International Institute of African Languages and Cultures*, London, Vol. 2, 1929, pp. 221–43, 352–78.

23. Field Museum of Natural History, Anthropological Series, Vol. 26, Chicago, 1937, pp. 325 ff.

24. New York, 1959.

25. See Chapter 3 "The Desert and the Sown."

26. Wissler, *The American Indian, op. cit.*, pp. 217–57; A. L. Kroeber, *Anthropology*, New York, 1923, pp. 335–39.

27. Cf. Henry Ayrout, *Fellahs d'Egypte*, Cairo, 1952, p. 171.

28. Max v. Oppenheim, *Die Beduinen*, 3 volumes, Leipzig, 1939—Wiesbaden, 1952.

29. Cf. R. Maunier, *The Sociology of Colonies*, London, 1949, II: 634.

30. E. F. Gautier, *Le Sahara*, Paris, 1928, pp. 209 ff.; C. G. Seligman, *Races of Africa*, London, 1930, pp. 142, 146–52; C. G. Feilberg, *La Tente Noire*, Copenhagen, 1944, p. 144; J. Greenberg, *The Influence of Islam on a Sudanese Religion*, New York, 1946, pp. 1–2; R. Patai, "Nomadism."

31. Murdock, *Africa, op. cit.*, pp. 14, 129; Joseph H. Greenberg, *Studies in African Linguistic Classification*, New Haven, 1955.

32. A. Vámbéry, *Skizzen aus Mittelasien*, Leipzig, 1868; *idem., Encyclopaedia of Religion and Ethics*, VIII: 888.

CHAPTER 3—

1. Cf. W. F. Albright, *From the Stone Age to Christianity*, Baltimore, 1940, pp. 120–21.

2. Genesis 13: 6. Cf. v. 2.

3. Albright, *op. cit.*, p. 121.

4. See below, Chapter 7, "Dual Organization."

5. E. Chiera, *Sumerian Religious Texts*, 1924, pp. 20 f.

6. Alec Kirkbride, "Changes in Tribal Life in Trans-Jordan," *MAN* March–April, 1945, No. 23, London.

7. K. S. Twitchell, *Saudi Arabia*, Princeton, 1953, pp. 47 ff., 171 ff. Ameen Rihani, *Ibn Saud of Arabia, His People and His Land*, London, 1928. Cf. also Dwight Sanderson, *The Rural Community*, 1932, Chapters 2 and 3, on transition from the nomadic tribe to the subagricultural state.

8. Jeremiah 35: 1–10.

9. Jeremiah 2: 2.

10. Joseph Braslawski, "The Composition of the Bedouin Tribes of the Negev," *Edoth, A Quarterly for Folklore and Ethnology*, ed. Raphael Patai and Joseph Rivlin, Jerusalem, 1946, Vol. 1, No. 2, in Hebrew with English summary.

11. *Op. cit.*, p. 95.

12. Cf. C. S. Jarvis, "Southern Palestine and Its Possibilities for Settlement," *Journal of the Royal Central Asian Society*, Vol. xxv, Jan. 1938, p. 205.

CHAPTER 4—

1. Charles W. Churchill, *The City of Beirut: A Socio-economic Survey*, Beirut, 1954, p. 4.

2. Hashemite Kingdom of Jordan, *1952 Census of Housing.*

3. Lebanese Ministry of National Economy, *Kasmie Rural Improvement Project*, Beirut, 1953, p. 8.

4. Government of Palestine, "Survey of Social and Economic Conditions in Arab Villages," *General Monthly Bulletin of Current Statistics*, 1945, p. 432.

5. Bryan Clarke, *Berber Village*, London, 1959, pp. 75–76.

6. Francis R. Rodd, *The People of the Veil*, London, 1926, pp. 148, 150; cf. 136.

7. Rom Landau, *Moroccan Journal*, London [1952], p. 55.

8. Gerald de Gaury, *Arabian Journey and Other Desert Travels*, London, 1950, p. 92.

9. Survey 1945: 435.

10. Ilse Lichtenstaedter, "An Arab-Egyptian Family," *The Middle East Journal*, Vol. 6, No. 4, Autumn 1952, p. 382.

11. Survey 1945: 436

12. Ian D. Suttie, *The Origins of Love and Hate*, New York, 1952, p. 105.

13. Lichtenstaedter, *op. cit.*, p. 385.

14. Koran 60: 10; Cf. Reuben Levy, *The Social Structure of Islam*, Cambridge, 1957, p. 103.

15. Cf. Fulanain, *The Marsh Arab*, Philadelphia, 1928, pp. 251–73.

16. Bräunlich, "Zur Gesellschaftsordnung der heutigen Beduinen," *Islamica*, Vol. vi, 1934, pp. 186–87.

17. Alois Musil, *Manners and Customs of the Rwala Bedouins*, New York, 1928, pp. 136–37, 139.

18. H. R. P. Dickson, *The Arab of the Desert*, London, 1949, pp. 140–41, 602–3.

19. Bertram Thomas, *Arabia Felix*, New York, 1932, p. 67; cf. G. Wyman Bury, *The Land of Uz*, London, 1911, p. 278.

20. A. C. Jewett, *An American Engineer in Afghanistan*, Minneapolis, 1948, p. 262.

21. Horace Miner, *The Primitive City of Timbuctoo*, Princeton, 1953, p. 180.

22. G. Wyman Bury, *op. cit.*, p. 278.

23. Hilma Granqvist, *Marriage Conditions in a Palestinian Village*, Helsingfors, 1931–35.

24. W. E. Lane, *Manners and Customs of the Modern Egyptians*, Everyman's Library, London–New York, Chap. xiii, p. 301.

25. Lichtenstaedter, *op. cit.*, p. 387.

26. Weulersse, *Paysans de Syrie et du Proche-Orient*, Paris, 1946, p. 221.

27. Kazem Daghestani, *Etude sociologique sur la famille Musulmane contemporaine en Syrie*, Paris, 1932, pp. 21–22; cf. below, Chapter 6, Cousin Marriage.

28. Burckhardt, *Arabic Proverbs*, London, 1830, p. 118.

29. *Encyclopaedia of Islam* (old edition), s.v. Arabia.

30. Bertram Thomas, *Arabia Felix*, New York, 1932, p. 97.

31. William S. Haas, *Iran*, New York, 1946, p. 58.

32. *Encyclopaedia of Islam* (old edition), s.v. Berbers.

32a. Lloyd Cabot Briggs, *Tribes of the Sahara*, Cambridge: Harvard University Press, 1960, p. 174.

33. Survey 1945: 443.

34. Cf. Survey of the Khiss-Finn Camp. U.N. Doc. No. ME/3S/20.

35. Cf. Abbas M. Ammar, *A Demographic Study of an Egyptian Province (Sharqiya)*, London, 1942, p. 36.

36. Churchill, *op. cit.*, p. 5.

37. Alois Musil, *Arabia Petraea*, Wien, 1908, Vol. III, p. 207; *idem.*, *Manners and Customs of the Rwala Bedouins*, p. 230. Cf. the story of Rachel, Leah, and the mandrakes, Genesis 30:14; cf. R. Patai, *Sex and Family in the Bible and the Middle East*, New York, 1959, pp. 43 ff.

38. Michel Feghali, "La famille Catholique au Liban," *Revue d'Ethnographie*, Paris, 1925, pp. 291 f.

39. Kingsley Davis, *Human Society*, New York, 1949, p. 51.

40. Sania Hamady, *Temperament and Character of the Arabs*, New York, 1960, pp. 28, 94.

41. Gertrude Joly, "The Woman of the Lebanon," *Journal of the Royal Central Asian Society*, Vol. 38, 1951, pp. 17 ff.

42. Kasmie 1953: 25.

43. Feghali, *op. cit.*, 292 f.

44. Survey 1945: 441.

45. *United Nations Demographic Yearbook*, 1958, pp. 321 ff. The marriage rates, that is, the number of marriages registered annually per 1,000 population, cannot serve as a basis of comparison. In the United States the marriage rate in 1957 was 8.9; in Jordan, 1957, 11.5; in Aden Colony, 1950, 16.1. In other Middle Eastern countries they are lower than in the United States: in Iraq, for example, as low as 3.8 in 1955, which only shows how incomplete is the registration of marriages, just as that of births and deaths. Cf. *loc. cit.*

46. U.N. Economic and Social Council Document No. E/CN.9/82, 24 April 1951.

47. *U.N. Demographic Yearbook* 1949–50.

48. Ammar, *op. cit.*, I:257.

49. Churchill, *op. cit.*

50. Survey 1945:440.

51. H. R. P. Dickson, *Kuwait and Her Neighbors*, London, 1956, pp. 84–86.

52. Survey 1945:442–43.

53. *U.N. Demographic Yearbook*, 1958, pp. 472 ff.

54. *Arab Women's Congress in Cairo 1944*:320.

55. Antonin Jaussen, *Coutumes des Arabes au Pays de Moab*, Paris, 1908, p. 20; Victor Muller, *En Syrie avec les Bedouins: Les Tribus du Désert*, Paris, 1931, p. 270.

56. A. H. Hourani, *Syria and Lebanon: A Political Essay*, London, 1946, p. 92.

57. Sources: *United Nations Demographic Yearbook* 1949–50, 1958; *Statistical Abstract of Palestine*, 1942, 1944–45.

58. U.N. Social Welfare Seminar, Cairo 1950:298.

59. Nadel, *The Nuba*, Oxford University Press, 1949.

60. United Nations General Assembly. Information from Non-Self-Governing Territories, Doc. No. A/1269, 20 July, 1950.

61. Cf. R. P. Davies, "Syrian Arabic Kinship Terms," *Southwestern Journal of Anthropology*, Vol. 5, 1949, pp. 244–52.

CHAPTER 5—

1. M. E. Hume-Griffith, *Behind the Veil in Persia and Turkish Arabia*, London, 1909, pp. 96–97.

2. Eleanor Bisbee, *The New Turks*, Philadelphia, 1951, pp. 23–24, 31.

3. Jewett, *Afghanistan*, p. 48.

4. For example, among the Copts in Egypt, Cf. Lane, *The Manners and Customs of the Modern Egyptians*, Everyman's Library, 537; C. B. Klunzinger, *Upper Egypt: Its People and Its Products*, London, 1878, p. 90; S. H. Leeder, *Modern Sons of the Pharaohs*, London (ca. 1918), p. 21. Among the Christian Arabs of Palestine and Syria, cf. F. J. Bliss, *The Religions of Modern Syria and Palestine*, New York, 1912, p. 284, note 1. Among the Jews in Egypt, cf. Lane, *op. cit.*, p. 559.

5. Bisbee, *op. cit.*, p. 37.

6. E.g. In Dhahran in Saudi Arabia, Cf. H. St. J. Philby, *Arabian Highlands*, New York, 1952, p. 389; Egypt: Lane, *op. cit.*, p. 561.

7. Cf. Sources adduced by Josef Henninger, "Die Familie bei den heutigen Beduinen," *Internationales Archiv für Ethnographie*, Leyden, 1943, Vol. 42, pp. 94–95.

8. *Ibid.*, p. 94.

9. *Ibid.*, p. 95.

10. The writer's observations in Palestine.

11. Henninger, *op. cit.*, p. 95; *Encyclopaedia of Islam* (old ed.), s.v. litham.

12. Klunzinger, *op. cit.*, pp. 41, 122; Winifred Blackman, *The Fellahin of Upper Egypt*, London, 1927, pp. 59–60; Ayrout, *Fellahs d'Egypte*, *op. cit.*, p. 99.

13. Rodd, *The People of the Veil*, *op. cit.*, p. 67.

14. Alois Musil, *Manners and Customs of the Rwala Bedouins*, New York, 1928, pp. 122–124.

15. H. R. P. Dickson, *The Arab of the Desert*, London, 1949, p. 155.

16. Dickson, *op. cit.*, pp. 154–55.

17. Charles M. Doughty, *Travels in Arabia Deserta*, Cambridge, 1888, I: 336.

18. G. Wyman Bury, *The Land of Uz*, London, 1911, pp. 198–99.

19. Freya Stark, *The Southern Gates of Arabia*, New York, 1936, p. 136.

20. H. St.-J. B. Philby, *Sheba's Daughters*, London, 1939, p. 211.

21. Bury, *op. cit.*, pp. 189–90; Stark, *op. cit.*, picture opp. p. 226.

22. Philby, *op. cit.*, p. 410.

23. Bertram Thomas, *Alarms and Excursions in Arabia*, p. 151.

24. Bertram Thomas, *Arabia Felix*, New York, 1932, p. 227.

25. George Haddad, *Fifty Years of Modern Syria and Lebanon*, Beirut, 1950, p. 198.

26. Leeder, *op. cit.*, pp. 21–22.

27. Donald N. Wilber, *Iran, Past and Present*, Princeton, 1955, p. 218.

28. Bisbee, *op. cit.*, pp. 23–24.

29. Doughty, *Arabia Deserta*, I: 350, 367.

30. E.g., Teyma, cf. Doughty, *op. cit.*, I: 336.

31. Philby, *op. cit.*, pp. 79, 211.

32. Musil, *Rwala*, p. 232.

33. Cf. Doughty, *op. cit.*, I: 365.

34. *Voyages d'Ibn Batouta*, ed. Defremery, Vol. iv, pp. 388 ff.

35. Musil, *Rwala*, p. 240; Philby, *Sheba's Daughters*, p. 356.

36. Lane, *Modern Egyptians*, Chap. iv, p. 184.

37. *Ibid.*, Chap. xxiv, p. 435–37.

38. Cf. A. M. Hasanein, *The Lost Oases*, London, 1925, p. 101, as quoted by Levy, *The Social Structure of Islam*, p. 109.

39. Cf. Walter Cline, *Notes on the People of Siwah and El Garah in the Libyan Desert*, General Series in Anthropology, No. 4, Menasha, Wis., 1936, pp. 42–43.

40. Cf. Patai, *Sex and Family*, *op. cit.*, pp. 138 ff.

41. Rodd, *People of the Veil*, *op. cit.*, pp. 173–75.

42. Cf. Henri Lhote, *Les Touaregs du Hoggar* (*Ahaggar*), Paris, 1944, pp. 288–94; cf. Count Byron Khun de Prorok, *In Quest of Lost Worlds*, New York, 1935, pp. 45–46.

42a. Lloyd Cabot Briggs, *Tribes of the Sahara*, Cambridge: Harvard University Press, 1960, pp. 220–21.

43. Horace Miner, *The Primitive City of Timbuctoo*, pp. 176–77, 192.

44. William S. Haas, *Iran*, New York, 1946, p. 58.

45. Gertrude Joly, "The Woman of the Lebanon," *Journal of the Royal Central Asian Society*, Vol. 38, 1951, pp. 179 ff.

46. "Arab Women's Congress in Cairo 1944," *Moslem World*, 1945, p. 322.

47. Feghali, "La famille Catholique au Liban," *op. cit.*, pp. 292 ff.

48. B. Yebamot 37*b*; B. Yoma 18*b*.

49. *Kitāb al-Aghāni*, VII, 18; as quoted by Reuben Levy, *The Social Structure of Islam*, Cambridge, 1957, p. 116.

50. *Muslim's Collection of Traditions with Nawawi's Commentary*, III, 309–14; as quoted by G. A. Wilken, *Das Matriarchat* (*Das Mutterrecht*) *bei den alten Araben*, Leipzig, 1884, pp. 11–14.

51. Cf. Count Carlo Landberg, *Etudes sur les dialectes de l'Arabie méridionale*, Leiden, 1909, II/2, p. 935.

52. Cf. Ignaz Goldziher, *Die Richtungen der Islamischen Koranauslegung*, Leyden, 1920, p. 13.

53. Cf. Wilken, *op. cit.*, pp. 23, 25.

54. Hamilton, *New Account of the East Indies*, I: 52–53 (about Ṣan'a, capital of Yemen); Guarmani, *Neged*, 113–16; Alois Musil, *The Northern Nejd*, New York, 1928, pp. 85, 253; Snouck Hurgronje, *Mekka*, II: 109 f.; Heffening, *Encyclopedia of Islam* (old ed.), III: 838*a*; Henninger, "Familie," p. 47; G.-H. Bousquet, *La morale de l'Islam et son ethique sexuelle*, Paris, 1953, p. 104.

55. Lane, *Modern Egyptians*, p. 384.

56. Harold Ingrams, *Geographical Journal*, Vol. 88 (1936), p. 537.

57. Arminius Vámbéry, *Meine Wanderungen . . . in Persien*, Pesth, 1867, p. 71; Dr. A. M. Djamdudi Djahausouzi, *Les Pelerinages de l'Islam Schiite*, Paris, 1930, p. 85; G.-H. Bousquet, *op. cit.*, pp. 103–4; S. G. W. Benjamin, *Persia and the Persians*, London, 1887, pp. 451–53; Marie Anastase, "*La Femme du désert autrefois et aujourd'hui*," *Anthropos*, Vol. 3 (1908), p. 186.

58. Reuben Levy, *The Social Structure of Islam*, Cambridge, 1957, p. 117, and sources there, in Notes 1 and 2.

59. *U.N. Demographic Yearbook* 1949–50, p. 254; *Census of Palestine* 1931.

60. *U.N. Demographic Yearbook* 1949–50.

61. Cf. "Conditions of Work in Syria and Lebanon," *International Labour Review*, April, 1939, p. 513, as quoted in ILO Regional Meeting for the Near and Middle East, Cairo, Nov. 1947, *Report on Protection of Industrial and Commercial Workers*, p. 21.

62. Cf. ILO Report of Regional Meeting for the Near and Middle East, Cairo, 1947, p. 32.

63. Widad Sakakini, "The Evolution of Syrian Women," *United Asia*, Bombay, May–June, 1949, Vol. 1, pp. 531 ff.

64. "Arab Women's Congress in Cairo 1944," 316 ff.

65. "Arab Women's Congress in Cairo 1944," 320.

66. Joly, *op. cit.*, p. 178.

CHAPTER 6—

1. Cf. Gait, *Census of India, 1911*, Vol. I (India) Report, pp. 252, 256; Matin uz-Zaman Khan, *Census of India, 1911*, Vol. XX (Kashmir), Report, p. 139; quoted after E. Westermarck, *History of Human Marriage*, Vol. II, p. 71.

2. Cf. Sibree, *The Great African Island*, p. 248; Grandidier, *Ethnographie de Madagascar*, Vol. II, p. 167.

3. Cf. Sibree, *Journal of the Royal Anthropological Institute* IX (1880), p. 50; quoted after Brenda Z. Seligman, "Studies in Semitic Kinship," *Bulletin of the School of Oriental Studies* III (1923–25), pp. 277–78.

4. G. McCall Theal, *The Yellow and Dark-Skinned People of Africa South of the Zambesi*, London, 1910, p. 219; *idem.*, *History of the Boers in South Africa*, pp. 16 ff., quoted after Westermarck, *op. cit.*, Vol. II, p. 71.

5. Cf. Westermarck, *op. cit.*, Vol. II, pp. 71–81.

6. Ayrton, Curelly, and Weigall, *Abydos*, III: 44; Pausanias, *Descriptio Graeciae*, I, 7, 1; Johannes Nietzold, *Die Ehe in Ägypten zur Ptolemaisch-Römischen Zeit*, Leipzig, 1903, pp. 12 ff.; Hastings, *Encyclopaedia of Religion and Ethics*, VIII: 444; Erman, *Life in Ancient Egypt*, p. 153; Westermarck, *op. cit.*, Vol. II, p. 91.

7. Nietzold, *op. cit.*, pp. 12 ff.; Erman, *op. cit.*, p. 153; Griffith, in Hastings, *Encyclopaedia of Religion and Ethics*, VIII: 444.

8. Cf. Nietzold, *op. cit.*, p. 14, and Song of Solomon 4:9.

9. In the royal family after the time of Cambyses, cf. Herodotus III: 31; Spiegel, *Eranische Altertumskunde* III: 678 f.; otherwise: Rapp, *Zeitschrift der deutschen morgenländischen Gesellschaft* XX: 112 f.; Hubschmann, *ibid.*, XLIII: 308 ff.; Gray, in Hastings, *Enclyclopaedia of Religion and Ethics* VIII: 457; Westermarck, *op. cit.*, Vol. II, p. 86.

10. Darab Dastur Peshotan Sunjana, *Next-of-kin Marriages in Old Iran*, p. 16 ff. and *passim*; Westermarck, *op. cit.*, Vol. II, p. 87.

11. West, *Sacred Books of the East*, XVIII: 427 f.; Moulton, *Early Zoroastrianism*, p. 207; Westermarck, *op. cit.*, Vol. II, p. 87.

12. Darab Dastur, *op. cit.*, p. 45; Westermarck, *op. cit.*, Vol. II, p. 89.

13. William Robertson Smith, *Kinship and Marriage in Early Arabia*, p. 163.

14. Cf. R. Patai, *Sex and Family*, *op. cit.*, pp. 23 ff.

15. Robertson Smith, *op. cit.*, p. 192, and also pp. 82, 138, 164, 285; Wellhausen, *Nachrichten der königlichen Gesellschaft der Wissenschaften*, Göttingen, 1893, No. 11, pp. 436 f.; Wilken, *Das Matriarchat bei den alten Arabern*, p. 59.

16. Krauss, *Sitte und Brauch der Südslaven*, pp. 221 f., quoted after Westermarck, *op. cit.*, Vol. II, p. 97.

17. Reuben Levy, *The Social Structure of Islam*, Cambridge, 1957, pp. 102 f.

18. Cf. Bruno Meissner, "Neuarabische Geschichten aus dem Iraq," *Beiträge zur Assyriologie*, Vol. v (1906), pp. 48–51; *idem.*, "Neuarabische

Gedichte aus dem Iraq." *Mitteilungen des Seminars für Orientalische Sprachen zu Berlin*, Vol. V, 2 (1902), p. 101; Enno Littman, "Märchen und Legenden aus der Syrisch-Arabischen Wüste," *Nachrichten von der königl. Gesellschaft der Wissenschaften und der Georg-August Universität zu Göttingen*, 1915, pp. 4–17; Schmidt und Kahle, *Volkserzählungen aus Palästina*, Vol. I, Göttingen, 1918, pp. 126–35, 158–61, 200, 203, 204 f.; Vol. II, Göttingen, 1930, pp. 72, 77, 95, 195; E. S. Stevens, *Folk Tales of Iraq*, Oxford–London, 1931, pp. 194, 233; T. Ashkenazi, *Tribus Semi-Nomades de la Palestine du Nord*, Paris, 1938, pp. 57 ff.; Leo Haefeli, *Die Beduinen von Beerseba*, Luzern, 1938, p. 106.

19. Eleanor Bisbee, *The New Turks*, Philadelphia, 1951, p. 41.

20. Among the Mandaeans of Iraq and Iran, cf. E. S. Drover, *The Mandaeans of Iraq and Iran*, Oxford, 1937, p. 59: "Marriages between cousins are usual, and the paternal cousin is preferred to the maternal cousin." In southern Arabia, cf. Landberg, *Etudes*, *op. cit.*, II/2 : 841 f.; Bent, *Southern Arabia*, London, 1900, p. 144. Among the Kababish, Beni Amer, and Hadendowa of Upper Egypt and the Sudan, cf. Brenda Z. Seligman, "Studies in Semitic Kinship," *op. cit.*, pp. 268, 279.

21. Ella C. Sykes, *Persia and Its Peoples*, New York, 1910, p. 201; cf. also *idem.*, "Persian Family Life," *Journal of the Royal Central Asian Society*, 1914, Pt. I, p. 7.

22. *'Aqd dukhtar 'amu wapesar 'amu ra dar behesht basta and;* communicated by a Persian student in Philadelphia to Mr. William Stockton, Jr., to whom the author is indebted for it.

23. C. Colliver Rice, *Persian Women and Their Ways*, London, 1923, p. 68; cf. Bess Allen Donaldson, *The Wild Rue*, London, 1938, p. 48: "Marriage between cousins is common." Cf. also Henri Massé, *Persian Beliefs and Customs*, New Haven, 1954, pp. 40–41: "Unions between cousins are quite frequent in the upper classes."

24. H. N. Hutchinson, *Marriage Customs in Many Lands*, New York, 1897, p. 67.

25. Ernest F. Fox, *Travels in Afghanistan, 1937–1938*, New York, 1943, p. 195.

26. Lane, *Modern Egyptians*, pp. 161–62.

27. Ilse Lichtenstadter, "An Arab-Egyptian Family," *The Middle East Journal*, Vol. 6, No. 4, Autumn 1952, p. 387.

28. Winifred Blackman, *The Fellahin of Upper Egypt*, London, 1927, p. 37.

29. C. G. and Brenda Z. Seligman, *The Kababish, A Sudan Arab Tribe*, Harvard African Studies, II, Cambridge, Mass., 1918, p. 131.

30. Oral information supplied by my Coptic student Mr. Fawzi Fahim Gadallah. Cf. also C. B. Klunzinger, *Upper Egypt*, London, 1878, p. 90; Brenda Z. Seligman, *op. cit.*, p. 276.

31. Cf. Walter Cline, *Notes on the People of Siwah and el Garah in the Libyan Desert*, General Series in Anthropology (ed. Leslie Spier), No. 4, Menasha, Wis., 1936, p. 46.

32. Adolf Erman und Hermann Ranke, *Aegypten und aegyptisches Leben im Altertum*, Tübingen, 1923, p. 180.

33. Cf. Gertrude H. Stern, *Marriage in Early Islam*, James G. Forlong Fund Vol. xviii, The Royal Asiatic Society, London, 1939, pp. 60, 65–66, 172, 177–78.

34. Henry Ayrout, *Fellahs d'Egypte*, *op. cit.*, p. 143.

35. Klunzinger, *Upper Egypt*, *op. cit.*, p. 196.

36. Georges Legrain, *Une Famille Copte de Haute Egypte*, Brussels, 1945, pp. 33–39.

37. Fredrik Barth, *Principles of Social Organization in Southern Kurdistan*, Oslo, 1954, p. 68.

38. Fredrik Barth, "Father's Brother's Daughter Marriage in Kurdistan," *Southwestern Journal of Anthropology*, Vol. 10, 1954, p. 167.

39. Hilma Granqvist, *Marriage Conditions in a Palestinian Village*, Helsingfors, 1931, Vol. I, pp. 82–83, 192–95.

39a. Horace M. Miner and George de Vos, *Oasis and Casbah: African Culture and Personality in Change*, Ann Arbor: University of Michigan, 1960, pp. 37, 43, 57, 61; Lloyd Cabot Briggs, *Tribes of the Sahara*, Cambridge, Harvard Univ. Press, 1960, pp. 86, 91, 198, 220.

40. Horace Miner, *The Primitive City of Timbuctoo*, Princeton, 1953, pp. 143–44.

41. *Ibid.*, p. 154.

42. Cf. for example Lane, *Modern Egyptians*, *op. cit.*, p. 166.

43. Ilse Lichtenstadter, *op. cit.*, p. 388.

44. Ayrout, *op. cit.*, p. 144.

45. Cf. John Lewis Burckhardt, *Notes on the Bedouins and Wahabys*, London, 1830, p. 154; Kazem Daghestani, *Etude sociologique sur la famille Musulmane contemporaine en Syrie*, Paris, 1932, p. 22.

46. Alois Musil, *Manners and Customs of the Rwala Bedouins*, New York, 1928, pp. 444–45; Cf. also Charles M. Doughty, *Travels in Arabia Deserta*, Cambridge, 1888, I : 491 (the Muwahib in northern Hijaz); P. Antonin Jaussen, *Coutumes Arabes au Pays de Moab*, Paris, 1908, pp. 46 f. (Moab in Transjordan).

47. Granqvist, *op. cit.*, I : 23–32, 69–71, 75 note 3, 122 f.; Daghestani, *op. cit.*, 22, 27; Khaled Chatila, *Le Mariage chez les Musulmans en Syrie*, Paris, 1933, pp. 184, 192.

48. Fredrik Barth, "Father's Brother's Daughter Marriage," *op. cit.*, pp. 167–71.

49. Cf. Josef Henninger, "Die Familie bei den heutigen Beduinen," *Internationales Archiv für Ethnographie*, Leiden, 1943 (Vol. 42), pp. 73 f.

50. Bertram Thomas, *Alarms and Excursions in Arabia*, London, 1931, p. 275.

51. Burckhardt, *Notes on the Bedouins and Wahabys*, London, 1830, pp. 64–65, 154. In a footnote Burckhardt refers to the Biblical parallel of Ruth 4 : 7–8.

52. Richard F. Burton, *Personal Narrative of a Pilgrimage to Al-Madinah and Meccah*, London, 1913, II : 84.

53. Doughty, *op. cit.*, I : 231, 236.

54. Lady Anne, Blunt, *A Pilgrimage to Nejd*, London, 1881, I : 42.

55. William Robertson Smith, *Lectures and Essays*, London, 1912, p. 563.

56. L. W. C. van den Berg, *Le Hadhramaut et les colonies Arabes dans l'Archipel Indien*, Batavia, 1886, p. 45; Theodore and Mrs. Bent, *Southern Arabia*, London, 1900, p. 144; Bertram Thomas, *Alarms and Excursions*, *op. cit.*, p. 275.

57. Bertram Thomas, *Arabia Felix*, *op. cit.*, p. 99.

58. Ailon Shiloh, private communication from Beit Mazmil, Israel, based on field observations among Yemenite Jewish immigrants.

59. S. D. Goitein, "Portrait of a Yemenite Weavers' Village," *Jewish Social Studies*, January 1955, p. 20.

60. Musil, *Rwala Bedouins, op. cit.*, pp. 137–140.

61. Lady Anne Blunt, *Bedouin Tribes of the Euphrates*, New York, 1879, p. 308 ; le Comte de Perthuis, *Le Désert de Syrie, l'Euphrate et la Mesopotamie*, Paris, 1896, pp. 98–102; L. Bouvat, "Le droit coutumier des tribus Bedouines de Syrie," *Revue de Monde Musulman*, Vol. 43, 1921, p. 39; Musil, *Rwala Bedouins, op. cit.*, 137.

62. Cf. J. G. Wetzstein, "Sprachliches aus den Zeltlagern der syrischen Wüste," *Zeitschrift der deutschen morgenländischen Gesellschaft*, xxii (1868), pp. 102–12; F. H. Weissbach, *Beiträge zur Kunde des Iraq-Arabischen*, Leipzig, 1908–30, pp. 41 f.; 25; Musil, *Rwala Bedouins, op. cit.*, 137 f.; *idem., Northern Negd*, New York, 1928, pp. 112 f.; Burckhardt, *Notes, op. cit.*, 64 f.; G. A. Wallin, "Probe aus einer Anthologie neuarabischer Gesänge in der Wüste gesammelt," *Zeitschrift der deutschen morgenländischen Gesellschaft*, iv, 1852, p. 125; Victor Muller, *En Syrie avec les Bedouins*, Paris, 1931, p. 227.

63. Perthuis, *op. cit.*, pp. 98–102.

64. Blunt, *Bedouin Tribes of the Euphrates*, pp. 308, 322–24.

65. Alois Musil, *Arabia Deserta*, New York, 1927, p. 175.

66. *Ibid.*, p. 285.

67. *Ibid.*, p. 240.

68. Alois Musil, *Arabia Petraea*, Wien, 1908, III : 174.

69. Antonin Jaussen, *Moab, op. cit.*, pp. 45–47; Jaussen and Savignac, *Coutumes des Fuqara*, Paris, 1914, p. 24.

70. Jaussen, *Moab, op. cit.*, p. 46.

71. *Ibid.*, pp. 46–47. The case happened in the Hajāya tribe.

72. P. Marie Anastase de St. Elie, "La femme du désert autrefois et aujourd'hui," *Anthropos*, Vol. 3, pp. 186, 189.

73. Jaussen, *Moab, op. cit.*, p. 47.

74. G. Robinson Lees, *The Witness of the Wilderness*, London, 1909, p. 121.

75. Omar el-Barghuthi, "Judicial Courts among the Bedouin of Palestine," *Journal of the Palestine Oriental Society*, Vol. 2, 1922, p. 28; Antonin Jaussen, *Coutumes Palestiniennes. I. Naplouse et son district*, Paris, 1927, p. 62; T. Canaan, "Unwritten Laws Affecting the Arab Woman of Palestine," *Journal of the Palestine Oriental Society*, Vol. 11, 1931, p. 178; Granqvist, *Marriage Conditions, op. cit.*, p. 72.

76. Canaan, *op. cit.*, p. 178; Musil, *Rwala Bedouins*, p. 137.

77. Barghuthi, *op. cit.*, p. 28.

78. Jaussen, *Coutumes Palestiniennes, op. cit.*, p. 62.

79. Philip J. Baldensperger, "Women in the East," *Palestine Exploration Fund Quarterly Statement*, London, 1900, p. 181; T. Ashkenazi, *Tribus semi-nomades de la Palestine du Nord*, Paris, 1938, p. 63.

80. F. A. Klein, "Mitteilungen uber Leben, Sitten und Gebräuche der Fellachen in Palästina," *Zeitschrift des deutschen Palästina Vereins*, 1883, p. 84; Philip J. Baldensperger, *The Immovable East*, London, 1913, p. 121; Jaussen, *Coutumes Palestiniennes, op. cit.*, p. 62; Granqvist, *op. cit.*, p. 72.

81. Granqvist, *op. cit.*, pp. 67–72.

82. Enno Littmann, *Neuarabische Volkspoesie*, Berlin, 1902, pp. 32–33 (Arabic text) and 119—120 (German translation).

83. Granqvist, *op. cit.*, pp. 72–75.

84. Daghestani, *Etude, op. cit.*, pp. 21–22; Jacques Weulersse, *Paysans de Syrie et du Proche-Orient*, Paris, 1946, p. 221.

85. Daghestani, *Etude, op. cit.*, p. 22; Musil, *Arabia Petraea*, p. 174.

86. Daghestani, *op. cit.*, pp. 21–23; cf. above, p. 152.

87. Chatila, *op. cit.*, p. 93.

88. *Ibid.*, pp. 91–94; Daghestani, *op. cit.*, pp. 21–22.

89. Leonard Bauer, *Volksleben im Lande der Bibel*, Leipzig, 1903, p. 98 ; Jaussen, *Coutumes Palestiniennes, op. cit.*, p. 66; Daghestani, *op. cit.*, pp. 18, 19, 173.

90. Daghestani, *op. cit.*, pp. 20, 23, 24, 32, 173; J. Castagné, "Le mouvement d'émancipation de la femme musulmane en Orient," *Revue de Monde Musulman*, Vol. 43, 1921, p. 261.

91. H. R. P. Dickson, *The Arab of the Desert, op. cit.*, p. 140; cf. also George L. Harris (ed.), *Iraq: Its People, Its Society, Its Culture*, New Haven, 1958, pp. 272 f.

92. Bruno Meissner, "Neuarabische Geschichten aus dem Iraq," *Beiträge zur Assyriologie*, Vol. 5, 1906, pp. 48–49, 74–75.

93. Jacob M. Landau, Private written communication from Jerusalem, based on field work.

94. John B. Glubb, "The Bedouins of Northern Iraq," *Journal of the Royal Central Asian Society*, London, Vol. 22, 1935, p. 24.

95. H. R. P. Dickson, *Kuwait and Her Neighbours*, London, 1956, pp. 228–235.

96. W. R. Hay, *Two Years in Kurdistan*, London, 1921, p. 45.

97. Barth, "Father's Brother's Daughter Marriage," pp. 167, 169; *idem.*, *Principles of Social Organization in Southern Kurdistan*, p. 26.

98. Hay, *op. cit.*, pp. 71–72.

99. Hellmut Ritter, "Aserbeidschanische Texte zur nordpersischen Volkskunde," *Der Islam*, Vol. 11, 1921, p. 185 (Turcic text) and 198 (German. translation).

100. C. G. Feilberg, *Les Papis*, Copenhagen, 1952, p. 136.

101. Burckhardt, *op. cit.*, pp. 154–55.

102. G. W. Murray, *Sons of Ishmael: A Study of the Egyptian Bedouin*, London, 1935, pp. 179–80.

103. Charles G. and Brenda Z. Seligman, *The Kababish*, p. 81.

104. *Ibid.*, p. 131; Brenda Z. Seligman, *op. cit.*, pp. 269–70.

105. Edward Westermarck, *Marriage Ceremonies in Morocco*, London, 1914, p. 53.

106. Cf. Major A. J. Tremearne, *The Ban of the Bori*, London, *n.d.* [1914], p. 121.

107. Dozy (ed.), *Commentaire historique sur le poème d'Ibn 'Abdan*, pp. 27, 29, as quoted by I. Goldziher, "Endogamy and Polygamy among the Arabs," *The Academy*, London, July 10, 1880, p. 26.

108. Cf. Julius Wellhausen, *Nachrichten der königl. Gesellschaft der Wissenschaften zu Göttingen*, 1893, No. 11, pp. 437 f.

109. *Kitāb al-'Aghāni*, ed. Bulaq, viii : 113, as quoted by I. Goldziher, *op. cit.*

110. E. W. Lane, *Arabian Society in the Middle Ages*, London, 1883, p. 227.

111. Lane, *Modern Egyptians, op. cit.*, pp. 161–62.

112. Chatila, *op. cit.*, p. 92.

113. J. R. Jewett, "Arabic Proverbs and Proverbial Phrases," *Journal of the American Oriental Society*, 15 (1893), p. 86.

114. Barghuthi, *op. cit.*, p. 28.

115. Snouck Hurgronje, *Mekkanische Sprichwörter*, Haag, 1886, p. 17.

116. Gertrude H. Stern, *Marriage in Early Israel*, *op. cit.*, pp. 60, 158 ff.

117. Chatila, *op. cit.*, p. 91; Westermarck, *op. cit.*, pp. 53–54; Ella C. Sykes, *Persia and Its Peoples*, *op. cit.*, p. 201; etc.

118. Barth, "Father's Brother's Daughter Marriage," *op. cit.*, pp. 167, 169, 171; *idem.*, *Principles*, *op. cit.*, pp. 69 f.

119. Goldziher, *op. cit.*, p. 26.

120. Wilken, *Matriarchat*, *op. cit.*, pp. 59, 61.

121. Ghazālī, *Iḥyā 'ulūm al-dīn*, Book xii, Chapter, ii; cf. the German translation by Hans Bauer, *Von der Ehe. Das 12. Buch von al-Gazali's "Neubelebung der Religionswissenschaften,"* Halle a.S., 1917, p. 66.

122. Westermarck, *op. cit.*, pp. 54–55.

123. Goldziher, *op. cit.*, p. 26.

124. Westermarck, *op. cit.*, pp. 54–55; *idem.*, *Ritual and Belief in Morocco*, London, 1926, I : 164.

125. Chatila, *op. cit.*, p. 93.

CHAPTER 7—

1. The following is a partial and incomplete list of the most important studies in which dual organization is treated and defined: W. H. R. Rivers, *Social Organization*, London, 1932, pp. 29–30; A. M. Hocart, *The Progress of Man*, London, 1933, pp. 238–44; R. Linton, *The Study of Man*, New York, 1936, p. 207; B. Malinowski, *Crime and Custom in Savage Society*, London, 1940, pp. 24–26; I. Schapera, in *Encyclopaedia Britannica*, 14th ed., Vol. 8, p. 70; M. D. W. Jeffreys, "Dual Organization in Africa," in *African Studies*, Vol. 5 (1946), p. 84; G. P. Murdock, *Social Structure*, New York, 1949, pp. 47, 90, 124–25.

2. Josef Haekel, "Die Dualsysteme in Afrika," *Anthropos*, 1950, pp. 13–24.

3. Again only a selective list can be given: India: W. Koppers, "India and Dual Organization," *Acta Tropica*, Basel, 1944, Vol. i, Heft 1–2; Ugric people: J. Haekel, "Idolkult und Dualsysten bei den Ugriern," *Archiv für Völkerkunde*, Wien, 1947, Bd. I; Indonesia, Oceania and North America: W. J. Perry, *The Children of the Sun*, London, 1923, *passim*; Negro Africa: Jeffreys, *op. cit.*; Haekel, *op. cit.*

4. Dominik Josef Woelfel, "Die Hauptprobleme Weissafrikas," *Archiv für Anthropologie*, Braunschweig, 1942, p. 118; Jeffreys, *op. cit.*, pp. 159–62; Haekel, *op. cit.*, p. 18.

5. Bräunlich, E., "Beiträge zur Gesellschaftsordnung der Arabischen Beduinenstämme," *Islamica*, Vol. 6, p. 185.

6. *Handbook of Arabia* (Naval Intelligence Division), Oxford–London, 1920, I : 43.

7. One is tempted to compare with this popular tendency the Biblical account of the ten generations from Adam to Noah, and the ten generations from Noah to Abraham, telescoping the entire history of the world from Genesis to the first ancestor of the Hebrews into a mere 20 generations.

8. Bräunlich, *op. cit.*, pp. 77–78.

9. *Ibid.*, p. 69.

10. Cf. Procopius, *History of the Wars*, I, xix. Loeb Classical Library, London, 1944, I : 181.

11. Wm. Robertson Smith, *Kinship and Marriage in Early Arabia*, Cambridge, 1885, pp. 7, 247.

12. *Ibid.*, p. 7.

13. E.g., Ḥaṣarmaweth, Hadhramaut; Sheba, Saba; Yeraḥ, Mahra, etc. Cf. Gunkel, *Genesis*, 4th ed., Göttingen, 1917, pp. 91–92.

14. Cf. *Encyclopaedia of Islam* (old edition), s.v. Ḳaḥṭān.

15. Cf. Wüstenfeld, *Genealogische Tabellen*, Göttingen, 1852, table A.

16. Cf. *Encyclopaedia of Islam* (old ed.), s.v. Ḳais-'Ailān; (new ed.), s.v. al-'Arab, Djazīrat, p. 544; Wüstenfeld, *Gen. Tab.*, D.

17. Cf. R. Dozy, *Spanish Islam*, London, 1913, p. 65; Philip K. Hitti, *History of the Arabs*, London, 1937, p. 32. It is remarkable that this important and patent fact escaped the authors of the otherwise thorough *Handbook of Arabia*; on p. 44 (Vol. I) both the Qaḥṭān and the Ishmaelite tribes are stated to be the descendants of Abraham. Prof. Majid Khadduri repeats the same statement in his *Area Handbook on Iraq*, xerographed preliminary edition, New Haven: Human Relations Area Files, 1956, p. 122.

18. *Encyclopaedia of Islam* (old ed.), s.v. Ḳaḥṭān: cf. also new ed. s.v. al-'Arab, Djazīrat, p. 545.

19. Cf. Philip K. Hitti, *Origins of the Druze People and Religion*, New York, 1928, p. 21.

20. Cf. Julius Wellhausen, *Das arabische Reich*, Berlin, 1902, pp. 44 f. I. Goldziher, *Muhammedanische Studien*, Halle, 1890, I : 94 ff.

21. Wellhausen, *op. cit.*, pp. 44 f.; *Encyclopaedia of Islam* (old ed.), s.v. Kais-'Ailān; Dozy, *Spanish Islam*, *op. cit.*, p. 68; Hitti, *History of the Arabs*, p. 280.

22. Charles M. Doughty, *Travels in Arabia Deserta*, New York, 1937, I : 282; cf. p. 418.

23. Hitti, *History of the Arabs*, *op. cit.*, p. 281.

24. *Encyclopaedia of Islam*, *loc. cit.*

25. Dozy, *Spanish Islam*, *op. cit.*, p. 126.

26. *Ibid.*, p. 66, quoting Abu al-Fidā' II : 64 and Ibn 'Idhāri's *Bayān*, II : 84; 265.

27. Hitti, *History of the Arabs*, *op. cit.*, p. 281.

28. S. B. Miles, *The Countries and Tribes of the Persian Gulf*, London, 1919, II : 419. The above account of Omani dual organization is based on data contained in this book. Cf. *Encyclopaedia of Islam* (new ed.), s.v. al-'Arab, Djazīrat, p. 545.

29. British Admiralty, *Handbook of Arabia*, London, 1916–17, p. 273.

30. *Handbook of Arabia*, *op. cit.*, pp. 240–41, 334–35; Bertram Thomas, *Arabia Felix*, New York, 1932, pp. 111–12, 273.

31. Thomas, *op. cit.*, p. 273.

32. *Ibid.*, p. 26.

33. Wüstenfeld, *Gen. Tab.* 1.

34. Thomas, *Arabia Felix*, *op. cit.*, p. 26; Harold Ingrams, *Arabia and the Isles*, London, 1942, pp. 179, 223, 312; *Handbook of Arabia*, *op. cit.*, I, 213.

35. S. B. Miles and M. W. Muenzinger, "Account of an Excursion into the Interior of Southern Arabia," *Journal of the Royal Geographical Society*, London, 1871, Vol. 41, pp. 234–36.

36. Landberg, *Arabica*, Leyden, 1897, IV : 12–16.

37. Landberg, *Arabica*, Leyden, 1898, V : 3, 5, 12; *Encyclopaedia of Islam* (new ed.), s.v. Bayḥān al-Ḳaṣāb.

38. Miles and Muenzinger, *op. cit.*, p. 234; Landberg, *Arabica*, Leyden, 1897, IV : 52; *Handbook of Arabia*, *op. cit.*, I : 214. But according to G. Wyman Bury (Abdullah Mansur), *The Land of Uz*, London, 1911, p. 164, "the Ba-Kazim with its numerous sub-divisions composes the entire tribal population of Lower Aulaki."

39. Bury, *Land of Uz*, *op. cit.*, p. 216.

40. Miles and Muenzinger, *op. cit.*, pp. 229, 234; Landberg, *Arabica*, V, Leyden, 1898, p. 230.

41. Sir Bernard Reilly, "The Aden Protectorate," *Journal of the Royal Central Asian Society*, London, April, 1941, p. 139; *Handbook of Arabia*, I, 229, 232.

42. Thus according to an early authority, S. B. Heines, "Memoir of the South and East Coasts of Arabia," *Journal of the Royal Geographical Society*, London, 1841, Vol. 15, p. 112; cf. Thomas, *Arabia Felix*, *op. cit.*, pp. 47–48, 142–43. Wüstenfeld, *Register*, 1853, 280.

43. Wüstenfeld, *Register*, p. 280. Although none of the three names appearing in the popular tribal genealogy of the Mahra is found in Wüstenfeld's list, the claim to be a Noahide tribe makes this genealogy more plausible than the alternative of 'Adnānī descent.

44. Ingrams, *op. cit.*, p. 223.

45. Wüstenfeld, *Gen. Tab.* 1 and 9, *op. cit.*

46. Thomas, *Arabia Felix*, *op. cit.*, p. 269, note.

47. Leo Hirsch, *Reisen in Südarabien, Mahra-Land und Hadramaut*, Leiden, 1897, p. 11.

48. *Handbook of Arabia*, *op. cit.*, I, p. 229; H. St. John Philby, *Sheba's Daughters*, London, 1939, p. 154.

49. Thomas, *Arabia Felix*, *op. cit.*, p. 36; Sir Bernard Reilly, *op. cit.*, p. 139.

50. Ingrams, *op cit.*, p. 204.

51. Miles II, *op. cit.*, p. 515; Ingrams, *op. cit.*, pp. 189–90; Philby, *Sheba's Daughters*, *op. cit.*, p. 167.

52. Miles II, *op. cit.*, p. 515; Thomas, *Arabia Felix*, *op. cit.*, pp. 4, 13, 112, 181, 269.

53. *Encyclopaedia of Islam* (new ed.), s.v. 'Awāmir.

54. Thomas, *Arabia Felix*, *op. cit.*, pp. 112, 142–43, 269, 273.

55. Philby, *Sheba's Daughters*, *op. cit.*, pp. 35, 60, 65, 66; Ingrams, *op. cit.*, pp. 288, 319, 320–22.

56. Philby, *op. cit.*, p. 218.

57. *Encyclopaedia of Islam* (old ed.), s.v. Hashid and Bakil; cf. Amin Rihani, *Arabian Peak and Desert*, Boston and New York, 1930, p. 235; Carl Niebuhr, *Beschreibung von Arabien*, Copenhagen, 1772, p. 260.

58. *Encyclopaedia of Islam*, *loc. cit.*

59. *Handbook of Arabia*, *op. cit.*, pp. 479 ff.

60. H. St. John Philby, *Arabian Highlands*, Ithaca: Cornell University Press, 1952, p. 161.

61. *Handbook of Arabia*, *op. cit.*, pp. 430, 441.

62. Wüstenfeld, *Genealogische Tabellen*, 4; *idem.*, *Register*, p. 132; Philby, *Arabian Highlands*, *op. cit.*, pp. 405, 494, 502, 503, 537–38, 561.

63. Philby, *Arabian Highlands*, *op. cit.*, pp. 36, 111, 116, 119, 121, 123, 124, 129, 130, 133, 139, 144, 177, 449, 454, 456, 458.

64. Wüstenfeld, *Gen. Tab.*, 4; Philby, *Arabian Highlands*, *op. cit.*, p. 225.

65. Philby, *Arabian Highlands*, *op. cit.*, pp. 225, 384, 388, 405.

66. *Ibid.*, pp. 150, 217, 225, 242, 245.

67. Oppenheim, *Die Beduinen*, Leipzig, 1952, Vol. III, pp. 142–43.

68. H. R. P. Dickson, *The Arab of the Desert*, London, 1949, pp. 264, 284, 363.

69. Philby, *Arabian Highlands*, *op. cit.*, p. 245.

70. Oppenheim, *op. cit.*, III : 149–50.

71. Harry W. Hazard, *Saudi Arabia*, Subcontractor's Monograph (xerographed), Human Relations Area Files, Inc., New Haven, Conn., 1956, pp. 58, 60, 61, 64.

72, H. St. John Philby, *Sheba's Daughters*, *op. cit.*, p. 19; *idem.*, *Arabian Highlands*, *op. cit.*, p. 405.

73. Cf. for example Bertram Thomas, *Arabia Felix*, 208 ff.; Philby, *Sheba's Daughters*, *op. cit.*, pp. 19, 26–27, 333.

74. Cf. *Encyclopaedia of Islam* (old ed.), s.v. Hilal.

75. Cf. *Handbook of Arabia*, *op. cit.*, p. 44.

76. Wüstenfeld, *Genealogische Tabellen*, F; and *Encyclopaedia of Islam*, s.v. Hilal.

77. Cf. H. St. John Philby, *The Heart of Arabia*, New York–London, 1923, II : 23, 217; *idem.*, *The Empty Quarter*, New York, 1933, Index, s.v. Murra; Thomas, *Arabia Felix*, *op. cit.*

78. Fu'ad Hamza, *Qalb Jezīret al-'Arab*, Cairo, 1352/1933, pp. 195 f., as quoted by Oppenheim, *Die Beduinen*, III : 159.

79. Oppenheim, *Die Beduinen*, *op. cit.*, III : 160–61.

80. *Ibid.*, III : 159.

81. Philby, *The Empty Quarter*, *op. cit.*, pp. 409 ff. (Table). A somewhat different account of the Murra divisions is given by H. R. P. Dickson, *Kuwait and Her Neighbours*, London, 1956, p. 96.

82. Cf. Oppenheim, *Die Beduinen*, *op. cit.*, III : 106; *Encyclopaedia of Islam* (old ed.), s.v. Kahtan.

83. Doughty, *Arabia Deserta*, *op. cit.*, I : 418; Philby, *Arabian Highlands*, *op. cit.*, 109.

84. Oppenheim, *Die Beduinen*, *op. cit.*, III : 112–15.

85. Philby, *Arabian Highlands*, *op. cit.*, pp. 18, 30, 34, 110, 128, 136, 144, 161, 181, 193, 196, 352, 366, 374, 442, 444, 445.

86. An older enumeration of the Qaḥṭān tribes of 'Asīr (Rufaydat el-Yemen, Benī Bishr, Senhān el-Hibab, 'Abidah, Wada'ah and Shereyf, six separate tribes), found in the *Handbook of Arabia*, I : 430, is also unsatisfactory.

87. Philby, *The Heart of Arabia*, *op. cit.*, II : 228–29. The inconsistencies between the structure of the Yām as appearing above and the one appearing in the 'Asīr district can be explained by the different tribal traditions prevalent in 'Asīr on the one hand and in inner Southern Arabia on the other.

88. Burckhardt, *Notes on the Bedouins*, London, 1831, I : 1, 10, 27; II : 6.

89. *Encyclopaedia of Islam* (old ed.), s.v. Harb.

90. Philby, *Arabia of the Wahhabis*, pp. 393–94; Oppenheim, *Die Beduinen*, *op. cit.*, III : 65–66, 362 f., 379.

91. Oppenheim, *op. cit.*, II : 362 ff., 379.

92. Harry W. Hazard, *op. cit.*, pp. 61–62, 64, 67.

93. Cf. Dozy, *Spanish Islam*, *op. cit.*, p. 68.

94. Cf. Robert Montagne, *Le Civilisation du Désert*, Paris, 1947, p. 51.

95. *Encyclopaedia of Islam* (new ed.), 1957, s.v. 'Anaza.

96. Cf. Oppenheim, *Die Beduinen*, *op. cit.*, I : 113, 114–23.

97. Cf. R. Patai (ed.), *The Republic of Syria*, HRAF Subcontractor's Monograph, New Haven, 1956, I : 160 ff., 170 ff., 181 ff.

98. Oppenheim, *Die Beduinen*, *op. cit.*, I : 159–63; Henry Field, *The Anthropology of Iraq* (Papers of the Peabody Museum of American Archaeology and Ethnology), Harvard University, Vol. 46, No. 1, Cambridge, Mass., 1951, pp. 19–21; Vol. 46, No. 2, 1952, pp. 89 f.

99. Oppenheim, *op. cit.*, I : 169, 176–77

100. Alois Musil, *Palmyrena*, New York, 1928, p. 151.

101. Oppenheim, *op. cit.*, I : 245 ff., 264–65, 335–36; II : 203 ff., 244 ff.; Frederick G. Peake, *History and Tribes of Jordan*, University of Miami Press, 1958, pp. 143–221; R. Patai (ed.), *Jordan*, Country Survey Series, Human Relations Area Files, New Haven, 1957, pp. 181–88.

102. Harry W. Hazard, *op. cit.*, p. 67.

103. H. R. P. Dickson, *Kuwait and Her Neighbours*, *op. cit.*, pp. 97–101.

104. Oppenheim, *op. cit.*, I : 196 ff., 211 ff.

105. Cf. Macalister and Masterman, *Palestine Exploration Fund Quarterly Statement*, 1905, p. 343; 1906, pp. 33–34.

106. Michael Assaf, *History of the Arabs in Palestine* (in Hebrew), Tel Aviv, 1941, II : 279.

107. Hitti, *History of the Arabs*, *op. cit.*, p. 281.

108. A. N. Haddad, *Journal of the Palestine Oriental Society*, I : 210–13; E. Robinson, *Biblical Researches in Palestine*, London 1841–1856, III : 283.

109. C. F. Volney, *Travels Through Syria and Egypt in the Years 1783, 1784, and 1785*, London, 1788, II : 325; Robinson, *op. cit.*, II : 17.

110. Cf. Robinson, *op. cit.*, II : 344.

111. Cf. Assaf, *op. cit.*, II : 279.

112. *Ibid.*, II : 278.

113. Volney, II : 177, as quoted by Gibb and Bowen, *Islamic Society and the West*, Oxford, 1950, I : 268, English translation, II : 302.

114. Volney, II : 203; English translation I : 325–26, 333–34; Gibb and Bowen, *op. cit.*, I : 268.

115. Cf. Elihu Grant, *The Peasantry of Palestine*, New York, 1907, pp. 159, 225.

116. Cf. Ya'qov Shim'oni, *'Arvē Ereṣ Yisrael*, Tel Aviv, 1947, p. 175; Omar el-Barghuthi, *Judicial Courts among the Bedouins of Palestine*, reprint from the *Journal of the Palestine Oriental Society*, Jerusalem, 1922, p. 9.

117. Mariam Zarour, 'Ramallah: My Home Town," *The Middle East Journal*, Autumn 1953, Vol. 7, No. 4, pp. 431–32.

118. Gibb and Bowen, *op. cit.*, I : 222.

119. Cf. Hitti, *The Origins of the Druze People and Religion*, *op. cit.*, p. 8; cf. also Niebuhr, *Reisebeschreibung nach Arabien und andern umliegenden Ländern*, Kopenhagen, 1778, II : 447.

120. Cf. Niebuhr, *loc. cit.*

121. Cf. R. Montagne, *La Civilisation du Désert*, *op. cit.*, p. 62.

122. Cf. Shim'oni, *op. cit.*, pp. 172–73; Granqvist, *Marriage Conditions in a Palestinian Village*, Helsingfors, 1935.

123. Mahmud, Bavār, *Kūh-Gīlūyē wa Ilāte ān* (Kūh-Gīlūyē and Its Tribes), Gachsārān, 1324 (1945), 158 pp.

124. *Ibid.*, 86 ff., 116 f., 130 ff.

125. C. S. Coon, *Caravan*, New York, 1951, pp. 217–18; Herbert H. Vreeland (ed.), *Iran.* Country Survey Series, Human Relations Area Files. New Haven, 1957, p. 42; *Encyclopaedia of Islam* (new ed.), s.v. Bakhtiyārī.

126. Cf. Henry Field, *The Anthropology of Iran*, p. 123, quoting Sykes.

127. *Encyclopaedia of Islam* (new ed.), s.v. Afghān, Afghānistān, and Abdālī; Donald N. Wilber, *Afghanistan*, Human Relations Area Files Subcontractors Monograph, New Haven, 1956, I : 73, 81–85; S. G. W. Benjamin, *Persia and the Persians*, London, 1887, pp. 142–43.

128. *Encyclopaedia of Islam* (new ed.), s.v. Balūčistān.

129. Cheikh Abd-el-Rahman el-Djabarti, *Merveilles Biographiques et Historiques ou Chroniques du* . . . Traduites de l'Arabe. . . . Le Caire, 1888, Tome I, pp. 50–54, 209; II : 157.

130. Gibb and Bowen, *op. cit.*, pp. 268–69, citing Girard, Chabrol, and Volney.

131. M. de Chabrol, *Essai sur les moeurs des habitants modernes de l'Egypte, Description de l'Egypte*, Paris, 1822, Tome Seconde, IIe partie, p. 372–73.

132. M. P. S. Girard, *Mémoire sur l'Agriculture, l'Industrie et le Commerce de l'Egypte, Description de l'Egypte*, Paris, 1823, Tome Seconde, p. 514.

133. Lane, *Modern Egyptians*, *op. cit.*, p. 202.

134. Oppenheim, *Die Beduinen*, *op. cit.*, I : 295.

135. G. W. Murray, *Sons of Ishmael: A Study of the Egyptian Bedouin*, London, 1935, pp. 253, 264–65.

136. Ibn Battuta, *Travels in Asia and Africa*, ed. Gibb, London, 1929, pp. 53–54.

137. *Encyclopaedia of Islam* (new ed.), s.v. Bedja.

138. Winifred Blackman, *The Fellahin of Upper Egypt*, London, 1927, pp. 129–31.

139. Cf. C. G. and Brenda Seligman, *The Kababish: A Sudan Arab Tribe*, Harvard African Studies, 1918, II : 113.

140. Hamed Ammar, *Growing Up in an Egyptian Village*, London, 1954, pp. vii, 44, 45, 47, 61.

141. *Encyclopaedia of Islam* (new ed.), s.v. Bishārīn.

142. Cf. G. Marçais, *Les Arabes en Berberie du xie au xive siecle*, Constantine & Paris, 1913, p. 59; E. E. Evans-Pritchard, *The Sanusi of Cyrenaica*, London, 1949, pp. 48, 49, 56.

143. Ibn Khaldun, *Histoire de Berberes*, Paris, 1934, Vol. iii, p. 181.

144. Ibn Khaldun, *op. cit.*, I : 168–69; III : 181.

145. Cf. Leo Africanus, *Description d'Afrique*, Paris, 1896–1898, I : 327; English edition: *History and Description of Africa*, London, 1896, 3 vols.

146. Cf. Henri Lhote, *Les Touaregs du Hoggar*, Paris, 1944, p. 115, referring to a note sent by a Marabout of the Tuareg tribe Kel es-Suq in 1907 to Captain Cortier and reprinted in the latter's volume *D'une rive a l'autre du Sahara*, p. 394.

147. Ibn Khaldun, *op. cit.*, I : 169, 170, 172; II : 11 ff.; III : 180, 181, 190, 300.

148. C. S. Coon, *Tribes of the Rif*, Harvard African Studies, Cambridge, Mass, Vol. ix, p. 17.

149. Cf. Eugène Guernier, *La Berberie, l'Islam et la France*, Paris, 1950, I : 338; Marçais, *op. cit.*, pp. 643–44, 709; Bryan Clarke, *Berber Village*, London, 1959, p. 96. The term *ṣoff*, in the form *ṣuff*, was met above as designating the factional alliances in Oman. The same term, pronounced *ṣaff*, is used by the Terābīn Bedouins of the Negev (today in Israel), for warlike alliances. Cf. Aaref el-Aaref, *The History of Beersheba and Her Tribes* (Hebrew translation), Tel Aviv, 1937, p. 65.

150. Robert Montagne, *Les Berberes et le Makhzen dans le sud au Maroc*, Paris, 1930, p. 197.

151. Coon, *Tribes of the Rif*, *op. cit.*, pp. 18, 169, 172–73.

152. Josef Haekel, "Die Dualsysteme in Afrika," *Anthropos*, 1950, p. 18, quoting Montagne, *Les Berberes*.

153. Coon, *Tribes of the Rif*, *op. cit.*, p. 19.

154. Montagne, *Les Berberes*, p. 197, 212; *idem.*, *La Civilisation du Desert*, 261.

155. Jean Despois, *L'Afrique du Nord*, Paris, 1949, p. 145; Haekel, *op. cit.*, p. 18.

156. Cf. Despois, *op. cit.*, p. 145; Haekel, *op. cit.*, p. 18; Montagne, *Les Berberes*, *op. cit.*, p. 197; Clarke, *loc. cit.*

157. Montagne, *Les Berberes*, p. 212; *idem.*, *La Civilisation du Desert*, p. 261.

158. R. Turnbull, *Sahara Unveiled*, London, 1940, p. 25, as quoted by Jeffreys, *African Studies*, Vol. 5 (1946), p. 159.

159. Dr. H. Barth, *Travels and Discoveries in North and Central Africa*, London, 1867, I : 99, 100, 148; as quoted by Jeffreys, *op. cit.*, p. 162.

160. Walter Cline, *Notes on the People of Siwah and El Garah in the Libyan Desert*, General Series in Anthropology, Menasha, Wis., 1936, No. 4, pp. 12, 46.

160a. Lloyd Cabot Briggs, *Tribes of the Sahara*. Cambridge: Harvard University Press, 1960, pp. 78–80.

161. E. E. Evans-Pritchard, *The Sanusi of Cyrenaica*, *op. cit.*, p. 58.

162. Edward Westermarck, *Ritual and Belief in Morocco*, London, 1926, I : 178.

162a. Lloyd Cabot Briggs, *Tribes of the Sahara*, *op. cit.*, pp. 195–96.

163. Doutté, *Magie et religion dans l'Afrique du Nord*, Alger, 1909, p. 509.

164. Westermarck, *op. cit.*, II : 72. On other ceremonial fights between children in Morocco, cf. *op. cit.*, I : 601; II : 65; between men and women, II : 72.

165. *Ibid.*, II : 73, 115, 131–33, 171, 188, 197–98, 272.

166. Ibn Khaldun, *op. cit.*, I : 273.

167. Francis R. Rodd, *The People of the Veil*, London, 1926, pp. 349–53; Lhote, *op. cit.*, p. 127.

168. Henri Duveyrier, *Les Touareg du Nord*, Paris, 1864, p. 329.

169. Lhote, *op. cit.*, p. 156.

170. Cf. H. Barth, *Travels in Central Africa*, London, 1859, IV : 552 f.

171. Rodd, *op. cit.*, p. 387.

172. Cf. Henri Lhote, *Les Touaregs du Hoggar* (*Ahaggar*), 2d ed., Paris, 1955, pp. 216–18, 239, 248.

173. Hocart, *The Progress of Man*, London, 1933, p. 241.

174. G. P. Murdock, *Social Structure*, New York, 1949, p. 80.

175. Perry, in Appendix III to Rivers, *Social Organization*, London, 1932, pp. 208 ff., maintains that the superiority of one moiety over the other was one of the original traits of ancient Egyptian dual organization which became diffused from there as an integral part of the "Archaic civilization."

CHAPTER 8—

1. Cf. H. R. P. Dickson, *The Arab of the Desert*, London, 1949, p. 515; Charles M. Doughty, *Travels in Arabia Deserta*, New York, 1937, I : 324 ff.; John B. Glubb, *The Sulubba and Other Ignoble Tribes of Southwestern Asia*, General Series in Anthropology (ed. Leslie Spier), Menasha, Wis., 1943, No. 9, p. 14.
2. Cf. Dickson, *op. cit.*, p. 516.
3. H. R. P. Dickson, *Kuwait and Her Neighbours*, London, 1956, p. 102.
4. John Lewis Burckhardt, *Notes on the Bedouins and Wahabys*, London, 1831, II : 19–20.
5. Alois Musil, *Manners and Customs of the Rwala Bedouins*, New York, 1928, p. 136.
6. Glubb, *op. cit.*, pp. 15–16.
7. Cf. G. W. Murray, *Sons of Ishmael*, London, 1935, pp. 269, 285.
8. Burckhardt, *op. cit.*, II : 15.
9. Cf. Carleton S. Coon, *Caravan, The Story of the Middle East*, New York, 1951, p. 200.
10. Bertram Thomas, *Arabia Felix*, New York, 1932, pp. 46 f.; Richard F. Burton, *The Land of Midian* (*Revisited*), London, 1879, I : 161.
11. Cf. E. E. Evans-Pritchard, *The Senusi of Cyrenaica*, Oxford, 1949, p. 51; G. W. Murray, *Sons of Ishmael*, *op. cit.*, pp. 273 ff.
12. Cf. Henri Lhote, *Les Touaregs du Hoggar*, Paris, 1944, p. 150; *Encyclopaedia of Islam* (new ed.), s.v. Ahaggar.
13. Cf. Max Freiherr von Oppenheim, *Die Beduinen*, Leipzig, 1939, I : 23.
14. Cf. Musil, *op. cit.*, p. 60.
15. *Ibid.*, p. 136.
16. Glubb, *op. cit.*, p. 16.
17. Burton, *op. cit.*, I : 170–71.
18. Musil, *op. cit.*, p. 137.
19. Murray, *op. cit.*, p. 245.
20. Doughty, *op. cit.*, I : 325.
21. W. B. Seabrook, *Adventures in Arabia*, New York, 1927, p. 53.
22. Glubb, *op. cit.*, p. 14.
23. Seabrook, *op. cit.*, p. 53.
24. Musil, *op. cit.*, p. 453.
25. Doughty, *op. cit.*, I : 324; also Musil, *op. cit.*, pp. 452–53.
26. Cf. Seabrook, *op. cit.*, p. 52.
27. Murray, *op. cit.*, p. 268.
28. Doughty, *op. cit.*, I : 325.
29. Glubb, *op. cit.*, p. 15.
30. Murray, *op. cit.*, p. 269.
31. Glubb, *op. cit.*, p. 15.
32. Murray, *op. cit.*, p. 268.
33. Dickson, *The Arab of the Desert*, *op. cit.*, p. 515.
34. Glubb, *op. cit.*, p. 14.

35. Burton, *op. cit.*, II : 118.
36. Dickson, *op. cit.*, pp. 571–72.
37. Glubb, *op. cit.*, p. 15.
38. Dickson, *op. cit.*, pp. 516–17.
39. Musil, *op. cit.*, pp. 136–37; Glubb, *op. cit.*, p. 16.
40. Cf. Ernest Main, *Iraq From Mandate to Independence*, London, 1935, pp. 253 ff.; John Van Ess, *Meet the Arab*, New York, 1943, pp. 69–70.
41. Cf. Musil, *op. cit.*, p. 282; Coon, *op. cit.*, p. 201.
42. Dickson, *op. cit.*, p. 516; Glubb, *op. cit.*, p. 14.
43. Burton, *Personal Narrative of a Pilgrimage to al-Madinah and Meccah*, London, 1893, II : 121.
44. Glubb, *op. cit.*, pp. 15, 16.
45. Pierre Ponafidine, *Life in the Moslem East*, New York, 1911, p. 133; Dickson, *op. cit.*, p. 517; Musil, *op. cit.*, pp. 118, 134, 325, 406–7; Coon, *op. cit.*, p. 200; Glubb, *op. cit.*, p. 15.
46. Glubb, *op. cit.*, pp. 15–16; Musil, *loc. cit.*
47. Musil, *op. cit.*, pp. 281–82; Coon, *op. cit.*, p. 200.
48. Bertram Thomas, *Alarms and Excursions in Arabia*, London, 1931, p. 152; *idem.*, *Arabia Felix*, p. 47.
49. Musil, *op. cit.*, pp. 278—81; Coon, *op. cit.*, p. 203; Murray, *op. cit.*, p. 285.
50. Murray, *op. cit.*, pp. 265–66.
51. Dickson, *op. cit.*, p. 518.
52. Burton, *op. cit.*, II : 121.
53. Cf. Dickson, *op. cit.*, pp. 516–17; Coon, *op. cit.*, p. 200; Jarvis, *Desert and Delta*, London, 1938, pp. 154–55; Seabrook, *op. cit.*, pp. 52–53; Ponafidine, *op. cit.*, p. 132; Gerald de Gaury, *Arabian Journey*, London, 1950, p. 140.
54. Jarvis, *op. cit.*, p. 153, Seabrook, *op. cit.*, p. 53.
55. Glubb, *op. cit.*, p. 14.
56. Coon, *op. cit.*, p. 200.
57. Cf. for example Murray, *op. cit.*, pp. 268–69: " . . . these Hiteim represent ancient broken clans, who have lost their independence. . . . Some may contain non-Arab elements, but these must be rare." Glubb, *op. cit.*, p. 16, says, " . . . they are known to be of base descent."
58. Coon, *op. cit.*, p. 200.
59. Musil, *op. cit.*, pp. 136–37, 282.
60. Glubb, *op. cit.*, pp. 15–16; Gerald de Gaury, *Arabia Phoenix*, London, 1946, p. 143.
61. Cf. Murray, *op. cit.*, p. 265; Jarvis, *op. cit.*, p. 119.
62. Thomas, *Arabia Felix*, *op. cit.*, pp. 46–47.
63. Fulanain, *The Marsh Arab*, Philadelphia, 1928, p. 254.
64. Dickson, *op. cit.*, pp. 550–51.
65. Cf. E. E. Evans-Pritchard, *op. cit.*, pp. 48 f.; Murray, *op. cit.*, pp. 272 ff.
66. Henri Lhote, *Les Touaregs du Hoggar* (*Ahaggar*), 2nd ed., Paris, 1955, pp. 145, 166, 188, 213–14, 239, 247.
67. Lloyd Cabot Briggs, *Tribes of the Sahara*, Cambridge: Harvard University Press, 1960, pp. 126–27, 136–38.
68. *Ibid.*, pp. 168–71.
69. *Ibid.*, pp. 194–95.
70. *Ibid.*, pp. 216–17, 219.

CHAPTER 9—

1. Raphael Patai, *The Kingdom of Jordan*, Princeton, N.J. 1958, pp. 186–98.

2. George A. Lipsky (ed.), *Saudi Arabia: Its People, Its Society, Its Culture*, New Haven, 1959, p. 64.

3. *Ibid.*, pp. 78–80.

4. *Ibid.*, pp. 212–13, 267.

5. Donald N. Wilber, *Afghanistan*, Subcontractor's Monograph, Human Relations Area Files, New Haven, 1956, Vol. I, p. 284; *idem*, *Iran Past and Present*, Princeton, N.J., 1958, p. 169.

6. Lipsky, *op. cit.*, p. 81.

7. *The Middle East: A Political and Economic Survey*, London and New York (Royal Inst. of Intern. Affairs), 3rd ed., 1958, p. 219; Doreen Warriner, *Land Reform and Development in the Middle East*, Oxford, 1962, p. 24.

8. Henry Ayrout, S. J., *The Egyptian Peasant*, Boston, 1963, p. 88.

9. Patai, *op. cit.*, pp. 122, 201.

10. Lipsky, *op. cit.*, p. 82.

11. *Ibid.*, p. 82.

12. Harold B. Barclay, *Buurri Al Lamaab; A Suburban Village in the Sudan*, Ithaca, N.Y., 1964, p. 4.

13. Jacques Weulersse, *Paysans de Syrie et du Proche-Orient*, Paris, 1946, pp. 234–35.

14. Wilber, *Iran Past and Present*, *op. cit.*, p. 170.

15. Wilber, *Afghanistan*, *op. cit.*, I, 286.

16. Hamed Ammar, *Growing Up in an Egyptian Village*, London, 1954, p. 45.

17. Manfred Halpern, *The Politics of Social Change in the Middle East*, Princeton, N.J., 1963, p. 81.

18. Wilber, *Iran*, *op. cit.*, pp. 241–42.

19. Gabriel Baer, *Population and Society in the Arab East*, London, 1964, p. 148; Weulersse, *op. cit.*, p. 124.

20. *Area Handbook for Pakistan.* DA Pam (Dept. of the Army Pamphlets) no. 550–48, Washington, D.C., 1965, pp. 382–83.

21. Nuri Eren, *Turkey Today and Tomorrow*, New York, 1963, p. 111.

22. U.N. sources, quoted in Baer, *op. cit.*, pp. 20–21.

23. Mirrit B. Ghali, *Siyasat al-ghad*, Cairo, 1944, pp. 58–62, as quoted by Baer, *op. cit.*, p. 21; Charles Issawi, *Egypt in Mid-Century*, London, 1954, p. 86.

24. George L. Harris (ed.), *Iraq: Its People, Its Society, Its Culture*, New Haven, Conn., 1958, p. 259.

25. *Ibid.*, p. 260.

26. Raphael Patai (ed.), *The Republic of Syria*, Subcontractor's Monograph, Human Relations Area Files, New Haven, 1956, Vol. II, p. 573.

27. Wilber, *Iran Past and Present*, *op. cit.*, p. 172.

28. Patai, *The Republic of Syria*, *op. cit.*, Vol. II, pp. 569–70.

29. A. K. S. Lambton, *Landlord and Peasant in Persia*, London, 1953, pp. 394–95.

30. A. Michael Critchley, "The Health of the Industrial Worker in Iraq," *British Journal of Industrial Medicine*, Vol. 12, 1955, as quoted by Halpern, *op. cit.*, p. 85.

31. Harris, *Iraq*, *op. cit.*, pp. 211, 260, 262.

32. Patai, *Syria*, *op. cit.*, Vol. II, pp. 577–85.

33. Doreen Warriner, *Land and Poverty in the Middle East*, London, 1948,

pp. 41–42, citing the investigations of Dr. Mohammed Abd el-Khalik; *The New York Times*, May 5, 1952, as quoted by *Halpern*, *op. cit.* p. 85.

34. Horace M. Miner and George de Vos, *Oasis and Casbah: Algerian Culture and Personality in Change*, Ann Arbor, 1960, p. 35.

35. Cf. Baer, *op. cit.*, pp. 21–22.

36. *Genesis* 29:15ff.; Raphael Patai, *Sex and Family in the Bible and the Middle East*, New York, 1958, pp. 60–61.

37. Halpern, *op. cit.*, p. 83.

38. Paul Stirling, *Turkish Village*, London, 1965, p. 237.

39. *Area Handbook for Morocco*, DA Pam (Dept. of the Army Pamphlets) no. 550–49, Washington, D.C., 1965, p. 95.

40. *Area Handbook for Pakistan*, *op. cit.*, pp. 95–96.

41. Majid Khadduri (ed.), *Iraq*. Subcontractor's Monograph, Human Relations Area Files, 1956, pp. 96–97, 104.

42. *Ibid.*, p. 107.

43. John Gulick, *Social Structure and Culture Change in a Lebanese Village*, New York, 1955, pp. 101–02.

44. Weulersse, *op. cit.*, p. 229; Gulick, *op. cit.*, pp. 100–01.

45. Stirling, *op. cit.*, pp. 182–83 and plates 11 and 12.

46. Wilber, *Afghanistan*, *op. cit.*, Vol. I, p. 268.

47. Stirling, *op. cit.*, pp. 238–46.

48. Carleton S. Coon, *Caravan: The Story of the Middle East*, New York, 1965, p. 181.

49. Wilber, *Iran*, *op. cit.*, p. 171.

50. Gulick, *op. cit.*, pp. 70–71.

51. *Ibid.*, p. 71.

52. Miner and de Vos, *op. cit.*, pp. 37–39. I changed the French spelling of the Arabic words used by the authors.

53. Barclay, *op. cit.*, pp. 43–45.

54. Stirling, *op. cit.*, p. 254.

55. Barclay, *op. cit.*, pp. 136, 209.

56. Harris, *op. cit.*, pp. 75–76; Khadduri, *op. cit.*, p. 106.

57. Barclay, *op. cit.*, p. 177.

58. Lloyd Cabot Briggs, *Tribes of the Sahara*, Cambridge, Mass., 1960, p. 101.

59. Ammar, *op. cit.*, pp. 187ff.

60. Wilber, *Iran*, *op. cit.*, p. 172.

61. Ammar, *op. cit.*, p. 20.

62. Wilber, *Afghanistan*, *op. cit.*, Vol. I, pp. 283, 288.

63. Cf. *The New York Times*, June 4, 1960, as summarized by Morroe Berger, *The Arab World Today*, New York, 1964, pp. 58–59.

64. Berger, *op. cit.*, pp. 68–69.

65. Daniel Lerner, *The Passing of Traditional Society*, Glencoe, Ill., 1958, as summarized by Nuri Eren, *op. cit.*, p. 165.

66. Stirling, *op. cit.*, pp. 168, 232, 233.

67. *Ibid.*, p. 231.

68. *Ibid.*, p. 29.

69. Gulick, *op. cit.*, p. 135.

70. *Ibid.*, p. 139.

71. *Ibid.*, p. 155.

72. Halpern, *op. cit.*, p. 86.

CHAPTER 10—

1. Gustave E. von Grunebaum, "The Structure of the Muslim Town," *Islam: Essays in the Nature and Growth of a Cultural Tradition.* Comparative Studies of Cultures and Civilizations, No. 4. The American Anthropological Association, Memoir No. 81, April, 1955, p. 142.

2. H. A. R. Gibb, and Harold Bowen, *Islamic Society and the West*, London, Royal Institute of International Affairs, 1950, Vol. I, p. 276.

3. W. E. Lane, *Modern Egyptians*, Everyman's Library, p. 4.

4. Cf. R. Patai (ed.), *The Republic of Lebanon.* Subcontractor's Monograph, Human Relations Area Files, New Haven, 1956, Vol. I, pp. 223 ff.

5. Cf. R. Patai (ed.), *The Republic of Syria.* Subcontractor's Monograph, Human Relations Area Files, New Haven, 1956, Vol. I, p. 341.

6. Lane, *op. cit.*

7. Freya Stark, *Winter in Arabia*, London, 1945, p. 44.

CHAPTER 11—

1. The author is indebted to Professors H. H. Rowley, F. S. C. Northrop, Edward J. Jurji, David Bidney, and Dr. Everett R. Clinchy for their comments on this chapter.

2. Cf. above, pp. 13 f.

3. Cf. above, Chapter 1, pp. 33 ff.

4. John Clark Archer, "Hinduism," in E. J. Jurji (ed.), *The Great Religions of the Modern World*, Princeton, 1947, p. 49.

5. Daniel and Alice Thorner, "India and Pakistan," in Ralph Linton (ed.), *Most of the World*, New York, 1949, pp. 571, 574, 577, 646.

6. A. K. Reischauer, "Buddhism," in *The Great Religions of the Modern World*, pp. 138, 105–06.

7. Lewis Hodous, "Taoism," in *The Great Religions*, pp. 41–42.

8. Hodous, *op. cit.*, pp. 24–43.

9. Hodous, "Confucianism," *op. cit.*, pp. 6–7.

10. *Ibid.*, pp. 7–18.

11. *Ibid.*, p. 20.

12. Joachim Wach, *Sociology of Religion*, Chicago, 1944, pp. 274 ff.

13. Cf. above, p. 36.

14. Rebecca West, *Black Lamb and Grey Falcon*, New York, 1943, p. 298; as quoted by F. S. C. Northrop, *The Meeting of East and West: An Inquiry Concerning World Understanding*, New York, 1946, p. 431.

15. B. L. Atreya, "Indian Culture; Its Spiritual, Moral and Social Aspects," in *Interrelations of Cultures*, UNESCO publication, Paris, 1953, p. 144.

16. Younghill Kang, *The Grass Roof*, New York, 1931, pp. 7, 12; *idem*, *East Goes West*, New York, 1937, p. 233; as quoted by Northrop, *op. cit.*, p. 314.

17. Kurt Singer, *The Idea of Conflict*, Melbourne, 1949, pp. 50–52.

18. Northrop, *op. cit.*, p. 388; cf. also p. 496, where in the closing sentence of the book the same statement is repeated with slight variations.

19. Arnold J. Toynbee, *A Study of History*, abr. ed., Oxford, 1947, p. 487.

20. Edward W. Lane, *The Manners and Customs of the Modern Egyptians*, Everyman's Library, p. 241.

21. Northrop, *op. cit.*, p. 401.
22. Archer, *op. cit.*, p. 51.
23. E. S. Geden, "God (Hindu)," in James Hastings (ed.), *Encyclopaedia of Religion and Ethics*, Vol. 6, p. 285; Archer, *op. cit.*, p. 76.
24. Passages followed by this reference number are based on written communications from Professor F. S. C. Northrop.
25. Reischauer, *op. cit.*, p. 139.
26. M. Anesaki, "Prayer (Buddhist)," in *Encyclopaedia of Religion and Ethics*, Vol. 10, p. 166.
27. One must carefully distinguish between this Western term and the Eastern concept of "transcendence." In the Eastern sense the Tao transcends sense objects. Cf. Northrop, "The Complementary Emphases of Eastern Intuitive and Western Scientific Philosopy," in *Philosophy—East and West*, ed. Charles Moore, Princeton, 1944, p. 219.
28. Hodous, *op. cit.*, pp. 24–25.
29. *Ibid.*, p. 40.
30. Edward Sell, "God (Muslim)," in *Encyclopaedia of Religion and Ethics*, Vol. 6, p. 300.
31. W. T. Davison, "God (Biblical and Christian)," *op. cit.*, Vol. 6, pp. 265 ff.
32. F. S. C. Northrop, *The Meeting of East and West*, *op. cit.*, p. 409.
33. Atreya, *op. cit.*, p. 126.
34. Max Weber, *Gesammelte Aufsätze zur Religionssoziologie*, 2d ed., Tübingen, 1923, Vol. 2, pp. 22, 24.
35. Raymond Kennedy, "Southeast Asia and Indonesia," in *Most of the World*, pp. 675, 677.
36. Francis L. Hsu, "China," in *Most of the World*, p. 766.
37. Northrop, *op. cit.*, pp. 409–10.
38. Hodous, *op. cit.*, p. 41.
39. Douglas G. Haring, "Japan and the Japanese," *Most of the World*, p. 856.
40. Reischauer, *op. cit.*, p. 90.
41. Northrop, *op. cit.*, p. 412.
42. Krishnalal Shridharani, *My India, My America*, New York, p. 298.
43. Toynbee, *op. cit.*, pp. 299–300.
44. *Ibid.*, p. 485.
45. Northrop, *op. cit.*, p. 411.
46. Toynbee, *op. cit.*, pp. 300–301.
47. *Op. cit.*, p. 553.
48. F. S. C. Northrop, *The Taming of the Nations: A Study of the Cultural Bases of International Policy*, New York, 1952, p. 77.
49. Hodous, *op. cit.*, pp. 1–23.
50. Northrop, *The Meeting of East and West*, p. 339.
51. Oral information supplied by my student, Mr. Timothy Lin.
52. Archer, *op. cit.*, pp. 62, 75, 88.
53. Reischauer, *op. cit.*, p. 97.
54. *Ibid.*, pp. 98–100, 103, 105.
55. Hodous, *op. cit.*, pp. 27, 32, 37, 39.
56. Singer, *op. cit.*, p. 52.

CHAPTER 12—

1. Prof. John B. Whitton of Princeton University, in the *Encyclopedia Americana*, article "Nationalism and Internationalism."

2. *Ibid.*

3. Hazem Zaki Nuseibeh, *The Ideas of Arab Nationalism*, Cornell University Press, Ithaca, N.Y., 1956, p. 203.

4. Cf. Hans Kohn, *A History of Nationalism in the East*, London, Routledge, 1929, pp. 231–32.

5. Philip K. Hitti, *History of Syria*, New York, Macmillan, 1951, p. 667.

6. After the above was written, my attention was directed to a statement by Shaykh Muṣṭafā al-Sibā'ī that expresses basically the same idea. Advocating "The Establishment of Islam as the State Religion of Syria," the shaykh says in an article published in the Syrian newspaper *al-Manār* (in February, 1950): "Although it is understood that the nationalism of Europe decrees as a fundamental tenet the expulsion of religion, that step is not incumbent on us, the Arabs. Nazi Germany may have found in Christianity a religion which was foreign to it. Turanian Turkey may find in Islam a religion foreign to it. But the Arabs will never find in Islam a religion foreign to them. In fact they believe that Arab nationalism was born only when they embraced Islam. . . ." Trans. R. B. Winder, *The Muslim World*, XLIV (1954), p. 223. Quoted also by G. E. von Grunebaum, "Problems of Muslim Nationalism," in Richard N. Frye (ed.), *Islam and the West*, The Hague, 1957, p. 22.

7. Cf. R. Patai, *The Kingdom of Jordan*, Princeton University Press, 1958, pp. 136 ff.; *Idem.*, *Sex and Family in the Bible and the Middle East*, New York, Doubleday, 1959, pp. 19 ff.

8. Cf. R. Patai, *The Kingdom of Jordan*, pp. 275, 287 f.

9. Cf. above, Chapter 7, "Dual Organization."

10. R. Patai, *Sex and Family*, *op. cit.*, p. 17.

11. Cf. for example Alexander Pallis, *In the Days of the Janissaries: Old Turkish Life as Depicted in the "Travel Book" of Evliya Chelebi*, London, 1951, p. 120.

12. Cf. R. Patai (ed.), *The Republic of Syria*, I : 154 ff.

13. Cf. Reuben Levy, *The Social Structure of Islam*, Cambridge University Press, 1957, p. 66.

14. Cf. below, p. 350.

15. Cf. above, p. 307.

16. Cf. Nabih A. Faris and Mohammed T. Husayn, *The Crescent in Crisis*, Lawrence, The University of Kansas, 1955, pp. 130 ff.

17. The creed of Pan-Arab nationalism has been summarized by G. E. von Grunebaum, *op. cit.*, pp. 15–16.

CHAPTER 13—

1. Cf. Melville J. Herskovits, *Man and His Works*, New York: Alfred A. Knopf, 1948, p. 523.

2. Cf. Raphael Patai, *Israel Between East and West*, Philadelphia; Jewish Publication Society 1953, pp. 27 ff.

3. Cf. above, Chapter 10, pp. 286 ff.

4. Arnold J. Toynbee, *A Study of History* (abr. ed.), New York and London, 1947, p. 377.

5. Carleton S. Coon, "The Impact of the West on Middle Eastern Institutions." An address before the Academy of Political Science, Columbia University, New York, 1952.

6. A. L. Kroeber, *The Nature of Culture*, Chicago, 1952, pp. 152 ff.

7. Cf. p. 36.

8. Cf. pp. 364–65.

9. Cf. p. 34.

10. Bernard Lewis, "Communism and Islam," *International Affairs*, Vol. 30 (January, 1954), pp. 1–12.

11. Cf. p. 34.

12. Ali Othman and Robert Redfield, "An Arab's View of Point IV." University of Chicago Round Table, No. 749, Aug. 5, 1952.

CHAPTER 14—

1. Typical and forceful expressions of these two opposing points of view were given in a meeting of the American Academy of Political and Social Science, held in Philadelphia in the spring of 1952. Cf. N. Saifpour Fatemi, "Tensions in the Middle East," and Ray Brock, "Report from the Middle East," in the *Annals of the American Academy of Political and Social Science*, July, 1952, pp. 53–59 and 64–68. The two quotations are found on pp. 57 and 65.

2. This was the experience, for example, of Mr. Abdel-Aziz Allouni working in Syria under the auspices of the Near East Foundation in the Village Welfare Service, and of Mr. Mohammed Shalabi working in Egyptian villages under the sponsorship of the Egyptian Association for Social Studies. (Oral communication from both.) These examples could easily be multiplied.

3. Raphael Patai, *On Culture Contact and Its Working in Modern Palestine*, Memoir No. 67, American Anthropological Association, October, 1947, p. 42.

4. Oral communication from Mr. Nuri Eren, Director of the Turkish Information Office in New York, and Mr. Farid Zeineddine, Permanent Representative of Syria to the United Nations.

5. Roderic D. Matthews and Matta Akrawi, *Education in the Arab Countries of the Near East*, Washington, 1948, pp. 540–41, and *passim*.

6. In Iran, for example, 28,991 children attended *Maktabs* (Koran-schools) in 1942–43, while no less than 152,168 attended modern schools. The total number of school-age population (children aged six to fourteen) in Iran was estimated at more than 3 millions. Cf. Abdullah Faryar, "Rural Education in Iran." *The Iran Review*, Jan.–Feb., 1950, p. 22; UNESCO Publication No. 133, p. 27.

7. Eleanor Bisbee, *The New Turks*, Philadelphia, 1951, p. 154; E. W. F. Tomlin, *Life in Modern Turkey*, London and New York, 1946, p. 63.

8. The entire issue of preference for the old and the new (Western) in music has received much attention in *The Passing of Traditional Society: Modernizing the Middle East*, by Daniel Lerner, Glenco, Ill., 1958.

9. Cf. *An Arab's View on Point IV:* an NBC Radio Discussion by Ali Othman and Robert Redfield, The University of Chicago Round Table, No. 749, August 3, 1952, p. 10, where the dispositions that developed in Arab kinship culture are discussed.

10. Cf. Sania Hamady, *Temperament and Character of the Arabs*, New York, 1960, p. 229.

11. F. S. C. Northrop, *The Meeting of East and West: An Inquiry Concerning World Understanding*, New York, 1947, p. 4.

12. This is shown statistically by the much higher numbers of boys enrolled in schools in all Middle Eastern countries as compared with those of girls.

13. G. E. von Grunebaum, "Problems of Muslim Nationalism," in Richard N. Frye (ed.), *Islam and the West*, The Hague, 1957, p. 23.

14. In many places, as for instance in Africa south of the Sahara, in Central Asia, in India, and in the East Indies, Muslim missions or missionaries have been more successful than Christian.

15. Northrop, *op. cit.*, p. 411.

16. Since the Middle East and the Western world have two different sets of etiquette, the Westerner may be behaving impeccably according to his own pattern, and still be regarded as offensively impolite by Middle Eastern standards which, of course, are the only ones a Middle Easterner can apply, unless he has had sufficient experience to become acquainted with what the Westerners regard as polite manners.

17. Cf. above, p. 34; Carleton S. Coon, "The Impact of the West on Middle Eastern Social Institutions," *The Academy of Political Science*, Columbia University, New York, 1952, p. 7: " . . . religion provides the dominant tone to Muslim civilization. . . ."

18. As an example of how conservative Middle Easterners view what we called above "superficial Westernization," let us quote a passage from an editorial in the conservative Pakistani paper, *Al-Islam: An Independent Exponent of Orthodox Islam* (Karachi, Pakistan, Jan. 1, 1955, Vol. 3, No. 1, p. 1; as quoted by G. E. von Grunebaum, *op. cit.*, pp. 23–24): "Our intelligentsia, utterly ignorant of the scientific implications of the progress made by the West, sing the praises of Western culture only because it gives them opportunities of indulging in frivolous and vulgar pursuits. . . ."

These phenomena are not confined to the Middle East. Very similar processes have been observed in Indonesia where the new factor making its impact on the old traditional native cultures of the islands is Islam. Cf. Justus van der Kroef, "Patterns of Western Influence in Indonesia," *American Sociological Review*, Vol. 17, No. 4 (August, 1952), pp. 421–30.

19. Robert Redfield, *The Primitive World and Its Transformations*, Ithaca, N.Y., 1953, p. 23.

20. *Ibid.*, p. 77.

21. Arnold J. Toynbee, *A Study of History*, abr. ed., New York and London, 1947, p. 394.

22. Redfield, *op. cit.*, p. 77.

CHAPTER 15—

1. Melville J. Herskovits, *op. cit.*, pp. 289–309.

2. J. S. Slotkin, *Social Anthropology*, New York, 1950, p. 440.

3. *Op. cit.*, p. 441, quoting Hilma Granqvist, *Marriage Conditions in a Palestinian Village*, II: 51.

4. Meyer Fortes, "The Structure of Unilineal Descent Groups," *American Anthropologist*, 1953, Vol. 55, pp. 17–41.

5. E.g., pp. 35, 37, 38.

6. E.g., pp. 24, 25, 26, 27, 28, 38.

7. Allan D. Coult, "Role Allocation, Position Structuring and Ambilineal Descent," *American Anthropologist*, Vol. 66, 1964, p. 35.

8. Raymond Firth, "A Note on Descent Groups in Polynesia," *Man*, Vol. 57, 1957, pp. 4–8.

9. George P. Murdock (ed.), *Social Structure in Southeast Asia*, Viking Fund Publications in Anthropology, No. 29.

10. *Op. cit.*, p. 36.

11. Sally Falk Moore, "Descent and Symbolic Filiation," *American Anthropologist*, Vol. 66, 1964, p. 1308.

12. *Op. cit.*, p. 1316.

13. Robert F. Murphy and Leonard Kasdan, "The Structure of Parallel Cousin Marriage," *American Anthropologist*, Vol. 61, 1959, p. 17.

14. George P. Murdock, "World Ethnographic Sample" *American Anthropologist*, Vol. 59, 1957, pp. 667, 687.

15. *Op. cit.*, pp. 677–78, 680, 685, 687.

16. Horace Miner, *The Primitive City of Timbuctoo*, p. 136.

17. Lloyd Cabot Briggs, *Tribes of the Sahara*, pp. 86, 91.

18. Walter Cline, *Notes on the People of Siwah and el Garah*, p. 46.

19. Edward Westermarck, *Marriage Ceremonies in Morocco*, p. 53; William D. Schorger, in Elman R. Service (ed.), *Profiles of Primitive Culture*, New York, 1958, pp. 396, 399; cf. above, p. 168.

20. Cf. above, pp. 147, 151–53.

21. Raphael Patai, *Sex and Family in the Bible and the Middle East*, pp. 27–31; above, pp. 137–38.

22. John Gulick, *Social Structure and Culture Change in a Lebanese Village*, p. 120.

23. Cf. above, pp. 141, 154, 155.

24. Paul Stirling, private communication in 1965.

25. Alois Musil, *The Manners and Customs of the Rwala Bedouins*, p. 256.

26. H. R. P. Dickson, *The Arab of the Desert*, pp. 57, 129, 174, 234.

27. Majid Khadduri (ed.), *Area Handbook on Iraq*, pp. 123–24.

28. George L. Harris (ed.), *Iraq*, pp. 271–73.

29. Government of Palestine, "Survey of Social and Economic Conditions in Arab Villages," *op. cit.*, p. 436; Patai (ed.), *The Republic of Syria*, I, pp. 376–77; Patai (ed.), *The Republic of Lebanon*, I: 259; Patai, *The Kingdom of Jordan*, p. 137.

30. Hamed Ammar, *Growing Up in an Egyptian Village*, pp. 137–39, and 53–54, 58.

31. Harold B. Barclay, *Buurri Al Lamaab*, pp. 109, 110, 228, 231.

32. George de Vos and Horace Miner, "Algerian Culture and Personality in Change," *Sociometry*, Vol. 21, 1958, p. 265; Miner and de Vos, *Oasis and Casbah*, p. 89.

33. Briggs, *op. cit.*, p. 171.

34. Donald N. Wilber (ed.), *Afghanistan*, pp. 200–01.

35. Cf. J. N. D. Anderson, *Islamic Law in the Modern World*, London, 1959, pp. 43–44, 47, as quoted by Gabriel Baer, *Population and Society in the Arab East*, p. 62.

36. Bertram Thomas, *Arabia Felix*, pp. 98–99.

37. As quoted by Arslan Humbaraci, *Algeria: The Revolution that Failed*, New York, 1966, p. 250.

38. *Le Monde*, August 15, 1965, as quoted by Humbaraci, *loc. cit.*
39. Abner Cohen, *Arab Border-Villages in Israel*, Manchester, 1965, pp. 71–93. The case itself took place in 1958.
40. Emanuel Marx, *Bedouin of the Negev*, New York, 1967, p. 228.
41. Cf. above, pp. 141–42, Cohen, *op. cit.*, p. 111; Barclay, *op. cit.*, pp. 119–20.
42. Fredrik Barth, *Principles of Social Organization in Southern Kurdistan*, p. 68.
43. Schorger, *op. cit.*, p. 396.
44. Barclay, *op. cit.*, 21.
45. Patai, "Musha 'a Tenure" *op. cit.*, pp. 438–39.
46. Raphael Patai, "The Middle East as a Culture Area," *The Middle East Journal*, Vol. 6, 1952, p. 6.
47. Ammar, *op. cit.*, pp. 57–60.
48. Barclay, *op. cit.*, p. 85.
49. Ammar, *op. cit.*, p. 55.
50. Raphael Patai, "Relationship Patterns among the Arabs," *Middle Eastern Affairs*, Vol. 2, 1951, p. 183.
51. Barclay, *op. cit.*, p. 112.
52. Ammar, *op. cit.*, pp. 56, 258.
53. Fortes, *op. cit.*, p. 33.
54. *Ibid.*
55. *Ibid*, p. 34.
56. 'Āref el 'Āref, *Die Beduinen von Beerseba*, Aus dem Arabischen übersetzt von Leo Haefeli, Luzern, 1938, p. 47.
57. Musil, *op. cit.*, pp. 48, 489.
58. Antonin Jaussen, *Coutumes des Arabes au Pays de Moab*, pp. 158–62, 220.
59. Fortes, *op. cit.*, p. 26.
60. *Ibid*, p. 24.
61. *Ibid.*
62. Cf. above, p. 352.
63. Fortes, *op. cit.*, p. 26.
64. Cf. above, pp. 177–250.
65. Fortes, *op. cit.*, p. 28.
66. *Ibid.*, p. 35.
67. *Ibid.*, p. 37.
68. *Ibid.*, pp. 25–26, 27, 28, 29, 31, 32, 36.
69. *Ibid.*, p. 32.
70. *Ibid.*
71. Patai, "Nomadism" *op. cit.*, p. 411; Patai, *The Republic of Syria*, I:190–93.
72. Fortes, *op. cit.*, p. 27.
73. Cf. above, p. 209.

CHAPTER 16—

1. A. Kardiner, "The Concept of Basic Personality Structure as an Operational Tool in the Social Sciences," in Ralph Linton (ed.), *The Science of Man in the World Crisis*, New York, 1945, pp. 107–22; J. W. W. Whiting and I. L. Child, *Child Training and Personality*, New Haven, Conn., 1953, pp. 61 ff.

2. The most important of these studies are Hamed Ammar, *Growing Up in an Egyptian Village*, London, 1954, *passim*, and especially pp. 99–106, and Edwin Terry Prothro, *Child Rearing in the Lebanon*, Harvard Middle Eastern Monographs VIII, Cambridge, Mass., 1961. Cf. also A.A. al-Qasīmī, *Hādhī hiya 'l-aghlāl* (These Are Our Chains), Cairo, 1946, p. 162; Hilma Granqvist, *Birth and Childhood among the Arabs*, Helsingfors, 1947, pp. 107 ff., 175 ff.; S. M. Zwemer, *Childhood in the Moslem World*, New York, 1915, pp. 15–16; Sania Hamady, *Temperament and Character of the Arabs*, New York, 1960, pp. 220–21.

3. Carlo Landsberg, *Proverbs et dictons du peuple Arabe*, Leiden, 1883, p. 104, as quoted by Hamady, *op. cit.*, p. 221; Granqvist, *op. cit.*, pp. 111, 171.

4. Granqvist, *op. cit.*, p. 165.

5. Hamady, *op. cit.*, p. 220–21.

6. As E. T. Prothro put it in his study of child rearing in several ethnic groups in the Lebanon (*op. cit.*, p. 66), "in every group boys were treated more warmly than were girls . . . the boys, on the average, received more warmth than did the girls."

7. Ammar, *op. cit.*, p. 101.

8. *Ibid.* Also Prothro found in his study of Lebanese child-rearing practice that mothers encouraged aggression in male children more than in female children (*op. cit.*, pp. 96–98, 121).

9. Anne H. Fuller, *Buarij: Portrait of a Lebanese Muslim Village*, Cambridge, Mass., Harvard University Press, 1961, p. 40.

10. Ammar, *op. cit.*, p. 105.

11. *Op. cit.*, p. 121.

12. Cf. Abdullah M. Lutfiyya, *Baytin, A Jordanian Village: A Study of Social Institutions and Social Change in a Folk Society.* University Microfilms, Ann Arbor, Mich., 1962, pp. 198–201.

13. *Herodotus* ii, 36, 37, 104; Encyclopaedia of Religion and Ethnics, III: 671–75.

14. Exodus 4:24–25; Genesis 17:10–14, 24–27; 21:4; 31:13–14; Joshua 5:2ff. Leviticus 12:3, etc.

15. Josephus Flavius, *Antiquity of the Jews*, I: 12:2; cf. Genesis 27:25.

16. Josephus, *op. cit.*, 13:9:1 and 13:11:3.

17. Reuben Levy, *The Social Structure of Islam*, p. 251.

18. Cf. Ploss-Bartels-Reitzenstein, *Das Weib*, 11th ed., Berlin, 1927, Vol. 1, p. 378, and sources there. The chapter dealing with the subject, *op. cit.*, pp.377–96, contains a large amount of information on excision, infibulation, and related practices in all parts of the world.

19. Strabo, *Geography*, 16:2:34,37; 16:4:9; 17:2:5, Loeb Classical Library ed., VII:281, 285, 323, and VIII:153. The notion that the ancient Hebrews practiced excision crops up in a lengthy footnote appended by Richard F. Burton to his *A Plain and Literal Translation of the Arabian Nights' Entertainments, etc.* Benares, 1885, V:279. Burton says, "This rite is supposed by Moslems to have been invented by Sarah, who so mutilated Hagar for jealousy and was afterwards ordered by Allah to have herself circumcised." Then Burton goes on to say, without adducing any proof, that he believes that excision is still practiced by several outlying or remote Jewish tribes.

20. Cf. Adrian Reland, *De Religione Mohammedica*, Ultrajecti, 1705, pp.58–59.

21. Cf. Edward William Lane, *An Arabic-English Dictionary*, London, 1863 s.v. *bazr.*

22. Cf. Lane, *ibid.*, and Reland, *op. cit.*

23. Cf. Kitāb al-Aghāni, XIX. 59, lines 11–12.

24. Julius Wellhausen, *Reste Arabischen Heidentums*, Berlin, 1897, p. 176; William Robertson Smith, *Kinship and Marriage in Early Arabia*, p. 76 n.; both quoting Diw. Hudh. 57,2 and 147,2.

25. Wellhausen, *op. cit.*, p. 176.

26. Cf. Henri Massé, *Persian Beliefs and Customs*, p. 31. Sir Thomas Herbert, *Some Years of Travels into Divers Parts of Africa and Asia the Great*, 4th impression, London, 1677, p. 306.

27. See Reland, *op. cit.*; Carsten Niebuhr, *Description de l'Arabie*, Amsterdam, 1774, pp. 70, 71.

28. E.g., Levy, *op. cit.*, p. 252; cf. also *Encyclopedia of Religion and Ethics*, III: 667, 679.

29. Cf. e.g. Klunzinger, *Upper Egypt*, p. 195; Charles Doughty, *Travels in Arabia Deserta*, London, 1936, I: 386, 437; Edward Westermarck, *Ritual and Belief in Morocco*, II: 433.

30. Doughty, *op. cit.*, I: 170,457; Snouck Hurgronje, *Mekka*, Haag, 1889, II: 141; Westermarck, *op. cit.*, II: 431. See also below.

31. Cf. sources in Westermarck, *op. cit.*, II: 431, and below.

32. Cf. sources in the long footnote of Westermarck, *op. cit.*, II: 431–32, to which have to be added the sources quoted further on in this section.

33. *Encyclopaedia of Islam*, 1st ed., 1925., s.v. Khitān.

34. Niebuhr, *op. cit.*, p. 71.

35. Fuller, *op. cit.*, pp. 41–42.

36. *Ibid.*, p. 42.

37. Cf. Patai, *Sex and Family*, pp. 201 ff.

38. Hilma Granqvist, *Birth and Childhood among the Arabs*, Helsingfors, 1947, pp. 184–209.

39. Cf. Antonin Jaussen, *Coutumes Palestiniennes*, pp. 40–41.

40. Cf. Alois Musil, *Arabia Petraea*, III: 219,222; Antonin Jaussen, *Coutumes des Arabes au Pays de Moab*, pp. 35, 351, 363–64.

41. Cf. Hurgronje, *op. cit.*, II: 141–43.

42. Eldon Rutter, *The Holy Cities of Arabia*, London and New York, 1928, pp. 55–56; Josef Henninger, "Eine eigenartige Beschneidungsform in Südwestarabien," *Anthropos*, 1938, pp. 952–58; Henninger, "Nochmals: Eine eigenartige Beschneidungsform in Südwestarabien," *Anthropos*, 1940–41, pp. 370–76; Philby, *Arabian Highlands*, pp. 449–50.

43. Bertram Thomas, *Arabia Felix*, pp. 71–72, 224 n.

44. Bertram Thomas, *Alarms and Excursions in Arabia*, p. 163.

45. H. R. P. Dickson, *The Arab of the Desert*, pp. 175–78, 518.

46. J. W. McPherson, *The Moulids of Egypt*, Cairo, 1941, pp. 52, 191, 205, 235–36, 245.

47. *Ibid.*, pp. 67–68, 191–92, 220.

48. Ammar, *op. cit.*, pp. 116, 118, 121, 122.

49. Jacques Berque, *Histoire Sociale d'un Village Egyptien au XXe Siècle*, Paris, 1957, p. 44.

50. Edward William Lane, *The Manners and Customs of the Modern Egyptians*, *op. cit.*, p. 60, 537, 541.

51. Marie Bonaparte, "Notes on Excision," in Géza Roheim (ed.), *Psychoanalysis and the Social Sciences*, New York, 1950, II: 70,82.

52. G. W. Murray, *op. cit.*, p. 176.

53. Barclay, *op. cit.*, pp. 241–43.

54. J. W. Crawfoot, "Customs of the Rubaṭāb," *Sudan Notes and Records*, 1918, I: 132–33.

55. Barclay, *op. cit.*, pp. 157–58, 237–38.

56. Barclay *op. cit.*, pp. 237–40, partly quoting P. D. R. MacDonald, "Female Circumcision in the Sudan: A Paper Delivered at the Sudan Branch British Medical Association" (mimeo, 1936).

57. Briggs, *Tribes of the Sahara*, pp. 128–29, 172, 198–99, 220.

58. Miner, *Timbuctoo*, pp. 158, 161, 164.

59. Westermarck, *op. cit.* I: 177; II: 417, 423, 426.

60. Cf. Herbert, *op. cit.*, pp. 306 ff.

61. *Voyages du Chevalier Chardin en Perse et autres Lieux de l'Orient*, nouvelle edition . . . par L. Langlés, Paris, 1811, III:165, as quoted by Massé, *op. cit.*, p. 31.

62. Cf. Jakob Eduard Polak, *Persien, das Land und Seine Bewohner*, Leipzig, 1865, I: 197–98.

63. Cf. H. Arakélian, "Les Kurdes en Perse," in *Verhandlungen des XIII. Internationalen Orientalisten Kongresses*, p. 150.

64. Massé, *op. cit.*, pp. 31–33.

65. Fredrik Barth, *Nomads of South Persia: The Basseri Tribe of the Khamseh Confederacy*, Boston, 1961, p. 138.

66. Bonaparte, *op. cit.*, p. 82.

67. Cf. Ammar, *op. cit.*, p. 118.

68. *Ibid.*

69. Paul Stirling, *Turkish Village*, p. 24.

70. Ammar, *op. cit.*, p. 206.

71. Gabriel Baer, *Population and Society in the Arab East*, pp. 49–50.

72. Cf. Charles Churchill, "The Arab World," in R. Patai (ed.), *Women in the Modern World*, New York, 1967, p. 117.

73. George A. Lipsky (ed.), *Saudi Arabia: Its People, Its Society, Its Culture*, New Haven: HRAF Press, 1959, p. 278.

74. Cf. Donald Wilber, *Afghanistan*, pp. 85, 93.

75. Cf. Lutfiyya, *op. cit.*, p. 85.

76. Cf. Fuller, *op. cit.*, pp. 58, 83.

77. Lutfiyya, *op. cit.*, pp. 89–90.

78. Cf. A. J. Tremearne, *The Ban of the Bori*, pp. 280 ff.; Tremearne, *The Tailed Headhunters of Nigeria*, London, 1912, pp. 254 ff.; Tremearne, *Hausa Supersititions and Customs*, London, 1913, pp. 145 ff.; Brenda Z. Seligman, in *Folk Lore*, Vol. 25, 1914, pp. 300 ff.

79. Cf. W. Ch. Plowden, *Travels in Abyssinia and the Galla Country*, London, 1868, pp. 259 ff.; J. Borelli, *Ethiopie méridionale*, reprinted by De Goeje, in *Zeitschrift der deutschen morgenländischen Gesellschaft*, 1890, p. 480; C. Conti Rossini, "Note sugli Agau," in *Giornale della Societa Asiatica Italiana*, Vol. 18, 1905; G. R. Sundström, *Le Monde Orientale*, 1909, III: 149–51; A. Z. Aešcoly, "Les noms magiques dans les apocryphes chrétiens des Ethiopiens," in *Journal Asiatique*, Vol. 220, 1932; Enrico Cerulli, *Etiopia Occidentala*, Rome, 1933,

Vol. II; *Encylcopaedia of Islam*, s.v. *Zār*; Leiris, "Le culte des Zars à Gondar," in *Aethiopica*, IV: 96–103, 125–36; Leiris, "La croyance aux génies zar en Ethiopie du nord," *Journal de Psychologie*, 1938, pp. 108–25; Wolf Leslau, An Ethiopian Argot of People Possessed by a Spirit," in *Africa*, Vol. 19, no. 3, London, July 1949, pp. 204–12 (includes a brief description of a *zār*-ceremony among the Falashas); Simon D. Messing, "Group Therapy and Social Status in the Zar Cult of Ethiopia," *American Anthropologist*, Vol. 60, no. 6, Dec. 1958, pp. 1120–26.

80. Cf. Enrico Cerulli, "Note sul movimiento musulmano in Somalia," in *Rivista degli Studii Orientali*, Vol. 10; *Encyclopaedia of Islam*, s.v. "Somaliland."

81. J. Spencer Trimingham, *Islam in the Sudan*, London, 1949, p. 174; Sophie Zenkovsky, "Zar and Tamboura as Practiced by Women in Omdurman," *Sudan Notes and Records*, Vol. 31, 1950, p. 68; Barclay, *op. cit.*, pp. 196–207.

82. Cf. Klunzinger, *op. cit.*, pp. 395–97; Jacoub Artin Pasha, in *Bulletin de l'Institut Egyptien*, II. 6, 1885, p. 185 (footnote); Karl Vollers, "Noch einmal der Zār," ZDMG, Vol. 45, 1891, pp. 343–51; Paul Kahle, "Zār Beschwörungen in Egypten," *Der Islam*, Vol. 3, 1912, pp. 1–41, 189–90, and literature there on p. 1; Brenda Z. Seligman, "Ancient Egyptian Beliefs in Modern Egypt," in *Essays and Studies Presented to William Ridgeway*, Cambridge, 1913, pp. 448–51; *id.*, "On the Origin of the Egyptian Zār," *Folk Lore*, Vol. 25, London, 1914, pp. 300–23.

83. Thomas, *Alarms and Excursions*, pp. 260–262; Thomas, *Arabia Felix*, pp. 194–97.

84. Cf. Doreen Ingrams, *A Survey of Social and Economic Conditions in the Aden Protectorate*, printed by the Government Printer, British Administration, Eritrea, 1949, pp. 58–59.

85. Hurgronje, *op. cit.*, II: 124–28, English translation, Leiden, 1931, pp. 100–03; De Goeje, ZDMG, vol. 44, 1890, p. 480; Arnold Nöldeke, ZDMG, *ibid*, p. 701; S. Zwemer, *The Influence of Animism on Islam*, London, 1920, and its review by G. Levi della Vida, in *Bilychis*, Vol. 10, 1921, pp. 75–79.

86. Cf. J. J. Hess, *Von den Beduinen des Innern Arabiens: Erzählungen, Lieder, Sitten und Gebräuche*, Zürich, 1938, pp. 158–59.

87. Hurgronje, *op cit.*, II: 124–28.

88. Cf. Thomas, *Alarms and Excursions* pp. 260–262. A similar *zār* ceremony among the Murra tribe of the Hadhramaut region (today Southern Yemen) is described by the same author in his *Arabia Felix*, pp. 194–97.

89. Barclay, *op. cit.*, pp. 196–97, 201–02, 204–05.

90. Quoted after Kahle, *op. cit.*, pp. 189–90.

91. Cf. Levy, *op. cit.*, pp. 140–41.

92. Cf. Emanuel Marx, *Bedouin of the Negev*, New York, 1967, pp. 185–86.

93. Cf. Ibrahim Abdulla Muhyi, "Women in the Arab East," *Journal of Social Issues*, 1959, no. 3; reprinted in Richard H. Nolte (ed.), *The Modern Middle East*, New York, 1963, pp. 135–40.

94. Hajji Shaykh Yusuf of Najaf and Gilan, *The Means of the Chastity of Women: A Volume on Chastity* (in Persian), Resht, Iran, 1926, pp. 294 ff., translated by C. R. Pittman, in *The Moslem World*, Vol. 33, 1943, pp. 203–12.

95. Cf. Baydāwī's commentary (13th century); Ibn Khaldun, *Prolegomena* (Paris, 1858 ff.), I: 354; as quoted by Levy, *op. cit.*, pp. 98–99.

96. Levy, *op. cit.*, p. 132.

97. Cf. Tullio Tentori, "Italy," in Patai (ed.), *Women in the Modern World*, p. 167.

98. Nermin Abadan, "Turkey," in Patai (ed.), *Women in the Modern World*, p. 93, quoting Serim Yurtören, "Fertility and Related Attitudes among Two Social Classes in Ankara" (unpublished Master's Thesis, Cornell University, 1965); cf. also Lutfiyya, *op. cit.*, p. 186.

99. Richard T. Antoun, "On the Modesty of Women in Arab Muslim Villages," *American Anthropologist*, Vol. 70, 1968, pp. 690–91.

100. Antoun, *op. cit.*, p. 679.

101. Antoun, *op. cit.*, pp. 678–79.

102. Ibrahim Abdulla Muhyi, *op. cit.*, p, 135.

103. Cf. Lutfiyya, *op. cit.*, pp. 203–04.

Statistical Appendix—

1. Cf. Gabriel Baer, *op. cit.*, p. 2.

2. Cf. Wilber, *op. cit.*, p. 33.

Index

Note: *Arabic proper names preceded by the article are listed under* al-, *even when in the text the spelling* el- *is used, in order to approximate more closely its pronunciation.*